Preface

With the theme "Smart Robotics for Sustainable Society", the 16th International Conference on Intelligent Robotics and Applications (ICIRA 2023) was held in Hangzhou, China, July 5–7, 2023, and designed to encourage advancement in the field of robotics, automation, mechatronics, and applications. It aimed to promote top-level research and globalize quality research in general, making discussions and presentations more internationally competitive and focusing on the latest outstanding achievements, future trends, and demands.

ICIRA 2023 was organized and hosted by Zhejiang University, co-hosted by Harbin Institute of Technology, Huazhong University of Science and Technology, Chinese Academy of Sciences, and Shanghai Jiao Tong University, co-organized by State Key Laboratory of Fluid Power and Mechatronic Systems, State Key Laboratory of Robotics and System, State Key Laboratory of Digital Manufacturing Equipment and Technology, State Key Laboratory of Mechanical System and Vibration, State Key Laboratory of Robotics, and School of Mechanical Engineering of Zhejiang University. Also, ICIRA 2023 was technically co-sponsored by Springer. On this occasion, ICIRA 2023 was a successful event after the COVID-19 pandemic. It attracted more than 630 submissions, and the Program Committee undertook a rigorous review process for selecting the most deserving research for publication. The Advisory Committee gave advice for the conference program. Also, they help to organize special sections for ICIRA 2023. Finally, a total of 431 papers were selected for publication in 9 volumes of Springer's Lecture Note in Artificial Intelligence. For the review process, single-blind peer review was used. Each review took around 2–3 weeks, and each submission received at least 2 reviews and 1 meta-review.

In ICIRA 2023, 12 distinguished plenary speakers delivered their outstanding research works in various fields of robotics. Participants gave a total of 214 oral presentations and 197 poster presentations, enjoying this excellent opportunity to share their latest research findings. Here, we would like to express our sincere appreciation to all the authors, participants, and distinguished plenary and keynote speakers. Special thanks are also extended to all members of the Organizing Committee, all reviewers for peer-review, all staffs of the conference affairs group, and all volunteers for their diligent work.

July 2023

Huayong Yang
Honghai Liu
Jun Zou
Zhouping Yin
Lianqing Liu
Geng Yang
Xiaoping Ouyang
Zhiyong Wang

Huayong Yang · Honghai Liu · Jun Zou ·
Zhouping Yin · Lianqing Liu · Geng Yang ·
Xiaoping Ouyang · Zhiyong Wang
Editors

Intelligent Robotics and Applications

16th International Conference, ICIRA 2023
Hangzhou, China, July 5–7, 2023
Proceedings, Part V

Editors

Huayong Yang
Zhejiang University
Hangzhou, China

Jun Zou (ID)
Zhejiang University
Hangzhou, China

Lianqing Liu (ID)
Shenyang Institute of Automation
Shenyang, Liaoning, China

Xiaoping Ouyang (ID)
Zhejiang University
Hangzhou, China

Honghai Liu (ID)
Harbin Institute of Technology
Shenzhen, China

Zhouping Yin
Huazhong University of Science
and Technology
Wuhan, China

Geng Yang (ID)
Zhejiang University
Hangzhou, China

Zhiyong Wang
Harbin Institute of Technology
Shenzhen, China

ISSN 0302-9743   ISSN 1611-3349 (electronic)
Lecture Notes in Artificial Intelligence
ISBN 978-981-99-6494-9   ISBN 978-981-99-6495-6 (eBook)
https://doi.org/10.1007/978-981-99-6495-6

LNCS Sublibrary: SL7 – Artificial Intelligence

This Springer imprint is published by the registered company Springer Nature Singapore Pte Ltd.
The registered company address is: 152 Beach Road, #21-01/04 Gateway East, Singapore 189721, Singapore

Paper in this product is recyclable.

Lecture Notes in Computer Science

Lecture Notes in Artificial Intelligence   14271

Founding Editor

Jörg Siekmann

Series Editors

Randy Goebel, *University of Alberta, Edmonton, Canada*
Wolfgang Wahlster, *DFKI, Berlin, Germany*
Zhi-Hua Zhou, *Nanjing University, Nanjing, China*

The series Lecture Notes in Artificial Intelligence (LNAI) was established in 1988 as a topical subseries of LNCS devoted to artificial intelligence.

The series publishes state-of-the-art research results at a high level. As with the LNCS mother series, the mission of the series is to serve the international R & D community by providing an invaluable service, mainly focused on the publication of conference and workshop proceedings and postproceedings.

Organization

Conference Chair

Huayong Yang   Zhejiang University, China

Honorary Chairs

Youlun Xiong   Huazhong University of Science and Technology, China
Han Ding   Huazhong University of Science and Technology, China

General Chairs

Honghai Liu   Harbin Institute of Technology, China
Jun Zou   Zhejiang University, China
Zhouping Yin   Huazhong University of Science and Technology, China
Lianqing Liu   Chinese Academy of Sciences, China

Program Chairs

Geng Yang   Zhejiang University, China
Li Jiang   Harbin Institute of Technology, China
Guoying Gu   Shanghai Jiao Tong University, China
Xinyu Wu   Chinese Academy of Sciences, China

Award Committee Chair

Yong Lei   Zhejiang University, China

Publication Chairs

Xiaoping Ouyang   Zhejiang University, China
Zhiyong Wang   Harbin Institute of Technology, China

Regional Chairs

Zhiyong Chen   University of Newcastle, Australia
Naoyuki Kubota   Tokyo Metropolitan University, Japan
Zhaojie Ju   University of Portsmouth, UK
Eric Perreault   Northeastern University, USA
Peter Xu   University of Auckland, New Zealand
Simon Yang   University of Guelph, Canada
Houxiang Zhang   Norwegian University of Science and Technology,
                             Norway
Duanling Li   Beijing University of Posts and
                             Telecommunications, China

Advisory Committee

Jorge Angeles   McGill University, Canada
Tamio Arai   University of Tokyo, Japan
Hegao Cai   Harbin Institute of Technology, China
Tianyou Chai   Northeastern University, China
Jiansheng Dai   King's College London, UK
Zongquan Deng   Harbin Institute of Technology, China
Han Ding   Huazhong University of Science and Technology,
                             China
Xilun Ding   Beihang University, China
Baoyan Duan   Xidian University, China
Xisheng Feng   Shenyang Institute of Automation, Chinese
                             Academy of Sciences, China
Toshio Fukuda   Nagoya University, Japan
Jianda Han   Nankai University, China
Qiang Huang   Beijing Institute of Technology, China
Oussama Khatib   Stanford University, USA
Yinan Lai   National Natural Science Foundation of China,
                             China
Jangmyung Lee   Pusan National University, Korea
Zhongqin Lin   Shanghai Jiao Tong University, China

Hong Liu	Harbin Institute of Technology, China
Honghai Liu	University of Portsmouth, UK
Shugen Ma	Ritsumeikan University, Japan
Daokui Qu	Siasun Robot and Automation Co., Ltd., China
Min Tan	Institute of Automation, Chinese Academy of Sciences, China
Kevin Warwick	Coventry University, UK
Guobiao Wang	National Natural Science Foundation of China, China
Tianmiao Wang	Beihang University, China
Tianran Wang	Shenyang Institute of Automation, Chinese Academy of Sciences, China
Yuechao Wang	Shenyang Institute of Automation, Chinese Academy of Sciences, China
Bogdan M. Wilamowski	Auburn University, USA
Ming Xie	Nanyang Technological University, Singapore
Yangsheng Xu	Chinese University of Hong Kong, China
Huayong Yang	Zhejiang University, China
Jie Zhao	Harbin Institute of Technology, China
Nanning Zheng	Xi'an Jiaotong University, China
Xiangyang Zhu	Shanghai Jiao Tong University, China

Contents – Part V

**Advanced Sensing and Control Technology for Human-Robot
Interaction**

Knowledge-Based Robot Decision-Making and Manipulation

Design and Control of Legged Robots

Pattern Recognition and Machine Learning for Smart Robots

Real-Time Detection and Tracking of Express Parcels Based on Improved YOLOv5+DeepSORT

Qikong Liu, Jian Wu(✉), Lei Yin, Wenxiong Wu, and Ziyang Shen

School of Mechanical Engineering, Nanjing University of Science and Technology, 210094 Nanjing, China
liuqikong0909@163.com, 2609995918@qq.com

Abstract. At present, the sorting of express parcels still requires manual participation in the operations of package supply, deviation correction and separation. In order to improve the automation of express parcel sorting, a multi-target tracking algorithm based on improved YOLOv5 and DeepSORT is proposed. Firstly, the SE attention mechanism is incorporated into the YOLOv5 network to enhance the model's feature extraction capability for express parcels. Secondly, the EIOU loss function is employed as an alternative to the original CIOU loss function used in YOLOv5, aiming to improve the model's convergence. Finally, the improved YOLOv5 model is utilized as the detector for DeepSORT to conduct multi-object tracking experiments on express parcels. Experimental results demonstrate that the improved YOLOv5 algorithm achieves a 4.5% improvement in mean average precision (mAP_0.5) compared to the original algorithm, along with a 1.3% increase in precision and a 6.3% increase in recall. When combined with Deep-SORT, the proposed approach enabled accurate tracking of express parcels with good real-time performance.

Keywords: Express parcels · YOLOv5 algorithm · DeepSORT algorithm

1 Introduction

In recent years, with the rise of online shopping and the development of the logistics industry, the volume of express parcels shipments has been steadily increasing. In 2022, the express parcels volume in China reached 110.58 billion pieces and has maintained a significant growth trend. Enhancing the automation of transportation and sorting for express parcels has become a prominent research direction. The current assembly line sorting of express parcels still has problems such as manual supply of packages, deviation of packages from the track, and manual separation of packages. With the rapid development of computer vision technology, object detection and object tracking technology based on deep learning provides a solution to these problems. Real-time detection and tracking of express parcels, combined with 3D camera positioning, can perform operations such as robotic arm supply, parcel deviation correction, and single-piece separation.

Currently, there have been many studies on multi-target tracking based on YOLO and DeepSORT. In literature [1], an improved YOLOv3 and DeepSORT algorithm is utilized for vehicle detection, tracking, and counting in traffic monitoring scenarios. The YOLOv3 backbone network is pruned to reduce network parameters. Additionally, to enhance detection of small objects, the header of YOLOv3 is improved, and the original 3-scale detection is extended to 4-scale detection. The algorithm is deployable on Jetson TX2 edge devices and demonstrates good real-time performance. Literature [2] proposes an algorithm for field fruit tracking and counting, which uses the improved YOLOv3 as a detector to enhance the detection of small targets by adjusting the network structure, and introduces the channel attention and spatial attention multi-scale fusion modules to fuse the semantic features and shallow texture detail features of deep networks. The algorithm has certain application value for fruit yield evaluation. Literature [3] proposes a multi-ship detection and tracking method based on YOLOv5x and DeepSort algorithm, which accelerates bounding box convergence by replacing the GIoU loss function with CIoU loss function, and uses DIoU-NMS instead of NMS to solve the problem of missing detection when the target is dense. The algorithm can provide effective technical support for the supervision of illegal mining and transportation of silicon energy bulk materials.

Object detection and tracking technology based on deep learning algorithm has achieved certain research results in industry, transportation, agriculture and other fields. In this paper, YOLOv5 and DeepSORT are also used to detect and track parcels, but due to the problems of YOLOv5 algorithm such as target loss, missed detection, and duplicate detection during tracking, further optimization is required. The DeepSort algorithm is able to accurately track multiple targets, so combining it with the YOLOv5 algorithm can improve the tracking and positioning accuracy of express parcels. Therefore, this study proposes an algorithm based on improved YOLOv5 and DeepSort, and the main work is as follows:

1) Add SE (Squeeze-and-Excitation) attention mechanism to the backbone network of YOLOv5 to improve the ability of the model to extract features.
2) Replacing the original CIOU (Complete Intersection over Union) loss function in YOLOv5 with EIOU (Enhanced Intersection over Union) to enhance model convergence.
3) Utilizing the improved YOLOv5 as the detector in DeepSORT for conducting tracking experiments on express parcels.

2   Improved YOLOv5 Algorithm

The improvement of YOLOv5 is mainly reflected in the addition of SE (Squeeze-and-Excitation Networks) [4] attention mechanism at the backbone network to increase the ability of the YOLOv5 network model to extract features. Additionally, the original CIoU loss function of YOLOv5 has been replaced with the EIOU loss function.

2.1   Improvement of YOLOv5 Network Structure

In order to enhance the extraction of target features by the network model, the SE attention mechanism module is introduced. By explicitly realizing the interdependence between each feature channel, the SE attention mechanism adaptively recalibrates the importance of the channel feature response, and then assigns a weight value to each feature channel according to the obtained importance, so that the neural network can focus on important feature channels and suppress unimportant feature channels.

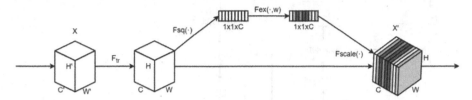

Fig. 1. Structure of the Squeeze-and-Excitation Networks

The structure of the SE attention mechanism module is shown in Fig. 1, the size of the SE module input feature map U is W × H × C, W represents the width of the picture, H represents the height of the picture, and C represents the number of channels. The specific working process of the SE module is as follows:

1. Squeeze. As shown in Eq. 1, the input feature map is pooled globally average, and a vector of $1 \times 1 \times C$ is obtained after each channel of the feature map is compressed accordingly.

$$z_c = F_{sq}(u_c) = \frac{1}{H \times W} \sum_{i=1}^{H} \sum_{j=1}^{W} u_c(i,j) \tag{1}$$

2. Excitation. To capture the interdependencies between channels, a simple gate mechanism with a sigmoid activation function is used for excitation. This process involves two fully connected layers. The first layer acts as a dimensionality reduction step, compressing the C-dimensional features to establish channel correlations. The second layer restores the dimensions. This is represented by Eq. 2.

$$s = F_{ex}(z, W) = \sigma(g(z, W)) = \sigma(W_2 \delta(W_1 z)) \tag{2}$$

where σ represents the Sigmoid activation function, δ represents the ReLU activation function, and W_1 and W_2 represent the weight parameters of the two fully connected layers, respectively.

3. Scale. The final output of the SE module is obtained by rescaling U using the stimulus s, as shown in Eq. 3.

$$\tilde{x}_c = F_{\text{scale}}(u_c, s_c) = s_c u_c \tag{3}$$

where $\tilde{x}_c$ and Fscale represent the channel product between scalar s_c and feature map u_c.

In order to reduce the impact of the attention mechanism on the network parameters, the SE module is added after the last C3 layer of the backbone network, and the mapping relationship between channels is established so that the network makes full use of the global features and improves the feature extraction ability of express parcels. The changed network structure is shown in Fig. 2.

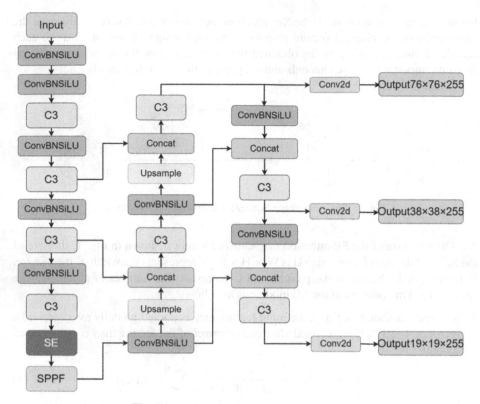

Fig. 2. Improved YOLOv5 network structure

2.2 Modify the Loss Function

The loss of YOLOv5 includes positioning loss, confidence loss and classification loss, and the overall loss is the weighted sum of the three, and the attention to a certain loss can be changed by adjusting the weight [5]. The YOLOv5 network uses the CIoU loss function by default, CIoU is improved from DIoU, on the basis of DIoU, considering the aspect ratio of the bounding box, the regression accuracy is improved. As shown in Eq. 4 is the DIoU loss function:

$$L_{DIoU} = 1 - IoU + \frac{\rho^2(b, b^{gt})}{C^2} \tag{4}$$

where b and b^{gt} represent the center position of the label box and prediction box, ρ^2 represents the Euclidean distance between the two center positions, and C^2 represents the square of the diagonal length of the smallest bounding box of the detection box and the prediction box.

In CIoU, an additional penalty term αv is introduced based on DIoU, as shown in Eq. 5:

$$L_{CIoU} = 1 - IoU + \frac{\rho^2(b, b^{gt})}{c^2} + \alpha v \tag{5}$$

where α is a weight coefficient defined as:

$$\alpha = \frac{v}{(1 - IoU) + v} \tag{6}$$

where v is the normalization of the predicted box and the ground truth box's width and height, defined as:

$$v = \frac{4}{\pi^2} \left(\arctan \frac{w^{gt}}{h^{gt}} - \arctan \frac{w}{h} \right)^2 \tag{7}$$

Although CIoU considers the intersection over union, the distance between center points, and the aspect ratios of the bounding boxes, the aspect ratio alone cannot accurately reflect the true difference in width and height between the predicted box and the ground truth box. Therefore, Zhang et al. [8] separated the width and height of the bounding boxes and proposed EIoU, as shown in Eq. 8:

$$L_{EIOU} = L_{IOU} + L_{dis} + L_{asp} = 1 - IOU + \frac{\rho^2(b, b^{gt})}{(w^c)^2 + (h^c)^2} + \frac{\rho^2(w, w^{gt})}{(w^c)^2} + \frac{\rho^2(h, h^{gt})}{(h^c)^2} \tag{8}$$

where w^c and h^c are the width and height of the minimum bounding box that surrounds the two anchor boxes, respectively. Because EIoU calculates the width and height of the prediction box separately from the width and height of the label box, the accuracy of the loss function is improved.

3 DeepSORT Algorithm

In order to obtain the location information of the express parcels, it is necessary to use the target tracking algorithm for tracking. DeepSORT [6] is an improvement over the SORT [7] algorithm. The SORT algorithm utilizes Kalman filtering and Hungarian matching for multi-object tracking of detected targets. In the SORT algorithm, to improve efficiency, the trajectories of occluded targets are eliminated. When a target is re-detected by the detector, it is assigned a new identity, leading to an increased number of ID switches in the SORT algorithm. Based on the SORT algorithm, the DeepSORT algorithm introduces appearance features and cascade matching, the detector enters the coordinates and confidence of the detection frame of the target, uses the Kalman filter to predict the trajectory motion state, and the Hungarian algorithm cascades the predicted trajectory with the current frame, which reduces the number of identity number conversions. DeepSORT uses an 8-dimensional spatial vector $(\mu, v, \gamma, h, \dot{x}, \dot{y}, \dot{r}, \dot{h})$ to describe the tracked target, where (μ, v) represents the central position coordinates of the input target detection box; γ indicates the aspect ratio of the detection frame; h represents the height of the detection frame. $(\dot{x}, \dot{y}, \dot{r}, \dot{h})$ represents the motion information of the target, that is, the speed in the respective image coordinates. The input of the DeepSORT algorithm is the Bounding Box, Confidence and Feature information detected by the detector as input, and the core of the algorithm is to use the Kalman filter algorithm to predict the target state and use the Hungarian algorithm for correlation matching, as shown in Fig. 3 for the workflow of DeepSORT.

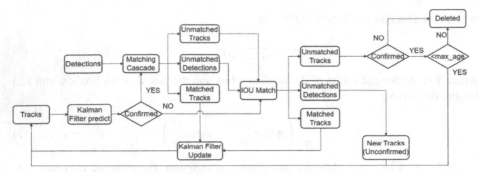

Fig. 3. DeepSORT tracking process

DeepSORT utilizes the Kalman filter to calculate the Mahalanobis distance between the predicted bounding box and the detected bounding box from the detector, representing the motion information of the target. The Mahalanobis distance is defined as shown in Eq. 9:

$$d^{(1)}(i,j) = (d_j - y_i)^T S_i^{-1} (d_j - y_i) \qquad (9)$$

where $d^{(1)}(i,j)$ is the degree of matching between the j-th detection frame and the i-th trajectory, d_j is the state of the j-th target detection frame, y_i is the state of the prediction box of the i-th tracker, and S_i is the covariance matrix between the i-th target prediction position and the detection position. The detection frame was filtered by Mahalanobis distance, and if the associated Mahalanobis distance $d^{(1)} < t^{(1)}$, it indicates a successful association of the motion states [9].

When an object is occluded, it is inaccurate to measure it using Mahalanobis distance. Therefore, the appearance feature is introduced and the re-identification network is added to extract the appearance information of the target. The minimum cosine distance between the trajectory and the detection frame in the appearance space is used to filter the detection frame, and the distance less than the threshold indicates that the tracking is successful, and the calculation formula is:

$$d^{(2)}(i,j) = min\left\{ 1 - r_j^T r_k^{(i)} \mid r_k^{(i)} \in R_k \right\} \qquad (10)$$

$d^{(2)}(i,j)$ represents the minimum cosine distance between the j-th detection frame and the i-th trajectory, r_j represents the appearance characteristic descriptor calculated for each detection frame d_j, and sets the $\|rj\| = 1$, $r_k^{(i)}$ represents the appearance descriptor of the i-th trajectory, R_k is the appearance library of the i-th target trajectory, containing the appearance information of 100 tracked targets.

Finally, the Mahalanobis distance based on motion information and the cosine distance based on appearance characteristics are linearly weighted as the final association, and the association formula is shown in Eq. 11:

$$C(i,j) = \lambda d^{(1)}(i,j) + (1 - \lambda)d^{(2)}(i,j) \qquad (11)$$

where $C(i,j)$ is the metric and λ is the weight value.

4 Experimental Results and Analysis

In order to verify the detection accuracy of the improved YOLOv5 algorithm and the accuracy of DeepSORT tracking, experimental verification was conducted. The experimental hardware platform configuration is: processor AMD Ryzen 7 6800H, GPU uses NVIDIA GeForce RTX3060; operating system: Windows64-bit operating system; software environment: PyTorch2.0.0, Python3.9, CUDA11.7.

4.1 Experimental Evaluation of Improved YOLOv5's Detection Performance

Dataset and Evaluation Metrics. Due to the absence of publicly available datasets for package detection, this paper uses a self-made dataset. The source of the self-made dataset includes 2194 images collected from express post stations, 473 images collected in daily life scenes, videos collected in the express sorting center and cut into frames, and the cut frames contain 2475 images. The data set contains a total of 5142 images. LabelImg software is used to label the collected pictures. In order to facilitate the operation of the express package by the robotic arm, according to the shape characteristics of the express, it is divided into box express (box), bag express (bag) and Stick-shaped express delivery (bar), and the three-segment code label (label) on the express delivery is also recognized, so that the identification label is upward when the robot arm supplies the package. Use the LabelImg annotation to generate an xml file, and use a Python script to convert the xml file into a txt file in YOLO format. The marked pictures are divided into training set, verification set and test set according to the ratio of 7:2:1. The training set has a total of 3600 images, the verification set has a total of 1028 images, and the test set has a total of 514 images.

The evaluation indicators mainly include detection speed (FPS), recall (Recall), precision (precision) and average accuracy (mAP) to evaluate the performance of the model. The recall formula is shown in Eq. 12:

$$\text{Recall} = \frac{TP}{TP + FN} \tag{12}$$

where TP represents the number of correctly detected samples, FP represents the number of samples that were falsely detected, and FN represents the number of samples that missed detection. Recall refers to the rate at which positive samples are correctly predicted. The formula for precision is shown in Eq. 13:

$$\text{Precision} = \frac{TP}{TP + FP} \tag{13}$$

Precision refers to the ratio of the number of correctly predicted samples to the total number of predicted samples. The average accuracy mAP equation is shown in Eq. 14:

$$mAP = \frac{\sum AP}{NC} \times 100\% \tag{14}$$

The mean average precision (mAP) is the accuracy of a single category divided by the overall number of categories, which is the main evaluation index of the model.

In addition, when comparing with other models, network parameters (Params) and weight size (Weight Size) are also used as evaluation indicators to comprehensively evaluate the performance of the model.

Ablation Experiments. In order to verify the effectiveness of the improved algorithm, based on the YOLOv5s network, the improved modules are added separately, and then the two are combined for experiments. In order to verify the effectiveness of the embedded SE attention mechanism, several commonly used attention mechanisms were added to the YOLOv5 network for comparison, including the coordinate attention mechanism CA (Coordinate attention) [10], the channel and spatial attention mechanism CBAM (Convolutional Block Attention Module) [11] and the channel attention mechanism ECA (Efficient Channel Attention) [12]. In order to compare the influence of different loss functions on the model, the CIOU loss function of the original YOLOv5 network, the DIOU loss function considering the aspect ratio of the prediction frame and the EIOU loss function used in this paper were selected for experiments, and the training process is shown in Fig. 4.

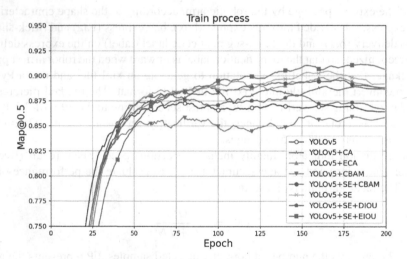

Fig. 4. Ablation experimental training process

From Fig. 4, it can be observed that except for the CBAM attention mechanism, which led to inferior training performance compared to the original YOLOv5 network, the other attention mechanisms showed improvements in mAP@0.5. Although the YOLOv5+SE+EIOU loss function used in this study exhibited slower convergence during training compared to other models, after approximately 100 epochs, it gradually achieved the highest mAP@0.5 among all the models. The comparative results of the ablation experiments are shown in Table 1.

In order to reflect the effect of the improved module in this paper more clearly, the training process of the improved module used in this paper is shown in Fig. 5.

It can be observed from Fig. 5 that after increasing the SE attention mechanism, the mAP@0.5 of the model has a significant improvement, and after replacing the loss

Table 1. Results of Ablation Experiments

Models	CA	ECA	CBAM	SE	CIOU	DIOU	EIOU	mAP50/%
YOLOv5	–	–	–	–	√	–	–	0.871
A	√	–	–	–	√	–	–	0.89
B	–	√	–	–	√	–	–	0.898
C	–	–	√	–	√	–	–	0.867
D	–	–	√	√	√	–	–	0.9
E	–	–	–	√	√	–	–	0.907
F	–	–	–	√	–	√	–	0.88
Ours	–	–	–	√	–	–	√	0.916

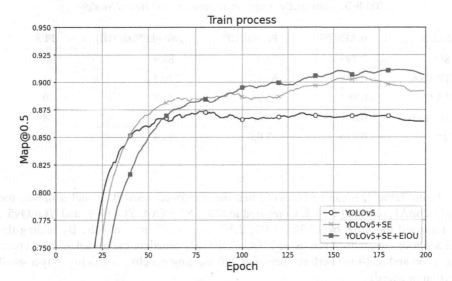

Fig. 5. Training Process of the Proposed Enhancement Module in this Study

function with EIOU, the mAP@0.5 of the model has a small increase. Table 2 shows the specific parameters after the model is improved.

Table 2. Experimental Results of the Improved Model

Models	Params/10^6	Precision	Recall	mAP50/%	FPS
YOLOv5	7.02	0.904	0.819	0.871	78
YOLOv5+SE	7.05	0.911	0.87	0.907	75
YOLOv5+SE+EIOU	7.05	0.917	0.882	0.916	75

As shown in Table 2, since the improved model increases the SE attention mechanism compared with the original YOLOv5 model, the parameters are increased by 3×104, but the accuracy is improved by 1.3%, the recall rate is increased by 6.3%, the mAP@0.5 is improved by 4.5%, and when the input image pixels are 640×480, the FPS of the improved model is 75, which has better real-time performance.

Comparative Experiment. In order to further verify the performance of the improved model in terms of speed and accuracy, the current popular models are selected for comparison, including SSD, YOLOv4, YOLOv7, YOLOv5s with default parameter configuration, and the model in this paper, the main parameters of the comparison include mAP@0.5, the number of model parameters, weight size, and the number of detection frames per second (the input image resolution is 640×480). The main experimental results are shown in Table 3.

Table 3. Comparative Experiment Results of Different Models

Models	mAP50/%	Params/10^6	Weight Size(MB)	FPS
SSD	0.793	24.2	87.9	25
YOLOv4	0.825	64.01	220.3	32
YOLOv7	0.893	36.50	74.8	60
YOLOv5s	0.871	7.02	14.4	78
Ours	0.916	7.05	14.4	75

From Table 3, it can be observed that the improved network model achieved the highest mAP, reaching 91.6%. Compared to SSD, YOLOv4, YOLOv7, and YOLOv5s, it improved the mAP by 12.3%, 9.1%, 2.3%, and 4.5%, respectively. By adding the SE attention mechanism and using EIOU as the loss function, the model achieved high precision and real-time performance after 200 training epochs, sacrificing only a small portion of speed.

To provide a more visual representation of the detection performance, two complex scenarios were selected for evaluation. As shown in Fig. 6, scenario A contains an occluded "bag" target, and the scenario B contains a large number of express parcels stacked.

From Fig. 6, it can be observed that in the scenario A, only the algorithm of this paper and YOLOv7 algorithm detect the partially occluded "bag" class, with a detection confidence of 0.81 for the proposed algorithm and 0.48 for YOLOv7. In the scenario B, only the algorithm of this paper, the YOLOv5s algorithm and the YOLOv7 algorithm successfully detected the two stacked "bag" express parcels in the middle of the picture, and the YOLOv5s and YOLOv7 algorithms failed to detect the labels that were blocked by the express parcels. Experiments show that the proposed algorithm can still maintain high detection accuracy in the occluded and stacked state.

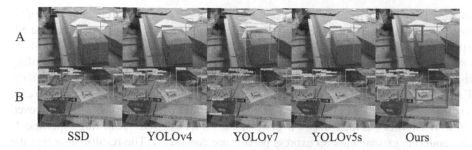

SSD   YOLOv4   YOLOv7   YOLOv5s   Ours

Fig. 6. Comparison of detection effects of different algorithms

4.2 Tracking Experiment for Express Parcels

The original YOLOv5 and the improved YOLOv5 were used as detectors for the Deep-SORT tracker to conduct tracking experiments on express parcels. A segment of the conveyor belt, lasting 28 s, was selected for detection and tracking. The effect is shown in Fig. 7 and Fig. 8.

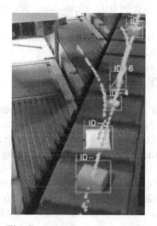

Fig. 7. YOLOv5+DeepSORT   **Fig. 8.** Improved YOLOv5+DeepSORT

From the comparison of Fig. 7 and Fig. 8, it can be observed that the improved model has much enhanced the extraction ability of express parcel features, and the semi-obscured express parcel in the upper left of Fig. 8 can still be detected by the improved YOLOv5 and assigned an ID for tracking. The unimproved YOLOv5 model did not detect the semi-obscured express package in time. Moreover, the tracking of the improved algorithm has real-time performance, which has certain practical value for the correction and separation of express parcels.

5 Conclusion

This paper proposes a tracking algorithm based on improved YOLOv5 and DeepSORT for the detection and tracking of express parcels. The algorithm enables stable tracking of identified express parcels and can be applied in various logistics processes such as parcel supply, correction, and separation. The proposed approach enhances the feature extraction capability of the YOLOv5 backbone network by incorporating the SE attention mechanism. Additionally, the EIOU loss function is employed instead of the original CIOU loss function in the YOLOv5 network to address the issue of disregarding the width and height losses during training, thereby improving the detection accuracy. Experimental results demonstrate that the improved algorithm achieves a 4.5% increase in mAP compared to the unimproved YOLOv5 algorithm. Lastly, by using the improved YOLOv5 network as the detector in conjunction with DeepSORT, tracking experiments and counting experiments on express parcels are conducted. The results show that the improved YOLOv5 and DeepSORT algorithm combination achieves excellent performance in terms of accuracy and real-time capability, effectively detecting and tracking express parcels.

References

1. Chen, C., Liu, B., et al.: An edge traffic flow detection scheme based on deep learning in an intelligent transportation system. IEEE Trans. Intell. Transp. Syst. **22**(3), 1840–1852 (2020)
2. Zhang, W.L., Wang, J.Q., et al.: Deep-learning-based in-field citrus fruit detection and tracking. Hortic. Res. **9**(3) (2022)
3. Jang, Q., Li, H.: Silicon energy bulk material cargo ship detection and tracking method combining YOLOv5 and DeepSORT. Energy Rep. **9**(2), 151–158 (2023)
4. Hu, J., Shen, L., Sun, G.: Squeeze-and-excitation networks. In: 31st IEEE/CVF Conference on Computer Vision and Pattern Recognition (CVPR), Salt Lake City, UT, pp. 7132–7141. IEEE (2018)
5. Duan, L.C., Tan, B.H., et al.: Defect detection for wine bottle caps based on improved YOLOv3. Electron. Meas. Technol. **45**(15), 130–137 (2022)
6. Wojke, N., Bewley, A., Paulus, D.: Simple online and realtime tracking with a deep association metric. In: IEEE International Conference on Image Processing (ICIP), Beijing, China, pp. 3645–3649. IEEE (2017). arXiv
7. Bewley, A., Ge, Z.Y., et al.: Simple online and realtime tracking. In: IEEE International Conference on Image Processing (ICIP), Phoenix, AZ, pp. 3464–3468. IEEE (2016). arXiv
8. Zhang, Y.F., Ren, W.Q., et al.: Focal and efficient IOU loss for accurate bounding box regression. Neurocomputing **506**, 146–157 (2021)
9. Chen, J.Q., Jin, X.H., et al.: Vehicle flow detection based on YOLOv3 and DeepSort. Acta Metrologica Sinica **42**(06), 718–723 (2021)
10. Hou, Q., Zhou, D.Q., Feng, J.S.: Coordinate attention for efficient mobile network design. In: 2021 IEEE/CVF Conference on Computer Vision and Pattern Recognition, CVPR 2021, pp, 13708–13717. IEEE Computer Society, Virtual, Online, United states (2021)
11. Woo, S., Park, J., Lee, J.Y., Kweon, I.S.: CBAM: convolutional block attention module. In: Ferrari, V., Hebert, M., Sminchisescu, C., Weiss, Y. (eds.) ECCV 2018. LNCS, vol. 11211, pp. 3–19. Springer, Cham (2018). https://doi.org/10.1007/978-3-030-01234-2_1
12. Wang, Q.L., Wu, B.G., et al.: ECA-Net: efficient channel attention for deep convolutional neural networks. In: 2020 IEEE/CVF Conference on Computer Vision and Pattern Recognition (CVPR), pp. 11531–11539. IEEE Computer Society, Virtual, Online, United states (2020)

Micro Speaker Quality Inspection Based on Time-Frequency Domain Feature Learning

Xianyi Chen[1,2], Hongyun Kong[1,2], Huiting Zha[1,2(✉)], and EnLai Zhang[1,2]

[1] Xiamen University of Technology, Xiamen, Fujian, China
chenxy@xmut.edu.com
[2] Xiamen Key Laboratory of Robot Systems and Digital Manufacturing, Xiamen, Fujian, China

Abstract. Because of the low efficiency, easy fatigue, and high cost of manual micro speaker quality inspection, intelligent quality inspection methods are urgently needed. This paper proposed an intelligent sound classifier based on the amplitude and frequency features of the micro speaker sound for the micro speaker quality inspection. The classifier includes amplitude feature parameters of crests and troughs in the time domain and frequency feature parameters in the frequency domain. The values of the feature parameters are obtained by machine learning and that would be the key basis for the classifier to detect whether the micro speaker is qualified or not. The quality inspection experimental results showed that the detection accuracy of the proposed method reaches 99.5%, which is 1.75% higher than that of the manual inspection. The detection time is only 1.5– 2 s, which is twice as efficient as the manual work. The proposed method can improve the quality and efficiency of micro speaker quality inspection.

Keywords: Quality Inspection · Time-Frequency Domain Feature · Machine Learning · Micro Speaker Sound

1 Introduction

Micro speaker is an important component of mobile phone, Pad, laptop, and other electronic products and widely used in the industry. So it is of great significance to improve the production efficiency and quality of the micro speaker. At present, the quality detection is mainly by manual through micro speaker sound. The length and width of the micro speaker are generally about 10 mm, and the height is are less than 4 mm. Because of its small size, workers who use hearing for quality detection for a long time are prone to auditory fatigue, which would reduce the accuracy of quality detection. In addition, the work is boring, so it is difficult to recruit suitable quality inspectors.

Therefore, the method of computer sound detection can be used for the quality detection. The research field of sound detection is relatively extensive, such as sound event detection [1–3], mechanical and electronic equipment health state monitoring [4,

Supplementary Information The online version contains supplementary material available at https://doi.org/10.1007/978-981-99-6495-6_2

5], non-contact fault diagnosis [6–8], etc. Pattern recognition is usually used for sound event detection in specific environmental scenes such as SVM [1], multi-task learning [3], etc. These methods perform sound event detection by pre-learning and constructing sound detection classifiers that provide references for the abnormal sound detection of the micro speaker. Actually, the most widespread application of sound detection is non-contact fault diagnosis in the industry, especially for the rotary machine such as bearings [8, 11], conveyor idlers [12], etc. For rotary machines, machine learning can be carried out by the time-frequency domain features of the different fault sounds, and a fault detection classifier can be constructed for fault detection. For more complex fault sound, it can be converted into Mel-image [9–11] and the richer image features can be extracted. In addition, image recognition technology such as deep learning method can be used for fault sound detection. Usually, unknown faults can appear in the process of the mechanical work, and the unsupervised mechanical sound fault detection method [13] can be applied to recognize and detect the new mechanical faults, such as deep adversarial transfer learning network [14]. In conclusion, sound-based event or mechanical fault detection methods are heavily dependent on the amplitude and frequency feature of sound. On this basis, machine learning, pattern recognition, and other methods can be used to construct the sound recognition classifiers and carry out sound detection.

The remainder of this paper is structured as follows, the sound data would be analyzed by positive and negative samples and the amplitude and frequency feature parameters are extracted in Sect. 2. In Sect. 3, the quality detection classifier is constructed with the feature parameters. In Sect. 4, the quality inspection experiments and the experimental results are analyzed. In the end, conclusions of this article are made in Sect. 5.

2 Sound Data Analysis and Amplitude-Frequency Features Extraction

A qualified micro speaker can make a right sound and it is recorded by a sound recorder as MP3 format. The sound data is parsed to obtain the time domain wave as shown in Fig. 1 and it is periodic. There are about 15000 data points in each periodic and the duration of a periodic sound is about 1.5 s.

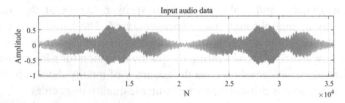

Fig. 1. The sound wave of a qualified micro speaker in the time-domain.

In order to analyze the sound of the micro speaker, the typical waves of the qualified and unqualified products are showed in Fig. 2. In this paper, the sound waves of qualified and unqualified products are marked as positive samples (OK-data) and negative samples (NG-data) respectively.

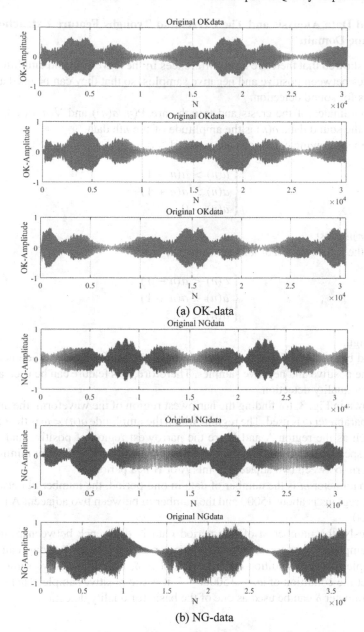

(a) OK-data

(b) NG-data

Fig. 2. The sound data in the time-domain. The OK-data is from the positive samples of qualified products and the NG-data is from the negative samples of unqualified products.

2.1 Sound Data Analysis and The Crests and Troughs Feature Extraction in Time Domain

The Fig. 2 showed that there are large differences in the waveform and amplitude of the sound waves between positive and negative samples, so that they can be used as one of the features for sound detection.

The coordinates of the crests and troughs are P(n, $a(n)$) and V(n, $a(n)$), n is the number of the sound data, $a(n)$ is the amplitude of the nth data.

When the following conditions are satisfied,

$$\begin{cases} a(n) > a(n-1) \\ a(n) > a(n+1) \\ a(n) > 0 \end{cases} \qquad (1)$$

The $a(n)$is crest.

When the following conditions are satisfied,

$$\begin{cases} a(n) < a(n-1) \\ a(n) < a(n+1) \\ a(n) < 0 \end{cases} \qquad (2)$$

$a(n)$ is trough.

It could be found in Fig. 2 that the position of the minimum amplitude is different between the positive and negative samples. Therefore, this feature can be used as one of the basis for quality detection.

As shown in Fig. 3, for finding the narrowest region of the waveform, the amplitude threshold parameter ω is used. The regions which the amplitude $a(n) < \omega$ is the narrowest region, such as the region A and B are the narrowest region of positive and negative samples respectively. In addition, the amplitude of the point P and V are minimum and the waveform between two adjacent points A or B is a period.

If the parameter m is the number of data in one period, the number m between two adjacent B regions is about 15000 and the number m between two adjacent A regions is below15000.

Obviously, the number m of one period data is difference between positive and negative samples. Therefore, the feature parameter δ for the number of data can be used. If the sample met the condition of $|m - 15000| > \delta$, it is the negative sample. If the sample met the condition of $|m - 15000| \leq \delta$, it is the positive sample. Therefore, this feature parameter δ can be used as one of the basis for quality detection.

2.2 Data Analysis in Frequency Domain and Feature Extraction

The Fig. 2(b) showed that the waveforms of the first and second negative samples are similar to the positive samples, and that would cause false detections. In order to improve the accuracy of sound detection, it is necessary to analyze and extract the features in frequency domain.

The sound data in time domain are needed to be transformed by FFT to obtain the spectrum diagram. Figure 4 showed the spectrum diagrams of four typical positive and

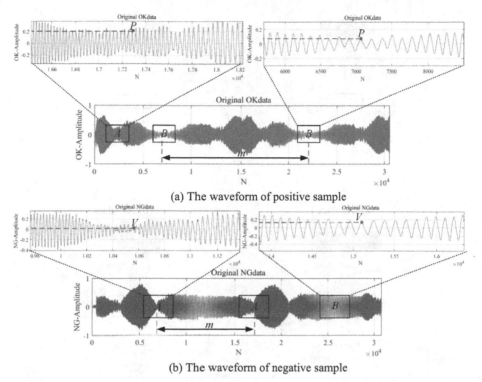

(a) The waveform of positive sample

(b) The waveform of negative sample

Fig. 3. The crest and trough features of the sound wave. The larger versions of Fig. 3 showed that the crests are less than 0.15.

negative samples respectively. The larger versions of Fig. 4 showed the amplitude of secondary frequencies.

It can be seen from the Fig. 4 that the primary frequencies of positive samples and negative samples are difficult to distinguish. However, the secondary frequencies made a clear difference. The parameter ψ is the amplitude of the secondary frequency, such as $\psi \approx 44$ in the positive sample in Fig. 4(a) and $\psi \approx 10$, $\psi \approx 18$, $\psi \approx 262$ respectively in the negative sample in Fig. 4 (b), (c), (d). It can be find that the frequency amplitude of negative samples is smaller or much larger than that of the positive samples. Therefore, the feature parameter α greater than 44 and the feature parameter β less than 44 can be defined to distinguish the positive and negative samples by setting appropriate thresholds.

3 Constructing the Quality Inspection Classifier

The Sect. 2 had analyzed and extracted the feature parameters of sound detection and they are the amplitude feature parameter ω, the feature parameter δ for the number of data, the amplitude thresholds parameter α and β in the frequency domain. Therefore, these parameter values must be trained to construct the quality detection classifier. So 100 positive samples are used to train the parameter values.

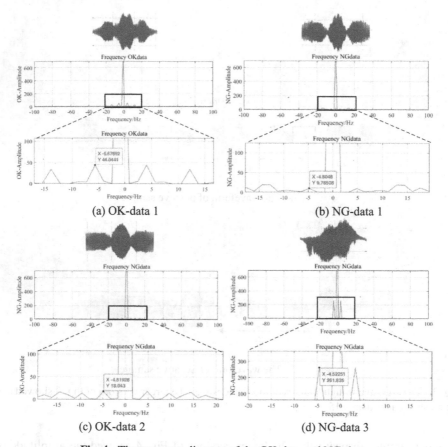

(a) OK-data 1   (b) NG-data 1

(c) OK-data 2   (d) NG-data 3

Fig. 4. The spectrum diagram of the OK-data and NG-data.

3.1 Training the Parameter Values

Firstly, the parameter values ω, δ are trained in the time domain. In Fig. 5, the flow diagrams showed the training process of the parameters ω, δ.

Secondly, as the Fig. 6 shown that the parameters α and β are trained in the frequency domain.

3.2 The Quality Inspection Classifier

After obtaining the parameter values ω, δ, α and β through training and they are used to construct the quality inspection classifier. As the Fig. 7 showed that the parts in the dotted box are the key steps for quality detection.

The working process of the classifier is described as follows. Firstly, the sound data with MP3 format of the micro speaker is parsed into a time domain wave diagram as the Fig. 1 shown. Secondly, through the amplitude feature parameter ω in the time domain, the number m of a periodic sound data is extracted. And then the initial sound detection is carried out by using the inequation $|m - 15000| \leq \delta$. At last, FFT is used to get

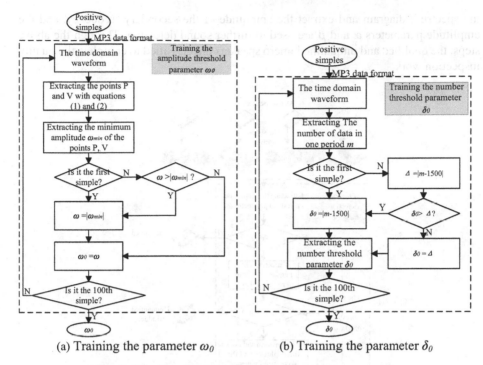

(a) Training the parameter ω_0

(b) Training the parameter δ_0

Fig. 5. The flow diagrams of training the parameters ω and δ.

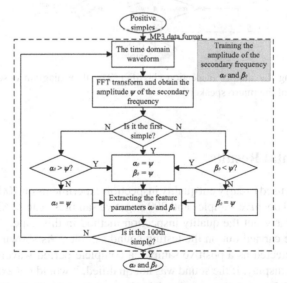

Fig. 6. The flow diagram of training the parameters α and β.

the spectrum diagram and extract the amplitude of the secondary frequency, and the amplitude parameters α and β are used to further sound detection. Through the above steps, the qualified and unqualified micro speakers are classified to complete the quality inspection work.

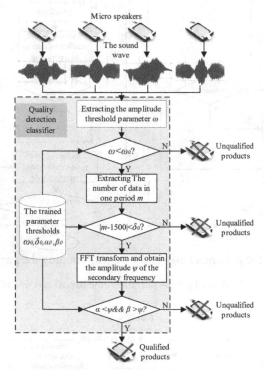

Fig. 7. Constructing the quality inspection classifier. The flow diagram describes the quality inspection process of the micro speaker.

4 Experimental Results

The classifier was used to carry out quality inspection experiments on 400 testing samples which having 200 positive samples and 200 negative samples. The MATLAB was used to program and carry out the quality inspection method in this paper. The recognition experiments were carried out on the testing sound samples. As shown in Fig. 8, when the sound was detected as a positive sample, a complete period waveform in the time domain would be display. If the sound was not qualified, it would not extract a complete period waveform.

The experimental results were shown in the Table 1.

$$\text{Accuracy} = \frac{\text{TP} + \text{TN}}{\text{TP} + \text{TN} + \text{FP} + \text{FN}} = 0.995$$

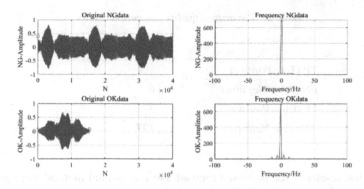

Fig. 8. The display interface of the detection results by using MATLAB.

Table 1. The quality inspection results.

	Results
TP (True Positive)	198
FN (False Negative)	2
FP (False Positive)	0
TN (True Negative)	200

$$\text{Precision} = \frac{\text{TP}}{\text{TP} + \text{FP}} = 1$$

$$\text{Recall} = \frac{\text{TP}}{\text{TP} + \text{FN}} = 0.99$$

It can be seen from the experimental results that the precision is 100% and the recall is 99%, which mean that the proposed method in this paper has a high reliability for the qualified products detection. The disadvantage is that there are 1% of qualified products which are wrongly detected, so that it would lose a small percentage of qualified products. This part of the products can be reinspected to reduce error rate.

To prove the proposed method was practical and advanced, the method was compared with manual quality inspection. The 400 samples were detected by manual, and the results are shown in Table 2.

$$\text{Accuracy} = \frac{\text{TP} + \text{TN}}{\text{TP} + \text{TN} + \text{FP} + \text{FN}} = 0.9775$$

$$\text{Precision} = \frac{\text{TP}}{\text{TP} + \text{FP}} = 0.985$$

$$\text{Recall} = \frac{\text{TP}}{\text{TP} + \text{FN}} = 0.97$$

Table 2. The manual quality inspection results.

	Results
TP (True Positive)	194
FN (False Negative)	6
FP (False Positive)	3
TN (True Negative)	197

The detection results of the proposed method and the manual method were compared and the results were showed in Table 3.

Table 3. Comparing the method and the manual method.

Quality Inspection Method	The Proposed Method	The Manual Method
Accuracy	99.5%	97.75%
Precision	100%	98.5%
Recall	99%	97%
Detection time	1.5–2 s	4–5 s

The experimental results showed the accuracy, precision and recall of the proposed method are improved by 1.75%, 1.5% and 2% respectively comparing with the manual method, and all the detection effects are improved. In addition, the manual quality inspection time is about 4–5 s and the method in this paper is less than 2 s, the efficiency is almost doubled. Therefore, the detection method in this paper can be well applied to the quality inspection of the micro speaker. In the future work, the deep learning algorithms will be used to improve the accuracy of the proposed method.

5 Conclusions

In this paper, the crest and trough features of the sound wave and the amplitude feature of the secondary frequency were used for quality inspection. The experimental results showed that the method achieved a good detection effect. The quality inspection success rate of qualified products is 100% and the precision and recall are 100% and 99% respectively. In addition, the accuracy, precision and recall of the proposed method are all improved and the efficiency of the quality inspection had also been doubled comparing with the manual method.

Acknowledgement. This work is supported by the Young Science Foundation of Xiamen, Fujian, China under Grant No. 3502Z20227069, the Talent Fund Project of Xiamen University of Technology under Grant No. YKJ22014R and YKJ22015R, the Natural Science Foundation of Fujian Province under Grant No. 2022J05280 and 2023J011437.

References

1. Lei, B., Mak, M.W.: Robust scream sound detection via sound event partitioning. Multimedia Tools Appl. **75**(11), 6071–6089 (2016)
2. Pandeya, Y.R., Bhattarai, B., Lee, J.: Visual object detector for cow sound event detection. IEEE Access **8**, 162625–162633 (2020)
3. Liang, H., Ji, W., Wang, R., et al.: A scene-dependent sound event detection approach using multi-task learning. IEEE Sens. J. **22**(18), 12483–17489 (2022)
4. Cui, P., Wang, J., Li, X., Li, C.: Sub-health identification of reciprocating machinery based on sound feature and OOD detection. Machines **9**, 179 (2021)
5. Shubita, R.R., et al.: Fault detection in rotating machinery based on sound signal using edge machine learning. IEEE Access **11**, 6665–6672 (2023)
6. Altaf, M., et al.: Automatic and efficient fault detection in rotating machinery using sound signals. Acoust. Aust. **47**, 125–139 (2019)
7. Mian, T., Choudhary, A., Fatima, S.: An efficient diagnosis approach for bearing faults using sound quality metrics. Appl. Acoust. **195**, 108839 (2022)
8. Shi, H., Li, Y., Bai, X., et al.: Sound-aided fault feature extraction method for rolling bearings based on stochastic resonance and time-domain index fusion. Appl. Acoust. **189**, 108611 (2022)
9. Tran, T., Lundgren, J.: Drill fault diagnosis based on the scalogram and mel spectrogram of sound signals using artificial intelligence. IEEE Access **8** (2020)
10. Nguyen, M.T., Huang, J.H.: Fault detection in water pumps based on sound analysis using a deep learning technique. Proc. Inst. Mech. Eng. Part E J. Process Mech. Eng. **236**(2), 298–307 (2022)
11. Brusa, E., Delprete, C., Di Maggio, L.G.: Deep transfer learning for machine diagnosis: from sound and music recognition to bearing fault detection. Appl. Sci. **11**, 11663 (2021)
12. Zhang, Y., Li, S., Li, A., et al.: Fault diagnosis method of belt conveyor idler based on sound signal. J. Mech. Sci. Technol. **37**(1), 69–79 (2023)
13. Wu, J., Yang, F., Hu, W.: Unsupervised anomalous sound detection for industrial monitoring based on ArcFace classifier and gaussian mixture model. Appl. Acoust. **203**, 109188 (2023)
14. Li, J., et al.: A deep adversarial transfer learning network for machinery emerging fault detection. IEEE Sens. J. **99**, 1 (2020)

Data Acquisition System for Energy Consumption Characteristics of Vibratory Rollers

Yulin Jiang, Guiqin Li$^{(\boxtimes)}$, Xin Xiong, and Bin He

Shanghai Key Laboratory of Intelligent Manufacturing and Robotics, Shanghai University,
Shanghai 200444, China
leeching@shu.edu.cn

Abstract. As a key construction machine in road construction, vibratory rollers play a vital role in the construction of highways, airports, ports, dykes and industrial building sites. With the rapid expansion of construction machinery ownership, the resulting environmental problems have become more and more prominent. In the background of "carbon neutral" era, the future development trend of construction machinery field will focus on energy saving and intelligence. The real-time and accurate collection of energy consumption data of vibratory rollers is the basis of energy saving and intelligence. In this paper, we study a data collection system for energy consumption characteristics of vibratory rollers, which is divided into two major parts: hardware and software. The hardware is the edge-end device, responsible for real-time data acquisition, and the software system visualizes and stores these data in real time.

Keywords: Vibratory rollers · Data acquisition · Energy saving · Hydraulic system · Vibration system

1 Introduction

Non-road mobile sources include railroad internal combustion locomotives, ships, construction machinery, agricultural machinery, aircraft, etc. Taking three emission indicators of hydrocarbons (HC), nitrogen oxides (NOx) and particulate matter (PM) as examples, as shown in Fig. 1. The emission contribution of construction machinery accounts for a large proportion of the multiple non-road mobile sources.

Construction machinery, including excavators, loaders, rollers and a dozen other machinery, with the rapid expansion of construction machinery holdings, the resulting environmental problems more and more prominent.

As a key construction machine in road construction, vibratory rollers play a crucial role in highways [1], embankments [2], municipal constructions [3] and construction site construction [4]. At home and abroad, a lot of research has been conducted on vibratory rollers in terms of dynamic response [5], compaction quality evaluation system [6], dynamic response of excitation system [7] and path tracking control [8] and the compaction performance of vibratory rollers has been greatly improved, but relatively little

H. Yang et al. (Eds.): ICIRA 2023, LNAI 14271, pp. 26–36, 2023.
https://doi.org/10.1007/978-981-99-6495-6_3

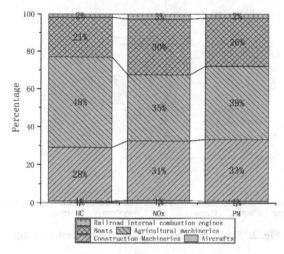

Fig. 1. Contribution rate of emissions from non-road mobile sources

research has been conducted on energy saving and consumption reduction of vibratory rollers, and data collection of energy consumption characteristics is very important.

Komatsu Corporation has developed Komtrax (Komatsu Tracking System) for general construction machinery and VHMS (Vehicle Health Monitoring System) for mining equipment [9]. Jonathan Downey et al. present a data acquisition system consisting of multiple sensors for acoustic emission, cutting force and vibration data from machine tools in a real-time production environment, along with automatic image acquisition [10]. Rowe et al. proposed an intelligent crane monitoring system to control the safe operation of cranes by monitoring crane operation data [11]. Humberto Henao et al. analyze and detect wire rope failures in crane winch systems by monitoring motor torque and current characteristics to avoid safety problems [12]. Donghai Liu et al. designed a cyber-physical system for collaborative control of multiple rollers, which can analyze and monitor the compaction parameters of each roller [13]. Jianwei Leng et al. developed a monitoring and management system for overhead cranes, where various parameters in the system can be set by the client computer to enhance the communication function between machines and equipment [14].

This paper studies a data acquisition system for energy consumption characteristics of vibratory rollers, using a combination of hardware and software to realize real-time data acquisition, visualization and storage.

2   Analysis of Energy Consumption Characteristics

The object of this research is a 26.5t fully hydraulic type double-drive single drum vibratory roller, whose structure schematic diagram is shown in Fig. 2.

The model vibratory roller is mainly composed of power system, hydraulic system, electrical system, and other parts. The main hydraulic components of the hydraulic system are hydraulic pump, hydraulic valve, hydraulic motor hydraulic cylinder and so on.

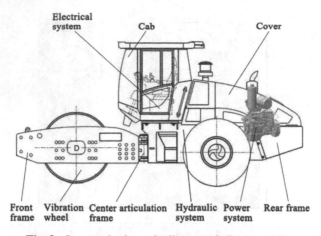

Fig. 2. Structural schematic diagram of vibratory roller

Hydraulic drive pump, hydraulic vibration pump and hydraulic steering pump 3 pumps through couplings in series on the same engine torque output shaft, to achieve the same speed rotation. The hydraulic pump will get the mechanical energy from the engine into the hydraulic energy of the hydraulic system, through the oil circuit and hydraulic valve transmission to the hydraulic cylinder, hydraulic motor and other executive components, again into mechanical energy to provide power for the vibratory road roller work devices.

2.1 Hydraulic System

The hydraulic drive system is a closed hydraulic drive system composed of a variable pump and a variable motor. The components in the system cooperate to complete the transmission and control of hydraulic energy. The driving pump is an axial piston variable displacement pump, and the displacement is adjusted by adjusting the angle of the swash plate. The hydraulic vibration system is a closed hydraulic system composed of an axial piston variable pump and an axial piston quantitative motor, and is equipped with dual-frequency, dual-amplitude exciting forces. The oil flow direction of the variable pump changes with the change of the angle of the swash plate. When the direction changes, the output shaft of the hydraulic motor realizes forward and reverse switching, resulting in two vibration frequencies. Steering is rarely used in the actual operation process, and it is generally compacted in a straight line. Steering is generally used for fine-tuning the direction, changing the operating route, and transferring the site. The steering hydraulic system is controlled by a combination of two single-rod double-acting cylinders.

2.2 Vibration Mechanical System

The core of the vibration mechanism is the eccentric block mechanism, as shown in Fig. 3. When the vibratory roller turns on the vibration mode, the eccentric block rotates to generate an exciting force and transmits it to the vibrating wheel, and the vibrating wheel contacts the ground again, so that the compacted ground is hit harder and the soil becomes more compacted.

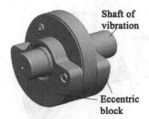

Fig. 3. Vibrating eccentric block mechanism

The exciting force F_e generated by the eccentric block is the component force of the centrifugal force generated when it rotates in the direction vertical to the ground, and the expression is as follows:

$$F_e = F_0 \sin \omega_e t \tag{1}$$

In the above equation, F_0 is the amplitude of the excitation force, that is, the centrifugal force; ω_e is the rotational angular velocity of the eccentric block.

2.3 Energy Flow Analysis

The energy loss of the vibratory roller mainly occurs in the hydraulic system and the mechanical system, mainly including mechanical energy loss, pipeline pressure loss, component efficiency loss, overflow loss, and improper engine-hydraulic pump power matching loss.

The energy transfer process of the vibratory roller is shown in Fig. 4.

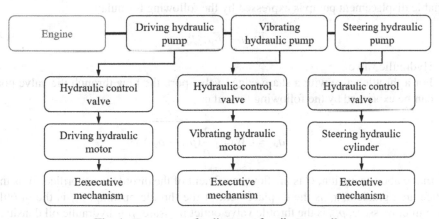

Fig. 4. Energy transfer diagram of a vibratory roller

During the operation of the vibratory roller, as shown in Fig. 5, it can be seen that the proportion of driving power and vibration power is relatively high, so this paper mainly collects the energy consumption characteristic data of the drive system and vibration system.

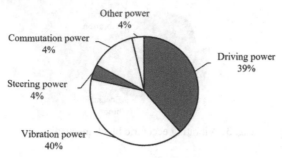

Fig. 5. The proportion of each power consumption

3   Mathematical Model

3.1   Mathematical Model of Hydraulic Components

(1) Variable pump

The torque balance equation of the variable displacement pump is expressed by the following formula:

$$T_{pin} - T_{pout} = J_p \frac{d\omega_p}{dt} + B_p \omega_p + T_{fp} \qquad (2)$$

In the above equation, T_{pin} is the output torque of the diesel engine, T_{pout} is the load torque of the variable displacement pump, J_p is the moment of inertia of the variable displacement pump, B_p is the damping coefficient of the variable pump, T_{fp} is the friction torque on the variable displacement pump. Among them, the load moment T_{pout} of the variable displacement pump is expressed by the following formula:

$$T_{pout} = K_p \gamma_p p_p \qquad (3)$$

(2) Hydraulic valve

For a throttle valve with a sharp-edged valve port, the flow through the valve port can be expressed by the following formula:

$$q_v = CWx_v \sqrt{\frac{2}{\rho}(p_{vi} - p_{vo})} \qquad (4)$$

In the above equation, C is the flow coefficient of the throttle valve orifice, W is the orifice area gradient, x_v is the displacement of the throttle opening, p_{vi} is the throttle valve inlet pressure, p_{vo} is the throttle valve outlet pressure, ρ is hydraulic oil density.

(3) Variable motor

The torque balance equation of the variable motor is:

$$T_{vmin} - T_{vmout} = J_{vm} \frac{d\omega_{vm}}{dt} + B_{vm} \omega_{vm} + T_{fvm} \qquad (5)$$

In the above equation, T_{vmin} is the input torque of the variable motor, T_{vmout} is the output torque of the variable motor, J_{vm} is the moment of inertia of the variable motor, B_{vm} is the variable motor damping coefficient, T_{fvm} is the friction torque on the variable motor. Among them, the load torque T_{vmout} of the variable motor is expressed as follows:

$$T_{vmin} = K_{vm} \gamma_{vm} P_{vm} \tag{6}$$

3.2 Mathematical Model of the Vibration Module

As shown in Fig. 6. The frame-steel wheel-vibrating soil model is shown, where m_1, m_2, and m_3 are the masses of the frame, vibrating wheel, and vibrating soil respectively, and the frame and vibrating wheel are connected by a shock absorber; x_1, x_2, and x_3 are the vibration displacements of the frame, steel wheel, and vibration-accompanied soil, respectively, and when there is no vibration jump, $x_2 = x_3$; k_1, k_3 are the composite stiffnesses of the shock absorber and the vibration-accompanied soil; c_1, c_3 are The damping of the shock absorber and the soil with vibration; F_e is the exciting force generated by the eccentric block, which is a sinusoidal function, denoted as:

$$F_e = F_0 \sin \omega_e t \tag{7}$$

F_0 is the amplitude of the exciting force, and ω_e is the rotational angular velocity of the eccentric block.

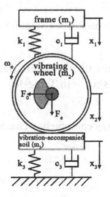

Fig. 6. Frame-steel wheel-vibration-accompanied soil dynamics model

The vibrating wheel is affected by multiple forces, namely gravity, the elastic force and damping force of the rubber shock absorber, the exciting force of the vibrating wheel and the contact force between the vibrating wheel and the soil. When the vibrating wheel is in contact with the vibrating soil, the vibration of the system should take into account the parasitic vibration effect of the soil, and the dynamic equation can be expressed as:

$$(m_2 + m_3)\ddot{x}_2 + c_1(\dot{x}_2 - \dot{x}_1) + k_1(x_2 - x_1) = F_e + (m_2 + m_3)g \tag{8}$$

It can be seen from formula (8) that the factors that affect the change of exciting force are: 1. The mass of the vibrating wheel and the soil with vibration; 2. The damping and composite stiffness of the shock absorber; 3. The frame and vibration The displacement of the wheel and the vibration acceleration of the vibrating wheel. And only vibration acceleration needs to be measured with a sensor.

4   Data Acquisition of Energy Consumption Characteristics

4.1   Data Acquisition Scheme

In practical engineering of vibratory rollers, the drive system and vibration system account for the largest proportion of power consumption. Its energy consumption characteristic parameters mainly include the following components: engine, hydraulic main pump, hydraulic motor, vibration wheel mechanism. A complete set of data acquisition system is constructed to ensure the smooth acquisition of energy consumption characteristic data of vibratory rollers. The system includes Sensors, Data Acquisition Instruments (DAI) and Computer equipment, etc. The architecture is shown in Fig. 7.

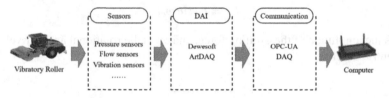

Fig. 7. Data acquisition system architecture

Through the above analysis, the characteristic data of energy consumption of the vibratory roller are determined as shown in Table 1.

Table 1. Energy consumption characteristic data

Data		Sensors	Signal type
hydraulic pump pressure		pressure sensors	analog
hydraulic pump flow		flow sensors	digital
hydraulic motor pressure		pressure sensors	analog
hydraulic motor flow		flow sensors	digital
drain flow		flow sensors	digital
vibration Acceleration		vibration sensors	analog
CAN	engine	rotating speed, fuel consumption, torque, load
	hydraulic system	control current of drive pump and vibration pump

Table 2. Detailed parameters of the sensor

Num.	Sensors	Range	Quantity	Output
1	pressure sensors	0–600bar	10	0–10 V
2	pressure sensors	0–60bar	6	0–10 V
3	flow sensors (42MPa)	9–300 L/min	4	frequency
4	flow sensors (42MPa)	15–600 L/min	3	frequency
5	vibration sensors	±50g	1	frequency
6	CAN	——	1	CAN

Details such as the type and quantity of the determined sensors are shown in Table 2. The sensor layout is shown in Fig. 8.

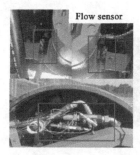 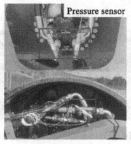 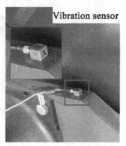

(a) Flow sensor layout

(b) Pressure sensor layout

(c) Vibration sensor layout

Fig. 8. Sensor layout

When the above sensors collect data, the output is the electrical signal corresponding to the actual data, and what is ultimately needed is the actual data, which requires the use of a data acquisition instrument to achieve signal conversion. The conversion process is shown in Fig. 9.

The data acquisition instrument (DAI) used in this paper is DEWEsoft integrated data acquisition instrument, which includes signal conditioning digital-to-analog conversion function, and can simultaneously acquire multi-channel and multi-type signals. The data acquisition hardware system of DEWEsoft is SIRIUS series.

According to the number of channels such as analog quantity, CAN bus and digital quantity in this project, the SIRIUS data acquisition system established initially adopts 2 pieces of data acquisition modules, including 24 channels Voltage/full bridge +8-channel frequency (digital) +2-channel CAN data acquisition (video signal). The data acquisition modules are connected by synchronous lines to realize the synchronous transmission of sampling data.

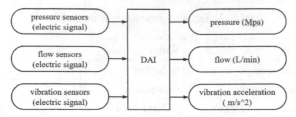

Fig. 9. DAI A/D conversion

4.2 Data Acquisition Working Condition

When collecting the energy consumption characteristic parameters of the vibratory roller, the OPC-UA (OLE for Process Control-Unified Architecture) communication protocol is used between the data logger and the edge device for data communication, and the sampling frequency is set to 500 Hz. The data acquisition instrument is shown in Fig. 10.

Fig. 10. Data acquisition instrument

According to the working characteristics of the vibratory roller, formulate the working conditions for collecting energy consumption characteristic data.

Working Condition 1: First turn on the data acquisition equipment, then start the engine, without walking or vibrating, and collect for 30 s.

Working Condition 2: Set the displacement of the hydraulic motor according to the compaction speed, and compact the road surface of the test site for 2 cycles according to the speed, with one cycle of forward compaction and one backward compaction. The test time of this working condition is about 120 s.

Working Condition 3: Set the displacement of the hydraulic motor according to the compaction operation speed, and perform 2 cycles of compaction according to the speed as described in working condition 2, and turn on the small vibration mode at the same time. The test time at this stage is about 120. The test time of this working condition is about 240 s.

Working Condition 4: Set the displacement of the hydraulic motor according to the transfer speed, and move forward and backward according to the speed for 30s each. The test time of this working condition is about 60 s.

Working Condition 5: The vehicle stops driving, the vibration is turned off, the engine is turned off, and the test is over. Among them, working condition 3 was tested twice separately.

The collected characteristic data of energy consumption of the vibratory roller are shown in Fig. 11.

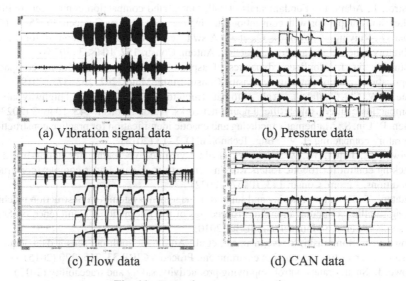

(a) Vibration signal data   (b) Pressure data

(c) Flow data   (d) CAN data

Fig. 11. Data of energy consumption

Therefore, the required characteristic data collection can be completed through the constructed vibratory roller energy consumption characteristic data collection platform.

5   Conclusion

This study analyzes the energy consumption characteristics of the vibratory roller, establishes the mathematical model of the hydraulic components and vibration modules, and determines that the hydraulic components mainly collect pressure, flow and vibration acceleration data of the vibrating wheel. After determining the energy consumption characteristic data to be collected and the required sensors and data acquisition instruments, a complete set of energy consumption characteristic data acquisition system for vibratory rollers is constructed. The system can collect the energy consumption characteristic data of vibratory rollers in real time and Data are visualized and saved on the software.

Acknowledgement. This research is partly supported by the National Key Research & Development Program of China (grant No. 2020YFB1709902).

References

1. Liu, D., Chen, J., Li, S.: Collaborative operation and real-time control of roller fleet for asphalt pavement compaction. Automa. Constr. **98**, 16–29 (2019)
2. Zhong, D., Li, X., Cui, B., et al.: Technology and application of real-time compaction quality monitoring for earth-rockfill dam construction in deep narrow valley. Autom. Constr. **90**, 23–38 (2018)
3. Pistrol, J., Adam, D.: Fundamentals of roller integrated compaction control for oscillatory rollers and comparison with conventional testing methods. Transp. Geotech. **17**, 75–84 (2018)
4. Yuan, J., Ruiying, Z., Ye-Hwa, C., et al.: A switched servo constraints control for the smart vibratory roller in unmanned compaction. Autom. Constr. **152**, 104883 (2023)
5. Wan, Y., Jia, J.: Nonlinear dynamics of asphalt–screed interaction during compaction: application to improving paving density. Constr. Build. Mater. **202**, 363–373 (2019)
6. Xuefei, W., Chi, C., Jiale, L., et al.: Automated monitoring and evaluation of highway subgrade compaction quality using artificial neural networks. Autom. Constr. **145**, 104663 (2023)
7. Shen, P., Lin, S.: Mathematic modeling and chaotic identification for practice construction in vibratory compacting. J. Vib. Eng. Technol. **6**(1), 1–13 (2018)
8. Shiwei, G., Jiajun, W., Xiaoling, W., et al.: Dynamic hyperparameter tuning-based path tracking control for robotic rollers working on earth-rock dam under complex construction conditions. Autom. Constr. **143**, 104576 (2022)
9. Kitatani, T.: Global monitoring and support management system for construction machinery using satellite communication. In: Proceedings of the International Conference on Service Systems & Service Management. IEEE (2010)
10. Downey, J., Bombiński, S., Nejman, M., et al.: Automatic multiple sensor data acquisition system in a real-time production environment. Procedia CIRP **33**, 215–220 (2015)
11. Rowe, J.: Smart crane control-improving productivity, safety and traceability (2012)
12. Henao, H., Fatemi, R., et al.: Wire rope fault detection in a hoisting winch system by motor torque and current signature analysis. IEEE Trans. Ind. Electron. **58**(5), 1727–1736 (2011)
13. Liu, D., Chen, J., Li, S.: Collaborative operation and real-time control of roller fleet for asphalt pavement compaction. Autom. Constr. **98**, 16–29 (2019)
14. Leng, J.W., Man, B.: Bridge crane monitoring and management control system. Appl. Mech. Mater. **644**, 693–696 (2014)

Robotic Tactile Sensation, Perception, and Applications

FBG Tactile Sensor Integrated on Bronchoscope for Force and Contact Position Sensing

Yingxuan Zhang, Qi Jiang$^{(\boxtimes)}$, Feiwen Wang, and Jie Wang

School of Control Science and Engineering, Shandong University, Jinan 210016, China
jiangqi@sdu.edu.cn

Abstract. During the transbronchial lung biopsy (TBLB), the bronchoscope may easily collide with the airway, which can cause damage. In order to improve the safety of the surgery, this paper puts forward a tactile sensor integrated at the end of the flexible bronchoscope. It can be used to detect the radial force, axial force and contact position of the bronchoscope when it enters the airway. The sensor is sandwich design, with 4 fiber Bragg grating (FBG) arranged in the middle flexible layer. Through theoretical analysis and simulation verification, it is obtained that the radial force and axial force are proportional to the change of FBG wavelength. And the contact position can be obtained from the relationship between the FBG wavelength variation. It is proved that the proposed sensor can be used for the force and position detection. It lays a foundation for the safe control of clinical bronchoscopy.

Keywords: Tactile Sensor · Bronchoscope · Force and Contact Position Sensing

1 Introduction

Transbronchial lung biopsy (TBLB) plays a significant role in judging tuberculosis, lung cancer, etc. However, during the process of bronchoscope insertion, it will inevitably collide with the tracheal wall, resulting in accidental bleeding. Existing bronchoscope devices cannot sense the contact force. Therefore, in order to ensure the safety of bronchoscopy, tactile sensing devices should be integrated [1].

Generally, the tactile sensing device can be mounted on the instrument installation interface, the wrist of the manipulator, the driving mechanism, the end of the instrument, etc. Although the sensor placed outside the body has lower requirements on size and insulation, it is more likely to lead to inaccurate results. The sensor integrated at the end of the instrument is often more accurate because it interacts directly with the tissue. Sensitive elements such as strain gauge [2], piezoresistive [3, 4], capacitance [5], piezoelectric [6] and optical fiber [8, 9] are often used. Nagatomo T et al. propose a tactile sensor based on strain gauge [2], which obtains information of contact forces in different directions by measuring 4 resistance changes. Jin et al. improve the safety of the robot-assisted system by equipping the cardiac catheter with a force sensor with pressure-sensitive rubber [4], which can detect the collision between the tip of the catheter and blood vessels. Kim U et al. propose a 6-axis capacitive micro force/moment sensor for robot-assisted

H. Yang et al. (Eds.): ICIRA 2023, LNAI 14271, pp. 39–50, 2023.
https://doi.org/10.1007/978-981-99-6495-6_4

minimally invasive surgery with simple structure and high durability [5]. Shaikh M O et al. propose a pen-like tactile sensor for palpation of oral cancer [6]. Piezoelectric film is used as the sensitive element, and the hardness information of tissue under contact can be obtained by piezoelectric effect. However, the above sensors are vulnerable to electromagnetic interference due to their activeness, which limits their clinical application [7]. As a passive component, optical fiber is increasingly used in surgical robots. Lai W et al. proposed a fiber-based triaxial force sensor [8] that can be integrated into the surgical arm for the clamp force perception. 3 fiber Bragg gratings (FBG) are embedded in the sensing structure to measure the tension and lateral forces. Du C et al. present an x-perca force sensing kit [9] that can be deployed in laparoscopic surgical robots. Triaxial force sensing with temperature compensation and dual-wire mechanism is achieved by combining a 3D-printed biocompatible joint design with 6 FBG layouts. At present, most of the related research focuses on the force sensing integrated with forceps and other instruments, and has not been integrated into the endoscope body for the force sensing between the instrument and tracheal walls.

In order to accurately perceive the contact force, this paper proposes a tactile sensor integrated at the end of the flexible bronchoscope, which can be used to detect the radial force, axial force and contact position of the bronchoscope in contact with the tracheal wall. The sensor is sandwich design, and 4 FBGs are arranged in the middle flexible layer. Through theoretical analysis and simulation verification, relationships between radial force, axial force, contact position and FBG wavelength variation are obtained, which proves the sensor's ability to detect force and contact position.

2 Structure of the Tactile Sensor

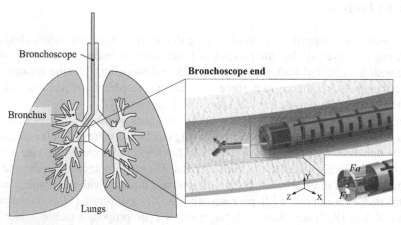

Fig. 1. Overview of the tactile sensor integrated on the bronchoscope.

The contact force that a bronchoscope may receive when it enters the bronchus is often composed of an axial force F_a caused by contact and friction and a radial force F_r, as both are the reaction forces generated by the sidewall of trachea on the bronchoscope when it comes into contact with the sidewall of trachea. The two forces often coexist and act on the same position of the sensor, as shown in Fig. 1. Based on the clinical application and demand, a small FBG tactile sensor integrated at the end of bronchoscope is designed, as shown in Fig. 1 and Fig. 2(a). The sensor can be integrated into the end of a flexible or rigid bronchoscope with an external diameter of only 6 mm, and allows lens, lights and biopsy tools to be passed through. The function of the existing bronchoscope is preserved to the maximum extent, and FBGs are embedded to detect the magnitude of contact force and contact position. Although the symmetrical arrangement of optical fibers is more intuitive and common, due to the structural limitations of the endoscope itself, the arrangement as shown in Fig. 2(c) is adopted.

The sensor is sandwich design, as shown in Fig. 2(b), composing of 3 layers, the end cover, PDMS deformable layer and the intermediate plate. 4 suspension FBGs are arranged in the middle flexible layer. In order to reduce friction and improve sensor sensitivity, the optical fiber adopts hanging arrangement instead of embedding in the flexible layer. The actual sensor integrated on the bronchoscope end is shown in Fig. 2(d).

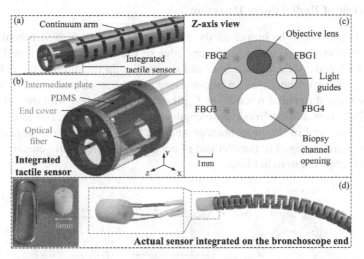

Fig. 2. (a) Overview of the bronchoscope with integrated tactile sensor (b) the integrated tactile sensor (c) Z-axis view of the sensor (d) actual sensor integrated on the bronchoscope end.

3   Detection Principle

FBG is sensitive to parameters that can cause its wavelength to change, such as strain, temperature, bending. Therefore, when an external force applies on the sensor, the middle flexible layer is deformed, driving the internal fiber strain. The position and magnitude of the force can be calculated by the different wavelength changes of the FBGs.

When the light from the wideband source is injected into the fiber, the specific Bragg wavelength is reflected, and the conditions are as follows [10]:

$$\lambda = 2n_{eff}\Lambda \tag{1}$$

where λ is the reflected Bragg wavelength, n_{eff} is the effective index of the fiber core, and Λ is the periodicity of the refractive index variation.

When the grating periodicity or effective refractive index of the core changes due to perturbation of FBG, the reflected Bragg wavelength also changes. The relationship between variation and strain and temperature is shown in Eq. (2) [11]:

$$\frac{\Delta\lambda}{\lambda} = \varepsilon\left\{1 - 0.5n_{eff}^2\left[p_{12} - v(p_{11} + p_{12})\right]\right\} + \zeta\Delta T \tag{2}$$

where $\Delta\lambda$ is the Bragg wavelength shift, p_{ij} is the strain-optic coefficients, v is the Poisson's ratio, ε is the induced fiber axial strain, ζ is the thermos-optic coefficient, and ΔT is the temperature shift.

Since the change of wavelength has a linear relationship with the change of temperature, it can be compensated in actual use, so the influence of the temperature is expressed in his paper.

3.1 Principle of Radial Force Detection

When the scope enters the bronchus, the end edge first contacts the tracheal wall, so in this discussion, the force acts on the end edge of the sensor, as shown in the Fig. 3. By fixing both ends of the optical fiber and suspending in the middle, the radial force on the end of the bronchoscope can be converted into the axial tensile strain. When the sensor is subjected to radial force F_x or F_y, the fiber is stretched with the deformation of the flexible layer, and the Bragg wavelength changes accordingly. Because the sensor integrated at the end of the bronchoscope and the flexible layer are cylindrical, the 4 optical fibers are arranged in parallel and of equal length, they will generate the same strain when subjected to radial force.

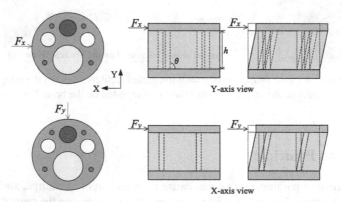

Fig. 3. Deformation of the sensor under the radical force.

Tensile strain ε_i (i = 1, 2, 3, 4) of the fiber can be expressed as:

$$\varepsilon_i = \frac{\text{enlongation of the fiber}}{\text{original lenth of the fiber}} = \frac{\Delta f}{h} = \frac{F_r \cos\theta}{(k_m + k_f \cos^2\theta)h} = a_0 F_r, (i = 1, 2, 3, 4) \tag{3}$$

where $\Delta f = \Delta f_1 = \Delta f_2 = \Delta f_3 = \Delta f_4$, F_r is the applied radical force, k_m is the stiffness of the flexible layer matrix, k_f is the stiffness of the fiber, the angle θ indicates the angle between the fiber and the PDMS layer, $a_0 = \frac{\cos\theta}{(k_m + k_f \cos^2\theta)h}$ is constant.

Substitute Eq. (3) into Eq. (2) to obtain the relationship between wavelength variation, force F_r and sensor parameters:

$$\frac{\Delta\lambda_r}{\lambda_r} = \frac{\cos\theta\left\{1 - 0.5n_{eff}^2\left[p_{12} - \nu(p_{11} + p_{12})\right]\right\}}{(k_m + k_f \cos^2\theta)h} \times F_r = aF_r \qquad (4)$$

where, $\frac{\Delta\lambda_r}{\lambda_r}$ is the wavelength change of FBG under the radial force F_r, and $a = \frac{\cos\theta\left\{1 - 0.5n_{eff}^2\left[p_{12} - \nu(p_{11} + p_{12})\right]\right\}}{(k_m + k_f \cos^2\theta)h}$ is a constant.

It can be seen that the wavelength variation is related to the external force F_r, the optical fiber sticking angle θ, the thickness of the flexible layer h and the hardness k_m. When the sensor parameter is constant, there is a linear relationship between the change of wavelength shift and F_r.

The change of wavelength also reflects the sensitivity of the sensor. Under the same radial force, the larger the change of wavelength, the higher the sensitivity. The sensitivity can be improved by the selection of structural parameters. Since the optical fiber hardness k_f is much larger than the PDMS layer hardness k_m, the wavelength variation is positively correlated to θ. And the maximum θ value is 90°, that is, the vertical arrangement. The wavelength variation is positively correlated with the thickness h. But thicker flexible layers can cause the end of the bronchoscope to become less stable and controllable. Overall, the thickness $h = 5$ mm is selected. The wavelength variation is negatively correlated with the hardness k_m of the flexible layer. But the low hardness can cause the end of the bronchoscope to destabilize, and may also cause damage to the internal fibers. In addition, the hardness of bronchus is about 0.8–1.4 MPa (22 ha–35 ha), and the sensitive layer that is similar to the tissue hardness can be selected to make the detection range close to the actual biological tissue hardness [12]. Therefore, the flexible layer with a hardness of 30 ha is selected.

3.2 Principle of Axial Force and Contact Position Detection

Since the contact force between the bronchoscope and the trachea wall is located at the edge of the end of the bronchoscope, the theoretical model of the axial force applied to the edge of the sensor is analyzed. As shown in Fig. 4, FBGs are strained when the sensor is subjected to an axial force F_z. The FBGs near the stress point undergo compression deformation and the FBGs far away from it undergo tensile deformation. Their deformation amounts are different from each other (except for the position of symmetry).

The axial compressive/tensile strain ε_i (i = 1, 2, 3, 4) of FBG can be expressed as:

$$\varepsilon_i = \frac{F_{ai}}{k_m} = b\frac{d_i}{k_m} \times F_a \qquad (5)$$

where, F_{ai} is the actual effective force of axial force F_a at FBG_i, d_i is the radial distance between FBG_i and the stress point, and b is the constant coefficient related to the sensor material.

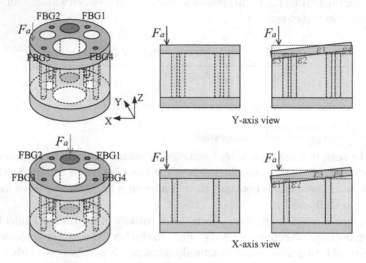

Fig. 4. Deformation of the sensor under the axial force.

It can be seen that the axial strain ε_i of the fiber is linearly related to the axial force F_a when the stress position is selected. The strain is also related to the stress position. As shown in Fig. 5, when the eccentric axial force F_a acts on point A at the edge of the sensor, the sensor as a whole overturns around the neutral axis. The distance between the projection of FBG on the cross-section a-a perpendicular to the central axis where F_a is located and point A is d_1, d_2, d_3 and d_4, respectively. When the force F_a is constant, the strain ε_i of FBG is positively correlated with the distance d_i.

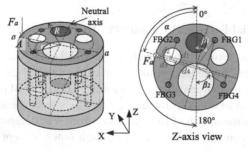

Fig. 5. Relationship between position of force F_a and distance d_i.

Because the sensor is symmetrical, only the left part is analyzed. When the stress position A changes from $0°$ to $180°$ as shown in Fig. 5, the relationship between distance d_i and point A (represented by angle α) is arranged as Eq. (6) according to the triangular relationship:

$$d_1 = R - r \cdot cos(\beta_1 + \alpha)$$
$$d_2 = R - r \cdot cos(\beta_1 - \alpha)$$
$$d_3 = R + r \cdot cos(\beta_2 + \alpha)$$
$$d_4 = R + r \cdot cos(\beta_2 - \alpha)$$

(6)

where R is the radius of the sensor, r is the radius of the circle where FBGs are located, β_1 is the angle between FBG1(FBG2) and $0°$, β_2 is the angle between FBG3(FBG4) and $180°$, α is the angle between the point A and $0°$.

Substituting Eq. (6) into (5) and (2):

$$\frac{\Delta\lambda_{a1}}{\lambda_{a1}} = \frac{b[R - r \cdot cos(\beta_1 + \alpha)]\left\{1 - 0.5n_{eff}^2\left[p_{12} - \nu(p_{11} + p_{12})\right]\right\}}{k_m} \times F_a = c[R - r \cdot cos(\beta_1 + \alpha)]F_a$$

$$\frac{\Delta\lambda_{a2}}{\lambda_{a2}} = \frac{b[R - r \cdot cos(\beta_1 - \alpha)]\left\{1 - 0.5n_{eff}^2\left[p_{12} - \nu(p_{11} + p_{12})\right]\right\}}{k_m} \times F_a = c[R - r \cdot cos(\beta_1 - \alpha)]F_a$$

$$\frac{\Delta\lambda_{a3}}{\lambda_{a3}} = \frac{b[R + r \cdot cos(\beta_2 + \alpha)]\left\{1 - 0.5n_{eff}^2\left[p_{12} - \nu(p_{11} + p_{12})\right]\right\}}{k_m} \times F_a = c[R + r \cdot cos(\beta_2 + \alpha)]F_a$$

$$\frac{\Delta\lambda_{a4}}{\lambda_{a4}} = \frac{b[R + r \cdot cos(\beta_2 - \alpha)]\left\{1 - 0.5n_{eff}^2\left[p_{12} - \nu(p_{11} + p_{12})\right]\right\}}{k_m} \times F_a = c[R + r \cdot cos(\beta_2 - \alpha)]F_a$$

(7)

where, $\frac{\Delta\lambda_{ai}}{\lambda_{ai}}$ ($i = 1, 2, 3, 4$) represents the wavelength variation of the 4 FBGs under axial force and $c = \frac{b\left\{1 - 0.5n_{eff}^2\left[p_{12} - \nu(p_{11} + p_{12})\right]\right\}}{k_m}$ is a constant.

When F_a is constant, the relationship between wavelength variation of each FBG and position α of force is visualized as shown in Fig. 6. It can be seen that when α changes at $[0°, 360°]$, the wavelength changes of the 2 FBGs closest to the stress point are the smallest. And the stress position can be preliminarily determined by the relationship between the wavelength changes. The difference of FBG wavelength variation changes with α, and the proportion of the them nearly linearly with α. This ratio is defined as W, $W = \frac{\frac{\Delta\lambda_i}{\lambda_i} - \frac{\Delta\lambda_j}{\lambda_j}}{\frac{\Delta\lambda_k}{\lambda_k} - \frac{\Delta\lambda_g}{\lambda_g}}$ ($i, j, k, g = 1, 2, 3, 4$), as shown in Fig. 6 ($i = 2, j = 1, k = 4, g = 2$).

When the sensor is subjected to combining force (axial force and radial force), the wavelength change is expressed as:

$$\frac{\Delta\lambda_i}{\lambda_i} = \frac{\Delta\lambda_r}{\lambda_r} + \frac{\Delta\lambda_{ai}}{\lambda_{ai}} = aF_r + cF_{ai} = \begin{cases} aF_r + c[R - r \cdot cos(\beta_1 + \alpha)]F_a, i = 1 \\ aF_r + c[R - r \cdot cos(\beta_1 - \alpha)]F_a, i = 2 \\ aF_r + c[R + r \cdot cos(\beta_2 + \alpha)]F_a, i = 3 \\ aF_r + c[R + r \cdot cos(\beta_2 - \alpha)]F_a, i = 4 \end{cases}$$

(8)

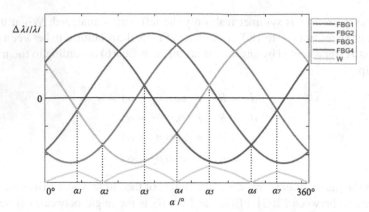

Fig. 6. Relation between wavelength variation and contact position under constant axial force. ($\alpha1 = 44°$, $\alpha2 = 79°$, $\alpha3 = 136°$, $\alpha4 = 180°$, $\alpha5 = 224°$, $\alpha6 = 281°$, $\alpha7 = 316°$)

The magnitude of axial force and radial force can only be calculated by obtaining the force position. Since the ratio W does not vary with the magnitude of forces, the exact contact position α can be obtained. Then, the values of radial force F_r and axial force F_a can be obtained by solving the Eq. (8):

$$F_r = \frac{R(\frac{\Delta\lambda_2}{\lambda_2} - \frac{\Delta\lambda_1}{\lambda_1}) + r[\frac{\Delta\lambda_1}{\lambda_1}\cos(\beta_1 - \alpha) - \frac{\Delta\lambda_2}{\lambda_2}\cos(\beta_1 + \alpha)]}{ra[\cos(\beta_1 - \alpha) - \cos(\beta_1 + \alpha)]}$$

$$F_a = \frac{\frac{\Delta\lambda_2}{\lambda_2} - \frac{\Delta\lambda_1}{\lambda_1}}{rc[\cos(\beta_1 + \alpha) - \cos(\beta_1 - \alpha)]} \qquad (9)$$

4 Verification of the Detection Ability

In order to verify the detection ability of the proposed sensor for radial force, axial force and contact position, static mechanical simulation of the sensor is carried out using finite element software.

4.1 Verification of Radial Force Detection

Firstly, the simulation of the sensor's radial force F_r detection is carried out, and the settings are shown in Fig. 7(a).

The intermediate plate and the end cover are set to stainless steel, the intermediate PDMS layer is set to mooney-rivlin flexible elastic material [13], and the optical fiber is set to quartz. The optical fibers do not contact the flexible layer, and other contact surfaces are set to bonding. The lower surface of the sensor is fixed and a 3N preload force is applied to the optical fiber. As examples, radial forces of 0–3N in X and Y directions and forces of 45° and 225° are applied to the upper surface of the sensor successively. Since the wavelength variation of FBG is proportional to the axial direction becoming εi, the z-direction strain of each fiber under different forces is recorded. The result is shown in Fig. 8.

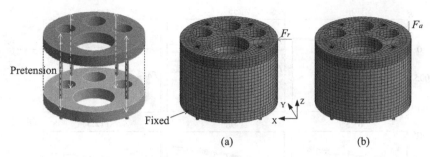

(a)   (b)

Fig. 7. Settings of simulation.

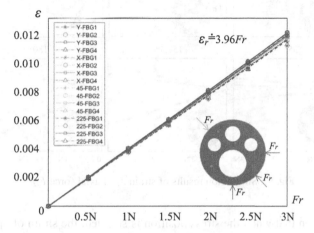

Fig. 8. Simulation results of strain ε_i and radical force F_r.

It can be seen that the effect of radial force has nothing to do with the position of the force, but only with the magnitude of the force. All of strains are linear with the radial force and have similar slope, which is consistent with the theoretical analysis. The fitting of the relationship between strain and radial force is as follows:

$$\varepsilon_{ri} = 3.96F_r, \ (i = 1, 2, 3, 4) \tag{10}$$

4.2 Verification of Axial Force Detection and Contact Position Detection

As shown in Fig. 7(b), an axial force of 0–3N is applied to the sensor, and the Z-direction strain of each fiber under different forces is recorded. The force point is shown in Fig. 9. A force point is taken at the outer edge of the upper surface of the sensor every 22.5°, so that the resolution is less than 1.2mm. Because the sensor is symmetrical, it is only analyzed in the range of 0°–180° on the left half. The relationship between strain and axial force is shown in Fig. 9.

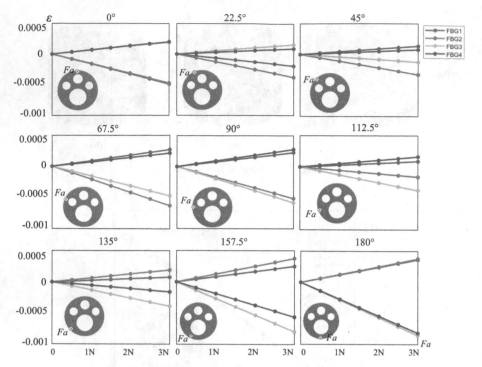

Fig. 9. Simulation results of strain ε_i of axial force F_a.

It can be seen that when the stress position is selected, the strain of optical fiber is linear with the axial force. A positive slope indicates the stretch length of the optical fiber, and a negative slope indicates that the optical fiber is compressed. The effect of axial force is related to the stress position, and the closer the fiber is to the stress point, the smaller the strain, which is consistent with the theory. The slopes are different at different stress positions.

The relationship between the strain under axial force and the stress position α at 1N is plotted as a curve shown in Fig. 10.

It can be seen that the strain of the 4 FBGs changes with the stress position. Since the strain is proportional to the change of wavelength, the trend and magnitude relationship of the wavelength variation are consistent with the theory. At 0° and 180°, FBG1 and FBG2, FBG3 and FBG4 are symmetric, so they have the same strain. However, in the simulation results, the position of the neutral axis with strain 0 is offset, which is considered to be affected by the elasticity and viscosity of the flexible layer. Since the determination of force position is not related to the absolute magnitude of strain, but only to the relative value, the neutral axis deviation has no influence on the calculation results. The stress position can be preliminarily judged by the relationship between wavelength variations, and then the exact position can be calculated by the ratio W. Then the corresponding axial force and radial force can be calculated by Eq. (9).

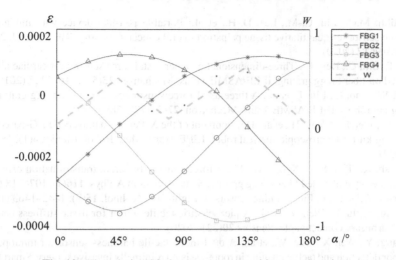

Fig. 10. The relationship between stress position α and strain ε_i

5 Conclusions

This paper proposes a tactile sensor integrated into the end of bronchoscope, which can be used to detect the radial force, axial force and contact position without affecting the use of bronchoscope imaging, lighting and biopsy tools. Through the relationship of wavelength variation of 4 FBGs under different force conditions, the contact position and force can be obtained. Through theoretical analysis and simulation verification, it is concluded that the radial force and axial force are proportional to the change of FBGs wavelength, and the contact position can be calculated by the magnitude relation of FBGs wavelength variation. The sensor is compatible with surgical instruments and integrated into the existing endoscope, which can reduce the learning time of the doctor. It can also be easily fused with the endoscope of the teleoperated surgical robot for force detection.

References

1. Juo, Y.Y., Abiri, A., Pensa, J., et al.: Center for advanced surgical and interventional technology multimodal haptic feedback for robotic surgery. In: Handbook of Robotic and Image- Guided Surgery, pp. 285–301 (2020)
2. Nagatomo, T., Miki, N.: A flexible tactile sensor to detect stiffness distribution without measuring displacement. In: International Conference on Solid-State Sensors, Actuators and Microsystems & Eurosensors XXXIII (Transducers & Eurosensors XXXIII), pp. 551–555 (2019)
3. Naidu, A.S., Patel, R.V., Naish, M.D.: Low-cost disposable tactile sensors for palpation in minimally invasive surgery. IEEE-ASME Trans. Mechatron. **22**(1), 127–137 (2017)
4. Jin, X., Guo, S., Guo, J., et al.: Total force analysis and safety enhancing for operating both guidewire and catheter in endovascular surgery. IEEE Sens. J. **21**(20), 22499–22509 (2021)
5. Kim, U., Kim, Y.B., Seok, D.-Y., et al.: A surgical palpation probe with 6-axis force/torque sensing capability for minimally invasive surgery. IEEE Trans. Ind. Electron. **65**(3), 2755–2765 (2018)

6. Shaikh, M.O., Lin, C.-M., Lee, D.-H., et al.: Portable pen-like device with miniaturized tactile sensor for quantitative tissue palpation in oral cancer screening. IEEE Sens. J. **20**(17), 9610–9617 (2020)

7. Li, T., Shi, C., Ren, H.: Three-dimensional catheter distal force sensing for cardiac ablation based on fiber bragg grating. IEEE/ASME Trans. Mechatron. **23**(5), 2316–2327 (2018)

8. Lai, W., Cao, L., Liu, J., et al.: A three-axial force sensor based on fiber bragg gratings for surgical robots. IEEE/ASME Trans. Mechatron. **27**(2), 777–789 (2022)

9. Du, C., Wei, D., Wang, H., et al.: Development of the X-Perce—a universal FBG-based force sensing kit for laparoscopic surgical robot. IEEE Trans. Med. Robot. Bionics **4**(1), 183–193 (2022)

10. Suresh, R., Tjin, S.C., Ngo, N.Q.: Shear force sensing by strain transformation using non-rectilinearly embedded fiber Bragg grating. Sens. Actuators A Phys. **116**(1), 107–118 (2004)

11. Kersey, A.D., et al.: Fiber grating sensors. J. Lightwave Technol. **15**(8), 1442–1463 (1997)

12. Zhang, Y., Ju, F., Wei, X., et al.: A piezoelectric tactile sensor for tissue stiffness detection with arbitrary contact angle. Sensors **20**(22) (2020)

13. Zhang, Y., Wei, X., Yue, W., et al.: A dual-mode tactile hardness sensor for intraoperative tumor detection and tactile imaging in robot-assisted minimally invasive surgery. Smart Mater. Struct. **30**(8) (2021)

Soft Humanoid Finger with Magnetic Tactile Perception

Xingyu Ding[1] , Jianhua Shan[1(✉)] , Ziwei Xia[2] , Fuchun Sun[3] ,

and Bin Fang[3(✉)]

[1] School of Mechanical Engineering, Anhui University of Technology, Ma'anshan, China
2931@ahut.edu.cn
[2] School of Engineering and Technology, China University of Geoscience, Beijing, China
xzw@email.cugb.edu.cn
[3] Department of Computer Science and Technology, Tsinghua University, Beijing, China
{fcsun,fangbin}@tsinghua.edu.cn

Abstract. The human skin is equipped with various receptors that sense external stimuli and provide tactile information to the body. Similarly, robots require sensors to perceive their environment and interact with it. Inspired by the bionics of human skin, we have developed a magnetic haptic tactile sensor that mimics the softness of the human finger skin. Our magnetic finger abdomen deforms when it comes in contact with an object, causing a change in magnetic flux density. The three-dimensional Hall sensor detects this change in magnetic field signal, allowing us to accurately measure the normal force applied to the sensor. There is a linear relationship between the z-axis magnetic field signal and the magnitude of the normal force ($R^2 > 0.988$). Our single bionic magnetic finger abdomen sensor has a Root Mean Squared Error of only 0.18N for the detection range of 0–10N, and force measurement accuracy of up to 95.5%. Our soft sensory skin is simple to manufacture, interchangeable, and customizable to meet the needs of haptic soft surfaces. Experimental results show that the sensor can accurately predict the normal force and the soft humanoid finger can stabilize the envelope grasp. This study provides a new idea for the design of magneto-tactile sensors, which is of great significance for the study of dexterous hand-grasping operations.

Keywords: Soft magnetic skin · Force sensing · Dexterous hand design

1 Introduction

As a fundamental part of the dexterous manipulation of robots [1–3], tactile sensors [4] play a key role in endowing robots human tactile perception [5–10], enabling precise manipulation, intelligent feedback, and control [11]. Traditional rigid tactile sensors such as piezoresistive [12], capacitive [13], etc., have been widely used in robot

This work was supported by the National Natural Science Foundation of China (Grant No. 62173197, U22B2042), Tsinghua University Initiative Scientific Research Program with 2022Z11QYJ002 and the Anhui Provincial Natural Science Foundation of China(Grant no. 2108085MF224).

grasping manipulation [14], such as texture detection, slip feedback, and fine control. However, due to their structural limitations, rigid sensors have low mechanical damping, making it difficult to adapt to complex and changing contact surfaces. This can result in incomplete contact with the object and an inability to collect complete contact information. Although rigid sensors can detect high-frequency dynamic stimuli with high sensitivity, their inability to adapt to varying surfaces can limit their effectiveness in certain robotic applications.

Flexible tactile sensors have the advantage of being able to adapt to different shapes of interacting surfaces due to their soft substrate and large deformability. However, traditional inorganic electronic materials are unable to meet the requirements of high mechanical flexibility due to their rigid characteristics. Advances in flexible and even stretchable materials, such as substrate materials and active materials, have made it possible to manufacture large-area flexible tactile sensors. One is substrate materials [15]. The substrate material, although not directly contributing to the sensing function, determines the flexibility of the tactile sensor. Conventional tactile sensors have used silicon, ceramic, and glass as substrates, but these materials are fragile, lack flexibility, and are not stretchable, limiting the flexibility required for tactile sensors to meet the actual operation. However, substrates such as polydimethylsiloxane (PDMS), polyurethane (Puu), and even paper and silk fibers have been developed for flexible tactile sensors, all of which show good performance and promise. In addition to the substrate material, the active layer needs to have excellent mechanical properties to meet the requirements of high-performance sensor devices. Carbon nanotubes (CNTs), graphene, hydrogels, and ionic gels have shown good cyclic stability, and high stretchability, and can detect deformation over a large and wide strain range. These active materials have great potential in the development of flexible tactile sensors that can provide accurate feedback for precise manipulation and control in robotics.

Soft tactile sensors that use multiple conduction methods face common barriers to scalability, such as complex manufacturing and integration techniques [8, 16–18], material and fluid leakage, and other issues. Additionally, the sensing principle of the sensor, external noise and interference, data processing methods, and algorithms present a difficult trade-off between resolution and sensing accuracy [19, 20], two important metrics for measuring the performance of robotic tactile sensors. Magnetic tactile sensors [21–24] offer advantages over traditional tactile sensors. They can support continuous sensing data, have high transmission response rates, have limited dependence on direct wires [25], and avoid the need for soft rigid electrical connections. Magnetic flux detection is only dependent on the distance to the magnetic field source, which makes it possible to use commercial magnetic field sensors that offer high sensitivity, high robustness, small size, ease of manufacture, and low price. We have developed a magnetic finger abdomen shape by mixing magnetic particles embedded in silicone rubber. When the magnetic finger abdomen comes into contact with an object and deforms, the magnetic field inside the magnetic finger abdomen changes accordingly due to the displacement and reorientation of the magnetic particles within it. These changes in magnetic flux can be measured directly without an electrical connection by a 3D Hall effect sensor, providing continuous changes that can be used to estimate contact position, force, contact shape, and other parameters. Soft magnetic tactile sensors can often be combined with discrete 3D Hall sensing chips via elastomeric layers, allowing for large-area sensing and meeting more design and manufacturing requirements. Our magnetic tactile sensor offers a promising approach to overcoming the limitations of traditional tactile sensors and can provide accurate feedback for precise manipulation and control in robotics.

Tactile sensors are critical components for robots to interact with the outside world, and they represent an essential research area in the field of intelligent robotics. Soft magnetic tactile sensors show great potential in dexterous hand manipulation and large area e-skin [26–30] and offer broad research prospects. Our proposed soft humanoid finger uses a magnetic finger abdomen that deforms upon contact with an object. Hall sensors can detect changes in magnetic flux density and fit the contact force based on abundant tactile feedback from the finger abdomen. This allows the soft humanoid finger to dynamically adjust the contact force and achieve precise grasping. Soft magnetic tactile sensors offer a promising approach to overcoming the limitations of traditional tactile sensors and can provide accurate feedback for precise manipulation and control in robotics. With further development, soft magnetic tactile sensors will continue to play a significant role in the advancement of intelligent robotics, enabling robots to interact with their environment in a more human-like manner.

2   Design and Materials

2.1   Structure

As shown in Fig. 1(a), the proposed soft humanoid finger comprises three magnetic finger abdomens and 3D Hall sensors paired with the designed finger as a substrate. The magnetic finger abdomen is made by mixing permanent magnetic particles (NdFeB, BY-Br-500, a permanent magnetic material with high residual magnetization strength) with silicone (Ecoflex 00–30, Smooth-on) and curing the mixture. The nylon substrate (7500, strong, producing very high-precision fine holes for cord drive) is modeled on the human hand and holds the magnetic finger abdomen and the 3D Hall effect sensor to enable enveloping grasping. The knuckle section is cast and cured in high-performance polyurethane rubber (PMC780, Smooth-on) for robustness and durability. The 3D Hall effect sensor (MLX90393, Melexis) is uniformly placed on the back of each finger, opposite the magnetic membrane of the finger abdomen, to detect changes in strength across the magnetic field.

This design provides a durable soft humanoid finger that can achieve enveloping grasping and provide abundant tactile feedback. The use of permanent magnetic particles and silicone in the magnetic finger abdomen allows for high residual magnetization strength and deformability, respectively, making it possible to adapt to different shapes of interacting surfaces. The 3D Hall effect sensors provide continuous sensing data and can detect changes in magnetic flux density with high sensitivity and accuracy, allowing for precise control and manipulation of the soft humanoid finger.

The following is the principle of our proposed soft humanoid finger with magnetic tactile perception:

– When the magnetic finger abdomen comes into contact with an object, the magnetic finger abdomen produces a contact deformation, which causes the permanent magnetic particles in it to move relative to their position, which in turn causes the magnetic field to change. The changing magnetic field values are collected by 3D Hall effect sensors. Analyzing the collected data, extracting tactile features, and fitting the contact force. At the same time, as the magnetic field decays with the third power of distance:

$$B \propto \frac{1}{R^3} \tag{1}$$

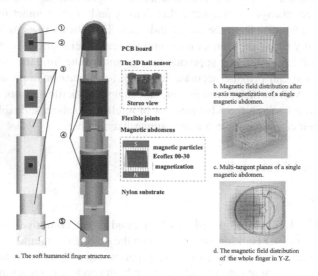

a. The soft humanoid finger structure.

PCB board

The 3D hall sensor

Stereo view

Flexible joints

Magnetic abdomens

magnetic particles
Ecoflex 00-30
magnetization

Nylon substrate

b. Magnetic field distribution after z-axis magnetization of a single magnetic abdomen.

c. Multi-tangent planes of a single magnetic abdomen.

d. The magnetic field distribution of the whole finger in Y-Z.

Fig. 1. Overall structure and simulation. Fig(a) is the soft humanoid finger structure. In order, 1–5 are the PCB board, 3D Hall sensor, flexible joint, magnetic abdomen, and nylon substrate support. Fig(b) is the Z-axis magnetization of the magnetic finger abdomen. Fig(c) is the multi-tangent planes of the finger abdomen after magnetization. Fig(d) is the magnetic field distribution of the whole finger in Y-Z.

2.2 Simulation

To verify whether the 3D Hall sensor can detect a stable magnetic field signal in our designed finger structure, we conducted a simulation using Comsol. In the simulation environment, we magnetized the magnetic finger abdomen in the z-axis direction and obtained the entire magnetic field distribution, as shown in Fig. 1 (b). We also obtained the magnetic field inside the magnetic finger abdomen in multi-tangent planes after unidirectional magnetization on the z-axis, as shown in Fig. 1 (c). Figure 1 (d) shows the decay of the magnetic field in the y-z plane. Based on the simulation results, we concluded that a steady magnetic field signal can be detected when the 3D Hall sensor is arranged on the back of the finger base. This ensures the effectiveness of the sensor arrangement and confirms that the 3D Hall sensor can detect a stable magnetic field signal in our designed finger structure. Overall, the simulation results provide further evidence that our proposed soft magnetic tactile sensor design is effective and can provide accurate feedback for precise manipulation and control in robotics.

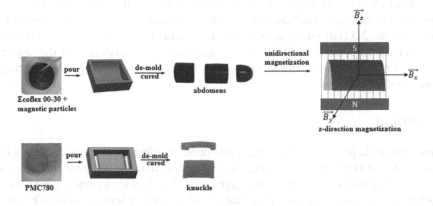

Fig. 2. The manufacturing process of magnetic finger abdomens and knuckles.

2.3   Fabrication and Assembly

Under the same conditions, the residual flux strength of soft magnetic materials mixed with permanent particles tends to be much smaller than that of hard magnets. For a 3D Hall effect sensor to receive stable magnetic field signals over the range, the residual flux strength in the magnetic finger abdomen must be sufficiently large. Also, considering the material properties of the magnetic finger abdomen, such as elasticity and recovery, we mix liquid silicone and permanent magnet particles at a 1:1 (weight ratio) as in Fig. 2(a), mix well, and pour into the finger abdomen mold we designed, then the mold containing the silicone rubber and permanent magnet particles is degassed in a vacuum machine and cures at room temperature for four hours (heating shortens the curing time). Once the magnetic finger abdomen is fully cured and molded, magnetized in a magnetizing machine, the molded finger abdomen is made magnetic. After magnetization, the finger abdomen becomes magnetic and provides information on the strength of the magnetic field. The finger abdomen is deformed when in contact with an object, the magnetic particles inside are displaced and reorganized, and the 3D Hall sensors detect the change in magnetic flux density. The magnetic finger abdomen is coated with silicone (DOWSIL™ 3145 RTV, Dow Corning) and bonds to a finger substrate.

Again, we mix PMC-780A and B at 2:1, stir well, and pour into our knuckle mold, then degauss the mold in a vacuum machine and cure it at room temperature for forty-eight hours (the increased temperature helps to accelerate the curing and reduces the curing time) then de-mold it, heat the cured rubber to 150F (65C) for 4 to 8 h will improve its physical properties. Then embed it in the knuckles. It is important to note that PMC780 requires a release agent (Universal release, Smooth-on). Before pouring the mixed liquid polyurethane rubber into the mold, ensure that the mold is completely dry by gently brushing a soft brush with the release agent over the surface of the mold or spraying a thin coat of the mold and drying for a further thirty minutes.

Finally, the small magneto-tactile sensor circuit board we designed is embedded into the back of the finger and assembled that mimics the human hand. In this case, three identical 3D Hall sensors transmit the response of the three Hall sensors to magnetic field changes simultaneously via an I^2C communication bus, ensuring a fast response of the 3D Hall sensor array to magnetic field changes. The overall size of the soft humanoid finger is 20*120*20 mm, the magnetic finger abdomen of the fingertip is 17*15*5 mm, the middle finger abdomen is 17*20*5 mm, and the proximal finger abdomen is 17*15*5 mm.

3 Method

When a magnetic finger abdomen comes into contact object, it produces contact deformation. The 3D Hall sensor can collect magnetic field data for different contact situations that cover information on contact forces, etc. The Machine Learning Technique is robust in characterizing the non-linear features of soft-touch sensors and can be effective in improving the performance and effectiveness of the model.

3.1 Multilayer Perceptron

It's easy for human individuals to learn from a priori, to quickly acquire the ability to learn new tasks on top of what they already have. For ANN, the weights and bias parameters can be adaptively adjusted based on the training data to achieve adaptive processing and feature extraction for better generalization ability and prediction accuracy, and still maintain better recognition and classification performance in the face of data perturbations such as noise and distortion. In addition, the obvious advantage of ANN over DNN is that it is friendly to small datasets. When the datasets are relatively small, ANN performs more consistently and reliably.

Based on the dataset we collect, we use a multilayer perceptron to train the magnetic soft humanoid finger, which adopts a backpropagation algorithm to learn and adjust the model parameters quickly. Combined with a grid search optimization algorithm, finding the optimal combination of hyperparameters, as shown in Table 1. Automatic adjustment of the model hyperparameters reduces the possibility of manual intervention and errors and improves model performance and prediction accuracy.

Table 1. The main optimal combination of hyperparameters by the grid search optimization algorithm.

Sensor position	activation	batch size	hidden layer sizes	learning rate
Fingertip	relu	50	(100, 100)	0.005
Middle knuckle	relu	50	(200, 50)	0.01
Proximal knuckle	relu	20	(150, 50)	0.01

3.2   Tactile Force

As shown in Fig. 3, we have processed the contact force fitting task as follows. If the single magnetic finger abdomen receives a contact deformation, the internal permanent magnet particles' position moves, and the magnetic field signal changes, the changing magnetic field values can be collected by the 3D Hall sensor. Establishing training and testing sets on the collected data, using an end-to-end feature extraction network to collect the raw magnetic field data and perform pre-processing operations to improve training effectiveness and stability. Magnetic field data (magnetic field strength values for 3D Hall sensors in the x, y, and z directions) is used as input to an ANN to train the model and output the contact forces.

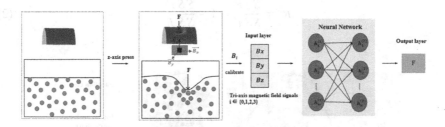

Fig. 3. Normal force estimation.

4   Experiment and Result

We build a data acquisition mobile platform and mount a spherical resin indenter (8200Pro, D=12mm) on a digital push-pull gauge as shown in Fig. 4. While the indenter is driven by the Z -axis of the mobile platform, the magnetic finger is pressed vertically downwards. To verify the soft humanoid finger, we design two experiments to test force detection and enveloping capability.

4.1   Data Collection

We fix the soft humanoid finger to the data acquisition mobile platform and collect information on the magnetic field data of the contact force. The spherical indenter is installed onto the force gauge, and the three parts of the soft humanoid finger are pressed down by it. Controlling the mobile platform to achieve the press between the indenter and the magnetic finger abdomen in the z-axis, the digital display push-pull meter reads the pressure data, and the sensor reads the raw magnetic field data. Collecting fifty sets of forces for each magnetic finger abdomen by pressing downwards in the vertical direction 0.1 mm at a time.

For the magnetic finger abdomen, we report the Mean Absolute Error (MAE) between the predicting and actual normal forces on a five-fold cross-validation set in Table 2. To ensure the accuracy of our analysis, we decided to only consider data with a force greater than 0.1 N. This threshold was chosen based on the resolution of the sensor and to eliminate any possible noise in the data. By focusing on data with a force above this threshold, we can ensure that our analysis is based on reliable and accurate data, which will improve the precision of our results. As shown in Fig. 5(a), the error bar graph between the loading and predictive forces indicates the detection of the contact force. The Root Mean Square Error (RMSE) is 0.18 N and has an accuracy of 98.2%. Furthermore, we find that the magnetic field signal and force are linearly well correlated in the Z-axis direction. We use R-Square to determine the linear fitting effect between the Z-axis magnetic field signal and force, whereby the closer the R-Square is to 1, the better the model fit and the stronger the linear correlation between the Z-axis magnetic field signal and force, as shown in Fig. 5(b), with $R^2 > 0.988$. Which:

$$R^2 = \frac{SSR}{SST} = 1 - \frac{SSE}{SST} \tag{2}$$

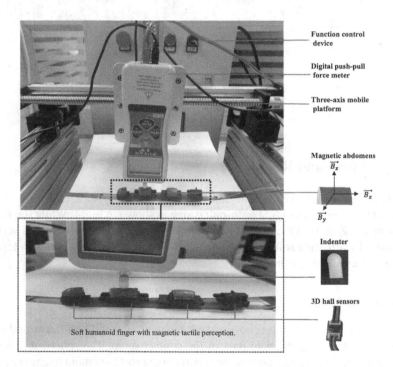

Fig. 4. Experimental platform. It mainly consists of a motion controller (CL-04K) and a digital push-pull gauge (DS2-20N, PUYAN)

Table 2. The Mean squared error on five-fold cross-validation.

Sensor position	Training set(N)	Testing set(N)
Fingertip	0.126 ± 0.121	0.259 ± 0.139
Middle knuckle	0.190 ± 0.026	0.316 ± 0.136
Proximal knuckle	0.184 ± 0.044	0.295 ± 0.199

If y_i is given as the actual measuring value, $\bar{y}$ as the actual measured average value, and $\bar{y}_i$ as the fitting value, the Sum of Squares Regression(SSR):

$$SSR = \sum_i^n (\hat{y}_i - \bar{y})^2 \tag{3}$$

The Sum of Squares Error(SSE):

$$SSE = \sum_i^n (y_i - \hat{y}_i)^2 \tag{4}$$

The Sum of Squares Total(SST):

$$SST = SSR + SSE = \sum_i^n (y_i - \bar{y})^2 \tag{5}$$

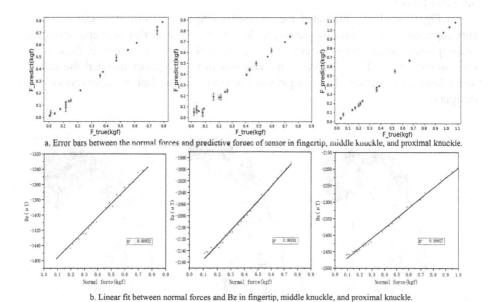

a. Error bars between the normal forces and predictive forces of sensor in fingertip, middle knuckle, and proximal knuckle.

b. Linear fit between normal forces and Bz in fingertip, middle knuckle, and proximal knuckle.

Fig. 5. The calibrate result. Fig(a) is the error bar graph between the normal forces and predictive forces from fingertip to finger root. Fig(b) is the linear fit between normal forces and Bz from fingertip to finger root.

Therefore, Eq. 2 can be expressed as:

$$R^2 = \frac{\sum_i^n (\hat{y}_i - \bar{y})^2}{\sum_i^n (y_i - \bar{y})^2} = 1 - \frac{\sum_i^n (y_i - \hat{y}_i)^2}{\sum_i^n (y_i - \bar{y})^2} \tag{6}$$

4.2 Force Measuring

Utilizing the experimental platform we build, we re-collect a batch of normal forces and magnetic field data and bring it into the model. The line graphs between the actual and predicted normal forces show a good correlation, the accuracies of normal force measurement are as high as 95.5%. This demonstrates that the magneto-tactile sensor we designed for the soft humanoid finger has a well-responsive prediction of contact force and can accurately characterize the magnitude of the normal force.

4.3 Envelope Grasping

Our dexterous hand design showcases the ability to grasp various shapes and display a high level of adaptability throughout the grasping process. The single humanoid finger is affixed to the base, which incorporates a miniature servo-electric cylinder integrated into the pedestal. Upon initiation of the servo-electric drive, the micro-servo-electric cylinder is inserted into the serial port, and the finger undergoes bending motion facilitated by the rope drive, enabling proximity to the object being grasped and achieving envelopment. The envelope-grasping capability is effortlessly attained by our soft humanoid finger.

In Fig. 6, we have illustrated the successful gripping of objects such as a coffee cup, tape, and hand cream by the finger. Moreover, our experimental endeavors have encompassed the grasping of numerous objects, including pens, small balls, and towels, among others. These experiments have unequivocally demonstrated the stability and self-adaptive nature of the single soft humanoid finger that we have meticulously designed.

Fig. 6. Enveloping grasp with a single soft humanoid finger.

5   Conclusion

The magnetic soft humanoid finger we proposed, with a structure closer to the human finger, has excellent prospects for dexterous hand-grasping operations. We have described the fabrication process of the sensor, which has been experimentally shown to fit the contact force more effectively during grasping. Additionally, we have used a multilayer perceptron combined with a grid search optimization algorithm to extract contact surface features and improve the generalization performance of this sensor. The artificial neural network (ANN) we used has high stability for small datasets and can achieve up to 95.5% accuracy in contact force estimation within the detection range of 0–10N. This approach offers a promising solution for improving the performance of soft magnetic tactile sensors and enabling them to perform more complex tactile recognition tasks, such as 3D reconstruction.

Although the magnetic finger abdomen sensor we designed has good tactile feature extraction capability, further research is needed to optimize the finger structure, sensor distribution, and quantity to improve its performance in complex tactile recognition tasks.

Overall, our magnetic soft humanoid finger provides a new design idea for soft magnetic tactile sensors, and with further development, it has the potential to significantly advance the field of intelligent robotics, enabling robots to interact with their environment in a more human-like manner.

Supplemental Funding. CIE-Tencent Robotics X Rhino-Bird Focused Research Program under Grant 2022-01.

References

1. Chin, L., Yuen, M.C., Lipton, J., Trueba, L.H., Kramer-Bottiglio, R., Rus, D.: A simple electric soft robotic gripper with high-deformation tactile feedback. In: 2019 International Conference on Robotics and Automation (ICRA), Montreal, QC, Canada, 2019, pp. 2765–2771 (2019). https://doi.org/10.1109/ICRA.2019.8794098
2. Chen, W., Khamis, H., Birznieks, I., Lepora, N.F., Redmond, S.J.: Tactile sensors for friction estimation and incipient slip detection-toward dexterous robotic manipulation: a review, IEEE Sensors J. **18**(22), 9049–9064 (2018)
3. Torres-Jara, E., Natale, L.: Sensitive manipulation: manipulation through tactile feedback, Int. J. Humanoid Robot. **15**(01), 1850012 (2018)
4. Tomo, T.P., et al.: A new silicone structure for uSkin-A soft, distributed, digital 3-axis skin sensor and its integration on the humanoid robot iCub. IEEE Robot. Autom. Lett. **3**(3), 2584–2591 (2018). https://doi.org/10.1109/LRA.2018.2812915
5. Bartolozzi, C., Natale, L., Nori, F.: Robots with a sense of touch. Nature Mater. **15**, 921–925 (2016). https://doi.org/10.1038/nmat4731
6. Soter, G., Conn, A., Hauser, H., Rossiter, J.: Bodily aware soft robots: integration of proprioceptive and exteroceptive sensors In: 2018 IEEE International Conference on Robotics and Automation (ICRA) (IEEE, 2018), pp. 2448–2453 (2018)
7. Chin, L., Lipton, J., Yuen, M.C., Kramer-Bottiglio, R., Rus, D.: Automated recycling separation enabled by soft robotic material classification. In: 2019 2nd IEEE International Conference on Soft Robotics (RoboSoft) (IEEE, 2019), pp. 102–107 (2019)

8. Thuruthel, T.G., Shih, B., Laschi, C., Tolley, M.T.: Soft robot perception using embedded soft sensors and recurrent neural networks. Sci. Robot. **4**, eaav1488 (2019)

9. Justus, K.B., et al.: A biosensing soft robot: autonomous parsing of chemical signals through integrated organic and inorganic interfaces. Sci. Robot. **4**, eaax0765 (2019)

10. Farrow, N., Correll, N.: A soft pneumatic actuator that can sense grasp and touch. In: 2015 IEEE/RSJ International Conference on Intelligent Robots and Systems (IROS) (IEEE), pp. 2317–2323 (2015)

11. Yan, Y., et al.: Soft magnetic skin for super-resolution tactile sensing with force self-decoupling. Sci. Robot. **6**, eabc8801(2021). abc8801 https://doi.org/10.1126/scirobotics

12. Shih, B., Mayeda, J., Huo, Z., Christianson, C., Tolley, M.T.: 3D printed resistive soft sensors. In: Proceedings of IEEE International Conference Soft Robotics, pp. 152–157 (2018)

13. Frutiger, A., et al.: Capacitive soft strain sensors via multicore-shell fiber printing, Adv. Mater. **27**(15), 2440–2446 (2015)

14. Homberg, B.S., Katzschmann, R.K., Dogar, M.R., Rus, D.: Robust proprioceptive grasping with a soft robot hand. Auton Robots. **43**(3), 681–96 (2019)

15. Majidi, C.: Soft-matter engineering for soft robotics. Adv. Mater. Technol. **4**, 1800477 (2019). https://doi.org/10.1002/admt.201800477

16. Lenz, J., Edelstein, S.: Magnetic sensors and their applications, IEEE Sensors J. **6**(3), 631–649 (2006)

17. Zhang, Q., Wang, Y.L., Xia, Y., Kirk, T.V., Chen, X.D.: Textile-only capacitive sensors with a lockstitch structure for facile integration in any areas of a fabric, ACS Sens. **5**, 1535–1540 (2020). https://doi.org/10.1021/acssensors.0c00210

18. Li, Y., et al.: Origami NdFeB flexible magnetic membranes with enhanced magnetism and programmable sequences of polarities, Adv. Funct. Mater. **29**, 1–10 (2019). https://doi.org/10.1002/adfm.201904977

19. Huang, Z., et al.: Three-dimensional integrated stretchable electronics. Nat. Electron. **1**(8), 473–480 (2018)

20. Piacenza, P., Sherman, S., Ciocarlie, M.: Data-driven super-resolution on a tactile dome. IEEE Robot. Autom. Lett. **3**, 1434–1441 (2018)

21. Homberg, B.S., Katzschmann, R.K., Dogar, M.R., Rus, D.: tactile identification of objects using a modular soft robotic gripper. In: Proceedings of IEEE/RSJ International Conference Intelligent Robots System, pp. 1698–1705 (2015)

22. Choi, C., Schwarting, W., DelPreto, J., Rus, D.: Learning object grasping for soft robot hands, IEEE Robot. Autom. Lett. **3**(3), 2370–2377 (2018)

23. Hellebrekers, T., Chang, N., Chin, K., Ford, M.J., Kroemer, O., Majidi, C.: Soft magnetic tactile skin for continuous force and location estimation using neural networks. IEEE Robot. Autom. Lett. **5**(3), 3892–3898 (2020). https://doi.org/10.1109/LRA.2020.2983707

24. Chi, C., Sun, X., Xue, N., Li, T., Liu, C.: Recent progress in technologies for tactile sensors Sensors **18**(4), 948 (2018)

25. Hu, H., Zhang, C., Pan, C., et al.: Wireless flexible magnetic tactile sensor with super-resolution in large-areas. ACS Nano **16**(11), 19271–80 (2022)

26. Wang, H., Totaro, M., Beccai, L.: Toward perceptive soft robots: progress and challenges. Adv. Sci. **5**, 1800541 (2018)

27. Chin, K., Hellebrekers, T., Majidi, C.: Machine learning for soft robotic sensing and control. Adv. Intell. Syst. **2020**, 1900171 (2020)

28. Shah, D.S., Yuen, M.C., Tilton, L.G., Yang, E.J., Kramer-Bottiglio, R.: Morphing robots using robotic skins that sculpt clay. IEEE Robot. Autom. Lett. **4**, 2204–2211 (2019)

29. Fang, B., Xia, Z., Sun, F., et al.: Soft magnetic fingertip with particle-jamming structure for tactile perception and grasping. IEEE Trans. Industr. Electron. **70**(6), 6027–35 (2023)

30. Xia, Z., Fang, B., Sun, F., et al.: Contact shape and pose recognition: utilizing a multipole magnetic tactile sensor with a metalearning model. IEEE Robot. Autom. Mag. **29**(4), 127–37 (2022)

Learning Tactilemotor Policy for Robotic Cable Following via Sim-to-Real Transfer

Chang Sun, Boyi Duan, Kun Qian$^{(\boxtimes)}$, and Yongqiang Zhao

School of Automation, Southeast University, Nanjing 210096, China
kqian@seu.edu.cn

Abstract. Manipulating deformable liner objects, such as following a cable, is easy for human beings but presents a significant challenge for robots. Moreover, learning strategies in real world can bring damage to sensors and pose difficulties for data collection. In this paper, we propose a Reinforcement Learning method to generalize cable following skills from simulation to reality. The agent uses an end-to-end approach, directly inputting raw sensor data into the framework to generate robot actions. Meanwhile, a Sim-to-Real network is applied to enable the tactilemotor policy transfer. In particular, we use different perception modalities and representations as components of the observations and investigate how these factors impact cable following results. Our extensive experiments in simulation demonstrate that the success rate of cable following can be up to 81.85% when both visual and tactile features are put into the policy, compared to using only one type of modality. The proposed method provides valuable insights for deformable objects manipulating scenarios.

Keywords: DLOs following · Sim-to-Real transfer · Tactile sensing

1 Introduction

For robots, object manipulation is fundamental to completing various complex tasks. Obtaining information about objects and perceiving the operating environment is a prerequisite for intelligent robot operation. With the advancement of visual sensors, some robot manipulation methods rely on vision based perception to quickly understand the environment. However, these methods may be affected by occlusion, lighting conditions and other factors, resulting in unreliable measurements. Tactile perception, on the other hand, has fewer such concerns. It can characterize the physical properties and spatial information of the objects in contact, enhancing robot performance and safety in various tasks such as grasping, exploration, and interaction. Robot tactile sensing can be achieved using different types of sensors, including capacitive [1], piezoelectric [2] and optical sensors [3, 4]. More and more robotic tasks will be completed with variety of sensing modalities.

Among robotic tasks, Deformable Linear Objects (DLOs) manipulation is challenging for artificial systems. A typical application scenario is cable following. With the

---

C. Sun and B. Duan—Contribute equally to this work.

© The Author(s), under exclusive license to Springer Nature Singapore Pte Ltd. 2023
H. Yang et al. (Eds.): ICIRA 2023, LNAI 14271, pp. 63–73, 2023.
https://doi.org/10.1007/978-981-99-6495-6_6

movement of the gripper, the state of the cable changes dynamically, potentially causing knotting and winding. To overcome these issues, some researches use additional constraints, e.g., placing a object on a table [5] or fixing the starting end of a cable [6].

Another concern is Sim-to-Real transfer of the learned tactile policy. Training in real scenarios can result in sensor damage and require large amounts of learning data. Therefore, most of RL policies are trained in simulation which can overcome the problems mentioned above. But it triggers a new issue that there is a significant performance decline when the policy is deployed in the reality directly because of the non-negligible domain gaps. Hence, transferring the policy from simulation to reality is hugely essential in order to maintain its performance as much as possible when the domain is different from that in training.

In this paper, we propose a Reinforcement Learning (RL) method to generalize cable following skills from simulation to reality. An RL agent is created in a simulated environment to learn the tactilemotor policy, equipped with both visual and tactile senses. Raw visual and tactile images are used as parts of the observations. To address the challenges posed by domain gaps, CTF-CycleGAN [7] is applied for the tactile image transfer. Through this Sim-to-Real method, the tactilemotor policy can be directly transferred to reality. Additionally, we investigate its performance in both simulator and real world, and study the impact of different modalities and their representations on results through extensive experiments.

2 Related Work

2.1 DLOs Manipulation

Most approaches on Deformable Linear Objects (DLOs) involve developing methods and techniques for manipulating and controlling these objects. This includes perceiving the state of the DLOs, controlling their shape, and planning its motion. An initial state estimate from a given point cloud can be refined to better align with the system dynamics [8, 9]. In [10] a novel tracking algorithm is proposed to observe and estimate the states of DLOs in real-time, especially when dealing with heavy occlusion situations and physical properties of different objects. For shape control, Yu et al. [11] propose an adaptive scheme with offline and online learning of unknown models. The offline learning aims to provide a good approximation prior to the manipulation task, while the online learning aims to compensate for errors due to insufficient training in the offline phase.

There also have been several studies concerning DLOs following that utilise tactile sensors. In [12], they use a RL approach to close a deformable ziplock bag using BioTac sensors. The authors train a deep neural net classifier to estimate the state of a zipper within a robot's pinch grasp and implement a Contextual Multi-Armed Bandit (C-MAB) RL algorithm to maximize cumulative rewards. She et al. [13] present a perception and control framework that uses a real-time tactile feedback from GelSight [4] to accomplish the task of cable following. The authors achieve the behavior by combining cable grip controller and cable pose controller. The problem of using vision and tactile inputs together to complete the task of DLOs has investigated for the first time in [6]. They created a RL agent using different sensing modalities and investigated how its behavior can be boosted using visual-tactile fusion, compared to using a single sensing modality.

2.2 Sim-to-Real Transfer of Robot Manipulation Skills

Sim-to-Real is an active area of research, as it can significantly reduce the time and cost of training robots for complex tasks. However, the domain gaps degrade the performance of the policies once the skills are transferred into real world. Multiple researches have proposed their methods to improve the transfer. The main methods at the moment can be categorized into these types: domain randomization, domain adaptation, imitation learning, meta-learning and knowledge distillation [14].

Domain randomization is highly used for learning transfer. Through randomizing parameters in the simulator, the policy can handle a range of system parameters. If the training data covers the real distribution of the real-world, the policy is able to generalize to reality. For instance, some dynamics parameters are randomized in [15] including the mass of each part of the robot and the joint interface damping. Andrychowicz et al. [16] also randomizes similar parameters in the simulator, such as robot link masses, surface friction coefficients an so on. For visual tasks, The method in [17] randomizes the texture of the objects and the shape and number of sundries, etc. James et al. [18] translate the randomized simulated image and real-world into the canonical sim images with another angle for domain randomization.

Domain adaptation methods make these two feature space from the source domain and target domain unified. [7, 19–21] use this approach to improve the performance of the model when it is applied on real-world. For instance, in our previous work [7], we propose pixel-level domain adaptation approach CTF-CycleGAN framework based on [21] and apply it to tactile image transfer. In this paper, we follow this method, extending its application to the cable following task.

3   Overview

The goal of cable following task in this paper is to grasp the cable at its beginning and follow it to its end using appropriate motion. As shown in Fig. 1, during this process, the gripper should be constantly close to the end and keep the cable in hand all the times. The starting point of the cable is fixed in 3D space, while its end is free.

In some ways, this task is similar to [6]: visual and tactile data are used as components of the observations to train the RL model in simulation. However, there are several key differences: If the cable falls from the gripper during following, it is regripped while [6] regards the training to be completed. Specifically, we employ an end-to-end approach in which sensor data is directly fed into the RL algorithm. This is different from [6], where perception and strategic learning are decoupled. Furthermore, we not only train and test the model in simulation, but also evaluate the tactilemotor policy in reality using a Sim-to-Real method.

Figure 2 illustrates an overview of our proposed method. For Sim-to-Real phase, unpaired simulated and real-world tactile images are used to train the transfer network CTF-CycleGAN [7]. In simulation, tactile images pretreated by CTF-CycleGAN generator of Sim-to-Real direction, along with other observations, are input into the RL network to learn the strategy.

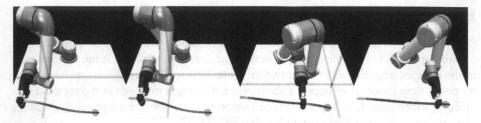

Fig. 1. The goal of task: the gripper should hold the cable at the fixed head position (left) and follow it until the end (right).

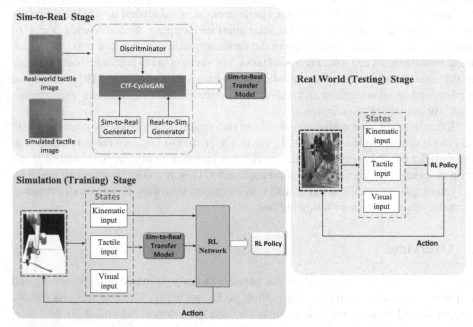

Fig. 2. An overview of our proposed framework. Sim-to-Real Stage presents the CTF-CycleGAN to get Sim-to-Real Transfer Model. Simulation (Training) Stage shows the robot manipulation policy learning in the simulator, and Real World (Testing) Stage shows the deployment of RL model in the real-world setting.

4   Sim-to-Real Skills Learning of Cable-Following Tasks

As outlined in Sect. 3, the component of our task involves setting up the scenarios in the simulator and learning the cable following strategy with RL method. This section will describe the above in detail.

4.1   Simulation Experiment Setup

MuJoCo [22] is used to construct an RL-based learning platform in simulation for robot cable manipulation skills, as shown on the left side of Fig. 3. To simulate DIGIT tactile sensors, we follow the GelSight simulation method in Taxim [23], using approximately 100 data points from the real sensor for optical calibration and 10 data points collected using a pin-indenter for shadow calibration. The accuracy of the MuJoCo physics engine simulation depends on parameter settings, which significantly impact strategy training. For instance, through several trials, we set solref = "0.01 1", solimp = "0.99 0.99 0.01" in our task to improve contact resolution. To increase the generalization of the strategy, the head point of the cable is randomly initialized within a five centimeter cube space. At the same time, the gripper is initially allowed to grasp the cable's starting position in a horizontal pose to avoid complicating the task.

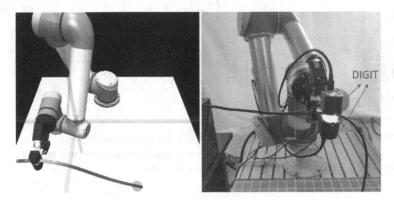

Fig. 3. Experiment setup in simulation (left) and real world (right).

4.2 Sim-to-Real Domain Adaptation Network Structure

Domain adaptation transferring is used for tactile images to realize Sim-to-Real of manipulation skill. We follow the method in our previous work [7]. The key point is CTF-CycleGAN, as shown in Fig. 4, a novel pixel-level unsupervised domain adaptation network that cascades CNNs and Transformer. Unpaired tactile images in simulation and reality are fed into the network to realize domain transferring, Sim-to-Real and Real-to-Sim. Specifically, in our work, the simulated tactile images captured from Mujoco are converted to fake real tactile images by the Sim-to-Real generator $G_{S \rightarrow R}$ of CTF-CycleGAN. More details please refer to [7].

4.3 Tactilemotor Policy Learning

In this paper, Soft Actor-Critic (SAC) [24, 25] RL algorithm is used to learn cable manipulation skill. SAC provides state-of-the-art performance in continuous control tasks, being able to combine sample efficient off-policy method with ability to operate in a continuous action and state spaces.

Observations. Specifically, observations include the gripper's pose, tactile and visual features.

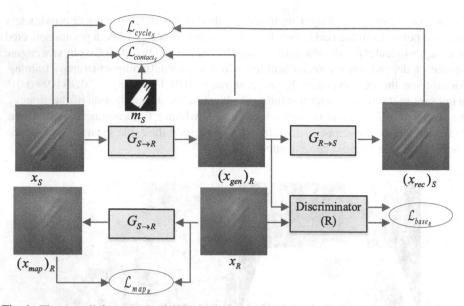

Fig. 4. The overall framework of CTF-CycleGAN. It includes both sim-real-sim and real-sim-real cycle generation pipelines, in which the generators and discriminators will be alternately and iteratively trained according to the weighted sum of all losses.

- Kinematic: It includes the position (3D coordinates) and posture (quaternion form) of the tool center point (TCP) of the end-effector in the world coordinate system. It is a one-dimensional array consisting of seven elements: $O_G = [p_x, p_y, p_z, q_w, q_x, q_y, q_z]$
- Tactile: The tactile features O_T consist of two components: tactile images O_{Tl}, O_{Tr} and the tactile signal O_{Ts}. Using an end-to-end approach, O_{Tl} is extracted directly from the DIGIT sensor on the left of the gripper and O_{Tr} from the right DIGIT sensor of the gripper. The tactile signal (O_{Ts}) is obtained by comparing these tactile images with a rendered background image and using a 1D array to represent whether the cable is in the hand.
- Visual: Scene image O_V is captured by a third perspective camera.

Action. Since the gripper should move freely in three-dimensional space, the action array comprises position and gesture displacements of the gripper: $O_G = [p_x, p_y, p_z, q_w, q_x, q_y, q_z]$.

Reward. The goal of the task in this paper is to enable the gripper to follow the cable from the initial position to the end. During this process, the cable may fall or the gripper fail to move towards cable's end. Taking these factors into account, the reward can be expressed as partial rewards and defined as follows:

$$R_t = \begin{cases} R_{\text{start}} + R_{\text{end}}, & \text{if } O_{Ts} = 1 \\ R_{\text{fall}}, & \text{if } O_{Ts} = 0 \end{cases} \qquad (1)$$

where R_{start} represents a reward for moving away from the beginning; R_{end} is a reward for being close to the end of the rope, and R_{fall} is a penalty for dropping it; The tactile signal O_{ts} is used to determine whether the cable is dropped or not.

The partial rewards R_{start} is defined as follows:

$$R_{start} = \alpha_0/D(P_{tcp}, P_{start}) \tag{2}$$

where α_0 is the weight of that reward; P_{tcp} is the current position of TCP in the world coordinate system; P_{start} is the position of the beginning of rope, and D represents the distance between two arguments.

R_{end} characterizes the reward with respect to the end position of the cable P_{end}. R_{end} is only awarded when the gripper is farther than distance d from the end of the rope and increases linearly as the gripper approaches the end. When the distance is less than the set value d, R_{end} is set to 0.

$$R_{end} = \begin{cases} \alpha_1 * D(P_{tcp}, P_{end}), & \text{if } D(P_{tcp}, P_{end}) > d \\ 0, & \text{otherwise} \end{cases} \tag{3}$$

In the work, P_{tcp}, P_{start} and P_{end} are available in the simulator. R_{fall}, α_0, α_1 and d are all hyperparameters, they are set to $R_{fall} = -1000$, $\alpha_0 = -0.5$, $\alpha_1 = -0.8$, d = 0.25.

5 Experiment

5.1 Robot Policy Learning Results

To evaluate the proposed method and investigate the impact of different observations on the cable following task, several experiments are conducted in the simulator. The number of timesteps for each training experiment is 2e5.

We first fix the gripper's posture and analyse the effect of single (tactile) and multi-modal (visual-tactile) perception as inputs on RL learning. Figure 5 shows the specific performance of the agent during the training process. When only tactile perception is available, the maximum success rate during the training phase in the simulator is 49%. In contrast, the maximum success rate reaches 59% when trained with visual-tactile multimodal inputs. This result is expected as the two modalities complement each other: tactus provides cable texture perception while vision provides external scene information. However, as can be observed, the success rate does not reach the ideal goal, It is speculated that since neither kinematic, tactile nor visual perception provides information about the end position of the DLO, the agent is more inclined to stop prematurely.

Based on the above analysis, the end position of DLO is then added to the observations. The agent is trained with different modal inputs to obtain control policies for ablation experiments. These policies are evaluated over 2000 timesteps with random DLO properties and configuration in the simulator. The performance of testing can be seen in Table 1. Specifically, the success rate represents the ratio of successful attempts to the total number of episodes over 2000 timesteps, while the mean reward indicates the average episode reward. According to the first two rows of Table 1, using $O_{Tl} + O_{Tr}$

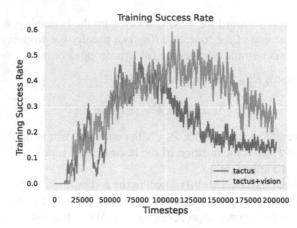

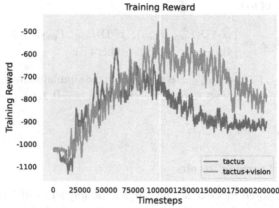

Fig. 5. The success rate curve (top) and reward curve (bottom) of training processes with two types of inputs.

$+ O_{Ts} + O_V$ as the modal input increases the success rate by 8.37% compared to using $O_{Tl} + O_{Tr} + O_{Ts}$. This result is consistent with Fig. 5. Visual data can capture the global information, such as the state of the cable, which is useful for cable following tasks. When only one tactile image and a tactile signal are used for perception, the success rate drops from 73.48% to 26.67% compared to the first row of Table 1. Tactile images are primarily used to perceive the cable posture, reducing them indicates that only one finger is able to perceive the cable while the other assists with gripping. When only a tactile signal is used (the fourth row of Table 1), the success rate drops to 3.19%. The tactile signal just manifests whether or not the cable is in the gripper. What the robot can learn from the tactile signal is insufficient to perceive the environment.

The above experiments are all conducted with the gripper's posture fixed. Upon removal of this constraint, as shown in the fifth row of Table 1, the success rate decreases to 14.17% when using $O_{Tl} + O_{Tr} + O_{Ts}$ as the modal input. The shape of the cable is complex and unpredictable during the robot's tracking process. In this study, relieving posture control means that the dimension of the action space increases. However, the available observations are insufficient for the robot to learn the control policy with the gripper's posture unrestricted.

Table 1. The success rate and mean reward of different modal information after adding the end position of the DLO to the observations in simulation.

Modal input	Success Rate	Mean reward
$O_{Tl} + O_{Tr} + O_{Ts}$	73.48%	−407.02
$O_{Tl} + O_{Tr} + O_{Ts} + O_v$	81.85%	−259.59
$O_{Tl} + O_{Ts}$	26.67%	−960.16
O_{Ts}	3.19%	−1103.74
$O_{Tl} + O_{Tr} + O_{Ts}$ (unrestricting posture)	14.17%	−1054.98

5.2   Real-World Experiment Results

In the real world, the system is consisted of a UR5 robot and a Robotiq 2F-85 gripper equipped with two DIGIT sensors, as shown in the right part of Fig. 2. Besides, Fig. 6 presents the process of experiments in reality.

Different from the settings in simulation, tactile features determine whether the gripper reaches the end of the cable. Simulation experiments demonstrate that visual data can capture scene information, which is useful for this task. Despite randomizing certain scene parameters in the simulator, such as the color of the background and cable, transferring visual images remains challenging due to domain gaps. Therefore, we combine kinematic data and $O_{Tl} + O_{Tr} + O_{Ts}$ as the observations for the robot and apply the tactilemotor policy to the real world. The use of cables with different diameters affect the experiments results. After 10 consecutive episodes of experiments, the overall task success rate reaches 60.00% with a 50-cm cable, however, the success rate is 70.00% when applying a 45-cm cable.

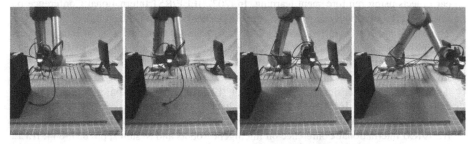

Fig. 6. Experimental snapshot in real-world scenarios.

6 Conclusion

In this paper, we propose a novel method for cable following task. In particular, the tactilemotor policy is not only completed in simulation, but also verified for the performance in real world through Sim-to-Real transfer. With the tactile perception, the robot has the ability to handle flexible objects with invisible textures. The proposed method has potential to be further applied to more complex tasks, e.g., untangling the cables and following the cable to find its plug-end. In the simulation experiments, ablation studies are conducted to show the importance of multimodality. In the future, to address the diversity of cables in real world, anchor points could be added to tactile images. This would reduce the impact of cable texture differences and improve the model's generalization ability.

Acknowledgments. This work is sponsored by the Natural Science Foundation of Jiangsu Province, China (No. BK20201264), Zhejiang Lab (No. 2022NB0AB02), and the National Natural Science Foundation of China (No. 61573101).

References

1. Ha, K.H., Huh, H., Li, Z., Lu, N.: Soft capacitive pressure sensors: trends, challenges, and perspectives. ACS Nano **16**(3), 3442–3448 (2022)
2. Lin, W., Wang, B., Peng, G., Shan, Y., Hu, H., Yang, Z.: Skin-inspired piezoelectric tactile sensor array with crosstalk-free row+ column electrodes for spatiotemporally distinguishing diverse stimuli. Adv. Sci. **8**(3), 2002817 (2021). https://doi.org/10.1002/advs.202002817
3. Lepora, N.F., Lin, Y., Money-Coomes, B., Lloyd, J.: DigiTac: a digit-tactip hybrid tactile sensor for comparing low-cost high-resolution robot touch. IEEE Robot. Autom. Lett. **7**(4), 9382–9388 (2022)
4. Yuan, W., Dong, S., Adelson, E.H.: GelSight: high-resolution robot tactile sensors for estimating geometry and force. Sensors **17**(12), 2762 (2017). https://doi.org/10.3390/s17122762
5. Yan, M., Zhu, Y., Jin, N., Bohg, J.: Self-supervised learning of state estimation for manipulating deformable linear objects. IEEE Robot. Autom. Lett. **5**(2), 2372–2379 (2020)
6. Pecyna, L., Dong, S., Luo, S.: Visual-tactile multimodality for following deformable linear objects using reinforcement learning. In: 2022 IEEE/RSJ International Conference on Intelligent Robots and Systems (IROS), pp. 3987–3994. IEEE, October 2022
7. Zhao, Y., Jing, X., Qian, K., Gomes, D.F., Luo, S.: Skill generalization of tubular object manipulation with tactile sensing and Sim2Real learning. Robot. Auton. Syst. **160**, 104321 (2023). https://doi.org/10.1016/j.robot.2022.104321
8. Javdani, S., Tandon, S., Tang, J., O'Brien, J.F., Abbeel, P.: Modeling and perception of deformable one-dimensional objects. In 2011 IEEE International Conference on Robotics and Automation, pp. 1607–1614. IEEE, May 2011
9. Lui, W.H., Saxena, A.: Tangled: learning to untangle ropes with RGB-D perception. In: 2013 IEEE/RSJ International Conference on Intelligent Robots and Systems, pp. 837–844. IEEE, November 2013
10. Khalifa, A., Palli, G.: New model-based manipulation technique for reshaping deformable linear objects. Int. J. Adv. Manuf. Technol., 1–9 (2022)

11. Yu, M., Zhong, H., Zhong, F., Li, X.: Adaptive control for robotic manipulation of deformable linear objects with offline and online learning of unknown models. arXiv preprint arXiv:2107. 00194 (2021)

12. Hellman, R.B., Tekin, C., van der Schaar, M., Santos, V.J.: Functional contour-following via haptic perception and reinforcement learning. IEEE Trans. Haptics 11(1), 61–72 (2017)

13. She, Y., Wang, S., Dong, S., Sunil, N., Rodriguez, A., Adelson, E.: Cable manipulation with a tactile-reactive gripper. Int. J. Robot. Res. 40(12–14), 1385–1401 (2021)

14. Zhao, W., Queralta, J.P., Westerlund, T.: Sim-to-real transfer in deep reinforcement learning for robotics: a survey. In: 2020 IEEE Symposium Series on Computational Intelligence (SSCI), pp. 737–744. IEEE, December 2020

15. Chebotar, Y., et al.: Closing the sim-to-real loop: adapting simulation randomization with real world experience. In: 2019 International Conference on Robotics and Automation (ICRA), pp. 8973–8979. IEEE, May 2019

16. Andrychowicz, O.M., et al.: Learning dexterous in-hand manipulation. Int. J. Robot. Res. 39(1), 3–20 (2020)

17. Niu, H., Hu, J., Cui, Z., Zhang, Y.: Dr2l: Surfacing corner cases to robustify autonomous driving via domain randomization reinforcement learning. In: Proceedings of the 5th International Conference on Computer Science and Application Engineering, pp. 1–8, October 2021

18. James, S., et al.: Sim-to-real via sim-to-sim: data-efficient robotic grasping via randomized-to-canonical adaptation networks. In: Proceedings of the IEEE/CVF Conference on Computer Vision and Pattern Recognition, pp. 12627–12637 (2019)

19. Church, A., Lloyd, J., Lepora, N.F.: Tactile sim-to-real policy transfer via real-to-sim image translation. In: Conference on Robot Learning, pp. 1645–1654. PMLR, January 2022

20. Jianu, T., Gomes, D.F., Luo, S.: Reducing tactile Sim2Real domain gaps via deep texture generation networks. In: 2022 International Conference on Robotics and Automation (ICRA), pp. 8305–8311. IEEE, May 2022

21. Chen, W., et al.: Bidirectional sim-to-real transfer for GelSight tactile sensors with CycleGAN. IEEE Robot. Autom. Lett. 7(3), 6187–6194 (2022)

22. Todorov, E., Erez, T., Tassa, Y.: MuJoCo: a physics engine for model-based control. In: 2012 IEEE/RSJ International Conference on Intelligent Robots and Systems, pp. 5026–5033. IEEE, October 2012

23. Si, Z., Yuan, W.: Taxim: an example-based simulation model for GelSight tactile sensors. IEEE Robot. Autom. Lett. 7(2), 2361–2368 (2022)

24. Haarnoja, T., Zhou, A., Abbeel, P., Levine, S.: Soft actor-critic: off-policy maximum entropy deep reinforcement learning with a stochastic actor. In: International Conference on Machine Learning, pp. 1861–1870. PMLR, July 2018

25. Haarnoja, T., et al.: Soft actor-critic algorithms and applications. arXiv preprint arXiv:1812. 05905 (2018)

Electric Fish-Inspired Proximity and Pressure Sensing Electronic Skin

Jiacheng Li, Xiaochang Yang, Chen Xu, Yansong Gai, and Yonggang Jiang(✉)

Insitute of Bionic and Micro-Nano Systems, School of Mechanical Engineering and
Automation, Beihang University, Beijing 100191, China
jiangyg@buaa.edu.cn

Abstract. In the field of human-robot interaction, there is a growing demand
for high-sensitivity proximity and pressure perception in sensor design. However, current sensing solutions often rely on the combination of several sensing
principles, which presents challenges in signal acquisition, flexibility, and array
integration. To overcome these challenges, we propose a flexible array of electronic skins, inspired by the electric field sensing mechanism in electric fish,
capable of proximity and pressure sensing. The electronic skin consists of several
key components, including an elastic layer, emitting electrodes, receiving electrodes, and a dielectric layer. By exploiting this simple yet effective our electronic
skin is capable of generating electric fields through the emitting electrodes and
detecting electric field disturbances through the receiving electrodes. This design
enables simultaneous bimodal perception of proximity and pressure, allowing for
a comprehensive understanding of the environment. One of the main advantages
of our approach is its simplicity. By leveraging the electric fields as the sensing
modality, we eliminate the need for complex combinations of multiple sensors.
This not only simplifies the overall system design, but also reduces manufacturing cost and enhances scalability. Additionally, the use of electric fields enables
real-time and accurate detection of both object proximity and applied pressure
on the robot, leading to improved environmental awareness. To demonstrate the
feasibility and effectiveness of our electronic skin, we conducted experiments on
a robotic arm. The results of these experiments demonstrate the successful implementation of basic human-robot interactions using our proposed technique. This
validation further emphasizes the potential and practicality of our approach.

Keywords: Electric field perception · Electronic skin · Human-computer
interaction

1 Introduction

With the rapid development of emerging technologies such as robotics, computer science, and electronics, intelligent robots have been widely applied in various domains,
including daily life and industrial production. There is an increasing demand for human-
robot interaction capabilities and safety in the use of machines and devices. Advances in

© The Author(s), under exclusive license to Springer Nature Singapore Pte Ltd. 2023
H. Yang et al. (Eds.): ICIRA 2023, LNAI 14271, pp. 74–80, 2023.
https://doi.org/10.1007/978-981-99-6495-6_7

robotics technology reflect a country's development in the field of intelligent manufacturing and serve as an indicator of its production and manufacturing capabilities [1].To achieve intelligence in robots, it is essential for them to have more sensitive perception of external environments and data analysis capabilities [2]. Flexible proximity sensors are one of the key areas of research in this regard [3].

Rong Zhu proposed a new theory for piezo-thermal sensing and a new mechanism for multimode sensing based on thermal induction [4]. Jia Zhang completed a theoretical analysis of proximity and tactile perception in a multi-level force sensitivity study of pressure capacitance/pressure resistance coupling [5]. Li Wen developed a flexible dual-mode intelligent skin based on a triboelectric nanogenerators and liquid metal sensing, enabling humans to teach soft robot locomotion by eye coordination [6].The electronic skin (e-skin) developed by Wei Gao is used to perceive and detect the surrounding environment; This kind of perception includes proximity, touch and temperature perception. The robot can also feedback and communicate with humans in real-time [7].

Flexible sensors can be installed on arbitrary surfaces, providing greater freedom in their usage [8]. However, existing proximity sensors face challenges such as insufficient flexibility, sensitivity affected by curvature, and weak resistance to interference [9]. In this paper, we study a highly flexible proximity sensor that addresses these challenges. We establish a signal acquisition system to collect and analyze information regarding object position and applied pressure [10]. Additionally, we develop a training algorithm to recognize object image information, which can be applied in areas such as obstacle avoidance, emergency stopping, and robotic gripper control. This highly flexible proximity sensor exhibits fast information processing, long detection range, and the ability to react promptly to obstacles, thereby minimizing risks.

Through the development and application of such advanced flexible proximity sensor, robots can achieve more precise and efficient interactions with the surrounding environment. This contributes to improved safety, productivity, and overall performance in various areas. Furthermore, the research and development of high-flexibility sensing technologies will promote the continuous advancement of robotics, enabling the realization of more sophisticated and intelligent robotic systems.

2 Result and Discussion

2.1 Design and Principle

The electric fish live in cluttered environments where the electro sense becomes a crucial tool for sensing surroundings. They use an electric organ to generate voltage pulses or oscillations and have voltage receptors on their skin to detect disturbances of the field [11], as shown in Fig. 1A. Based on the electric field principle [12], we propose a flexible array e-skin, capable of proximity and pressure sensing. The electronic skin consists of several key components, including an elastic layer, transmit electrodes, receiver electrodes, shield layer, and a dielectric layer. By incorporating e-skin technology into the robotic arm, simple interactions with humans can be realized, as shown in Fig. 1B. Transmit electrode apply alternating voltages to generate electrical field. We use four receiver electrodes to detect the variations in the electrical field. The electric field is distorted when the hand is close to the electronic skin, and when the hand is pressed against the

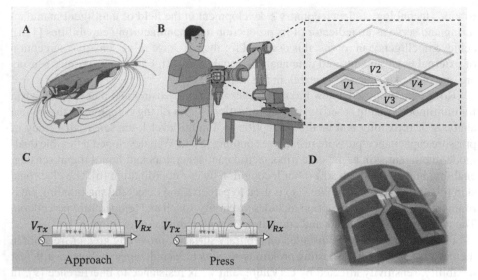

Fig. 1. Schematic of the e-skin. (A) Bio-inspired principle of weakly electric fish. (B) Application scenarios of e-skin. (C) Principle of e-skin. The transmitting electrode generates an electric field, and the receiving electrode perceives electric field disturbances in space (D) Digital picture of as-prepared e-skin.

sensor surface, the elastic layer is deformed and the distance between the hand and the electrode changes, so that the electric field is distorted, as shown in Fig. 1C. The digital picture of the as-prepared e-skin is illustrated in Fig. 1D.

2.2 Sensing Performances

We tested the response ability of the sensor with a copper block. As shown in Fig. 2A, scatter points of finger distance and electrode voltage within 0–160 mm were collected through a measurement platform, and fitted to form the sensor distance and electrode potential ΔV. From the response curve, we can see that the varying voltage increases exponentially as the distance between the finger and the sensor gradually shrinks. In practical applications of human-computer interaction, the signal received by sensors varies nonlinearly with distance. Therefore, we move the copper block from left to right at a height of 40 mm, and the electrode potential changes, as shown in Fig. 2B. The electrode potential is higher near the electrode, and the consistency of the four receiver electrode signals is good.

When an object touches the sensor, it exerts pressure on the sensor. Therefore, we conducted the third stage of testing on the sensor. Changes in electrode potential and sensor stability were tested when the sensor was subjected to a pressure of 0−20 kPa, as shown in Fig. 3A. Under the same conditions, we tested the electrode potential of the sensor under forces of 10 N, 20 N, and 30 N, and repeated the test four times for each force, as shown in Fig. 3B. It can be seen that the electrode potential measured many times under the same force, ΔV is basically the same, and the repetition accuracy is very small, indicating that the sensor has a stable ability to judge the magnitude of the force.

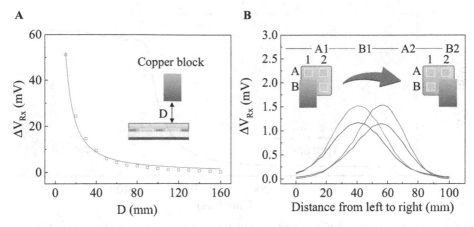

Fig. 2. Response ability testing of e-skin under proximity conditions. (A) The relative voltage response of the e-skin to finger approaching. (B) The finger moves from left to right, the voltage of the e-skin changes.

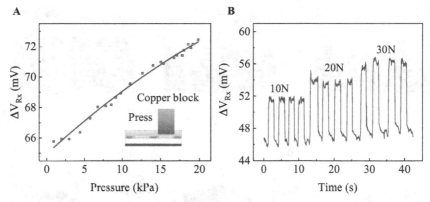

Fig. 3. Response ability and stability testing of sensors under pressure conditions. (A) Sensor to electrode potential within a pressure of 0−20 kPa.(B) Test the electrode potential of the sensor 4 times under a force of 10 N, 20 N, and 30 N.

We record the changes in sensor output electrode potential ΔV during the two stages of the sphere's falling approaching and pressing, as shown in Fig. 4. In the first stage, the sphere starts approaching the sensor from its initial height. The sphere enters the detection range of the sensor, resulting in electrode potential ΔV drops from 0 to 64.3 mV. In the second stage, the sphere contacts the sensor. Electrode potential ΔV further decreased from 64.3 mV to 73.5 mV.

As shown in Fig. 5, the 3D histogram distribution of a finger at the top left, middle and bottom right positions 8 cm away from the sensor. It can be seen that the 3D histogram corresponding to each sensor unit is exactly the same as the finger position. This result shows that proximity sensing sensors have the ability to detect multiple points or positions.

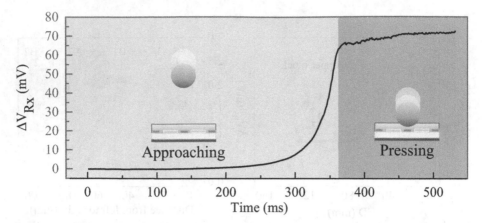

Fig. 4. The variation of variable electrode potential Δ V in two stages under the approaching and pressing of a sphere (with an approaching distance of 160 mm).

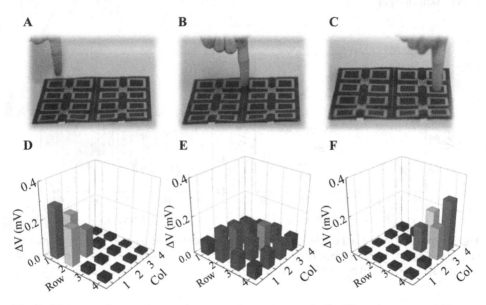

Fig. 5. The macro button chooses the correct format automatically. Finger image acquisition at three positions 8 cm above the sensor. (A)Finger points at the top left. (B) Finger points at the middle. (C)Finger points at the bottom left. (D)The 3D histogram of a finger at the top left. (E) The 3D histogram of a finger at the middle. (F) The 3D histogram of a finger at the bottom left.

2.3 Electric Skin Application

As shown in Fig. 6A, we installed a proximity sensor on the six degrees of freedom (6-DoF) manipulator. Due to the good flexibility of the sensors, we can easily install the proximity sensors on the robot, and design a feedback control system for the manipulator for obstacle avoidance test, as shown in Fig. 6B. Firstly, the proximity sensing sensors detect the approaching signals of objects in real-time, and send the position and force information to the robot arm controller. The controller processes the signal. When the detected signal is greater than the initial set safety threshold the robotic arm will timely trigger its safety control (braking) to achieve obstacle avoidance effect. Conversely, when the detected signal is less than the safety threshold, the robot arm does not respond. Figure 6C shows the signal curve detected when only the arm is used to apply proximity to approach the robot arm, which is the response of the robot arm to the obstacle avoidance control. A human hand approaches the running robot arm. When the detected signal the initial set threshold, the robot triggers a braking response. The results show that the peak proximity reaches about 90 mm, and the robot arm can brake after the approach occurs.

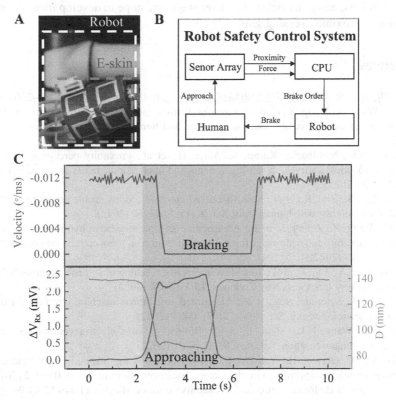

Fig. 6. Proximity sensing sensors are applied to robotic arm systems for obstacle avoidance testing. (A) Prototype of a robotic arm equipped with sensing sensors. (B) Schematic diagram of the feedback control system of the robotic arm for obstacle avoidance testing. (C) The response of the robotic arm system when only force detection is used in obstacle avoidance testing.

3 Conclusion

Based on the principle of weak electric field fish, we propose a flexible sensing array that mimics the proximity and pressure sensing of electric field fish. With this array, we have designed a proximity sensing sensor. This sensor is suitable for obstacle avoidance, emergency stopping, and other functions of robotic arms or robots due to its transparency, flexibility, and long detection distance. In this project, we demonstrated through the collection of proximity and force information, image acquisition, and application testing of proximity sensors on robotic arms that proximity sensors can achieve the goal of quickly completing obstacle avoidance and safety control, effectively reducing unnecessary collisions and accidents, improving safety in use, and can be used in industrial production, intelligent robots, and other fields. At a later stage, we hope to develop more directions for the use of proximity sensing sensors.

References

1. 谢广明, 郑君政, 王晨.:水下仿生电场感知综述. 系统仿真学报**32**(12), 2289–2305 (2020)
2. Jin, J., Wang, S., Wang, Y., et al.: Progress on flexible tactile sensors in robotic applications on objects properties recognition, manipulation and human-machine interactions. Soft Sci. (2023)
3. Navarro, S.E., Muhlbacher-Karrer, S., Alagi, H., et al.: Proximity perception in human-centered robotics: a survey on sensing systems and applications. IEEE Trans. Robot. **38**(3), 1599–1620 (2022)
4. Li, G., Liu, S., Zhu, R., et al.: Multifunctional electronic skins enable robots to safely and dexterously interact with human. Adv. Sci. **9**(11), 2104969 (2022)
5. Ge, C., Wang, Z., Zhang, J., et al.: A capacitive and piezoresistive hybrid sensor for long-distance proximity and wide-range force detection in human–robot collabo-ration. Adv. Intell. Syst. 2100213 (2022)
6. Liu, W., Duo, Y., Liu, J., et al.: Touchless interactive teaching of soft robots through flexible bimodal sensory interfaces. Nat. Commun. **13**(1), 5030 (2022)
7. Yu, Y., Li, J., Solomon, S.A., et al.: All-printed soft human-machine interface for robotic physi-cochemical sensing. Sci. Robot. **7**(67), 0495 (2022)
8. Guo, Z.H., Wang, H.L., Shao, J., et al.: Bioinspired soft electroreceptors for artificial precontact somatosensation. Sci. Adv. **8**(21), 5201 (2022)
9. Gottwald, M., Herzog, H., Von Der Emde, G., et al.: A bio-inspired electric camera for short-range object inspection in murky waters. Bioinspir. Biomim. **14**(3), 035002 (2019)
10. Yoo, Y., Choi, B.D.: Readout circuits for capacitive sensors. Micromachines **12**(8), 960 (2021)
11. Von Der Emde, G., Bousack, H., Huck, C., et al.: Electric fish as natural models for technical sensor systems. Bioeng. Bioinspired Syst. **73650B**, 102–112 (2009)
12. Dai, Y., Gao, S.: A flexible multi-functional smart skin for force, touch position, proximity, and humidity sensing for humanoid robots. IEEE Sens. **21**(23), 26355–26363 (2021)

A Novel Tactile Palm for Robotic Object Manipulation

Fuqiang Zhao[1], Bidan Huang[2], Mingchang Li[3], Mengde Li[4], Zhongtao Fu[5], Ziwei Lei[1], and Miao Li[1,4(✉)]

[1] The School of Power and Mechanical Engineering, Wuhan University, Wuhan, China
[2] Tencent Robotics X, Shenzhen, Guangdong Province, China
[3] Department of Neurosurgery, Renmin Hospital of Wuhan University, Wuhan, China
[4] The Institute of Technological Sciences, Wuhan University, Wuhan, China
miao.li@whu.edu.cn
[5] School of Mechanical and Electrical Engineering, Wuhan Institute of Technology, Wuhan, China

Abstract. Tactile sensing is of great importance during human hand usage such as object exploration, grasping and manipulation. Different types of tactile sensors have been designed during the past decades, which are mainly focused on either the fingertips for grasping or the upper-body for human-robot interaction.

In this paper, a novel soft tactile sensor has been designed to mimic the functionality of human palm that can estimate the contact state of different objects. The tactile palm mainly consists of three parts including an electrode array, a soft cover skin and conductive sponge. The design principle are described in details, with a number of experiments showcasing the effectiveness of the proposed design. (This work was supported by Suzhou Key Industry Technology Innovation Project under the grant agreement number SYG202121 and by the Fundamental Research Funds for the Central Universities under the grant agreement number 2042023kf0110).

Keywords: Tactile Sensor · Robotic Grasping and Manipulation · Robot Tactile Palm

1 Introduction

Tactile sensing is one of the most important modalities that endows the human hands with incomparable dexterity to explore, grasp and manipulate various objects [1–3]. These tasks involve physical contacts with the real world, which requires the tactile information to guide the sequence of actions for the task accomplishment [4]. Taking robotic grasping as an example, vision can inform the robot about the placement of the hand and the finger configuration, but ultimately the tactile information is still required to predict the contact state in terms of contact locations, contact forces and the grasp stability as well.

H. Yang et al. (Eds.): ICIRA 2023, LNAI 14271, pp. 81–92, 2023.
https://doi.org/10.1007/978-981-99-6495-6_8

During the past decades, a large variety of tactile sensors have been designed for different robotic applications [5–7], which can be roughly categorized into two groups: the tactile sensors installed on the fingertips for robotic grasping and dexterous manipulation [8,9], and the tactile (artificial) skin for human-robot interaction [10,11]. The former group requires the tactile sensor to be compact and with high-resolution, similar to the human fingertips [4]. Conversely, the latter group is usually used for human-robot interaction, where only a limited number of interaction patterns are required to be recognized in a human-like manner. Therefore the tactile skin must be soft and even stretchable in order to cover a large area with the compromise of the spatial resolution.

To summarize, previous studies of tactile sensors in robotics have focused mostly on the fingertips sensing and the tactile skin for the humanoid robot body. However, the palm is also an indispensable part for object manipulation, particularly in-hand manipulation [2,12]. In this work, we propose a biomimetic design of an inexpensive robotic tactile palm that can provide the object contact information such as contact position and contact forces during in-hand manipulation. The tactile palm comprises three main components: an array of sensing electrodes, a soft cover skin and a conductive sponge, as shown in Fig. 1.

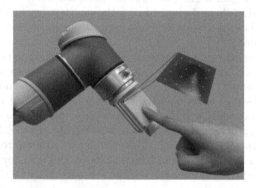

Fig. 1. The robotic tactile palm mounted on the UR5 robot arm. The top right window shows the tactile response to the corresponding contact state, where the filled yellow circles represent the positions of the 16 sensing electrodes. (Color figure online)

1.1   Robot Palm for Soft Grasping

The superior performance of soft hands is achieved at the expense of dexterity and precision. Many recent works have developed active palms to improve the dexterity of soft hand through implementing an additional degree of freedom to the palm [13–19]. For example, the palm-object interaction is actively controlled through varying the friction force by either changing the coefficient of friction or the normal load [20]. Jamming-based palm has been designed to actively adapt its shape for different objects geometry with variable stiffness [21,22].

While these new designs can help the soft hands to grasp more diverse objects with better stability, they still lack of the ability to estimate the contact state between the object and the hand. In another word, the grasp stability is passively guaranteed by the mechanical design of the hand.

1.2   Tactile Palm for In-Hand Object Manipulation

For in-hand object manipulation, the goal is to move the object to a desired state rather than to secure the object. To this end, it is extremely important to acquire the information about the object contact state. Previous studies have mostly focused on using vision and hand proprioception to estimate the object state or hand-object configuration [23–25]. This is partly due to the difficulty to design and integrate inexpensive but robust tactile sensor with the hand. Tactile dexterity is proposed for dexterous manipulations that render interpretable tactile information for control [26,27]. The tactile pad used for manipulation is largely adapted from two vision-based tactile sensors that use a camera to measure tactile imprints-GelSlim [28] and GelSight [29]. The vision-based tactile sensors have the advantages of low-cost and robust for physical interactions. However, vision-based tactile sensing has two intrinsic issues of non-uniform illumination and a strong perspective distortion, both of which require a careful calibration process.

In this paper, inspired by the work [30] and our previous work [31], we propose a novel design of an inexpensive robotic tactile palm, which can be used to estimate the contact state of the object during grasping and in-hand manipulation. For the sake of clarity, in this work we present:

– a novel design and fabrication method of a soft tactile palm consisting of an array of sensing electrodes, a soft cover skin inside and the conductive sponge.
– a systematic approach to estimate the contact positions and contact forces for the proposed tactile palm.

The rest of this paper is organized as follows: The design details and fabrication process are described in Sect. 2, while the methods used for contact position and contact forces estimation are given in Sect. 3. The experimental results are presented in Sect. 4 to demonstrate the effectiveness of this tactile palm, with a discussion and a conclusion in Sect. 5.

2   Design and Fabrication

2.1   Design Principle and Overall Structure

Similar to the design principle in [30], the proposed tactile palm consists of a rigid electrode board covered by conductive dielectric contained within an elastomeric skin. Multiple electrodes including the excitation electrodes and the sensing electrodes are mounted on board and connected to an impedance-measuring circuitry as shown in Fig. 2.

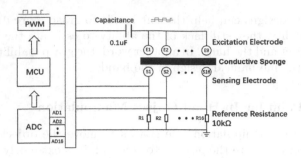

Fig. 2. The architecture of the electric circuitry to measure the electrode array impedance.

When external force is applied to the elastomeric skin, the conductive dielectric around the corresponding electrodes will deform. Therefore the measured impedance changes accordingly, which contains information about the external force and contact location as well.

For the conductive dielectric, we selected a conductive sponge composed of polymer, which is a porous composite material that exhibits excellent resilience and conductivity. The conductive sponge is placed around the electrodes. When pressure is applied to the skin, the conductive sponge deforms and alters the conductivity of the adjacent electrode points. The elastomeric skin is made by 3D printing using TPU material, which encapsulates all the devices inside the skin.

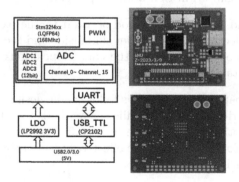

Fig. 3. The microcontroller(Stm32F4x) embedded with three 12-bit ADCs. Here, the excitation pulse is given through pulse width modulation (PWM) at a rate of 10000 Hz.

2.2 Fabrication and Assembly

Sensor Base and Skin: Both the base of sensor and the the skin are fabricated using 3D printing with an accuracy of $0.02mm$. (3D printer: UltiMaker Extended+, material: TPU).

Data Acquisition Module: For the data acquisition and processing module, we chose STM32F4x series chip[1] to design a simple analog-to-digital conversion (ADC) microcontroller with a sampling rate of 200 Hz. STM32F4 has frequency 168Mhz, embedded with three 12-bit ADCs. Each ADC module shares 16 external channels. Through the interface and soft wire, the microcontroller sends pulse-width modulation (PWM) signals at a frequency of 10000 Hz after capacitive filtering as an excitation signal to the excitation electrode. The signals collected by the sensing electrodes are then transmitted back to the microcontroller. The microcontroller uses a USB to TTL level serial module to communicate with the host computer and send the collected voltage values. The PCB consists of two layers, with most of the devices placed on the top layer. The overall size of the sensor contact acquisition module is 50mm*40mm, as shown in Fig. 3.

Assembly: The assembly consists of a base, a PCB, a conductive sponge, an isolation pad, and a soft skin, all arranged in layers as shown in Fig. 4 and Fig. 5. The isolation pad serves the purpose of isolating the conductive sponge from the electrode points on the PCB when no contact force is applied. The total fabrication cost of our tactile palm, including the data acquisition card, is less than 200 dollars.

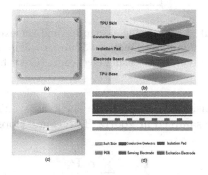

Fig. 4. The overall structure of the proposed tactile palm. It consists of an electrode board covered by conductive sponge contained within an elastomeric skin. Multiple electrodes including the excitation electrodes and the sensing electrodes are mounted on board and connected to an impedance-measuring circuitry.

3 Contact State Estimation

3.1 Contact Position Estimation

Our tactile palm has 16 sensing electrodes as shown in Fig. 6, $\{\mathbf{P}_i\}_{i=1...16}$, which are used as the anchor points to estimate the contact location. Once contacted

---

[1] https://atta.szlcsc.com/upload/public/pdf/source/20140801/1457707197138.pdf.

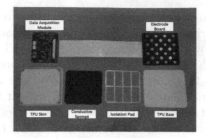

Fig. 5. The assembly of the tactile palm.

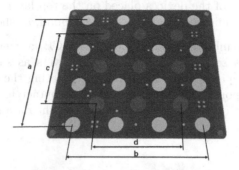

Fig. 6. The spatial layout of the sensing electrodes and the excitation electrodes. The design parameters are: a=45mm, b=45mm, c=30mm, d=30mm. Red represent excitation electrode, and yellow represent sensing electrode. (Color figure online)

with objects, 16 dimensional raw pressure data $S = \{S_i\}_{i=1...16}$ from the 16 sensing electrodes were sampled at 200Hz. The contact position is estimated as:

$$\mathbf{P}_c = \sum_{i=1}^{m} \alpha_i \mathbf{P}_i \tag{1}$$

where m is the number of activated electrodes that generally locate close to the contact points. α_i is the coefficient of the ith electrode, which can be computed as follows:

$$\alpha_i = \frac{\beta_i}{\sum_{1}^{m} \beta_i}, \quad \beta_i = 1 - e^{-\frac{2(S_i - S_{bi})^2}{\sigma_i^2}} \tag{2}$$

where S_{bi} and σ_i are the baseline of pressure and range of variation for the ith electrode, respectively. To test the accuracy of the contact position estimation, we use two 3D printed models as shown in Fig. 7 to test the position accuracy at several given points as well as along a given straight line. The average accuracy of the estimated contact position is around 2.7mm in practice and the maximal estimation error of position is 4.5mm. The position estimation and the straight line estimation is shown in Fig. 8.

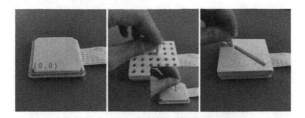

Fig. 7. Left: the coordinate system of the tactile palm; Middle: printed model to test the position accuracy at several given points; Right: printed model to test the position accuracy along a given straight line.

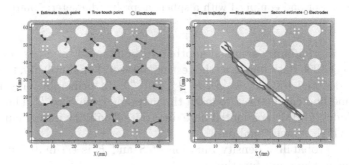

Fig. 8. Left: The contact position estimation for several given points. The average accuracy of the estimated position is around 2.7mm and the maximal estimation error of position is 4.5mm; Right: The straight line estimation during three trials. A printed probe is moving along a given slot for two times as shown in Fig. 7 (right) and the estimated traces are shown with different colors.

3.2   Contact Force Estimation

The tactile palm can provide 16 dimensional raw pressure data $\{S_i\}_{i=1\ldots16}$ from 16 sensing electrodes distributed as in Fig. 6. The goal of contact forces estimation is to predict the contact forces from these raw data. To this end, an ATI net Force/Torque sensor is used to measure the contact forces $\{F_i\}_{i-1\ldots3}$ between the tactile palm and the force sensor, while the contact forces are varied by the robot to take all the possible contact situations into account. The setup for the contact force estimation is shown in Fig. 9.

We uniformly sampled 28 points on the tactile palm. For each point, we first move the robot to a home position that is 20mm above the sampled point. Then we move the robot downwards until the contact is detected by the tactile sensor. Then the robot is moving downwards for a distance of 4mm in position control mode and both the force and tactile data are collected during this pressing procedure. Finally, the robot moves upwards to the home position. This process is repeated 5 times for each points.

The sampling rates for both tactile palm and force sensor are down-sampled to 100 Hz. $28 \times 5 \times 700 = 98000$ data points are collected as the training dataset.

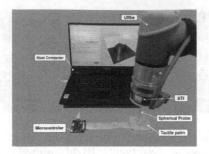

Fig. 9. The robot setup for the contact force estimation. The robot is mounted with a force/torque sensor and equipped with a spherical probe (diameter: 5mm)

In addition, we randomly sampled another 10 points and used the same procedure to collect 7000 data points as the testing dataset. For simplicity, the training data set is denoted by $\{X_i^j = [S^j, F^j]\}_{i=1...27}^{j=1...98000}$. In principle , any nonlinear regression method can be used to learn the mapping from S to F. The Gaussian Mixture Model (GMM) is adopted here due to its flexibility in modeling density function for high dimensional data.

The joint probability density function of S and F is estimated by a GMM composed of K Gaussian functions:

$$p(X) = \sum_{k=1}^{K} \pi_k \mathcal{N}(X|\boldsymbol{\mu}_k, \boldsymbol{\Sigma}_k) \tag{3}$$

where π_k is the prior of the kth Gaussian component and $\mathcal{N}(\boldsymbol{\mu}_k, \boldsymbol{\Sigma}_k)$ is the Gaussian distribution with mean $\boldsymbol{\mu}_k$ and covariance $\boldsymbol{\Sigma}_k$. The number of Gaussian functions K is selected by Bayesian information criterion (BIC), in this work $K = 7$. Other parameters $\{\pi_k, \boldsymbol{\mu}_k, \boldsymbol{\Sigma}_k\}$ are learned using EM algorithm.

With the trained model, now given a new tactile response S^*, the contact forces can be predicted as $F^* = E[F|S^*]$, which can be easily computed using Gaussian Mixture Regression (GMR). The Root Mean Square Error (RMSE) is 0.38N and the testing result is shown in Fig. 10.

As a comparison, we also applied SVR (Support Vector Regression) and DNN (Deep Neural Network) for the contact force estimation. The best performance of the estimation in terms of RMSE is 0.54N for SVR and 0.42N for DNN, respectively. This can be explained by the fact that SVR and DNN attempt to learn the regression between the force and the tactile data directly, which is a quite strict constraint and is also sensitive to sensory noise. As a comparison, GMM attempts to model the joint density between the contact force and the tactile information, from which the mapping to predict the contact force can be implicitly inferred.

4 Experiment and Result

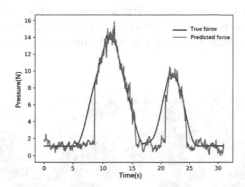

Fig. 10. The force calibration along the normal direction. The Root Mean Square Error (RMSE) of the estimated contact force is 0.38N. Force Unit: Newton.

In the experiment, we tested the tactile response to different everyday objects, as shown in Fig. 11. For small and light object like earphone, the proposed tactile palm can still generate a very clear tactile pattern. It is worth mentioning that the sensitivity of the tactile palm can still be improved by using a softer elastomeric skin and more electrodes.

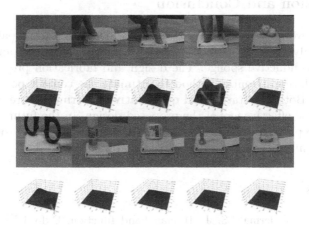

Fig. 11. The tactile responses to different objects. From the left to right: touch by one finger, touch by two fingers, touch by three fingers, earphone, stone, clip, charger, screw, solid glue, 3D printed workpiece.

The experimental results demonstrate promising applications of the proposed tactile palm in robotic manipulation and object exploration. For example, as discussed in [3], one can use the palm as an intermediate step to change the state of the object, in order to accomplish the sequential more complex manipulation task, such as the in-hand manipulation task in [24]. These potential applications will be further investigated in our future work. In addition, from the details of the fabrication process, it can be known that more complex shaped tactile sensor can be designed. For example, a cylindrical shaped tactile pad can be developed to cover the link of a robot arm, which will possibly pave a new direction for whole body tactile sensing. One example would be bimanual tactile manipulation as shown in Fig. 12.

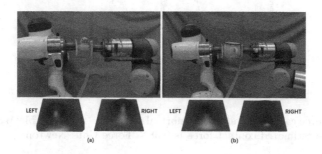

Fig. 12. Bimanual tactile manipulation (a) Grasping a rubber object (b) Grasping a water cup.

5   Discussion and Conclusion

In this paper, we proposed a novel biomimetic design of tactile palm. The tactile palm mainly consists of three parts: an array of electrodes, an elastomeric skin and the conductive sponge. The design and fabrication process are given in details, with a systematic method to estimate the contact position and the contact force. Both qualitative and quantitative experiments are conducted to demonstrate the effectiveness of the proposed design. In the future, we will further study the problem of how to combine the tactile palm with robot arm and fingers to accomplish more complex object manipulation tasks.

References

1. Jones, L. A., Lederman, S. J.: Human hand function. Oxford University Press (2006)
2. Castiello, U.: The neuroscience of grasping. Nat. Rev. Neurosci. **6**(9), 726–736 (2005)
3. Billard, A., Kragic, D.: Trends and challenges in robot manipulation, Science **364**(6446), eaat8414 (2019)
4. Johansson, R.S., Flanagan, J.R.: Coding and use of tactile signals from the fingertips in object manipulation tasks. Nat. Rev. Neurosci. **10**(5), 345–359 (2009)
5. Bartolozzi, C., Natale, L., Nori, F., Metta, G.: Robots with a sense of touch. Nat. Mater. **15**(9), 921–925 (2016)

6. Dahiya, R.S., Metta, G., Valle, M., Sandini, G.: Tactile sensing-from humans to humanoids. IEEE Trans. Rob. **26**(1), 1–20 (2009)
7. Kappassov, Z., Corrales, J.-A., Perdereau, V.: Tactile sensing in dexterous robot hands. Robot. Auton. Syst. **74**, 195–220 (2015)
8. Yousef, H., Boukallel, M., Althoefer, K.: Tactile sensing for dexterous in-hand manipulation in robotics-a review. Sens. Actuators A **167**(2), 171–187 (2011)
9. Luo, S., Bimbo, J., Dahiya, R., Liu, H.: Robotic tactile perception of object properties: a review. Mechatronics **48**, 54–67 (2017)
10. Argall, B.D., Billard, A.G.: A survey of tactile human-robot interactions. Robot. Auton. Syst. **58**(10), 1159–1176 (2010)
11. Silvera-Tawil, D., Rye, D., Velonaki, M.: Artificial skin and tactile sensing for socially interactive robots: a review. Robot. Auton. Syst. **63**, 230–243 (2015)
12. Stival, F., Michieletto, S., Cognolato, M., Pagello, E., Müller, H., Atzori, M.: A quantitative taxonomy of human hand grasps. J. Neuroeng. Rehabil. **16**(1), 1–17 (2019)
13. Wang, H., Abu-Dakka, F.J., Le, T.N., Kyrki, V., Xu, H.: A novel soft robotic hand design with human-inspired soft palm: achieving a great diversity of grasps. IEEE Robot. Autom. Mag. **28**(2), 37–49 (2021)
14. Capsi-Morales, P., Grioli, G., Piazza, C., Bicchi, A., Catalano, M.G.: Exploring the role of palm concavity and adaptability in soft synergistic robotic hands. IEEE Robot. Autom. Lett. **5**(3), 4703–4710 (2020)
15. Yamaguchi, A., Takemura, K., Yokota, S., Edamura, K.: A robot hand using electro-conjugate fluid: Grasping experiment with balloon actuators inducing a palm motion of robot hand. Sens. Actuators A **174**, 181–188 (2012)
16. Meng, J., Gerez, L., Chapman, J., Liarokapis, M.: A tendon-driven, preloaded, pneumatically actuated, soft robotic gripper with a telescopic palm. In: 2020 3rd IEEE International Conference on Soft Robotics (RoboSoft), pp. 476–481. IEEE (2020)
17. Subramaniam, V., Jain, S., Agarwal, J., y Alvarado, P.V.: Design and characterization of a hybrid soft gripper with active palm pose control. Int. J. Robot. Res. **39**(14), 1668–1685 (2020)
18. Sun, Y., Zhang, Q., Chen, X.: Design and analysis of a flexible robotic hand with soft fingers and a changeable palm. Adv. Robot. **34**(16), 1041–1054 (2020)
19. Pagoli, A., Chapelle, F., Corrales, J.A., Mezouar, Y., Lapusta, Y.: A soft robotic gripper with an active palm and reconfigurable fingers for fully dexterous in-hand manipulation. IEEE Robot. Autom. Lett. **6**(4), 7706–7713 (2021)
20. Teeple, C., Aktas, B., Yuen, M. C.-S., Kim, G., Howe, R. D., Wood, R.: Controlling palm-object interactions via friction for enhanced in-hand manipulation. IEEE Robot. Autom. Lett. **7**, 2258–2265 (2022)
21. Lee, J., Kim, J., Park, S., Hwang, D., Yang, S.: Soft robotic palm with tunable stiffness using dual-layered particle jamming mechanism. IEEE/ASME Trans. Mechatron. **26**(4), 1820–1827 (2021)
22. Li, Y., Wei, Y., Yang, Y., Chen, Y.: A novel versatile robotic palm inspired by human hand. Eng. Res. Express **1**(1), 015008 (2019)
23. Choi, C., Del Preto, J., Rus, D.: Using Vision for Pre- and Post-grasping Object Localization for Soft Hands. In: Kulić, D., Nakamura, Y., Khatib, O., Venture, G. (eds.) ISER 2016. SPAR, vol. 1, pp. 601–612. Springer, Cham (2017). https://doi.org/10.1007/978-3-319-50115-4_52
24. Andrychowicz, O.M., et al.: Learning dexterous in-hand manipulation. Int. J. Robot. Res. **39**(1), 3–20 (2020)

25. Hang, K., Bircher, W.G., Morgan, A.S., Dollar, A.M.: Hand-object configuration estimation using particle filters for dexterous in-hand manipulation. Int. J. Robot. Res. **39**(14), 1760–1774 (2020)
26. Hogan, F.R., Ballester, J., Dong, S., Rodriguez, A., Tactile dexterity: manipulation primitives with tactile feedback. In: IEEE International Conference on Robotics and Automation (ICRA). IEEE, vol. 2020, pp. 8863–8869 (2020)
27. Hogan, F. R., Bauza, M., Canal, O., Donlon, E., Rodriguez, A.L.: Tactile regrasp: grasp adjustments via simulated tactile transformations. In: 2018 IEEE/RSJ International Conference on Intelligent Robots and Systems IROS, pp. 2963–2970. IEEE (2018)
28. Donlon, E., Dong, S., Liu, M., Li, J., Adelson, E., Rodriguez, A.: Gelslim: a high-resolution, compact, robust, and calibrated tactile-sensing finger. In: 2018 IEEE/RSJ International Conference on Intelligent Robots and Systems (IROS), pp. 1927–1934. IEEE (2018)
29. Yuan, W., Dong, S., Adelson, E.H.: GelSight: high-resolution robot tactile sensors for estimating geometry and force. Sensors **17**(12), 2762 (2017)
30. Wettels, N., Santos, V.J., Johansson, R.S., Loeb, G.E.: Biomimetic tactile sensor array. Adv. Robot. **22**(8), 829–849 (2008)
31. Lei, Z., et al.: A biomimetic tactile palm for robotic object manipulation. IEEE Robot. Autom. Lett. **7**(4), 11 500–11 507 (2022)

Tactile-Based Slip Detection Towards Robot Grasping

Yuru Gong[1], Yan Xing[2], Jianhua Wu[1(✉)], and Zhenhua Xiong[1]

[1] State Key Laboratory of Mechanical System and Vibration, School of Mechanical Engineering, Shanghai Jiao Tong University, Shanghai 200240, China
wujh@sjtu.edu.cn
[2] Beijing Institute of Control Engineering, Beijing 100000, China

Abstract. Precise grasp is a vital application in robot manipulation while real-time slip detection can help the control system to monitor grasp force and compensate for position deviation. However, commonly-used robots hardly have slip detection modules, and the lack of real-time slip information obstructs the robot from making timely force or position adjustments. This paper proposes a real-time slip detection method using 2D images and surface height maps provided by a tactile sensor. Marker-centered sub-height maps, which indicate the local tangential and normal deformation of the sensor surface, are compared based on fast normalized cross correlation (NCC). The object status is determined from the integration of all the local slips. The experiment validates the proposed method with the average classification accuracy of 88.89% for 21 daily objects in 90 grasp trials, including translational slip, rotational slip, and stable trials. Frame detection accuracy of 94.56% for slip frames and 98.81% for stable frames are achieved. The real-time capability of the algorithm is also tested. The proposed method demonstrates the feasibility of detecting slip using the dual-modal outputs from single tactile sensor which can be installed on robot grippers. Moreover, real-time classification results can be used to monitor force or position regulation strategies and assist precise manipulation, including assembly work and deformable objects operation.

Keywords: Slip detection · Tactile sensor · Robot grasping

1 Introduction

One of the essential endeavors in robotics is to enable robot manipulators to grasp various objects with dexterity and accuracy [1]. Some industrial robots need to maintain the tools' stability and compensate for disturbance to finish assembly work, and robots in the agriculture or service industry are required to

This research was supported in part by the Science and Technical Innovation 2030-Artificial Intelligence of New Generation under Project2018AAA0102704 and the State Key Laboratory of Mechanical System and Vibration (Grant No. MSVZD202205).

grasp non-rigid or deformable objects without excessive force [18]. These tasks are simple for humans with the help of tactile sensing, as we monitor the force to stabilize the grasped object when we feel the slip intention of it [2]. Considering the robot precision manipulation, robots can use the real-time slip signals to overcome uncertainty and compensate for external disturbance, similar to the human fingers [12]. As slip is a subtle and rapid process, real-time slip detection is vital to ensure that the robot obtains the object's status in time to make adjustments and prevent further failure. However, slip detection is difficult to reproduce in the robots as they rarely have the sensing system to detect contact information with the environment [23]. Therefore, it is necessary to integrate the robot with the proper sensor to realize real-time slip detection.

Various sensors have been deployed to detect slip including uniaxial or triaxial force sensors and accelerometers. As contact force is the direct factor to detect slip, Cavallo et al. [3] modeled the contact behavior between a compliant force sensor and a manipulated object based on a Kalman filter to detect slip. However, this method hypothesized a constant friction coefficient of the object surface throughout the experiment. To avoid the impact of the objects surface parameters on the slip detection algorithm, Stachowsky et al. [14] further proposed a method that was immune from the different object properties or changes in the contact area. Cross-covariance of normal forces measured by two force sensors was applied in a force-regulation model to manipulate fragile objects. Physical models are usually necessary to process the force sensors data. Alternatively, vibration measured by accelerometers can be used directly to detect slip. Chathuranga et al. [4] employed five accelerometers to detect the high-frequency vibration caused by contact of the object and manipulator, and used the derivatives of signals to detect slip. However, installing all the accelerometers on the manipulator was cumbersome, and the linear acceleration could affect the vibration signal processing

Although these sensors mentioned above enabled practical slip detection methods, they were limited in the physical modeling relying on objects' properties and the vulnerability to external disturbance [12]. To overcome these deficiencies, researchers developed various tactile sensors to directly sense the contact information, and use machine learning algorithms to detect slip [13]. Veiga et al. [17] designed a tactile sensor called BioTac, resembling human fingers. The sensor was equipped with thermal, force, and vibration sensors. A random forest classifier processed the sensor's high-dimensional information and classifed the object status, reaching a success rate of 74.28% when grasping seven objects. Like BioTac, James et al. [7] developed a biomimetic tactile sensor named TacTip. The displacements of pins embedded in the sensor were used to detect slip with the support vector machines. Nevertheless, they only tested the method's effectiveness on simple stimuli rather than performing on daily objects. Meanwhile, the aforementioned tactile sensors were designed for the humanoid fingertip, limiting their application on industrial grippers with paralleled fingers. Tomo et al. [15] produced a soft tactile sensor called USkin, which was able to be integrated with industrial grippers. Each Uskin module measures the applied 3D force vector using a Hall effect sensor and a magnet. Yan et al. [20] used this sensor's raw data to classify the slip and stable grasping trials on 52 daily objects using a spatio-temporal network. Although their method reached an 81.38% accuracy, it was difficult to meet real-time requirements, and dataset collection was time-consuming.

Researchers tried to endow tactile sensors to "see" the changes on the sensor's surface. Johnson et al. [8] designed a vision-based optical tactile sensor named Gelsight. The sensor's surface is a soft elastomer painted with a reflective membrane, which deforms to the object's shape upon contact. Underneath this elastomer is a webcam to record the deformed gel illuminated by RGB LEDs from different edges. This 2D image data can indicate the tangential deformation of the elastomer with the added markers as displacement reference. The shear force exerted on the sensor surface is estimated from the marker displacement [22]. Therefore, Yuan et al. proposed a slip detection method based on the friction theory using the marker displacement distribution as a slip indicator [22]. However, the friction effect during slip can hardly be reflected from the high-dense marker array when grasping objects with a small contact area, which still not covering enough reference markers. Additionally, this method was less robust and accurate due to the large proportion of marker center detection in the subtle marker displacement. Considering these potential defects, Dong et al. [6] replaced the sensor's surface material and combined three methods to detect slip: the movement of the object texture, marker displacement distribution, and the loss of contact area. These methods achieved an average 77.7% accuracy on the slip detection of 37 objects. Each of the methods was discussed for a different type of contact situation, including obvious texture and texture-less objects. However, the relative movement detection of the objects texture contradicted with the marker displacement distribution method since the relative movement was determined by using markers as a static reference and may fail when markers displaced. The combination of these two methods may reduce the system's robustness. The main reason for the contradiction was that the 2D image can only reflect the tangential deformation of the elastomer, but the methods managed to measure the object texture movement and marker displacement simultaneously. Therefore, a second modal of information, which refers to the height map indicating the normal elastomer deformation, should be introduced to slip detection. The height map is generated by photometric stereo methods [21].

In this paper, a real-time slip detection method using a commercial tactile sensor Gelsight Mini is proposed. By fusing the marker images captured by internal camera and contact height maps indicating surface normal deformation, relative movement between the sensor and the object is quantified by calculating the NCC [5], and is used to classify the objects' status to slip or stable. The proposed method can potentially provide the real-time slip detection result for robotic grasping in an uninstructed environment without the knowledge of objects features. The rest of this paper is organized as follows. Section 2 describes the detailed proposed slip detection method. Experiments are shown in Sect. 3. Subsequently, experiment results and the discussion are provided in Sect. 4. Finally, conclusions and future works are demonstrated in Sect. 5.

2 Proposed Method

This section describes the proposed real-time slip detection method consisting of three parts: (1) the detection of the contact condition between the tactile sensor and the object; (2) an NCC-based method to detect object slip by fusing the sensor's tangential and normal deformation information; (3) the real-time slip detection system architecture. Each grasping trial is divided into three stages: non-contact, stable-contact, and lifting. During the lifting stage, the object's status S^t at frame t is classified to slip or stable. Slip status is identified when object moves relative to the sensor surface.

The tactile sensor Gelsight Mini is installed on the robot gripper, providing 25 Hz dual-modal information at each frame t (Fig. 1): the 320*240 RGB colored image G^t indicating the tangential deformation of the sensor elastomer from the marker centers' displacement and the same size height deformation map H^t extracted by the sensor's built-in algorithm indicating normal deformation. There are 7*9 black markers manufactured on the elastomer surface. The markers would deform, and their centers would shift as the elastomer deforms. Due to the illumination condition at the edge of the image, the colored image was resized to 265*235, while available markers reduce to 7*8.

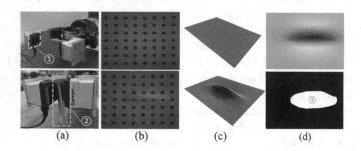

Fig. 1. Demonstration of the contact between the sensor and the object. (a) Gelsight① before (upper) and after (down) contact with the object②. (b) Marker image without (upper) and with (down) contact. (c) Height map without and with contact. (d) Changes in the height map resulted by contact (upper) and the resulted contact-area③(down).

2.1 Contact Area, Frame, and Active Markers Detection

In the non-contact stage, the height map H^t is close to zero. As the object contacts the sensor, the deformation of the sensor's surface results in the height map changes (Fig. 1(c)). Considering the elastomer thickness of 4 mm [21] and the membrane's elasticity, the areas with more than 1 mm indentation in the height map H^t are recognized as the contact area A. Considering the possible noise disturbance, two consecutive images and height maps are analyzed to determine the stable-contact frame. Three features are chosen to determine the stable-contact frame: each height map's mean and standard variance, and the two images' structural similarity (SSIM) index. The SSIM index indicates the similarity between compared images in the scope of their brightness, contrast, and structure [19]. The latter frame of the two consecutive images is regarded as the stable-contact frame t_{sc} if the means and standard variances of two images are close and the SSIM index is close to one.

During the stable-contact period, objects of different sizes may have limited contact area on the tactile sensor, therefore only markers located within the possible contact area A_{pc} are analyzed to improve the algorithm's real-time performance. The possible contact area A_{pc} is dilated from the stable-contact area A_{sc}, which is conservatively determined by $h^t > 1$ mm. The markers located within the A_{pc} are recognized as active markers, denoted as K_{am} (Fig. 2(b)(c)). The centers of the markers $(x^m_{c_k}, y^m_{c_k})$ are calculated from the grayscale image of G^t by centroid calculation algorithm.

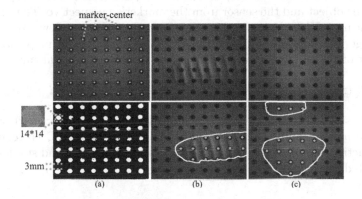

Fig. 2. Demonstration of marker center detection and the active markers of different objects. (a) Marker center detection for 56 marker (upper) and marker contours (down). Active markers represented by blue dots for (b) screwdriver, (c) bottle. (Color figure online)

2.2 Detection of Slip Based on NCC of Sub-Height Maps

Displacements of the active markers can reflect elastomer deformation and indicate slip [6]. However, the marker displacements are prone to be a misleading signal when the sensor surface is stretched under the grasping load (Fig. 3). The markers displace along with the object's movement while keeping the relatively static position, and this situation should be recognized as a stable grasp.

To avoid this problem, sub-height map H^t_k is extracted from the H^t within active marker k-centered square window (Eq.(1)). H^t_k fuses the information from

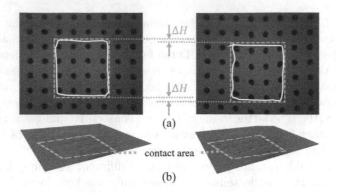

Fig. 3. Demonstration of the sensor's stretch due to the object's movement.(a) White box is the contact area, markers in yellow box are identical markers. Markers and contact area are moving at this moment while they are relatively static. (b) Height maps which correspond to the images remain the same. (Color figure online)

the image G^t and the height map H^t, indicating the local relative displacement between the object and the sensor from the marker's perspective. The size of the sub-height map H_k^t is determined by the squared marker window size $w_m = 21$, as the larger w_m can extend the perception scope of the height map changing at the center of the active markers, but increase the computational time,

$$H_k^t (i,j) = H^t \left(x_{c_k}^m - 0.5w_m + i, y_{c_k}^m - 0.5w_m + j\right), 0 \le i,j \le w_m \qquad (1)$$

where H^t is the height map at the frame t; $\left(x_{c_k}^m, y_{c_k}^m\right)$ is the k marker center; w_m is the marker sub-height map width. Therefore, the NCC correlation R_k^t between active marker$k$-centered sub-height maps at frame t and stable-contact is calculated as [16]

$$R_k^t (x,y) = \frac{\sum\limits_{i,j=0}^{w_{ncc}} H_k^t (x+i, y+j) \bullet H_k^{sc} (x+i, y+j) - w_{ncc}^2 \mu_t \mu_{sc}}{\sqrt{\sigma_t \sigma_{sc}}} \qquad (2)$$

where H_k^t and H_k^{sc} are active marker$k$-centered sub-height maps at frame t and stable-contact, respectively; w_{ncc} is the NCC sliding window width; and

$$\mu_t = \frac{1}{w_{ncc}^2} \sum\nolimits_{i,j} H_k^t (x+i, y+j)$$
$$\sigma_t = \sum\nolimits_{i,j} H_k^{t\,2} (x+i, y+j) - w_{ncc}^2 \mu_t \qquad (3)$$

μ_{sc} and σ_{sc} are similar to μ_t and σ_t but replace the t with sc.

Since the sub-height map H_k^t stands for the local elastomer deformation at the center of the active marker k at time t, the change of H_k^t indicates the possible local slip of the object. To quantify this change, NCC is applied to the

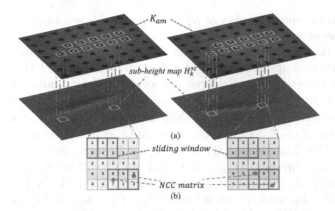

Fig. 4. Demonstration of the NCC calculation between height maps. (a) Sub-height maps extraction at active markers. (b) The NCC matrix calculation between sub-height maps with the sliding window.

sub-height maps. NCC is widely applied to the image pattern matching field due to its reliability and simplicity. This area-based matching calculates the dot product of the sliding windows from two images [9]. The sub-height map H_k^{sc} extracted from the stable-contact height map H^{sc} is regarded as the template in NCC calculation. At each frame t, the NCC matrix R_k^t of active marker k is calculated (Fig. 4, Eq.(2)) to evaluate the local relative displacement. Values r_k^t from R_k^t indicate the local correlation between two corresponding sliding windows. Therefore, a small value of r_k^t could be considered as a possible slip indicator. The sliding window size w_{ncc} controls the comparing precision of the H_k^t, as the algorithm with smaller w_{ncc} is more sensitive to small changes, but becomes less robust and computationally efficient. The w_{ncc} was set to 10. Due to the identical size of two comparing images in the algorithm, the integral image method can optimally fasten the NCC calculation (Eq.(4)) and promote the algorithm to the real-time level.

$$\sum_{i,j=0}^{w_{ncc}} H_k^t (x+i, y+j) \bullet H_k^{sc} (x+i, y+j) =$$

$$1/2 \left\{ \sum_{i,j} \left(H_k^t (x+i, y+j) + H_k^{sc} (x+i, y+j) \right)^2 - \sum_{i,j} H_k^{t^2} (x+i, y+j) \right.$$

$$\left. - \sum_{i,j} H_k^{sc2} (x+i, y+j) \right\} \tag{4}$$

where $\sum_{i,j} \left(H_k^t + H_k^{sc} \right)^2$, $\sum_{i,j} H_k^{t^2}$ and $\sum_{i,j} H_k^{sc2}$ can be efficiently calculated by the integral images.

$$d_{slip} = cnt_r \Big/ K_{am} \left(w_m - w_{ncc} + 1 \right)^2 \tag{5}$$

where cnt_r is the count number of R_k^t value r which is less than $r_{th} = 0.8$; K_{am} is the number of selected active markers.

Because the objects vary in size and trials vary in slip patterns, not the entire sub-height map nor all the sub-height maps can detect the local height map changes caused by slip. However, less local correlation can indicate a larger possibility of slip. Therefore, the slip index d_{slip}^t is proposed to evaluate the local slip proportion in each frame. Slip index d_{slip}^t at frame t is defined as the proportion of small NCC values r_k^t in the total NCC values from all active markers (Eq.(5)). The status of the frame S^t will be set to slip once the slip index d_{slip}^t reaches the threshold $D_{slip} = 0.4 \times 0.4$, which will be discussed further in the Discussion part. D_{slip} consists of two parts: the small NCC values proportion D_{slip}^1 and the "slip marker" proportion D_{slip}^2. D_{slip}^1 stands for the proportion threshold of small NCC values in each NCC matrix to identify the "slip marker". D_{slip}^2 stands for the proportion threshold of "slip markers" in all active markers. The algorithm process described in this part is shown in Algorithm 1.

Algorithm 1. Detection of Local Slip Based on the NCC of Sub-height Maps

---

Require: Frame t active markers K_{am}, marker centers $\left(x_{c_k}^m, y_{c_k}^m\right)$, height maps H_k^t;
Stable-contact frame marker centers $\left(x_{c_k}^{sc}, y_{c_k}^{sc}\right)$, height maps H_k^{sc}
Ensure: Frame t slip index $d_{k_{slip}}^t$ of each marker k
1: $cnt_r = 0$;
2: **for** $k \in K_{am}$ **do**
3:     **Calculate** sub-height maps H_k^t, H_k^{sc} with H^t, H^{sc};   ▷ Eq.(1)
4:     **Calculate** R_k^t with H_k^t, H_k^{sc};   ▷ Eq.(2),(4)
5:     **for** $r \in R_k^t$ **do**
6:         **if** $r < r_{th}$ **then**
7:             cnt_r ++;
8:         **end if**
9:     **end for**
10: **end for**
11: **Calculate** $d_{k_{slip}}^t$ with cnt_r;   ▷ Eq.(5)
12: **Return** $d_{k_{slip}}^t$;

2.3   Real-Time Slip Detection System Architecture

The real-time slip detection process is structured as Algorithm 2: in the contact stage, the changes in the height map are used to detect the contact area. Once the stable-contact frame is detected, the stable-contact area is dilated to determine active markers. In the lifting stage, sub-height maps at active marker centers are obtained, and the sub-height maps in the stable-contact area are used as templates. Then the slip index of sub-height maps calculated by the NCC algorithm is compared with the slip index threshold, and the object's status at frame$t$ is eventually classified as slip or stable.

3 Experiment

3.1 Experimental Setup

The robot grasp experiments with a robot system composed of a JAKA Zu 6DOF arm and a Robotiq 2F-140 paralleled gripper was conducted. Two Gelsight Mini sensors were installed on each of the fingers (Fig. 5(a)), while only the left-side sensor's data was collected and processed. The right-side sensor was installed to maintain grasping balance. The working radius of the robot arm was 1327 mm, and the repeatability was 0.03 mm. Robotiq 2F-140 can provide grasp force from $10N$ to $125N$. A connector was customized to maintain its stroke of 140 cm.

Algorithm 2. Real-time Slip Detection with Gelsight Input

Require: Frame t Gelsight image G^t, height map H^t
Ensure: Frame t Slip index d_{slip}^t and object status S^t
1: **while** Grasping **do**
2:     **Calculate** contact area A with H^t;
3:     **if** stable-contact at frame t_{sc} **then**
4:         **Set** H^{sc} as NCC template
5:         **Dilate** contact area A_{sc} to A_{pc};
6:         **Compute** marker centers $\left(x_{c_k}^m, y_{c_k}^m\right)$ with grayed G^t;
7:         **Determine** active markers K_{am} located in A_{pc};
8:         **while** $d_{k_{slip}}^t < D_{slip}$ **do**
9:             **Calculate** slip index $d_{k_{slip}}^t$ with Algorithm 1;
10:         **end while**
11:         **Set** object status $S^t \Rightarrow Slip$;
12:         **Return** $d_{k_{slip}}^t$ and S_{slip};
13:     **end if**
14: **end while**

The grasp experiments were performed on 21 objects that were commonly seen in daily life (Fig. 5(b)). These objects were chosen based on their material, mass, shape, and surface texture. As the objects' shapes could directly affect the elastomer's deformation, these objects were further classified into 5 categories according to their shapes: cylinder, spheric, irregular, long-thin, and cuboid, and objects in the first three categories generate more significant elastomer deformation. In this experiment, each object was grasped several times with different grasp forces related to the distance between the gripper's parallel fingers. The object was also lifted at different velocities with each grasp force. Some grasp forces were insufficient to lift the object stably, while others could lift the same object without slipping.

3.2 Data Collection

During the experiment, the robot was set to the initial position, and the Gelsight sensor began to capture its surface image with markers and obtain height map

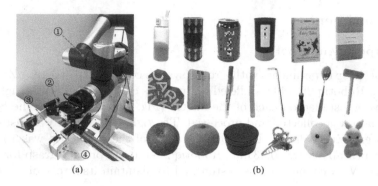

(a)   (b)

Fig. 5. Experimental Setup. (a) JAKA Zu 6DOF arm①, Robotiq 2F-140 paralleled②gripper, Two Gelsight Mini tactile sensor③ customized connector④. (b) 21 daily objects used for experiment.

by the built-in algorithm. The robot started to lift the object when the gripper grasped the object and reached the pre-determined distance between two fingers. The experiment during the grasping and lifting process were recorded for further manual analysis. For most objects, we obtained approximate transitional-slip, rotational-slip and stable trial numbers. However, we only collect rotational slip and stable trials for long and thin objects, which are not prone to slip vertically.

In total, 90 grasp trials were collected, including 52 slip trials (23 translational slip and 29 rotational slip) and 38 stable trials. Each trial and frame were manually labeled as slip or stable according to the experiment videos and Gelsight images. The status of the grasped object is clearly shown in the experiment videos and human observer can indicate the objects' status from these videos and the recorded sensor images. Eventualy, 52 slip trials and 38 stable trials were labeled by frames containing 2076 slip frames and 2358 stable frames, respectively.

4 Experiment Results and Discussion

4.1 Slip Detection Accuracy

Generally, the algorithm achieved 88.89% accuracy in detecting slip trials (Table 1), and achieved 94.56% and 98.81% accuracy in the classification of slip and stable frames, respectively (Fig. 6). The proposed method has outperformed the previous research with the accuracy of 77.77% [6] and 80.26% [11]. For cylinder, spheric, long-thin, and irregular objects, the detection accuracy reached 96.15%, 92.13%, 90%, and 100%, respectively. However, the accuracy on trials dropped to 66.67% when grasping cuboid objects, which usually contacted the sensor elastomer with a flat and texture-less surface. These results indicate that the NCC calculation-based detection accurately captures the subtle slip for objects that apply significant deformation on elastomer, but may struggle to detect the slip of cuboid objects. The similar problem was also mentioned in [6,7]. This deficiency is related to the sensor's construction and an alternative detection method should be applied.

Table 1. Numbers of objects and grasp trails in each category, and results of classification accuracy. L and T represents slip and stable trials, respectively.

	Cylinder	Cuboid	Spheric	Long&Thin	Irregular	Total
Objects Count	5	4	3	6	3	21
Trials Count(L+T)	26(17+9)	18(10+8)	13(9+4)	20(10+10)	13(6+7)	90(52+38)
Successful Trial(L+T)	25(17+8)	12(6+6)	12(8+4)	18(9+9)	13(6+7)	80(47+33)
Accuracy(%)	96.15	66.67	92.13	90	100	88.89

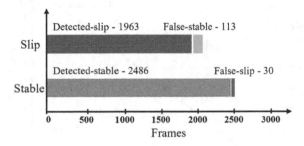

Fig. 6. Frame classification accuracy. Detected-stable and detected-slip frames are frames of objects status accurately detected. False-stable frames are slip frames misclassified to stable. False-slip frames are stable frames misclassified to slip.

The proposed method is also capable of stable trial detection. Stable trials could be misclassified as slip trials in [10] as the markers could shift under the shear force. Considering the complicated marker deformation and center displacements, we proposed the method based on the sub-height maps at the marker-centered windows. Therefore, only the normal deformation relative to the markers was considered, essentially describing the object-elastomer slip and avoiding the marker shift problem. The detection accuracy by frames in Fig. 6 showed the relatively low misclassified probability in stable frames. The false-slip detection may cause more damage comparing to the false-stable. If the classification result serves as a signal for the robot to adjust grasp force, the false-slip signal leads to the force enhancement without changing the height map value distribution, and the misclassified result cannot be corrected. The force enhancement infinite loop can cause damage to the object and the control system. False stable frames usually happen in the early stage of the slip where the objects move marginally. This false could be corrected once the slip has accumulated. Luckily, this method only performed 30 false slip frames, mainly from cuboid trials out of 2486 frames.

4.2 Algorithm Real-Time Capability Evaluation

The potential of the proposed method for real-time applications was tested with an Intel core i5-10500 CPU and 16 GB RAM. Since slip detection time for each frame was related to the number of active markers, we analyzed several grasp trials with the different numbers of active markers and calculated the average execution time of each frame (Fig. 7). The average slip detection execution time is 16.9 ms, and most trials have only 13 active markers due to the limited contact area. Compared to the Gelsight's camera's 25 Hz output rate, the object's status at the current frame can be classified before the next frame is captured. Therefore, the slip detection output can be the signal for the robot to make timely adjustments of grasp force and position, which is significant for robot precision manipulation.

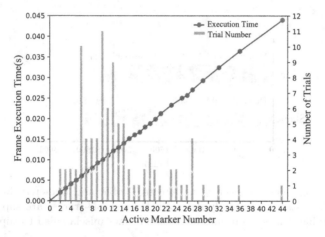

Fig. 7. Average frame execution time and trial counts with different number of active markers. The dot and line represent the average execution time for each frame, the bar represents the number of trials. The average frame execution time is 16.9 ms.

4.3 Slip Index Threshold

The high classification accuracy has proved the validity of the slip index threshold value D_{slip}. To further discuss the robustness of the slip index threshold, the slip index change throughout the trials of two typical grasped objects are analyzed (Fig. 8). The slip index remained close to zero in the contact stage, and slightly increased at the beginning of the lifting stage but was still smaller than the slip index threshold, indicating the movement of the sensor's surface caused by shear force. During the lifting stage, the slip index in slip trials demonstrated significant change, but remained relatively small in stable trials. Moreover, the slip index in slip trials increased as the slip of the object became severe. Due to the significant step in slip trials when the slip happened, the value of the slip index should be robust enough for the application.

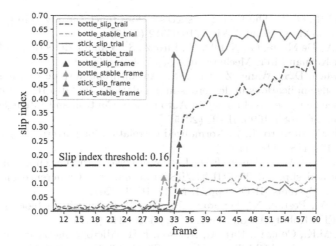

Fig. 8. Slip index of each frame in the chosen trials

5   Conclusions

In this paper, a slip detection method is proposed, using the marker images and height maps provided by Gelsight Mini tactile sensor. Dual-modal information of images and height maps indicates the tangential and normal deformation caused by contact. The local relative movement of the object and the sensor is quantified by NCC metrics, and elements in the NCC matrix are used to determine the object status as slip or stable. The method's feasibility is proved by experiments of 90 grasp trials and 4592 frames for 21 objects in 5 categories, and slip classification of each frame achieved satisfactory accuracy. However, slip detection performance for cuboid objects with flat and texture-less surface are restricted due to the sensor's capability. The proposed slip detection method can help the robot perceive interactions with the external environment, which is meaningful in force adjustments, grasping strategy selection, and precision manipulations. For future work, we plan to detect slip angles of rotational slip, which is vital for precision manipulation, and use machine learning methods to enhance the robustness and accuracy, especially for objects with a flat surface. The robot perceive interactions with the external environment, which is meaningful in force adjustments, grasping strategy selection, and precision manipulations. For future work, we plan to detect slip angles of rotational slip, which is vital for precision manipulation, and use machine learning methods to enhance the robustness and accuracy, especially for objects with a texture-less surface.

References

1. Al-Mohammed, M., Adem, R., Behal, A.: A switched adaptive controller for robotic gripping of novel objects with minimal force. IEEE Trans. Control Syst. Technol. **31**(1), 17–26 (2022)

2. Calandra, R., et al.: The feeling of success: Does touch sensing help predict grasp outcomes? arXiv preprint arXiv:1710.05512 (2017)
3. Cavallo, A., De Maria, G., Natale, C., Pirozzi, S.: Slipping detection and avoidance based on Kalman filter. Mechatronics **24**(5), 489–499 (2014)
4. Chathuranga, D.S., Wang, Z., Hirai, S.: An anthropomorphic tactile sensor system with its applications in dexterous manipulations. In: 2015 IEEE International Conference on Cyber Technology in Automation, Control, and Intelligent Systems (CYBER), pp. 1085–1090. IEEE (2015)
5. Dickey, F.M., Romero, L.A.: Normalized correlation for pattern recognition. Opt. Lett. **16**(15), 1186–1188 (1991)
6. Dong, S., Yuan, W., Adelson, E.H.: Improved gelsight tactile sensor for measuring geometry and slip. In: 2017 IEEE/RSJ International Conference on Intelligent Robots and Systems (IROS), pp. 137–144. IEEE (2017)
7. James, J.W., Pestell, N., Lepora, N.F.: Slip detection with a biomimetic tactile sensor. IEEE Robot. Autom. Lett. **3**(4), 3340–3346 (2018)
8. Johnson, M.K., Cole, F., Raj, A., Adelson, E.H.: Microgeometry capture using an elastomeric sensor. ACM Trans. Graph. (TOG) **30**(4), 1–8 (2011)
9. Lewis, J.P.: Fast template matching. In: Vision interface. vol. 95, pp. 15–19. Quebec City, QC, Canada (1995)
10. Li, J., Dong, S., Adelson, E.: Slip detection with combined tactile and visual information. In: 2018 IEEE International Conference on Robotics and Automation (ICRA), pp. 7772–7777. IEEE (2018)
11. Li, L., Sun, F., Fang, B., Huang, Z., Yang, C., Jing, M.: Learning to detect slip for stable grasping. In: 2017 IEEE International Conference on Robotics and Biomimetics (ROBIO), pp. 430–435. IEEE (2017)
12. Reinecke, J., Dietrich, A., Schmidt, F., Chalon, M.: Experimental comparison of slip detection strategies by tactile sensing with the biotac® on the DLR hand arm system. In: 2014 IEEE International Conference on Robotics and Automation (ICRA), pp. 2742–2748. IEEE (2014)
13. Romeo, R.A., Zollo, L.: Methods and sensors for slip detection in robotics: a survey. Ieee Access **8**, 73027–73050 (2020)
14. Stachowsky, M., Hummel, T., Moussa, M., Abdullah, H.A.: A slip detection and correction strategy for precision robot grasping. IEEE/ASME Trans. Mechatron. **21**(5), 2214–2226 (2016)
15. Tomo, T.P., et al.: A modular, distributed, soft, 3-axis sensor system for robot hands. In: 2016 IEEE-RAS 16th International Conference on Humanoid Robots (Humanoids), pp. 454–460. IEEE (2016)
16. Tsai, D.M., Lin, C.T., Chen, J.F.: The evaluation of normalized cross correlations for defect detection. Pattern Recogn. Lett. **24**(15), 2525–2535 (2003)
17. Veiga, F., Peters, J., Hermans, T.: Grip stabilization of novel objects using slip prediction. IEEE Trans. Haptics **11**(4), 531–542 (2018)
18. Vysocky, A., Novak, P.: Human-robot collaboration in industry. MM Sci. J. **9**(2), 903–906 (2016)
19. Wang, Z., Bovik, A.C., Sheikh, H.R., Simoncelli, E.P.: Image quality assessment: from error visibility to structural similarity. IEEE Trans. Image Process. **13**(4), 600–612 (2004)
20. Yan, G., et al.: SCT-CNN: A spatio-channel-temporal attention CNN for grasp stability prediction. In: 2021 IEEE International Conference on Robotics and Automation (ICRA), pp. 2627–2634. IEEE (2021)
21. Yuan, W., Dong, S., Adelson, E.H.: Gelsight: high-resolution robot tactile sensors for estimating geometry and force. Sensors **17**(12), 2762 (2017)

22. Yuan, W., Li, R., Srinivasan, M.A., Adelson, E.H.: Measurement of shear and slip with a gelsight tactile sensor. In: 2015 IEEE International Conference on Robotics and Automation (ICRA), pp. 304–311. IEEE (2015)
23. Zou, L., Ge, C., Wang, Z.J., Cretu, E., Li, X.: Novel tactile sensor technology and smart tactile sensing systems: a review. Sensors **17**(11), 2653 (2017)

A Faster and More Robust Momentum Observer for Robot Collision Detection Based on Loop Shaping Techniques

Zhongkai Duan[1], Zhong Luo[1,4(✉)], Yuliang Liu[2,3], Yuqiang Wu[2,3], and Wenjie Chen[2,3(✉)]

[1] School of Mechanical Engineering and Automation, Northeastern University, Shenyang 110819, China
zhluo@mail.neu.edu.cn
[2] Midea Corporate Research Center, Foshan 528311, China
chenwj42@midea.com
[3] Blue-Orange Lab, Midea Group, Foshan 528300, China
[4] Foshan Graduate Innovation School of Northeastern University, Foshan 528312, China

Abstract. Fast and robust collision monitoring is crucial to guarantee safe human-robot collaboration. In this paper, the loop shaping technique is used to improve the performance and robustness of conventional collision detection observers. External force estimated by the state-of-the-art first-order observer is fed to a lead-lag compensator for further processing, which results in a high-order observer. The lead compensator improves response speed in low-frequency range while the lag compensator enhances high-frequency noise attenuation of the observer. The effectiveness of utilizing the loop shaping technique is validated through simulation and experiments. The results show that the proposed observer has the fastest response speed and best noise attenuation performance compared with previous observers.

Keywords: Collision detection · High-order momentum observer · Loop shaping technique

1   Introduction

With the proportion of robots in automated production applications increasing year by year, the trend of expanding from industrial production applications to the service industry, medical and other fields is increasingly obvious. The robot workspace in this situation has also changed from the formerly closed workspace to a shared human-robot workspace, so monitoring collisions is crucial to ensure the safety of human-robot collaboration [1].

The safety of robots has been the subject of much research in recent years. In industrial robotics, safety thresholds are set for each joint motor of the robot and the torque exceeds the threshold when a collision occurs thus causing alerts [2], but this approach limits the effective output of the robot and is not conducive to

© The Author(s), under exclusive license to Springer Nature Singapore Pte Ltd. 2023
H. Yang et al. (Eds.): ICIRA 2023, LNAI 14271, pp. 108–120, 2023.
https://doi.org/10.1007/978-981-99-6495-6_10

the human-robot collaboration process [3]. Buondonno et al. introduced a six-dimensional moment sensor at the end of the robot to achieve accurate estimation of the contact force between the robot and the external environment [4]. However this approach only enables end force estimation, and human-robot collaboration in the service industry requires the robot to have the ability to force-sense its entire body.

The DLR laboratory in Germany has earlier achieved full-arm collision detection on the light collaborative arm using only the combined information collected by each joint torque sensor and applied it to KUKA's LWR series [5,6]. The current collision detection method based on momentum observer proposed by DLR has been extended more. Chang-Nho Cho et al. proposed a collision algorithm to further differentiate collision signals by introducing a second-order observer in the form of a band-pass filtered transmission [7], so that intentional contact and accidental collisions can be distinguished, but the proposed algorithm is not accurate for the identification of high-frequency torque and is not applicable to tasks such as deburring. Joonyoung Kim et al. proposed a collision detection method with parallel estimation by monitoring external forces simultaneously by two observers based on low-pass filtered and high-pass filtered transmission forms for the detection of fast and slow collisions [8], but the single observer has some problems for the noise disturbance. Jie Wang et al. further optimized the second-order observer using the second-order damping model [9], and the collision detection is faster with the same bandwidth, but there is also greater overshoot and difficulty in tuning the parameters. In terms of modelling, Li et al. accurately simulated the gravitational acceleration in dynamical modeling and verified the correctness [10,11], which provides certain reference.

In view of the shortcomings of the above observers, the loop shaping technique is used to improve the performance and robustness of conventional collision detection observers in this paper. Thus a collision detection algorithm based on high-order observer is proposed based on loop shaping technique, the lead compensator improves response speed in low-frequency range while the lag compensator enhances high-frequency noise attenuation of the observer. The feasibility of new algorithm is finally verified by simulation and experiment.

The framework of this paper is roughly as follows: Sect. 1 introduces the history of collision detection development, Sect. 2 introduces the conventional collision detection algorithm, Sect. 3 proposes new collision detection algorithm based on high-order observer. In Sect. 4 is simulation and experiments, and the final section summarizes the conclusions.

2 Conventional Collision Detection Algorithms

2.1 Collision Modeling

In n-degree of freedom tandem robots, the dynamic equations of the robot in the event of a collision can be expressed as follows:

$$M(q)\ddot{q} + C(q,\dot{q})\dot{q} + G(q) = \tau_i + \tau_{\text{ext}} \tag{1}$$

where τ_i consists of the motor torque and the friction torque together, namely $\tau_i = \tau_{mot} + \tau_f$, and external disturbance force is denoted by τ_{ext} ; the generalized coordinate, velocity and acceleration vectors of robot are denoted as q, $\dot{q}$, $\ddot{q} \in R^n$ respectively. $M(q)$, $G(q)$ denote the mass matrix and gravity matrix of the robot respectively, and $C(q, \dot{q})$ consists of a matrix of Koch forces and centrifugal forces.

The friction torque can be compensated by a generalized friction model, and the coulomb-viscosity model [12] used here is compensated. The expressions are as follows:

$$\begin{cases} \tau_f = \tau_c sgn(\dot{q}) + \tau_v(\dot{q}), if \, |\dot{q}| > \xi \\ \tau_v = \alpha_1 \dot{q} + \alpha_2 \dot{q}^2 \end{cases} \tag{2}$$

where τ_c denotes Coulomb friction, τ_v denotes viscous friction, and ξ denotes the maximum current noise of joint velocity, where α_1, α_2 are the coefficients of viscous friction.

To avoid the large signal noise caused by the direct introducing of acceleration $\ddot{q}$, we use a generalized momentum observer to indirectly obtain the collision moment. Generalized momentum can be defined as:

$$p = M(q)\dot{q} \tag{3}$$

Derivation of Eq. 3 yields:

$$\dot{p} = M(q)\ddot{q} + \dot{M}(q)\dot{q} \tag{4}$$

In Ref. 5, $C(q, \dot{q})\dot{q}$ of Eq. 1 can be written as [5]:

$$C(q, \dot{q})\dot{q} = \dot{M}(q)\dot{q} - C^T(q, \dot{q})\dot{q} \tag{5}$$

Let $v(q, \dot{q}) = C^T(q, \dot{q})\dot{q} - G(q)$, and further obtain the generalized momentum equation of the robot as follows:

$$\dot{p} = v(q, \dot{q}) + \tau_i + \tau_{ext} \tag{6}$$

where external disturbance force τ_{ext} is the value to be observed, defined as r, so that the estimated value of momentum $\hat{p}$ is expressed as follows:

$$\dot{\hat{p}} = \hat{v}(q, \dot{q}) + \tau_i + r \tag{7}$$

2.2   Conventional Observer Implementation

First-order observer: define the derivative of the residual [5] as:

$$\dot{r} = K(\dot{p} - \dot{\hat{p}}) \tag{8}$$

where K is the constant gain matrix, and assuming $\hat{v}(q, \dot{q}) = v(q, \dot{q})$, integrating Eq. 8 and substituting into $\hat{p}$ yields the observed value in the time domain:

$$r(t) = K \left[p - \int_0^t (\hat{v}(q, \dot{q}) + \tau_i + r) \, dt \right] \tag{9}$$

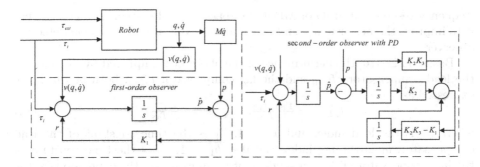

Fig. 1. First-order and Second-order observer algorithms.

To verify the stability, the Laplace transform of the derivatives of the residuals yields Eq. 10, for a first-order filter apparently stable.

$$r_i(s) = \frac{K_i}{s + K_i} \tau_{ext,i}(s), \quad i = 1, ..., n \tag{10}$$

Second-order observer: second-order observer with PD optimization [9] is introduced as a comparison group for the validation of the new algorithm, and its transfer function model is as follows:

$$\frac{r_i}{\tau_{ext,i}} = \frac{(K_{3,i}s + 1) K_{2,i}}{s^2 + K_{1,i}s + K_{2,i}}, \quad i = 1, ..., n \tag{11}$$

Converting it to the time domain yields:

$$r(t) = \int \left[K_2 \int (\tau_{ext} - r) \, dt + K_2 K_3 (\tau_{ext} - r) + (K_2 K_3 - K_1) r \right] dt \tag{12}$$

Substituting $\dot{p}$ and the estimated value $\dot{\hat{p}}$ yields the final expression:

$$r(t) = \int \left[K_2 p(t) - K_2 \int \hat{p} dt + (K_2 K_3 - K_1) r - K_2 K_3 \dot{\hat{p}} \right] dt + K_2 K_3 p(t) \tag{13}$$

The implementation of Eqs. 9 and 13 is shown in Fig. 1

3   Collision Algorithm Based on High-Order Observer

3.1   High-Order Observer Design

In Sect. 2.2, first-order observer is simple but has few adjustable parameters, and second-order observer has oscillation and overshoot; both are difficult to meet the observation requirements of specific frequency bands. Thus combine design ideas from Sect. 2.2 to reverse the design of new observer by loop shaping technique. The loop shaping technique is usually used to shape open-loop frequency response of SISO or MIMO feedback control system, and here we use it to improve the performance and robustness of conventional collision detection observers.

Based on Eq. 10, the performance of the observer is improved by introducing the lead compensator tf_{lead} and the lag compensator tf_{lag}, both of which are expressed as:

$$tf_{lead} = \frac{1+a_1 T_1 s}{1+T_1 s}, \quad tf_{lag} = \frac{1+b_1 T_2 s}{1+T_2 s} \tag{14}$$

where a_1 is the lead index and $a_1 > 1$, T_1 is the time constant of the lead compensator; b_1 is the lag index and $0 < b_1 < 1$, T_2 is the time constant of the lag compensator. Taking a single joint as an example, the expression for the high-order observer is as follows:

$$\frac{r}{\tau_{ext}} = tf_{lead} \times \frac{K_1}{s+K_1} \times tf_{lag} \tag{15}$$

Let $K_2 = T_1$, $K_3 = a_1 T_1$, $K_4 = T_2$ and $K_5 = b_1 T_2$, simplify and expand to obtain:

$$\frac{r}{\tau_{ext}} = \frac{K_1 K_3 K_5 s^2 + (K_1 K_5 + K_1 K_3) s + K_1}{K_2 K_4 s^3 + (K_4 + K_1 K_2 K_4 + K_2) s^2 + (1 + K_1 K_2 + K_1 K_4) s + K_1} \tag{16}$$

For simplicity of expression, let $a = K_2 K_4$, $b = K_4 + K_1 K_2 K_4 + K_2$, $c = 1 + K_1 K_2 + K_1 K_4$, $d = K_1$, $e = K_1 K_3 K_5$, $f = K_1 K_5 + K_1 K_3$ and the final transfer function form of the observer can be expressed as:

$$\frac{r_i(s)}{\tau_i(s)} = \frac{e_i s^2 + f_i s + d_i}{a_i s^3 + b_i s^2 + c_i s + d}, \quad i = 1, ..., n \tag{17}$$

The expression of new observer in the time domain can be written as:

$$r(t) = \frac{1}{a} \int \left[e\tau - br + \int \left(f\tau - cr + d \int (\tau - r) dt \right) dt \right] dt \tag{18}$$

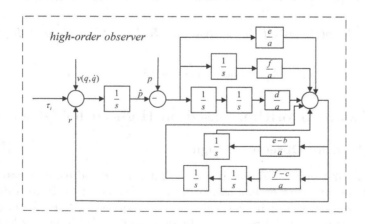

Fig. 2. High-order observer algorithm.

where vectors $b, c, d, e, f, \frac{1}{a} \in R^{n \times n}$ are diagonal gain matrices larger than 0. Simplifying Eq. 18 yields the following equation:

$$
r(t) = \frac{1}{a} \int \left[e(\tau - r) + \int \left(f(\tau - r) + d \int (\tau - r) dt \right) dt \right] dt \\
+ \int \left(\frac{e}{a} r + \int \frac{f - c}{a} r dt \right) dt
\tag{19}
$$

Due to $\hat{v}(q, \dot{q}) \approx v(q, \dot{q})$, $\tau - r$ in Eq. 19 can be written as $\tau - r = \dot{p} - \dot{\hat{p}}$, and substituting $\dot{p} = v(q, \dot{q}) + \tau_i + \tau_{\text{ext}}$, $\dot{\hat{p}} = \hat{v}(q, \dot{q}) + \tau_i + r$, the implementation algorithm of the new observer is shown in Fig. 2.

3.2 Observer Parameters Setting

Table 1. Parameter gain setting.

observer	$a(K_1)$	$b(K_2)$	$c(K_3)$	d	e	f
first-order	47.12	–	–	–	–	–
second-order	43.59	1530.2	0.00118	–	–	–
high-order	6.14×10^{-5}	0.027	2.14	47.2	4.34×10^{-5}	1.5

The specific parameters of all observers are selected as shown in Table 1. The low-frequency range is chosen 5 Hz $\sim$ 7.5 Hz for high-order observer, taking $a_1 = 1.5$ and $T_1 = \frac{1}{15\pi}$, and the high-frequency range is chosen 55 Hz $\sim$ 5.5 kHz, taking $b_1 = 0.01$ and $T_2 = \frac{1}{110\pi}$. The cutoff frequency of original first-order observer is chosen to be $7.5Hz$, namely $w_c = 15\pi \text{Rad/s}$, so original first-order observer gain value is taken as $K_1 = 15\pi$. For comparison, first-order and second-order observer cutoff frequencies are kept the same, both at $7.5Hz$.

The transfer function models of three observers are plotted in Bode diagrams according to Table 1. It can be seen that the high-order observer has much smaller

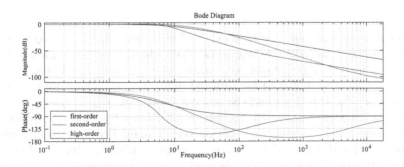

Fig. 3. Bode diagram for observers.

lag and better response speed than the others. As shown in Fig. 3, it also decays faster on the high-frequency range and has better high-frequency noise attenuation performance. The specific collision detection performance is verified by simulation and experiment in the next section.

4   Algorithm Verification

4.1   Simulation Verification

Robot simulation platform is built using Simulink, consisting of trajectory planning module, controller, robot system and the observer. The trajectory planning module gives a section of excitation to the robot arm, and the planning joint 1, 3 and 5 are planned from $0°$ to $10°$, $20°$ and $30°$ respectively, and all the following simulations are performed under this trajectory.

To verify the rapidity of high-order observer in the low-frequency range, a step signal is used to simulate the input of collision force and observe the time to reach the detection threshold. In order to verify the high-frequency range characteristics of high-order observer, the current noise signal input is simulated and the noise attenuation ratio of each observer is compared.

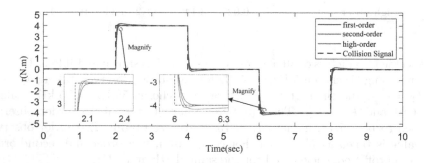

Fig. 4. The diagram of step signal simulation in joint 3. Simulating step signals to compare speed of observers, it can be seen that high-order observer has the fastest response speed.

Low-frequency performance verification: as Fig. 4, step force is added to joint 3 for both positive and negative segments. Since the simulation is an ideal environment, namely, default model is accurate, the collision signal (black dashed line) is used here as threshold for collision detection, and then the time for all three to reach the threshold and the amount of overshoot are observed.

High-frequency performance verification: Fig. 5 shows that two ramp waves of opposite amplitude are used for collision signal simulation, meanwhile current noise is introduced during the collision occurrence, where a sinusoidal signal of amplitude 0.5 and frequency 1KHz is used as noise input superimposed on the motor torque output.

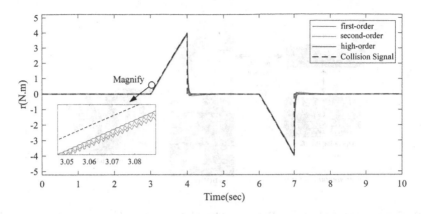

Fig. 5. The diagram of high-frequency noise simulation in joint 3. Simulating two ramp collision signals at the addition of high-frequency noise, it can be seen that high-order observer has the best reproduction of the collision signal, while the other observers are more affected by noise.

The collision signals are detected by each observer in Fig. 5, but the attenuation for high-frequency noise is different. To further describe the high-frequency attenuation performance, the following evaluation index is introduced:

$$\|E\|_{RMS} = \sqrt{\frac{1}{N-1} \sum_{i=1}^{N} \|E\|^2} \tag{20}$$

where E represents the error value of the detection signal and the collision signal and N represents the number of sampling points for the simulation.

The detection time and overshoot in Fig. 4 are counted in Table 2. Error E in Fig. 5 is extracted and described by $\|E\|_{RMS}$ in the table and evaluated by $'+'$, the more the number, the better the performance.

Comprehensive Table 2, high-order observer in low-frequency range has the fastest response time of 45ms compared to the low-order, and overshoot is also smaller than the second-order, without oscillation, and the adjustment time is shorter. In the high-frequency range, high-order attenuation of high-frequency noise is more pronounced under the same premise of current noise, and the error evaluation index $\|E\|_{RMS}$ is 0.0013 .

Table 2. Simulation results.

Observer	Low-frequency test				High-frequency test	
	1st-detection	overshoot	2nd-detection	overshoot	$\|E\|_{RMS}$	evaluation
first-order	165ms	0	165ms	0	0.0055	++
second-order	62ms	5%	62ms	4.5%	0.0059	+
high-order	45ms	2.5%	45ms	2.25%	0.0013	+++

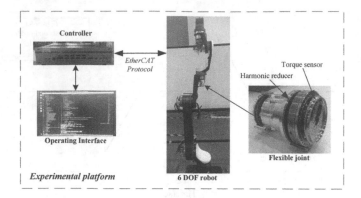

Fig. 6. Experimental platform diagram. The platform mainly consists of a controller and a flexible jointed robot, both of which are communicated through EtherCAT.

4.2 Experimental Verification

Experimental platform and collision threshold setting. In Fig. 6, collision experimental platform is built for verification based on Midea's self-developed AMR-PT1 flexible-joint robot, and the platform consists of controller, operating interface, and 6 DOF robot. In the experiment, choosing five polynomial plans excite joints 1, 2 and 3 from 0° to 20° of cyclic motion, and using the arm to randomly crash link 3 for interaction. Figure 7 depicts the limit position of the robot in the experiment and the location where the collision occurred, because here the simulated collision occurred at link 3, so joint 2 and 3 are taken as the detection index.

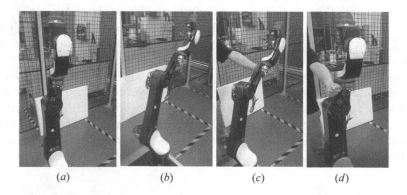

Fig. 7. Experimental test diagram. The $(a)(b)$ diagram on the left shows the two limit joint positions of the trajectory excitation, and the diagram $(c)(d)$ on the right indicates the position where the collision occurred in the test.

Due to robot model in the experimental environment cannot be completely accurate, namely, the value of observer is not 0 in the no-collision situation. Let the robot run in a non-collision situation for a period of time, and use high-order observer to detect the moments of 2,3 joints, and take the maximum value of each joint as the collision threshold,and eventually the thresholds of joints 2 and 3 are selected as $[-13, 5]$, $[-10, 4]$N.

Collision detection experiment and result. The robot sampling period in the experiment is $1ms$, and the sampling period in the figure is taken as $10ms$ in order to data simplicity. In order to better describe the experimental effect, only the collision detection effect of the first-order and high-order observers are compared here, and the specific first-order, second-order, and high-order differences are shown in Table 2. In (c)(d) of Fig. 7, joint 3 are randomly given multiple positive and negative low-frequency collision forces and high-frequency impulsive forces. As shown in Fig. 8 and 9, the observations of first-order and high-order observers are compared to analyze the response time and detection effect.

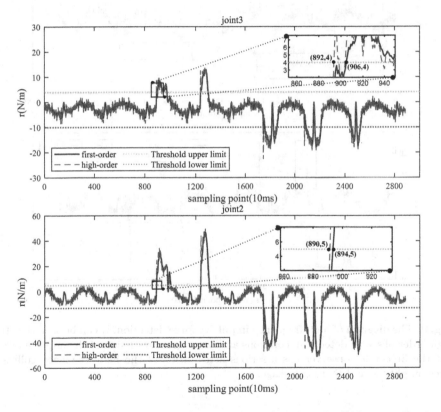

Fig. 8. The diagram of low-frequency collision force detection. It can be seen that both observers can detect the occurrence of collisions, but the high-order observer responds more rapidly, 140ms and 40ms faster on joints 3 and 2, respectively.

Figure 8 shows that in low-frequency collision test, both joints 2 and 3 can successfully detect the collision occurrence, and two measured collision forces are very close to each other, which further verified that the high-order observer designed in this paper has a good effect on the reversion of the collision force. Taking the first positive collision as an example, high-order observer in joint 3 detected the collision 140ms faster than first-order observer, and 40ms faster in joint 2, which reflects the rapidity advantage of high-order observer. And the difference in detection time between the two is due to the different collision sensitivity of joints 2 and 3.

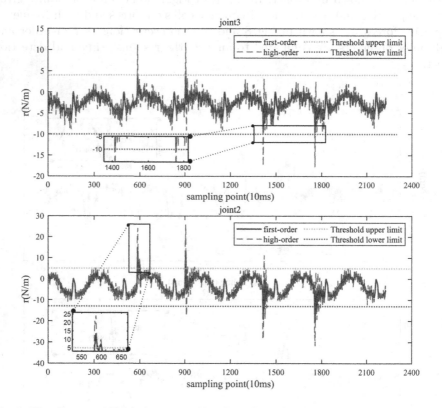

Fig. 9. The diagram of high-frequency impulsive force detection. It can be seen that the high-order observer detects all collisions and has a great reversion of the impulse force, but the first-order observer has a serious attenuation of the high-frequency collision force amplitude and there is leakage.

As shown in Fig. 9, in high-frequency impulse test, first-order observer in joints 2 and 3 has a large attenuation of the observed amplitude of the high-frequency impulse, and the last two collisions of joint 3 are not detected, and some safety concerns exist as a result of the missed detection phenomenon. High-order observer detects all collisions and reacts sensitively to high frequencies, faster detection of collision occurrence and stopping, which can better ensure collaboration safety.

Combined with the above experiments and analysis, high-order observer designed in this paper has faster response to low-frequency and high-frequency collision signals compared to the conventional observers, while the reversion to high-frequency impact force signals is higher, more sensitive detection and has less leakage detection. Furthermore, it is experimentally verified that the high-order observer has more rapidity and accuracy, improving the collision detection performance.

5 Conlusion

In order to better ensure the safety of human-robot collaboration, the loop shaping technique is used to improve the performance and robustness of conventional collision detection observers in this paper. A collision detection algorithm based on high-order observer is proposed based on loop shaping technique, the lead compensator improves response speed in low-frequency range while the lag compensator enhances high-frequency noise attenuation of the observer. And then the simulation verifies that high-order momentum observer has the fastest response speed of 45ms and the best high-frequency attenuation performance($\|E\|_{RMS} = 0.0013$) under the same conditions. Then the feasibility of the new algorithm is further verified through experiments, which not only detect collision at least 40ms faster than the original observer but also have a better reversion of the impulse collision signal, avoid the leakage detection phenomenon of the first-order observer, and can ensure human-robot collaboration safety better under the same threshold setting.

Acknowledgements. This work was supported by the Basic and Applied Basic Research Foundation of Guangdong Province [grant number 2020B1515120015]; the National Science Foundation of China [grant numbers 12272089, U1908217]; and the Fundamental Research Funds for the Central Universities of China [grant numbers N2224001-4, N2003013].

References

1. Haddadin, S., De Luca, A., Albu-Schäffer, A.: Robot collisions: a survey on detection, isolation, and identification. IEEE Trans. Robot. **33**(6), 1292–1312 (2017)
2. Maurtua, I., Ibarguren, A., Kildal, J., Susperregi, L., Sierra, B.: Human-robot collaboration in industrial applications: safety, interaction and trust. Int. J. Adv. Rob. Syst. **14**(4), 1729881417716010 (2017)
3. Zinn, M., Khatib, O., Roth, B., Salisbury, J.: Playing it safe [human-friendly robots]. IEEE Robot. Autom. Mag. **11**(2), 12–21 (2004)
4. Buondonno, G., De Luca, A.: Combining real and virtual sensors for measuring interaction forces and moments acting on a robot. In: 2016 IEEE/RSJ International Conference on Intelligent Robots and Systems (IROS), pp. 794–800 (2016)

5. De Luca, A., Albu-Schaffer, A., Haddadin, S., Hirzinger, G.: Collision detection and safe reaction with the DLR-III lightweight manipulator arm. In: 2006 IEEE/RSJ International Conference on Intelligent Robots and System, pp. 1623–1630 (2006)

6. Albu-Schäffer, A.O., Haddadin, S., Ott, C., Stemmer, A., Wimböck, T., Hirzinger, G.: The DLR lightweight robot: design and control concepts for robots in human environments. Ind. Robot. **34**, 376–385 (2007)

7. Cho, C.N., Kim, J.H., Kim, Y.L., Song, J.B., Kyung, J.H.: Collision detection algorithm to distinguish between intended contact and unexpected collision. Adv. Robot. **26**(16), 1825–1840 (2012)

8. Kim, J.: Collision detection and reaction for a collaborative robot with sensorless admittance control. Mechatronics **84**, 102811 (2022)

9. Wang, J., Zhu, H., Guan, Y., Song, Y.: Sensitive collision detection of second-order generalized momentum flexible cooperative joints based on dynamic feedforward control. In: 2021 IEEE International Conference on Robotics and Biomimetics (ROBIO), pp. 1682–1687 (2021)

10. Luo, Z., Li, L., He, F., Yan, X.: Partial similitude for dynamic characteristics of rotor systems considering gravitational acceleration. Mech. Mach. Theory **156**, 104142 (2021)

11. Li, L., Luo, Z., Wu, F., He, F., Sun, K.: Experimental and numerical studies on partial similitude of rotor system considering the vibration consistency. Mech. Mach. Theory **183**, 105270 (2023)

12. Lee, S.D., Kim, M.C., Song, J.B.: Sensorless collision detection for safe human-robot collaboration. In: 2015 IEEE/RSJ International Conference on Intelligent Robots and Systems (IROS), pp. 2392–2397 (2015)

Dynamic and Static Performance Analysis of a Linear Solenoid Elastic Actuator with a Large Load Capacity

Chuchao Wang[1], Wenyin Mo[1], Shizhou Lu[1,2](✉), Zeying Jing[1], Quan Zhang[1], and Junda Li[1]

[1] Mechanical, Electrical and Information Engineering, Shandong University, Weihai 264209, China
lushizhou@sdu.edu.cn

[2] WeiHai Research Institute of Industrial Technology of Shandong University, Weihai 264209, China

Abstract. In order to increase the electromagnetic force and improve the load resistance of micro and small robots, a linear solenoid elastic actuator (LSEA) with a magnetic ring is designed. The static and dynamic performance of the LSEA is analyzed. First, the magnetic field distribution and the function of the electromagnetic force are presented. The nonlinear vibration equation is obtained by dynamic modeling. Second, the averaging method is employed to obtain analytical results of the system parameters including equivalent stiffness, natural frequency, and damping coefficient. The transient network is constructed with the Simulink software to numerically solve the nonlinear equation. Finally, the dynamic test and the resistance load test on the LSEA are performed. The displacement curves and performance indicators obtained by the theoretical, simulation and experimental methods are compared. The maximum errors of setting time and stable displacement are 55.1 ms and 0.25 mm, respectively. The LSEA can resist a load of 10 g and produce a displacement of 4.7 mm at the voltage of 4.5 V. The mass of the load is 5.6 times that of the mover in the LSEA.

Keywords: Electromagnetic actuator · Elastic actuator · Nonlinear vibration

1 Introduction

Due to their small size, low cost, high accuracy, and high speed, micro and small robots have enormous potential in medicine [1], bioengineering [2], detection [3], rescue [4], and other fields. Several different types of miniature actuators, such as piezoelectric actuators (PZAs) [5], shape memory alloy (SMA) actuators [6], electroactive polymer (EAP) actuators [7], and electromagnetic actuators (EMAs) [2], have been widely used in microrobots. EMAs have a high response speed and can generate large displacements without excessive voltage, which have been widely used in microrobots. They also have a small resistance, simple control, and low cost. Considering the size and weight of robots, EMAs mainly consist of coils and ferromagnetic components. According to different moving parts, EMAs can be divided into moving magnet actuators (MMAs) [8], voice coil actuators (VCAs) [9] and electromagnets [10]. Linear EMAs (LEMAs) can generate thrust directly on the end effector, which have better dynamic performance and higher reliability. As a kind of LEMAs, LSEAs contain a magnetic plunger that is wrapped with electrically conductive wires, that can fully utilize the magnetic field to generate a large displacement [11].

Micro-robots with LSEAs often take advantage of high-frequency vibration generated by the actuators [12]. For example, LSEAs were used to design a multi-segmented robot [13, 14]. Each segment of the miniaturized robot was actuated by a pair of LSEAs. This robot can move linearly and turn by mimicking the peristaltic plane locomotion of earthworms. Modular LSEAs with actuation and sensing functions by using voice coils and magnets were designed [15, 16]. They can navigate complex unstructured environments and carry out inspection tasks. Increasing the electromagnetic force generated by LSEAs is of great significance for improving the load capacity of the robots, improving the dynamic and static response performance, and realizing various motion functions for the robots. On the one hand, the size parameters in the original structure can be optimized to achieve a larger driving force. Ebrahimi et al. [17] designed and optimized a soft LSEA to generate a larger force. On this basis, the geometry of the coil was optimized so that the magnetic field and force of the actuator can be maximized [18]. On the other hand, improving the original stator structure can also increase the magnetic field and the electromagnetic force, such as setting armatures to the outside or inside of the coil. For example, a novel tubular moving magnet linear oscillating actuator was designed [19]. The stator assembly is composed of a modular C-core structure to prevent flux cancelation. The mover assembly accommodates permanent magnets that contribute to high thrust force generation. Besides, an improved topology of the linear oscillation actuator was designed [20]. The improved C-core adopts double-sided stators and one active mover. However, the volume and mass of the LSEA with armatures also increase significantly. The heating caused by eddy currents is serious, which limits its application in micro and small robots.

In this paper, a kind of LSEA with a parallel magnetic ring is designed. Without changing the stator of the LSEA, adding a magnetic ring at the end of the magnets enables the mover to make full use of both the axial and radial magnetic field generated by the coil. Improve the electromagnetic force by optimizing the structure of the mover in the LSEA. Section 2 introduces the structural composition, functional principle and applications of the LSEA. Section 3 describes the establishment process of the electromagnetic model and nonlinear dynamic model in the LSEA. Section 4 presents the analysis of the displacement varying with the time of the LSEA under the step voltage using analytical and numerical methods. The system parameters for evaluating the dynamic and static performance of the nonlinear system are concluded. Section 5 describes the experiments including the dynamic performance test and the resistance load test on the LSEA. Transient curves and indicators of the LSEA obtained by the theoretical, simulation and experimental methods are compared and analyzed. The load capacity of the LSEA with and without the magnetic ring is compared.

2 Design of the LSEA

The 3D structure of the LSEA is shown in Fig. 1(a). The effective length is 23 mm, and the width is 11 mm. The coil is set on the outer wall of the inner sleeve, which is maintained relatively fixed with the shell to form the stator. The magnetic ring is squeezed into the outer sleeve. The magnet, magnetic bar and magnetic ring are arranged in the same order as the magnetic poles to form a mover. A compression spring is connected in parallel between the magnetic bar and the inner sleeve. A buffer spring with a larger stiffness is fixed to the bottom of the inner sleeve. A certain gap is left between the magnet and the inner sleeve. It is assumed that the maximum displacement of the magnets is 9 mm. The parallel spring maintains its natural length when the actuator keeps its initial state. The shell, inner sleeve, outer sleeve and back cover are manufactured by 3D printing with photosensitive resin.

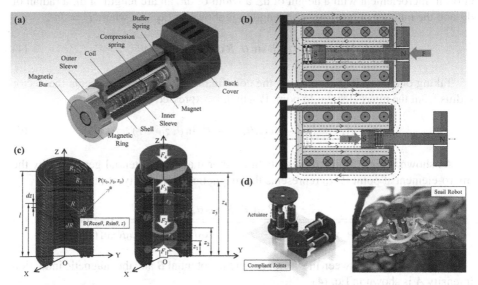

Fig. 1. The structure and function diagram of the LSEA. (a) 3D structure diagram. (b) Functional schematic. (c) Simplified model of the LSEA. (d) Application of the LSEA.

As shown in Fig. 1(b), it is assumed that the N pole is located on the right sides of the magnets, respectively, and the S pole is located on their left sides. From right to left, when a counterclockwise current is applied, a magnetic field from left to right can be generated inside the coil, and a right-to-left magnetic field can be generated outside the coil. Since the magnetic bar is located inside the coil, it moves forward and squeezes the parallel spring by the repulsive force. The parallel spring provides buffering, stores energy, and improves stability. Similarly, when a current in the opposite direction is applied, the magnetic bar retracts. During this movement, the energy of the parallel compression spring is released, and the spring placed at the bottom can effectively be a buffer. The electromagnetic system is abstracted into the model as shown in Fig. 1(c). The system consists of a coil and three magnets. The driving force on the magnets is the result of the interaction between the magnetic fields. Miniature-compliant joints and a bionic snail robot composed of LSEAs are shown in Fig. 1(d).

3   Mathematic Modeling of the LSEA

3.1   Electromagnetic Modeling of the LSEA

As shown in Fig. 1(c), R_1 and R_2 represent the inner and outer radii of the coil, respectively. l represents the height of the coil. r_1 and r_2 represent the radii of the magnetic bar and magnet, respectively. z_i ($i = 1$–4) represent the axial coordinates of the lower surfaces on the magnet, the intersection between the magnetic bar and the magnet, the lower surface on the magnetic ring, and the upper surface on the magnetic bar in the established coordinate system, respectively. I represents the current through the coil. A current microelement with a height of dz, a width of dR, an arc length of dl, a radian of $d\theta$ and the number of turns per unit length n is shown in Eq. (1), where $I' = In^2$.

$$I'\overrightarrow{dl} = In^2(-R\sin\theta, R\cos\theta, z)\,dzdRd\theta \tag{1}$$

Taking one point P (x_0, y_0, z_0) in the coordinate system, $\overrightarrow{r(z)}$ represents the vector radius from the microelement to point P, which is expressed in Eq. (2).

$$\overrightarrow{r(z)} = (x_0 - R\cos\theta, y_0 - R\sin\theta, z_0 - z) \tag{2}$$

As shown in Eq. (3), $\overrightarrow{dA}$ represents the vector magnetic potential generated by the micro-element at point P. μ_0 represents the magnetic permeability of the vacuum.

$$\overrightarrow{dA} = \frac{\mu_0 In^2}{4\pi} \frac{(-R\sin\theta, R\cos\theta, z)}{\sqrt{x_0^2 + y_0^2 + R^2 + (z - z_0)^2 - 2x_0R\cos\theta - 2y_0R\sin\theta}} d\theta dzdR \tag{3}$$

The relationship between the vector magnetic potential B and the magnetic induction intensity A is shown in Eq. (4).

$$B = \nabla \times A = \begin{vmatrix} i & j & k \\ \dfrac{\partial}{\partial x} & \dfrac{\partial}{\partial y} & \dfrac{\partial}{\partial z} \\ A_x & A_y & A_z \end{vmatrix} \tag{4}$$

After substituting Eq. (3) into Eq. (4), the axial magnetic induction intensity B_z generated by the current microelement is integrated over the circumferential, axial, and radial directions of the coil to obtain the axial magnetic induction intensity generated by the coil, as shown in Eq. (5).

$$B_z = \frac{\mu_0 n^2 I}{4\pi} \int\limits_{R_1}^{R_2} \int\limits_{0}^{l} \int\limits_{0}^{2\pi} \frac{R^2 - x_0R\cos\theta - y_0R\sin\theta}{\sqrt[3]{x_0^2 + y_0^2 + R^2 + (z - z_0)^2 - 2x_0R\cos\theta - 2y_0R\sin\theta}} d\theta dzdR \tag{5}$$

As shown in Fig. 1(c), the received total axial force is the sum of the electromagnetic forces on the four end surfaces, which are recorded as F_i ($i = 1, 2, 3, 4$) from bottom to top. F_1 and F_3 are upward repulsive forces. F_2 and F_4 are downward attractive forces when the magnets move upward. It is assumed that the surface remanence of the magnet and the magnetic bar is set to B_1, and the surface remanence of the magnetic ring is set to B_2. According to the magnetic charge model, the electromagnetic force F_i can be calculated according to Eqs. (6)–(9).

$$F_1 = \frac{B_1 n^2 I}{2} \int_0^l \int_0^{2\pi} \int_{R_1}^{R_2} \int_0^{r_1} \frac{Rr(R-r)\sin\theta}{r^3(z_1)} dr dR d\theta dz \tag{6}$$

$$F_2 = \frac{B_1 n^2 I}{2} \int_0^l \int_0^{2\pi} \int_{R_1}^{R_2} \int_{r_2}^{r_1} \frac{Rr(R-r)\sin\theta}{r^3(z_2)} dr dR d\theta dz \tag{7}$$

$$F_3 = \frac{B_2 n^2 I}{2} \int_0^l \int_0^{2\pi} \int_{R_3}^{R_4} \int_{r_3}^{r_4} \frac{Rr(R-r)\sin\theta}{r^3(z_3)} dr dR d\theta dz \tag{8}$$

$$F_4 = \frac{n^2 I}{2} \int_0^l \int_0^{2\pi} \int_{R_3}^{R_4} \left[B_1 \int_0^{r_2} \frac{r(R-r)\sin\theta}{r^3(z_4)} dr + B_2 \int_{r_3}^{r_4} \frac{r(R-r)\sin\theta}{r^3(z_4)} dr \right] R dR d\theta dz \tag{9}$$

The total electromagnetic force F_{Bz} generated by LSEA can be calculated by Eq. (10).

$$F_{Bz} = F_1 - F_2 + F_3 - F_4 \tag{10}$$

3.2 Dynamic Modeling of the LSEA

When the current is passed through the coil of the actuator, the magnets are forced to produce a reciprocating motion. The system can be abstracted into a spring-mass-damping model. Through the analysis of electromagnetic force, the displacement can be obtained from the differential equation as shown in Eq. (11). In this equation, m, c, k, and f represent the mass of the system, the viscous damping coefficient, the stiffness of the parallel spring, and the external load, respectively. x, $\dot{x}$ and $\ddot{x}$ represent the displacement, velocity, and acceleration of the magnets with time t, respectively.

$$m\ddot{x} + c\dot{x} + kx = f \tag{11}$$

The size and structural parameters of the coil, magnets are shown in Fig. 2(a). The magnet and magnetic bar (N35, Shenzhen Lala Magnetic Material, China) with the remanence of 1.18 T are selected. The magnetic ring (N38, Guangzhou Xingsheng Magnetic Industry, China) with the remanence of 1.22 T is selected. When a current of 1 A is applied to the coil, Eqs. (6)–(10) are used to calculate F_{Bz} and F_i ($i = 1$–4), and the results are shown in Figs. 2(b)–(f). The quartic polynomial function is used to fit the force-displacement relationship described by Eq. (10).

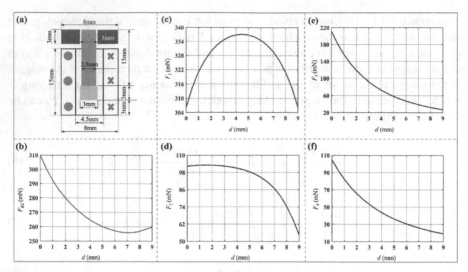

Fig. 2. (a) Size parameters of main components in the LSEA. Electromagnetic forces including (b) F_{BZ}, (c) F_1, (d) F_2, (e) F_3 and (f) F_4.

The polynomial fitting function is substituted into Eq. (11). The vibration equation is shown in Eq. (12). In Eq. (12), C_i ($i = 0, 1, 2, 3, 4$) represents the coefficient corresponding to the i-th degree, and g represents the acceleration of gravity. When the input current is 1 A, the C_i calculated by Eq. (12) is shown in Table 1.

$$m\ddot{x} + c\dot{x} + (k - IC_1)x - IC_2x^2 - IC_3x^3 - IC_4x^4 = IC_0 - mg \tag{12}$$

Table 1. The fitting coefficients in Eq. (12)

C_0	C_1	C_2	C_3	C_4
309.8	−20.26	3.233	−0.303	0.01396

4   Transient Response Analysis of the LSPEA

Equation (12) can be abstracted into Eq. (13) by introducing a small parameter ε, where w_0 represents the natural frequency of the system without considering damping.

$$\ddot{x} + w_0^2 x = A_0 + \varepsilon f(x) = A_0 + \varepsilon(A_2x^2 + A_3x^3 + A_4x^4) \tag{13}$$

In Eq. (13), it is assumed that $A_i = IC_i/m$ ($i = 2, 3, 4$). w_0 and A_0 are calculated according to Eqs. (14) and (15), respectively.

$$w_0 = \sqrt{\frac{k - IC_1}{m}} \tag{14}$$

$$A_0 = \frac{IC_0}{m} - g \qquad (15)$$

When the value of ε is set to 0, the solved result of the vibration equation described by Eq. (13) under the zero initial conditions is shown in Eq. (16), where x_0 represents the displacement without considering the nonlinearity, a_0 and ψ_0 represent the amplitude and phase of x_0, respectively.

$$x_0 = a_0(1 - \cos\psi_0) = \frac{A_0}{w_0^2}(1 - \cos w_0 t) \qquad (16)$$

The averaging method is first used to solve the problem, where the amplitude a and phase ψ are considered as the functions of the time. In Eq. (17), x represents the displacement changing with time. $\dot{a}$ represents the first derivative of the amplitude with time. $\dot{\psi}$ represents the first derivative of the phase with time. $a_1(a)$ and $w_1(a)$ represent the functions of the amplitude.

$$\begin{cases} x = a(1 - \cos\psi) \\ \dot{a} = \varepsilon a_1(a) \\ \dot{\psi} = w_0 + \varepsilon w_1(a) \end{cases} \qquad (17)$$

By substituting Eq. (17) into Eq. (13), the first-order derivatives of the amplitude $\dot{a}$ and phase $\dot{\psi}$ can be obtained as shown in Eqs. (18) and (19), respectively.

$$\dot{a} = \frac{\varepsilon}{2\pi w_0}\int_0^{2\pi}\left[f(x) + A_0 - aw_0^2\right]\frac{\sin\psi}{1 - \cos\psi}\,d\psi = 0 \qquad (18)$$

$$\dot{\psi} = w_0 - \frac{\varepsilon}{2\pi a w_0}\int_0^{2\pi}\left[f(x) + A_0 - aw_0^2\right]d\psi$$

$$= w_0 - \frac{\varepsilon}{a w_0}\left[\frac{3A_2 a^2}{2} + \frac{5A_3 a^3}{2} + \frac{35A_4 a^4}{8} + (A_0 - aw_0^2)\right] \qquad (19)$$

According to Eqs. (17)–(19), the displacement x_1 is obtained, as shown in Eq. (20).

$$x\_1 = a_0 - a_0\cos\left\{\left[w_0 - \frac{\varepsilon}{w_0}\left(\frac{3A_2 a_0}{2} + \frac{5A_3 a_0^2}{2} + \frac{35A_4 a_0^3}{8}\right)\right]t\right\} \qquad (20)$$

In Eq. (20), the natural frequency w_n is shown in Eq. (21).

$$w_n = w_0 - \frac{1}{w_0}\left(\frac{3A_2 a_0}{2} + \frac{5A_3 a_0^2}{2} + \frac{35A_4 a_0^3}{8}\right) \qquad (21)$$

The equivalent stiffness k_e can be obtained as shown in Eq. (22).

$$k_e = w_n^2 m \qquad (22)$$

The damping coefficient c can be calculated. σ represents the overshoot.

$$c = 2m\left[w_0 - \frac{1}{w_0}\left(\frac{3A_2a_0}{2} + \frac{5A_3a_0^2}{2} + \frac{35A_4a_0^3}{8}\right)\right]\sqrt{\frac{(\ln^\sigma)^2}{(\ln^\sigma)^2 + \pi^2}} \quad (23)$$

Next, Simulink software in MATLAB can be used to solve Eq. (13), and the transient network was built as shown in Fig. 3.

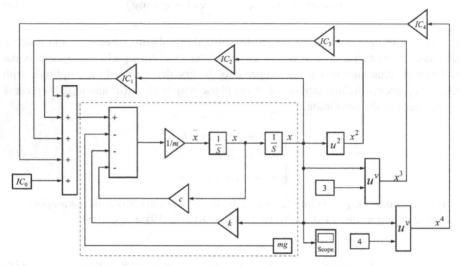

Fig. 3. The transient network of the electromagnetic system built in the Simulink software.

5   Experiments of the LSEA

5.1   Dynamic Performance Experiment of LSEA

The required experimental equipment for the dynamic performance test is shown in Fig. 4. It is assumed that G represents the shear modulus of the material, d corresponds to the wire diameter of the spring, n corresponds to the effective number of turns in the spring, and D corresponds to the middle diameter of the spring. The stiffness parameters of the compression spring and buffer spring are shown in Table 2. A laser displacement sensor is used to measure the displacement of the actuator. An oscilloscope is used to display the whole transient process of the magnets.

The transient curves obtained by the transient network in Fig. 3 are shown in Fig. 5(a). The transient curves obtained by the Adams software and the experimental method are shown in Figs. 5(b) and (c), respectively. When the relative error between the actual displacement and the stable displacement reaches 2.5%, the time is regarded as the setting time. When the LSPEA becomes stable, the stable displacement is calculated by taking the average of the actual displacements. The setting time and stable displacement can reflect the dynamic and steady-state performance of the LSEA, which are shown in Figs. 5(d) and (e), respectively. The setting time obtained by the theory and simulation is smaller than that obtained by the experimental method, because there is damping during the rising of the magnets. Due to the existence of the assembly gap, the axial distance between the upper surface of the lower magnet and the inner surface of the shell is greater than the length of the compression spring. The stable displacement obtained by the experimental method is larger than that obtained by the theory and simulation. Due to the existence of friction, the oscillation times of the transient curves obtained by the experiment is smaller than that obtained by other methods. The maximum errors of setting time and stable displacement are 55.1 ms and 0.25 mm, respectively.

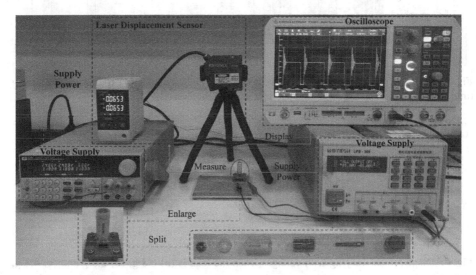

Fig. 4. Experimental equipment of dynamic performance test.

Table 2. Stiffness parameters in the springs

	d (mm)	N	G (GPa)	D (mm)	k (N/m)
Compression Spring	0.1	8	74.023	2.9	4.78

5.2 Load Resistance Test of LSEA

As shown in Fig. 6, the axial displacement under different loads is also obtained by the laser displacement sensor. The fitting curves of the axial displacement and voltage based on a third-order polynomial function are shown in Figs. 6(a), (b) and (c), when the load is 0.8 g, 2.8 g and 4.8 g, respectively. It can be seen that the output displacement of

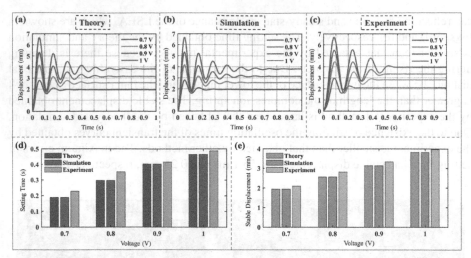

Fig. 5. Transient curves obtained by the (a) theory, (b) simulation, and (c) experiment. (d) Setting time and (e) stable displacement obtained by the different methods.

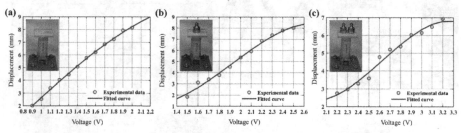

Fig. 6. Displacement varying with voltages when the load is (a) 0.8 g, (b) 2.8 g and (c) 4.8 g, respectively.

LSEA increases nonlinearly with the increase of input voltage. The voltage stiffness of LSEA shows a tendency to increase and then decrease with increasing voltage.

As shown in Fig. 7(a), the load resistance ability of LSEA with a magnetic ring (#1) and LSEA without magnetic rings (#2) is compared below. The displacement of #1 LSEA is larger than that of #2 LSEA at the same step voltage and load. The mass of the mover in #1 LSEA is 1.8 g. It can resist a load of 10 g and produce a displacement of 4.7 mm at the voltage of 4 V. As shown in Fig. 7(c), the electromagnetic force varies with the displacement of the magnets. The electromagnetic force generated by #1 LSEA and #2 LSEA rises and falls monotonically with increasing displacement, respectively. For #2 actuator, the electromagnetic force is maximum when the displacement of the magnetic bar is in the initial state. The average electromagnetic force generated by #1 LSEA is higher than that generated by #2 LSEA under the same voltage.

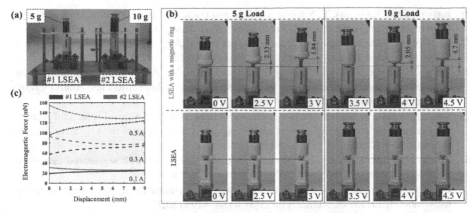

Fig. 7. Comparative analysis of the load resistance for the LSEAs. (a) LSEAs for testing. (b) Displacement response of LSEAs. (c) Electromagnetic forces of varying with displacement.

6 Conclusion

In this paper, an LSEA capable of resisting large loads is designed. This LSPEA can achieve a theoretical displacement of 9 mm and reach a steady state within 0.5 s. It can withstand a load of 10 g and generate a displacement of 4.7 mm at the voltage of 4 V. The electromagnetic force generated by the LSEA is proportional to the current. There is a nonlinear functional relationship between the electromagnetic force and the displacement. The transient curves and performance indicators are obtained by the experiment and simulation. The transient curves under the step voltages can reflect the dynamic processes including overshoot, damped oscillation, and stabilization. The maximum errors of setting time and stable displacement are 55.1 ms and 0.25 mm, respectively. Analytical expressions of system parameters including natural frequency and equivalent stiffness can reflect the performance within a certain error. The output displacement of the LSEA increases nonlinearly with the increase of input voltage through the load resistance test. The electromagnetic force generated by the LSEA without and with the magnetic ring rises and falls with increasing displacement, respectively. The average electromagnetic force generated by the LSEA with a magnetic ring is larger.

References

1. Ijaz, S., et al.: Magnetically actuated miniature walking soft robot based on chained magnetic microparticles-embedded elastomer. Sens. Actuator A Phys. **301**, 111707 (2020)
2. Yang, Z., Zhang, L.: Magnetic actuation systems for miniature robots: a review. Adv. Intell. Syst. **2**(9), 2000082 (2020)
3. Wang, H., et al.: Biologically inspired electrostatic artificial muscles for insect-sized robots. Int. J. Rob. Res. **40**(6–7), 895–922 (2021)
4. Ng, C.S.X., Tan, M.W.M., Xu, C., Yang, Z., Lee, P.S., Lum, G.Z.: Locomotion of miniature soft robots. Adv. Mater. **33**(19), 2003558 (2021)
5. Gao, X., et al.: Piezoelectric actuators and motors: materials, designs, and applications. Adv. Mater. Technol. **5**(1), 1900716 (2020)

6. Hasan, M.M., Baxevanis, T.: Structural fatigue and fracture of shape memory alloy actuators: Current status and perspectives. J. Intell. Mater. Syst. Struct. **33**(12), 1475–1486 (2022)
7. Bar-Cohen, Y., Anderson, I.A.: Electroactive polymer (EAP) actuators—background review. Mech. Soft Mater. **1**(1), 1–14 (2019). https://doi.org/10.1007/s42558-019-0005-1
8. Wang, C., Zhang, W., Zou, Y., Meng, R., Zhao, J., Wei, M.: A sub-100 mg electromagnetically driven insect-inspired flapping-wing micro robot capable of liftoff and control torques modulation. J. Bionic Eng. **17**(6), 1085–1095 (2020)
9. Sabzehmeidani, Y., Mailah, M., Hing, T.H., Abdelmaksoud, S.I.: A novel voice-coil actuated mini crawler for In-pipe application employing active force control with iterative learning algorithm. IEEE Access **9**, 28156–28166 (2021)
10. Zhang, R., Shen, Z., Wang, Z.: Ostraciiform underwater robot with segmented caudal fin. IEEE Robot. Autom. **3**(4), 2902–2909 (2018)
11. Bhushan, P., Tomlin, C.: Design of an electromagnetic actuator for an insect-scale spinning-wing robot. IEEE Robot. Autom. Lett. **5**(3), 4188–4193 (2020)
12. Bhushan, P., Tomlin, C.: An insect-scale self-sufficient rolling microrobot. IEEE Robot. Autom. Lett. **5**(1), 167–172 (2019)
13. Song, C.W., Lee, S.Y.: Design of a solenoid actuator with a magnetic plunger for miniaturized segment robots. Appl. Sci. **5**(3), 595–607 (2015)
14. Song, C.-W., Lee, D.-J., Lee, S.-Y.: Bioinspired segment robot with earthworm-like plane locomotion. J. Bionic Eng. **13**(2), 292–302 (2016). https://doi.org/10.1016/S1672-6529(16)60302-5
15. McKenzie, R.M., Sayed, M.E., Nemitz, M.P., Flynn, B.W., Stokes, A.A.: Linbots: soft modular robots utilizing voice coils. Soft Rob. **6**(2), 195–205 (2019)
16. Sayed, M.E., Roberts, J.O., McKenzie, R.M., Aracri, S., Buchoux, A., Stokes, A.A.: Limpet II: a modular, untethered soft robot. Soft Rob. **8**(3), 319–339 (2021)
17. Ebrahimi, N., Schimpf, P., Jafari, A.: Design optimization of a solenoid-based electromagnetic soft actuator with permanent magnet core. Sens. Actuator A Phys. **284**, 276–285 (2018)
18. Ebrahimi, N., Guda, T., Alamaniotis, M., Miserlis, D., Jafari, A.: Design optimization of a novel networked electromagnetic soft actuators system based on branch and bound algorithm. IEEE Access **8**, 119324–119335 (2020)
19. Khalid, S., Khan, F., Ullah, B., Ahmad, Z., Milyani, A.H., Alghamdi, S.: Electromagnetic and experimental analyses of a low-cost miniature tubular moving magnet linear oscillating actuator for miniature compressor applications. IET Electr. Power Appl. **17**(1), 58–67 (2023)
20. Zhang, H., et al.: Electromagnetic calculation of tubular permanent magnet linear oscillation actuator considering corrected air gap permeance. IEEE Trans. Mag. **59**(5), 8000305 (2023)

Fully Tactile Dexterous Hand Grasping Strategy Combining Visual and Tactile Senses

Jian Ma, Qianqian Tian, Kuo Liu, Jixiao Liu[✉], and Shijie Guo

School of Mechanical Engineering, Hebei University of Technology, Tianjin 300401, China
liujixiao@hebut.edu.cn

Abstract. Robotic dexterous hands need to rely on both visual and tactile information for grasping during grasping and interaction. The position and type of objects are identified by visual information, and stable grasping is accomplished by tactile information. In this paper, a solution based on visual-tactile fusion control is proposed. At the same time, the data set is established by the method of tactile teaching to complete stable grasping. The tactile teaching approach is inspired by adults teaching children to write by hand. The "hand-held" grip method enables a more natural and convenient grip teaching. By fusing visual and tactile information, the perceptual capability and control accuracy of the robot's dexterous hand are improved. Using the proposed method, a series of grasping tasks were tested in an experimental environment. The results show that the method can not only effectively improve the grasping success rate of the robot dexterous hand on objects of different shapes, but also achieve stable interaction between the robot dexterous hand and the objects.

Keywords: Dexterous Hand · Visual-tactile Fusion · Tactile Teaching

1 Introduction

The humanoid design of the robot dexterous hand in terms of structure and function is a prerequisite for complex tasks and human-robot interaction. When humans perform grasping action, they first observe the spatial position of the object and its shape and size through their eyes. The next step is to adjust the hand posture in the process of moving the human hand to the object, so that the human hand posture is suitable for grasping the target object, and finally grasping to complete the whole process. Similarly, the robot dexterous hand needs to adjust the hand posture close to the operating object according to the different operating objects in the process of grasping or interaction [1]. And in the grasping process, it needs to ensure that the operating object will not deform or slip to complete a stable grasp.

Through computer vision technology, the robot dexterous hand can capture images of the surrounding environment to achieve a wide range of movement control. However, due to the influence of environmental factors such as illumination and occlusion, vision control requires good illumination of the surrounding environment and the absence of any occlusion, otherwise it will have a large impact on the control accuracy of the

© The Author(s), under exclusive license to Springer Nature Singapore Pte Ltd. 2023
H. Yang et al. (Eds.): ICIRA 2023, LNAI 14271, pp. 133–143, 2023.
https://doi.org/10.1007/978-981-99-6495-6_12

robotic dexterous hand. At the same time, due to the problem of target detection error, the robot dexterous hand will inevitably make wrong grasping and operation. Among the dexterous hands that are controlled using only monocular cameras, hundreds of thousands of grasping trainings are required to form the grasping data set [2–4].

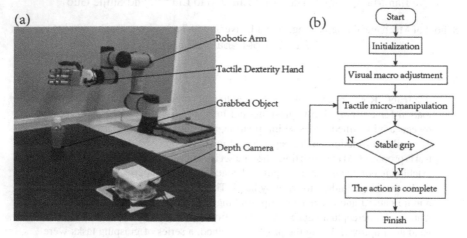

Fig. 1. (a)Experimental platform; (b) control flow

In order to avoid spending a lot of time to build the grasping dataset and at the same time to improve the accuracy of the dexterous hand grasp, this paper proposes a combined visual-tactile full-tactile dexterous hand control method. As shown in Fig. 1(a), the experimental platform takes a depth camera for visual control. The dexterous hand completes the adjustment of grasping posture through the robotic arm, and achieves more accurate tactile control through the full-coverage tactile sensor on the hand. As shown in Fig. 1(b), the shape of the grasped object is judged visually in the early stage of grasping so as to adjust the grasping posture [5], and the tactile information is used to judge whether the stable grasping process is completed during the grasping process. [6, 7] This paper adopts the control method of tactile teaching to establish the teaching data set. The dexterous hand is helped to complete the grasping in the teaching stage by the form of "hand-holding", and then the dexterous hand completes the grasping task by calling the teaching dataset in the process of autonomous grasping.

In this paper, we design three control modes for the robot dexterous hand to cope with different scenarios. They are: manual mode, demonstration mode and autonomous grasping mode. Manual mode: It is mainly used for the experimenter to debug the motor and check whether the sensor is working properly. Teaching mode: In this mode, the information priority of the sensor of the back of the hand is greater than that of the palm. This mode is mainly used for the experimenter to control the manipulator to operate the target object through the sensor of the back of the hand in the demonstration mode. That is, after the sensor in the back of the hand direction detects the contact force exceeding the set threshold, the corresponding joint of the finger unit is controlled to move along the direction of the force. At the same time, the experimenter judges whether the grasp is stable or not, and records the data of the sensor in the direction of the palm of the hand from the beginning of the action to the stable grasp process, as well as the motor operation state at the corresponding moment, and builds up the data set.

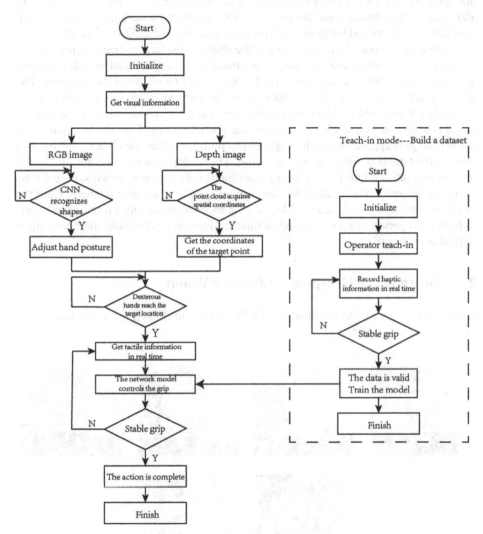

Fig. 2. Control flow diagram of the robot dexterous hand

Autonomous grasping mode: This mode will call the database established in the demonstration mode as the basis, and the control flow of the robot dexterous hand autonomous grasping mode is shown in Fig. 2. The first stage is from the initial position to before contacting the target object. In this stage, the sense of touch is not involved in the control, and the interaction with the outside world is done based on visual information. At the beginning of the experiment, the robot dexterous hand was mounted on the robot arm, and both the hand position and the robot arm were in the initial state. After placing the target object, two-dimensional and three-dimensional images are taken using the Kinect depth camera. The 2D image is used to identify the shape and name of the target object by CNN neural network. The shape of the target object is used to adjust the hand position of the robot's dexterous hand when it touches the target object. In addition, the two-dimensional image circles the boundary of the target object through contour recognition, and integrates with the three-dimensional image to obtain the spatial coordinates of the boundary. According to the shape of the target object, it moves to the corresponding position, and according to the name of the target object, it calls the stable grasping method and pressure range of the corresponding object in the database. The second stage is the state of the last moment of the previous stage to grip stabilization. Vision is not involved in the control in this stage, and the interaction with the outside world is done based on tactile information. The spatial position from the last moment of the first stage is approached to the target object until it touches the object. This triggers the grasp/interaction signal to start gripping. The motor running state and the tactile information are fed into the multi-input and multi-output neural network in real time to obtain the prediction result of the motor running state in the next moment. Until the tactile information is judged as stable grasping then the motor stops running and starts to hold for a period of time, a period of time are grasping stable state, then the grip is judged to be completed.

2   Adjustment of Grasping Posture by Vision

Based on the image contours identified by the algorithm [8–10], the adjustment of the grasping pose is started.

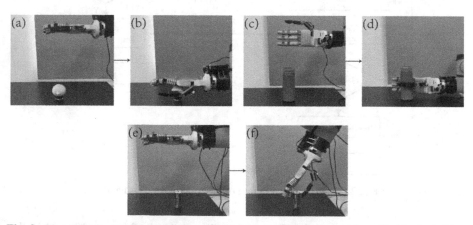

Fig. 3. Pose adjustment of grasping process (a) spherical object recognition; (b) spherical object pose adjustment; (c) cylindrical/prismatic object recognition; (d) cylindrical/prismatic object pose adjustment; (e) smaller volume object recognition; (f) smaller volume object pose adjustment

If the shape of the target object is recognized as a ball, as shown in Fig. 3(a). It is necessary to detect the spatial coordinates of the points on the upper edge of the target object outline. And the palm of the robot dexterous hand is turned downward, with the thumb at an angle of 30° to the palm of the hand. The robot arm drives the robot's dexterous hand to a distance of 10 cm from the upper edge of the target object. After that, it slowly moves downward until the palm of the hand partially touches the target object, as shown in Fig. 3(b).

If the shape of the target object is recognized to be a cylinder/prism, as shown in Fig. 3(c). The spatial coordinates of the upper right point of the target object outline and the midpoint coordinates of the right boundary need to be detected. And the palm of the robot dexterous hand is oriented toward the object with the thumb at an angle of 0 degrees to the palm. The robot arm drives the robot dexterous hand to the upper edge of the target object at a distance of 10 cm and moves the thumb to the opposite side of the palm. After that, it slowly moves downward until the robot dexterous hand reaches the midpoint coordinate of the right border and starts grasping, as shown in Fig. 3(d).

If the shape of the target object is recognized as a small volume object, as shown in Fig. 3(e). The spatial coordinates of the points on the upper edge of the target object outline need to be detected. And the fingertips of the robot dexterous hand are brought down close to the target object, with the thumb on the opposite side of the hand. The robot arm drives the robot dexterous hand to a distance of 10 cm from the upper edge of the target object. After that, it slowly moves downward until the fingertips reach the upper edge of the target object, and then controls the index finger and middle finger to start pinching, as shown in Fig. 3(f).

This completes the posture adjustment of the robot's dexterous hand during grasping by visual information.

3   Stable Grasping Through Tactile Sensation

3.1   Demonstration and Teaching Mode to Build Tactile Information Data Set

At this point the robot dexterous hand reaches the initial position ready for grasping. The teaching process for the cylinder/prism class, shown in Fig. 4(a), contains the action flow diagram and the pressure distribution diagram of key frames for each object teaching process. In the moments I and II before the experiment, the arm drives the robot dexterous hand to reach the top of the object. And moves down along the contour line until the appropriate position for grasping. Then the thumb is rotated to 90°. No pressure is applied during this process. At Moment III, the tactile teaching process begins. The operator touches the dorsal part of the robot's dexterous hand and the pressure on B1 triggers the teaching grasp mode. The triggered area Bx then instructs the corresponding motor to bend the finger, which causes the robot hand to grasp the target object. At the IV moment, the signal appears in the palm area. The operator begins to determine whether the robotic hand has reached a stable grasp and whether to stop applying force. At moment V, a stable grasp is judged to be reached and the operator leaves the robotic dexterous hand. At time VI, the robot arm moves the object being grasped to test if the grasp is stable. If the object does not slide and is not deformed. Then the tactile data at time T and all the motor operating states at time T + 1 are recorded and added to the database as a set of data during the whole teaching process.

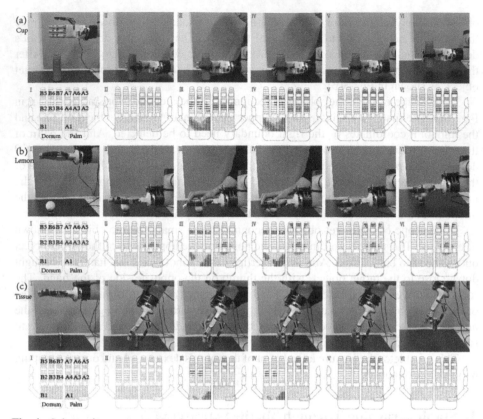

Fig. 4. Schematic process and keyframe diagram of (a) spherical object; (b) cylindrical/prismatic object; (c) small volume object.

A total of twelve everyday objects were used for the experiments during the demonstration. Each object was grasped twenty times and the data were processed. The motor state at T + 1 and the tactile information at T + 1 are stored separately, and the motor state at T + 1 is predicted using a multi-input multi-output neural network, which is divided into a training set train and a test set. The training set contains eighteen successful and stable grasps of each experimental object, and the test set contains two successful and stable grasps of each experimental object.

The process of teaching a sphere is basically the same as that of a cylinder/prism. The only difference is the way of approaching the object when grasping and the position of the thumb. The teaching process of the sphere-like object is shown in Fig. 4(b). The grasping result of the teaching process shows that the grasping action for the sphere-like object is more oriented towards a palm-down four-finger grasp. In this process, the distal and proximal knuckles of the middle finger cooperate with the palm of the hand. The little finger and the index finger bend to apply force on the side of the target object, forming an envelope around the target object to complete a stable grasp.

The teaching process for small objects is basically the same as the teaching process for cylinders/prisms. The only difference is the way of approaching the object and the position of the thumb when grasping. The teaching process for small objects is shown in Fig. 4(c). The grasping posture shows a preference for pinching for small objects. The index finger and the middle finger work directly with the thumb to complete a stable grasp.

3.2   Multi-output Neural Network Action Classification

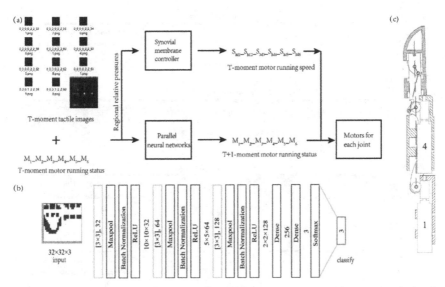

Fig. 5. (a) Neural network control model; (b) FashionNet network architecture; (c) index finger motor number

During the grasping process, we need to control the operation status of six motors based on the tactile information. But using six neural networks cannot guarantee synchronization and real-time, so this paper uses Keras for multiple output classification. It is compiled using Tensorflow version 2.0. In this paper, the crawling process needs to control six motors. So the input is a 32 * 32 2D image at time T and the running state of the motor at that time, and the output type is the state of 6 motors at time T + 1, as shown in Fig. 5(a). In order to predict multiple outputs, a special network architecture of FashionNet is used in this paper. This architecture divides the model into six "subnetworks" for parallel processing, which are responsible for controlling the operating states of six motors in the finger part of the robot dexterous hand. The network structure of each branch is shown in Fig. 5(b). There are six disjoint fully connected heads at the end of the network, and each fully connected head is responsible for its own classification duty. Each branch performs its own convolution, activation, pooling, and other operations until the final correct prediction is obtained [11, 12].

As shown in Fig. 5(c), the motor numbers corresponding to the index finger are 1 and 4, and the other two fingers in turn. The data set created in the demonstration mode was put into this multi-output neural network for training, and the accuracy and loss output results were obtained as shown in Fig. 6. After performing more than thirty training sessions, it is guaranteed that the motor control accuracy is higher than 80% in all cases.

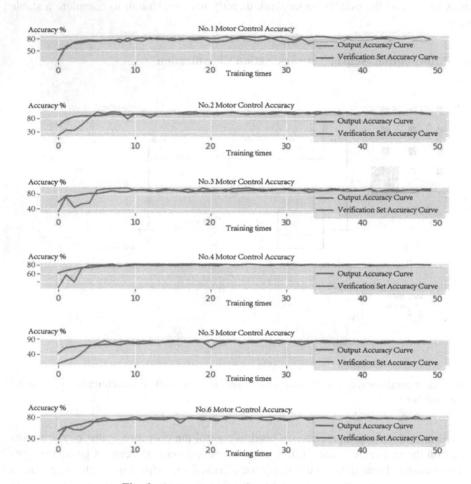

Fig. 6. Accuracy curve of multi-output network.

3.3 Dexterous Hand Autonomous Grasping Experiment

After the training of the data set for the demonstrative grasping is completed and the accuracy rate meets the requirements, the robot dexterous hand is controlled to start the autonomous grasping of the target object. The robot arm is reset with each finger unit of the robot before grasping. The robot arm is controlled by vision information to move the robot dexterous hand to the corresponding position.

First is the autonomous grasping experiment for cylindrical/prismatic objects, as shown in Fig. 7(a). According to the experimental results, it can be seen that in the autonomous grasping process, the thumb and proximal phalanges of the robot's dexterous

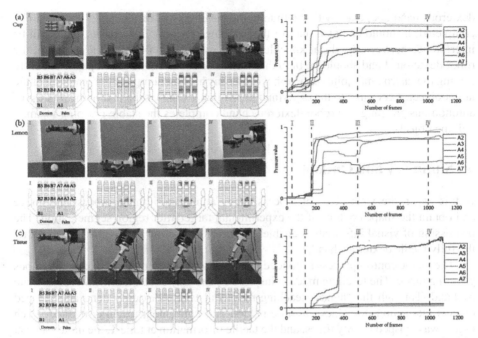

Fig. 7. Key frames of the autonomous grasping process with pressure variations (a) cylindrical/prismatic objects; (b) spherical objects; (c) small volume objects.

hand first touch the target object and form an envelope. Then the middle finger drives the proximal phalanges to bend and completely envelop the object to complete stable grasping [13]. In this process, due to the stretching state of the sensor electrode in the back of the hand direction of the robot dexterous hand, the compression state of the sensor electrode in the palm direction, and the operation of electromagnetic interference from the motor operation, there will be some degree of interference with the tactile sensor. The collected data will have some jump in value. At this point, it is necessary to extend the judgment time of the controller to avoid the occurrence of misjudgment.

The next experiment is for the autonomous grasping of sphere-like objects, as shown in Fig. 7(b). For the sphere-like object grasping, the robot's dexterous hand needs to work with other fingers downward to form an envelope space. Since the far knuckle of the robot dexterous hand needs to reach the bottom of the target object and the size of the robot dexterous knuckle is large, it is necessary to add a small-sized shelf to raise the target object during the experiment. The space at the bottom of the target object is left empty so that the distal knuckle of the robot dexterous hand can reach the bottom of the target object to facilitate the grasping task. Based on the experimental results, it can be seen that during the autonomous grasping process, the palm of the robot's dexterous hand first touches the target object. Then it bends with the other three fingers to form an envelope to complete a stable grasp.

Finally, the experiment of autonomous grasping for small volume objects is shown in Fig. 7(c). For the grasping of small volume objects, it is sufficient to tilt the palm of the robot's dexterous hand. As long as the middle finger and index finger of the robot dexterous hand cooperate with the thumb, the envelopment of the target object can be completed. It should be noted that for the grasping of low height objects, there will be interference between the distal knuckle and the experimental table. The thumb of the robot dexterous hand should be brought into contact with the target object first before driving the interpalmar joint of the robot dexterous hand to complete the pinching of the target object. According to the experimental results, it can be seen that in the process of autonomous grasping, the robot dexterous hand completes the stable grasping of small volume objects.

4 Summary and Outlook

In this paper, the visual control process uses Canny algorithm to process the image and obtain the shape contour of the experimental target after region segmentation. The processing of visual information enables the fast localization of the grasped object by the fully tactile dexterous hand.

The tactile control process is divided into a demonstration mode and an autonomous grasping mode. The teaching mode is inspired by the way adults teach children to write by hand. Through the "hands" teaching robot full tactile dexterity hand and grasped objects interaction, to achieve a more natural and convenient teaching method. Each object was grasped twenty times, and the tactile information at time T, the motor state at time T, and the motor state at time T + 1 were stored. After the training of the teaching data set is completed, the autonomous grasping performed by the dexterous hand can complete the grasping task stably and rapidly.

This paper assembles tactile sensors and tactile information acquisition cards into the designed fully tactile robot dexterous hand according to the self-designed control flow. The experimental data set of three different shapes of experimental objects is built and validated, and the experiments of autonomous grasping can be done according to the data set. In this paper, a tactile hand control method based on tactile information is proposed. The task of autonomous grasping of daily objects and human-machine collaboration is accomplished. The control effect of "visual macro-regulation and tactile micro-operation" is achieved.

References

1. Feix, T., Romero, J., Schmiedmayer, H.B., Dollar, A.M., Kragic, D.: The grasp taxonomy of human grasp types. IEEE Trans. Hum.-Mach. Syst. **46**(1), 66–77 (2016)
2. Levine, S., Pastor, P., Krizhevsky, A., Ibarz, J., Quillen, D.: Learning hand-eye coordination for robotic grasping with deep learning and large-scale data collection. Int. J. Robot. Res. **37**(4–5), 421–36(2017)
3. Lenz, I., Lee, H., Saxena, A.: Deep learning for detecting robotic grasps. Int. J. Robot. Res. **34**(4–5), 705–24(2015)
4. Redmon, J., Angelova, A.: Real-time grasp detection using convolutional neural networks. In: International Conference on Robotics and Automation (ICRA), pp. 26–30.IEEE (2015)
5. Song, F., Zhao, Z., Ge, W., Shang, W., Cong, S.: Learning optimal grasping posture of multi-fingered dexterous hands for unknown objects. In: International Conference on Robotics and Biomimetics (ROBIO), pp. 12–15. IEEE (2018)

6. Matak, M., Hermans, T.: Planning visual-tactile precision grasps via complementary use of vision and touch. IEEE Robot. Autom. Lett. **8**(2), 768–75 (2023)

7. Jara, C.A., Pomares, J., Candelas, F.A., Torres, F.: Control framework for dexterous manipulation using dynamic visual servoing and tactile sensors' feedback. Sensors (Basel), **14**(1), 1787–804 (2014)

8. Reddy, R.V., Raju, K.P., Kumar, M.J., Kumar, L.R., Prakash, P.R., Kumar, S.S.: Comparative analysis of common edge detection algorithms using pre-processing technique. Int. J. Electr. Comput. Eng. (IJECE) **7**(5), 2574–2580 (2017)

9. Selvakumar, P., Hariganesh, S.: The performance analysis of edge detection algorithms for image processing. In: International Conference on Computing Technologies and Intelligent Data Engineering (ICCTIDE'16), pp. 7–9 (2016)

10. Deng, C.X., Wang, G.B., Yang, X.R.: Image edge detection algorithm based on improved canny operator. In: International Conference on Wavelet Analysis and Pattern Recognition, pp.14–17 (2013)

11. Lambeta, M., et al.: Digit: a novel design for a low-cost compact high-resolution tactile sensor with application to in-hand manipulation. IEEE Robot. Autom. Lett. **5**(3), 3838–3845 (2020)

12. Lampe, T., Riedmiller, M.: Acquiring visual servoing reaching and grasping skills using neural reinforcement learning. In: International Joint Conference on Neural Networks (IJCNN), pp.4–9 (2013)

13. Shaw-Cortez, W., Oetomo, D., Manzie, C., Choong, P.: Tactile-based blind grasping: a discrete-time object manipulation controller for robotic hands. IEEE Robot. Autom. Lett. **3**(2), 1064–1071 (2018)

Intelligent Tactile System and Human-Robot Interaction for Collaborative Robots

Xiujuan Liang, Hang Gao, Peng Wang, Jixiao Liu[(✉)], and Shijie Guo

School of Mechanical Engineering, Hebei University of Technology, Tianjin 300401, China
liujixiao@hebut.edu.cn

Abstract. Robot tactile intelligence is an important means for robots to perceive and recognize external collaborative interactions. It ensures safety, comfort, and friendliness during human-robot collaboration. In order to enable collaborative robots to achieve large-scale perception of the environment or tactile interaction with humans, a tactile sensor and intelligent system with large coverage were designed, prepared, and tested. The tactile sensor covers 75% of the surface area of the collaborative robot. These tactile sensors can conform to non-uniform curved surfaces, addressing the limitation of traditional flexible sensors in achieving large-area conformity to non-uniform curved surfaces. The tactile intelligent system is capable of simultaneously recognizing 12 types of human-machine interaction actions and determining the position and direction of contact points. By integrating the tactile intelligent system with collaborative robots, the collaborative robots can perceive the intentions, positions, and directions of human body movements, enabling the robots to provide corresponding response and feedback. Human-robot interaction experiments were designed, and the results demonstrated that the robot was able to perceive human intentions and perform appropriate movements using the tactile sensors, thereby improving the safety, comfort, and friendliness of human-robot collaboration.

Keywords: Tactile sensor · Position mapping · Robot

1 Introduction

The application of robots has made significant progress, and the current focus is gradually shifting towards robots handling objects in the real world in any environment, working safely with humans, and assisting them [1]. Among them, robot tactile sensing plays an irreplaceable and important role in the human-robot physical interaction process. It is an essential means for robots to perceive the objects they touch and the external environment. It ensures the safety, comfort, and friendliness of the human-robot contact process. It is a technical prerequisite for robots to achieve high-level intelligence and perform challenging tasks that involve direct interaction with humans, such as assistance, carrying, and supporting walking.

Currently, the development of robotic haptic sensing and detection technology has made significant progress. However, conventional flexible haptic sensors face challenges in fitting well on the curved surfaces of robots. As a result, sensory interfaces that provide

© The Author(s), under exclusive license to Springer Nature Singapore Pte Ltd. 2023
H. Yang et al. (Eds.): ICIRA 2023, LNAI 14271, pp. 144–155, 2023.
https://doi.org/10.1007/978-981-99-6495-6_13

conformal, full-body coverage and can record and analyze interactions across the entire body have not been fully developed. Such haptic sensors capable of conforming to shaped surfaces can be used to equip robots with electronic skins for human-robot collaboration [2]. Furthermore, haptic sensors covering the entire robot body are crucial for ensuring the safety, accuracy, and robustness of human-robot interaction and control.

The application of flexible tactile sensors on large-area irregular surfaces still presents numerous challenges, such as the inability to achieve conformal contact on irregular surfaces, complex signal processing, dealing with intricate wiring, and limited information transmission capability [3]. In order to achieve extensive coverage of tactile sensors on surfaces, there are generally two approaches: array-based structures [4, 5] and modular structures [6–8]. Zhiqiu Ye et al. developed a robot skin composed of force sensing unit arrays and serpentinite structure substrates, both made of porous materials. The serpentinite structure imparts stretchable properties to the developed skin, and finite element analysis has validated its ability to conform to complex surfaces of robots with small local stresses [9]. RobotSkin adopts a modular structure approach [10, 11]. The robot skin system utilizes triangular skin modules with 12 capacitive force sensors. These skin modules can be assembled into larger structures to cover arbitrary surfaces. This allows for flexible deployment, reduces wiring, and contains faults within the modules. Although good spatial resolution has been achieved, the frequent use of rigid components prevents full flexibility and complicates the manufacturing process. The issue of achieving full conformity between tactile sensors and the irregular surfaces of robots is a pressing challenge in human-robot collaboration that needs to be addressed.

In the field of human-robot interaction, recent research advances have focused on inferring human states, action intentions [12, 13], and ensuring collaborative safety [14] based on tactile feedback information. Tactile sensors applied to robots have been able to achieve action recognition. When humans interact with robots, the robots can perceive the types of actions performed by humans [15]. However, in order for robots to perceive human intentions, mere action recognition is not sufficient; it is also necessary for the robots to constantly sense the spatial locations being touched or contacted.

To achieve more intelligent collaborative robots, two main aspects need to be addressed. Firstly, a set of tactile sensors that conform to the robot's surface needs to be established. These sensors enable the collaborative robot to perceive external or human contact information through the assembled tactile sensors. Second, the tactile sensor enables the mapping of tactile units to the surface positions of the robot, allowing the robot to perceive the spatial location of contact. In this study, the tactile sensor on the collaborative robot's link 2 was selected to achieve the mapping of tactile unit positions, combined with action recognition, enabling the robot to perceive human intentions and control its movements accordingly. Experimental verification was conducted to validate the effectiveness of the designed robot tactile sensor, aiming to enhance the safety, comfort, and friendliness of human-robot collaboration.

2 Six Degree-of-Freedom Robot Tactile Sensor

2.1 Tactile Sensor Area Design

A set of tactile sensors was designed based on the shell configurations of various parts of the AUBO-i3 robot, dividing the robot into four regions. As shown in Fig. 1, the four regions are the red end region, yellow forearm region, blue upper arm region, and gray shoulder region. To accommodate the different shell configurations of joints and linkages in each region, both irregular surface flexible tactile sensors and conventional flexible tactile sensors were designed.

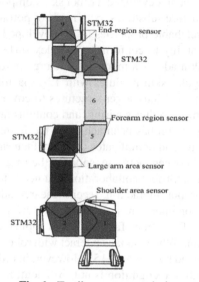

Fig. 1. Tactile sensor area design

As shown in Table 1, the tactile sensor adopts an array-type structure. Taking the forearm area as an example, there are 13 rows for part 5 and 11 rows for part 6. Both parts have 21 columns, forming a total of 504 tactile units. The column electrodes of each part in each region are connected in parallel, while the row electrodes are connected in series, and they are connected to the same intelligent module circuit. Four intelligent module circuits are designed on the side wings of the joint shell, reducing the number of wiring and intelligent module circuits in this way.

2.2 Tactile Sensor Design

The designed tactile sensors are divided into irregular surface flexible tactile sensors and conventional flexible tactile sensors. Both types of sensors utilize the principle of capacitive sensing and are composed of upper and lower electrode layers and a dielectric layer. The row and column electrodes are placed in a cross pattern, forming capacitive sensing units at each intersection point. The upper electrode layer and lower electrode

Table 1. Number of rows and columns for each part of tactile sensors

Region	Sensor row number	Sensor column number
End (7, 8, 9)	8 + 8 + 8	21
Forearm (5, 6)	13 + 11	21
Big arm (3, 4)	10 + 11	22
Shoulder (1, 2)	11 + 11	27

layer each consist of m and n electrodes, respectively, and the electrodes on the upper and lower layers intersect vertically in space [4]. Thus, the sensor is composed of an array of m × n individual units. As shown in Fig. 2(a), the designed conventional flexible tactile sensor is a cylindrical tactile sensor on link 2, with 13 rows and 21 columns, forming a total of 273 tactile units. In order to enable the columns of the tactile sensors in different parts of the same region to be connected in series, two column connection terminals were designed for each part.

The difference lies in the preparation of the irregular surface flexible tactile sensor, which requires the production of an irregular surface substrate. According to different surface configurations, molds are designed to cast the flexible substrate solution into the mold, resulting in an irregular surface substrate with a thickness of approximately 0.5 mm. By adhering conductive tape to the irregular surface substrate, the upper electrode layer and lower electrode layer are formed. At the same time, each electrode is led out through the designed FPC lead contact point to create an electrode terminal. The design of FPC requires selecting areas where the irregular surface can be unfolded, and in order to achieve series connection, the FPC lead is also designed with two electrode terminals. Ion fiber is chosen as the dielectric layer, and finally, the sensors are encapsulated using adhesive. As shown in Fig. 2(b), the tactile sensors at joints 4, 5, and 6 in the end region are well fitted to the irregular surface. The same approach can be applied to prepare irregular surface tactile sensors in other regions as well.

Fig. 2. (a) Cylindrical sensor. (b) Irregular surface sensors

Based on the existing intelligent module circuit in the laboratory and the Labview display upper computer, the prepared end region tactile sensor and cylindrical tactile sensor were connected for testing, as shown in Fig. 3. The tactile sensors completely conform to the irregular surfaces of the robot, verifying the feasibility of designing a set of collaborative robot tactile sensors.

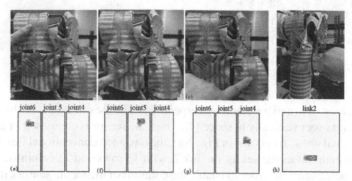

Fig. 3. (a–c) represents pressing different parts of the irregular surface tactile sensor, corresponding to the testing shown in (e–f). (d) represents pressing the cylindrical tactile sensor, corresponding to the testing shown in (h).

3   Tactile Information Recognition and Human Motion Intention Inference

Tactile sensors applied to robots have been able to achieve action recognition. When humans interact with robots, the robots can perceive the types of actions performed by humans [15]. But merely achieving action recognition is not enough. To accomplish the robot's understanding of human body motion intentions, it is necessary for the robot to perceive the location and orientation of the interaction.

3.1   Cylindrical Tactile Unit Position Calculation

The designed cylindrical surface tactile sensor on linkage 2 is installed on the robot, and a coordinate system is established as shown in Fig. 4. The robot joint coordinate system 3 is selected as the base coordinate system for all tactile units. The array of the cylindrical surface tactile sensor consists of 13 rows and 21 columns, resulting in a total of 273 tactile units. Each tactile unit has its own reference coordinate system, and the coordinate system of each tactile unit is defined as follows: $(x_{i,j}, y_{i,j}, z_{i,j})$, where i represents the column number ranging from 1 to 21, and j represents the row number ranging from 0 to 12, indicating 13 rows.

The two-dimensional and three-dimensional diagrams in Fig. 4 show that the tactile units on the cylindrical surface are uniformly distributed in the circumferential direction. The base coordinate system 3 rotates around its own x-axis and then moves along the x, y, and z axes to align with the reference coordinate systems of each tactile unit. In other words, by applying rotation and translation transformations, the spatial positions of each tactile unit relative to the base coordinate system 3 can be obtained.

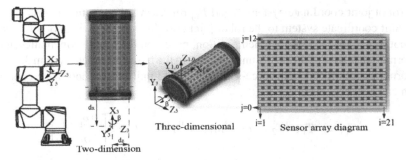

Fig. 4. Sensor coordinate system

The transformation matrix of the reference coordinate system of all tactile units in the first row (j = 0) of the cylindrical surface sensor is:

$$M_{3i}(\beta, d_z, d_x, d_y) = Rot(x, \beta) \cdot Trans(0, 0, d_z) \cdot Trans(d_x, 0, 0) \cdot Trans(0, d_y, 0) \quad (1)$$

By using Solidworks software, the transformation parameters of the reference coordinate system for the first row of 21 tactile units of the cylindrical surface sensor were obtained by measuring the i3 robot model. The rotation angle is β, and the distances moved along the x, y, and z axes are d_x, d_y, and d_z, respectively.

$$\beta = (360/21)\, i, \; d_x = 0.06976 \, \text{m}, \; d_y = 0, \; d_z = 0.03343 \, \text{m} \quad (2)$$

Given the reference coordinate system of all tactile unit points in the first row, it is possible to directly transform to the reference coordinate systems of other rows based on a pattern. In the sensor array diagram shown in Fig. 4, the resolution of the cylindrical surface sensor is 0.01 m. This means that from the first row to the second row, the coordinate system only moves along the x-axis by 0.01 m. Therefore, the transformation matrix of all tactile units relative to the base coordinate system 3 can be ex-pressed using the following formula, representing their spatial positions.

$$^{3}M_{i,j} = M_{3i}(\beta, d_z, d_x, d_y) \cdot M_{3i}(0, 0_z, 0.01 \cdot j, 0) \quad (3)$$

$$^{3}M_{i,j} = \begin{bmatrix} ^{3}R_{i,j} & P_{i,j} \\ 0 & 1 \end{bmatrix} \quad (4)$$

of which:

$$P_{i,j} = \begin{bmatrix} P_x \\ P_y \\ P_z \end{bmatrix} = \begin{bmatrix} d_x + 0.01j \\ d_y \cos \beta - d_y \sin \beta \\ d_z \cos \beta + d_y \sin \beta \end{bmatrix}, \quad ^{3}R_{i,j} = \begin{bmatrix} 1 & 0 & 0 \\ 0 & \cos \beta & -\sin \beta \\ 0 & \sin \beta & \cos \beta \end{bmatrix} \quad (5)$$

For j = 0 to 12, representing the 13 rows of electrodes, and i = 1 to 21, representing the column numbers of the electrodes, different combinations can be used to calculate the spatial positions of the corresponding tactile units relative to the base coordinate system 3. Meanwhile, $^{3}R_{i,j}$ represents the rotation matrix from the tactile unit coordinate system to the robot joint coordinate system 3, and $P_{i,j}$ represents the position matrix from the tactile unit coordinate system to the robot joint coordinate system 3. In order to enable the robot to perceive the user's touch position, based on the robot's kinematics and the transformation matrix of the tactile units relative to the base coordinate system 3, the total transformation matrix of each force-sensitive tactile unit in the robot base coordinate system can also be solved.

$$^{0}T_{i,j} = {}^{0}T_1 \cdot {}^{1}T_2 \cdot {}^{2}T_3 \cdot {}^{3}M_{i,j} = {}^{0}T_3 \cdot {}^{3}M_{i,j} = \begin{bmatrix} {}^{0}R_F & P_F \\ 0 & 1 \end{bmatrix} \tag{6}$$

$^{0}R_F$ represents the rotation matrix from the tactile unit coordinate system to the robot's base coordinate system under the influence of force. P_F represents the position matrix from the tactile unit coordinate system to the robot's base coordinate system under the influence of force.

3.2 Calculation of Human-Computer Interaction Equivalent Point Position and Direction

The transformation matrix of the tactile units, computed from 3.1, represents the pose matrix of all tactile units with respect to the robot joint coordinate system 3. The pose matrix of the tactile units is matched with the tactile data matrix, as shown in Fig. 5. When the tactile sensor is subjected to an action, the spatial positions of all contact points can be obtained through the corresponding relationship.

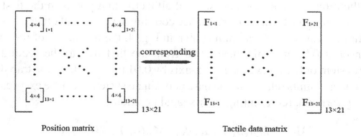

Fig. 5. Location mapping diagram

When the user applies an action to the robot and assumes that n tactile units perceive the contact, the equivalent centroid of the n tactile units can be calculated. Given the measured values F_n of the n tactile units, the centroid of all contact points can be determined using the following formula:

$$P_F = \begin{bmatrix} X \\ Y \\ Z \end{bmatrix} = \begin{bmatrix} \dfrac{\sum\limits_{n=1}^{n} F_n \cdot P_{xn}}{\sum\limits_{n=1}^{n} F_n} & \dfrac{\sum\limits_{n=1}^{n} F_n \cdot P_{yn}}{\sum\limits_{n=1}^{n} F_n} & \dfrac{\sum\limits_{n=1}^{n} F_n \cdot P_{yn}}{\sum\limits_{n=1}^{n} F_n} \end{bmatrix}^{T} \tag{7}$$

By using the above equation, we can equivalently represent all contact points as a single point, enabling joint 3 of the robot to perceive the position of the user's applied action. Similarly, in the reference coordinate system of the tactile unit, the direction of the contact force is $(0, 0, F_n)$. By performing coordinate transformation, the direction and magnitude of the equivalent contact point force can be determined. Additionally, it is possible to calculate the contact position and direction in the robot's base coordinate system.

4 Experimental Design and Results

In order to verify that the cylindrical surface tactile sensor on link 2 can enhance the safety, comfort, and user-friendliness of human-robot collaboration, and enable the robot to effectively perceive human intentions and perform corresponding movements, an experimental platform was built.

4.1 Building Experimental Prototypes

As shown in Fig. 6(a), a prototype of a tactile intelligent system based on the AUBO-i3 robot is constructed. The cylindrical tactile sensor is assembled on the link 2 of the robot, and a ribbon cable is used to connect the tactile sensor to the intelligent module circuit. For aesthetic and neatness considerations, the intelligent module circuit is arranged on the side of the joint housing, and the ribbon cable is bundled and adhered. The intelligent module circuit is connected to the upper computer control system software via a mini USB to USB data cable. The AUBO-i3 robot establishes data communication with the upper computer control system software through an Ethernet cable.

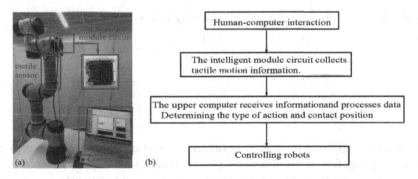

Fig. 6. (a) Experimental prototype. (b) The control flowchart

The workflow of the entire experimental system, as shown in Fig. 6(b), involves the intelligent module circuit collecting action contact information from tactile sensors. It utilizes a neural network model and action features to calculate and discriminate the recognition results. Then, the intelligent module circuit transmits the action recognition results and the collected tactile data matrix to the host computer. Finally, the robot control software Python in the upper computer reads the action recognition results and the tactile data matrix, enabling the calculation of the position centroids for all contact points. This allows for the determination of the position information applied to Link 2, and based on the different actions applied by the user, the robot is controlled to perform corresponding movements.

Table 2 presents the control settings for human-robot collaboration experiments. Python reads the tactile data matrix and action type information from the intelligent module circuit. The tactile data matrix corresponds to the position matrix of tactile units, enabling the calculation of the centroid coordinates (X, Y, Z) of the contact points. In this experiment, four types of human-robot interaction actions were selected: poking, pushing, pulling, and pinching.

If it is a poking action, the centroid (X, Y, Z) of the poking action is calculated. If Y > 0, the robot's joint 3 rotates in the negative direction at a speed of V = 0.1 rad/s, rotating X radians. The robot is poked at different heights on the cylindrical surface, resulting in different rotation angles of the robot. The higher the poking height, the greater the robot's rotation angle, indicating an increase in the robot's rotation speed.

If it is a pinching action, regardless of the robot's pose, it returns to the zero posture at a speed of V = 1.0 rad/s.

If it is a pushing action, the centroid (X, Y, Z) of the pushing action is calculated. If Y > 0, the robot's joint 3 rotates in the negative direction at a speed of V = 1 rad/s, rotating 0.15 radians.

If it is a pulling action, it simultaneously checks if the centroid of the pulling action has Y < 0. If so, the robot's joint 3 rotates in the positive direction at a speed of V = 0.8 rad/s, rotating 0.15 rad.

Table 2. Different action response feedback settings

Type of action	Position (X.Y.Z)	Velocity(rad/s)	Radian of rotation
Poke	Y > 0	0.1	−X
Push	Y > 0	1	−0.15
Pull	Y < 0	0.8	0.15
Pinch	—	1	Zero posture

After setting up the experimental apparatus, we first conducted action recognition experiments using four types of actions: poking, pushing, pulling, and pinching. The confusion matrix for the actual recognition test of the cylindrical surface is shown in Table 3.

4.2 Experimental Results

Finally, through human-robot interaction experiments, it was verified that the tactile intelligent system can perceive the user's intention and perform specific movements by sensing the spatial position of the interaction action type and contact point when the user interacts with the robot.

Table 3. The confusion matrix of the actual recognition test

Type of action	Pull	Poke	Push	Pinch
Pull	45	5	0	0
Poke	0	45	0	5
Push	0	1	49	0
Pinch	0	0	0	50

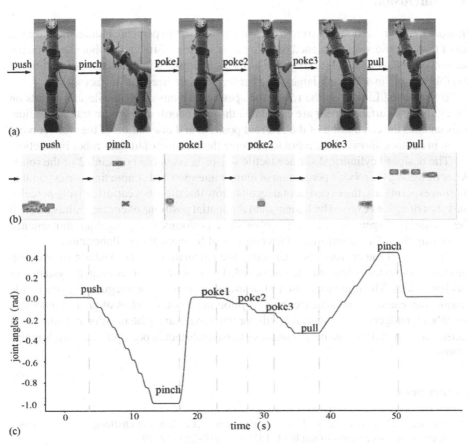

Fig. 7. (a) Actual experimental process(b) Applied motion tactile image display(c) Curve of joint 3 radians over time

Figure 7(a) shows the predetermined sequence of applied actions in the experiment, including pushing, pinching, poking 1, poking 2, poking 3, pulling, and pinching. It demonstrates the specific movements performed by the robot in response to the user's interactive actions.

Figure 7(b) displays the interface of the planar image of the region. Figure 7(c) depicts the entire experimental process and displays the variation curve of joint 3 angle when the user interacts with the robot. When the user continuously pushes the robot, the robot quickly rotates in the negative direction by approximately 0.15 radians. When the user pulls the robot, the robot quickly rotates in the positive direction by approximately 0.14 radians. When the user pinches the robot, regardless of the initial pose of the robot, it rapidly returns to the zero posture at a speed of 1 rad/s. When the user pokes the robot at different positions, the robot's response varies. The higher the position where it is poked on link 2, the greater the angle of rotation of the robotic arm.

5   Conclusion

In order to integrate robots into our lives and enable them to perceive human intentions, a set of tactile sensors was designed based on a six-degree-of-freedom robot. These tactile sensors can better conform to irregular surfaces, addressing the limitation of traditional flexible sensors in achieving large-scale conformance to irregular surfaces.

By selecting Link 2 on the robot, the spatial positions of all tactile unit points on the cylindrical surface sensor are calculated through coordinate system transformation. This enables the calculation of the centroid position and orientation of the contact point when in contact, allowing the robot to perceive the location of human-robot interaction.

The designed cylindrical surface tactile sensor is assembled on Link 2 of the robot. After designing the robot's perception of human intention and conducting corresponding motion experiments, the experimental results show that the robot can effectively perceive the types of actions exerted by humans and the spatial positions of contact points through the tactile intelligent system. The robot then performs corresponding movements, improving the safety, comfort, and friendliness of human-robot collaboration.

However, at the current research stage, the calculation of the position of irregular surface tactile sensors has not been achieved. The robotic tactile intelligent system still has limitations. The implementation of position calculation for irregular surface tactile sensors can enable large-scale tactile perception in robots, which is of great importance for robot intelligence. This research will continue to advance the position calculation of tactile units on irregular surfaces to achieve large-scale tactile perception in collaborative robots.

References

1. Dahiya, R., Yogeswaran, N., Liu, F.: Large-area soft e-skin: the challenges beyond sensor designs. In: Proceedings of the IEEE **107**(10), 2016–2033 (2019)
2. Luo, Y., Li, Y., Sharma, P.: Learning human–environment interactions using conformal tactile textiles. Nat. Electr. **4**(3), 193–201 (2021)
3. Dahiya, R., Navaraj, W.T., Khan S.F.: Developing electronic skin with the sense of touch. Inf. Display **31**(4), 6–10 (2015)
4. Liu, J., Wang, M., Wang, P.: Cost-efficient flexible supercapacitive tactile sensor with superior sensitivity and high spatial resolution for human-robot interaction. IEEE Access **8**, 64836–64845 (2020)
5. Hirai, Y., Suzuki, Y., Tsuji, T.F.: Tough, bendable and stretchable tactile sensors array for covering robot surfaces. In: 2018 IEEE International Conference on Soft Robotics, pp. 276–281. IEEE, Livorno, Italy (2018)

6. Kaboli, M., Cheng, G.: Robust tactile descriptors for discriminating objects from textural properties via artificial robotic skin. IEEE Trans. Robot. **34**(4), 985–1003 (2018)
7. Dean-Leon, E., Pierce, B., Bergner, F.: TOMM: tactile omnidirectional mobile manipulator. In: 2017 IEEE International Conference on Robotics and Automation, pp. 2441–2447. IEEE, Singapore (2017)
8. Cheng, G., Dean-Leon, E., Bergner, F.: A comprehensive realization of robot skin: sensors, sensing, control, and applications. Proc. IEEE **107**(10), 2034–2051 (2019)
9. Ye, Z., Pang, G., Xu, K.: Soft robot skin with conformal adaptability for on-body tactile perception of collaborative robots. IEEE Robot. Autom. Lett. **7**(2), 5127–5134 (2022)
10. Cannata, G., Maggiali, M., Metta, G.F.: An embedded artificial skin for humanoid robots. In: 2008 IEEE International conference on Multisensor Fusion and Integration for Intelligent Systems, pp. 434–438. IEEE, Seoul, Korea (South) (2018)
11. Albini, A., Cannata, G.: Pressure distribution classification and segmentation of human hands in contact with the robot body. Int. J. Robot. Res. **39**(6), 668–687 (2020)
12. Hughes, D., Lammie, J., Correll, N.: A robotic skin for collision avoidance and affective touch recognition. IEEE Robot. Autom. Lett. **3**(3), 1386–1393 (2018)
13. Chen, Y., Yu, M., Bruck, H.A.: Compliant multi-layer tactile sensing for enhanced identification of human touch. Smart Mater. Struct. **27**(12), 125009 (2018)
14. Cirillo, A., Ficuciello, F., Natale, C.F.: A conformable force/tactile skin for physical human–robot interaction. IEEE Robot. Autom. Lett. **1**(1), 41–48 (2015)
15. Wang, P., Liu, J., Hou, F.: F.: Organization and understanding of a tactile information dataset TacAct for physical human-robot interaction. In: International Conference on Intelligent Robots and Systems. IEEE, pp. 7328–7333. Prague, Czech Republic, IEEE (2021)

Tacformer: A Self-attention Spiking Neural Network for Tactile Object Recognition

Jiarui Hu[1,2,3], Zhipeng Wang[1,2,3], Ping Lu[1,2,3], Philip F. Yuan[4], and Yanmin Zhou[1,2,3]([⊠])

[1] Department of Control Science and Engineering, College of Electronics and Information Engineering, Tongji University, Shanghai 201804, China
{2132976,wangzhipeng,pinglu,yanmin.zhou}@tongji.edu.cn
[2] National Key Laboratory of Autonomous Intelligent Unmanned Systems, Shanghai 201210, China
[3] Frontiers Science Center for Intelligent Autonomous Systems, Shanghai 201210, China
[4] College of Architecture and Urban Planning, Tongji University, Shanghai 201804, China
philipyuan007@tongji.edu.cn

Abstract. Tactile sensor plays an important role in the human-robot interaction by providing environmental information to robots. How to effectively use the haptic information of array sensors to encode and extract haptic features for object recognition is the focus of current research. Previous studies have provided methods to construct array sensors in order to acquire tactile information efficiently. New advances in event-driven array sensors could capture spatial spiking tactile data, which include rich spatial information. In this paper, we propose a Residualized Graph Self-attention Spiking Neural Network (Tacformer) for tactile object recognition. The proposed Tacformer pays attention to both the spatial properties and the temporal sensing values of each sensor point in event-driven array sensors. Experimental results on two tactile datasets show that the accuracy, precision, recall and F1-value of the method in this paper are improved. On the EvTouch-Objects dataset, Tacformer has improved the accuracy by 8.34% compared with the GNN-SNN based a baseline approach. On the EvTouch-Containers dataset, Tacformer also has increased the accuracy by 16.17%. The Tacformer could be applied to facilitate robot tasks like grasping and sorting.

Keywords: tactile perception · spiking neural network · graph neural network · self-attention mechanism

1 Introduction

It is well known that the sense of touch is one of the important information sources for both humans and robots to perceive the object properties. With

H. Yang et al. (Eds.): ICIRA 2023, LNAI 14271, pp. 156–168, 2023.
https://doi.org/10.1007/978-981-99-6495-6_14

the obtained tactile information, human can easily judge the type of an object and operation classification [1]. When we use hands to grip an object, spatial changes in skin deformation provide important cues for fine object recognition [2]. In the exploratory procedure, human pays attentions to the points that give more excitement rather than treating the whole contacting region equally. For instance, to distinguish a Lego brick and a normal brick as illustrated in Fig. 1, the studs of Lego provide more cures than a smooth surface of normal brick. When we want to distinguish the types of Lego bricks, the different points on our hands are inspired by these studs. These points could construct a tactile graph by real physical space location. The information of graph is sent to our brains to recognize the types. It makes sense to use graphical mechanism and attention mechanism to describe an object.

Fig. 1. Tactile Selective Mechanism

To have robots assist our daily life such as sorting objects [3–5], it is important to provide the tactile information of objects [6]. For example, if robots are able to distinguish whether a cylinder is a glass cup or chip bucket, the column can be better sorted and placed. Inspired by human skin, event-driven tactile array sensors have been used to enable robots the sense of touch [7,8]. When the points of event-driven array sensors interact with an object, sensors asynchronously sense changes and thus, provide event-based spike sequences. The spatial construct of points in event-driven array sensors is crucial to interpreting the objects as well as their sensor values. Algorithms are then required to extract both of the spatial and temporal information of tactile perception.

In this paper, we propose a Residualized Graph Self-attention Spiking Neural Network (Tacformer) for tactile object recognition. We use GCN to acquire the spatial information and implement attention mechanism to a SNN model to study the importance of each point based on event-driven array sensors. The Tacformer has two key advantages: firstly, the model can better exploit the spatial properties of array sensors. Secondly, SNN is event-driven and can directly process the spike-based data; this bypasses potentially transformations from discrete events to real-valued frames. The experiments show that our Tacformer boosts the objects recognition accuracy to a large extent.

2   Related Works

In this section, we will first review works on methods of tactile sensing and recognizing, followed by a discussion of attention mechanism.

2.1   Methods of Tactile Sensing and Recognizing

Tactile information has played a key role in object recognition as it conveys important pressure characteristics, given by the shape, size and density of its elementary parts [3,4]. Various approaches have been proposed in the literature to retrieve the object information from the collected tactile data [9].

Tactile Sensing and Recognizing

Array sensing pixels are widely applied by tactile sensors, such as the Gelsight [10] and TacTip [11], to sense the micro-structure patterns of object. In [10], deep learning models were applied to extract features collected by Gelsight. Garcia et al. [12] used haptic information from array sensors to predict the stability of grip. They described the actual position of points on array sensors by graph. By using GCN, the spatial information was fed to determine whether the grip appears to slide. Gu et al. [13] proposed a tactile object recognition method based on event-driven tactile array sensors. They manually constructed a haptic graph based on the spatial location of the sensors. They used GCN and SNN to build their model and tested the model on two datasets. In such approaches, the tactile spatial information collected by array sensors was used to discriminate objects through deep learning methods.

Graph Convolutional Network

The convolution operation of GCN could be conducted in the spectral domain via trainable graph filters [14], fitting the position information of each point in the space [15,16]. To reduce the computational cost of decomposition and projection in the frequency domain, graph filters are usually approximated using finite order polynomials. In this study, we use the TAGConv and GENConv to perform convolution on the tactile data due to their computational efficiency and demonstrated performance [17].

Spiking Neural Network

Davies et al. [18] proposed that SNN is more biologically plausible than deep neural networks. SNN has the similar network topology as DNN, but use different neuron models. Commonly-used neuron models for SNN include the IF, LIF [19]. In this work, we use SNN as it is able to directly handle spiking tactile data [20].

2.2   Attention Mechanism

Attention mechanism was firstly proposed to improve the performance of machine translation. Since then, it has been popular in solving various problems in the field of NLP [21]. Recently, many visual self-attention models have been proposed [22,23]. These models are able to automatically locate the important regions in order to better capture differences between images. By introducing the self-attention mechanism, the model provided in this work could pay more attention to the important points of sensors when processing the tactile data of array sensors.

3   Research Methods

In this section, we provide a description of graph and attention approach for learning the tactile data from event-driven array sensors. The Tacformer receives multichannel tactile sequences collected by event-driven array sensors. It outputs a predicted label which refers to the category of the contacted objects. As illustrated in Fig. 2, the model consists of four parts: 1)A tactile graph connects the array points and forms the input multichannel sequences according to the Euclidean distance. 2)The ResTAG acts as an embedding layer of Tacformer to fit the node-to-node features. 3)The Tacformer Encoder Block uses attention mechanism to learn the different importance between different points. 4)The Header layer decodes the vector features and generates spike train as the output layer of the Tacformer.

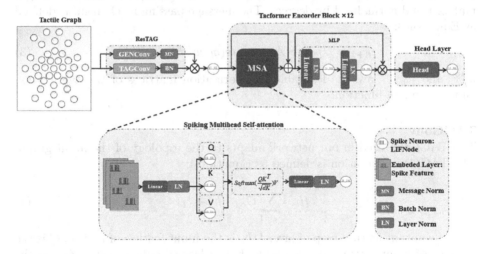

Fig. 2. Structure of Tacformer

3.1   Residual Graph Neural Network

This network is an embedding layer. As illustrated in Fig. 3, the multichannel spiking tactile data is firstly fed into TAGConv to extract the spatial features. TAGConv can better match the topology of the input graph and fit the features of vertex with neighboring points. The residual operation is implemented by

GENConv to reduce problems such as vanishing gradients and excessive smoothing. These problems can cause the local features of the GCN to converge to the same value. Finally, Features are mapped by the linear layer and LIF to the high-dimensional space.

GCN

GCN represents the information of point v by feature vector [24]. The features of a graph G can be represented by connecting the features of all points:

$$h_G = [h_{v1}, h_{v2}, ...h_{vN}]^T \in R^{N \times D} \tag{1}$$

The graph convolution operation is divided into two parts. One is the aggregation operation, which aggregates the point feature and the features of neighboring points; the other is the update operation, which updates the next node information based on the previous aggregation operation. GCN is mathematically defined as Equation 2:

$$hv_l = \sum_{u_l \in N(v_l)} \frac{1}{\sqrt{\deg(v_l)} \cdot \sqrt{\deg(u_l)}} (\Theta \cdot h_{u_{l-1}}) \tag{2}$$

where $\deg(v_l)$ and $\deg(u_l)$ represent the degrees of point v and its neighboring point u, respectively. The features hu_{l-1} of u are multiplied with the weight matrix t and normalized by degrees. The message passing mechanism is defined as Equation 3:

$$g_{l+1} = Update(Aggregate(g_l, w_l^{agg}), w_l^{update}) \tag{3}$$

w_l^{agg} and w_l^{update} are the learnable transformation matrices of the aggregation and the update function.

TAGConv

The TAGConv used in our network adapts to the topology of the input graph. The TAGConv operation is defined as Equation 4:

$$H_l = \sum_{c=1}^{C} G_{c,l} * h_c + b_l \tag{4}$$

H is the output feature map of layer l. h_c is the input feature of node c. C is the number of input features of each node. b_l is a learnable bias vector. $G_{c,l}$ is the convolution kernel. To make the convolution operation work for arbitrary graph topologies, the graph filter needs to be carefully designed. One approach is to define the graph filter with the normalized adjacency matrix of the graph,

$$G_{c,l} = \sum_{k=0}^{K} g_{c,f,k} A^k \tag{5}$$

where $g_{c,f,k}$ is the polynomial coefficient of the graph filter, A is the normalized adjacency matrix.

ResTAG

Although the TAGConv has greater advantages in processing non-regular spatial data, there are some problems such as vanishing gradients and excessive smoothing. These problems are more pronounced in the case of small samples. To address these problems, this paper introduces the residual connection structure to construct ResTAG as Eq. 6. The proposed method also has a good performance to deal with the small samples situation.

$$g_{l+1} = F(g_l, w_l) + P(g_l, w_l) = g_l + g_l^{res} \tag{6}$$

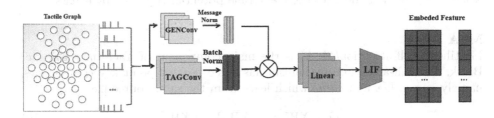

Fig. 3. Structure of ResTAG

3.2 Self-attention Spiking Neural Network

The network is used as the feature learning layer of the Tacformer. An overview of Tacformer Encoder Block is depicted in Fig. 1. In the tactile graph, the importance of different nodes tends to be different. In order to emphasize the importance of points in array sensors, we develop a spatial attention model to assign higher weights to crucial points, whereas lower weights are assigned to the points that contain less information.

The input features, passed to Tacformer Encoder Block, are spike sequences $X \in R^{B \times C \times D}$ from ResTAG. In MSA, we combine the multi-head self-attention mechanism with SNN to handle X [25]. Residual connections are applied in both the MSA and MLP block. We use the LIF as the activating neuron in the network, which is a popular model for describing the dynamics of spiking neurons [26]. Output features generated by the network are sent to the fully-connected-layer to get the prediction label.

LIF Activation

Compared with traditional neural networks, SNN can deal with spike sequences directly and reduce the link of converting impulse data into matrices [27]. As the basic unit of the SNN, LIF receives stimuli and accumulates membrane potentials. LIF compares the accumulated membrane potential to a threshold value to determine whether a pulse should be generate. Here is the update of the membrane potential description:

$$H(t) = V(t-1) + \frac{1}{\tau}[X(t) - (V(t-1) - V_{\text{reset}})] \tag{7}$$

$$S(t) = \theta[H(t) - V_t h] \tag{8}$$

$$V(t) = H(t)[1 - S(t)] + V_{reset}S(t) \tag{9}$$

where τ is the membrane time constant and $X(t)$ is the input current at time step t. The spiking neuron will trigger a pulse when the membrane potential $H(t)$ exceeds the trigger threshold. S(t) is the step function, which equals to 1 when $\theta(t) \geq 0$. $V(t)$ denotes the membrane potential triggered by events.

MSA Block

Multihead Self-attention(MSA) is the main component of Tacformer Encoder Block. The self-attention mechanism has three floating-point key components, namely *query*, *key* and *value* which learn from the same source [28].

$$Q = XW, K = XW, V = XW \tag{10}$$

The output of self-attention can be computed as Eq. 11:

$$MSA(Q, K, V) = Soft\max(QK^T)V \tag{11}$$

However, the calculation of MSA is not applicable in SNN for two reasons: 1) The float-point matrix multiplication of Q, K and softmax function which contains exponent calculation and division operation, do not comply with the calculation rules of SNN. 2) The quadratic space and time complexity of the sequence length of MSA do not meet the efficient computational requirements of SNN. To address these problems, we add the linear layer after LIF, which could make SNN suitable for MSA. Inspired by vanilla self-attention [29], we add a scaling factor $\sqrt{dk}$ to control the large value of the matrix multiplication result. As shown in Fig. 4, the spike-friendly MSA is defined as :

$$Q, K, V = LN(Linear(LIF(LN(Linear(X, W))))) \tag{12}$$

$$MSA'(Q, K, V) = Soft\max(\frac{QK^T}{\sqrt{dK}})V \tag{13}$$

$$MSA = LN(Linear(LIF(MSA'))) \tag{14}$$

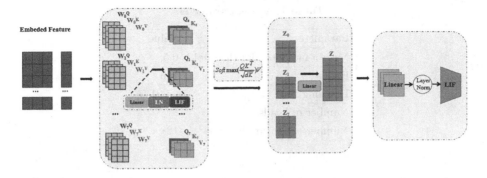

Fig. 4. Structure of Self-attention Spiking Neural Network

3.3 Output Layer

The output layer consists of a fully connected layer and a LIF neuron. The output is a one-dimensional spike train after the activation of LIF. It is not necessary to get the position with the highest probability in the output. We can directly get the position index with element value 1. MSELoss, as the loss function, compares the index value with label and calculates the difference. The difference is used to train the whole model. The parameters are learned by the GCN and linear layers.

$$y_p re = [0, 1, 0, 0, ...]_{[batch\_size, 1]} \tag{15}$$

4 Experiment

In our experiments, we aim to test whether spatial structure and attention mechanism can improve the performance of tactile object recognition. To do this, we conduct a study with different neural network frameworks to learn how these properties help the recognition task. We first apply GNN-SNN on tactile sequences. Subsequently, we add the spatial model(ResTAG) to the GNN-SNN to learn the spatial features. In a further step, both spatial model and self-attention mechanism are included to form the Tacformer.

4.1 Experimental Preparation

The experiments are conducted with two datasets of EvTouch-Objects and EvTouch-Containers collected from household items by event-driven array sensors. EvTouch-Objects includes 720 samples from 36 types of objects. EvTouch-Containers includes 300 samples from 4 types of containers. Every sample is consisted by multichannel tactile sequences.

The model hyperparameter settings are shown in Table 1.

Four commonly used machine learning validation metrics are selected to measure model performances. *Accuracy* refers to the proportion of correctly classified

Table 1. Model Parameters

Parameters	Value
Membrane potential threshold	0.5
Epoch	100
Learning Rate	0.001
Number of heads	8
Number of Linear channels	128

samples to all samples; *Precision* refers to the proportion of correctly identified positive samples to all identified positive samples; *Recall* refers to the proportion of correctly identified positive samples to all positive samples; the $F1$ -value reflects overall model performance. TP and TN represent the number of correct classifications of positive and negative samples respectively, and FP and FN represent their number of their misclassifications, respectively. The calculation methods of the above verification index are as following formulas:

$$Accuracy = \frac{TP + TN}{TP + TN + FN + FP} \tag{16}$$

$$Precision = \frac{TP}{TP + FP} \times 100\% \tag{17}$$

$$Recall = \frac{TP}{TP + FN} \times 100\% \tag{18}$$

$$F1 = \frac{1}{n} \sum_{i=1}^{n} \frac{2 \times Precision \times Recall}{Precision + Recall} \times 100\% \tag{19}$$

4.2   Experimental Results

We use GNN-SNN, TAGConv-SNN, ResTAGConv-SNN, Tacformer and ResTAG-Tacformer to conduct experiments on two datasets - EvTouch-Containers and EvTouch-Objects. These two datasets contain tactile data for 36 different objects and tactile data for 4 different containers with different volumes of objects. During the data collection, the robot gripper grasped each object to lift it 5 cm off the table. Every dataset is divided into a training set (80%) and a test set (20%). The performance of these models on the above two datasets is compared through 100 epochs. As shown in Fig. 5, the train loss of Tacformer decreases rapidly on two datasets at the beginning, tends to converge after the fifteenth training round. The best accuracy also appears on the 15th epoch for EvTouch-Containers. For EvTouch-Objects, the best accuracy occurs after 60 rounds.   As shown in Table 2 and Table 3, we can see that our proposed Tacformer model achieves the best recognition performance. Compared with the baseline GNN-SNN, the recognition accuracy of the Tacformer has increase by 8.34% on EvTouch-Objects and 16.17% on EvTouch-Containers.   With both

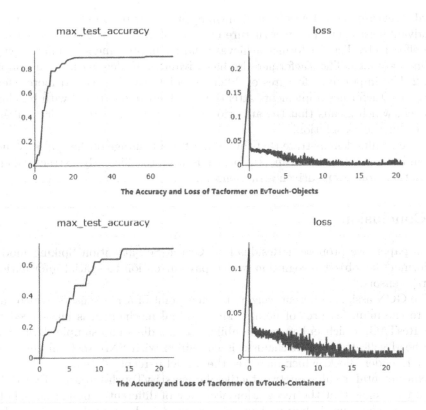

Fig. 5. The Accuracy and Loss of Tacformer curves

Table 2. The results of Tacformer on EvTouch-Objects

Model	Accuracy	Precision	Recall	F1-value
GNN-SNN	0.8514	0.8402	0.8922	0.8424
TAGConv-SNN	0.8944	0.8889	0.9332	0.8938
ResTAGConv-SNN	0.9161	0.8681	0.9159	0.8724
TAGConv-Tacformer	0.9236	0.8839	0.9289	0.8874
ResTAG-Tacformer	**0.9375**	**0.9198**	**0.9523**	**0.9158**

Table 3. The results of Tacformer on EvTouch-Containers

Model	Accuracy	Precision	Recall	F1-value
GNN-SNN	0.5833	0.5850	0.6130	0.5836
TAGConv-SNN	0.6417	0.6361	0.9332	0.6400
ResTAGConv-SNN	0.6634	0.5867	0.6192	0.5803
TAGConv-Tacformer	0.7333	0.6192	0.6564	0.6228
ResTAG-Tacformer	**0.7500**	**0.6830**	0.8051	**0.7372**

spatial structure and attention mechanism applied, our proposed Tacformer has two advantages: 1)The points structure features of array sensors can be learned more effectively. The Tacformer achieves a larger improvement compared with baseline approach. The Tacformer also has advantage to deal with small sample data. 2)The importance features of different points can be learned more effectively. The Tacformer implements attention mechanism compared with baseline approach, which means that the attention mechanism can help to select salient features for the recognition.

These results demonstrate that, by taking the advantage of the spatial structure and attention mechanism, Tacformer is able to efficiently extract salient information from event-driven array sensors.

5   Conclusion

In this paper, we propose a Residualized Graph Self-attention Spiking model (Tacformer) for object recognition, which pays attention to spatial information of array sensors.

The GCN assigns different weights to each point of array sensors, which can capture the main features of points. The residual mechanism is introduced to build ResTAG, which enhances the ability to handle small-sample data. The multi-head self-attention mechanism is combined with SNN to form the Tacformer Encoder Block, which increases the model perceptual field.

Experimental results on two tactile datasets(EvTouch-Objects, EvTouch-Containers) show that the recognition accuracy of different common household objects and container is better than existing models, laying the foundation for subsequent natural interaction and human-computer integration based on tactile information.

Acknowledgement. This work was supported in part by the National Natural Science Foundation of China (No. U2013602, 51975415, 61825303, 62088101), in part by the National Key Research and Development Program of China (No. 2020AAA0108905), in part by the Science and Technology Commission of Shanghai Municipality (No. 2021SHZDZX0100, 22ZR1467100), and in part by the Fundamental Research Funds for the Central Universities. (Corresponding author: Yanmin Zhou)

References

1. Das, A., Alagirusamy, R.: Improving tactile comfort in fabrics and clothing, in Improving Comfort in Clothing, pp. 216–244 (2011)
2. Bensmaïa, S., Hollins, M.: Pacinian representations of fine surface texture. Perception Psychophys. **67**(5), 842–854 (2005)
3. Kappassov, Z., Corrales, J.-A., Perdereau, V.: Tactile sensing in dexterous robot hands. Robot. Auton. Syst. **74**, 195–220 (2015)
4. Navarro, S.E., Gorges, N., Wörn, H., Schill, J., Asfour, T., Dillmann, R.: Haptic object recognition for multi-fingered robot hands. IEEE Haptics Symposium (HAPTICS). IEEE **2012**, 497–502 (2012)

5. Soh, H., Su, Y., Demiris, Y.: Online spatio-temporal Gaussian process experts with application to tactile classification. In: Intelligent Robots and Systems (IROS), 2012 IEEE/RSJ International Conference on. IEEE, 2012, pp. 4489–4496 (2012)

6. Wang, P., Liu, J., Hou, F., et al.: Organization and understanding of a tactile information dataset TacAct for physical human-robot interaction. In: 2021 IEEE/RSJ International Conference on Intelligent Robots and Systems (IROS). IEEE, 2021 7328–7333 (2021)

7. Taunyazov, T., et al.: Event-driven visual-tactile sensing and learning for robots. In: Proceedings of Robotics: Science and Systems (2020)

8. Pfeiffer, M., Pfeil, T.: Deep learning with spiking neurons: opportunities and challenges. Front. Neurosci. **12**(774), 1–18 (2018)

9. Zapata-Impata, B.S., Gil, P., Torres, F. Non-matrix tactile sensors: How can be exploited their local connectivity for predicting grasp stability? arXiv preprint arXiv:1809.05551, 2018

10. Yuan, W., Dong, S., Adelson, E.H.: Gelsight: High-resolution robot tactile sensors for estimating geometry and force, Sensors **17**(12), 2762 (2017)

11. Ward-Cherrier, B., et al.: The TacTip family: Soft optical tactile sensors with 3D-printed biomimetic morphologies, Soft Robot. 5(2), 216–227 (2018)

12. Garcia-Garcia, A., Zapata-Impata, B.S., Orts-Escolano, S., Gil, P., Garcia-Rodriguez, J.: Tactilegcn: A graph convolutional network for predicting grasp stability with tactile sensors. In: 2019 International Joint Conference on Neural Networks (IJCNN). IEEE, pp. 1–8 (2019)

13. Gu, F., Sng, W., Taunyazov, T., et al.: Tactilesgnet: a spiking graph neural network for event-based tactile object recognition. In: 2020 IEEE/RSJ International Conference on Intelligent Robots and Systems (IROS). IEEE, pp. 9876–9882 (2020)

14. Kipf, T.N., Welling, M.: Semi-supervised classification with graph convolutional networks, arXiv preprint arXiv:1609.02907 (2016)

15. Bruna, J., Zaremba, W., Szlam, A., LeCun, Y.: Spectral networks and locally connected networks on graphs, arXiv preprint arXiv:1312.6203 (2013)

16. Bianchi, F.M., Grattarola, D., Livi, L., Alippi, C.: Graph neural networks with convolutional arma filters, arXiv preprint arXiv:1901.01343, 2019

17. Du, J., Zhang, S., Wu, G., Moura, J.M., Kar, S.: Topology adaptive graph convolutional networks, arXiv preprint arXiv:1710.10370, 2017

18. Davies, M., et al.: Loihi: a neuromorphic many core processor with on-chip learning. IEEE Micro **38**(1), 82–99 (2018)

19. Wu, Y., Deng, L., Li, G., Zhu, J., Shi, L.: Spatio-temporal backpropagation for training high performance spiking neural networks. Front. Neurosci. **12**, 331:1–12 (2018)

20. Shrestha, S.B., Orchard, G.: Spike layer error reassignment in time. Adv. Neural Inform. Process. Syst. **31** (2018)

21. Rush, A.M., Chopra, S., Weston, J.: A neural attention model for abstractive sentence summarization In: EMNL (2015)

22. Dosovitskiy, A., et al.: An image is worth 16x16 words: Transformers for image recognition at scale. arXiv preprint arXiv:2010.11929 (2020)

23. Liu, Z., Lin, Y., Cao, Y., et al.: Swin transformer: hierarchical vision transformer using shifted windows. In: Proceedings of the IEEE/CVF International Conference on Computer Vision, pp. 10012–10022 (2021)

24. Xie, Y., Xu, Z., Kankanhalli, M.S., Meel, K.S., Soh, H.,: Embedding symbolic knowledge into deep networks. In: Advances in Neural Information Processing Systems, pp. 4235–4245 (2019)

25. Cordonnier, J.B., Loukas, A., Jaggi, M.: On the relationship between self-attention and convolutional layers[J]. arXiv preprint arXiv:1911.03584 (2019)
26. Gerstner, W., Kistler, W.M.: Spiking neuron models: Single neurons, populations, plasticity. Cambridge University Press (2002)
27. Lee, J.H., Delbruck, T., Pfeiffer, M.: Training deep spiking neural networks using backpropagation. Front. Neurosci. **10**, 508 (2016)
28. Devlin, J., Chang, M.W., Lee, K., et al.: Bert: Pre-training of deep bidirectional transformers for language understanding[J]. arXiv preprint arXiv:1810.04805 (2018)
29. Vaswani, A., Shazeer, N., Parmar, N., et al.: Attention is all you need. Adv. Neural Inform. Process. Syst. **30** (2017)

MC-Tac: Modular Camera-Based Tactile Sensor for Robot Gripper

Jieji Ren[1,2], Jiang Zou[1,2], and Guoying Gu[1,2(✉)]

[1] Robotics Institute, School of Mechanical Engineering, Shanghai Jiao Tong University, 200240 Shanghai, China
{jiejiren,zoujiang,guguoying}@sjtu.edu.cn
[2] School of Mechanical Engineering, State Key Laboratory of Mechanical System and Vibration, Shanghai Jiao Tong University, 200240 Shanghai, China
guguoying@sjtu.edu.cn

Abstract. Camera-based tactile sensors provide a convenient and low-cost approach for robot tactile perception. However, existing sensors are customized and only suit limited robots, which retards tactile applications. In this work, we proposed a modular design for camera-based tactile sensor to facilitate their integration on various robot grippers and fingers. Specifically, we disassemble tactile sensors into sense module for sensing surface interaction, receptor module for arranging camera, illumination, and structure elements, and adapter module for connection with robot gripper. Experiments show the proposed sensors can adopt various robot grippers and achieve high tactile perception performance.

Keywords: Tactile · Perception · Robot Sensor

1 Introduction

Perception abilities provide robots with the physical properties of the real world. Although visual sensing has achieved amazing performance, it is limited by darkness, occlusion, opaque and many other situations that make the vision perception dramatically degrade. Besides, appearance observation is not enough to obtain complete information for robot. Tactile perception [28] provides powerful complementary for robots and can improve their surface perception, grasping, and manipulation performance. Compared with electrical based sensors, camera-based tactile sensors provide high-density surface signals with related simple fabrication process and low hardware cost [32].

Researchers have proposed various camera-based tactile sensors, which can provide surface geometric details, interaction force distribution, and dynamic information, such as slip. Gel-Sight family is the most famous camera-based tactile sensors, which covers the range from tabletop size [8], portable size [9] and gripper size [13, 14, 23, 25]. They provide classical structure of camera-based

This work was partly supported by the NSFC No. 52275024, and in part by Natural Science Foundation of Shanghai under Grant 23ZR1435500. Project designs can be found at: https://github.com/Tacxels/MC-Tac.

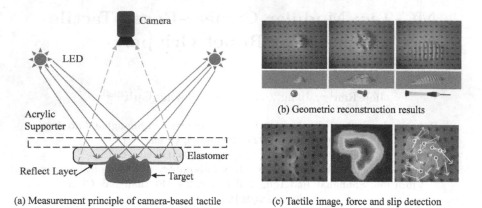

(a) Measurement principle of camera-based tactile

(b) Geometric reconstruction results

(c) Tactile image, force and slip detection

Fig. 1. Tactile sensing mechanism, measured geometric maps and force distribution [22].

tactile sensor, which contains camera, illumination, soft sensing elastomer and an additional transparent supporter layer. To improve the adaptation for robot gripper, Gel-Slim [6,16,22] family continues reducing the sensor size and simplifying the manufacturing process, and iterates to 3.0 version [22] already. With these inspirations, various novel sensors [2,10,17] are also proposed for special robots or tasks.

However, most of existing sensors are designed for special robot, which make them difficult to be applied on variety of grippers. Besides, their illuminations are specially designed PCB board, which impede the generalities and accessibility for researchers to fabricate and assemble tactile sensors into customs system.

To overcome these limitations and promote the applications of tactile sensor, we proposed a modular designed, flexible-integration, accessible, low-cost, and camera-based tactile sensor MC-Tac, with small size and high performance. We dissemble camera-based tactile sensor into modules and specially designed a connection module to suit for wide range of robot grippers. Furthermore, to lower the fabrication obstacles of camera-based tactile sensor, we choose easy-purchased commercial elements to fabricate our sensor, which dramatically reduce the difficulty of the making process. Experiments show the MC-Tac has flexible compatibility, as well as good sensing abilities and surface perception performance.

2   Related Works

Camera-based tactile sensors utilize the camera to capture the deformation between the soft elastomer and the target surface under various illuminations (color/directions), which can encode surface geometry by reflection intensity and color. Based on photometric stereo theory, one can calibrate the mapping between observed pixel and surface gradient and obtain the surface gradient map (Gx, Gy) in practice [28]. Finally, they calculate the surface depth by Fast

Poisson Solver. With these sensing mechanisms, diverse sensors are designed and integrated into robotic applications [6]. With the high-density image-like information, tactile sensor can greatly improve robot performance in texture classification, force perception, and even object 3D reconstruction by touch, as well as robust grasping and dexterous manipulation [4,20,21,24,26].

2.1   Camera-Based Tactile Sensing

Soft gel-based surface sensing mechanism is first introduced by GelSight [8]. Sensors with different varieties are proposed and applied in surface measurement, texture recording, and tactile. Camera-based tactile sensors take the soft elastomer layer to capture geometric details on target surface in the interaction process, place LEDs to illumination the elastomer layer inside, and utilized camera to record the image intensity variations, then decode the geometry from images based on photometric stereo. To enhance the deformation observation of elastomer, various sensor structures, illumination configurations, gel softness, reflection layer recipes, and optical path designs are explored.

2.2   Gel-Sight and Gel-Slim Family

GelSight [8] are the earliest and the most famous serials. The early table version [8] verifies the effectiveness and performance of the proposed method. Then, high-precision and portable version are proposed for surface micro-geometric measurement [9]. In order to apply tactile to robot grasp and manipulation tasks, fingertip [11] version is designed with small and compact size. Slip detection is also introduce in another version [5]. These sensors inspire the following research and provide preliminary designs for camera-based tactile sensor. Besides, Gel-Slim family also focuses on sensors for gripper, and designed GelSlim 1.0 [6] for optimizing optical path and reducing size, GelSlim 2.0 [16] for additional maker layers and dense force estimation, and GelSlim 3.0 [22] for integrate and compact design, and open source to the community.

In order to extend into more tasks and improve tactile performance, researchers developed new configurations to expand the perception range and manipulation abilities. To overcome the field of view (FOV) and the limitation of planar sensing gel, multi-sensors are integrated [27], and finger-like [7,19] round gel structure is introduced. Besides, full view tactile sensor [23] is also developed to provide 360 degrees tactile sensor for gripper. For more convenient grasping and manipulating, soft fin-like structure [13] are proposed to adapt more diverse target objects, as well as the more compact version [14]. Besides, tactile sensors are also integrated into soft-hand [15] and can provide very flexible manipulation, even playing Rubik's Cube.

2.3   Unique-Designed Camera-Based Tactile Sensors

Besides previous sensors, many other camera-based structures are also in vigorous development. DenseTact [2,3] utilizes a semi-sphere gel as contact layer

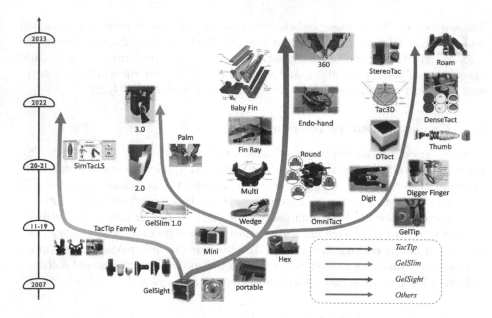

Fig. 2. Evolutionary tree of camera-based tactile sensors.

to reduce sensors size and achieve real-time reconstruction. Dtact [12] adopts reflection property of semitransparent elastomer to reconstruct 3D geometry by observing the tactile image darkness with singe image. To integrate sensor into dexterous hand, fingertip size sensor, named Digit [10], are designed and achieved impressive manipulation performance. Besides, GelTip [7] expand sensing range to whole fingertip; Minsight [1] improves the contact force sensing performance. Stereo vision is also introduced by Tac3D [31] and stereoTac [18]. Complex pattern [30] and compound eyes [34] are also explored. Besides dexterous grasping and manipulation, tactile sensors are also applied in object identification inside granular media [17] and fossil detection [33]. We concluded existing camera-based tactile sensors as evolutionary tree in Fig. 2, to present their development more clearly.

These sensors describe the blueprint and potential applications of camera-based tactile sensor, however nearly all of them are special designed and lack adeptness and flexibility. To improve wider applications of tactile sensor, we proposed a new tactile sensor MC-Tac with modular design and sample fabricate process.

3   Design and Fabrication of MC-Tac

There are various robot gripper and dexterous hands with different size, shape, and motion trace, redesigning the tactile sensor for each of them is time-consuming and laborious. To improve the flexibility and adeptness, we disassemble the tactile sensor into modules and redesign whole structure with more

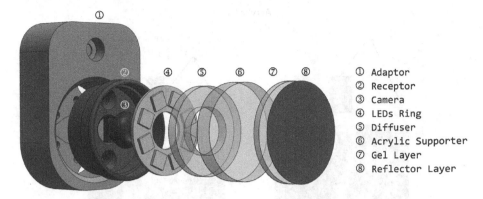

① Adaptor
② Receptor
③ Camera
④ LEDs Ring
⑤ Diffuser
⑥ Acrylic Supporter
⑦ Gel Layer
⑧ Reflector Layer

Fig. 3. The technical structure skeleton of MC-Tac (colors are added for more clear presentation).

accessible components. It is mainly divided into adapter and receptor module, where the adapter is customized connector to various grippers and actuators, and the receptor holds camera, illumination, elastomer, and accessories to provide general tactile image. The design criteria of MC-Tac is modularity and generality, which make the receptor reusable for all configuration (concentrate on core function iteration without wheel making repeatedly) and make adapter accessible for various robot with simple adjustment. The following section will introduce the design details and manufacturing process for the previous proposed MC-Tac.

3.1 Modular Designs

As shown in Fig. 3, the adapter provides connection to gripper and acts as holder for the receptor. Taking the Franka Gripper as an example, we design a slot to place gripper and a screw hole to tightly fixed them together. Holes on the bottom reduce weight and provide passway for electric line. With slight adjustment in CAD, the adapter can suit various two-finger grippers easily.

For receptor design, we first choose the global shape as a circle. The isoperimetric inequality shows the circle has the smallest geometric size under same sensing area, which helps improve the minimization design. Considering the size of gripper, illumination component and camera, we set the radium of receptor around 15 mm. In this cylinder-like receptor, we first put and fixed the camera in the center. The small lens connects CMOS base through the hole on the bottom of receptor structure. Considering the distortion and FOV, we choose 120° compact camera.

Then, a commercial LED ring is placed on the bottom of receptor. LEDs can illuminate from any direction on the circle. We choose WS2812 programmable LED with 5050 package and 8 lights ring as our illumination, which can be conveniently brought from e-commercial website and has uniform size, and eliminates the customized LED PCB board design and long-term fabrication. Besides,

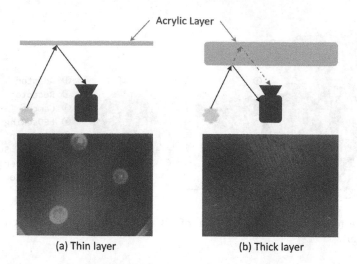

Fig. 4. Light reflection with different thickness of acrylic. Thicker layer may alleviate the inner reflection and increase image quality.

because the intensity and color are tunable separately, we can configure the sensor work under various illumination modes as necessary.

On the top of camera and LED ring, we design a step to place the acrylic piece, which provides support for elastomer in contact deformation and optical transparency for imaging process. However, because LEDs on the bottom, emitted shiny light may directly reflect into camera by the lower surface of acrylic piece, and leads the image quality degrade. To attenuate the reflection, we first add a frosted acrylic ring as diffuse layer to produce more uniform illumination, and increase the thickness of acrylic piece to increase incident angle (by reducing the distance between LEDs and its lower surface).

At last, the soft elastomer with reflect layer is putted on the upper surface of acrylic and stuck by glue. Reflect layer provide a uniform appearance layer to various target materials and geometries, and help sensor encode the surface details into intensity and color.

To prevent the elastomer adhere to target surface and increase its operation life, we also spray ultra-thin layer of micro powder. Unlike silicon-gel ink need vulcanization reaction to adhere with gel-layer, micro powder just adsorption on the surface to adjust friction. With previous design, MC-Tac can provide flexibility and maintain high-performance tactile sensing.

3.2 Fabrication Pipeline

To increase the accessibility of camera-based tactile sensor, we choose more common equipment, materials, and fabricate process in stand of advanced techniques (with little sacrifice of performance).

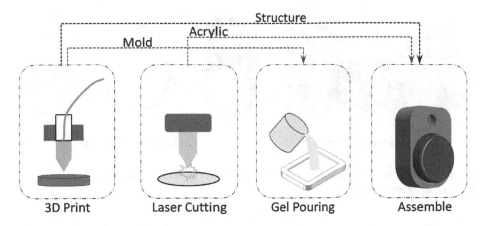

Fig. 5. Fabrication pipeline. We take 3D printer fabricate the gel mold and sensor structure, and use laser to cut acrylic piece and ring. Finally, we assemble components into MC-Tac.

For the structure building, we choose fused deposition modeling (FDM) 3D printer with polylactic acid fiber (PLA) to make the adaptor and receptor body. The camera is fixed with its lens and hot-melt adhesive (HMA), the LEDs ring is snap-fitted on the bottom and also fixed by HMA. The acrylic piece (D: 30 mm, h: 5 mm) and ring (D: 28 mm, d: 15 mm, h: 3 mm) are cut by general laser cutter. We take 120 grit sandpaper to process the ring into a diffuse surface.

Finally, we utilized soft transparent PDMS (hardness: C-0030) and gray silicon-gel ink to spray reflective layer. We choose 2 mm gel layer [29] which can cover most tactile-related surface details. After pouring into mode, the gel needs 4 h–6 h curing time under 55°C. To provide uniform and diffuse reflection layer, we spray silicon-gel ink on the upper surface of gel. Because the median of RGB is gray, so we choose the gray color to act as background to increase imaging stability and appearance. The ink can cure under 100°C in 1 h. Finally, we stick the painted gel, acrylic piece together and fix them on the top of receptor. The whole fabrication process is illustrated in Fig. 5.

4 Experiment on Surface Perception

We mount design sensor on Franka Gripper to test the adeptness. Besides, we also design various versions of MC-Tac to show the generalities of proposed design. Details are shown in Fig. 6.

To test the performance of proposed sensor, we utilize one version of MC-Tac test on various ordinary objects, such as screw, pen, and cylinder. Figure 7 shows tactile results. The geometric details are clearly detected and shown. With these tactile images, the robot can clearly discriminate the different objects

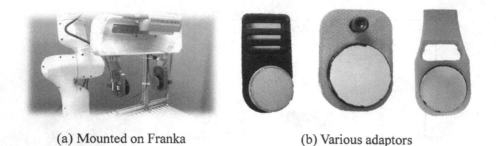

(a) Mounted on Franka   (b) Various adaptors

Fig. 6. MC-Tac is mounted on Franka Gripper (left). Verious versions of MC-Tac for different gripper(right).

with geometric details. It is worth mentioning that the original tactile image may affect by the illumination intensity, we improve the image quality by post-processing. Furthermore, compared with previous sensor, we placed the LED ring in the bottom. This sample design eliminates complex calculation and fabrication while leading inadequate mixing of RGB lights. However, this does not degrade perception performance which is based on the discrepancy of target objects. Besides, we also can achieve surface reconstruction by dense calibration and learning-based methods.

On the other hand, surface texture and roughness also influence the perception ability. We then test the tactile results on various sanding sponges with different grit number and diverse clothes to test MC-Tac sensing abilities. As shown in Fig. 8, MC-Tac can observe details of clothes and the tiny difference between sand sponges.

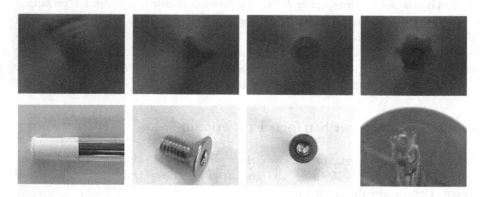

Fig. 7. Tactile images various objects, which include details on cylinder, screws thread, allen screw hole, and star-like pen.

Fig. 8. Perception tactile image on diverse fabrics (scouring pad, dishcloth, and towel) and sanding sponge with #60, #100, and #400 grit from left to right (zoom in for better view).

5   Conclusion

We proposed a modular camera-based tactile sensor MC-Tac, which has a small size and provides adaptive connectors to various grippers. We adopt a simple fabrication process and standard industrial components to reduce the manufacturing threshold of tactile sensor. In addition, we also demonstrated the perception abilities on various objects and surface texture. In future work, we will improve the LEDs arrangement to eliminate non-uniform illuminations and develop a new calibration method to generate accurate surface geometric details.

References

1. Andrussow, I., Sun, H., Kuchenbecker, K.J., Martius, G.: Minsight: a fingertip-sized vision-based tactile sensor for robotic manipulation. Adv. Intell. Syst. 2300042 (2023)
2. Do, W.K., Jurewicz, B., Kennedy III, M.: DenseTact 2.0: Optical tactile sensor for shape and force reconstruction. arXiv preprint arXiv:2209.10122 (2022)
3. Do, W.K., Kennedy, M.: DenseTact: optical tactile sensor for dense shape reconstruction. In: 2022 International Conference on Robotics and Automation (ICRA), pp. 6188–6194. IEEE (2022)
4. Dong, S., Jha, D., Romeres, D., Kim, S., Nikovski, D., Rodriguez, A.: Tactile-RL for insertion: Generalization to objects of unknown geometry. In: 2021 IEEE International Conference on Robotics and Automation (ICRA) (2021). https://arxiv.org/pdf/2104.01167.pdf
5. Dong, S., Yuan, W., Adelson, E.H.: Improved gelsight tactile sensor for measuring geometry and slip. In: 2017 IEEE/RSJ International Conference on Intelligent Robots and Systems (IROS), pp. 137–144. IEEE (2017)
6. Donlon, E., Dong, S., Liu, M., Li, J., Adelson, E., Rodriguez, A.: GelSlim: a high-resolution, compact, robust, and calibrated tactile-sensing finger. In: 2018 IEEE/RSJ International Conference on Intelligent Robots and Systems (IROS), pp. 1927–1934. IEEE (2018)
7. Gomes, D.F., Lin, Z., Luo, S.: GelTip: a finger-shaped optical tactile sensor for robotic manipulation. In: 2020 IEEE/RSJ International Conference on Intelligent Robots and Systems (IROS), pp. 9903–9909. IEEE (2020)

8. Johnson, M.K., Adelson, E.H.: Retrographic sensing for the measurement of surface texture and shape. In: 2009 IEEE Conference on Computer Vision and Pattern Recognition, pp. 1070–1077. IEEE (2009)

9. Johnson, M.K., Cole, F., Raj, A., Adelson, E.H.: Microgeometry capture using an elastomeric sensor. ACM Trans. Graph. (TOG) **30**(4), 1–8 (2011)

10. Lambeta, M., et al.: Digit: a novel design for a low-cost compact high-resolution tactile sensor with application to in-hand manipulation. IEEE Robot. Autom. Lett. **5**(3), 3838–3845 (2020)

11. Li, R., et al.: Localization and manipulation of small parts using gelsight tactile sensing. In: IEEE/RJS International Conference on Intelligent Robots and Systems (2014)

12. Lin, C., Lin, Z., Wang, S., Xu, H.: DTact: A vision-based tactile sensor that measures high-resolution 3d geometry directly from darkness. arXiv preprint arXiv:2209.13916 (2022)

13. Liu, S.Q., Adelson, E.H.: Gelsight Fin Ray: Incorporating tactile sensing into a soft compliant robotic gripper. In: 2022 IEEE 5th International Conference on Soft Robotics (RoboSoft), pp. 925–931. IEEE (2022)

14. Liu, S.Q., Ma, Y., Adelson, E.H.: GelSight Baby Fin Ray: a compact, compliant, flexible finger with high-resolution tactile sensing. In: 2023 IEEE International Conference on Soft Robotics (RoboSoft), pp. 1–8. IEEE (2023)

15. Liu, S.Q., Yañez, L.Z., Adelson, E.H.: GelSight EndoFlex: a soft endoskeleton hand with continuous high-resolution tactile sensing. In: 2023 IEEE International Conference on Soft Robotics (RoboSoft), pp. 1–6. IEEE (2023)

16. Ma, D., Donlon, E., Dong, S., Rodriguez, A.: Dense tactile force estimation using gelslim and inverse fem. In: 2019 International Conference on Robotics and Automation (ICRA), pp. 5418–5424. IEEE (2019)

17. Patel, R., Ouyang, R., Romero, B., Adelson, E.: Digger finger: gelsight tactile sensor for object identification inside granular media. In: Siciliano, B., Laschi, C., Khatib, O. (eds.) ISER 2020. SPAR, vol. 19, pp. 105–115. Springer, Cham (2021). https://doi.org/10.1007/978-3-030-71151-1_10

18. Roberge, E., Fornes, G., Roberge, J.P.: StereoTac: a novel visuotactile sensor that combines tactile sensing with 3D vision. arXiv preprint arXiv:2303.06542 (2023)

19. Romero, B., Veiga, F., Adelson, E.: Soft, round, high resolution tactile fingertip sensors for dexterous robotic manipulation. In: 2020 IEEE International Conference on Robotics and Automation (ICRA), pp. 4796–4802. IEEE (2020)

20. She, Y., Wang, S., Dong, S., Sunil, N., Rodriguez, A., Adelson, E.: Cable manipulation with a tactile-reactive gripper. Int. J. Robot. Res. **40**(12–14), 1385–1401 (2021)

21. Sunil, N., Wang, S., She, Y., Adelson, E., Garcia, A.R.: Visuotactile affordances for cloth manipulation with local control. In: Conference on Robot Learning, pp. 1596–1606. PMLR (2023)

22. Taylor, I.H., Dong, S., Rodriguez, A.: GelSlim 3.0: High-resolution measurement of shape, force and slip in a compact tactile-sensing finger. In: 2022 International Conference on Robotics and Automation (ICRA), pp. 10781–10787. IEEE (2022)

23. Tippur, M.H., Adelson, E.H.: GelSight360: An omnidirectional camera-based tactile sensor for dexterous robotic manipulation. In: 2023 IEEE International Conference on Soft Robotics (RoboSoft), pp. 1–8. IEEE (2023)

24. Wang, C., Wang, S., Romero, B., Veiga, F., Adelson, E.: SwingBot: Learning physical features from in-hand tactile exploration for dynamic swing-up manipulation. In: 2020 IEEE/RSJ International Conference on Intelligent Robots and Systems (IROS), pp. 5633–5640. IEEE (2020)

25. Wang, S., She, Y., Romero, B., Adelson, E.: GelSight Wedge: measuring high-resolution 3D contact geometry with a compact robot finger. In: 2021 IEEE International Conference on Robotics and Automation (ICRA), pp. 6468–6475. IEEE (2021)
26. Wang, S., et al.: 3D Shape Perception from Monocular Vision, Touch, and Shape Priors. In: IEEE/RSJ International Conference on Intelligent Robots and Systems (IROS) (2018)
27. Wilson, A., Wang, S., Romero, B., Adelson, E.: Design of a fully actuated robotic hand with multiple gelsight tactile sensors. arXiv preprint arXiv:2002.02474 (2020)
28. Yuan, W., Dong, S., Adelson, E.H.: GelSight: high-resolution robot tactile sensors for estimating geometry and force. Sensors 17(12), 2762 (2017)
29. Yuan, W., et al.: Tactile measurement with a gelsight sensor. Ph.D. thesis, Massachusetts Institute of Technology (2014)
30. Zhang, G., Du, Y., Yu, H., Wang, M.Y.: DelTact: a vision-based tactile sensor using a dense color pattern. IEEE Robotics and Automation Letters 7(4), 10778–10785 (2022)
31. Zhang, L., Wang, Y., Jiang, Y.: Tac3D: A novel vision-based tactile sensor for measuring forces distribution and estimating friction coefficient distribution. arXiv preprint arXiv:2202.06211 (2022)
32. Zhang, S., et al.: Hardware technology of vision-based tactile sensor: a review. IEEE Sensors J. 22(22), 21410–21427 (2022)
33. Zhang, S., Yang, Y., Shan, J., Sun, F., Fang, B.: A novel vision-based tactile sensor using lamination and gilding process for improvement of outdoor detection and maintainability. IEEE Sensors J. 23(4), 3558–3566 (2023)
34. Zhang, Y., Chen, X., Wang, M.Y., Yu, H.: Multidimensional tactile sensor with a thin compound eye-inspired imaging system. Soft Rob. 9(5), 861–870 (2022)

Advanced Sensing and Control Technology for Human-Robot Interaction

Integrated Direct/Indirect Adaptive Robust Control for Electrical Driven Injection Machine Mold Closing with Accurate Parameter Estimations

Jianfeng Liao[1,2(✉)], Shiqiang Zhu[1,2], Qiwei Meng[1,2], Wei Song[1,2], and Jason Gu[2,3]

[1] Research Center for Intelligent Robotics, Zhejiang Engineering Research Center for Intelligent Robotics, Zhejiang Lab, Hangzhou, Hangzhou, China
weisong@zhejianglab.com
[2] Zhejiang University, Hangzhou, China
jfliao@zhejianglab.com
[3] Department of Electrical and Computer Engineering, Dalhousie University, Halifax, Canada

Abstract. In this paper, the control issue of the mold closing system of Injection machine is studied. In actual application, there are two major control problems needed to be addressed in controller design: to ensure the quality of products, the precision of mold needs to be guaranteed; the operation parameters of the machines are willing to be recorded for analysis, such as health monitoring and prognosis. However, the existing controllers usually rely on the servo motor, where the dynamics of the mold closing system is not taken into consideration, that may lead to degraded tracking performances. Moreover, the uncertain model parameters are usually ignored or simply treated as disturbances. Instead in this paper, the nonlinear dynamic model of mold closing system is first proposed including parameter uncertainties and disturbances for controller design. Subsequently, an integrated direct/indirect adaptive robust control law(DIARC) is proposed that not only achieves excellent tracking performance but also attenuates the parameter uncertainties with accurate parameter learning. Comparative experiments are carried out to verify our proposed approach and the results demonstrate the effectiveness of the integrated direct/indirect adaptive robust control.

Keywords: Injection machine · adaptive control · robust control

1 Introduction

The injection machine is an essential equipment widely used in industry for manufacturing plastics, including automotive, aerospace and medical equipment. Generally, the injection machine can be divided into two types: electrical and hydraulic by the actuators [12]. Since the high accuracy, electrical injection molding machine has attracted a lot of attention from industry and academic [23].

© The Author(s), under exclusive license to Springer Nature Singapore Pte Ltd. 2023
H. Yang et al. (Eds.): ICIRA 2023, LNAI 14271, pp. 183–196, 2023.
https://doi.org/10.1007/978-981-99-6495-6_16

The mold closing system is one of the major systems in injection machine, which can drive the mold to the desired position and clamp the mold. Thus, the heated plastic is injected into the mold by the injection system. Then the mold opens and we capture the products. This paper mainly pays attention on the controller design of mold closing system.

At present, many controllers are designed for injection machine, some researcher propose position controller [17], where the artificial neural network is trained. The controller with fuzzy logic is also proposed [6]. However, most of the existing controllers applied in practice for electrical driven injection machine simply depend on servo motor, where the influence from the dynamics of injection machine can not be taken into consideration [11]. Thus, the controller can also to be synthesized with the dynamic model of injection machine. Since the injection machine is usually used in harsh environment, a perfect dynamic model can't be obtained with hand-crafted model design and parameter identification. Uncertainties could degrade the control performance, leading to unexpected control accuracy [10,15]. To reduce negative influence, lots of control techniques are proposed such as adaptive controller [9], robust controller [18,22]. In addition, Yao proposed an adaptive robust control law(ARC) theoretic framework for precision motion control with application to several equipment [3–5,16]. Therefore, the ARC framework [2,20,21] can be adopted for the injection machine mold closing process to improve the tracking performance, where the gradient type adaptation law is usually used in the ARC design(DARC).

In addition, in practice, the operation states such as friction, external forces, are expected to be estimated for monitoring the system or health diagnosis [13,14,24]. For example, the frictions can be used to determine when to add lubrication oil, which helpful to mold protection system [8]. However, such a direct ARC(DARC) control law only focuses on the objective of reducing the tracking error [7], which may lead to controller that the estimated parameters will not converge to their true values. These practical limitations demonstrates that the estimated parameters could not be used for secondary purpose that need reliable and accurate parameters such as operation monitoring and fault detection. Thus, the indirect adaptive robust control (IARC) with accurate least square parameter estimates is a choice to overcome the drawbacks of DARC, where the parameter estimation and robust control law is designed separately. Though IARC designs have much better parameter estimation performance than DARC. However, the IARC may have a poorer tracking performance than DARC. To obtain a good tracking performance and accurate parameter estimations, the integrated direct/indirect adaptive robust control is then proposed [1]. Many applications verity the superior control performance of DIARC.

In this paper, the trajectory tracking control of injection machine mold closing process is studied. Apart from the controller design in practice, the proposed DIARC controller is synthesized with the dynamics of whole mold closing process. To validate the effectiveness of the proposed method, it is compared with the controller used in practice. Comparative experimental results show that the proposed controller can not only achieve high tracking performance but also accurate parameter estimations.

2   System Dynamic and Problem Formulation

2.1   Nonlinear Mold Closing Dynamic Model

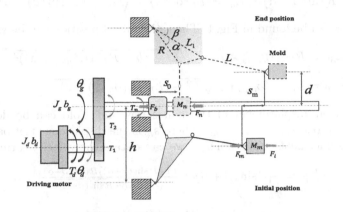

Fig. 1. Schematic of injection machine mold closing system.

The schematic of mold closing system is shown in Fig. 1. To establish a general nonlinear dynamic model, it's initial position and end position are depicted in the figure, the dynamics of the driving motor is yield

$$J_d \ddot{\theta}_d + b_d \dot{\theta}_d + f_d + T_1 = T_d \tag{1}$$

where the $T_d = u_d$ is the driving torque, J_d is total inertia of driving motor, b_d is the viscous damping ratio, θ_d is the rotation angle of the driving motor, f_d is the torque from coulomb friction acting on driving motor, T_1 is the reaction torque from the gear. The relationships of the gear meshing process can be described as $\theta_d = i_g \theta_g, T_2 = i_g T_1$, where T_2 is the input torque of the big gear which is resulted from gear meshing, i_g is the reducer ratio of the gear meshing process, θ_g is the rotation angle of the big gear. Similarly, dynamics of the big gear can be derived as

$$J_g \ddot{\theta}_g + b_g \dot{\theta}_g + f_g + T_n = T_2 \tag{2}$$

where J_g is the inertia of big gear, b_g is viscous coefficient of big gear, f_g is the coulomb friction torque, T_n is the torque acting on the ballscrew. The relationship between the rotary input and the liner force is given as $F_b = \frac{2\pi v T_n}{l}, \theta_g = \frac{2\pi}{l} s_n = i_n s_n$, where T_n is torque applied to screw, F_b is linear force applied, l is ball screw lead and v is ball screw efficiency, s_n is the linear displacement of ball screw system. The dynamics of the ballscrew can be obtained as

$$M_n \ddot{s}_n + b_n \dot{s}_n + f_n + F_n = F_b \tag{3}$$

where M_n is the lumped mass of ballscrew system, b_n is the viscous coefficient, f_n is coulomb friction. For the mold, the dynamics can be written as

$$M_m \ddot{s}_m + b_m \dot{s}_m + f_m + F_l = F_m \tag{4}$$

where M_m is the mass of mold, b_m is the viscous coefficient, f_m is the coulomb friction, f_l is the external forces, F_m represents the forces applied to the mold. The position of the ball screw and mold is given as $x_n = R\cos{(\beta + \alpha)} - \sqrt{L^2 - (h - R\sin{(\beta + \alpha))^2}}, x_m = L_1\cos{(\beta)} + \sqrt{L^2 - (L_1\sin{(\beta)} - d)^2}$, where R, L, L_1, β, α can be found in Fig. 1. Then, the initial position can be written as

$$x_{n0} = R\cos{(\beta_{max} + \alpha)} - \sqrt{L^2 - (h - R\sin{(\beta_{max} + \alpha))^2}}$$

$$x_{m0} = L_1\cos{(\beta_{max})} + \sqrt{L^2 - (L_1\sin{(\beta_{max})} - d)^2} \tag{5}$$

Thus, the linear displacement of the ball screw and mold can be derived as $s_n = x_n - x_{n0}, 1ex, s_m = x_m - x_{m0}$, where s_n is the displacement of ball screw, s_m is the displacement of mold. Then, we can obtain the velocity formula

$$\frac{\partial s_n}{\partial \beta} = -[R\sin{(\beta + \alpha)} + \frac{(h - R\sin{(\beta + \alpha)})R\cos{(\beta + \alpha)}}{\sqrt{L^2 - (h - R\sin{(\beta + \alpha))}}}]$$

$$\frac{\partial s_m}{\partial \beta} = -[L_1\sin{(\beta)} + \frac{(L_1\sin{(\beta)} - d)L_1\cos{(\beta)}}{\sqrt{L^2 - (L_1\sin{(\beta_{max})} - d)}}] \tag{6}$$

Thus, we can obtain the velocity relationships between ball screw and mold

$$\dot{s}_n = \frac{[R\sin{(\beta + \alpha)} + \frac{(h - R\sin{(\beta + \alpha)})R\cos{(\beta + \alpha)}}{\sqrt{L^2 - (h - R\sin{(\beta + \alpha))}}}]}{[L_1\sin{(\beta)} + \frac{(L_1\sin{(\beta)} - d)L_1\cos{(\beta)}}{\sqrt{L^2 - (L_1\sin{(\beta_{max})} - d)}}]}\dot{s}_m = i_m\dot{s}_m \tag{7}$$

where i_m is the reducer ratio. We then can obtain the relationship $F_m = i_mF_n$. From Eqs. (1)–(7), we obtain the general nonlinear dynamics of injection mold closing process

$$M_E\ddot{s}_m + b_E\dot{s}_m + f_E + F_l = T_E \tag{8}$$

where $M_E = J_di_g^2i_n^2i_m^2 + J_gi_n^2i_m^2 + M_ni_m^2 + M_m$ represents the equal mass of the mold closing process, $b_E = b_di_g^2i_n^2i_m^2 + b_gi_n^2i_m^2 + b_ni_m^2 + b_m$ denotes the equal viscous coefficient of mold closing process, $f_E = f_di_gi_ni_m + f_gi_ni_m + f_ni_m + f_m$ is the equal coulomb friction force of the mold closing system, F_l represents external forces, $T_E = i_gi_ni_mT_d$.

2.2   Problem Statement

In actual application, the task of the mold closing process is to make the s_m reach the user set position, where the controller design is a trajectory tracking problem. And to synthesize the control law, the coulomb friction can be roughly modeled as $f = A_fsgn(\dot{x})$ instead. Thus, the dynamic model Eq. (8) can be rewritten as

$$M_E\ddot{s}_m + b_E\dot{s}_m + A_fsgn(\dot{s}_m) + F_E = T_E + \tilde{\Delta} \tag{9}$$

where $F_E = F_l + \tilde{\Delta}$, F_E represents the nominal disturbances. In general, the M_E, b_E, f_E and the external load T_l are time varying and there true value can't be known a priori. We then adopt the adaptation law with parameters online learning to attenuate the influence from parameter uncertainties, where the unknown parameters are defined as $\boldsymbol{\theta} = [\theta_1, \theta_2, ..., \theta_4]^T = [M_E, b_E, A_f, F_E]^T$. Thus, the dynamics Eq. (9) can be written as a linear regression.

To design the control law with the parameter uncertainties, we can have the following assumptions.

Assumption 1. *The extent of the parametric uncertainties and uncertain non-linearities is known, i.e.,*

$$\boldsymbol{\theta} \in \Omega \triangleq \{\boldsymbol{\theta} : \boldsymbol{\theta}_{min} \leq \boldsymbol{\theta} \leq \boldsymbol{\theta}_{max}\} \tag{10}$$

$$\tilde{\Delta} \in \triangleq \{\tilde{\Delta} : |\tilde{\Delta}| \leq \delta_d\} \tag{11}$$

where $\boldsymbol{\theta}_{min} = [\theta_{1min}, \theta_{2min}, ..., \theta_{4min}]^T$, $\boldsymbol{\theta}_{max} = [\theta_{1max}, \theta_{2max}, ..., \theta_{4max}]^T$ and δ_d are known.

Based on the dynamics and statement, an adaptive robust controller with accurate parameter estimations is proposed in this paper, such that the mold closing process can achieve a good tracking performance.

3   Controller Design

3.1   Overall Control Architecture

The main challenge is to synthesize a control law that can achieve a good tracking performance, and attenuate the parameter uncertainties simultaneously. To deal with the stated problem, an indirect adaptive robust control method with accurate parameter estimation is proposed in this paper, as shown in Fig. 2. a) A parameter adaptation law is introduced to estimate the uncertain parameters online, where $\boldsymbol{\theta}$ can be estimated accurately, and then be fed to the model compensation part to improve the control performance; b) Robust feedback control law is synthesized to attenuate the disturbances.

3.2   Discontinuous Projection

Define $\hat{\boldsymbol{\theta}}$ as the estimation of uncertain parameter $\boldsymbol{\theta}$, and the parameter estimation error can be obtained as $\tilde{\boldsymbol{\theta}} = \hat{\boldsymbol{\theta}} - \boldsymbol{\theta}$. The following adaptation law with discontinuous projection modification can be adopted

$$\dot{\hat{\boldsymbol{\theta}}} = Proj_{\hat{\boldsymbol{\theta}}}(\boldsymbol{\Gamma}\boldsymbol{\tau}) \tag{12}$$

where $\boldsymbol{\Gamma} > 0$ is a diagonal matrix, τ is an adaptation function. The projection mapping is defined as

$$Proj_{\hat{\theta}_i}(\bullet_i) = \begin{cases} 0, & if \quad \hat{\theta}_i = \theta_{imax} \quad and \quad \bullet_i > 0 \\ 0, & if \quad \hat{\theta}_i = \theta_{imin} \quad and \quad \bullet_i < 0 \\ \bullet_i, otherwise \end{cases} \tag{13}$$

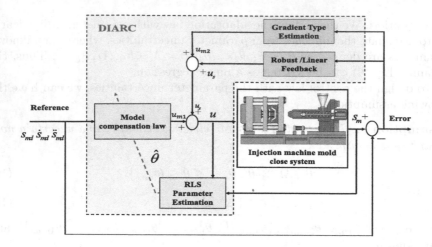

Fig. 2. Overall control structure of injection machine mold closing system.

The following properties are guaranteed for any adaptation function τ

$$\textbf{P1)} \ \theta \in \Omega \triangleq \{\theta : \theta_{min} \leq \theta \leq \theta_{max}\} \tag{14}$$

$$\textbf{P2)} \ \tilde{\theta}(\Gamma^{-1}Proj_{\hat{\theta}}(\Gamma\tau) - \tau) \leq 0, \forall \tau \tag{15}$$

3.3   Integrated Direct/indirect Adaptive Robust Control Law

Denote s_d, $\dot{s}_d$ and $\ddot{s}_d$ as the desired trajectory, and its first and second order derivatives respectively. Thus, the tracking error is defined as $e = s_m - s_d$. For simplicity, we define the following switching-function-like variable

$$p = \dot{e} + \lambda e \tag{16}$$

where $\lambda > 0$ is a feedback gain. Then, we choose the following Lyapunov function

$$V = \frac{1}{2}M_E p^2 \tag{17}$$

Differentiate Eq. (17) and refer to Eq. (9)

$$\begin{aligned}
\dot{V} &= p[u - b_E \dot{s}_m - A_f sgn(\dot{s}_m) - F_l + \Delta - M_E \ddot{s}_d + M_E \lambda \dot{e}] \\
&= p[u + \boldsymbol{\phi}^T \boldsymbol{\theta} + \Delta]
\end{aligned} \tag{18}$$

where $\boldsymbol{\phi} \in R^4$ is the regressor vector. Then, we can design the integrated direct/indirect adaptive robust control law(DIARC) as

$$\begin{aligned}
u = u_m + u_s, u_m = u_{m1} + u_{m2}, u_{m1} = -\boldsymbol{\phi}^T \hat{\boldsymbol{\theta}}, u_{m2} = -\hat{d}_c \\
u_s = u_{s1} + u_{s2}, u_{s1} = -kp
\end{aligned} \tag{19}$$

where u_m represents the model compensation control input, u_{m1} is the model compensation with least square parameter estimations $\hat{\boldsymbol{\theta}}$, u_{m2} is a model compensation term with stochastic gradient descent approach, u_s denotes the feedback control law, where $u_{s1} = kp$ is a proportional feedback law and k is the proportional gain; u_{s2} is a feedback law to ensure the robust performance, which will be designed below. With the control law Eq. (19), the Eq. (18) can be rewritten as

$$\dot{V} = p[-kp + u_{s2} + u_{m2} - \boldsymbol{\phi}^T \tilde{\boldsymbol{\theta}} + \Delta] \tag{20}$$

Define a constant d_c and time varying $\Delta^*(t)$ such that

$$d_c + \Delta^*(t) = -\boldsymbol{\phi}^T \tilde{\boldsymbol{\theta}} + \Delta \tag{21}$$

The adaptation law $\hat{d}_c$ is designed as

$$\dot{\hat{d}}_c = Proj(\gamma_d p) \tag{22}$$

where $\gamma_d > 0$ and $|\hat{d}_c| \leq d_{cm}$, d_{cm} is the pre-set upper bound. Then, we have

$$\begin{aligned}
\dot{V} &= p[-kp + u_{s2} + u_{m2} + d_c + \Delta^*(t)] \\
&= p[-kp + u_{s2} - \tilde{d}_c + \Delta^*(t)]
\end{aligned} \tag{23}$$

where $\tilde{d}_c = d_c - \hat{d}_c$. The robust feedback part can be designed to satisfy the following two conditions

$$\begin{aligned}
&1) p(u_{s2} - \tilde{d}_c + \Delta^*) = p[u_{s2} - \hat{d}_c - \boldsymbol{\phi}^T \hat{\boldsymbol{\theta}} + \Delta] \leq \epsilon \\
&2) p u_{s2} \leq 0
\end{aligned} \tag{24}$$

where ϵ is arbitrarily small.

Theorem 1. *With the DIARC law, the theoretical results are obtained, all signals are bounded. Furthermore, the positive definite function $V(t)$ is bounded above by*

$$V(t) \leq exp(-\lambda t) V(0) + \frac{\epsilon}{\lambda}[1 - exp(-\lambda t)] \tag{25}$$

where $\lambda = 2k/\theta_{1max}$.

Proof. Noting Eq. (24), the function Eq. (23) then becomes

$$\begin{aligned}
\dot{V} &= p[-kp + u_{s2} - \tilde{d}_c + \Delta^*(t)] \\
&\leq -kp^2 + p[u_{s2} - \tilde{d}_c + \Delta^*(t)] \leq -kp^2 + \epsilon \\
&\leq -\lambda V(t) + \epsilon
\end{aligned} \tag{26}$$

where $\lambda = 2k/\theta_{1max}$. Thus, Theorem 1 can be proved.

3.4   Accurate Parameter Estimation Algorithm

Referred to Eq. (19), the integrated direct/indirect adaptive robust control law is derived. The remain task is to design the accurate parameter estimation algorithm such that a good tracking performance can be achieved. In this section, a recursive least square law is introduced to estimate the uncertain parameters $\boldsymbol{\theta}$. For this purpose, an assumption is made that the uncertainties $\Delta = 0$ in model dynamics Eq. (9), so that the model dynamics can be written as

$$u = \boldsymbol{\varphi}^T \boldsymbol{\theta} \tag{27}$$

where $\boldsymbol{\varphi} = [\ddot{s}_m, \dot{s}_m, sgn(\dot{s}_m), 1]^T$ The predicted output of the linear regression is obtained as

$$u_p = \boldsymbol{\varphi}^T \hat{\boldsymbol{\theta}} \tag{28}$$

Define the prediction error $\xi = u - u_p$. And then the online parameter estimations $\boldsymbol{\theta}$ can be derived with the recursive least square estimation(RLSE) method.

$$\dot{\hat{\boldsymbol{\theta}}} = \boldsymbol{\Gamma}(t)\boldsymbol{\varphi}(t)\xi \tag{29}$$

where the covariance matrix is updated by

$$\dot{\boldsymbol{\Gamma}}(t) = \begin{cases} \mu\boldsymbol{\Gamma}(t) - \frac{\boldsymbol{\Gamma}(t)\boldsymbol{\varphi}(t)\boldsymbol{\varphi}(t)^T\boldsymbol{\Gamma}(t)}{1+\boldsymbol{\varphi}(t)^T\boldsymbol{\Gamma}(t)\boldsymbol{\varphi}(t)} & if \quad \sigma(\boldsymbol{\Gamma}(t)) < \rho_M \\ 0 & otherwise \end{cases} \tag{30}$$

where μ denotes the forgetting factor, $\sigma_M\cdot$ is used to calculate the maximum eigenvalue; ρ_M represents the pre-set upper bound.

Theorem 2. *Given the proposed DIARC law Eq. (19) and RLSE parameter estimation (29)(30), if the following PE condition is satisfied*

$$\exists T, t_0, \epsilon_p, s.t. \int_t^{t+T} \boldsymbol{\varphi}\boldsymbol{\varphi}^T d\nu \geq \epsilon_p I_p, \forall t \geq t_0 \tag{31}$$

the parameter estimates $\hat{\boldsymbol{\theta}}$ asymptotically converge to their true values and the asymptotic output tracking is achieved in the presence of parametric uncertainties only.

Proof. Select a positive definite Lyapunov function V_a as

$$V_a = V(t) + \frac{1}{2}\gamma_d^{-1}p^2 \tag{32}$$

Noting the robust condition (24) and the property (15), the derivative of V_a is

$$\begin{aligned} \dot{V} &= p[-kp + u_{s2} - \tilde{d}_c] + \gamma_d^{-1}\tilde{d}_c\dot{\tilde{d}}_c \\ &\leq -kp^2 + \gamma_d^{-1}\tilde{d}_c\dot{\tilde{d}}_c \\ &\leq -\lambda V(t) \end{aligned} \tag{33}$$

By Barbalat's lemma, asymptotic tracking can be achieved.

4 Results

4.1 Experiment Setup

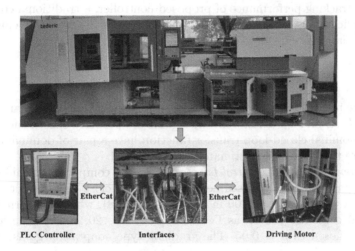

Fig. 3. Experimental platform of the injection machine mold closing system.

To test the proposed controller, experiments are carried out on an inject machine. The mold structure is driven by a servo motor through a gear and ball-screw structure, with about 0.35 m travelling distance and maximum 1 m/s velocity. The position signal of the mold is measured with a encoder sensor of the driving motor, and the velocity is directly obtained by differentiating the position signal with respect to time. The control law is implemented on a PLC controller and EtherCat communication interfaces with sampling time $t_s = 1$ ms.

Some nominal values are estimated by offline system identification with square signals that satisfy the PE condition, as shown in the following Table 1.

Table 1. Nominal parameters estimated offline.

M_E	b_E	A_f	F_l
$140uc/(m/s2)$	$500uc/(m/s)$	$55uc/(m/s)$	$12uc$

4.2   Comparison Controllers

To verify the performance of the proposed controller, the following two control algorithms are applied to the injection machine.

C1 *Proportional-integral-differential(PID) Controller for Driving Motor*: To verify the tracking performance of proposed controller, a traditional control law in real application is compared, which is the most used in actual implementation. The PID controller can be written as

$$u = -k_p e - k_i \int edt - k_d \dot{e} \tag{34}$$

For the the mold closing system driving motor, the controller gains are properly chosen as k_p, k_i and k_d. These controller gains are properly chosen such that the resulting nominal closed-loop transfer function have a pair of dominant poles at -50, where the parameters estimated offline is used.

C2 *Proposed DIARC Control Law*: To make the comparison meaningful, the controller gains of the proposed controller are set close to **C1**. The gains are chosen as $\lambda = 50$ and $k = 8700$ in Eq. (16) and (18), which is referred to [19]. The initial gains are chosen as $\Gamma = diag[500, 3000, 20, 26000]$. The forgetting factor are chosen as $\mu = 0.05$. The gradient type adaptation gains are set as $\gamma_d = 20$.

4.3   Experimental Results

The following two test sets are applied to verify the effectiveness of the proposed method.

Set 1: The trajectory tracking performance is tested on the injection machine experimental setup. Testing the trajectory tracking performance of both **C1** and **C2**.

For **Set1**, the desired trajectory is presented in Fig. 3, testing the trajectory tracking performance of both **C1** and **C2**. The tracking errors are plotted in Fig. 4. Apparently, both C1 and C2 achieve a acceptable performance, where the tracking error is less than 0.2mm. And the tracking error of C2 is less than C1, demonstrating that the performance is improved of the proposed controller with accurate parameter estimations. However, it is also found that the transient performance seems poorer than the traditional method. The reason is that for injection machine the accurate parameter estimation and steady error are more important than transient performance. And to improve the transient performance, a larger value of γ_d can be set. The typical histories of the parameter estimations are presented in Fig. 5, where the mass, friction and external forces are estimated during experiments and the parameters are converging. Moreover, from the results presented in Fig. 5 the online estimated parameters all converges close to the offline estimated values, which verify the capacity of the online accurate estimation.

Set 2: Since the true value of the parameters can't be known, it is difficult to tell whether the parameters converge to true values. To test the ability of

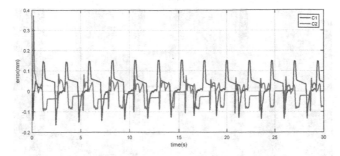

Fig. 4. Tracking errors of the experimental Set 1 .

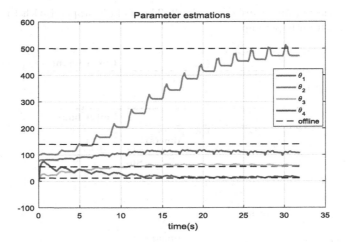

Fig. 5. Parameter estimations of the experimental Set 1.

the accurate parameter estimations, the experiment is designed as Fig. 6. In the experiment, the mold is moving forward the paper cup, where if the estimated parameter θ_4 violate pre-set bound, the machine will stop. The pre-set bound is estimated by offline experiments, where the upper bound is set as 20 and the lower bound is set as 10. As shown in Fig. 6, the mold closing procedure is presented, where the mold stop before the paper cup is destroyed. Referred to 7, when the mold touches the paper cup, the external acting on the mold is changed which leads the estimated parameter θ_4 violates the preset bound. And the injection machine is transfer to "Stop" from "Operation", where the driving force is set to zero. As we known, since the forces from the paper cup can't be very large, the experimental results demonstrate that the parameter estimation is sensitive to the external forces. It also infers that the controller with accurate parameter estimation can be used as health monitoring.

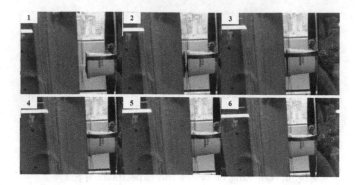

Fig. 6. Mold closing procedure of the Set 2. The mold is stopped with the estimated external forces from paper cup.

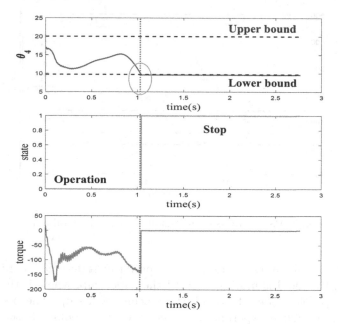

Fig. 7. State transfer of Set 2.The estimated parameter violates the preset bound, and then the machine stop

5   Conclusion

In this paper, the precision control problem of the electrical driven injection machine is studied. A nonlinear dynamic model is first developed including the gear mesh, ball screw process and the reduced order control oriented dynamic model is then derived. With the dynamics, an integrated DIARC controller that achieves not only excellent tracking performance but also accurate parameter estimations is developed and applied on an injection machine mold closing system. In the controller, to achieve accurate parameter estimations, the online adaptation law is designed separately with the recursive least-squares algorithms. To preserve the excellent tracking performance, the gradient type parameter estimations is also introduced. The stability and tracking performance of this integrated direct/indirect adaptive robust control scheme are theoretically guaranteed. Comparative experiments with traditional methods are carried out, and the experimental results show the better performance of our proposed scheme.

Acknowledgement. This research was supported by Zhejiang Provincial Natural Science Foundation of China Grant No. LQ23F030009 and also supported by Key Research Project of Zhejiang Lab (No. G2021NB0AL03).

References

1. Chen, Z., Li, C., Yao, B., Yuan, M., Yang, C.: Integrated coordinated/synchronized contouring control of a dual-linear-motor-driven gantry. IEEE Trans. Industr. Electron. **67**(5), 3944–3954 (2019)
2. Chen, Z., Pan, Y., Gu, J.: Integrated adaptive robust control for multilateral teleoperation systems under arbitrary time delays. Int. J. Robust Nonlinear Contr. **26**(12), 2708–2728 (2016)
3. Chen, Z., Pan, Y.J., Gu, J.: A novel adaptive robust control architecture for bilateral teleoperation systems under time-varying delays. Int. J. Robust Nonlinear Control **25**(17), 3349–3366 (2015)
4. Chen, Z., Yao, B., Wang, Q.: Accurate motion control of linear motors with adaptive robust compensation of nonlinear electromagnetic field effect. IEEE/ASME Trans. Mechatron. **18**(3), 1122–1129 (2013)
5. Chen, Z., Yao, B., Wang, Q.: μ-synthesis-based adaptive robust control of linear motor driven stages with high-frequency dynamics: a case study. IEEE/ASME Trans. Mechatron. **20**(3), 1482–1490 (2015)
6. Cui, Z.h., Li, S.l.: Speed control of the all electric injection molding machine based on the grey prediction fuzzy pid. J. Shandong Univ. Technol. (Natural Science Edition) (2015)
7. Hu, C., Yao, B., Wang, Q.: Integrated direct/indirect adaptive robust contouring control of a biaxial gantry with accurate parameter estimations. Automatica **46**(4), 701–707 (2010)
8. Kumar, S., Park, H.S., Lee, C.M.: Data-driven smart control of injection molding process. CIRP J. Manuf. Sci. Technol. **31**, 439–449 (2020)
9. Li, C., Li, C., Chen, Z., Yao, B.: Adaptive thrust allocation based synchronization control of a dual drive gantry stage. Mechatronics **54**, 68–77 (2018)
10. Liao, J., Chen, Z., Yao, B.: Model-based coordinated control of four-wheel independently driven skid steer mobile robot with wheel-ground interaction and wheel dynamics. IEEE Trans. Industr. Inf. **15**(3), 1742–1752 (2018)
11. Liao, J., Yuan, H., Song, W., Gu, J.: Adaptive robust fault detection and control for injection machine mold closing process with accurate parameter estimations. In: 2021 IEEE International Conference on Mechatronics (ICM), pp. 1–6. IEEE (2021)
12. Lin, C.Y., Shen, F.C., Wu, K.T., Lee, H.H., Hwang, S.J.: Injection molding process control of servo-hydraulic system. Appl. Sci. **10**(1), 71 (2020)

13. Moreira, E.E., et al.: Industry 4.0: Real-time monitoring of an injection molding tool for smart predictive maintenance. In: 2020 25th IEEE International Conference on Emerging Technologies and Factory Automation (ETFA), vol. 1, pp. 1209–1212. IEEE (2020)

14. Pierleoni, P., Palma, L., Belli, A., Sabbatini, L.: Using plastic injection moulding machine process parameters for predictive maintenance purposes. In: 2020 International Conference on Intelligent Engineering and Management (ICIEM), pp. 115–120. IEEE (2020)

15. Sun, W., Tang, S., Gao, H., Zhao, J.: Two time-scale tracking control of nonholonomic wheeled mobile robots. IEEE Trans. Control Syst. Technol. **24**(6), 2059–2069 (2016)

16. Sun, W., Zhao, Z., Gao, H.: Saturated adaptive robust control for active suspension systems. IEEE Trans. Indust. Electron. **60**(9), 3889–3896 (2013)

17. Veligorskyi, O., Chakirov, R., Khomenko, M., Vagapov, Y.: Artificial neural network motor control for full-electric injection moulding machine. In: 2019 IEEE International Conference on Industrial Technology (ICIT), pp. 60–65. IEEE (2019)

18. Xiong, L., Han, W., Yu, Z.: Adaptive sliding mode pressure control for an electrohydraulic brake system via desired-state and integral-antiwindup compensation. Mechatronics **68**, 102359 (2020)

19. Yao, B., Jiang, C.: Advanced motion control: from classical PID to nonlinear adaptive robust control. In: 2010 11th IEEE International Workshop on Advanced Motion Control (AMC), pp. 815–829. IEEE (2010)

20. Yao, J., Jiao, Z., Ma, D.: Extended-state-observer-based output feedback nonlinear robust control of hydraulic systems with backstepping. IEEE Trans. Industr. Electron. **61**(61), 6285–6293 (2014)

21. Yao, J., Jiao, Z., Ma, D., Yan, L.: High-accuracy tracking control of hydraulic rotary actuators with modeling uncertainties. IEEE/ASME Trans. Mechatron. **19**(2), 633–641 (2014)

22. Yong, K., Chen, M., Shi, Y., Wu, Q.: Flexible performance-based robust control for a class of nonlinear systems with input saturation. Automatica **122**, 109268 (2020)

23. Yu, S., Zeng, L.: Control strategy of screw motion during plasticizing phase for all-electric injection molding machine. Int. J. Autom. Technol. **12**(2), 215–222 (2018)

24. Zhang, Y., Xi, D., Yang, H., Tao, F., Wang, Z.: Cloud manufacturing based service encapsulation and optimal configuration method for injection molding machine. J. Intell. Manuf. **30**(7), 2681–2699 (2019)

Admittance Control of Flexible Joint with Dual-Disturbance Observer

Hongyu Wan[1,2], Silu Chen[1,2]([✉]), Chi Zhang[1,2], Chin-Yin Chen[1,2], and Guilin Yang[1,2]

[1] Ningbo Institute of Materials Technology and Engineering, Chinese Academy of Sciences, Ningbo 315201, China
{wanhongyu,chensilu}@nimte.ac.cn
[2] University of Chinese Academy of Sciences, Beijing 100049, China

Abstract. A high-performance inner position controller and accurate interaction torque sensing capability are essential for the admittance control of the flexible joint. To achieve this, most of the prior works use the lumped disturbance observer based on a single encoder with an installed force sensor. This brings a burden to system integration. In this paper, a novel dual-disturbance observer based on dual-encoder feedback is proposed on top of the conventional feedforward and feedback composite control, so that the friction and external torque are estimated and compensated separately. Better disturbance rejection ability is achieved with the proposed inner-loop position controller. In addition, the estimated external torque is fed into the admittance controller, thereby achieving compliant control of the flexible joint without the torque sensor. Real-time experiments are performed to demonstrate the practical appeal of the proposed method.

Keywords: Flexible joint · Admittance control · Disturbance observer · Force estimation

1 Introduction

Flexible joint is the core component of collaborative robots, which is regarded as a series elastic actuator (SEA) due to the introduction of harmonic drive and torque sensor [1,2]. This configurations bring many attractive features such as high tolerance to shock, low mechanical output impedance [3]. Since the flexible joint inevitably interact with the external environment [4], various admittance control methods are proposed for human-robot interaction scenario [5–7].

Inner-loop position controller is essential for the admittance control, but the tracking accuracy of the position control is deteriorated due to various forms of disturbances such as plant model uncertainties, friction and load variation [8,9]. A simple and effective method to deal with the low-frequencies disturbances is to combine a disturbance observer (DOB) [10,11]. The DOB is applied to

Supported by in part the National Key Research and Development Program of China under Grant 2022YFB4702500 and in part National Natural Science Foundation of China under grant U20A20282, U21A20121, 92048201, and U1913214.

compensate the model errors from time-varying rotary SEA based on the motor-side encoder [12,13]. To safely render a wide range of impedance, a DOB based on torque control architecture using link-side encoder has been adopted for SEA [14, 15]. Generally speaking, the slow disturbances exist in the motor side, while the disturbances in link side are fast. This causes that the position tracking accuracy is limited if only the motor-side position or the link-side position is utilized. It should be noted that the traditional DOBs are to estimate the disturbances in a lumped manner. The external torque serving the admittance controller is not obtained unless a force sensor is installed [16]. Hence, it is desirable to design a DOB by merging the signals from the motor side and link side, meanwhile such a DOB can extract the external torque for the compliant control.

In this paper, a novel admittance control architecture for the flexible joint is designed with a high-performance inner position loop. On the basis of traditional feedforward and feedback controllers, a novel dual-disturbance observer (DDOB) is proposed to estimate and compensate the friction torque and the external torque separately. Such a novel 3-degree-of-freedom (3-DOF) position controller not only obtains the better position control performance, but also serves the admittance control without the torque sensor. Real-time experiments validate that the proposed control scheme can achieve stable robot-environment interaction and high admittance rendering accuracy.

2   Problem Formulation

2.1   Dynamics Modeling

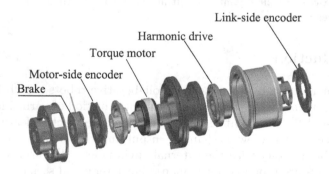

Fig. 1. Exploded view of flexible joint.

As shown in Fig. 1, the flexible joint is mainly composed of the brake, the motor-side encoder, the torque motor, the harmonic drive and the link-side encoder, etc. The motor-side inertia J_m and the link-side inertia J_l are separated by the joint flexibility with the stiffness K and the damping D. In addition, J_m and J_l are subjected to the viscous damping B_m and B_l. The command current is input into the motor to generate the torque τ_t. With the motor position θ_m and the link position θ_l, the dynamic model of the flexible joint is expressed as

$$\tau_t - \tau_j/N + \tau_f = J_m \ddot{\theta}_m + B_m \dot{\theta}_m \tag{1a}$$

$$\tau_j = K \left(\theta_m/N - \theta_l \right) + D \left(\dot{\theta}_m/N - \dot{\theta}_l \right) \tag{1b}$$

$$\tau_j + \tau_{ext} = J_l \ddot{\theta}_l + B_l \dot{\theta}_l \tag{1c}$$

where N is denoted as the reduction ratio of the harmonic drive, τ_{ext} is the actual interactive torque from the external environment, τ_j is the joint torque, and τ_f is the friction torque on the motor side.

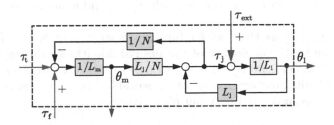

Fig. 2. Block diagram of dynamic model for flexible joint.

The above dynamic model in (1) is shown in Fig. 2, where $L_m(s) = J_m s^2 + B_m s$, $L_j(s) = K + Ds$, $L_l(s) = J_l s^2 + B_l s$. Therefore, the transfer function $P_{mt}(s)$ from τ_t to θ_m is derived as $P_{mt}(s) = N^2(L_l(s) + L_j(s))/[L_l(s)L_j(s) + N^2 L_m(s)(L_l(s) + L_j(s))]$. Similarly, the transfer function $P_{ml}(s)$ from θ_m to θ_l is written as $P_{lm}(s) = L_j(s)/[N(L_l(s) + L_j(s))]$, and the transfer function $P_{l,ext}(s)$ from τ_{ext} to θ_l is given as

$$P_{l,ext}(s) = (N^2 L_m(s) + L_j(s))/[L_l(s)L_j(s) + N^2 L_m(s)(L_l(s) + L_j(s)), \tag{2}$$

Hence, the transfer function $P_{lt}(s)$ from τ_t to θ_l is yielded as

$$rclP_{lt}(s) = NL_j(s)/[L_l(s)L_j(s) + N^2 L_m(s)(L_l(s) + L_j(s))]. \tag{3}$$

2.2 Control Objective

Our goal is to let such an SEA interact with the external environment with a desired admittance model G, where

$$rclG(s) = \frac{\theta_c}{\tau_{ext}} = \frac{1}{M_d s^2 + D_d s + K_d}, \tag{4}$$

In (4), M_d, D_d, and K_d are the desired inertia, damping and stiffness parameters, and $\theta_c = \theta_a - \theta_r$ is the difference between the reference trajectory θ_r and the

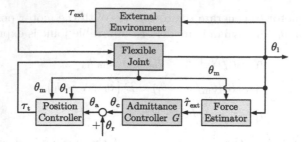

Fig. 3. Overview of the proposed compliant control architecture.

actual trajectory θ_a in Fig. 3. Notably, only τ_t, θ_m and θ_l are measurable in our case.

Denote $H_{l,ext}(s)$ as the transfer function from τ_{ext} to θ_l, i.e. $H_{l,ext}(s) = \theta_l/\tau_{ext}$. To render higher fidelity of the desired admittance during interaction with the environment, we try to make $H_{l,ext}(s)$ be as close to $G(s)$ as possible up to a band limit. However, τ_{ext} is not measurable due to the absence of a force sensor. Hence, as shown in Fig. 3, our objectives are

(i). To replace τ_{ext} with its estimation $\hat{\tau}_{ext}$ within the cut-off frequency of the estimator. Hence, the desired admittance is given as $G(s) = \theta_c/\hat{\tau}_{ext}$;

(ii). To design an inner-loop position controller to track the non-priori known interacting trajectory θ_a. Equivalently, to let $\hat{H}_{l,ext}(s) = \theta_l/\hat{\tau}_{ext} \approx G(s), \forall \omega \in (\omega_1, \omega_2)$.

3   Compliant Control Architecture Based on a Novel 3-DOF Position Control

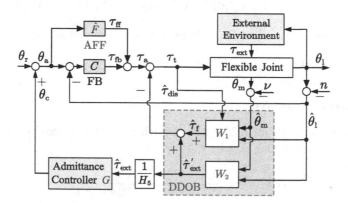

Fig. 4. Overview of the proposed admittance control architecture based on AFF+FB+DDOB.

In this section, as shown in Fig. 4, a novel admittance control structure is proposed. In the inner loop, a dual-disturbance observer (DDOB) based on the dual-encoder feedback, an approximate feedforward (AFF) subcontroller, and a feedback (FB) subcontroller form a novel 3-DOF position control. In the outer loop, a desired admittance controller G is given to achieve the compliant motion.

3.1 Feedback and Approximate Feedforward Controller

The FB controller is denoted as $C(s)$, and it is a proportional-derivative controller,

$$rlC(s) = k_p + \frac{k_d \cdot k_n}{[1 + k_n/s]} \tag{5}$$

where k_p, k_d, k_n are the proportional, derivative and filter coefficients, respectively.

The feedforward (FF) controller is denoted as the inverse nominal plant model, i.e. $F(s) = \bar{P}_{\mathrm{lt}}(s)^{-1}$. The human-robot interaction trajectory is unpredictable since the admittance controller is introduced in the outer loop. This makes the feedforward controller unimplementable. From (5), we know that $F(s) = (k_s s^4 + k_j s^3 + k_a s^2 + k_v s)/\rho(s)$, where $k_s = N^2 \bar{J}_m \bar{J}_1, k_j = N^2 \bar{J}_1 \bar{B}_m + N^2 \bar{J}_m(\bar{B}_1 + \bar{D}) + \bar{J}_1\bar{D}, k_a = N^2 \bar{B}_m(\bar{B}_1 + \bar{D}) + N^2 \bar{J}_m \bar{K} + \bar{J}_1 \bar{K} + \bar{B}_1 \bar{D}, k_v = N^2 \bar{B}_m \bar{K} + \bar{B}_1 \bar{K}, \rho(s) = N(\bar{K} + \bar{D}s)$. Since s is not realizable in real physical systems, s is approximated by the transfer function $h(s) = s/(cs+1)$, where c is a small coefficient. Here, c is equal to 0.008. Thus, the approximate feedforward controller (AFF) $\hat{F}(s)$ is given as follows

$$rl\hat{F}(s) = (k_s h^4 + k_j h^3 + k_a h^2 + k_v h)/\rho(s). \tag{6}$$

3.2 DDOB for Compensation and Force Estimation

Since the frictional torque τ_f is mainly concentrated on the motor side, a disturbance observer W_1 in Fig. 5 is designed to compensate such disturbance. Denote $(\bullet)$ to be the nominal version of an expression of parameter $(\bullet)$. ν and n are the measurement noises from the motor side and the link side. From (1a) and (1b), the estimation of τ_f is given as

$$rl\hat{\tau}_f = Q_1(s)\left(-\tau_t + H_1(s)\hat{\theta}_m + H_2(s)\hat{\theta}_1\right) \tag{7}$$

where $H_1(s) = (N^2 \bar{L}_m(s) + \bar{L}_j(s))/(N^2)$, $H_2(s) = -\bar{L}_j(s)/N$, $\hat{\theta}_m = \theta_m - \nu$, $\hat{\theta}_1 = \theta_1 - n$. $Q_1(s)$ is a low-pass filter (LPF) with the relative degree being not less than 2, which is used to guarantee physical realizability of W_1.

For estimating the external torque τ_{ext} on the link side, so the second disturbance observer W_2 in Fig. 5 is designed. Similarly, from (1b) and (1c), the estimation of τ_{ext} that acts on the link side is given by

$$rl\hat{\tau}_{\mathrm{ext}} = Q_2(s)\left(H_3(s)\hat{\theta}_m + H_4(s)\hat{\theta}_1\right) \tag{8}$$

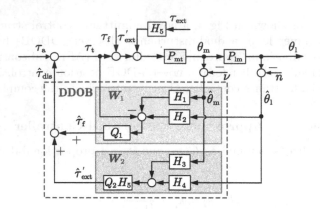

Fig. 5. Structure of the proposed DDOB for the flexible joint.

where $H_3(s) = -\bar{L}_j(s)/N$, $H_4(s) = (\bar{L}_1(s) + \bar{L}_j(s))$, $Q_2(s)$ is a LPF for ensuring the realizability of W_2. Remarkably, such $\hat{\tau}_{\text{ext}}$ is not only used to compensate for the exogenous disturbance, but is also utilized as the input to the desired admittance model $G(s)$.

To compensate for the disturbance using the motor torque, the exerting point of $\hat{\tau}_{\text{ext}}$ should be moved from the link side to the motor side. This yields the estimation of equivalent matched disturbance $\hat{\tau}'_{\text{ext}}$. By assigning nominal parameter values into $P_{1,\text{ext}}(s)$, the nominal transfer $\bar{P}_{1,\text{ext}}(s)$ is formed. Meanwhile, denote $\bar{P}'_{1,\text{ext}}(s)$ to be the nominal transfer from $\hat{\tau}'_{\text{ext}}$ to θ_1. Thus, the transfer H_5 from $\hat{\tau}_{\text{ext}}$ to $\hat{\tau}'_{\text{ext}}$ is expressed as

$$rlH_5(s) = \bar{P}_{1t}^{-1}\bar{P}_{1,\text{ext}} = (N^2\bar{L}_m(s) + \bar{L}_j(s))/(N\bar{L}_j(s)) \qquad (9)$$

Hence, $\hat{\tau}'_{\text{ext}} = H_5(s)\hat{\tau}_{\text{ext}}$. By (8) and (9), the relative degree of $Q_2(s)$ is not less than 3.

3.3 Stability of Admittance Control

As shown in Fig. 4, the inner-loop position controller is composed of AFF, FB and DDOB. This is denoted as "AFF+FB+DDOB". Afterwards, the admittance control is realized by utilizing the estimated external torque $\hat{\tau}_{\text{ext}}$, so that the flexible joint can interact with the environment. The transfer function $H_{1,\text{ext}}(s)$ from τ_{ext} to θ_1 is derived as

$$rclH_{1,\text{ext}}(s) = \frac{P_{1,\text{ext}} - Q_1\Omega_1 - Q_2\Omega_2}{1 + P_{1t}C - Q_1(1 - \Upsilon_1) - Q_2\Upsilon_2} \qquad (10)$$

where $P_{1,\text{ext}}$ is given in (2), $\Omega_1(s) = (N^2H_1(s) + L_j(s) + N^2L_1(s))/[L_1(s)L_j(s) + N^2L_m(s)(L_1(s) + L_j(s))]$, $\Omega_2(s) = NP_{1t}H_3(s)[(\hat{F}(s) + C(s))G(s) - H_5(s)]/L_j(s)$, $\Upsilon_1(s) = H_1P_{mt} + H_2P_{1t}$, $\Upsilon_2(s) = [(\hat{F} + C)G - H_5](P_{mt}H_3 + P_{1t}H_4)$.

Define $\hat{S}_{er}(s) = (1 - P_{lt}(s)\hat{F}(s))/(1 + P_{lt}(s)C(s))$, and

$$\Phi_2(s) = \Upsilon_2(s)/(1 + P_{lt}(s)C(s)) \tag{11}$$

The following Proposition concludes the stability of the entire system under admittance control.

Proposition 1. *Suppose $P_{lt}(s)$ in (3) can be stabilized by 2-DOF position control FB $C(s)$ in (5) and AFF $\hat{F}(s)$ in (6). Thereafter, the DDOB as in (7) and (8) is added, so that admittance control (4) is realized with $\hat{\tau}_{ext}$ in (8). Hence, the stability of the admittance control with AFF+FB+DDOB is guaranteed if $\sup_\omega |Q_1\Phi_1| < 1$ and $\sup_\omega |Q_2\Phi_2| < 1$ hold.* ∎

Proof of Proposition 1: The transfer $\hat{H}_{er}(s)$ from θ_e to θ_r is derived as $\hat{H}_{er}(s) = (\hat{S}_{er} - Q_1\Phi_1 - Q_2\Phi_2)/(1 - Q_1\Phi_1 - Q_2\Phi_2)$. We notice that the closed-loop stability of admittance control is equivalent to the stability of $\hat{H}_{er}(s)$. Thus, the stability of $\hat{H}_{er}(s)$ is guaranteed by the stability of $\hat{S}_{er}$, $Q_1\Phi_1$ and $Q_2\Phi_2$. Obviously, $\hat{S}_{er}$ is stable, since the 2-DOF closed-loop control is stable. Hence, the stability of $Q_1\Phi_1$ and $Q_2\Phi_2$ are granted by the small gain theorem, if $\sup_\omega |Q_1\Phi_1| < 1$ and $\sup_\omega |Q_2\Phi_2| < 1$. This proves Proposition 1. □

Proposition 1 can be used to guide the design of the desired admittance model $G(s)$.

4   Real-Time Experiment

In this section, a series of experiments are conducted to verify the effectiveness of the proposed method. The experimental setup is shown in Fig. 6. The CAPRO-S076030 incremental encoder and the DS-90 absolute encoder are installed in the motor and link sides of the flexible joint, respectively. The reduction ratio N is 160. The torque motor is connected to an Elmo driver configured in the current mode. It receives the commands from the Speedgoat Real-Time Target Machines. All control algorithms are programmed by MATLAB/Simulink with a sampling rate of 1 kHz. Two 7.5-kg payloads are attached to both sides of the end link of the flexible joint. To verify the accuracy of the estimation of the external torque, a Sunrise Instruments six-axis F/T sensor is fixed to measure the actual external torque.

The identified dynamic parameters are given in Table 1 for the experiments. $Q_1(s)$ and $Q_2(s)$ are designed as 2nd- and 3rd-order Butterworth filters in the proposed 3-DOF control, while $Q(s)$ in traditional 3-DOF control [15] is the same as $Q_2(s)$. In the FB controller, $k_p = 16, k_d = 0.5, k_n = 100$. For fairness of comparison, their cutoff frequencies are set as $\omega_c = 40$ rad/s and the controller parameters in different control methods are the same.

4.1   Performance of Inner Position Loop

Assume that a preset human-joint interaction trajectory θ_r is given in Fig. 7(a), thus the FF controller is implementable. To validate the superiority

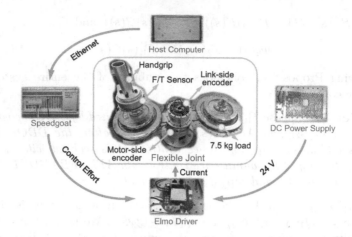

Fig. 6. Experimental setup of flexible joint.

Table 1. Identified system dynamics parameters.

Parameters	Values	Unit	Parameters	Values	Unit
$\bar{J}_\mathrm{m}$	92×10^{-6}	kg · m^2	$\bar{D}$	6.5	Nm · s/rad
$\bar{B}_\mathrm{m}$	0.003	Nm · s/rad	$\bar{J}_\mathrm{l}$	0.58	kg · m^2
$\bar{K}$	20648	Nm/rad	$\bar{B}_\mathrm{l}$	0.3	Nm · s/rad

of the proposed control structure, three control strategies are implemented for comparison:

C1: FF+FB-the traditional FF and FB (2-DOF) controllers.

C2: FF+FB+DOB-the DOB based on the link position on top of the FF and FB controllers [15].

C3: FF+FB+DDOB-the proposed DDOB based on the motor and link position on top of the FF and FB controllers.

As shown in Fig. 8, the mean and maximum tracking errors are 0.20mrad and 1.76 mrad by using FF+FB+DDOB, while they are 0.31 mrad and 2.13 mrad by using conventional FF+FB+DOB. The maximum tracking error of the link

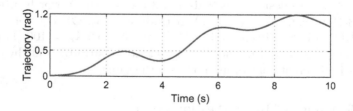

Fig. 7. Postulated trajectory during human-joint interaction.

position is reduced at least by 17.4% using FF+FB+DDOB. This verifies the superiority of the proposed inner-loop position control.

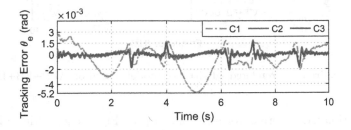

Fig. 8. Comparison of tracking errors.

4.2 Performance of Admittance Control

The interaction scenario is assumed to be the flexible joint performs a point-to-point task, i.e. the original trajectory in Fig. 9(a), and then the human user applies a force to the handgrip of F/T sensor in the link side by pulling and pushing. The link can comply with the external torque and generate an actual trajectory in Fig. 9(a). When the external torque is withdrawn, the joint continues to perform its task. Figure 9(b) shows that the estimated external torque is basically consistent with the measured torque from F/T sensor, the estimation errors mainly come from some nonlinear disturbances in the harmonic drive. In general, the proposed estimation method is feasible. This achieves task (i) in Sect. 2.2.

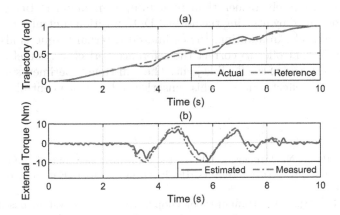

Fig. 9. Human-joint interaction. (a) The trajectory. (b) The external torque.

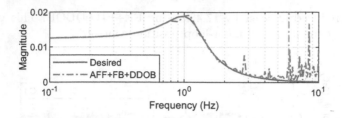

Fig. 10. Desired and rendered admittance models based on AFF+FB+DDOB.

The estimated external torque from W_2 in Fig. 4 enters the admittance controller to obtain the corrected trajectory θ_c. Set the desired parameters as $M_d = 1.6, B_d = 8, K_d = 80$ in G according to Proposition 1. To track desired admittance model G, the inner-loop AFF+FB+DDOB is utilized in Fig. 4. The magnitude response of $\hat{H}_{1,ext}$ is that the fast fourier transform (FFT) of $(\theta_1 - \theta_r)$ over to FFT of $\hat{\tau}_{ext}$. With the same $\hat{\tau}_{ext}$, the admittance control based on the proposed methods are performed. The magnitude response $A(G)$ and $A(\hat{H}_{1,ext})$ are shown in Fig. 10. To evaluate the task (ii) in Sect. 2.2, we denote the matching percentage of desired admittance model as $(1 - \sum_{\omega_1}^{\omega_2} [A(\hat{H}_{1,ext}) - A(G)] / \sum_{\omega_1}^{\omega_2} A(G)) \times 100\%$. As shown in Fig. 10, the fitness by using AFF+FB+DDOB is 88.33% when $\omega_1 = 0.1\,\text{Hz}$ and $\omega_2 = 6\,\text{Hz}$. The high model fidelity is achieved, thus verifies the effectiveness of the proposed method.

5   Conclusions

In this paper, a novel dual-disturbance observer (DDOB) is designed for the flexible joint, so that the friction and the external torque are estimated and compensated separately rather than in a lump-sum manner. Better tracking accuracy is obtained by utilizing the novel 3-DOF position control compared with traditional methods. In addition, the estimated external torque is also fed into the admittance controller to correct the reference trajectory, thereby achieving the compliant control of the flexible joint. The real-time experiments on a flexible joint validate the effectiveness of this sensorless admittance control.

References

1. Zhao, Y., Paine, N., Jorgensen, S.J., Sentis, L.: Impedance control and performance measure of series elastic actuators. IEEE Trans. Industr. Electron. **65**(3), 2817–2827 (2017)
2. Herbin, P., Pajor, M.: Human-robot cooperative control system based on serial elastic actuator bowden cable drive in Exoarm 7-DOF upper extremity exoskeleton. Mech. Mach. Theory **163**, 104372 (2021)
3. Li, X., Pan, Y., Chen, G., Yu, H.: Adaptive human-robot interaction control for robots driven by series elastic actuators. IEEE Trans. Rob. **33**(1), 169–182 (2016)

4. Sariyildiz, E., Chen, G., Yu, H.: A unified robust motion controller design for series elastic actuators. IEEE/ASME Trans. Mechatron. **22**(5), 2229–2240 (2017). https://doi.org/10.1109/TMECH.2017.2719682

5. Zhong, H., Li, X., Gao, L., Li, C.: Toward safe human-robot interaction: a fast-response admittance control method for series elastic actuator. IEEE Trans. Autom. Sci. Eng. **19**(2), 919–932 (2021)

6. Keemink, A.Q., van der Kooij, H., Stienen, A.H.: Admittance control for physical human-robot interaction. Int. J. Robot. Res. **37**(11), 1421–1444 (2018)

7. Kang, G., Oh, H.S., Seo, J.K., Kim, U., Choi, H.R.: Variable admittance control of robot manipulators based on human intention. IEEE/ASME Trans. Mechatron. **24**(3), 1023–1032 (2019)

8. Sariyildiz, E., Chen, G., Yu, H.: An Active Disturbance Rejection controller design for the robust position control of Series Elastic Actuators. In: 2016 IEEE/RSJ International Conference on Intelligent Robots and Systems (IROS), pp. 266–272 (Oct 2016). https://doi.org/10.1109/IROS.2016.7759065

9. Zhao, W., Sun, L., Yin, W., Li, M., Liu, J.: Robust position control of series elastic actuator with backstepping based on disturbance observer. In: 2019 IEEE/ASME International Conference on Advanced Intelligent Mechatronics (AIM), pp. 618–623 (Jul 2019). https://doi.org/10.1109/AIM.2019.8868550

10. Sariyildiz, E., Ohnishi, K.: Stability and robustness of disturbance-observer-based motion control systems. IEEE Trans. Industr. Electron. **62**(1), 414–422 (2015). https://doi.org/10.1109/TIE.2014.2327009

11. Yin, W., Sun, L., Wang, M., Liu, J.: Robust position control of series elastic actuator with sliding mode like and disturbance observer. In: 2018 Annual American Control Conference (ACC), pp. 4221–4226 (Jun 2018). https://doi.org/10.23919/ACC.2018.8431653

12. Kong, K., Bae, J., Tomizuka, M.: Control of rotary series elastic actuator for ideal force-mode actuation in human-robot interaction applications. IEEE/ASME Trans. Mechatron. **14**(1), 105–118 (2009)

13. Haninger, K., Asignacion, A., Oh, S.: Safe high impedance control of a series-elastic actuator with a disturbance observer. In: 2020 IEEE International Conference on Robotics and Automation (ICRA), pp. 921–927. IEEE (2020)

14. Mehling, J.S., Holley, J., O'Malley, M.K.: Leveraging disturbance observer based torque control for improved impedance rendering with series elastic actuators. In: 2015 IEEE/RSJ International Conference on Intelligent Robots and Systems (IROS), pp. 1646–1651 (Sep 2015). https://doi.org/10.1109/IROS.2015.7353588

15. Yun, J.N., Su, J., Kim, Y.I., Kim, Y.C.: Robust disturbance observer for two-inertia system. IEEE Trans. Industr. Electron. **60**(7), 2700–2710 (2012)

16. Yang, C., Peng, G., Cheng, L., Na, J., Li, Z.: Force sensorless admittance control for teleoperation of uncertain robot manipulator using neural networks. IEEE Trans. Syst., Man, Cybern.: Syst. **51**(5), 3282–3292 (2019)

Physical Reality Constrained Dynamics Identification of Robots Based on CAD Model

Lin Yang[1,2], Wenjie Chen[1,2(✉)], Che Hou[1,2], Yuqiang Wu[1,2], and Xiaoqiang Chen[1,2]

[1] Blue-Orange Lab, Midea Group, Foshan 528300, China
{yanglin23,chenwj42}@midea.com
[2] Midea Corporate Research Center, Foshan 528300, Shanghai, China

Abstract. Physical feasibility constraints play an important role in robot dynamics parameter identification. However, in practical robot development, not only physical feasibility is required, but also mapping the real inertial properties of each link. In this work, the latter requirement is called physical reality constraints. To address this problem, a two-step identification method for identifying the complete set of inertial parameters is adopted to guarantee the identified result is optimal in both static and dynamic environments while considering physical reality. To fulfill physical reality constraints, the dynamic parameters retrieved from the robot CAD model are used as the initial guesses in the optimization process, and the parameters' lower and upper boundaries are decided by adding and subtracting a suitable value respectively. The proposed approach is validated on a six-DOF collaborative robot.

Keywords: Parameter Identification · Physical Feasibility · Physical Reality · CAD Model · Robot Dynamics

1 Introduction

Robot dynamic model has a wide range of applications: model-based controller design which can effectively improve the static and dynamic performance of robots; motion planning considering dynamical constraints to maximize moving efficiency of robots; implementation of hand guiding, collision detection, and force control for collaborative robots also requires dynamic model. Thus, collecting high accuracy dynamic parameters of robots is fundamental in many robotic applications.

There are mainly three ways [1, 2] to identify robot dynamics, i.e. (1) Physical experiment method: the robot is disassembled into multiple links, and the inertia parameters of each linkage are measured by experiment. (2) Computer-aided design (CAD) meth-od: It uses the geometric and material properties designed in CAD software to deter-mine the desired robot dynamic parameters. (3) Dynamic model identification meth-od: It is based on the analysis of the "input/output" behavior of the robot's planned motion and estimates the parameter values by minimizing the differences between the variable functions and their mathematical models.

For the first method, it has high accuracy, however it requires amounts of engineering work, special measurement equipment, long measurement time and high measurement

H. Yang et al. (Eds.): ICIRA 2023, LNAI 14271, pp. 208–219, 2023.
https://doi.org/10.1007/978-981-99-6495-6_18

cost, which may be only feasible for robot manufacturers; While Retrieving dynamic parameters from robot CAD model is quite direct, the availability of the model could be a problem due to confidentiality. Even if it has an open access, the accuracy of parameters is in doubt due to mismatch between digital model and physical robots. The last method has no availability or high cost problem, it has attracted interest from many researchers.

The literature [3] used the Newton-Euler modeling approach to model the SCARA robot dynamics, and identified the base parameters set of robot dynamics by the least squares method. This is the most common identification method, but the base parameter set does not consider physical feasibility constraints. The literature [4] proposed an identification method for nonlinear optimization problems based on artificial bee colony algorithm, its identification parameters also did not consider physical feasibility constraints. The literature [5, 6] first calculated the base parameter set, and on this basis, it adopted an optimization method considering the physical feasibility constraints to obtain all the dynamic parameters, however, it ignored physical feasibility constraints when computing the base parameter set. The literature [7] proposed a method based on LMI-SDP to address the physical feasibility of estimated robot base inertial parameters, but it did not extend the constraint to each link.

Based on the above problems, this paper proposes an identification method with complete set of parameters considering physical reality constraints for each link based on CAD model. It designs optimal excitation trajectories for both quasi-static and dynamics models; substitutes the data which collected and processed during the trajectory execution into the identification model. The optimal robot dynamic parameter values are calculated by using genetic algorithm with applying reasonable constraints on the parameters based on CAD model. Finally, the accuracy and effectiveness of the identification method are verified through experiments.

The remainder of this paper is as follows. Section 2 formulates robot dynamic model in linear form and regroups inertial parameters into minimum set. Section 3 illustrates robot dynamics identification procedure considering physical reality constraints. In Sect. 4, the proposed approach is validated by an identification experiment. Finally, the conclusion is presented in Sect. 5.

2   Robot Dynamics Modeling

The dynamic equation of the $n-$ dof robot is:

$$M(q)\ddot{q} + C(q,\dot{q})\dot{q} + G(q) = \tau - \tau_f \tag{1}$$

where $M(q) \in \mathbb{R}^{n \times n}$ is the inertia matrix, $C(q,\dot{q}) \in \mathbb{R}^{n \times n}$ is the vector of the Coriolis and centrifugal forces, $G(q) \in \mathbb{R}^n$ is the gravity vector, $q\ \dot{q}\ \ddot{q} \in \mathbb{R}^n$ are respectively the joint positions, velocities and accelerations, $\tau \in \mathbb{R}^n$ is the torque vector, $\tau_f \in \mathbb{R}^n$ is the friction vector, each joint friction [8] can be expressed by the follow:

$$\tau_{fi} = f_{ci}\,\text{sgn}(\dot{q}_i) + f_{vi}\dot{q}_i \tag{2}$$

where f_{ci} is the Coulomb friction parameter and f_{vi} is the viscous friction parameter.

The Eq. (1) can be rewritten in linear form

$$Y(q, \dot{q}, \ddot{q})P = \tau - \tau_f \tag{3}$$

where $Y(q, \dot{q}, \ddot{q})$ is $n \times 10n$ matrix, $P = [p_1, p_2, \cdots, p_n]^T$ is $10n \times 1$ dynamic parameter vector, and p_i is

$$p_i = [m_i, m_i x_i, m_i y_i, m_i z_i, I_{ixx}, I_{ixy}, I_{ixz}, I_{iyy,}, I_{iyz}, I_{izz}]^T \tag{4}$$

Since the $Y(q, \dot{q}, \ddot{q})$ matrix is not of full rank, which contains zero columns and linearly related columns, using the QR decomposition method [9], the system of linear equations can be described

$$YP = [Y_b \ Y_d] \begin{bmatrix} P_b \\ P_d \end{bmatrix} = [Q_b \ Q_d] \begin{bmatrix} R_b \ R_d \\ 0 \ 0 \end{bmatrix} \begin{bmatrix} P_b \\ P_d \end{bmatrix} \tag{5}$$

where Y_b is the linearly independent submatrix between the columns of the Y matrix and P_b is the corresponding dynamic parameter vector; Y_d is the remaining submatrix composed of invalid columns and P_d is the remaining dynamic parameter vector, Q_b and Q_d are the orthogonal matrices, R_b is $n_b \times n_b$ upper triangular matrix, R_d is $n_d \times n_d$ upper triangular matrix; n_b denotes the number of underlying kinetic parameters.

Writing Y_d as a linear combination of Y_b

$$Y_d = Y_b K_d = Q_b R_d = Q_b R_b K_d \tag{6}$$

Substituting Eq. (6) into Eq. (5)

$$YP = Y_b [1 \ K_d] \begin{bmatrix} P_b \\ P_d \end{bmatrix} = Y_b (P_b + K_d P_d) = \hat{Y}\hat{P} \tag{7}$$

where $\hat{Y} = Y_b$ is the simplified regression matrix, $\hat{P} = (P_b + K_d P_d)$ is the minimum set of inertia parameters after reorganization.

3 Dynamic Parameter Identification

In order to improve the accuracy of identification parameters, this paper adopts a step-by-step identification method. First, the mass and center of mass parameters of the links are identified in the quasi-static environment with low speed, on this basis, the inertia parameters are further identified under dynamic conditions.

3.1 Quasi-static Gravity Parameter Identification

In the low-speed quasi-static environment, assuming $\dot{q} \approx 0$, $\ddot{q} \approx 0$, the Eq. (7) can be written as

$$\hat{Y}_g(q)\hat{P}_g(m, \vec{r}) + \tau_{fs}(f_c) = H_g(q, \dot{q})P_g(m, \vec{r}, f_c) = \tau_g \tag{8}$$

where $\hat{P}_g(m, \vec{r})$ is a vector about the mass of the link and the center of mass. $m = [m_1 \; m_2 \; \cdots \; m_n]^T$ and $\vec{r} = [\vec{r}_1 \; \vec{r}_2 \; \cdots \; \vec{r}_n]^T$ where $\vec{r}_i = [x_i \; y_i \; z_i]^T$ is the center of mass for link i, the friction model degenerates to $\tau_{fsi} = f_{ci}\text{sgn}(\dot{q}_i)$.

On the one hand, the weight of the robot body m_{rob} can be obtained by actual measurement. On the other hand, we can get the information about m_{cad} and $\vec{r}_{cad}$ from the CAD software.

The problem of gravity parameter identification can be transformed into finding nonlinear optimization equations

$$\min_x f_1(x) = \left\| H_g(q, \dot{q})P_g[x(m, \vec{r}, f_c)] - \tau_g \right\|^2$$
$$s.t. \, m_i > 0, \, i = 1, \cdots, n$$
$$(1 - \alpha)m_{i,\text{cad}} \leq m_i \leq (1 + \alpha)m_{i,\text{cad}}, \, i = 1, \cdots, n \qquad (9)$$
$$(1 - \beta)m_{\text{rob}} \leq \sum_{i=1}^{n} m_i \leq (1 + \beta)m_{\text{rob}}$$
$$(1 - \gamma)\vec{r}_{i,\text{cad}} \leq \vec{r}_i \leq (1 + \gamma)\vec{r}_{i,\text{cad}}, \, i = 1, \cdots, n$$

where α, β, γ are the constraint factors of inequality equations and their value ranges are all within [0 1] except their original CAD values are quite small.

Since the cost function $f_1(x)$ contains multiple local minima, we take genetic algorithms (GA) as the global optimization method which uses multi-point parallel computation, and each iteration generates new individuals by swapping and mutation, expanding the exploration range and easily finding the global optimal solution.

4 Dynamic Inertia Parameter Identification

In the dynamic motion environment, the Eq. (7) can be written as

$$\hat{Y}_m(q, \dot{q}, \ddot{q})\hat{P}_m\left(m, \vec{r}, J\right) + \tau_{fd} = H_m(q, \dot{q}, \ddot{q})P_m(m, \vec{r}, J, f_c, f_v) = \tau_m \qquad (10)$$

where $J = [I_1 \; I_2 \; \cdots \; I_n]^T$ and I_i is the inertia tensor which contains the elements of $[I_{ixx}, I_{ixy}, I_{ixz}, I_{iyy}, I_{iyz}, I_{izz}]^T$ and friction model $\tau_{fdi} = f_{ci}\text{sgn}(\dot{q}_i) + f_{vi}\dot{q}_i$.

The link mass, center of mass position and Coulomb friction parameters are obtained through quasi-static identification. On this basis, the inertia parameters of the robot can be identified through calculating the nonlinear optimization equations by using GA algorithm with considering physical consistency [10–12].

$$\min_x f(x) = \left\| H_m(q, \dot{q}, \ddot{q})P_m[x(J, f_v)] - \tau_m \right\|^2$$
$$s.t. \, I_i \succ 0, \, i = 1, \cdots, n$$
$$\frac{\text{tr}(I_i)}{2} - \lambda_{\max}(I_i) > 0, \, i = 1, \cdots, n \qquad (11)$$
$$(1 - \varphi)I_{i,\text{cad}} \leq I_i \leq (1 + \varphi)I_{i,\text{cad}}, \, i = 1, \cdots, n$$

where I_i is the inertia tensor of link i, the $\succ 0$ means the left-hand side is a positive definite matrix, φ is the constraint factor in the range [0 1].

5 Experiments

5.1 Excitation Trajectory Design

In order to improve the convergence speed and noise resistance of the recognition algorithm, a reasonable excitation trajectory needs to be designed. In this paper, we adopt the Fourier series-based excitation trajectory design method proposed by Swevers [13]. The trajectory of the $i-th$ joint can be defined as

$$q_i(t) = \left[\sum_{l=1}^{L} \frac{a_l^i}{\omega_f l} \sin(\omega_f lt) - \frac{b_l^i}{\omega_f l} \cos(\omega_f lt) \right] + q_{i,0} \tag{12}$$

where q_i is the joint angular displacement; ω_f is the basic frequency; a_l^i and b_l^i are the amplitudes of the sine and cosine terms respectively; L is the number of harmonic terms of the Fourier series, and each Fourier series contains $2L + 1$ parameters.

The observation matrix $\delta(q, \dot{q}, \ddot{q})$ is composed of K sampled time-point regression matrices $\widehat{Y}(q, \dot{q}, \ddot{q})$

$$\delta(q, \dot{q}, \ddot{q}) = \begin{bmatrix} \widehat{Y}(q_1, \dot{q}_1, \ddot{q}_1) \\ \widehat{Y}(q_2, \dot{q}_2, \ddot{q}_2) \\ \vdots \\ \widehat{Y}(q_K, \dot{q}_K, \ddot{q}_K) \end{bmatrix} \tag{13}$$

By setting the minimum condition number of the observation matrix as the objective function, the design problem of the optimal excitation trajectory is described as (14) and the trajectory can be get by using optimization algorithm.

$$
\begin{aligned}
&\min \mathrm{cond}(\delta(q, \dot{q}, \ddot{q})) \\
&s.t.\, q_{i,\min} \leq q_i(t) \leq q_{i,max} \\
&|\dot{q}_i(t)| \leq \dot{q}_{i,\max} \\
&|\ddot{q}_i(t)| \leq \ddot{q}_{i,\max} \\
&q_i(t_1) = 0 \\
&\dot{q}_i(t_1) = 0 \\
&\ddot{q}_i(t_1) = 0 \\
&\tau_{\min} \leq \delta(q, \dot{q}, \ddot{q})\widehat{P}\left(m, \vec{r}, J\right) \leq \tau_{\max}
\end{aligned} \tag{14}
$$

where $q_{i,\min}$ and $q_{i,\max}$ are the lower and upper joint limits respectively, $\dot{q}_{i,\max}$ and $\ddot{q}_{i,\max}$ are the maximum values of velocity and acceleration, $\tau_{\min}$ and $\tau_{\max}$ are the upper and lower limits of the torque constraints.

5.2 Identification Experiments

This experiment adopts the offline identification method, using a self-developed six-degree-of-freedom collaborative robot with its link frames shown in Fig. 1. Its modified D-H parameters are shown in Table 1.

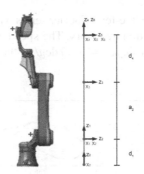

Fig. 1. Self-developed robot

Table 1. Modified D-H parameters

i	a_{i-1}	α_{i-1}	d_i	θ_i
1	0	0	d_1	q_1
2	0	$\pi/2$	0	q_2
3	a_2	0	0	q_3
4	0	$\pi/2$	d_4	q_4
5	0	$-\pi/2$	0	q_5
6	0	$\pi/2$	0	q_6

In the quasi-static parameter identification mode, according to formula (14), a five-term Fourier series with a basic frequency of 0.002 Hz is used as the excitation trajectory, where the velocity and acceleration constraints for each axis are $\dot{q}_{i,\max}=2$ deg/s, $\ddot{q}_{i,\max} = 10$ deg/s^2, the excitation trajectory is shown in Fig. 2.

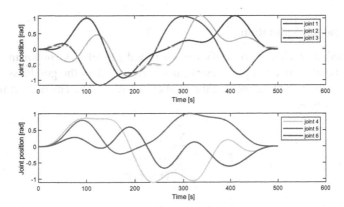

Fig. 2. Quasi-static excitation trajectory

In dynamic motion mode, a five-term Fourier series with a fundamental frequency of 0.05 Hz was used as the excitation trajectory. The speed and acceleration constraints of each axis are $\dot{q}_{i,\max}=100$ deg/s, $\ddot{q}_{i,\max} = 1000$ deg/s^2, the excitation trajectory is shown in Fig. 3.

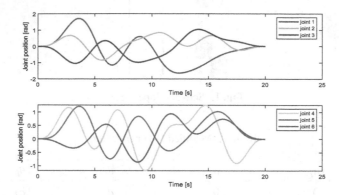

Fig. 3. Dynamic excitation trajectory

5.3   Identification Results

During the experiment, the position, velocity and torque information of each axis of the robot are collected and the acceleration are computed by speed differentiation. In order to prevent noise interference, the Butterworth filter with zero-phase filter technology is used to filter the speed, acceleration and torque data.

According to the quasi-static dynamic parameter identification method proposed in Sect. 3.1, the gravity parameter identification results are shown in Table 2.

On the above basis, according to the dynamic inertia parameter identification method proposed in Sect. 3.2, the inertia parameter identification results are shown in Table 3.

5.4   Experimental Validation

Selecting another trajectory to verify the identified model. As shown in Fig. 4, the accuracy of the identification parameters can be measured by the goodness of fit index (GFI) between the actual torque and the predicted torque. The calculation formula for the goodness of fit is

$$R^2= 1-\frac{\sum_{i=1}^{n} (\tau_i-\hat{\tau}_i)^2}{\sum_{i=1}^{n} (\tau_i-\overline{\tau}_i)^2} \tag{15}$$

where $\hat{\tau}_i$ is the calculated torque from the model, and $\overline{\tau}_i$ is the mean value of τ_i. R^2 is the measure of how well the model predicts the data, with value between 0 and 1. The higher the value of R^2, the more accurately the model predicts the data.

Table 2. Mass and centroid values of the links

parameter	CAD value	Ident value	units
m_1	4.5446544	4.5446544	kg
m_2	7.6946679	7.7234102	kg
m_3	3.4841589	3.3300834	kg
m_4	1.3983491	1.3635973	kg
m_5	1.9881453	1.9641976	kg
m_6	0.7265573	0.7614272	kg
c_{1x}	0.0000015	0.0000015	m
c_{1y}	0.0407862	0.0407862	m
c_{1z}	−0.0245280	−0.0245280	m
c_{2x}	0.2220000	0.1763876	m
c_{2y}	0.0000182	−0.0039570	m
c_{2z}	−0.1153757	−0.1094170	m
c_{3x}	0.0000286	−0.0028960	m
c_{3y}	−0.0648532	0.0595758	m
c_{3z}	0.1202963	0.1091569	m
c_{4x}	0.0000064	0.0079962	m
c_{4y}	0.0349615	0.0045047	m
c_{4z}	−0.0909967	0.0000145	m
c_{5x}	0.0000264	−0.0185760	m
c_{5y}	−0.0399124	−0.0088710	m
c_{5z}	0.0147045	−0.0567860	m
c_{6x}	0.0000000	0.0711218	m
c_{6y}	0.0000059	0.0039401	m
c_{6z}	0.1129660	0.1149079	m

In Fig. 5, the CAD model and the identified model are used for torque prediction respectively. The goodness of fit index (GFI) of the two methods is also shown in Fig. 6. The results can be seen that the GFI of each joint for the identified model is larger than 0.95 which represents a pretty high degree of fit. It shows that the predicted torques with identified model and the actual torques have a higher matching degree than the torques predicted with CAD model.

Table 3. Inertia elements of the links

parameter	CAD value	Ident	units
I_{1xx}	0.0281400	0.0322523	kg·m^2
I_{1xy}	−0.0000003	−0.0000003	kg·m^2
I_{1xz}	0.0000002	0.0000002	kg·m^2
I_{1yy}	0.0165634	0.0194073	kg·m^2
I_{1yz}	−0.0018998	−0.0017877	kg·m^2
I_{1zz}	0.0211343	0.0170308	kg·m^2
I_{2xx}	0.1157787	0.1389344	kg·m^2
I_{2xy}	−0.0000346	−0.0000282	kg·m^2
I_{2xz}	0.1979008	0.1601878	kg·m^2
I_{2yy}	0.8183498	0.6546798	kg·m^2
I_{2yz}	0.0000202	0.0000162	kg·m^2
I_{2zz}	0.7202942	0.5772736	kg·m^2
I_{3xx}	0.0999568	0.0857998	kg·m^2
I_{3xy}	0.0000138	0.0000159	kg·m^2
I_{3xz}	−0.0000197	−0.0000174	kg·m^2
I_{3yy}	0.0582624	0.0699140	kg·m^2
I_{3yz}	0.0375534	0.0304156	kg·m^2
I_{3zz}	0.0475440	0.0380352	kg·m^2
I_{4xx}	0.0241628	0.0289929	kg·m^2
I_{4xy}	−0.0000007	−0.0000007	kg·m^2
I_{4xz}	0.0000005	0.0000004	kg·m^2
I_{4yy}	0.0213209	0.0024769	kg·m^2
I_{4yz}	0.0011960	0.0011551	kg·m^2
I_{4zz}	0.0039753	0.0031803	kg·m^2
I_{5xx}	0.0081298	0.0097558	kg·m^2
I_{5xy}	0.0000010	0.0000009	kg·m^2
I_{5xz}	0.0000001	0.0000001	kg·m^2
I_{5yy}	0.0022990	0.0024769	kg·m^2
I_{5yz}	0.0001365	0.0001638	kg·m^2
I_{5zz}	0.0073778	0.0088532	kg·m^2
I_{6xx}	0.0095914	0.0115088	kg·m^2
I_{6xy}	−0.0000001	−0.0000001	kg·m^2

(*continued*)

Table 3. (*continued*)

parameter	CAD value	Ident	units
I_{6xz}	0.0000000	0.0000000	kg·m^2
I_{6yy}	0.0095916	0.0115097	kg·m^2
I_{6yz}	−0.0000004	−0.0000004	kg·m^2
I_{6zz}	0.0005189	0.0005154	kg·m^2

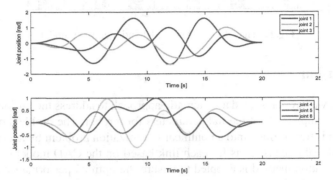

Fig. 4. The trajectory of validation

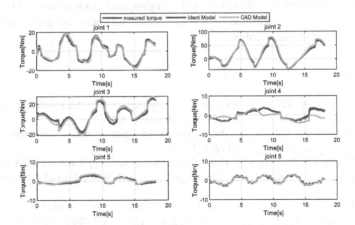

Fig. 5. Predicted torques of each joint by CAD model and identified model

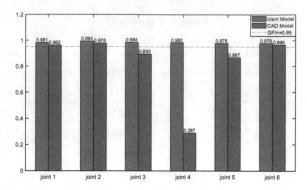

Fig. 6. The GFI of CAD model and identified model

6   Conclusion

In this paper, we have presented a systematic approach to address the physical reality of estimating a complete set of inertial parameters for a robot. The problem of parameter identification is transformed into a nonlinear optimization problem by adding a reasonable physical reality constraints for each link based on the CAD model parameters. A global optimization method is adopted to ensure the optimal performance of the identification results. In the low-speed quasi-static mode, the robot gravity parameters are identified, which could be used in some low-speed control modes. Based on this, the robot inertia parameters are identified in the high-speed motion mode. The accuracy and effectiveness of the identified model have been validated by experiments on the self-developed collaborative robot.

References

1. Jun W., Jinsong W., Zheng Y.: An overview of dynamic parameter identification of robots. Robot. Comput.-Integr. Manufactur. **26**(5), 414–419 (2010)
2. Huang W., Min H., Guo Y., Liu M.: A review of dynamic parameters identification for manipulator control. Cobot **1**(5), 5 (2022)
3. Zhang, T., Liang, X.H., Qin, B.B.: Dynamic parameter identification of SCARA robots based on Newton-euler method. J. South China Univ. Technol. (Nat. Sci. Ed.) **45**(10), 129–136+143 (2017)
4. Xi, W.Q., Chen, B., Ding, L.: Dynamic parameter identification for robot manipulators with nonlinear friction model. Transactions Chin. Soci. Agri. Mach. **48**(2), 393–399 (2017)
5. Gaz, C., Flacco, F., De Luca, A.: Extracting feasible robot parameters from dynamic coefficients using nonlinear optimization methods. In: 2016 IEEE International Conference on Robotics and Automation (ICRA), pp. 2075–2081. IEEE (2016)
6. Gaz, C., Cognetti, M., Oliva, A., Robuffo, G.P., De Luca, A.: Dynamic identification of the Franka Emika panda robot with retrieval of feasible parameters using penalty-based optimization. IEEE Robot. Autom. Lett. **4**(4), 4147–4154. IEEE (2019)
7. Sousa, C.D., Cortesao, R.: Physical feasibility of robot base inertial parameter identification: a linear matrix inequality approach. Int. J. Robot. Res. **33**(6), 931–944 (2014)
8. Liu, L.L., Liu, H.Z., Wu, Z.Y., Wang, Z.M.: An overview of friction models in mechanical systems. Adv. Mech. **154**(02), 201–213 (2008)

9. Zhang, T., Qin, B.B., Zou, Y.B.: Identification methods for robot payload dynamical parameters. Chin. J. Eng. **39**(12), 1907–1912 (2017)
10. Sousa, C.D., Cortesão, R.: Inertia tensor properties in robot dynamics identification: a linear matrix inequality approach. IEEE/ASME Trans. Mechatron. **24**(1), 406–411. IEEE (2019)
11. Mata, V., Benimeli, F., Farhat, N., Valera, A.: Dynamic parameter identification in industrial robots considering physical feasibility. Adv. Robot. **19**(1), 101–119 (2005)
12. Traversaro, S., Brossette, S., Escande, A., Nori, F.: Identification of fully physical consistent inertial parameters using optimization on manifolds. In: 2016 IEEE/RSJ International Conference on Intelligent Robots and Systems (IROS), pp. 5446–5451. IEEE (2016)
13. Swevers, J., Ganseman, C., Tukel, D.B., de Schutter, J., Van Brussel, H.: Optimal robot excitation and identification. IEEE Trans. Robot. Autom. **13**(5), 730–740. IEEE (1997)

Constant Force Tracking Using Dynamical System with External Force Estimation

Junyu Lai, Yuhang Chen, Jiexin Zhang, Pingyun Nie, and Bo Zhang$^{(\boxtimes)}$

State Key Laboratory of Mechanical System and Vibration, School of Mechanical Engineering, Shanghai Jiao Tong University, Shanghai 200240, China
b_zhang@sjtu.edu.cn

Abstract. Constant force tracking control strategies are becoming increasingly popular due to their wide range of applications in interactive tasks. These tasks require robots to be able to respond effectively to environmental disturbances. Disturbances in contact tasks are typically divided into two types: large disturbances caused by human-robot interaction, and small disturbances caused by deviations in contact surface position or environmental stiffness. This article proposes an impedance control method using the dynamical system for constant force tracking. Unlike existing solutions, the contact force is estimated through a generalized momentum observer. Therefore, the proposed method can effectively deal with large and small disturbances without requiring additional force/torque sensors on the end-effector. This method enhances the accuracy of constant force tracking under small disturbances and demonstrates excellent robustness and replanning capabilities for trajectories when facing large disturbances. The proposed method's advantages are demonstrated through constant force tracking verification experiments conducted on a six-degree-of-freedom collaborative robot.

Keywords: Force Tracking Control · Dynamical System · Contact Force Estimation · Disturbance Rejection

1 Introduction

In recent years, compliant control technology has enabled robots to complete increasingly complex manipulation tasks [1–5]. Constant force tracking, which involves maintaining a specific contact force during contact, is widely studied due to its application value in robot-environments or human-robot interaction scenarios. Examples of such scenarios include polishing [1], grinding [2], and robotic massage [3], where the robots are required to move along a specific trajectory while maintaining a certain force during contact. The representative approach for achieving force tracking of robots is impedance control [6–9]. It adjusts the dynamic relationship between interaction force and motion position deviation by setting up a virtual mass-spring-damper system. However, its performance is limited when facing unknown disturbances, which results in a loss of stability and accuracy in contact control.

As shown in Fig. 1, disturbances in the contact task are typically divided into two types: large disturbances and small disturbances [10]. Small disturbances are caused by

H. Yang et al. (Eds.): ICIRA 2023, LNAI 14271, pp. 220–231, 2023.
https://doi.org/10.1007/978-981-99-6495-6_19

deviations in surface position or environmental stiffness, which can affect the precision of contact force control. Large disturbances are introduced by human interaction. The robots are required to have the ability to fast react and re-plan in order to resume the original task when faced with such large disturbances.

Many studies have been conducted on impedance control methods to improve the real-time anti-small disturbance ability of robots. Seul Jung et al. [11] proposed an adaptive impedance control method which can effectively compensate for environmental position and dynamic uncertainty. A new class of admittance-coupled dynamic movement primitives that addresses environmental changes was presented in [12]. Recently, a high force tracking accuracy was demonstrated in the constant force tracking control scheme based on an impedance controller using online stiffness and reverse damping force, as proposed in [13]. Although the aforementioned works have contributed to the improvement of force tracking performance, they only consider the effect of small disturbances and do not involve the large disturbances in the task.

Dynamical system (DS) has been widely used to achieve invariant control, in order to enable robots to have fast reactivity and the ability to re-plan the trajectories of the task when facing large disturbances [10, 14]. W. Amanhoud et al. [10] proposed a passive interaction control method that enables the robot to re-plan after experiencing large disturbances. The energy tank theory was developed to address the issue of passivity loss. However, the theory does not account for small disturbances in force tracking, as contact force is controlled in an open loop manner. In addition, a learning method based on Radial Basis Functions (RBF) is used to modulate the DS and compensate for the lumped disturbance [14]. However, this method requires the robot to be equipped with the force/torque (F/T) sensors mounted on the end-effector.

This paper proposes an impedance control method using the DS for constant force tracking. In particular, the contact force is estimated through a generalized momentum observer (GMO). Therefore, this method can achieve modulation of the DS and compensation of system disturbances without the need for additional F/T sensors on the end-effector. This method enhances the accuracy of constant force tracking under small disturbances and demonstrates excellent robustness and replanning capabilities for trajectories when facing large disturbances.

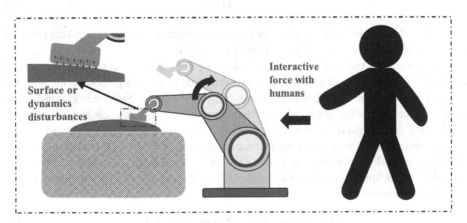

Fig. 1. Disturbances in contact tasks

2 Proposed Method

The diagram of the proposed method is shown in Fig. 2. In this section, we first present the DS impedance controller. Then, the development of DS modulation based on GMO is derived in detail.

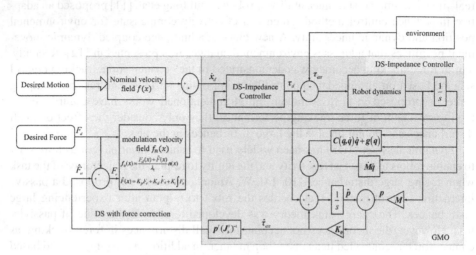

Fig. 2. Diagram of the proposed method

2.1 Dynamical System Impedance Control

The DS that describes the contact force tracking task can be defined as a velocity vector field, which represents the expected velocity of the robot at any given position in space during the manipulation task. The nominal DS enables the end-effector to follow the desired trajectory, which can be defined as:

$$\dot{x}_d = f(x) \tag{1}$$

where $x \in \mathbb{R}^3$ represents Cartesian space position coordinate, $f(x)$ represents the nominal DS that generates the vector field of desired velocity $\dot{x}_d$.

To ensure that the nominal velocity field does not affect the control of the normal contact force, it is necessary to maintain an orthogonal relationship between the nominal velocity field and the surface normal vector, (i.e. $f(x)^T n(x) = 0$ where $n(x)$ denotes the normal vector of the surface to be contacted at position x) when in contact.

During the process of surface force tracking, trajectory tracking is mainly carried out in the translational space. Assuming that the orientation of the end-effector changes only slightly during the force tracking process, it can be considered quasi-static. Therefore, the robot's task space dynamics can be simplified by only considering the influence of translational coordinates.

$$\Lambda(x)\ddot{x} + \mu(x, \dot{x})\dot{x} + F_g(x) = F_\tau + F_{ext} \tag{2}$$

where $\Lambda(x) \in \mathbb{R}^{3\times3}$, $\mu(x, \dot{x}) \in \mathbb{R}^{3\times3}$, $F_g(x) \in \mathbb{R}^3$, $F_\tau \in \mathbb{R}^3$, $F_{ext} \in \mathbb{R}^3$ represents the inertia matrix, Coriolis/centripetal matrix, gravity term, input forces of actuator and external forces, respectively.

By utilizing the desired translational velocity $\dot{x}_d$ as the input to the impedance controller, the control law F_τ for the DS impedance control can be expressed as:

$$F_\tau = F_g(x) + D(x)(\dot{x}_d - \dot{x}) \tag{3}$$

where $D(x)$ is the positive definite damping matrix.

Considering a set of orthonormal basis vectors $\xi_1, \xi_2, \xi_3 \in \mathbb{R}^3$ where the first basis vector $\xi_1 = \frac{\dot{x}_d}{\|\dot{x}_d\|}$, the damping coefficient of each basis vector can be set by configuring the damping eigenvalue matrix $D_\lambda = \mathrm{diag}([\,\lambda_1\ \lambda_2\ \lambda_3\,])$. The damping matrix is designed through a similarity transformation on D_λ:

$$D(x) = Q(x)D_\lambda Q(x)^T \tag{4}$$

where $Q(x) = [\,\xi_1\ \xi_2\ \xi_3\,]$.

Substituting Eq. (4) into Eq. (3) yields the following equation:

$$F_\tau = F_g(x) + \lambda_1\dot{x}_d - D(x)\dot{x} \tag{5}$$

In this paper, DS-impedance control only considers the design of translation control. As for the end-effector's orientation, the primary objective is to ensure that end-effector is aligned with the surface normal vector $n(x)$. The orientation error is represented by $\tilde{R} = RR_d^{-1}$ where R and R_d denote the rotation matrix of the real and the desired orientation respectively. Since the pose variation is assumed to be a quasi-static process, a Proportional-Derivative (PD) controller is applied to the orientation of the end-effector:

$$F_{\tau_r} = F_{g_r} - K_{d_r}\tilde{\omega} - D_{d_r}\dot{x}_r \tag{6}$$

where, $F_{\tau_r} \in \mathbb{R}^3$ represents the input forces, F_{g_r} denotes the gravity compensation term, $\tilde{\omega}$ is the axis-angle representation of the rotation error matrix $\tilde{R}$, $\dot{x}_r \in \mathbb{R}^3$ denotes the rotational velocity of the end effector, $K_{d_r} \in \mathbb{R}^{3\times3}$ and $D_{d_r} \in \mathbb{R}^{3\times3}$ respectively denote the stiffness matrix and damping matrix. The subscript r represents the rotational part.

By transforming the wrench from task space to joint space through the Jacobian matrix $J \in \mathbb{R}^{6\times N}$, the expected joint torque τ_d can be expressed as:

$$\tau_d = J^T \begin{bmatrix} F_\tau \\ F_{\tau_r} \end{bmatrix} = g(q) + J^T \begin{bmatrix} \lambda_1\dot{x}_d - D(x)\dot{x} \\ -K_{d_r}\tilde{\omega} - D_{d_r}\dot{x}_r \end{bmatrix} \tag{7}$$

where $g(q)$ denotes the gravity compensation term.

To control the contact force, it is necessary to introduce a modulation velocity field, denoted as $f_n(x)$, in addition to the nominal velocity field $f(x)$. Typically, by directly inputting the modulation velocity field in an open-loop manner, the desired contact force can be achieved without considering the position error between the end-effector and the surface. The open-loop DS is designed as:

$$\begin{aligned} \dot{x}_d &= f_t(x) = f(x) + f_n(x) \\ f_n(x) &= F_d(x)n(x)/\lambda_1 \end{aligned} \tag{8}$$

where $f_t(x)$ represents the total DS, including the nominal velocity field and the modulation velocity field $f_n(x)$, and F_d represents the desired contact force.

The modulation term actually applies an open-loop desired contact force to the end effector, which may not lead to a good force tracking accuracy as there is no feedback from contact force.

2.2 Dynamical System Modulation With Force Estimation Feedback

Force Estimation Based on Generalized Momentum Observer

The generalized momentum observer was first proposed in [15], and has been widely used in robotics [16]. In this work, we use GMO to estimate the external contact force.

According to the dynamics of the robot, the expression of the external torque τ_{ext} can be obtained as:

$$\tau_{ext} = M(q)\ddot{q} + C(q, \dot{q})\dot{q} + g(q) - \tau \tag{9}$$

where τ denotes the input torque of joints, q denotes the joint angle, $M(q)\ddot{q}, C(q, \dot{q})\dot{q}, g(q)$ denotes the mass term, the Coriolis/centripetal term and the gravity term, respectively. The generalized momentum is defined as follows:

$$p = M(q)\dot{q} \tag{10}$$

Using Eq. (9), the time-derivate of generalized momentum can be computed as:

$$\dot{p} = \tau + \dot{M}(q)\dot{q} - C(q, \dot{q})\dot{q} - g(q) + \tau_{ext} \tag{11}$$

The observer for generalized momentum p and external torque τ_{ext} can be constructed as:

$$\hat{p} = \int \left(\tau + \dot{M}(q)\dot{q} - C(q, \dot{q})\dot{q} - g(q) + \hat{\tau}_{ext}\right)dt$$
$$\hat{\tau}_{ext} = K_0(p - \hat{p}) \tag{12}$$

where $\hat{p}$ and $\hat{\tau}_{ext}$ respectively represent the estimated values of generalized momentum and external torque, and diagonal matrix $K_0 \in \mathbb{R}^{N \times N}$ the gain of observer.

Substituting Eq. (11) into Eq. (12), and Differentiating $\hat{\tau}_{ext}$ yields:

$$\dot{\hat{\tau}}_{ext} = K_0(\tau_{ext} - \hat{\tau}_{ext}) \tag{13}$$

Based on the estimated external torque, an estimation for the normal contact force can be obtained as follows:

$$\hat{F}_{ct} = p^T (J_b^T)^{-1} \hat{\tau}_{ext} \tag{14}$$

where $p = \begin{bmatrix} 0 & 0 & -1 & 0 & 0 & 0 \end{bmatrix}^T$, $J_b \in \mathbb{R}^{6 \times N}$ denotes the Jacobian matrix under the end-effector coordinate system.

Equation (13) indicates that the estimated contact force resulting from generalized momentum observer is, in essence, the outcome of a first-order low-pass filter of the actual contact force.

Improved Dynamical System with Force Correction

Based on the feedback from the estimated contact force $\hat{F}_{ct}$, a closed-loop correction for the DS can be constructed using a Proportional-Integral-Derivative (PID) control strategy.

$$f_n(x) = (F_d(x) + \tilde{F}(x))n(x)/\lambda_1$$
$$F_e(x) = F_d(x) - \hat{F}_{ct}(x) \tag{15}$$
$$\tilde{F}(x) = K_p F_e(x) + K_d \dot{F}_e(x) + K_i \int F_e(x)$$

where $\tilde{F}(x) \in \left[-\tilde{F}_{max}(x), \tilde{F}_{max}(x)\right]$ represents the feedback correction term whose boundary is denoted as $\tilde{F}_{max}(x)$, the coefficients for the proportional, differential, and integral terms are represented by K_p, K_d and K_i, respectively.

The estimated contact force is the first-order low-pass filtered version of the actual normal contact force:

$$\hat{F}_{ct}(s) = \frac{K_0}{s + K_0} F_{ct}(s) \tag{16}$$

Projecting Eq. (2) along the normal direction, one obtains:

$$F_{ct} = -n(x)^T \left(\Lambda(x)\ddot{x} + (D(x) + \mu(x, \dot{x}))\dot{x}\right) + \lambda_1 f(x)^T n(x) + \lambda_1 f_n(x)^T n(x) \tag{17}$$

Define the lumped disturbances as d_{ct}, which is caused by robot dynamics, direction error of the nominal DS and $n(x)$, and other factors such as dynamic parameter accuracy.

$$d_{ct} = -n(x)^T \left(\Lambda(x)\ddot{x} + (D(x) + \mu(x, \dot{x}))\dot{x}\right) + \lambda_1 f(x)^T n(x) \tag{18}$$

Substituting Eq. (15) and Eq. (16) into Eq. (17), and applying Laplace transform leads to:

$$F_{ct}(s) = G_{Fd}(s)F_d(s) + G_{ct}(s)d_{ct}(s) \tag{19}$$

where

$$G_{Fd}(s) = \frac{(s + K_0)(K_d s^2 + (K_p + 1)s + K_i)}{(K_0 K_d + 1)s^2 + (K_0 K_p + K_0)s + K_0 K_i}$$

$$G_{ct}(s) = \frac{s^2 + K_0 s}{(K_0 K_d + 1)s^2 + (K_0 K_p + K_0)s + K_0 K_i}$$

The effect of the disturbances on the actual contact force can be analyzed in terms of the response of F_{ct} to the dumped disturbance d_{ct}, as shown in Fig. 3. The controller parameters are selected as $K_p = 5.0$, $K_i = 1.0$, $K_d = 3$, and $K_0 = 50$.

According to the amplitude response curve of the lumped disturbance shown in the left plot of Fig. 3, the PID controller can effectively suppress the disturbances of the normal contact force. Therefore, it can be concluded that the contact force estimation based on the generalized momentum observer and the improved modulation velocity field can solve the problem of small disturbances caused by position error and dynamic parameter inaccuracy.

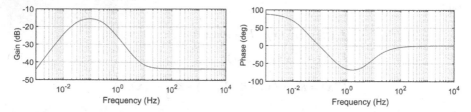

Fig. 3. The response of contact force to the dumped disturbance

Moreover, passivity is a sufficient condition for ensuring the stability of the robot while performing contact tasks in a passive environment. To maintain passivity, the tank-based approach is introduced to modify the original control system. The passivity of the whole system can be guaranteed using energy tanks, as described in [10].

3   Experiments

3.1   Experiments Setup

To verify the effectiveness of the proposed method, experiments are conducted on a 6-DOF collaborative robot. The experiment platform is shown in Fig. 4.

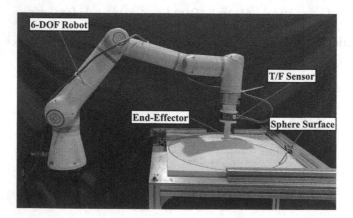

Fig. 4. Experiment platform

The robot configures with encoders to collect joint position signals. The joint velocities are obtained through numerical differentiation and filtering. The torque sensors are installed on each joint of the robot to acquire joint torque. For comparison, a F/T sensor is mounted on the end effector to measure the actual contact force. Moreover, a spherical surface is used as the target contact surface. Communication between the robot and the upper computer is achieved using the TwinCAT 3 interface with a communication frequency of 1 kHz.

In the experiment, the desired trajectory is selected as a circle on the sphere with a radius of 0.1 m. Assuming that $p_c = \begin{bmatrix} x_c & y_c & z_c \end{bmatrix}^T$ is the center of the desired circular trajectory, to obtain the desired circular trajectory generated by nominal DS, we firstly define a velocity field of circular motion f_{cir}:

$$f_{\mathrm{cir}}(x) = \begin{pmatrix} v_t(r - R)x - v_w y \\ v_t(r - R)y + v_w x \\ v_z(z_c - z) \end{pmatrix}$$

$$R = \sqrt{(x - x_c)^2 + (y - y_c)^2} \tag{20}$$

where, $x = \begin{bmatrix} x & y & z \end{bmatrix}^T$ denotes the position of end-effector, r denotes the radius of the circular trajectory, v_t, v_w, and v_z represent the weights of normal velocity, tangential velocity, and velocity along the Z-axis direction, respectively.

The nominal DS is constructed as:

$$\hat{f}_{\mathrm{cir}} = f_{\mathrm{cir}} - \left(n^T(x) f_{\mathrm{cir}} \right) n(x)$$

$$f(x) = v_0 \hat{f}_{\mathrm{cir}} / \left\| \hat{f}_{\mathrm{cir}} \right\| \tag{21}$$

where v_0 represents the preset end-effector target velocity.

Under the influence of the nominal DS, the end effector will ultimately converge to the circular trajectory and move along it. The parameters of controller are shown in Table 1.

Table 1. The parameters utilized in the experiments

parameter	value	parameter	value
D_λ	$\mathrm{diag}\begin{pmatrix} 250 & 250 & 250 \end{pmatrix}$	K_p	3
K_{d_r}	$\mathrm{diag}\begin{pmatrix} 100 & 100 & 100 \end{pmatrix}$	K_i	0.001
D_{d_r}	$\mathrm{diag}\begin{pmatrix} 1 & 1 & 1 \end{pmatrix}$	K_d	0.01
F_d	15 N	$\tilde{F}_{\max}$	10 N
K_0	$\mathrm{diag}\begin{pmatrix} 10 & 10 & 10 & 10 & 10 & 10 \end{pmatrix}$	v_0	0.05 m/s

3.2 Force Tracking Experiments

To validate the effect of the modulated DS corrected by contact force feedback on small disturbance rejection, experiments are conducted to track a surface with constant force. Two groups with different normal modulation velocity fields are used for the experiments. One group employs the original open-loop modulation DS, as given in Eq. (8), without force feedback. The other group uses the modulation DS based on contact force estimation feedback, as given in Eq. (15).

Figure 5 shows a comparison of the measured and GMO estimated contact force in the open-loop DS experiment. The trend of the GMO estimated values is basically identical to that of the F/T sensor values. However, due to factors such as the identification accuracy of the dynamic parameters, there is a certain deviation between the observation value and the measurement value of the contact force.

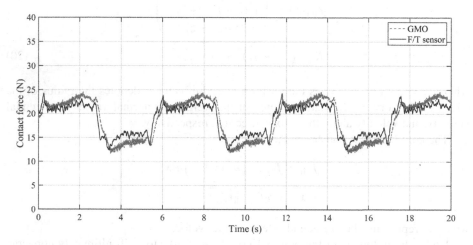

Fig. 5. Experiment results for contact force estimation

Figure 6 shows the results of two experimental groups. As we can see, the steady-state error of the group using the DS based on estimated force feedback is significantly reduced. The root mean squared error (RMSE) of the open-loop DS is 4.85, while the RMSE of the closed-loop DS is 1.41. This shows that the total DS improved by the estimated value of contact force can effectively suppress the small disturbances caused by model disturbances and position error in the surface constant force tracking.

3.3 Replanning Experiments in Face of Large Disturbances

To verify the re-planning ability of proposed DS-based impedance control in the face of the large disturbances, contact force tracking using closed-loop DS experiments are conducted. Artificial disturbances are introduced at the robot end-effector. Specifically, a human introduces an external force disturbance in the Z-axis direction from 3 to 8 s, in the X-axis direction from 13 to 17 s, and in the Y-axis direction from 23 to 27 s. Figure 7 details the experimental process during the replanning process of the robot.

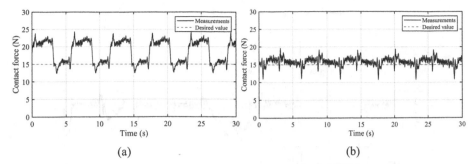

Fig. 6. Experiment results for force tracking using (a) open-loop DS, (b) closed-loop DS

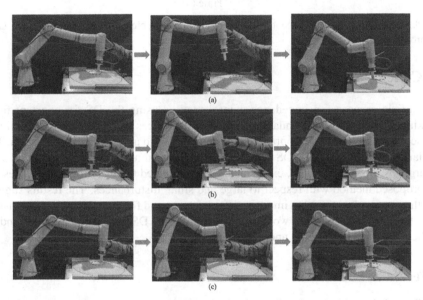

Fig. 7. Experiments for task replanning process after large disturbances (a) z-axis large disturbance (b) y-axis large disturbance (c) x-axis large disturbance; the red dashed circle denotes the desired trajectory

Moreover, the variation of contact force during force tracking is depicted in Fig. 8. When subjected to the z-axis disturbance, the end-effector detaches from the surface, resulting in a contact force of zero. Once the disturbance subsides, the robot enters a replanning state and returns to the surface constant force tracking task again using the DS. Similarly, when disturbances are applied in the X-axis and Y-axis directions, the robot's end-effector deviates from the desired trajectory. After the disturbances disappear, the robot's end-effector gradually approaches the desired trajectory again under the influence of DS. The replanning process is smooth without any unstable phenomena, indicating the replanning ability in face of large disturbances and the robustness of the control method.

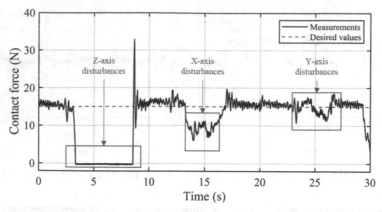

Fig. 8. Experiment results of contact force tracking using closed-loop DS in face of large disturbances

4   Conclusion

This article proposes an impedance control method using the DS for constant force tracking. To improve the attenuation of small disturbances without requiring additional F/T sensor, we estimate the contact force using GMO and use it for DS modulation. The re-planning capability of the DS enables the robot to resume the original task in the face of large disturbances. Finally, experiments are conducted to verify the effectiveness of the proposed method with respect to large and small disturbances. The results suggest that the proposed method can improve the robustness and force accuracy in the constant force tracking task. In future work, we will explore the DS generation methods and its applications such as grinding and polishing.

References

1. Xie, Q., Zhao, H., Wang, T., Ding, H.: Adaptive impedance control for robotic polishing with an intelligent digital compliant grinder. In: Yu, H., Liu, J., Liu, L., Ju, Z., Liu, Y., Zhou, D. (eds.) ICIRA 2019. LNCS, vol. 11745, pp. 482–494. Springer, Cham (2019). https://doi.org/10.1007/978-3-030-27529-7_41
2. Wang, T., Zhao, H., Xie, Q., Li, X., Ding, H.: A path planning method under constant contact force for robotic belt grinding. In: Yu, H., Liu, J., Liu, L., Ju, Z., Liu, Y., Zhou, D. (eds.) ICIRA 2019. LNCS, vol. 11745, pp. 35–49. Springer, Cham (2019). https://doi.org/10.1007/978-3-030-27529-7_4
3. Dong, H., Feng, Y., Qiu, C., Chen, I.-M.: Construction of interaction parallel manipulator: towards rehabilitation massage. IEEEASME Trans. Mechatron. **28**(1), 372–384 (2023). https://doi.org/10.1109/TMECH.2022.3202694
4. Zhang, J., Nie, P., Zhang, B.: An improved IDA-PBC method with link-side damping injection and online gravity compensation for series elastic actuator. Proc. Inst. Mech. Eng. Part C J. Mech. Eng. Sci. **236**(2), 1244–1254 (2022). https://doi.org/10.1177/09544062211008486
5. Zhang, J., Zhang, B.: An iterative identification method for the dynamics and hysteresis of robots with elastic joints. Nonlinear Dyn. (2023). https://doi.org/10.1007/s11071-023-085 97-2

6. Seraji, H., Colbaugh, R.: Force tracking in impedance control. Int. J. Robot. Res. **16**(1), 97–117 (1997). https://doi.org/10.1177/027836499701600107

7. Duan, J., Gan, Y., Chen, M., Dai, X.: Adaptive variable impedance control for dynamic contact force tracking in uncertain environment. Robot. Auton. Syst. **102**, 54–65 (2018). https://doi.org/10.1016/j.robot.2018.01.009

8. Roveda, L., Iannacci, N., Vicentini, F., Pedrocchi, N., Braghin, F., Tosatti, L.M.: Optimal impedance force-tracking control design with impact formulation for interaction tasks. IEEE Robot. Autom. Lett. **1**(1), 130–136 (2016). https://doi.org/10.1109/LRA.2015.2508061

9. Lin, Y., Chen, Z., Yao, B.: Unified motion/force/impedance control for manipulators in unknown contact environments based on robust model-reaching approach. IEEEASME Trans. Mechatron. **26**(4), 1905–1913 (2021). https://doi.org/10.1109/TMECH.2021.3081594

10. Amanhoud, W., Khoramshahi, M., Billard, A.: A dynamical system approach to motion and force generation in contact tasks. In: Robotics: Science and Systems XV, Robotics: Science and Systems Foundation, June 2019. https://doi.org/10.15607/RSS.2019.XV.021

11. Jung, S., Hsia, T.C., Bonitz, R.G.: Force tracking impedance control of robot manipulators under unknown environment. IEEE Trans. Control Syst. Technol. **12**(3), 474–483 (2004). https://doi.org/10.1109/TCST.2004.824320

12. Kramberger, A., Shahriari, E., Gams, A., Nemec, B., Ude, A., Haddadin, S.: Passivity based iterative learning of admittance-coupled dynamic movement primitives for interaction with changing environments. In: 2018 IEEE/RSJ International Conference on Intelligent Robots and Systems (IROS), pp. 6023–6028, October 2018. https://doi.org/10.1109/IROS.2018.859 3647

13. Wahballa, H., Duan, J., Dai, Z.: Constant force tracking using online stiffness and reverse damping force of variable impedance controller for robotic polishing. Int. J. Adv. Manuf. Technol. **121**(9), 5855–5872 (2022). https://doi.org/10.1007/s00170-022-09599-x

14. Amanhoud, W., Khoramshahi, M., Bonnesoeur, M., Billard, A.: Force adaptation in contact tasks with dynamical systems. In: 2020 IEEE International Conference on Robotics and Automation (ICRA), Paris, France, pp. 6841–6847. IEEE, May 2020. https://doi.org/10.1109/ICRA40945.2020.9197509

15. De Luca, A., Mattone, R.: Actuator failure detection and isolation using generalized momenta. In: 2003 IEEE International Conference on Robotics and Automation (Cat. No.03CH37422), vol. 1, pp. 634–639, September 2003 https://doi.org/10.1109/ROBOT.2003.1241665

16. Zhang, J., Nie, P., Chen, Y., Zhang, B.: A joint acceleration estimation method based on a high-order disturbance observer. IEEE Robot. Autom. Lett. **7**(4), 12615–12622 (2022). https://doi.org/10.1109/LRA.2022.3220501

Demonstration Shaped Reward Machine for Robot Assembly Reinforcement Learning Tasks

Ruihong Xiao[1] , Hong Zhan[1] , Yiming Jiang[2] , and Chenguang Yang[1(✉)]

[1] School of Automation Science and Engineering, South China University of
Technology, Guangzhou, China
cyang@ieee.org
[2] School of Robotics, Hunan University, Changsha, China

Abstract. Reinforcement Learning has been proven to be successfully applied in robotic manipulation tasks, but it has been confronted with problems about interacting with the dynamic environment and generating high-level policies. Existing reward functions include sparse and shaped reward, and other way to view the reward functions as black boxes and then discover the best strategies by interacting with the environment. In this paper, a reward machine with demonstration definition for robot assembly is presented, which is a finite state machine that supports generating the specified reward function from the demonstration data and displays the reward function structure. By dividing the task demonstration data, extracting the key points of the task and defining the state of the robot, a reward function based on state migration is generated. The robot chooses the best reward according to the current state, which is conducive to using the reward structure to improve the sample efficiency and the quality of the result strategy. In this paper, we focus on the robot assembly reinforcement learning task. The structure of the proposed method is used to carry out experiments in the robot simulator. We compare the design methods with different reward functions and it proves that the proposed method can effectively improve the training efficiency of robot reinforcement learning.

Keywords: Reward Machine · Reinforcement Learning · Demonstration · Robot Assembly

1 Introduction

Reinforcement Learning (RL), a subfield of machine learning used for strategy formulation and motion control, has been applied to the learning of robot manipulation skills. For different tasks, we need to design a specific reward function,

This work was supported in part by National Nature Science Foundation of China (NSFC) under Grant U20A20200 and 62003136 and Major Research Grant No. 92148204, in part by Guangdong Basic and Applied Basic Research Foundation under Grants 2019B1515120076 and 2020B1515120054, in part by Industrial Key Technologies R&D Program of Foshan under Grant 2020001006308 and Grant 2020001006496, and in part by the Open Research Fund from Guangdong Laboratory of Artificial Intelligence and Digital Economy (SZ) under Grant No. GML-KF-22-14.

H. Yang et al. (Eds.): ICIRA 2023, LNAI 14271, pp. 232–244, 2023.
https://doi.org/10.1007/978-981-99-6495-6_20

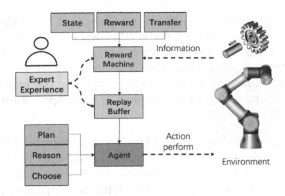

Fig. 1. The robot assembly skill learning system framework.

so that the robot can automatically learn the best strategy to maximize rewards on its own. A standard assumption in reinforcement learning is that the agent does not know the accurate environmental models [1], which means RL mainly studies the realization of a certain goal by an agent in complex and unknown environments. Artificial agents cannot inherently perceive reward from the environment, so that we ought to program the reward functions. By concretizing and digitizing the task, the reward is like a special language that enables communication between the targets and the algorithms. The quality of the reward function reflects its deep understanding of task logic and determines whether the intelligent agent can ultimately learn the expected skills. An agent that had access to the specification of the reward function might be able to use efficient information to learn optimal policies faster. We consider to do so in this work (Fig. 1).

In order to obtain the optimal strategy, robots need to extract information from tasks and experiences more efficiently for learning. Learning from Demonstration (LfD) has been proven to be a useful way for robot skill learning, which allows robots to quickly obtain reliable skill models from expert experience of human teaching, such as Behavior Clone (BC) [2] and Generative Adversarial Imitation Learning (GAIL) [3]. In contrast, RL can also learn various special skills on its own through exploration and interaction. Adding teaching experience to robot reinforcement learning can help robots learn the required skills faster, such as DQfD [4] and DDPGfD [5]. However, it is still difficult for robots to obtain effective empirical data in the high-level tasks with a simple and sparse reward functions. Recently, some researchers use demonstration data to define the reward function and achieve good results, such as Inverse Reinforcement Learning (IRL) [6] and Reward Machine (RM) [7]. Among these, reward machines decompose the task at an abstract level, inform the agent about their current stage along task completion, and guide them via dense rewards, which is well suited for high-level reinforcement learning tasks. In this work, we successfully adapt it to the high level assembly task and generate good performance.

By comparing with different methods, we show that RM help DDPG learn the optimal policy in each abstract state. The agent can learn from low-level tasks to high-level tasks through RM. Their policies are more robust, manifest higher success rate, and are learned with fewer training steps. The benefits of RM are more evident in long-horizon tasks. We carry out our experiments in the MuJoCo simulator. The primary contributions of this paper can be summarized as follows:

1) A demonstration defined reward machine for assembly reinforcement learning method is proposed. The reward machine can display the structure of rewards or automatically generate dense rewards. Experiments have shown that reward machines can generate policy with better performance.
2) A reinforcement learning with demonstration experience method is adopted, which significantly promoting the training effect of reinforcement learning. We put the teaching experience into the experience playback pool and samples it based on the sampling probability during training.
3) Two robot assembly reinforcement learning environments are developed on the MuJoCo simulation platform. We selected two representative assembly tasks: peg-in-hole assembly and gear assembly, and used UR3 robot with two-finger gripper to perform the assembly task.

The rest of the paper is organized as follows. In the next section, we will introduce recent research on the related work. Section 3 presents the proposed method and introduces each part of it in detail. Section 4 shows the details of the experimental results. Finally, we draw up our conclusions in Sect. 5. Our studies show great performance of the proposed methods on data efficiency and optimization strategy.

2   Related Work

Assembly is the subsequent process of product production and plays a very important role in the manufacturing industry. There are still some unresolved issues in robot assembly technology, such as high requirements for assembly equipment and environment, low assembly efficiency, and lack of perception and adaptive capabilities. Recently, new technologies in the areas of robotic and machine learning have the potential to accelerate the application of robot assembly. [8] proposed a robust multi-modal policy for industrial assembly via reinforcement learning and demonstrations on the recently established NIST assembly benchmark. The recently established NIST assembly benchmark [9] design several assembly task boards which enable objective comparisons with different methods in the measured results. These all indicate that the application of reinforcement learning in the field of robot assembly industry has great potential.

Reinforcement Learning is the third machine learning paradigm besides supervised learning and unsupervised learning. A reinforcement learning system generally consists of four elements: policy, reward, value, and environment.

Almost all reinforcement learning problems can be transformed into Markov Decision Process (MDP). Markov Property, also called Markov Chain, is a memoryless stochastic process, which can be represented by a tuple (S, P), where S is a finite number of state sets and P is a state transition probability matrix. The Markov Decision Process has three additional sets of actions A, reward R, discount parameter r, which is a tuple: (S, A, P, R, r). The existing RL algorithms applied in the field of robotics include TD3 [10], DDPG [11], PPO [12], SAC [13] and so on. In this paper, we apply DDPG, a model-free and off-policy RL algorithm, to realize the robotic manipulation task. Model-free RL methods are capable of training an agent to act directly on the environment. And the offline reinforcement learning is more convenient to add the demonstration experience.

In recent years, there are some researches of joining demonstration to reinforcement learning. DAPG [14] bootstraps the policy using behavior cloning and combines demonstrations with an on-policy policy gradient method. DDPGfD [5] successfully combine RL with demonstrations by incorporating the demonstrations into the training data. It is suited for off-policy RL method by adding them to the replay buffer. IRL [6] firstly infers the reward function based on demonstration, and then optimizes the policy based on the reward function.

In addition to introducing teaching experience from training data, reinforcement learning can also introduce teaching data through reward functions. The design of reward functions is also a crucial step in reinforcement learning. Some simple robot manipulation tasks can be obtained through sparse reward learning. Sparse rewards typically define a binary reward that returns only when the task is successful [5]. Therefore, the agent does not immediately receive a reward after each action, resulting in low utilization of data. Sparse rewards can quickly train low-level policies, but when encountering high-level or multi-level tasks, it is difficult to train well. Some researchers discussed how to enhance exploration and improve exploration efficiency in sparse rewards. Hindsight Experience Replay (HER) [15] allows sample-efficient learning from rewards which are sparse and binary and therefore avoid the need for complicated reward engineering by setting additional goals used for replay. Inverse Reinforcement Learning (IRL) [6] refers to an algorithm that deduces the reward function of MDPs in reverse, given an optimal or not strategy or some operational demonstrations, allowing agents to learn how to make decisions on complex problems through expert trajectories. Reward Machine (RM) [7] is a novel type of finite state machine that supports the specification of reward functions while exposing reward function structure. A reward machine takes abstracted descriptions of the environment as input, and outputs reward functions which allows for composing different reward functions in flexible ways. Reward machine decompose problems into a set of high-level states and define transitions using if-like conditions defined by the change of state. It is a mealy automaton, and its reward only depends on the current state and label. Among them, the label is obtained from the labeling function and is related to the historical state, current state, and current action. It is able to converge faster and achieve better results by designing specific state transition reward functions for specific tasks.

3 Methods

3.1 Reinforcement Learning from Demonstration

To begin with, we should collect a set of data from a designed trajectory and generate the state, action, reward and target state data. The demonstration datas are put into the replay buffer pool, and the segmentation and classification results are used for generating reward machines. While training, the agent sample from the demonstration replay buffer with a probability for policy updates. We adapt Deep Deterministic Policy Gradient (DDPG), which is an actor-critic, model-free, off-policy RL algorithm based on the deterministic policy gradient that can operate over continuous action spaces (Fig. 2). The environment generates new transitions $e = (s, a, r = R(s,a), s'\ P(.|s,a))$ by acting $a = \pi(s|\theta^\pi) + N$, where N is a random process allowing exploration. And then we add the data into the replay buffer. While training, we sample a batch of data to calculate the loss:

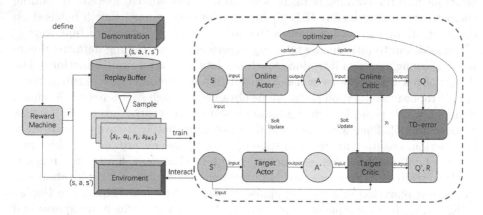

Fig. 2. DDPGfD with reward machine

$$L_1(\theta^Q) = E_{(s,a,r,s')\sim D}[R_1 - Q(s, a|\theta^Q)]^2 \tag{1}$$

where D is a distribution over transitions e and $R_1 = r + \lambda Q'(s', \pi'(s')|\theta^{\pi'})|\theta^{Q'})$. Here $Q'(.|\theta^{Q'})$ and $\pi'(.|\theta^{\pi'})$ are the target networks. The gradient step is taken as follow:

$$\delta_{\theta^\pi} J(\theta^\pi) \approx E_{(s,a)\sim D}[\delta_a Q(s, a|\theta^Q)_{a=\pi(s|\theta^Q)} \delta_{\theta^\pi} \pi(s|\theta^\pi)] \tag{2}$$

DDPGfD uses prioritized replay to sample experience from demonstration and exploring data. The probability of sampling a particular transition i is proportional to its priority:

$$P(i) = \frac{p_i^\alpha}{\sum_k p_k^\alpha} \tag{3}$$

where p_i is the priority of the transition.

$$p_i = \delta_i^2 + \lambda |\nabla_a Q(s_i, a_i | \theta^Q)|^2 + \epsilon + \epsilon_D \qquad (4)$$

where δ_i is the last TD error, the second term is the loss applied to the actor, ϵ is a small positive constant, ϵ_D is a positive constant for demonstration, and λ is used to weight the contributions.

Algorithm 1: DDPGfD with Reward Machine

---

input : *Env* Environment, D Demonstration, *RB* Replay Buffer, Q Critic Network, π Actor Network, Q' Target Critic Network, π' Target Actor Network, *RM* Reward Machine

output: $Q(.|\theta^Q)$ Critic function, $\pi(.|\theta^\pi)$ Actor function

1   *Initialize Policy Q, π, Q', π' parameter;*

2   *Initialize Reward Machine through Demonstration RM $\leftarrow$ D;*

3   *Initialize Replay Buffer with Demonstration $RB_D \leftarrow D$;*

4   *Pre-train network Q, π, Q', π' with Initialized Replay Buffer RB_D;*

5   **for** $i = 0$ *in Episodes* **do**

6   *Reset Environment Env;*

7   **for** *step = 0 in EpisodeSteps* **do**

8   *Get State s from Env and Get Action a from Actor π;*

9   *Env step Action a and generate next State s';*

10   *Get Value v from Critic Q;*

11   *Update Reward Machine RM base on Current State s';*

12   *Get Reward r from RM;*

13   *Add data (s, a, r, s') into replay buffer RB;*

14   *Calculate sample probability P_i for Demonstration sample;*

15   *Sample a mini-batch from replay buffer RB and RB_D with P_i ;*

16   *Calculate loss L;*

17   *Update critic Q parameter θ^Q with loss L;*

18   *Update actor π parameter θ^π through policy gradient;*

19   **if** *i%UpdateLength = 0* **then**

20   *Update target actor π' and target critic Q' parameter* $\theta^{Q'} \leftarrow \theta^Q, \theta^{\pi'} \leftarrow \theta^\pi;$

21   **if** *i%StoreLength = 0* **then**

22   *Store target actor and target critic as critic function $Q(.|\theta^Q)$ and actor function $\pi(.|\theta^\pi)$;*

Our experiments made use of several general techniques from the deep RL literature which significantly improved the overall performance of DDPG on our test domains. As we discussed in Sect. 5, these improvements had a particularly large impact when combined with demonstration data. We use two policy networks and two value networks. All of the neural networks have three linear hidden layers with 512, 512 and 512 units respectively. The ReLU activation function is used in all hidden layers. The input state is 7-dimensional, the output action is 3-dimensional, and the output value is 1-dimensional. The state space and the action space are defined as follows:

$$S_t = [x_e, y_e, z_e, x_t, y_t, z_t, s_m]$$
$$A_t = [\delta x, \delta y, \delta z] \tag{5}$$

where, (x_e, y_e, z_e) is the position of the end-effector and (x_t, y_t, z_t) represents the target position of the assembly object. s_m is generated from the state machine. $(\delta x, \delta y, \delta z)$ is the displacement of the end-effector. We normalize the action output by a Tanh layer.

3.2   Reward Machine from Demonstration

Task Decomposition in RL reduces tasks into subtasks that an agent can efficiently learn independently and in parallel. A state machine can semantically define the state of a robot based on current information, while also defining the conditions for state transfer, achieving higher-level description of robot tasks, and transforming high-level robot task descriptions into robot basic motion language. Reward Machine is a method used for reinforcement learning of high-level task reward descriptions, which allows agents to learn from low-level tasks to high-level tasks. The RM is also able to compute a potential function and shape a dense reward function.

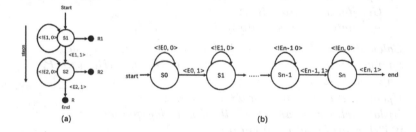

Fig. 3. A simple reward machine and a reward machine from demonstration

We present a method to construct RM from demonstrations that encourage a DDPG agent to achieve such goals. An RM takes abstracted descriptions of the environment as input, and output reward functions. Hence, an RM can be used to define temporally extended tasks and behaviours. The reward machine is defined over a set of propositional positions which represent the key position of the relevant high-level events from the task. We manually map the demonstrations into sequences of abstract states. And than we equip such state with a reward function to obtain a RM. As shown in Fig. 3, S_i represent the state of the robot. $< E_i, 1 >$ means that the machine will transition from S_i to S_{i+1} and output a reward of one. Intuitively, this machine outputs a reward of one if and only if the agent successfully transfer to the next state.

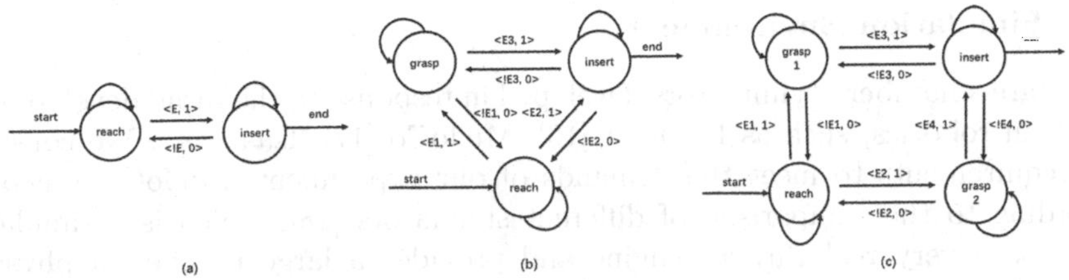

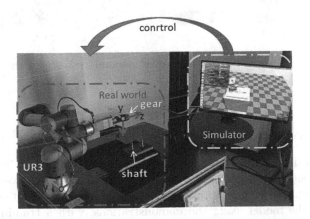

Fig. 4. Reward machines for high-level assembly

For high-level tasks, we need to define higher-level states and then define a reward function based on each state, which can be sparse rewards, shaped rewards or new reward machines. In this way, we can design new reward functions combined with existing knowledge and experience (Fig. 4).

4   Experiments

The computer environment is Ubuntu 16.04 LTS-64 bit platform, the processor is Intel(R) Core(TM) i5-8500, the main frequency is 3.0 GHz, and the GPU is GeForce GTX 2080 Ti. We also develop RL algorithms by using OpenAI Gym and Pytorch, which is utilized as a convenient toolkit for RL algorithms. In our experiments below, we find that DDPGfD can improve their data efficiency and training speed by joining the expert experience. Abstract states in RM serve the same purpose: they signal certain state properties that are correlated with optimal actions (Fig. 5).

Fig. 5. The assembly system in the real world.

4.1   Simulation Environment

There are a number of simulators developed in response to the rapid development of RL in robotics, such as Pybullet [16], MuJoCo [17], Isaac, etc. We consider the requirements to meet the demands of our experiment. MuJoCo is chosen according to the comparison of different simulators [18], which is a simulator that has a very real Physics engine and provides a large number of physical computing interfaces to facilitate simulation training and learning. The experimental environment consists of three main parts: simulator, robot and assembled objects. We use UR3, a 6-DOF robot with a two-finger gripper. In the simulator, we implement the joint control of the robot with the designed PD controller. Besides, controllers transform the high-level actions into low-level virtual motor commands that actuate the robots with the inverse kinematics of the robot. The URDF file of the robot is used to import the joint information of the robot, and the required robot end position is obtained to calculate the IK solution of the robot. As shown in Fig. 6, we generated two typical reinforcement learning environments for assembly: peg-in-hole assembly and gear assembly. The object of the peg-in-hole assembly is a cube with 2 cm length, 2 cm width, and 6 cm height, as well as a square hole with a side length of 2.3 cm. The gear assembly task consists of two main parts: the gear and the shaft. In this paper, two different gears are used, each mounted on a different shaft. The outer diameters of the gears are 40 mm and 30 mm respectively and both inner diameters are 10 mm. The diameters of the shafts are 8 mm.

(a)   (b)

Fig. 6. The peg-in-hole task and gear assembly task in the simulator.

4.2   Reinforcement Learning Result

The UR3 robotic arm was kinesthetically force controlled by a human demonstrator to collect the demonstration data. For each experiment, we collected 100 episodes of human demonstrations which were on average about 50 steps long. We pre-train the model using the demonstrations, with a training step count of 10000 steps before training. Batch training was performed by sampling uniformly from an experience replay buffer of size 100000, include a buffer of size 5000 filled with demonstrations. The learning rate is 0.0005. The reward decay is 0.00001. The batch size is 4096. The reward discount is 0.9. The action noise std is 0.1. The const demo priority is 0.99 and the minimal priority is 0.001.

For providing demonstration for the training tasks we used the same setup, we demonstrate by dragging the end of the robotic arm. For each experiment, we collected 100 episodes of human demonstrations which were on average about 50 steps long. We measure reward against environment interaction time. For each training session, we trained the policy with 2000 episodes and each lasting 50 steps under different conditions. We generate 6 charts to show the training result, including: the sampling probability of demonstration data, the loss of the actor, the average reward per episode, the loss of the critic, the running time per episode, and the length of each episode. Among them, reward is the most important indicator for evaluating reinforcement learning strategies.

We evaluate and discuss the performance of DDPG with demonstration or without demonstration in a simple reach task. As shown in Fig. 7, reinforcement learning perform better with the demonstration. The reward reach the top after nearly 200 episodes with demonstration. But without demonstration, the agent generate a policy with about 1000 episodes. Without demonstration data, it cost more episodes for the agent to learn a simple skill model. The results show that DDPGfD out-performs DDPG and DDPGfD exhibits a better training behaviour.

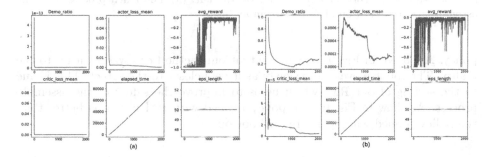

Fig. 7. The training results of DDPG without demonstration and DDPG with demonstration in the robot reach task. (a) Without demonstration; (b) With demonstration.

We evaluate and discuss the performance of DDPGfD with RM in a gear assembly task. The agent greatly outperformed the other ablations with the RM. As shown in Fig. 8, the reward reach the top after nearly 500 episodes with RM. But with sparse reward, the agent will generate a policy with about 1300 episodes. Overall, the results on these experiments show that exploiting the RM structure can greatly increase the sample efficiency and the performance of the policies for assembly task.

For sim-to-real transfer, we also adapt domain randomization to improve the adaptability and robustness of intelligent agents. Besides, we achieve real-time communication between simulation and reality through UDP to quickly obtain the status of real robots and update the robots in the simulation. At the same time, we can also control real robots in real-time through simulator and training

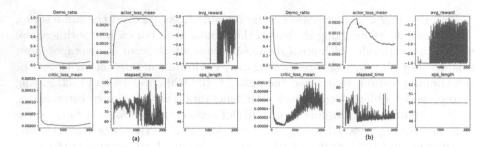

Fig. 8. The training results of training wit sparse reward and RM. (a) Sparse reward; (b) Reward machine.

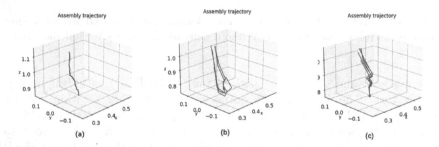

Fig. 9. The assembly process performed in the real world. The image on the right is a close-up of the corresponding image on the left. (a) The reach process; (b) The assembly process; (c) Complete the assembly task.

policy. As shown in Fig. 9, we can see that our method can well transfer to the reality. The robot moves more slowly as it gets closer to the target. This is due to the setting of our RM, which helps to improve the safety of the assembly process. As show in Fig. 10, the policy trained with RM performs better than the policy trained with sparse reward obviously.

Fig. 10. The assembly trajectories. (a) The demonstration reference; (b) The trajectories generated by the policy trained with the sparse reward; (c) The trajectories generated by the policy trained with the reward machine from demonstration.

5   Conclusion

In this paper, we propose a robot assembly skill RL learning method with expert demonstrations and reward machine which is put forward to make full use of human prior knowledge and improve the training efficiency and performance for robot assembly task. Specifically, the reward machine allows us to design a higher-level reward function that can be easily extended. We design the reward machine and adapt an adaptive experience replay method to sample experience from exploration and expert experience for policy update. A comprehensive comparison with different reward functions and different environments validates that the proposed method can achieve a higher success rate and stronger security to complete the assembly task more reasonably. We also successfully and safely transfer the policy from simulator to the real world. For future work, we will try to develop a more reliant and robust framework by joining more sensor information which is significant in the assembly task.

References

1. Sutton, R.S., Barto, A.G.: Reinforcement Learning: An Introduction. MIT Press, Cambridge (2018)
2. Torabi, F., Warnell, G., Stone, P.: Behavioral cloning from observation. arXiv preprint arXiv:1805.01954 (2018)
3. Ho, J., Ermon, S.: Generative adversarial imitation learning. In: Advances in Neural Information Processing Systems, vol. 29 (2016)
4. Hester, T., et al.: Deep Q-learning from demonstrations. In: Proceedings of the AAAI Conference on Artificial Intelligence, vol. 32 (2018)
5. Vecerik, M., et al.: Leveraging demonstrations for deep reinforcement learning on robotics problems with sparse rewards. arXiv preprint arXiv:1707.08817 (2017)
6. Arora, S., Doshi, P.: A survey of inverse reinforcement learning: challenges, methods and progress. Artif. Intell. **297**, 103500 (2021)
7. Icarte, R.T., Klassen, T., Valenzano, R., McIlraith, S.: Using reward machines for high-level task specification and decomposition in reinforcement learning. In: International Conference on Machine Learning, pp. 2107–2116. PMLR (2018)
8. Luo, J., et al.: Robust multi-modal policies for industrial assembly via reinforcement learning and demonstrations: a large-scale study. arXiv preprint arXiv:2103.11512 (2021)
9. Kimble, K., et al.: Benchmarking protocols for evaluating small parts robotic assembly systems. IEEE Robot. Autom. Lett. **5**(2), 883–889 (2020)
10. Fujimoto, S., Hoof, H., Meger, D.: Addressing function approximation error in actor-critic methods. In: International Conference on Machine Learning, pp. 1587–1596. PMLR (2018)
11. Lillicrap, T.P., et al.: Continuous control with deep reinforcement learning. arXiv preprint arXiv:1509.02971 (2015)
12. Schulman, J., Wolski, F., Dhariwal, P., Radford, A., Klimov, O.: Proximal policy optimization algorithms. arXiv preprint arXiv:1707.06347 (2017)
13. Haarnoja, T., et al.: Soft actor-critic algorithms and applications. arXiv preprint arXiv:1812.05905 (2018)

14. Rajeswaran, A., et al.: Learning complex dexterous manipulation with deep reinforcement learning and demonstrations. arXiv preprint arXiv:1709.10087 (2017)
15. Andrychowicz, M., et al.: Hindsight experience replay. In: Advances in Neural Information Processing Systems, vol. 30 (2017)
16. Coumans, E., Bai, Y.: Pybullet, a python module for physics simulation for games, robotics and machine learning (2016)
17. Todorov, E., Erez, T., Tassa, Y.: Mujoco: a physics engine for model-based control. In: 2012 IEEE/RSJ International Conference on Intelligent Robots and Systems, pp. 5026–5033. IEEE (2012)
18. Collins, J., Chand, S., Vanderkop, A., Howard, D.: A review of physics simulators for robotic applications. IEEE Access 9, 51416–51431 (2021)

The Construction of Intelligent Grasping System Based on EEG

Mengdi Wang, You Wu, Tao Ding, Xingwei Zhao[✉], and Bo Tao

School of Mechanical Science and Engineering, Huazhong University of Science and
Technology, Wuhan, China
zhaoxingwei@hust.edu.cn

Abstract. Brain-Computer Interfaces (BCI) can help disabled people to improve
human-environment interaction and rehabilitation. Grasping objects with EEG-
based BCI has become popular and hard research in recent years. The traditional
steady-state visual evoked potential (SSVEP)-based EEG signal classification is
offline, which involves conducting experiments first and then analyzing the overall
data. However, for robotic arm grasping tasks, real-time signal analysis is required
to obtain control signals. We propose and design a system for controlling robotic
arm grasping based on online SSVEP-based EEG signals classification by modified FBCCA with weighted signal template and conducted online and offline
analysis on the collected EEG signals. The experimental results show that our
modified classification algorithm has higher accuracy than the traditional classification algorithm FBCCA, and our designed online SSVEP-based BCI robotic
arm controlling system achieves an effective performance in grasping.

Keywords: BCI · SSVEP · Modified FBCCA · Robot Arm Grasping

1 Introduction

Brain–computer interface (BCI), which can directly communicate brain activities and
computer control signals, has been applied for people with severe motor disabilities to
communicate, control, and even restore their motor disabilities [1]. To some extent, it
can bypass the patient's damaged motor pathways by decoding the brain's intentions
and converting them into control commands that can be recognized by computers and
external devices [2–4]. With the integration of robotic arms and BCI, these people are
able to interact with the surrounding environment by equipped BCI systems, such as
having robotic arms help with water cups or food, opening and closing doors, tidying
up and organizing desks, and so on [5–7].

The steady-state visual evoked potential (SSVEP) based BCIs is widely praised for
providing a safe, natural, and intuitive human-computer interaction method for elderly
and disabled individuals with limited mobility, while avoiding the risks and high costs
of craniotomy surgery, and it has the characteristics of not demanding specific training

---

M. Wang and Y. Wu—These authors are co-first authors of the article.

© The Author(s), under exclusive license to Springer Nature Singapore Pte Ltd. 2023
H. Yang et al. (Eds.): ICIRA 2023, LNAI 14271, pp. 245–256, 2023.
https://doi.org/10.1007/978-981-99-6495-6_21

from the user [8]. In non-invasive brain computer interface technology, due to the characteristics of easy collection, high security, low price, and high time resolution of scalp EEG, research based on scalp EEG has made rapid progress in recent years. Compared to the P300-BCI and MI-BCI paradigms, the signals obtained by SSVEP have higher signal-to-noise ratio and higher information transmission rate.

In human-computer interaction, the control strategies of brain computer interface robots are mainly divided into three categories based on the degree of automation and intelligence, namely: direct-control, advanced-control, and shared-control [9, 10]. Among them, the "Advanced Control" strategy will delegate some low-level tasks to robots, and automatically complete path planning through data interaction between multiple sensors and the environment. It is usually suitable for rehabilitation training of limbs in stroke patients.

In this paper, we aim to propose and design a system of Advanced Control for controlling robotic arm grasping based on online SSVEP-based EEG signals classification by modified FBCCA with weighted signal template, which performs effectively and had some advantages. Firstly, we analyze the modified FBCCA recognition algorithm based on correction factors using offline collected SSVEP-based EEG signals to verify its higher accuracy compared to traditional FBCCA algorithm. Then we extract and segment the blocks in the depth camera's field of view through computer vision, and select the target block to grasp the blocks by SSVEP. Finally, the control command is transmitted to the robotic arm to complete the grasping action of the desired target for the subject. Repeat these steps until all the blocks are accurately captured.

The rest of the paper is organized as follows. The Pipeline of EEG-Based BCI For Grasping is illuminated in Sect. 2, which includes a modified FBCCA identification algorithm based on correction factors, vision-guided grasp and camera eye-in-hand calibration, and image contour extraction. Section 3 displays experiment configuration and provides the results of SSVEP recognition rate, calibration results, and image processing results. Finally, we give a conclusion in Sect. 5.

2   Method

There are three steps for the EEG-based BCI robot arm grasping system: classification of EEG signals, block extraction and segmentation in images, Robot arm and camera hand-eye calibration and grasping.

The first step is to classify the EEG signals. We proposed the modified FBCCA identification algorithm based on correction factors, which considers the frequency of position adjacent and numerical adjacent and correct the single filter bank generally used by traditional FBCCA algorithm. The second step is to extract and segment object blocks in the image. Each object block in the scene is obtained by a RealSense depth camera, which simultaneously accepts aligned RGB and depth maps. After image processing, the object blocks in the camera's field of view are extracted and the target pose of the object block to be grasped by the robotic arm is calculated based on this. Based on the classification results of the SSVEP-based EEG signals, specific object blocks are identified and displayed. The next step is to perform eye-in-hand calibration on the camera at the robotic arm's end. After obtaining the representation of the target grasping posture of the object block in the camera coordinate system, the calibration result matrix is converted to the representation of the robotic arm base coordinate system, and based on this, the robotic arm reverse solves the target posture of the robotic arm in joint space for grasping path planning to control the robotic arm to complete the grasping action of the identified target.

2.1 Modified FBCCA Identification Algorithm Based on Correction Factors

The SSVEP recognition is based on filter bank canonical correlation analysis (FBCCA) that can capture the inter-relationship between predictor and response variables.

First of all, we use type I Chebyshev filters to break down original EEG signals into N sub-bands: $X_1, X_2, \cdots, X_N$. Then, the standard CCA algorithm is applied to each sub-band to obtain correlation coefficients corresponding to all stimulus frequencies. The correlation coefficients corresponding to Y_k is represented by the vector $\vec{\rho_k}$, which contains correlation coefficient values for N sub-bands. The correlation coefficients vector $\vec{\rho_k}$ can be represented as

$$
\vec{\rho_k} = \begin{bmatrix} \rho_1 \\ \rho_2 \\ \vdots \\ \rho_N \end{bmatrix} = \begin{bmatrix} \rho(X_1^T w_X (X_1 Y_k), Y_k^T w_Y (X_1 Y_k)) \\ \rho(X_2^T w_X (X_2 Y_k), Y_k^T w_Y (X_2 Y_k)) \\ \vdots \\ \rho(X_N^T w_X (X_N Y_k), Y_k^T w_Y (X_N Y_k)) \end{bmatrix}, k = [1, 2, \cdots, S] \tag{1}
$$

When using a single frequency sinusoidal signal template for FBCCA, the frequency of position adjacent and numerical adjacent has a negative impact on the actual stimulus response. So, for the target frequency, we superimposed the physical distance and frequency distance to obtain the integration distance, as shown in the Fig. 1.

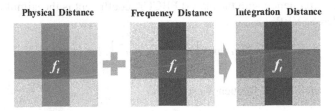

Fig. 1. The integration distance of target frequency

Therefore, a modified reference signal template is proposed to further improve the classification accuracy of FBCCA. The template signal Y_k can be represented as

$$
Y_k = \begin{bmatrix} \text{Vec}(W)^T \text{Vec}[sin(2\pi F \cdot n)] \\ \text{Vec}(W)^T \text{Vec}[cos(2\pi F \cdot n)] \\ \vdots \\ \text{Vec}(W)^T \text{Vec}[sin(2\pi M \cdot F \cdot n)] \\ \text{Vec}(W)^T \text{Vec}[cos(2\pi M \cdot F \cdot n)] \end{bmatrix}, n = \begin{bmatrix} \dfrac{1}{f}, \dfrac{2}{f} \cdots, \dfrac{L}{f} \end{bmatrix} \tag{2}
$$

where Vec() is the vectorization operator of the matrix, W is the correction factor matrix, M is the number of harmonics of EEG data, L is the data length of EEG in the direction of time, f is the sampling frequency, and F is a 3×3 connected frequency matrix. W can be represented as

$$W = \begin{bmatrix} w_3 & w_1 & w_3 \\ w_2 & 1 & w_2 \\ w_3 & w_1 & w_3 \end{bmatrix} \tag{3}$$

F can be represented as

$$F = \begin{bmatrix} f_i - 4 & f_i - 3 & f_i - 2 \\ f_i - 1 & f_i & f_i + 1 \\ f_i + 2 & f_i + 3 & f_i + 4 \end{bmatrix} \tag{4}$$

Therefore, the N sub-bands components ρ_n in $\overrightarrow{\rho_k}$ can be fused as a weighted sum of squares.

$$\widetilde{\rho_k} = \sum_{n=1}^{N} w(n) * \rho_n^2 \tag{5}$$

The weighted function $w(n)$ can be represented as

$$w(n) = n^{-a} + b, n \in [1, N] \tag{6}$$

where a and b are both constants. Their values are determined by the optimal performance of the classification. In practical applications, we can determine them by gird search in offline experiments [11].

Finally, the frequency with the largest FBCCA coefficient is the stimulus frequency of the recorded SSVEP.

$$f_{target} = \underset{f_i}{argmax} \left\{ \widetilde{\rho_1}, \widetilde{\rho_2}, \cdots, \widetilde{\rho_S} \right\}, i \in [1, S] \tag{7}$$

where f_{target} is the SSVEP frequency estimation.

2.2 Vision-Guided Grasp and Camera Eye-in-Hand Calibration

In the eye-in-hand calibration system for robots and cameras, H_{gij} represents the relative pose homogeneous transformation matrix between the end coordinate systems of the robotic arm, H_{cij} represents the relative pose homogeneous transformation matrix between camera coordinate systems, H_{cg} represents the homogeneous transformation matrix of the relative pose between the camera and the end of the robotic arm [12]. The above three matrices satisfy the following relationship

$$H_{gij} H_{cg} = H_{cg} H_{cij} \tag{8}$$

The basic equation of hand eye calibration can be obtained by decomposing the homogeneous transformation matrix into the rotation matrix part and the translation vector part, as shown in (9):

$$\begin{cases} R_{gij}R_{cg} = R_{cg}R_{cij} \\ (R_{gij} - I)T_{cg} = R_{cg}T_{cij} - T_{gij} \end{cases} \tag{9}$$

To solve the Eq. 9, first by calculating the rotation matrix, and convert the rotation matrix into rotation vector using Rodrigues transformation:

$$\begin{cases} r_{gij} = rodrigues(R_{gij}) \\ r_{cij} = rodrigues(R_{cij}) \end{cases} \tag{10}$$

Next, we normalize the rotation vector to N_{gij} and N_{cij}, and then rephrase the pose transformation with the modified Rodriguez parameters:

$$\begin{cases} P_{gij} = 2sin\frac{\theta_{gij}}{2}N_{gij} \\ P_{cij} = 2sin\frac{\theta_{cij}}{2}N_{cij} \end{cases} \tag{11}$$

Using the formulas proposed and proven by Tsai Lenz:

$$skew(P_{gij} + P_{cij})P_{cg}' = P_{cij} - P_{gij} \tag{12}$$

$$P_{cg} = \frac{2P_{cg}'}{\sqrt{1 + |P_{cg}'|^2}} \tag{13}$$

$$(R_{gij} - I)T_{cg} = R_{cg}T_{cij} - T_{gij} \tag{14}$$

Finally, the hand-eye relationship matrix between the end of the robotic arm and the camera can be obtained.

2.3 Image Contour Extraction

The image collected by the camera will still contain noise even after threshold segmentation, which will interfere with the image contour extraction, so the image needs to be denoised by Gaussian blur first. According to the two-dimensional Gauss distribution, the points at different positions in the convolution kernel of Gaussian blur are weighted. The Gaussian distribution of the two-dimensional variable $X = (x_1, x_2)$ is:

$$f(X) = \frac{1}{2\pi|\Sigma|^{1/2}}e^{-\frac{1}{2}(X-u)^T\Sigma^{-1}(X-u)} = \frac{1}{2\pi\sigma^2}e^{-(x_1^2+x_2^2)/2} \tag{15}$$

where the $u = (u_1, u_2) = (\mu, \mu)$ is mean matrix, and the $\Sigma = \begin{bmatrix} \delta_{11} & \delta_{12} \\ \delta_{21} & \delta_{22} \end{bmatrix} = \begin{bmatrix} \sigma^2 & 0 \\ 0 & \sigma^2 \end{bmatrix}$ is covariance matrix.

Using the convolution kernel coordinates (x, y) as the variable X, the Gaussian 3x3 convolution kernel can be calculated. The image denoising process can be expressed as the following formula for convolution of probability density $f(X)$ and image I:

$$G = f(X) \otimes I \tag{16}$$

Edge detection requires the use of image gradient information to determine edges. The Sobel operator can be used to perform convolution operations with the image in both horizontal and vertical directions to obtain the amplitude and direction of the image gradient:

$$G_x = \begin{bmatrix} -1 & 0 & 1 \\ -2 & 0 & 2 \\ -1 & 0 & 1 \end{bmatrix} \otimes I, G_y = \begin{bmatrix} 1 & 2 & 1 \\ 0 & 0 & 0 \\ -1 & -2 & -1 \end{bmatrix} \otimes I \tag{17}$$

$$G = \sqrt{G_x^2 + G_y^2}, \theta = tan^{-1}\left(\frac{G_y}{G_x}\right) \tag{18}$$

The gradient direction of the image is perpendicular to the edge direction, and it is necessary to use non maximum suppression methods to remove non edge points. Calculate the gradient amplitude at the edge in the gradient direction of each pixel point in the neighborhood of 8 and compare it with the gradient amplitude of that pixel point. Then preserve pixels with the maximum gradient amplitude in the neighborhood as edge points. After that, set the strength threshold of the boundary gradient, and take the pixels whose gradient value is greater than the strength threshold or between the strength threshold, and whose 8 neighborhoods have boundary point as boundary point, thus completing the image edge detection and extraction.

3   Experiments Setup

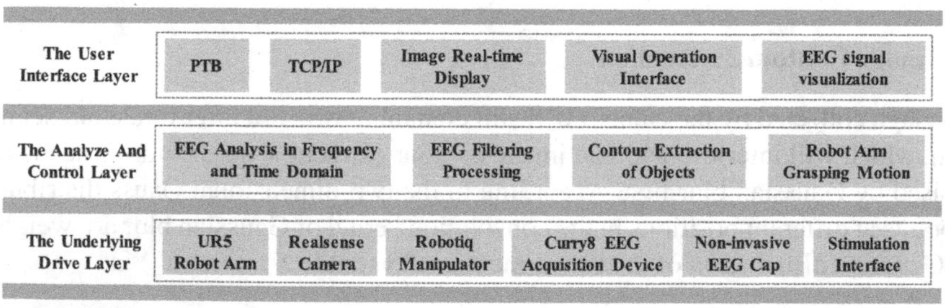

The User Interface Layer	PTB	TCP/IP	Image Real-time Display	Visual Operation Interface	EEG signal visualization

The Analyze And Control Layer	EEG Analysis in Frequency and Time Domain	EEG Filtering Processing	Contour Extraction of Objects	Robot Arm Grasping Motion

The Underlying Drive Layer	UR5 Robot Arm	Realsense Camera	Robotiq Manipulator	Curry8 EEG Acquisition Device	Non-invasive EEG Cap	Stimulation Interface

Fig. 2. The overall communication framework of the BCI-based grasping system

The overall communication framework of the BCI-based grasping system is shown in the Fig. 2. In the intelligent BCI-based grasping system, the EEG acquisition device is Neroscan Grael. In the Ubuntu control system, we install ROS Melodic to control robot arm. In the Windows system, we install CURRY8 to acquire EEG data.

As shown in Fig. 3, with the help of the psychological toolbox in Matlab [13], we can display the image obtained by the depth camera connected to the end of the manipulator on the screen. The objects to be grasped in the field of view flash at a certain frequency. We utilize the network cable to connect the EEG acquisition device to the computer of the Ubuntu system. We connect Windows and Ubuntu systems via a cable and interconnect them via ROS to transmit image, manipulator and gripper control information. In the Ubuntu system, we utilize ROS to control the depth camera to obtain pictures and perform the motion control, and use OpenCV library to process images.

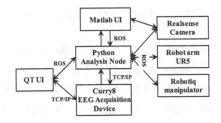

Fig. 3. The device-to-device communication

4   Experimental Results and Discussions

4.1   Weighted Template Signal Performance

We utilized Neuroscan EEG system with 34-channel electric potentials from the scalp of the user wearing an EEG cap and 4-channel electrooculography representing eye movements. The sampling rate is 2048 Hz. The distribution of EEG acquisition cap electrodes is shown in Fig. 4.

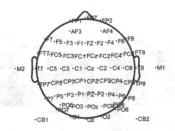

Fig. 4. The distribution of EEG electrodes

Fig. 5. The nine targets stimulus

SSVEP detection for object selection was performed every 500ms. We chose EEG signals from nine channels ("CPz", "P7", "P3", "Pz", "P4", "P8", "O1", "Oz", "O2") and filtered signals within the range of 7–70 Hz by type I Chebyshev filter.

To verify superiority of weighted signal template, offline analysis was performed of the collected data from 10 replicates by SSVEP. The subject gazed at nine patches in the Fig. 5. And the EEG data was collected. And the accuracies are shown in Table 1. To simplify the calculation, we let $w_1 = w_2 = w_3 = w$. In order to find the well-performing weight coefficient, we iteratively solve with a range of -0.1 to 0 and a step size of 0.02, and compare the accuracy of the classification results under different weight coefficients. It can be seen that, compared to the traditional $w = 0$ case, when the weight coefficient is -0.08, the classification accuracy is improved to a certain extent, and the highest accuracy can reach 95.56% with a data length of 4.25 s.

Table 1. Results in SSVEP Detection with w

w	2.00s	2.25s	2.50s	2.75s	3.00s	3.25s	3.50s	3.75s	4.00s	**4.25s**	Average Accuracy
0	22.22	31.11	38.89	47.78	61.11	72.22	**80.00**	84.44	91.11	93.33	62.22%
−0.02	23.33	30.00	38.89	48.89	60.00	72.22	78.89	85.56	91.11	95.56	62.44%
−0.04	23.33	30.00	37.78	48.89	62.22	**73.33**	78.89	85.56	91.11	95.56	62.67%
−0.06	**24.44**	30.00	40.00	48.89	63.33	72.22	78.89	85.56	90.00	95.56	62.89%
−0.08	23.33	**33.33**	**41.11**	**51.11**	**64.44**	71.11	78.89	**85.56**	91.11	**95.56**	**63.56%**
−0.1	23.33	32.22	42.22	51.11	63.33	71.11	78.89	84.44	**92.22**	94.44	63.33%

4.2 Camera Eye-in-Hand Calibration

Firstly, the robotic arm takes photos of the calibration board in seven pose states, so that the pose information of the calibration board relative to the camera in each pose can be obtained. And then, by calculating the pose transformation of the calibration plate in the camera and robot arm's end coordinate system, the hand eye calibration matrix can be accurately calculated (Fig. 6).

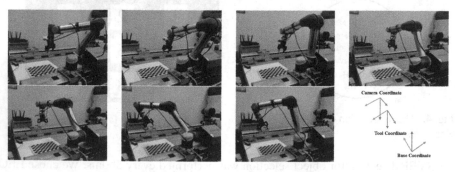

Fig. 6. The processing of the eye-in-hand calibration

The final hand-eye calibration result matrix is:

$$H_{cg} = \begin{pmatrix} R_{cg} & T_{cg} \\ 0\ 0\ 0 & 1 \end{pmatrix} = \begin{pmatrix} 0.99965 & -0.02318 & -0.00078 & -0.03285 \\ 0.02333 & 0.99985 & 0.00507 & -0.09764 \\ 0.00065 & -0.00522 & 0.99993 & 0.02395 \\ 0 & 0 & 0 & 1 \end{pmatrix}$$

4.3 Image Contour Extraction and Block Segmentation

After obtaining the RGB image captured by the depth camera, we performed a threshold segmentation algorithm and an edge extraction algorithm on the image. The obtained image segmentation results, segmented image contour extraction results, and final object block extraction results are shown in Fig. 7.

Fig. 7. The result of image contour extraction and block segmentation

It can be seen that the algorithms we adopted can accurately segment and extract the blocks in the camera's field of view. Each segmented and extracted block is represented by its minimum containment green rectangular box, and its center green dot is represented as the target point grasped by the robotic arm. The coordinates of the target points of each object block in the image coordinate system and their minimum bounding rectangle rotation angle results are shown in Table 2.

Table 2. The position and angle of the extracted blocks.

	Block1	Block2	Block3	Block4
x	346.70	526.22	359.68	170.01
y	83.07	220.93	344.12	353.31
Rotation Angle	−44.19°	+23.63°	−89.47°	+10.78°

After obtaining the depth information of the corresponding green dots in the depth image matched with the RGB image, the robotic arm's grasping trajectory planning and motion control are carried out accordingly. In the experiment, our robotic arm was able to grasp the target object block recognized by the subject's gaze (regardless of the accuracy of EEG signal classification results), and the success rate of grasping reached 100%, thus verifying the correctness of the camera's hand-eye calibration results and the feasibility of the algorithm we used.

4.4 Grasping Experiments

In this stage, a RealSense depth camera fixed just above the object is utilized for object recognition and extraction. The image shows four objects and each object with green flashing spots. After image representing selection of each object is generated by the RealSense depth camera, the user is instructed to just look for the object that they want to grasp by EEG. Then the target object turns red in potential selection. Concretely it can be selected based on SSVEP. The subject focuses on the virtual LED image above each object that oscillated at given 9 Hz, 10 Hz, 11 Hz, 12 Hz frequency, as shown in Fig. 8.

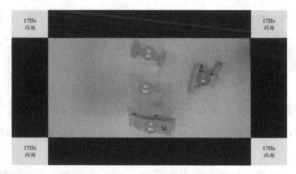

Fig. 8. Object selection by SSVEP. There are four objects and four different frequencies flashing LED above them. When we focus on the target object 4, the algorithm detects 12 Hz frequency and object 2 turns red. (color figure online)

The experiment platform was based on Robotiq 2-finger hand and UR5 6-joint arm. We chose four objects and placed them arbitrarily into scenes within the field of view of the RealSense depth camera. The four blocks corresponded to stimulus frequencies of 9 Hz, 10 Hz, 11 Hz, 12 Hz (Fig. 9).

Fig. 9. The grasping experiments with EEG-based brain-computer interfaces

When the experiment began, the white patches in all four corners of the screen flashed at 17 Hz. The subject gazed at the white patch. After detecting the result, the camera acquired a picture of the scene and displayed it on the screen. Each block on the screen flashed at a certain frequency.

When the subject gazed at the object he wanted to catch, the object turned red. Then, the robotic arm automatically planned the path, grabbed the target object and placed it in the basket. During the process of grabbing the object, the subject no longer looked at the flashing block, and the EEG data was constantly updated but did not output the classification result. After the object was placed in the basket, the robotic arm returned to its original position and waited for the next command.

5   Conclusions

In this paper, we propose and design a system for controlling robotic arm grasping based on online SSVEP-based EEG signals classification. We conducted online and offline analysis on the collected EEG signals and compared the results. The results of experiment demonstrate that the EEG-based BCI with weighted signal template can achieve selection and grasping task efficiently.

During the experiment, we found that SSVEP performed higher accuracy with weighted signal template. When the weight coefficient is -0.08, the accuracy can be improved according to offline analysis of EEG data. Considering efficiency and accuracy about the experiment, we chose 2s data to perform analysis. Four repetitions of the result were used to judge whether to grasp object, which can also improve the accuracy of grasping.

Acknowledgements. This work was supported by the National Science Foundation of China under Grant 52275020, 62293512, and the Fundamental Research Funds for the Central Universities, HUST: YCJJ202201005, YCJJ20230214.

References

1. Ang, K.K., Guan, C.: Brain-computer interface in stroke rehabilitation. J. Comput. Sci. Eng. **7**(2), 139–146 (2013)
2. Chaudhary, U., Birbaumer, N., Ramos-Murguialday, A.: Brain-computer interfaces for communication and rehabilitation. Nat. Rev. Neurol. **12**(9), 513 (2016)
3. Ortiz-Rosario, A., Adeli, H.: Brain-computer interface technologies: from signal to action. Rev. Neurosci. **24**(5), 537–552 (2013)
4. Wolpaw, J.R., Birbaumer, N., Heetderks, W.J., et al.: Brain-computer interface technology: a review of the first international meeting. IEEE Trans. Rehabil. Eng. **8**(2), 164–173 (2000)
5. Collinger, J.L., Wodlinger, B., Downey, J.E., et al.: High-performance neuroprosthetic control by an individual with tetraplegia. The Lancet **381**(9866), 557–564 (2013)
6. Wodlinger, B., Downey, J.E., Tyler-Kabara, E.C., et al.: Ten-dimensional anthropomorphic arm control in a human brain-machine interface: difficulties, solutions, and limitations. J. Neural Eng. **12**(1), 016011 (2014)

7. Zhang, W., Sun, F., Liu, C., Su, W., Liu, S.: A hybrid EEG-based BCI for robot grasp controlling. In: 2017 IEEE International Conference on Systems, Man and Cybernetics (SMC). IEEE (2017)
8. Ortner, R., Allison, B.Z., Korisek, G., et al.: An SSVEP BCI to control a hand orthosis for persons with tetraplegia. IEEE Trans. Neural Syst. Rehabil. Eng. **19**(1), 1–5 (2011)
9. Fernández-Rodríguez, Á., Velasco-Álvarez, F., Ron-Angevin, R.: Review of real brain-controlled wheelchairs. J. Neural Eng. **13**(6), 061001 (2016)
10. Wang, Y., Chen, X., Gao, X., et al.: A benchmark dataset for SSVEP-based brain–computer interfaces. IEEE Trans. Neural Syst. Rehabil. Eng. **25**(10), 1746–1752 (2016)
11. Zhang, D., Liu, S., Wang, K., et al.: Machine-vision fused brain machine interface based on dynamic augmented reality visual stimulation. J. Neural Eng. **18**(5), 056061 (2021)
12. Tsai, R.Y., Lenz, R.K.: A new technique for fully autonomous and efficient 3d robotics hand/eye calibration. IEEE Trans. Robot. Autom. **5**(3), 345–358 (1989)
13. Brainard, D.H., Vision, S.: The psychophysics toolbox[. Spatial Vision **10**(4), 433–436 (1997)

Comparing of Electromyography and Ultrasound for Estimation of Joint Angle and Torque

Zhongyi Ding, Jianmin Li, and Lizhi Pan[✉]

Key Laboratory of Mechanism Theory and Equipment Design of Ministry of Education, School of Mechanical Engineering, Tianjin University, Tianjin 300350, China
melzpan@tju.edu.cn

Abstract. Electromyography (EMG) signals and ultrasound sensing have been widely studied to estimate movement intentions in the human-machine interface (HMI) field. In this study, we compared the EMG and ultrasound for estimation of the positions and torque of the wrist joint. The estimation performance of EMG and ultrasound were compared and analyzed. EMG, ultrasound, and torque signals were collected from 8 able-bodied subjects. The subjects were instructed to conduct isometric contraction of the wrist flexion/extension at 13 different angular positions. Linear regression (LR) was adopted to estimate isometric contraction torque while support vector machine (SVM) was employed to identify different angular positions. Regarding isometric contraction torque estimation, the average Pearson's correlation coefficient (r) values across all subjects was 0.95 and 0.84 for EMG and ultrasound, respectively. Regarding angular position classification, the average classification accuracy (CA) across all subjects of EMG and ultrasound was 17.78% and 91.05%, respectively. The results demonstrated that the EMG outperformed the ultrasound in estimating torque while the ultrasound outperformed the EMG for angular position classification. Our study demonstrated the advantages of the different types of signals to achieve the estimation of the joint angle and torque.

Keywords: Joint angle · joint torque · electromyography · ultrasound

1 Introduction

Human-machine interfaces (HMI) have been studied for decades [1]. The positions and force of human joints changed during human-object interactions. Therefore, the current design of HMI should consider the positions and torque of joints simultaneously [2,3].

Electromyography (EMG) and ultrasound were studied to decode limb kinematics or kinetics [4,5]. Although both kinematics and kinetics need to be considered in the design of interactive machines, only one of them was considered in most EMG-based or ultrasound-based control applications. Kinematic data was obtained with the subject have no resistance to movement and kinetic data was obtained with the subject's joint entirely restricted. The control strategies described above may be considered less useful in interactive environments, which typically drive both positions and force.

Surface EMG (sEMG) containing rich physiological information was often adopted to decipher movement intentions [6]. The time-domain (TD) and frequency-domain (FD) features were extracted from EMG signals to realize pattern recognition, which make discrete motion decoding feasible [7]. With the development of EMG interface, a variety of methods have been adopted to realize the estimation of continuous finger and hand joints movement [8,9]. There were several studies focusing on the simultaneous estimation methods of joint angles and torque based on EMG signals [10,11]. Despite these methods could effectively decipher the movement intentions, the estimation accuracy was relatively low. The deep muscle activities were difficult to be captured through sEMG signals, leading to the decrease performance in deciphering deep muscle related movement intentions [12].

Ultrasound can detect more useful information of both superficial and deep muscles with respect to the EMG. Therefore, ultrasound has been employed to decode human movement intentions in recent years. There are many different kinds of ultrasound, such as A-mode, B-mode, and M-mode ultrasound. A novel method was proposed to simultaneously predict wrist rotation and finger gestures based on wearable A-mode ultrasound signals [13]. B-mode ultrasound has been widely studied to identify wrist movements and finger gestures [5]. The performance of EMG and B-mode ultrasound in recognizing discrete finger movements and predicting continuous finger angles were compared [14]. B-mode ultrasound had superior performance for prediction than EMG. The ability of M-mode ultrasound to identify wrist and finger motion was demonstrated [15].

The wrist has multiple degrees of freedom (DOFs) and can provide considerable torque, which is essential for a variety of hand movements. Therefore, it is necessary to study the change of positions and torque when the wrist joint interacts with the environment. We compared the performance of EMG and ultrasound for estimating the continuous torque and identifying the angular position when the wrist did isometric contraction at different angular positions. Each type of signal source has its pros and cons. For instance, EMG signals are easy to collect and process, and ultrasound may better solve the estimation of joint angle [14]. During the experiment, all signals were collected simultaneously to ensure the fair comparison of different data sources.

2   Method

2.1   Subjects

Eight limb-intact subjects (8 males, age range: 20 to 25 years) were recruited in this study. None of the subjects had neuromuscular diseases. All subjects signed informed consent forms. The experiment was approved by the Ethics Committee of Tianjin University (Approval No. TJUE-2021-114). All experimental procedures were in accordance with the latest version of the Declaration of Helsinki.

2.2 Experiments Setup

To achieve the torque measurement at different angular positions, a one DOF measuring platform for the wrist torque with multiple adjustable angles was developed. The platform contained a bottom support, a clamping mechanism, a rotating platform, and a torque sensor. A rigid coupling connection was installed between the torque sensor and the rotating platform. The platform allows subjects to conduct isometric contractions at a specific joint angle. The device structure is shown in Fig. 1 (a). The main processing material of the device was aluminum alloy 6066 to reduce the weight of the entire device. The rotating platform was reduced in size to mitigate the effect of gravity on measurement accuracy. The clamping mechanism employed quick-releases to achieve fast clamping positioning. The static torque sensor had a range of 0–25 Nm.

As shown in Fig. 1(b), all subjects were instructed to sit in a chair and place their arm on the measuring platform. Two EMG sensors were attached to the extensor carpi radialis (ECR) and flexor carpi radialis (FCR) muscles to acquire EMG signals [2]. The ultrasound probe was placed on the forearm, approximately 10 cm to the elbow.

The rotating platform could be set to $-60°$, $-50°$, $-40°$, $-30°$, $-20°$, $-10°$, $0°$, $10°$, $20°$, $30°$, $40°$, $50°$, and $60°$ with respect to the neutral position of the wrist. The angular position $0°$ indicated the neutral position of the wrist. As shown in Fig. 1 (c), the palm of the hand was constrained by the rigid body and

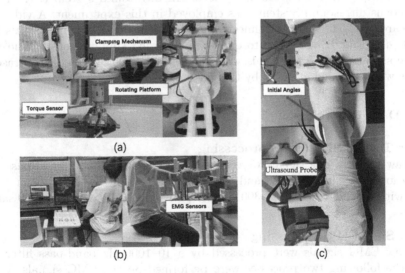

Fig. 1. (a). The structure of one degree-of-freedom torque measuring platform. (b). Experimental scene and the experimental setup used to simultaneously record EMG signals, ultrasound images and torque. (c). The palm of the hand was constrained by the rigid body and the forearm was tied to the support of the rotating platform tightly by Velcro straps.

the forearm was tied to the support of the rotating platform tightly by velcro straps to guarantee the isometric contraction of wrist flexion and extension.

The 13 angular positions were conducted in the following order: $-60°$, $-50°$, $-40°$, $-30°$, $-20°$, $-10°$, $0°$, $10°$, $20°$, $30°$, $40°$, $50°$, and $60°$. In each angular position, there were two types of trials: (1) Rhythm trials; (2) Random trials. In rhythm trials, the subjects were conducted cyclical isometric contractions in either direction for wrist flexion/extension at $1/4$ Hz frequency. In random trials, the subjects were conducted isometric contractions in a random direction at a variable force. There were three trials in each motion. The duration of each trial was 13 s with the first second reminding the subject to start the experiment. After 1st second, the subjects conducted isometric contractions. A maximum voluntary contraction (MVC) was conducted by the subjects to determine the MVC of wrist torque, EMG signals, and ultrasound images at each angular position. During the experiment, the EMG signals, the wrist joint torque, and the ultrasound images were collected simultaneously. A rest period of 3 min was provided to avoid muscle fatigue between two consecutive trials.

2.3 Data Acquisition

Torque signals and EMG signals were synchronously recorded by a data acquisition card (NI-USB6002). The EMG sensors (Noraxon Desktop DTS-16) were attached to ECR and FCR. Before placing the electrodes on the skin, an alcohol pad was wiped to reduce the impedance. An ultrasound system (BK Medical Flex Focus ultrasound System) was employed in this experiment. A video capture card (TC-540N1) was connected to the ultrasound system. Signals from EMG, ultrasound, and wrist torque were recorded simultaneously. The wrist torque signals and EMG signals were sampled at 3000 Hz Hz. The ultrasound videos were recorded at 30 Hz by the video capture card.

2.4 Data Preprocessing

Wrist Torque Signals Preprocessing
The raw wrist torque signals were processed by a 10–1000 Hz band-pass filter and a low-pass filter at 5 Hz, and then filtered by a moving root mean square filter with a window length of 300 sample points and a increment of 100 sample points.

EMG Signals Preprocessing
The raw EMG signals were processed by a 10–1000 Hz band-pass filter, and then the following two processes were performed on the EMG signals. 1. The EMG signals were full-wave rectified, low-pass filtered at 5 Hz, moving root mean square filtered with a window length of 300 sample points and a increment of 100 sample points, and normalized according to the EMG signals recorded during MVC [16]. 2. The EMG signals were segmented into multiple analysis windows to extract TD features. The analysis window was set to 300 sample points and the increment was set to 100 sample points. Four TD features were extracted from

the EMG signals: Mean Absolute Value (MAV), Zero Crossings (ZC), Slope Sign Changes (SSC), and Waveform Length (WL) [17]. Features were extracted from the two channels and then connected to form an 8-dimensional feature vector [18].

The EMG signals processed in the method 1 were adopted to estimate wrist torque while the EMG features extracted in the method 2 were employed to classify angular position. The EMG signals were processed in two different ways was due to the fact that the different EMG features needed for angular position classification and torque estimation [16,17].

B-Mode Ultrasound Images Preprocessing

The B-mode ultrasound images were cropped frame by frame from the ultrasound video. The parts with no useful information were removed from the ultrasound images. The columns 91 to 990 and the rows 11 to 370 of the images were retained. The size of the reserved images were 360×900 pixels. The first-order spatial feature was extracted from the reserved images. [19]. We divided the ultrasound images into uniform rectangular regions, each serving as a region of interest (ROI). The size of the ROI was 30×30 pixels. There were 360 ROI in total. The 900 pixels of each ROI were converted to 900 spatial points (x_i, y_i, z_i) for further analysis, where z_i represented the image gray at the pixel point's location (x_i, y_i). Then, a first-order plane fitting was applied for each ROI. The plane fitting formula was shown in equation (1). Each ROI has 3 plane fitting coefficients α, β, γ. All plane fitting coefficients form a 1080-dimensional feature vectors. Then, principal components analysis (PCA) was adopted to avoid the curse of dimensionality. The dominant 95 % of the variance was retained.

$$z_i = \alpha \cdot x_i + \beta \cdot y_i + \gamma \tag{1}$$

A data processing flow chart is shown in Fig. 2.

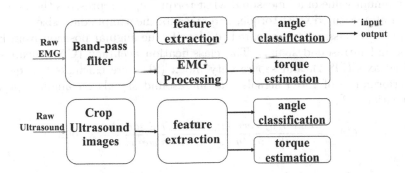

Fig. 2. The processing of comparing the performance of EMG and ultrasound. The performance of the same color were compared.

2.5 Algorithms Modeling

The LR was adopted to estimate the continuous isometric contraction torque [20,21] while the SVM was employed to classify the angular position [15] in this study. Three-fold cross-validation was employed in this study. For each subject, the data of the experiment was equally divided into 3 portions (each portion have a rhythm trial and a random trial). Two portions were chosen as the training dataset while the remaining portion was used as the testing dataset.

2.6 Evaluation Metrics

The LR was adopted to estimate the wrist torque from ultrasound signals and EMG signals. Pearson's correlation coefficient (r) and normalized root mean square error (NRMSE) between the measured and estimated joint torque for each angular position were calculated to quantify the performance of the EMG signals and ultrasound signals.

$$r_{a,b} = \frac{\sum\limits_{j=1}^{n} (a_j - \bar{a}) \cdot (b_j - \bar{b})}{\sqrt{\sum\limits_{j=1}^{n} (a_j - \bar{a})^2 \cdot (b_j - \bar{b})^2}} \tag{2}$$

$$NRMSE_{a,b} = \frac{\sqrt{\frac{1}{n} \cdot \sum\limits_{j=1}^{n} (a_j - b_j)^2}}{a_{max} - b_{min}} \tag{3}$$

where a_j represents the jth measured wrist torque, b_j represents the jth estimated wrist torque, $\bar{a}$ represents the average value of all measured wrist torque, $\bar{b}$ represents the average value of all estimated wrist torque, a_{max} represents the maximum value of all measured wrist torque, a_{min} represents the minimum value of all measured wrist torque, n represents the sample data size.

The SVM classifier was adopted to identify the angular position from EMG signals and ultrasound signals. The classification accuracy (CA), mean semi-principal axis (MSA), and separability index (SI) were calculated to quantify the performance of EMG signals and ultrasound signals on angular position classification [22].

$$CA = \frac{number\ of\ correctly\ classified\ samples}{number\ of\ the\ whole\ tests\ samples} \times 100\% \tag{4}$$

2.7 Statistical Analysis

A two-way repeated measures ANOVA was conducted on r and NRMSE. The two variables were angular position (13 Angles) and signal type (EMG signals and ultrasound signals). The Johnson transformation was applied to the r values and NRMSE values to ensure that the data obeyed a normal distribution. Then observed whether there was a significant interaction between the two independent variables. If no significant interaction was discovered between the two variables. One-way repeated measures ANOVA was conducted on angular position and signal type as independent variables respectively to observe r and NRMSE. Post hoc was conducted by the Tukey test to observe whether there were significant difference among the levels of factors. One-way ANOVA was conducted on the CA, SI, and MSA. The factor was signal type (EMG signals and ultrasound signals). The Johnson transformation was conducted to ensure that the data obeyed a normal distribution. Post hoc was conducted by the Tukey test to observe whether there were significant difference among the levels of factors. The significance level was set at p = 0.05.

3   Results

Figure 3 (a) shows the average r values of each subject in the estimation of wrist torque from EMG and ultrasound. The average r values of 8 subjects were 0.95 and 0.84 for EMG and ultrasound, respectively. The two-way ANOVA indicated that there was no significant interaction between the angular position and the signal type (p = 0.362). ANOVA with only main effects showed that angular position and signal type had a significant effect on r (angular position: p <0.01, signal type: p <0.001). The average r values of the EMG outperformed the ultrasound by 0.11.

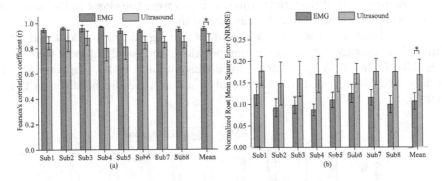

Fig. 3. (a) Pearson's correlation coefficient (r) between measured and estimated joint torque of the EMG and ultrasound for each subject. (b) NRMSE between measured and estimated joint torque of the EMG and ultrasound for each subject. * represents p<0.05. Error bars represent the standard deviation.

Figure 3 (b) shows the average NRMSE values of each subject in the estimation of wrist torque from EMG and ultrasound. The average NRMSE values of all subjects were 0.11 and 0.17 for EMG and ultrasound, respectively. The two-way ANOVA indicated that there was no significant interaction between

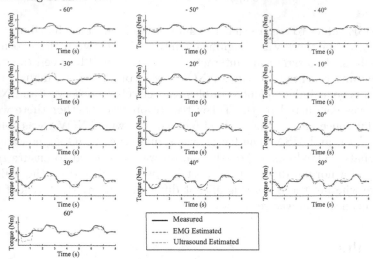

Fig. 4. The measured and estimated torque of the wrist at 13 angular positions for the subject 1.

angular position and signal type (p = 0.685). ANOVA with only main effects showed that angular position and signal type had a significant effect on NRMSE (angular position: p <0.001, signal type: p <0.001). The average NRMSE values of the EMG was 0.06 lower than that of the ultrasound.

Figure 4 shows the measured and estimated torque of the wrist for the two different signal types at 13 angular positions for the subject 1. The estimated trend and amplitude of the wrist torque for EMG were the closer to the measured torque when compared to that for the ultrasound.

Figure 5 illustrates the CA comparison of two signal types (EMG and ultrasound). The average CA of 13 angular positions across all subjects were 91.07 % ± 0.35 % and 15.51 % ± 0.99 % for ultrasound and EMG, respectively. The one-way ANOVA revealed that the signal type has a significant effect on CA (p <0.001).

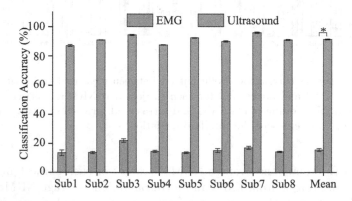

Fig. 5. CA of the EMG and ultrasound for each subject. * represents p <0.05. Error bars represent the standard deviation.

Figure 6 shows the average confusion matrices across all subjects of ultrasound and EMG with the SVM classifier. Regarding ultrasound, the wrist joint position was less correctly classified at $-40°$, $-30°$, and $-20°$. Misclassification of the different angular positions occurred mainly at the angular position adjacent to them. Regarding EMG, the CA for the different angular positions of the wrist were low, with only 7 % and 6 % for $0°$ and $30°$, respectively.

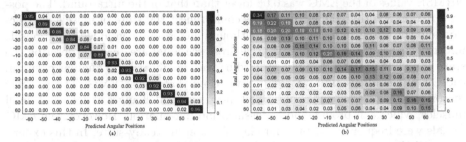

Fig. 6. (a) Confusion matrices of the average CA of the 13 different wrist angular positions across all subjects for the ultrasound. (b) Confusion matrices of the average CA of the 13 different wrist angular positions across all subjects for the EMG.

Figure 7 shows the values of SI and MSA of the EMG feature and ultrasound feature. For the SI values, the ultrasound was higher than the EMG. The one-way ANOVA revealed the signal type has a significant effect on SI (p <0.001). For the MSA values, the one-way ANOVA revealed the signal type has no significant effect on MSA (p = 0.745).

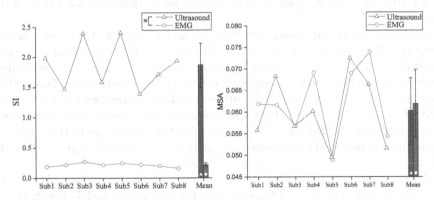

Fig. 7. (a) Comparative analysis of SI between EMG and ultrasound across all subjects. (b) Comparative analysis of MSA between EMG and ultrasound across all subjects. * represents p <0.05. Error bars represent the standard deviation.

4   Discussion

EMG or ultrasound has been adopted to decipher movement intentions focused on kinematics or kinetics. In this study, we compared the performance of EMG and ultrasound for estimating the continuous torque and identifying the angular position when the wrist did isometric contraction at different angular positions.

Our study demonstrated the following points. EMG signals were demonstrated with stronger correlation with joint torque, while ultrasound could better solve the estimation of joint angle. Regarding the estimation of torque, the average r values of the EMG outperformed the ultrasound by 0.11. The average NRMSE values of the EMG was 0.06 lower than that of the ultrasound. The possible reason was that the EMG signals could reflect the state of muscle contraction and the change of muscle force. Although ultrasound contained more muscle information, only the change of muscle cross-sectional area cannot describe the state of muscle contraction fully. Regarding the classification of angular position, the CA of the ultrasound was way better than that of the EMG. The possible reason was that ultrasound could detect morphological changes of deep and small muscles, which can provide more classification information. However, the EMG signals were frequently adopted for classification in steady-state. In this experiment, EMG signals were acquired when the subject's wrist performed isometric contractions. Therefore, the EMG signal was non-stationary and had a significant effect on CA. This indicated that the robustness of ultrasound was better than EMG signals. Recently, Kim et al. used EMG signals to simultaneously estimate joint positions and torque. The decoding method achieved good performance in kinetic (i.e., joint torque) and kinematic (i.e., joint angle) estimation [2]. The experimental results showed that EMG signals performed better in estimating joint torque than in estimating joint angles. Huang et al. demonstrated that the accuracy of ultrasound estimation of finger movements has greater advantages than EMG [14]. The findings in these studies were consistent with that of our current study.

Each type of signal source has its pros and cons. The EMG signals outperformed the ultrasound in estimating torque while the ultrasound performed better than the EMG in identifying angular position. Although the angle estimation was to classify 13 different angular positions, the discrete angle classification was equivalent to continuous angle estimation if the angle interval was reduced to infinitesimal. Therefore, a high CA was the basis for high continuous movement estimation. In the future, We can combine the advantages of the EMG and ultrasound signals to simultaneously estimate positions and torque of the wrist joint.

The SI and MAS were calculated to quantify the feature space of these signals. The ultrasound attained higher SI when compared to EMG. The potential explanation for this phenomenon was that the cross-sectional image change of the muscle during the isometric contraction was slight. Therefore, the SI of the ultrasound was relatively high. However, the isometric contraction of the muscle induced huge variance of the EMG, which led to a low SI of the EMG signal. The MSA of ultrasound and EMG had no significant difference. However, this was not reflected in the CA of the joint angular position. This indicated that EMG and Ultrasound have similar intra-class distances in the feature space.

This study had several limitations. Firstly, the experimental setup was not a continuous joint angular movement. In the future, we will improve our experimental setup, such as designing a torque measurement platform with impedance control, which can simultaneously measure the continuous angular movement and continuous torque of the wrist joint. Secondly, the current study was an offline analysis. We will conduct experiments during real-time environmental interaction with the robotic arm in future work. Finally, since the current study only employed the classic decoding algorithms to directly demonstrate the performance of signal sources, we will investigate more sophisticated algorithms to further compare the estimation performance.

5 Conclusion

In this study, we compared EMG and ultrasound for estimating positions and torque of the wrist joint. EMG signals were demonstrated with stronger correlation with joint torque, while ultrasound could better solve the estimation of joint angle. The average r values of the EMG estimated torque achieved 0.95. The CA of ultrasound for angular position classification achieved 91.05 %. The result demonstrated the advantage of EMG and ultrasound to estimate joint positions or torque.

Acknowledgments. The authors thank all participants who took part in the study. This work was supported in part by National Natural Science Foundation of China (Grant No. 52005364, 52122501). This work was also supported by the Key Laboratory of Mechanism Theory and Equipment Design of Ministry of Education (Tianjin University).

References

1. Zhu, M., et al.: Haptic-feedback smart glove as a creative human-machine interface (HMI) for virtual/augmented reality applications. SCI ADV **6**(19), eaaz8693 (2020)
2. Kim, D., et al.: EMG-based simultaneous estimations of joint angle and torque during hand interactions with environments. IEEE Trans. Biomed. Eng. (2021)
3. Dong, S., et al.: Predicting EMG with generalized Volterra kernel model. In: 2008 30th Annual International Conference of the IEEE Engineering in Medicine and Biology Society (2008)
4. Saridis, G.N., Gootee, T.P.: EMG pattern analysis and classification for a prosthetic arm. IEEE Trans. Biomed. Eng. **6**, 403–412 (1982)
5. Ravindra, V., Castellini, C.: A comparative analysis of three non-invasive human-machine interfaces for the disabled. Front. Neurorobot. **8**, 24 (2014)
6. Li, K., Zhang, J., Wang, L., Zhang, M., Li, J., Bao, S.: A review of the key technologies for sEMG-based human-robot interaction systems. Biomed. Signal Process. Control **62**, 102074 (2020)
7. Too, J., Abdullah, A., Zawawi, T.T., Saad, N.M., Musa, H.: Classification of EMG signal based on time domain and frequency domain features. Int. J. Human Technol. Interact. (IJHaTI) **1**(1), 25–30 (2017)

8. Smith, L.H., Kuiken, T.A., Hargrove, L.J.: Evaluation of linear regression simultaneous myoelectric control using intramuscular EMG. IEEE Trans. Biomed. Eng. **63**(4), 737–746 (2016)
9. Hahne, J.M., et al.: Linear and nonlinear regression techniques for simultaneous and proportional myoelectric control. IEEE Trans. Neural Syst. Rehabil. Eng. **22**(2), 269–279 (2014)
10. Chen, C., Yu, Y., Sheng, X., Farina, D., Zhu, X.: Simultaneous and proportional control of wrist and hand movements by decoding motor unit discharges in real time. J. Neural Eng. **18**(5), 056010 (11pp) (2021)
11. Rao, S., Carloni, R., Stramigioli, S.: Stiffness and position control of a prosthetic wrist by means of an emg interface. In: 2010 Annual International Conference of the IEEE Engineering in Medicine and Biology, pp. 495–498. IEEE (2010)
12. Li, G., Schultz, A.E., Kuiken, T.A.: Quantifying pattern recognition-based myoelectric control of multifunctional transradial prostheses. IEEE Trans. Neural Syst. Rehabil. Eng. **18**(2), 185–192 (2010)
13. Yang, X., Yan, J., Fang, Y., Zhou, D., Liu, H.: Simultaneous prediction of wrist/hand motion via wearable ultrasound sensing. IEEE Trans. Neural Syst. Rehabil. Eng. **28**(4), 970–977 (2020)
14. Huang, Y., Yang, X., Li, Y., Zhou, D., He, K., Liu, H.: Ultrasound-based sensing models for finger motion classification. IEEE J. Biomed. Health Inform. **22**(5), 1395–1405 (2017)
15. Li, J., Zhu, K., Pan, L.: Wrist and finger motion recognition via m-mode ultrasound signal: a feasibility study. Biomed. Signal Process. Control **71**(19), 103112 (2022)
16. Pan, L., Ding, Z., Li, J.: Comparing EMG continuous movement decoding with joints unconstrained and constrained. IEEE Robot. Autom. Lett. **7**(4), 9613–9619 (2022)
17. Pan, L., Liu, K., Li, J.: Effect of subcutaneous muscle displacement of flexor carpi radialis on surface electromyography. IEEE Trans. Neural Syst. Rehabil. Eng. **30**, 1244–1251 (2022)
18. Xiong, C., Liu, H., Huang, Y., Xiong, Y.: Intelligent robotics and applications. Lecture Notes in Computer Science 5315 (2008)
19. Castellini, C., Passig, G., Zarka, E.: Using ultrasound images of the forearm to predict finger positions. IEEE Trans. Neural Syst. Rehabil. Eng. **20**(6), 788–797 (2012)
20. Zhang, X., Wang, D., Yu, Z., Chen, X., Li, S., Zhou, P.: EMG-torque relation in chronic stroke: a novel EMG complexity representation with a linear electrode array. IEEE J. Biomed. Health Inform. **21**(6), 1562–1572 (2017)
21. Bhadane, M., Liu, J., Rymer, W.Z., Zhou, P., Li, S.: Re-evaluation of EMG-torque relation in chronic stroke using linear electrode array EMG recordings. Sci. Rep. **6**(1), 28957 (2016)
22. Pan, L., Zhang, D., Liu, J., Sheng, X., Zhu, X.: Continuous estimation of finger joint angles under different static wrist motions from surface EMG signals. Biomed. Signal Process. Control **14**, 265–271 (2014)

An Efficient Robot Payload Identification Method Based on Decomposed Motion Experimental Approach

Che Hou[1,2,3], Jianda Han[3], Wenjie Chen[1,2(✉)], Lin Yang[1,2], Xiaoqiang Chen[1,2], and Yanhao He[1,2]

[1] Blue-Orange Lab, Midea Group, Foshan 528300, China
chenwj42@midea.com
[2] Midea Corporate Research Center, Foshan 528300, China
[3] College of Artificial Intelligence, Nankai University, Tianjin 300350, China

Abstract. For most industrial/collaborative robot applications of model-based control, an accurate dynamic model is crucial to achieve good performance of the controller. Depending on the needs of different tasks, robots are often equipped with a variety of end effectors with various dynamic parameters (mass, center of mass and inertia), which could make the overall dynamics of the robot uncertain. This paper aims to identify the dynamic parameters of robot payload in its application by developing a new method with a 4-step motion, where only one joint needs to move in each step. Thanks to this particular motion with single joint, the robot dynamics can be decoupled and only the data of three joints which near the end-effector need to be collected. For each motion step, the adoption of a simplified dynamic model with fewer payload parameters is facilitated by the design of a special initial position and trajectory for a single joint, so that the impact of parameter on the accuracy of identification is significantly reduced compared with existing methods where multiple parameters are excited at the same time. Furthermore, a solving method of payload parameters based on the least squares method. The experimental results with a 6R industrial robot show the effectiveness of the proposed method for identifying different kinds of unknown payloads.

Keywords: dynamic parameters identification · payload identification of robot · parameter estimation

1 Introduction

Model-based control is widely used to improve control accuracy and robustness. In practice, the performance of these control methods often depends on the accuracy of the model.

In the field of robotics research, the control methods based on robot dynamics are often used in applications such as robot-human interaction and robot performance improvement. For example, researchers need accurate dynamic models to design observers to observe the unexpected contact forces of robots in motion, and then design

H. Yang et al. (Eds.): ICIRA 2023, LNAI 14271, pp. 269–279, 2023.
https://doi.org/10.1007/978-981-99-6495-6_23

impedance control methods to achieve flexible contact based on robot dynamic models. All of these require an accurate dynamic model.

In practical applications, one robot may be equipped with a variety of end effectors with different weight, center of mass, and inertia for different tasks, and it is difficult for users to measure all these payload parameters which leads to model uncertainty. Therefore, in order to guarantee the accuracy of the whole robot dynamics model, a fast way to obtain the dynamic parameters of random loads is demanded.

For an arbitrary end-effector, the dynamic parameters of interest are the mass, centroid position and inertia parameters. Although one could obtain the results from CAD data with sufficient accuracy, it is usually difficult for end users to access the accurate CAD model.

Alternatively, these parameters could be directly measured with specific instruments, such as mass scales for measuring the mass and center of mass of the end-effector, and air float tables for the inertia, etc. However, the availability of the corresponding measuring devices for the parts of different sizes is often problematic, and it is impractical to prepare them on site in the real application scenario.

Dynamic parameter identification is considered to be the more convenient and effective method to help users quickly obtain the parameters through experiments on site. At present, many robot dynamics identification methods have been proposed whose main idea is to obtain the joint sensor data including joint position and torque in the process of motion experiment. The main steps of dynamic parameter identification include: firstly, the calculation model of parameters is obtained based on dynamic model, including parameter linearization and QR decomposition to obtain the minimum set of parameters. The second step is usually to design the excitation trajectory to make the results more accurate and robust. Finally, with the collected experimental data, many solution methods are used to calculate the dynamic parameters, including least square method [1, 2], Kalman filtering method [3–5] and maximum-likelihood method [6, 7].

Most of the existing researches on robot dynamics parameter identification solve the parameters through the complete robot dynamics model and therefore the experimental data of all the robot joints are required. For a 6R manipulator, there are more than 70 dynamic parameters. Although these methods can theoretically obtain all the parameters through only one experiment, coupled model and insufficient motion excitation could lead to convergence and accuracy problems in reality [8].

Many other payload identification methods are based on the idea of using the whole robot dynamic model and the data of all joint positions and torques to solve the load parameters [9–12]. But there are far fewer (only no more than 13) payload dynamic parameters than the robot dynamic parameters to be calculated, and it is actually unnecessary to use the whole dynamic model and all the joint information to solve the payload parameters. Proper simplification treatments can be adopted to improve convergence performance and accuracy. For example, under the excitation of the motion trajectory, the mass of robot payload may induce torques in all joints, but the torque effect on some joints can be much smaller than the others. In this case, inputting all joint torques into the calculation model may amplify the influence of measurement noise on the results.

To solve the above issues, this paper presents an idea of using single joint excitation trajectories to reduce the coupling of dynamic parameters, and using a part of the dynamic model to calculate the payload parameters in order to reduce the number of noise channels and the impact of parameter coupling on the results. The experimental process of payload identification based on this idea is designed, and a novel method is proposed based on part of the robot dynamics model which only three joints' data of position and torque are used in the payload identification.

2 Preliminaries

Through the Newton Euler method, a robot dynamics model with n degrees of freedom (DoF) without payload is obtained as

$$M(q)\ddot{q} + C(q, \dot{q})\dot{q} + G(q) = \tau \tag{1}$$

$q \in \mathbb{R}^n$ is the vector of joint position, which can be collected by the encoders, and $\tau \in \mathbb{R}^n$ is the vector of joint torque, which can be calculated by motor current or obtained directly by the torque sensors for some cobots like KUKA iiwa and Franka Emika. $M(q) \in \mathbb{R}^{n \times n}$ represents the inertia term, $C(q, \dot{q})\dot{q} \in \mathbb{R}^n$ represents the Coriolis and centrifugal term, and $G(q) \in \mathbb{R}^n$ is the gravity term.

The vector of robot dynamic parameters with n links is expressed as

$$P = \begin{pmatrix} p_1 \, p_2 \cdots p_n \end{pmatrix}^{\mathrm{T}}, \tag{2}$$

$$\begin{aligned} p_i &= \begin{pmatrix} m_i & r_i & I_i \end{pmatrix}^{\mathrm{T}}, i = 1, \ldots, n, \\ {}^i r_{\mathrm{c}} &= \begin{pmatrix} r_{x,i} & r_{y,i} & r_{z,i} \end{pmatrix}^{\mathrm{T}}, \\ {}^i I_{\mathrm{c}} &= \begin{pmatrix} I_{xx,i} & I_{yy,i} & I_{zz,i} & I_{xy,i} & I_{xz,i} & I_{yz,i} \end{pmatrix}, \end{aligned} \tag{3}$$

here, ${}^i r_{\mathrm{c}}$ and ${}^i I_{\mathrm{c}}$ are respectively the position of the center of mass (CoM) with respect to the i-th link frame and the symmetric inertia tensor relative to the CoM of link i.

The dynamic model (1) can be transformed into the parameterized form of P, as [11]

$$Y(q, \dot{q}, \ddot{q})\pi(P) = \tau \tag{4}$$

The vector $\pi \in \mathbb{R}^p$ of dynamic coefficients appears linearly in the dynamic model (2), multiplied by the regressor matrix $Y \in \mathbb{R}^{n \times p}$ of known time-varying functions. Moreover, it can be easily shown that only linear combinations of the dynamic parameters in (2) will appear in the dynamic coefficients π.

Consider the dynamic model with payload as following [12]:

$$Y_{\mathrm{L}}(q, \dot{q}, \ddot{q})\pi(P, P_{\mathrm{L}}) = \tau_{\mathrm{total}}, \tag{5}$$

$$\tau_{\mathrm{total}} = \tau + \tau_{\mathrm{L}} \tag{6}$$

The vector of total torque with payload $\tau_{\mathrm{total}} \in \mathbb{R}^n$ is composed by τ and $\tau_{\mathrm{L}} \in \mathbb{R}^n$ which is only contributed by payload. τ and τ_{L} can be obtained with and without a payload in the experiment. Since it can also be computed by the accurate dynamics model (4), so that there is no need to perform experiments without the payload.

The vector P_L is a set of payload dynamic parameters, which is composed by mass m_L, CoM with respect to flange frame $r_L \in \mathbb{R}^3$, and the symmetric inertia tensor relative to the CoM of payload $I_L \in \mathbb{R}^3$, expressed as

$$P_L = \left(m_L \; r_L \; I_L \right)^T,$$
$$r_L = \left(x_c \; y_c \; z_c \right), I_L = \left(I_{xx} \; I_{yy} \; I_{zz} \right)^T$$

Here, for simplicity, only the principal inertial parameters are considered in the vector of I_L.

Let the symbolic difference vector be expressed as

$$\varepsilon(P_L) = \pi(P, P_L) - \pi(P_L) \tag{7}$$

With Eq. (6), we can rewrite the dynamic model (5) as

$$Y_L \pi(P) + Y_L \varepsilon(P_L) = \tau_{total} \tag{8}$$

where Y_L is the same regressor matrix with Y, evaluated under the action of the torque τ_{total} and in the presence of the payload. In the identification of P_L, Y_L should be kept with full rank by methods of [12]. Equation (8) reveals a superposition property when adding a payload, given the linearity in the dynamic coefficients, and with Eq. (6) it can be re-arranged as

$$Y_L \varepsilon(P_L) = \tau_L \tag{9}$$

In the experiment of payload identification, by stacking Eq. (9) with k sampling points of q and τ_{total} from the motion of experiment, one can obtain

$$\underbrace{\begin{pmatrix} {}^{(1)}Y_L({}^{(1)}q, {}^{(1)}\dot{q}, {}^{(1)}\ddot{q}) \\ {}^{(2)}Y_L({}^{(2)}q, {}^{(2)}\dot{q}, {}^{(2)}\ddot{q}) \\ \vdots \\ {}^{(k)}Y_L({}^{(k)}q, {}^{(k)}\dot{q}, {}^{(k)}\ddot{q}) \end{pmatrix}}_{\overline{Y}_L} \pi(P) + \underbrace{\begin{pmatrix} {}^{(1)}Y_L({}^{(1)}q, {}^{(1)}\dot{q}, {}^{(1)}\ddot{q}) \\ {}^{(2)}Y_L({}^{(2)}q, {}^{(2)}\dot{q}, {}^{(2)}\ddot{q}) \\ \vdots \\ {}^{(k)}Y_L({}^{(k)}q, {}^{(k)}\dot{q}, {}^{(k)}\ddot{q}) \end{pmatrix}}_{\overline{Y}_L} \varepsilon(P_L) = \underbrace{\begin{pmatrix} {}^{(1)}\tau_{total} \\ {}^{(2)}\tau_{total} \\ \vdots \\ {}^{(m)}\tau_{total} \end{pmatrix}}_{\overline{\tau}_{total}} \tag{10}$$

3 Payload Identification Method with Part of Dynamic Model

The estimated the value $\hat{\varepsilon}(P_L)$ can be obtained by using least square method as

$$\hat{\varepsilon}(P_L) = \overline{Y}_L^{\#} \underbrace{\left(\overline{\tau}_{total} - \overline{Y}_L \pi(P) \right)}_{\overline{\tau}_L} \tag{11}$$

The unknown parameters of payload can be obtained from Eq. (11), but the problem is that it needs too many input channels to solve the unknown parameter of payload. For 6R industrial robots, 12 input channels are required which are composed by $q \in \mathbb{R}^6$

and $\tau_L \in \mathbb{R}^6$. If 2000 points are collected in each channel, there are 24,000 sets of input data which may lead to an ill-conditioned matrix $\overline{Y}_L$ when the excitation motion is insufficient. The accuracy of the results may be affected by noise.

In order to solve the problems of payload identification, the dynamic model must be simplified and the input channels should be reduced. In this chapter, the method using the data collected from only three joints to identify the payload parameters by decoupling the dynamic model in special motion will be shown. 4 steps of motion are designed in the identification, with each step moving only one joint with the specified initial position of robot. In order to make the data more reliable, the sensor data of the joints as close as possible to the load are collected.

For simplicity without loss of generality, a 6R robot is used for the discussion in this section. To be specific, an ER10 robot as shown in Fig. 1 is used with the position of [0 0 90 0 −90 0](°). Define the initial position as [0 0 90 0 0 0](°) in order to ensure the y axis in the flange coordinate frame and the z axis in the coordinate frame of Joint 5 are parallel to the ground.

Step 1: Let the robot start from the initial position and Joint 5 perform reciprocating motion with sufficient speed and acceleration in the process of motion. During this process, the other joints do not move.

Since with Eq. (9), the parameters of links are no longer relevant, the relationship between payload parameters and joint data can be focused on. In this step, all the other joints are stationary except Joint 5. Therefore, the relationship between the motion of Joint 5 and the payload torque of Joint 5 and 6 can be expressed as

$$\underbrace{\begin{pmatrix} Y_5(q_5, \dot{q}_5, \ddot{q}_5) \\ Y_6(q_5, \dot{q}_5, \ddot{q}_5) \end{pmatrix}}_{Y_{\text{step1}}} \cdot \underbrace{\begin{pmatrix} \varepsilon_5(P_{\text{step1,5}}) \\ \varepsilon_6(P_{\text{step1,6}}) \end{pmatrix}}_{\varepsilon_{\text{step1}}} = \underbrace{\begin{pmatrix} \tau_{\text{step1,5}} \\ \tau_{\text{step1,6}} \end{pmatrix}}_{\tau_{\text{step1}}}, \tag{12}$$

where $Y_i(q_5, \dot{q}_5, \ddot{q}_5)$, $i = 5$, 6, and ε_i are the parts of Y_L and ε, respectively. The corresponding $\tau_{\text{step1},i}$ is the torque of Joint i in the motion of Step 1. And

$$P_{\text{step1,5}} = \left(m, x_c, z_c, I_{yy}\right)^T, P_{\text{step1,6}} = (mx_c y_c, my_c z_c, my_c)^T$$

are the payload parameters associated with the torque of Joint 5 and Joint 6. In this case, Y_i and $\varepsilon_i(i = 5, 6)$ can be obtained as

$$\varepsilon_5 = \begin{pmatrix} mx_c^2 + mz_c^2 + I_{yy} + md_7^2 + 2d_7 mz_c \\ mgd_7 + mz_c g \\ mx_c g \end{pmatrix}, \varepsilon_6 = \begin{pmatrix} mx_c y_c \\ my_c z_c \\ my_c \end{pmatrix} \tag{13}$$

$$Y_5(q_5, \dot{q}_5, \ddot{q}_5) = \left(\ddot{q}_5 \cos(q_5) \sin(q_5), \right)$$
$$Y_6(q_5, \dot{q}_5, \ddot{q}_5) = \left(\dot{q}_5^2 \ddot{q}_5 d_7 \ddot{q}_5 + g \cos(q_5)\right)$$

where g is the acceleration of gravity, d_7 is the distance between axis x from the coordinate frame of Joint 6 to the coordinate frame of the flange.

In the set of parameters in Step 1, only I_{yy} is involved in the calculation of the inertia parameters of the payload. Then, further motion needs to be designed to make I_{xx} and I_{zz} present in the calculation.

Step 2. In order to excite the parameter I_{zz}, the motion is designed as a repeated point-to-point motion of Joint 6 with enough speed and acceleration while other joints stay still, and the initial position is the same with Step 1.

Similar to Step 1, from the motion of Step 2, the dynamics of Joint 6 with the payload can be obtained as

$$\underbrace{Y_6(q_6, \dot{q}_6, \ddot{q}_6)}_{Y_{step2}} \cdot \underbrace{\varepsilon_6(P_{step2,6})}_{\varepsilon_{step2}} = \underbrace{\tau_{step2,6}}_{\tau_{step2}}, \tag{14}$$

where

$$\begin{aligned} Y_{step2}(q_6, \dot{q}_6, \ddot{q}_6) &= (\ddot{q}_6 \cos(q_6) \sin(q_6)), \\ \varepsilon_{step2} &= (mx_c^2 + my_c^2 + I_{zz} \ my_c g \ mx_c g)^T. \end{aligned} \tag{15}$$

It is obvious that of all the inertia parameters, only I_{zz} is present in Eq. (14) because of the special motion in this step, just as Eq. (12), where only I_{yy} is involved. The payload parameters are decoupled by Step 1 and Step 2. By this idea, it is straightforward to design the motion of Step 3 in order to solve I_{xx}.

Step 3: In order to excite the parameter of I_{xx}, the initial pose is adjusted by rotating Joint 6 by 90° so that the axis x of the flange is horizontal, and then Step 1 is repeated with only Joint 5 moving while the other joints keeping stationary. Then, the dynamic model of Joint 6 in Step 3 can be expressed as

$$\underbrace{Y_5(q_5, \dot{q}_5, \ddot{q}_5)}_{Y_{step3}} \cdot \underbrace{\varepsilon_5(P_{step3})}_{\varepsilon_{step3}} = \tau_{step3,6}, \tag{16}$$

where

$$Y_{step3}(q_5, \dot{q}_5, \ddot{q}_5) = (\ddot{q}_5 \ \dot{q}_5^2 \cos(q_5) \sin(q_5)),$$

$$\varepsilon_{step3} = \begin{pmatrix} my_c^2 + I_{xx} + (d_7 m + mz_c)(z_c + d_7) \\ my_c(z_c + d_7) - d_7 my_c - my_c z_c \\ d_7 mg + mz_c g \\ my_c g \end{pmatrix}. \tag{17}$$

Now Eq. (12), Eq. (14) and Eq. (16) are obtained, and each equation only includes the parts of robot dynamic model related to one or two joints, resulting in a simplified dynamics of the robot. In order to establish further equations to fully solve the parameter set, a Step 4 motion is designed.

Step 4: In the initial state of robot, let Joint 3 repeat the PTP motion with enough speed and acceleration and other joints remain stationary.

In Step 4, similar to Step 1 to 3, a group of new equations can be obtained as

$$\underbrace{Y_3(q_3, \dot{q}_3, \ddot{q}_3)}_{Y_{step4}} \cdot \underbrace{\varepsilon_3(P_{step4})}_{\varepsilon_{step4}} = \tau_{step4,3} \tag{18}$$

$$P_{\text{step4}} = \begin{pmatrix} I_{yy} & m & x_c & z_c \end{pmatrix}$$

$$Y_{\text{step4}} = \begin{pmatrix} \ddot{q}_3 \sin(q_3 + \tfrac{\pi}{2}) & \cos(q_3 + \tfrac{\pi}{2}) \end{pmatrix}$$

$$\varepsilon_{\text{step4}} = \begin{pmatrix} I_{yy} + mx_c^2 + mz_c^2 + (a_3^2 + d_7^2 + d_4^2 + 2d_4 d_7)m - 2a_3 mx_c + 2(d_4 + d_7)mz_c \\ (d_4 + d_7 + z_c)mg \\ (a_3 + x_c)mg \end{pmatrix} \tag{19}$$

where a_i, d_i are the D-H parameters of the i-th link except $i = 7$ which is one of the D-H parameter in the flange coordinate frame.

4 Parameter Calculation

For each step, similar to the calculation process (11), the payload parameters of linear combination by stacking $\overline{Y}_{\text{step}i}$ and $\overline{\tau}_{\text{step}i}$ using the collected data of Step i can be obtained as

$$\overline{Y}_{\text{step}i} \cdot \varepsilon_{\text{step}i} = \overline{\tau}_{\text{step}i}, i = 1, \ldots, 4 \tag{20}$$

Then, the results of linear combination of payload parameters for each step is calculated with

$$\hat{\varepsilon}_{\text{step}i} = \overline{Y}_{\text{step}i}^{\#} \overline{\tau}_{\text{step}i} \tag{21}$$

Here, $\hat{\varepsilon}_{\text{step}i}$ expresses the estimated value of $\varepsilon_{\text{step}i}$, $i = 1, \ldots, 4$.

Furthermore, with the estimated value of $\varepsilon_{\text{step}i}$, the payload parameters can be obtained by Eq. (13), (15), (17) and Eq. (19) as

$$\begin{cases} \hat{\varepsilon}_{\text{step1}}^{(1)} = \varepsilon_{\text{step1}}^{(1)}(I_{yy} + mx_c^2 + mz_c^2, mz_c, m) \\ \hat{\varepsilon}_{\text{step1}}^{(2)} = \varepsilon_{\text{step1}}^{(2)}(m, mz_c) \\ \hat{\varepsilon}_{\text{step1}}^{(3)} = \varepsilon_{\text{step1}}^{(3)}(mx_c) \\ \hat{\varepsilon}_{\text{step4}}^{(1)} = \varepsilon_{\text{step4}}^{(1)}(I_{yy} + mx_c^2 + mz_c^2, mx_c, mz_c) , \\ \hat{\varepsilon}_{\text{step1}}^{(6)} = \varepsilon_{\text{step1}}^{(6)}(my_c) \\ \hat{\varepsilon}_{\text{step2}}^{(1)} = \varepsilon_{\text{step2}}^{(1)}(I_{zz}, my_c^2, mz_c^2) \\ \hat{\varepsilon}_{\text{step3}}^{(1)} = \varepsilon_{\text{step3}}^{(1)}(I_{xx} + my_c^2 + mx_c^2, mz_c) \end{cases} \tag{22}$$

where $\varepsilon_{\text{step}i}^{(j)}$ is the j-th element of vector $\varepsilon_{\text{step}i}$, $i = 1, \ldots, 4$.

At this point, all the dynamic parameters of payload can be obtained by solving Eq. (22). In the whole calculation process from Eq. (12) to Eq. (22), only the data of less than three joints need to be collected, which is a significant simplification of the dynamic model. A case study of the process and the results of calculation will be shown in detail by using an ER10 robot in the next chapter.

5 Experiments

The Effort ER 10 industrial robot is used in the experiments. The joint torque can be calculated based on the motor current. Figure 1 shows the robot with the initial joint angles [0 0 90 0 0 0], together with the link frames. The D-H parameters are shown in Table 1.

Table 1. D-H Parameters of ER 10 Robot

i	$\alpha(i-1)$	$a(i-1)$	$d(i)$	$\theta(i)$
1	0	0	422	0
2	90	195	0	0
3	0	680	0	90
4	90	175	744.5	0
5	−90	0	0	0
6	90	0	0	0
flange	0	0	117.5	180

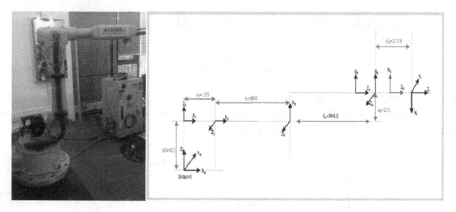

Fig. 1. ER 10 robot and its coordinate system definition

The payload used in the experiment is shown in Fig. 2. Some additional payloads can be installed on the main payload to simulate various uncertain parameters of the payload in practice. The physical parameters of the payloads are accurately measured before experiments. The nominal values of the dynamic parameters of the main payload are

$$m_L = 5.25\text{kg}, r_L = \begin{pmatrix} 0 & 0 & 138 \end{pmatrix}\text{mm},$$
$$I_L = \begin{pmatrix} 6.8317\text{e}^{-3} & 1.2532\text{e}^{-3} & 6.0329\text{e}^{-3} \end{pmatrix}\text{kg} \cdot \text{m}^2$$

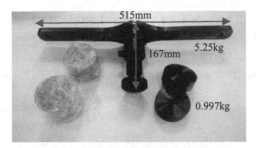

Fig. 2. Payload structure with detachable mass module used in the identification experiment

Within each step, the moving joint repeats the motion via a Point-To-Point (PTP) command, sweeping with the max velocities and accelerations of ± 70 deg/s and ± 150 deg/s2, respectively. Each trajectory lasts for 10 s and is performed with and without the payload. Joint positions and torques are recorded by the robot controller with the EtherCAT cycle time of 1ms, and filtered off-line using a low-pass zero phase shifting filter with a cutoff frequency of 50 Hz in MATLAB. Joint velocities and accelerations are obtained by numerical differentiation from the filtered positions. Finally, 10000 samples are collected in each step of identification.

First, the main payload without any additional load blocks is installed. With the step 1 to 4 and the process from Eq. (12) to Eq. (22), the equations to solve the payload parameters are established as

$$
\begin{cases}
I_{yy} + mx_c^2 + mz_c^2 + 0.235mz_c + 0.01380625m = \hat{\varepsilon}_{\text{step1}}^{(1)} \\
0.1175mg + mz_c g = \hat{\varepsilon}_{\text{step1}}^{(2)} \\
mx_c = \hat{\varepsilon}_{\text{step1}}^{(3)} \\
I_{yy} + mx_c^2 + mz_c^2 - 0.35mx_c + 1.724mz_c + 0.773669m = \hat{\varepsilon}_{\text{step4}}^{(1)} , \\
my_c = \hat{\varepsilon}_{\text{step1}}^{(6)} \\
I_{zz} + my_c^2 + mx_c^2 = \hat{\varepsilon}_{\text{step2}}^{(1)} \\
my_c^2 + I_{xx} + (0.1175m + mz_c)(z_c + 0.1175) = \hat{\varepsilon}_{\text{step3}}^{(1)}
\end{cases}
\tag{23}
$$

where

$$
\left(\hat{\varepsilon}_{\text{step1}}^{(1)} \quad \hat{\varepsilon}_{\text{step1}}^{(2)} \quad \hat{\varepsilon}_{\text{step1}}^{(3)} \quad \hat{\varepsilon}_{\text{step4}}^{(1)} \quad \hat{\varepsilon}_{\text{step1}}^{(6)} \quad \hat{\varepsilon}_{\text{step2}}^{(1)} \quad \hat{\varepsilon}_{\text{step3}}^{(1)} \right)^{T} =
\begin{pmatrix}
0.3558 \\
13.4934 \\
0.1101 \\
5.5286 \\
0.0075 \\
0.0063 \\
0.3621
\end{pmatrix}
\tag{24}
$$

The results are shown in Table 2 which are reasonably accurate compared with the nominal values. The remaining errors are attributed to the simplification of the inertial parameters because only the parameters of principal inertia tensor are concerned in this paper, and noise in both the joint torque and acceleration measurement is another non-negligible factor.

Table 2. Results of Identification With The Main Payload

Payload parameters	Nominal value	Estimated value
m(kg)	5.25	5.342
x_c(mm)	0	2.1
y_c(mm)	0	1.4
z_c(mm)	138.0	140.1
I_{xx}(kg·m^2)	$6.8317e^{-2}$	$7.8406e^{-2}$
I_{yy}(kg·m^2)	$1.2532e^{-2}$	$1.6247e^{-2}$
I_{zz}(kg·m^2)	$6.0329e^{-2}$	$6.4434e^{-2}$

Then, the payload is changed by installing some extra weights on the main pay-load, and the center of mass is offset in this case. The experiments of payload identification are repeated, and Table 3 shows the results compared with nominal values. As reported in Table 3, even with this added uncertainty, the mass and the position of the center of mass are estimated with high precision.

Table 3. Results of Identification With an Asymmetric Payload

Payload parameters	Nominal value	Estimated value
m(kg)	7.42	7.13
x_c(mm)	61.4	59.5
y_c(mm)	0	2.4
z_c(mm)	156.2	152.3
I_{xx}	$1.9806e^{-2}$	$2.2806e^{-2}$
I_{yy}	$15.4617e^{-2}$	$15.7898e^{-2}$
I_{zz}	$14.0100\,e^{-2}$	$13.9972\,e^{-2}$

6   Conclusions

This paper focuses on the problem of identifying the dynamic parameters of an unknown payload held by the robot end effector, and proposes a method that relies on 4 steps of experiments where only the motion with a single joint is required for each step. The changes of dynamics that occur in the specified robot initial position and motion for each step have been exploited, so that the decoupling of parameters in dynamics is realized. To simplify the calculation, a simplified dynamics model involving fewer data of joints near the end effector is used. The result produced by the proposed method is accurate enough when handling different payloads according to experiments.

References

1. Khalil, W., Gautier, M., Lemoine, P.: Identification of the payload inertial parameters of industrial manipulators. In: Proceedings of the 2007 IEEE International Conference on Robotics and Automation, Roma, Italy, pp. 4943–4948, April 2007
2. Jiang, J., Zhang, Y.: A revisit to block and recursive least squares for parameter estimation. Comput. Electr. Eng. **30**(5), 403–416 (2004)
3. Hu, J., Xiong, R.: Contact force estimation for robot manipulator using semiparametric model and disturbance Kalman filter. IEEE Trans. Ind. Electron. **65**(4), 3365–3375 (2017)
4. Jung, J., Lee, J., Huh, K.: Robust contact force estimation for robot manipulators in three-dimensional space. Proc. Inst. Mech. Eng. Part C J. Mech. Eng. Sci. **220**(9), 1317–1327 (2006)
5. Rigatos, G.G.: Derivative-free nonlinear Kalman filtering for MIMO dynamical systems: application to multi-DOF robotic manipulators. Int. J. Adv. Robot. Syst. **8**(6), 72 (2011)
6. Olsen, M.M., Swevers, J., Verdonck, W.: Maximum likelihood identification of a dynamic robot model: imple mentation issues. Ae Int. J. Robot. Res. **21**(2), 89–96 (2002)
7. Swevers, J., Ganseman, C., Tukel, D.B., De Schutter, J., Van Brussel, H.: Optimal robot excitation and identification. IEEE Trans. Robot. Autom. **13**(5), 730–740 (1997)
8. Duan, J., Liu, Z., Bin, Y., Cui, K., Dai, Z.: Payload identification and gravity/inertial compensation for six-dimensional force/torque sensor with a fast and robust trajectory design approach. Sensors **22**, 439 (2022)
9. Dong, Y., et al.: An efficient robot payload identification method for industrial application. Ind. Robot. **45**, 505–515 (2018)
10. Swevers, J., Verdonck, W., Naumer, B., Pieters, S., Biber, E.: An Experimental robot load identification method for industrial application. Int. J. Robot. Res. **21**(8), 701–712 (2002)
11. Gaz, C., Flacco, F., De Luca, A.: Identifying the dynamic model used by the KUKA LWR: a reverse engineering approach. In: Proceedings of the IEEE International Conference on Robotics and Automation, pp. 1386–1392 (2014)
12. Gaz, C., Luca, A.D.: Payload estimation based on identified coefficients of robot dynamics — with an application to collision detection. In: IEEE/RSJ International Conference on Intelligent Robots & Systems, pp. 3033–3040. IEEE (2017)

A Force Exertion Method for Redundant Mobile Manipulators Safely Operating in Small Spaces

Guanyi Zhao[1], Yuqiang Wu[2,3,4], Che Hou[2,3,4], Wenjie Chen[2,3,4(✉)], and Chenguang Yang[1(✉)]

[1] School of Automation Science and Engineering, South China University of Technology, Guangdong, China
cyang@ieee.org
[2] Midea Corporate Research Center, Foshan 528300, China
[3] Midea Corporate Research Center, Shanghai 201702, China
[4] Blue-Orange Lab, Midea Group, Foshan 528300, China
chenwj42@midea.com

Abstract. Mobile manipulator is increasingly expected to undertake tasks in intelligent automated factories. However, when facing resistance tasks in small spaces, it is a challenge to ensure the safety of target objects and robots without using high-precision positioning sensors. To address this issue, we propose a force exertion method for redundant mobile manipulators. To improve force exertion capability, the force manipulability ellipsoid of the mobile manipulator is optimized by exploiting its redundancy under a whole-body controller. Furthermore, a hybrid force-impedance control strategy is developed to guarantee safe operation in compact-space resistance tasks. The proposed method is validated by performing a turn-on-switch experiment.

Keywords: Redundant Mobile Manipulator · Hybrid Force-impedance Control · Force Manipulability Optimization

1 Introduction

Mobile manipulator with both mobility and handling capabilities is increasingly popular with the rapid development and growth of intelligent factories. They are used in a variety of applications, such as machine operation, assembly, sorting, and inspection [9,12]. A mobile manipulator is generally a redundant robotic system with more than 6 Degrees of Freedom (DoF), which creates more possibilities for task optimization. For example, paper [7] applied multi-objective optimization and constrained optimization methods to achieve obstacle avoidance for the

This work was supported in part by National Nature Science Foundation of China (NSFC) under Grant U20A20200 and Major Research Grant No. 92148204, in part by Guangdong Basic and Applied Basic Research Foundation under Grant 2020B1515120054, in part by Industrial Key Technologies R & D Program of Foshan under Grant 2020001006308 and Grant 2020001006496.

H. Yang et al. (Eds.): ICIRA 2023, LNAI 14271, pp. 280–290, 2023.
https://doi.org/10.1007/978-981-99-6495-6_24

mobile manipulator, paper [1] optimized the manipulability of mobile manipulators, and research [10] enhanced the force exertion capability but without taking the obstacle avoidance into account. By exploiting the redundancy, it is possible to customize different optimization objectives for specific tasks.

In the procedure of industrial manufacture, the mobile manipulator may inevitably need to undertake some resistance tasks such as operating mechanical switches, assembling nails, etc. [5], which are operated in quite small task spaces. Therefore, locating the task space is critical to the safety of objects and robots. There are some researches devoted to developing more accurate sensors and positioning algorithms based on high precision cameras [3]. However, these kinds of sensors are difficult to be obtained widely because of their high cost. On the other hand, directly applying position or force control may cause damage to both environment and robot if there is a large positioning error.

Impedance control and force control establish a relationship between force and position and shows superior performance in terms of sensitive force and compliance with unknown contact environments [6]. Many studies have demonstrated that the application of compliance or force control can help execute tasks in a much safer way [8]. For example, paper [11] completed the socket plugging task with impedance control, and an impedance policy learning method for the peg-in-hole task was given in [4].

For resistance tasks where task space is very small and cannot be precisely located, a force exertion method is proposed in this work, which mainly contains two parts: 1) An optimization solution to enhance force exertion capability while under collision avoidance constraints is designed for redundant mobile manipulators; 2) An exploration method based on hybrid force-impedance control to approach the task space is proposed. With the proposed approach, resistance tasks in small spaces like switch flipping, can be safely operated.

The remainder of this paper is organized as follows. Section 2 establishes the kinematic model of a mobile manipulator. In Sect. 3, a whole-body controller with force ellipsoid optimization is presented. Section 4 elaborates the flow of the impedance control-based force exertion method. Section 5 verifies the method through an air-switch-flipping experiment. Section 6 concludes this work.

2   Kinematic Modeling of Mobile Manipulator

As shown in Fig. 2, the mobile manipulator is composed of two parts: a velocity-controlled differential wheeled mobile chassis and a 6-DoF position-controlled manipulator. $\{w\},\{m\},\{b\}$, and $\{ee\}$ represent the world reference frame, mobile base frame, manipulator base frame, and end-effector frame, respectively. Since the velocity command can be converted to a position command easily, we choose velocity as the control input of this whole-body system.

For the manipulator, the relation between the Cartesian velocity of the end-effector w.r.t $\{b\}$ and the manipulator joint velocity is:

$$^b V_{ee} = \begin{bmatrix} ^b v_{ee} \\ ^b \omega_{ee} \end{bmatrix} = {}^b J_r \dot{q}_r \tag{1}$$

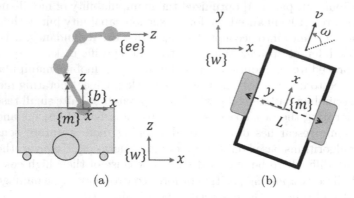

Fig. 1. Kinematic model of the mobile manipulator. (a)The whole-body model; (b)The model of the differential wheeled mobile chassis.

where $^b v_{ee} \in \mathbb{R}^3$ represents the linear velocity and $^b \omega_{ee} \in \mathbb{R}^3$ represents the angular velocity. $^b J_r \in \mathbb{R}^{6 \times 6}$ is the geometric Jacobian matrix of the manipulator w.r.t $\{b\}$. $\dot{q}_r \in \mathbb{R}^6 = [\dot{q}_1, \dot{q}_2, ..., \dot{q}_6]^T$ represents the joint velocities. Describing the end-effector velocity in task space (frame $\{w\}$) is expressed as:

$$V_{ee} = \begin{bmatrix} v_{ee} \\ \omega_{ee} \end{bmatrix} = \begin{bmatrix} ^w R_b & 0 \\ 0 & ^w R_b \end{bmatrix} \begin{bmatrix} ^b v_{ee} \\ ^b \omega_{ee} \end{bmatrix} = \begin{bmatrix} ^w R_b & 0 \\ 0 & ^w R_b \end{bmatrix} {}^b J_r \dot{q}_r = J_r \dot{q}_r \qquad (2)$$

where

$$J_r = \begin{bmatrix} ^w R_b & 0 \\ 0 & ^w R_b \end{bmatrix} {}^b J_r \qquad (3)$$

represents the manipulator Jacobian w.r.t $\{b\}$. $^w R_b = {}^w R_m {}^m R_b \in \mathbb{R}^{3 \times 3}$ is the rotation matrix from $\{b\}$ to $\{w\}$.

The differential mobile chassis can be regarded as a 2-DoF robot generally, whose motion can be described by the linear velocity of the center of the mobile chassis v and yaw angular velocity w, which relates to the speed of the wheels as follows:

$$\begin{bmatrix} v \\ \omega \end{bmatrix} = \begin{bmatrix} \frac{1}{2} & \frac{1}{2} \\ \frac{1}{L} & -\frac{1}{L} \end{bmatrix} \begin{bmatrix} v_r \\ v_l \end{bmatrix} \qquad (4)$$

where v_r and v_l denotes the speeds of the right wheel and the left wheel, respectively. L is the distance between the two wheels. Assuming that the manipulator is in the static state, the position vector of the manipulator base w.r.t $\{m\}$ is $^m P_b \in \mathbb{R}^3$, and the position vector of the end-effector w.r.t $\{b\}$ is $^b P_{ee} \in \mathbb{R}^3$ which can be obtained according to the manipulator forward kinematics. Then the relation between the end-effector velocity V_{ee} and the chassis motion velocity $\dot{q}_m = [v, w]^T$ is given as follows:

$$V_{ee} = J_m \dot{q}_m \qquad (5)$$

with the Jacobian of the chassis J_m defined as:

$$J_m = \begin{bmatrix} \cos(\theta) & \sin(\theta) & 0\ 0\ 0\ 0 \\ -P_{m,ee}(2) & P_{m,ee}(1) & 0\ 0\ 0\ 1 \end{bmatrix}^T \tag{6}$$

where $P_{m,ee} = {}^w R_m({}^m P_b + {}^m R_b{}^b P_{ee})$ means the vector from the origin of $\{m\}$ to the origin of $\{ee\}$ w.r.t $\{w\}$.

Therefore, the whole-body differential kinematic model of the 8-DoF mobile manipulator system can be obtained by combining Eq.(2) and Eq.(5):

$$V_{ee} = J\dot{q} = \begin{bmatrix} J_m & J_r \end{bmatrix} \begin{bmatrix} \dot{q}_m \\ \dot{q}_r \end{bmatrix} \tag{7}$$

where $J \in \mathbb{R}^{6 \times 8}$ is the whole-body Jacobian matrix. $\dot{q} = [\dot{q}_m^T, \dot{q}_r^T]^T \in \mathbb{R}^8$.

3   Whole-Body Controller

When given a desired end-effector velocity, the joint velocities of this redundant robotic system can generally be resolved using an optimization method with the cost function written as:

$$\min \frac{1}{2}(\dot{q} - \dot{q}_0)^T W(\dot{q} - \dot{q}_0) \qquad \text{s.t. } V_{ee} = J\dot{q} \tag{8}$$

where $W \in \mathbb{R}^{8 \times 8}$ is a positive definite and symmetric weighting matrix which determines the motion contribution of each joint, and $\dot{q}_0 \in \mathbb{R}^8$ is the desired joint velocity. Then the solution of $\dot{q}$ can be derived as:

$$\dot{q} = J^\dagger V_{ee} + (I - J^\dagger J)\dot{q}_0 \tag{9}$$

where $J^\dagger = W^{-1}J^T(JW^{-1}J^T)^{-1}$ is the weighted pseudo-inverse of J, $I \in \mathbb{R}^{8 \times 8}$ is an identity matrix. The first term of the Eq.(9) is relative to minimum norm joint velocities, and the second one is the homogeneous solution which attempts to satisfy the additional constraint by reflecting the specific vector $\dot{q}_0$ into null space. A typical choice of $\dot{q}_0$ is:

$$\dot{q}_0 = k_0 (\frac{\partial y(q)}{\partial q})^T, \quad k_0 > 0 \tag{10}$$

which attempts to maximize the objective function $y(q)$, and k_0 is a factor.

Torques in joint space $\tau \in \mathbb{R}^6$ and forces in task space $f \in \mathbb{R}^6$ are mapped as follows:

$$\tau = J_r^T f \tag{11}$$

Base on Eq.(11), force ellipsoid, which is a kind of index that can be used to describe the force exertion capability of the manipulator in a certain pose, is defined as [2]:

$$\tau^T\tau = f^T(J_r J_r^T)f \leq 1 \tag{12}$$

The volume of the force ellipsoid is proportional to the force capability, the principle axis of the force ellipsoid coincide with the eigenvectors of $(\boldsymbol{J}_r \boldsymbol{J}_r^T)^{-1}$, and the length of the principle axis is equal to the square root of the corresponding eigenvalue. Consider only a specific direction $\boldsymbol{u} \in \mathbb{R}^3$ and try to maximize the distance from the center to the surface of the force ellipsoid along it, so the objective function can be written as

$$y(\boldsymbol{q}) = \left[\boldsymbol{u}^T (\boldsymbol{J}_r \boldsymbol{W}_\tau^T \boldsymbol{W}_\tau \boldsymbol{J}_r^T) \boldsymbol{u}\right]^{-\frac{1}{2}} \tag{13}$$

where $\boldsymbol{W}_\tau = diag(\frac{1}{\tau_{m1}}, \frac{1}{\tau_{m2}}, ..., \frac{1}{\tau_{m6}})$ is a scaling matrix to normalize the joint torques, and τ_{m2} denotes the maximum torque of the ith joint.

Replace the weighted matrix $\boldsymbol{W}$ in Eq.(8) with $\boldsymbol{W}_c = \boldsymbol{W}^{-1}$, and $\boldsymbol{W}_c \in \mathbb{R}^{8 \times 8}$ is designed as:

$$\boldsymbol{W}_c = \begin{bmatrix} \frac{d-\varepsilon}{d-\varepsilon+1} \boldsymbol{I}_{2 \times 2} & \boldsymbol{0}_{2 \times 6} \\ \boldsymbol{0}_{6 \times 6} & \boldsymbol{I}_{6 \times 6} \end{bmatrix} \tag{14}$$

where d represents the distance between the chassis and the obstacle, and ε is a safety threshold. If the chassis is far away from the obstacle, $\frac{d-\varepsilon}{d-\varepsilon+1}$ is close to 1, indicating that the chassis can be fully involved in the motion. Conversely, when the chassis is too close to the safety line, i.e., $d - \varepsilon = 0$, it will stop to avoid a collision.

4   Force Exertion Method

In this section, a trial method based on impedance control is proposed to cope with resistance tasks with small task space. The flow chart of the method is shown in Fig. 2.

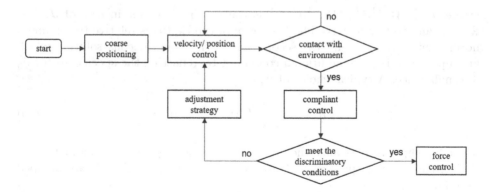

Fig. 2. The flow chart of the proposed method.

The method begins with coarse positioning of the target, and the robot approaches the target with velocity/position control mode and force ellipsoid optimization algorithm. Once being in contact with the environment, i.e. there existing a Cartesian external force $\boldsymbol{f}_{\text{ext}} \in \mathbb{R}^3$ acting on the end-effector, the robot will change into impedance control mode, generally defined as:

$$\boldsymbol{f}_{\text{ext}} = \boldsymbol{M}\ddot{\boldsymbol{e}} + \boldsymbol{B}\dot{\boldsymbol{e}} + \boldsymbol{K}\boldsymbol{e} \tag{15}$$

where $\boldsymbol{M} \in \mathbb{R}^{3\times3}$, $\boldsymbol{B} \in \mathbb{R}^{3\times3}$ and $\boldsymbol{K} \in \mathbb{R}^{3\times3}$ are the mass, damping and stiffness matrices, respectively. And $\boldsymbol{e} = \boldsymbol{x}_d - \boldsymbol{x} \in \mathbb{R}^3$ represents the error between the desired position and the actual position in Cartesian space. Compliant control can regulate the relationship between external forces and position, thus avoiding violent collisions between the end-effector of the robot and the environment. After that, some discriminatory conditions are used to distinguish the target from environmental obstacles, which are designed through pre-testing. In some cases where the target objects can be modeled as a spring, for example, the presenting stiffness of which is not the same as the surrounding fixed obstacles, which can be regarded as a discriminatory condition. Impedance-based force control is performed to complete the final resistant task when the conditions are met, which is defined as follows:

$$\boldsymbol{f}_{\text{ext}} - \boldsymbol{f}_d = \boldsymbol{M}\ddot{\boldsymbol{e}} + \boldsymbol{B}\dot{\boldsymbol{e}} + \boldsymbol{K}\boldsymbol{e} \tag{16}$$

where $\boldsymbol{f}_d \in \mathbb{R}^3$ represents the desired force required for specific tasks. Compared with position control, force control is more compliant which can increase operational safety to some extent. If the conditions are not met, the robot will take an adjustment strategy to get as close to the target as possible.

5   Experiment

The proposed method was validated through an experiment of flipping an air switch with a mobile manipulator. Air switches are widely used in factory workshops due to their role in protecting the safety of electricity. Research on this task will help to realize automatic inspection of unmanned factories and promote intelligent production. As shown in Fig. 3, the air switch has the following characteristics: a) The switching area (task space) is very near to the obstacle area with only 5 mm in width; b) The force required to turn on the switch upwards is more than 50N, which brings pressure that can not be ignored for the common manipulator, while the turn-off force is much smaller; c)The resistance gradually increases during the upward turning of the switch, reaching a maximum in the middle position and then followed by a sudden drop. Therefore, we aim to successfully push the switch upwards in this experiment while ensuring the safety of the switch and the robot.

The experimental setup is shown in Fig. 4, which consists of a controller, a mobile manipulator, and an air switch fixed on the wall. The mobile chassis is equipped with a depth camera to get the distance to the wall, and the manipulator is equipped with torque sensors. The controller communicates with the mobile manipulator through EtherCAT with a control cycle of 1 ms. In the

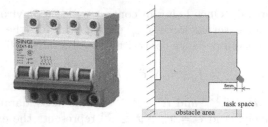

Fig. 3. The diagram of the air switch. The left one is the item photo, and the right one is its left view which is divided into two parts: obstacle areas and switch area (task space).

experiment, the end-effector of the manipulator will push the switch by moving along the Z-axis of $\{w\}$. Given an approximate location of the switch, the mobile manipulator is required to optimize the pose firstly to increase its force exertion capability, and then find the exact location via compliant control and finally turn on the switch by force control.

Fig. 4. Experiment setup of a mobile manipulator turning on air switch.

5.1 Experiment for Force Ellipsoid Optimization

In this experiment, the optimization direction is set $u = {}^{b}\boldsymbol{R}_{w}[0,0,1]^{T}$, safety distance ε is 0.05 m, and the matrix $\boldsymbol{W}_{\tau}$ equals $diag(1,1,1,2.5,2.5,2.5)$. Figure 5(a) and Fig. 5(b) show the robot postures before and after force ellipsoid optimization, and the chassis stops in front of the wall. The force ellipsoid increases during the optimization process, as shown in Fig. 5(c), and the distance between the chassis and the wall is shown in Fig. 5(d). When pushing the switch at the same speed of 5 mm/s, the corresponding experiment results of joint torques of the two postures are shown in Fig. 5(e) and Fig. 5(f), respectively. The maximum joint torques after optimization are significantly reduced than before, especially the second joint, the third joint, and the fifth joint, which means the force exertion capability and the operation safety of the manipulator are improved effectively.

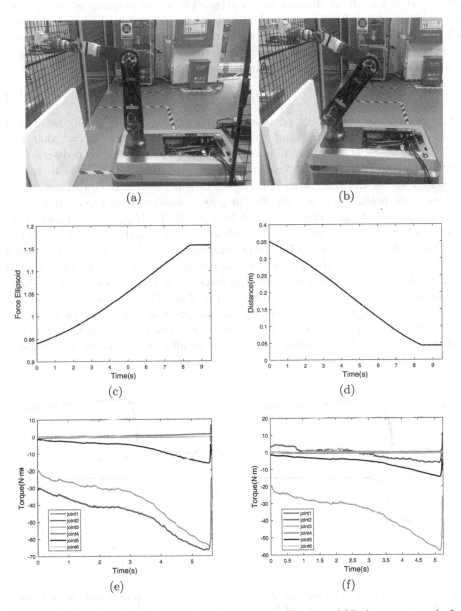

Fig. 5. Experiment results of force ellipsoid optimization. (a)Robot posture before optimization. (b)Robot posture after optimization. (c)Force ellipsoid during the optimization process. (d)The distance between the chassis and the wall. (e)Joint torques of the robot before optimization. (f)Joint torques of the robot after optimization.

5.2   Experiment for Force Exertion Method

In this experiment, we first conducted a compliant control test on the switch area and the obstacle area respectively in 1-DoF with the same parameters: $M = 1$, $B = 100$, $K = 40$, and $x_d = 0.02\,\mathrm{m}$. The corresponding external force and position along Z-axis w.r.t $\{w\}$ are shown in Fig. 6. The processes include velocity control stage ① with a speed of 0.5 mm/s and the compliant control stage ②. Generally, the environment in one direction can be modeled as a one-dimensional linear spring model with stiffness k_e, which is defined as

$$f_{\mathrm{ext}} = k_e(x - x_e) \tag{17}$$

where x_e is the environment position. Therefore, the corresponding estimated stiffness of the switch area and the obstacle area is about $k_e = 2000$ and $k_e = 5000$, which is distinctly different and can be considered as a discriminatory condition. To simplify the calculations, we set an external force threshold $f_h = 25N$ as the discriminatory condition which is essentially equivalent to the stiffness threshold. Once the end-effector gets in contact with the environment, it should record the maximum external force f_m in 3 s. If $f_m > f_h$, the environment would be regarded as an obstacle. Otherwise, it would be considered as the target switch. The position adjustment strategy is designed as moving towards the task area for 3 s with a speed of 5 mm/s in both horizontal and vertical downward directions. The desired force in force control mode is set to $f_d = 60N$. The experimental performance is shown in Fig. 7 and the force result is shown in Fig. 8. Stage ① represents the velocity control process, stage ② represents the compliant control process, stage ③ represents the position adjustment process, and stage ④ is the force control process. The results show that the manipulator successfully turns on the switch after two attempts.

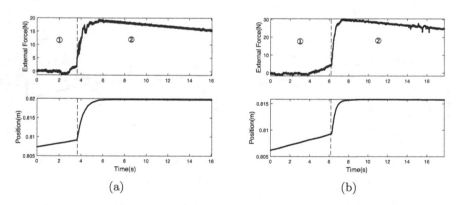

Fig. 6. Experimental results of compliant control test of switch area and obstacle area. ① is the velocity control stage and ② is the compliant control stage. (a)External force and position results of the switch area; (b)External force and position results of the obstacle area.

Fig. 7. Experimental process with the force exertion method.

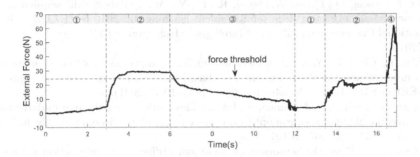

Fig. 8. External force of the turn-on-switch experiment. ① is the velocity control stage; ② is the compliant control stage; ③ is the position adjustment stage; ④ is the force control stage.

6   Conclusion

In this paper, we propose a force exertion method for resistance tasks with small task space based on mobile manipulator whole-body control and impedance control. Leveraging the redundancy of the mobile manipulator, the posture of the manipulator is optimized according to the force ellipsoid to enhance the force exertion capability while avoiding collision. The effectiveness is demonstrated by comparing the performance before and after optimization in the experiment, where the latter had smaller torques when executing the same task. Besides, an algorithm based on compliance control and force control is used to probe the location of the target in a safe way. The air switch flipping experiment verifies the feasibility of the method, where the manipulator turned on the switch without accurate positioning sensors. Our future work will focus on combing motion planning and this method to build a more complete system.

References

1. Bayle, B., Fourquet, J.Y., Renaud, M.: Manipulability of wheeled mobile manipulators: application to motion generation. Int. J. Robot. Res. **22**(7–8), 565–581 (2003)
2. Chiu, S.: Control of redundant manipulators for task compatibility. In: Proceedings. 1987 IEEE International Conference on Robotics and Automation. vol. 4, pp. 1718–1724. IEEE (1987)

3. Jiang, T., Cui, H., Cheng, X., Tian, W.: A measurement method for robot peg-in-hole prealignment based on combined two-level visual sensors. IEEE Trans. Instrum. Meas. **70**, 1–12 (2020)
4. Kozlovsky, S., Newman, E., Zacksenhouse, M.: Reinforcement learning of impedance policies for peg-in-hole tasks: Role of asymmetric matrices. IEEE Robot. Autom. Lett. **7**(4), 10898–10905 (2022). https://doi.org/10.1109/LRA.2022.3191070
5. Li, F., Jiang, Q., Quan, W., Song, R., Li, Y.: Manipulation skill acquisition for robotic assembly using deep reinforcement learning. In: 2019 IEEE/ASME International Conference on Advanced Intelligent Mechatronics (AIM), pp. 13–18. IEEE (2019)
6. Lin, Y., Chen, Z., Yao, B.: Unified motion/force/impedance control for manipulators in unknown contact environments based on robust model-reaching approach. IEEE/ASME Trans. Mechatron. **26**(4), 1905–1913 (2021)
7. Ram, R., Pathak, P.M., Junco, S.: Inverse kinematics of mobile manipulator using bidirectional particle swarm optimization by manipulator decoupling. Mech. Mach. Theory **131**, 385–405 (2019)
8. Roveda, L., Piga, D.: Sensorless environment stiffness and interaction force estimation for impedance control tuning in robotized interaction tasks. Auton. Robot. **45**(3), 371–388 (2021). https://doi.org/10.1007/s10514-021-09970-z
9. Wurll, C., Fritz, T., Hermann, Y., Hollnaicher, D.: Production logistics with mobile robots. In: ISR 2018; 50th International Symposium on Robotics, pp. 1–6. VDE (2018)
10. Xing, H., Torabi, A., Ding, L., Gao, H., Deng, Z., Tavakoli, M.: Enhancement of force exertion capability of a mobile manipulator by kinematic reconfiguration. IEEE Robot. Autom. Lett. **5**(4), 5842–5849 (2020)
11. Yang, C., Zeng, C., Liang, P., Li, Z., Li, R., Su, C.Y.: Interface design of a physical human-robot interaction system for human impedance adaptive skill transfer. IEEE Trans. Autom. Sci. Eng. **15**(1), 329–340 (2018). https://doi.org/10.1109/TASE.2017.2743000
12. Zhou, K., et al.: Mobile manipulator is coming to aerospace manufacturing industry. In: 2014 IEEE International Symposium on Robotic and Sensors Environments (ROSE) Proceedings, pp. 94–99. IEEE (2014)

Prediction of Elbow Torque Using Improved African Vultures Optimization Algorithm in Neuromusculoskeletal Model

Yunli Xia[1], Haojie Liu[1], Chang Zhu[1], Wei Meng[1], and Min Chen[2]([✉])

[1] Artificial Intelligence and Rehabilitation Robotics Laboratory, School of Information Engineering, Wuhan University of Technology, Wuhan 430070, China

[2] Network Information Center, Wuhan University of Technology, Wuhan 430070, China
minch@whut.edu.cn

Abstract. Surface electromyography (sEMG) plays a crucial role in prediction of elbow torque for human-robot interaction. However, accurately predicting joint torque still experiences a critical challenge, including the complexity of the human neuromuscular system, limitations in sensor technology, and real-time constraint. This study proposes an improved African vulture optimization algorithm (IAVOA) to calibrate the neuromusculoskeletal (NMS) model. To enhance the diversity of the population and prevent the algorithm from converging to local optima, the tent chaotic mapping and cauchy variation are integrated into the algorithm, based on AVOA. The conjugate gradient (CG) algorithm is also integrated into the algorithm to accelerate the convergence rate. The experimental results indicate that IAVOA is highly effective, with the global determination coefficient greater than 0.914 and root mean square error lower than 0.37 N·m. These results demonstrate the potential of proposed approach as a promising method for improving human-robot interaction in rehabilitation robotics.

Keywords: sEMG · Hill Muscle Model · Parameter Identification · Chaotic Map · African Vultures Optimization Algorithms

1 Introduction

Based on the recent "World Health Organization (WHO) Global Burden of Disease" report, stroke affects a staggering 86 million individuals worldwide [1] and can result in severe motor and cognitive dysfunction [2]. Robotic rehabilitation offers a customized and consistent approach to traditional rehabilitation methods, providing patients with effective training interventions that can facilitate nerve repair and functional recovery. Designing a control system with fast response performance that can predict joint torque in real-time can aid in achieving coordination and adaptability in human-robot interactions. [3]. Joint torque prediction has significant implications for limb quantitative rehabilitation, exoskeleton robots, and sports training evaluation [4,5].

H. Yang et al. (Eds.): ICIRA 2023, LNAI 14271, pp. 291–302, 2023.
https://doi.org/10.1007/978-981-99-6495-6_25

The 'black box' method, which uses machine learning algorithms is a common method for predicting joint torque. Zhang et al. presented a novel approach that utilizes artificial neural networks (ANN) to predict ankle joint torque from sEMG. [6]. Li et al. proposed a shoulder joint torque estimation method based on sEMG and CNN-LSTM [7]. However, it has limitations, including ignoring physiological information, poor generalization and possible overfitting.

Another approach to joint torque estimation is to develop a NMS model using the Hill muscle model as a basis. This model employs muscle activation as an input to replicate both the physiological and mechanical properties of power muscle contraction, which is a popular method for estimating skeletal muscle forces. Zhao et al. adopted genetic algorithm to identify physiological parameters in muscle model, and then estimated joint impedance for variable impedance control of wrist exoskeleton robot [8]. Lian et al. proposed a three-step muscle parameter identification model based on the Hill muscle model of an exoskeleton robot, and used Adam optimizer to calibration parameters [9]. However, the NMS modeling method still has some shortcomings.

The paper is organized as follows: Sect. 2 introduces the Hill model and proposes a collaborative calibration algorithm based on IAVOA, which is used to indentify the parameters of the Hill model. Section 3 introduces the experimental subjects and experimental scheme. Section 4 shows the analysis of algorithm calibration results and algorithm comparison results. Section 5 makes detailed conclusions.

2   Methods

This paper proposes a method for predicting elbow torque that is composed of three parts: inverse dynamics model, forward dynamics model and optimization of model parameters.

Figure 1 depicts the framework of the proposed method, which involves three main steps. Firstly, the torque of the elbow joint is calculated as the reference torque by establishing a two-link model of the upper limb. Next, a Hill muscle model is developed. Finally, the parameters of the Hill model are identified by utilizing the IAVOA algorithm.

2.1   Hill-Based NMS Model

Joint torque is difficult to directly measured by sensors [10]. Many researchers will conduct flex movement elbow wrist is simplified to two connecting rod structure rigidity, as shown in Fig. 2, and most researchers will establish dynamic equation based on Lagrange dynamics method. The elbow torque can be calculated:

$$\begin{aligned}
\tau_1 = {} & (m_1 d_1^2 + m_2 l_1^2 + m_2 d_2^2 + 2m_2 l_1 d_2 \cos(\theta_2) + J_1 + J_2)\ddot{\theta}_1 \\
& + (-m_2 d_2^2 - m_2 l_1 d_2 \cos(\theta_2) + J_2)\ddot{\theta}_2 \\
& + (-2m_2 l_1 d_2 \sin(\theta_2))\dot{\theta}_1 \dot{\theta}_2 + (m_2 l_1 d_2 \sin(\theta_2))\dot{\theta}_2^2 \\
& + m_1 g d_1 \cos(\theta_1) + m_2 g(l_1 \cos(\theta_1) + d_2 \cos(\theta_1 - \theta_2))
\end{aligned} \tag{1}$$

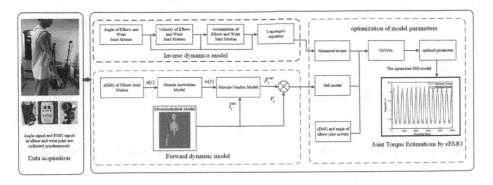

Fig. 1. The framework of the proposed method

where m_1, m_2, l_1, l_2, d_1 and d_2 are respectively the weight, length and center of mass of the forearm and palm, respectively. J_1 and J_2 are respectively the moment of inertia of the forearm and the palm with respect to its centroid axis. θ_1, θ_2, $\dot{\theta}_1$, $\dot{\theta}_2$, $\ddot{\theta}_1$, $\ddot{\theta}_2$ are the angles, angular velocities and angular accelerations of the forearms and palms, respectively.

The Hill model a three-element model that describes skeletal muscle function as shown in the Fig. 3. The muscle activation level $a(u)$ is expressed as

$$a(u) = \frac{e^{Au} - 1}{e^{A} - 1} \tag{2}$$

where u is the neural activation [11], A is the shape factor. Muscle force can be expressed as

$$F^m = (f_a(l) \cdot f_p(v) \cdot a + f_p(l)) \cdot F^m_{\max} \tag{3}$$

where $F^m_{\max}$ represents the maximum isometric force of muscle, $f_a(l)$ represents the relationship between active force and muscle fiber length, $f_p(v)$ represents the relationship between passive force and the contraction rate of muscle fibers, $f_p(l)$ represents the relationship between passive force and muscle fiber length. These relationships can be shown in reference [12]. The elbow torque is the sum of the torques of all contributing muscles

$$T_e = \sum_{i=1}^{N} F^{mt}_i r_i = \sum_{i=1}^{N} F^m_i r_i \cos\phi_i \tag{4}$$

where r_i represents the moment arm of the ith muscle, F^m_i represents the max isometric force of the ith muscle, and ϕ_i represents the pinnation angle of the ith muscle.

To capture the subject-specific characteristics of the NMS model, The parameter optimization problem of Hill model can be described as follows. The input vector is designed as

$$\begin{aligned} X = (d, c_{1,1}, c_{2,1}, A_1, k_{r,1}, \lambda_1, k^m_{s,1}, k_{v,1}, k^{mt}_{s,1}, F^m_{o,1} \cdots \\ c_{1,N}, c_{2,N}, A_N, k_{r,N}, \lambda_N, k^m_{s,N}, k_{v,N}, k^{mt}_{s,N}, F^m_{o,N}) \end{aligned} \tag{5}$$

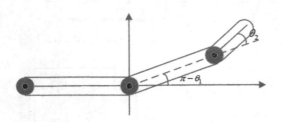

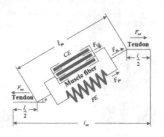

Fig. 2. Upper limb two-link model   **Fig. 3.** Hill NMS Model

where N is the number of muscles participated in flexion and extension of elbow joint. d, $c_{1,i}$, $c_{2,i}$ and A_i is the neural activation parameter. $k_{r,i}$ is the maximum neural activation. λ_i is the optimal muscle fiber length parameter. $k_{s,i}$ is the muscle fiber length parameter. $k_{v,i}$ is the the parameter of muscle contraction speed. $k_{s,i}^{mt}$ is the muscle-tendon length parameter. $F_{o,i}^m$ is the max isometric force.

The objective function of design in the process of parameter identification is

$$F(X) = \sum_{k=1}^{K} (T_{e,k} - T_{m,k})^2 \tag{6}$$

where $T_{m,k}$ represents the torque of the elbow at the sampling point k, , which can be obtained from (1). $T_{m,k}$ represents the torque of the elbow at the sampling point k, $T_{e,k}$ represents the elbow torque at the sampling point k obtained by the NMS model, K is the total number of sampling points.

To make sure that the optimized parameters are physiologically valid, it is important to impose appropriate constraints on their range of values. The following are the constraints for each parameter.

$$\begin{array}{lll} -1 \le c_{1,i} \le 1, & -1 \le c_{2,i} \le 1, & 10ms \le d \le 100ms, \\ -3 \le A \le 0, & 1.2 \le k_{r,i} \le 3, & -0.5 \le \lambda_i \le 0.75, \\ 0.8 \le k_{s,i}^m \le 1.3, & 0.8 \le k_{s,i}^{mt} \le 1.3, & 1.2 \le k_{v,i} \le 2 \end{array} \tag{7}$$

2.2 Collaborative Calibration Algorithm Based on IAVOA

AVOA algorithm is a meta-heuristic algorithm with fast convergence and stable performance [13]. The diversity of the population can significantly impact both the convergence speed and the quality of feasible solutions obtained [14]. Tent chaotic mapping has been found to generate sequences that are relatively flat and uniform, making it more conducive to the convergence of the algorithm [15,16], which can be represented by (8).

$$x^{t+1} = tent(x^t) = \begin{cases} 2x^t & 0 \le x^t < 0.5 \\ 2(1 - x^t) & 0.5 \le x^t \le 1 \end{cases} \tag{8}$$

When the initial value of the tent map is set to any value in the sets of either $\{0, 0.2, 0.4, 0.6, 0.8\}$ or $\{0, 0.25, 0.5, 0.75, \}$, the tent map becomes trapped in a non-random loop, necessitating its regeneration in both cases.

CG algorithm is a common method for solving optimization problems [17]. It has the advantages of small storage space and fast convergence. In order to improve the convergence speed of AVOA algorithm, AVOA algorithm is combined with CG algorithm. Specifically, AVOA randomly generates the initial position of each iteration, and CG algorithm is used to further optimize the initial position to get a better solution according to (6).

The process of using CG algorithm to optimize the position of African vultures in the iteration is as follows:

Step 1: AVOA randomly generates the initial position of African vultures in the population within the given range as the optimal position of CG algorithm.

Step 2: The CG algorithm is utilized to obtain a new position for each valture according to (6).

Step 3: If the position of vulture obtained by the CG algorithm is better than the initial optimization, the global optimal value is replaced by the position of vulture optimized by CG algorithm, and the position of vulture is generated again.

Step 4: After updating the positions of all vultures, if the algorithm reaches the stop condition, stop. Otherwise, go to step 2.

To avoid the stagnation phenomenon that may occur during the algorithm, a stagnation check on the optimal population value is conducted in the later stage of the algorithm. Additionally, the Cauchy variation algorithm is integrated to prevent the algorithm from being trapped in local optimal values. [18,19].

$$X_i^{t+1} = X_{best}(t) + cauchy(0, 1) \cdot X_{best}(t) \tag{9}$$

The IAVOA algorithm for parameter optimization can be described in Algorithm 1. Where X represents the parameter to be optimized, n_p represents the number of African vulture population, t represents the number of the current iteration, s is the s th vulture in the population, $X_{s,t}$ represents the position of the s th vulture in the t th iteration, $f_{o,t}$ represents the objective function of the s th vulture in the tth iteration, which is calculated by (6), $f_{s,t,n}$ represents the objective function of the sth vulture in the tth iteration at the nth iteration in CG algorithm, $X_{s,t,n}$ represents the position of the s th vulture in the t th iteration at the n th interation in CG algorithm, f_t^p represents the local best objective function in the t th iteration, $pBest_t$ represents the local best position in the t th iteration, f^g represents the global best objective function, and $gBest$ represents the global best position.

Algorithm 1 IAVOA Algorithm

Input: sEMG of two muscles, torque and angles of the elbow joint
Output: the optimal parameters
1: **initialize:** Set the constraints of X, IAVOA parameters: population of African vultures n_p and the maximum number of iterations for IAVOA and CG as $iter_{max}^{IAVOA}$, $iter_{max}^{CG}$, etc.

2: Set $s = 0$
3: **initialize population:** Generate a random number $a_0 \in [0, 1]$
4: **for** $s < n_p$ **do**
5: 　　Update a_s by (8)
6: 　　**while** $a_s \in \{0, 0.25, 0.5, 0.75\}$ **do**
7: 　　　$a_s = a_s + \epsilon$;
8: 　　**end while**
9: 　　$X_s = a_s(ub - lb) + lb, s \leftarrow s + 1$
10: **end for**
11: Set $t = 1, s = 0$, $gBest = INF$, $pBest = INF$
12: **while** $t < iter_{max}$ **do**
13: 　　**while** $s \leq n_p$ **do**
14: 　　　　Calulate $f_{s,t}$ by (6) for sth vulture
15: 　　　　set $X_{s,t}$ as the best vulture of CG, n = 1
16: 　　　　**while** $n < iter_{max}^{CG}$ **do**
17: 　　　　　update $X_{s,t,n}$ using CG algorithm
18: 　　　　　**if** $f_{s,t} > f_{s,t,n}$ **then**
19: 　　　　　　update $X_{s,t} \leftarrow X_{s,t,n}$
20: 　　　　　**end if**
21: 　　　　**end while**
22: 　　　　**if** $f_{s,t} < f_t^p$ **then**
23: 　　　　　$pBest_t = X_{s,t}, f_t^p = f_{s,t}$
24: 　　　　**end if**
25: 　　　　**if** $f_t^p < f^g$ **then**
26: 　　　　　$gBest = pBest_t, f^g = f_t^p$
27: 　　　　**end if**
28: 　　　　$s \leftarrow s + 1$
29: 　　**end while**
30: 　　Update $X_{s,t+1}$ by AVOA algorithm
31: 　　**if** $pBest_t$ has almost no change continuously **then**
32: 　　　Update $X_{s,t+1}$ by (9)
33: 　　**end if**
34: 　　$t \leftarrow t + 1$
35: **end while**

3　Experiments Setup

3.1　Subjects and Experimental Scheme

In this study, six healthy volunteers with an average age of 23 ± 2 are recruited to perform elbow flexion and extension exercises using their right hand with their palm slightly clenched but not forcefully. To ensure the accuracy and reliability of sEMG signals, all volunteers rest fully before the experiment to minimize the potential impact of muscle fatigue.

To ensure accurate data collection, we synchronize the Trigno and Qualisys systems using external buttons and follow established protocols for electrode placement. Additionally, the skin of all volunteers is cleaned by alcohol pads to reduce signal noise and improve electrode adherence.

The experiment is divided into two parts: (1) collecting data on maximum voluntary contractions (MVC) and (2) collecting data on elbow flexion and extension exercises.

During the maximum voluntary contraction (MVC) data acquisition experiment, volunteers are asked to move their elbow joint to the limit without causing any pain or discomfort, while keeping their shoulder joint stable and motionless. They do this three times, with a three-minute rest between each repetition. The mean value of the recorded sEMG signal is used to normalize the subsequent sEMG signals obtained during elbow flexion and extension exercises. During the data collection experiment, volunteers perform elbow flexion and extension exercises for 60 s, taking a three-minute rest between each repetition.

A second-order Butterworth high-pass filter with a cutoff frequency of 20 Hz is applied to remove low-frequency noise from the original EMG signals caused by equipment, skin movement, and DC drift during movement. Then we perform full-wave rectification, followed by normalization with the MVC EMG signals. Finally, a second-order Butterworth low-pass filter with a cutoff frequency of 3 Hz is applied to remove any remaining physiological factors.

3.2   Muscle Selection

Elbow flexion and extension movement is completed by the synergistic action of many muscles. If all the muscles involved in elbow flexion and extension movement are selected, the model parameters need to be optimized and the calculation amount is complex. Moreover, some muscles have little influence on elbow movement, so the muscle synergy theory should be used to select muscles.

Muscle synergy theory which is show in Fig. 4, decomposed muscle activation into a linear combination of muscle synergy elements and activation coefficient sequences

$$
\begin{aligned}
\mathbf{V}_{N \times T} &= \mathbf{W}_{N \times K} \times \mathbf{H}_{K \times T} \\
&= \begin{bmatrix} \mathbf{W_1} \ \mathbf{W_2} \cdots \mathbf{W_k} \end{bmatrix} \times \begin{bmatrix} \mathbf{H_1} \ \mathbf{H_2} \cdots \mathbf{H_k} \end{bmatrix}^T \\
&= \sum_{i=1}^{K} \mathbf{W_i H_i}
\end{aligned}
\tag{10}
$$

where, $\mathbf{V}_{N \times T}$ is muscle activation in target exercise, $\mathbf{W}_{N \times K}$ is muscle synergy matrix, and $\mathbf{H}_{K \times T}$ is activation coefficient matrix. N is the number of muscle channels; K is the number of sample points of signals; T is the number of synergetic elements; $\mathbf{W}_i = \left(W_{1i} \ W_{2i} \cdots W_{Ni} \right)^T$ represents a synergetic element; w_{ij} represents the contribution degree of i th muscle to the j th synergetic element; $\mathbf{H}_i = \left(h_1(t) \cdots h_i(T) \right)$ represents the activation coefficient sequence of the synergetic element of i th over time during the whole movement process. Where $h_i(t)$ represents the activation coefficient of the i th coelement at time t.

The contribution degree of each muscle to a particular elbow movement is

$$WD_i = \frac{W_i}{\sum\limits_{i=1}^{N} W_i} \tag{11}$$

where WD_i represents the contribution degree of the i th muscle to the action. PCA belongs to the category of factorial method. It is a common method to solve the synergistic effect of muscle.

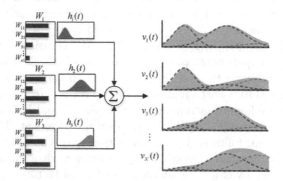

Fig. 4. Muscle synergy model

4   Results and Analysis

4.1   Muscle Selection Results

According to the two independent movements of elbow extension/elbow flexion, the EMG signal is collected and the contribution degree is analyzed for the six muscle tissues of the main muscles of the upper limb: biceps(BIC), triceps(TRI), brachioradialis(BR), flexor carpi radialis (FCR), flexor carpi ulnaris(FCU) and extensor carpi radialis(ECR). Figure 5(a) shows the contribution degree of each muscle in a single elbow extension and Fig. 5(a) shows the contribution degree of each muscle in a single elbow flexion. As can be seen from the Fig. 5, TRI contributes the most in elbow extension and BIC contributes the most in elbow flexion. Therefore, BIC and TRI are selected as the main muscle tissues of elbow movement to predict joint torque.

4.2   IAVOA Algorithm Calibration Results

The calibrated NMS model is used to predict joint torque, and the results are visualized in Fig. 6(a). The error between prediction and measurement is shown in Fig. 6(b). The global determination coefficient(R^2), root mean square error

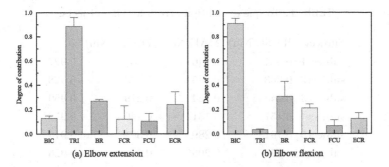

Fig. 5. The degree of Contribution for elbow extension and flexion

(RMSE), maximum error (MAXE), and mean absolute error (MAE) are introduced to evaluate the effectiveness of the proposed method.

Table 1 presents the results of testing the calibrated model's ability to predict elbow torque in six subjects. The results both in Fig. 6 and in Table 1 show that the error between between prediction and measurement can be kept in a small range and has a strong agreement, suggesting that the calibrated model performed well in accurately predicting joint torque.

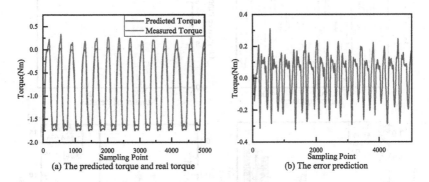

Fig. 6. The result using IAVOA algorithm

4.3   The Models Designed for Comparison

The IAVOA algorithm is compared to three other algorithms from the literature: the genetic algorithm(GA) [8], AVOA algorithm and NM-CO algorithm [20] to

Table 1. Torque estimation errors for six subjects.

Subject	RMSE(Nm)	MAE(Nm)	MAXE(Nm)	R^2
subject1	0.371	0.346	0.689	0.927
subject2	0.368	0.335	0.943	0.928
subject3	0.145	0.124	0.279	0.959
subject4	0.157	0.131	0.240	0.952
subject5	0.191	0.289	0.384	0.914
subject6	0.229	0.206	0.245	0.926
mean	0.244	0.238	0.462	0.934

evaluate the performance in calibrating sEMG-driven torque estimation models. Set the population size as 30 and the number of iterations as 30. 30 repeated experiments are conducted to verify the stability of IAVOA.

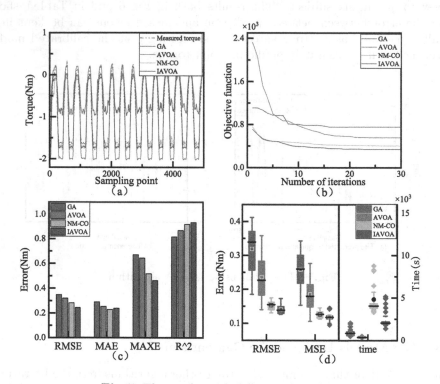

Fig. 7. The results with different algorithms

As shown in Fig. 7(a), the predicted torque values obtained using the IAVOA algorithm exhibit smoother patterns than those obtained using the other algorithms. As shown in Fig. 7(b), the proposed IAVOA algorithm achieves the smallest objective function at the beginning of the iteration process, indicating that it is able to quickly and accurately converge to the optimal solution. As shown in Fig. 7(c), the IAVOA algorithm outperforms the other three algorithms in terms of both RMSE, MAXE and R^2. The 30 repeated experiments's results are shown in Fig. 7(d). The results show the superiority of the proposed algorithm in model calibration and running time.

5   Conclusion

This paper proposes a collaborative calibration algorithm based on IAVOA algorithm, which is used to calibrate parameters simultaneously from three aspects: muscle activation model, muscle contraction model and musculoskeletal geometric model. Experimental results demonstrate that this method outperforms the comparison method in terms of prediction accuracy and running time, indicating the effectiveness of the proposed algorithm. The proposed method has potential applications in human-robot interactive control of rehabilitation robots, facilitating the prediction of patient's motion intentions and abilities, as well as enhancing the comfort and efficacy of rehabilitation training.

Acknowledgement. This work is supported by the National Natural Science Foundation of China under Grant 52075398 and 52275029.

References

1. Cieza, A., Causey, K., Kamenov, K., Hanson, S.W., Chatterji, S., Vos, T.: Global estimates of the need for rehabilitation based on the global burden of disease study 2019: a systematic analysis for the global burden of disease study 2019. The Lancet **396**(10267), 2006–2017 (2020)
2. Admoni, H., Srinivasa, S.S.: Predicting user intent through eye gaze for shared autonomy. In: Proceedings of AAAI '16 Fall Symposium on Shared Autonomy in Research and Practice, pp. 298–303 (2016)
3. Wang, W., et al.: Neuromuscular activation based sEMG-torque hybrid modeling and optimization for robot assisted neurorehabilitation. In: Gedeon, T., Wong, K.W., Lee, M. (eds.) ICONIP 2019. LNCS, vol. 11954, pp. 591–602. Springer, Cham (2019). https://doi.org/10.1007/978-3-030-36711-4_50
4. Chai, Y., Liu, K., Li, C., Sun, Z., Jin, L., Shi, T.: A novel method based on long short term memory network and discrete-time zeroing neural algorithm for upper-limb continuous estimation using semg signals. Biomed. Signal Process. Control **67**, 102416 (2021)
5. Yang, N., Li, J., Xu, P., Zeng, Z., Cai, S., Xie, L.: Design of elbow rehabilitation exoskeleton robot with semg-based torque estimation control strategy. In: 2022 6th International Conference on Robotics and Automation Sciences (ICRAS), pp. 105–113 (2022)
6. Zhang, L., Li, Z., Hu, Y., Smith, C., Farewik, E.M.G., Wang, R.: Ankle joint torque estimation using an EMG-driven Neuromusculoskeletal model and an artificial neural network model. IEEE Trans. Autom. Sci. Eng. **18**(2), 564–573 (2020)

7. Li, C., Zhang, X., Li, H., Xu, H.: Continuous sEMG estimation method of upper limb shoulder elbow torque based on CNN-LSTM. In: 2021 IEEE International Conference on Robotics and Biomimetics (ROBIO), pp. 1390–1395 (2021)

8. Zhao, Y., et al.: Adaptive cooperative control strategy for a wrist exoskeleton using model-based joint impedance estimation. IEEE/ASME Trans. Mechatron. **28**(2), 748–757 (2023)

9. Lian, P., Ma, Y., Zheng, L., Xiao, Y., Wu, X.: A three-step hill neuromusculoskeletal model parameter identification method based on exoskeleton robot. J. Intell. Robot. Syst. **104**(3), 44 (2022)

10. Bueno, D.R., Montano, L.: Neuromusculoskeletal model self-calibration for on-line sequential Bayesian moment estimation. J. Neural Eng. **14**(2), 026011 (2017)

11. Buchanan, T.S., Lloyd, D.G., Manal, K., Besier, T.F.: Neuromusculoskeletal modeling: estimation of muscle forces and joint moments and movements from measurements of neural command. J. Appl. Biomech. **20**(4), 367–395 (2004)

12. Ao, D., Song, R., Gao, J.: Movement performance of human-robot cooperation control based on EMG-driven hill-type and proportional models for an ankle power-assist exoskeleton robot. IEEE Trans. Neural Syst. Rehabil. Eng. **25**(8), 1125–1134 (2016)

13. Abdollahzadeh, B., Gharehchopogh, F.S., Mirjalili, S.: African vultures optimization algorithm: A new nature-inspired metaheuristic algorithm for global optimization problems. Comput. Indust. Eng. **158**, 107408 (2021)

14. Bangyal, W.H., Nisar, K., Ag. Ibrahim, A.A.B., Haque, M.R., Rodrigues, J.J., Rawat, D.B.: Comparative analysis of low discrepancy sequence-based initialization approaches using population-based algorithms for solving the global optimization problems. Appl. Sci. **11**(16), 7591 (2021)

15. Chen, A., Peng, H., Zhong, Y., Ren, H.: Improved seagull optimization algorithm incorporating golden sine and tent chaotic perturbations. In: 2022 IEEE 6th Advanced Information Technology, Electronic and Automation Control Conference (IAEAC), pp. 1879–1884 (2022)

16. Liu, M., Zhang, Y., Yao, D., Guo, J., Chen, J.: An improved lion swarm optimization algorithm based on tent-map and differential evolution. In: 2022 IEEE 5th International Conference on Computer and Communication Engineering Technology (CCET), pp. 1–6 (2022)

17. Jabbar, N., Mitras, B.: Modified chimp optimization algorithm based on classical conjugate gradient methods. J. Phys.: Conf. Series **1963**, 012027 (07 2021)

18. He, Q., Lin, J., Xu, H.: Hybrid cauchy mutation and uniform distribution of grasshopper optimization algorithm. Kongzhi yu Juece/Control and Decision **36**, 1558–1568 (07 2021)

19. MAO Qinghua, Z.Q.: Improved sparrow algorithm combining cauchy mutation and opposition-based learning. J. Front. Comput. Sci. Technol. **15**(6), 1155 (2021)

20. Wang, W., et al.: Prediction of human voluntary torques based on collaborative neuromusculoskeletal modeling and adaptive learning. IEEE Trans. Industr. Electron. **68**(6), 5217–5226 (2020)

Usability Evaluation of FURS Robot Control Panel Interface Design Based on SUS

Yong You[1,3], Lai Wei[2], Shiqiang Zhu[3], Yongwu Yu[4], Yunxiang Jiang[5,6], Xiaolei Liu[4], Jianda Han[3,7(✉)], Lingkai Chen[3(✉)], and Wei Song[3(✉)]

[1] Design Innovation Center, China Academy of Art, Hangzhou 310024, China
[2] L'École de Design Nantes Atlantique, China Academy of Art, Hangzhou 310024, China
[3] Research Center for Intelligent Robotics, Research Institute of Interdisciplinary Innovation, Zhejiang Laboratory, Hangzhou 311100, China
hanjianda@nankai.edu.cn, {clk,weisong}@zhejianglab.com
[4] Hangzhou Yunphant Network Technology Co. Ltd., Hangzhou, China
[5] State Key Laboratory of Robotics, Shenyang Institute of Automation, Chinese Academy of Sciences, Shenyang 110016, China
[6] Institutes for Robotics and Intelligent Manufacturing, Chinese Academy of Sciences, Shenyang 110169, China
[7] College of Artificial Intelligence and Tianjin Key Laboratory of Intelligent Robotics, Institute of Robotics and Automatic Information Systems, Nankai University, Tianjin 300350, China

Abstract. The objective of this study is to compare the interfaces of two FURS (Flexible Ureterorenoscopy) robotic operation consoles across generations. Analyzing functional requirements during surgery, the first-generation interface was designed. Evaluation of the first-generation interface, combined with user needs and design principles, informed the design of the second-generation interface, which aimed to improve the usability of the console during surgery. Both interface generations were assessed for usability and user experience using the System Usability Scale (SUS). The results indicate improvement in usability and user satisfaction following interface iteration.

Keywords: Medical device · interface design · system usability scale · usability evaluation

1 Introduction

1.1 A Subsection Sample

Flexible Ureterorenoscopy (FURS) has become an important technique in modern urological surgery [1]. In response to growing demand for minimally invasive surgery and endoscopic technology [2], medicine and robotics have made significant progress in recent decades [3], culminating in the development of robotic systems with control capabilities for ureteroscopy.

© The Author(s), under exclusive license to Springer Nature Singapore Pte Ltd. 2023
H. Yang et al. (Eds.): ICIRA 2023, LNAI 14271, pp. 303–312, 2023.
https://doi.org/10.1007/978-981-99-6495-6_26

The interface of the robotic operating console plays a crucial role as a control and information feedback component. It provides an intuitive visual interface, control functions for the ureteroscope, video imaging, and recording capabilities, enhancing user interaction and real-time feedback efficiency.

The current interface design of the Avicenna FURS robot by Elmed, Turkey, is function-oriented. The multi-functional touchscreen display interface of the Avicenna FURS robot includes a range of features, such as ureteroscope mode adjustment (U.S. or European), rotation and forward speed control, Ho: YAG laser fiber movement, irrigation flow rate adjustment, rotation and deflection angle display [4].

As a research team focusing on the FURS robot, our goal is to broaden our research on functionality-based interface design. Hence, evaluating the usability of the iterative design of the FURS robot interface is crucial.

We adhere to the principles of "design based on design goals, reliance on design strategies, using design methods based on design principles, and assessing whether the methods meet design goals through the required design indicators." during the design process. We initially develop the system based on functionality and subsequently focus on interface design. Proper layout and utilization enhance the readability and visibility of the interface, enabling users to identify functions and information. Finally, we employ the system quantization analysis table as an experimental tool, relying on SUS scores to evaluate the feasibility, usability, and learnability of the two interface versions, eliciting a series of conclusions.

2   FURS Robot Interface Design Theories and Examples

2.1   FURS Robot Operating Console Interface Design Theory

User-Centered Design (UCD) is a design methodology that centers around users, emphasizing their needs, abilities, and experiences. Designers thoroughly comprehend doctors' requirements, capabilities, and operational habits to develop robot interfaces and control systems that better align with their expectations [5]. Information Architecture (IA) concentrates on organizing and arranging the interface to allow users to quickly comprehend and discover the information they need. Effective IA reduces user alienation and frustration caused by technology [6]. IA design involves arranging surgical data, patient records, and robot control interface information in a logical manner, with the aim of achieving an organized and clear interface layout that provides effective ways to access the required information. This assists doctors in accurately accessing and interpreting relevant information during surgery. User-centered approaches to design can guide teams toward an understanding of users and aid teams in better posing design problems [7]. Much of the work of user-centered design (UCD) practitioners involves some type of interviewing. Interviewing is used, for example, when you are performing the following tasks: Selecting participants for research Moderating usability studies Briefing and debriefing during usability evaluations, etc. [8].

Visual Design focuses on the visual effects and aesthetics of the interface, utilizing elements such as colors, icons, fonts, and layouts to convey information and guide users' attention. A well-designed graphic interface ensures consistent and predictable behavior for all represented objects in the system [9].Visual elements on the interface help doctors rapidly access key information such as surgical status, patient indicators, and robot operation, permitting them to make accurate decisions and undertake operations.

2.2   User Interface Case

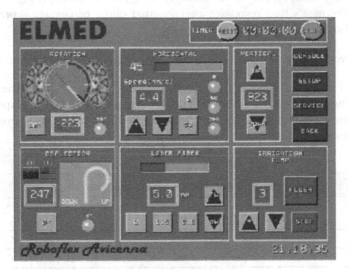

Fig. 1. Avicenna Interface.

"Since 2012, Elmed (Ankara, Turkey) has been utilized as a robot console for operation and a multifunctional touch screen interface for FURS treatment." [4]. The implementation of a multifunctional touch screen in medical devices enables doctors to possess increased operational flexibility and control capabilities. It incorporates several functions and adjustment options to increase the accuracy, safety, and personalization of the surgical process. The interface's primary focus is on function, combining multiple features and customization options to improve surgical personalization, accuracy, and safety. It provides users with an intuitive and user-friendly experience, facilitating efficient and accurate task execution. "The interface utilizes features such as ureteroscope mode adjustment (U.S. or European), rotation and forward speed control, holmium laser fiber forward and backward movement, irrigation flow rate adjustment, rotation and offset display" [4]. Professional teams subjected this surgery-related information to multiple simulated tests to determine and maintain surgical safety. Furthermore, the use of effective visual patterns and real-time data analysis feedback enables doctors to properly analyze and interpret surgical data from a visual and data analysis perspective (Fig. 1).

3   Interface Design and Evaluation Methods

3.1   System Usability Scale (SUS)

"The SUS (System Usability Scale), created by Brooke (1996), met an urgent need within the usability community for a tool that quickly and easily measures a user's subjective rating of a product's usability" [10]. The scale comprises ten statements, consisting of five positive and five negative descriptions. Categorized by Lewis and Sauro (2009), eight items were included in Usable, which contains two factors: Usable (eight items) and Learnable (two items, specifically Item 4 and Item 10). These new scales have acceptable reliability, with an alpha coefficient of .91 and .70, respectively [11]. Using a 5-point rating scale, ranging from "Strongly Disagree" to "Strongly Agree," the SUS is scored. The user's final responses are converted into a percentage score using the following formula:

$$[\Sigma(\text{Positive description score} - 1) + \Sigma(5 - \text{Negative description score})] * 2.5 \quad (1)$$

(Where 1 stands for Strongly Disagree and 5 means Strongly Agree). The total score must be multiplied by the multiplier such that a perfect score of 100 corresponds to 40, which suggests a multiplier of 2.5. Consequently, the SUS score ranges from 0 to 100 in increments of 2.5 (Fig. 2).

	Standard version of the SUS system availability scale	Very much agree			Strongly disagree	
		1	2	3	4	5
1	I am willing to use this system frequently	O	O	O	O	O
2	I found the system needn't be so complicated	O	O	O	O	O
3	I think the system is easy to use	O	O	O	O	O
4	I think I will need technical support to use this system	O	O	O	O	O
5	I think the functions in Tether are well integrated	O	O	O	O	O
6	I think the system is too inconsistent	O	O	O	O	O
7	I can imagine that most people can quickly learn to use the system	O	O	O	O	O
8	I found the system extremely clumsy to use	O	O	O	O	O
9	I feel very confident when using this system	O	O	O	O	O
10	I need to learn a lot before I can use the system	O	O	O	O	O

Fig. 2. Standard version of the SUS system usability scale.

3.2 USE Questionnaire

The USE questionnaire, developed by Amie Lund in 2001, represents Usefulness, Satisfaction, and Ease of use [12].

In the medical interface design domain, the USE questionnaire evaluates users' experience and satisfaction with a particular system or interface. It furnishes quantitative and qualitative data on the perceived usefulness, satisfaction, and usability of the system (Fig. 3).

Effectiveness	Ease of learning
it makes my work more efficient it makes me more productive it is useful It happens to allow me to manage my daily work and activities very well It makes it easier for me to get things done It saves me time when using it met my needs	I can quickly learn to use it i easily remember how to use it easy to learn Soon I will be able to practice using it
Ease of use	Satisfaction
it is easy to use it is easy to operate it is user friendly It helps me do what I need to do with few steps It is flexible effortless to use I can use it without written instructions During use, I did not notice any inconsistencies Users will love to use it no matter how often it is used When something goes wrong, it is quick to recover from the wrong operation	i am happy with it I will recommend it to my friends fun to use it works the way I expect it's good i feel i need to have it pleasant to use

Fig. 3. USE self-report scale.

3.3 PSSUQ Overall Usability Questionnaire

Lewis (1995) developed the Post-Study System Usability Questionnaire (PSSUQ) as a research tool for scenario-based usability evaluation at IBM [13]. The PSSUQ tool evaluates the usefulness, information quality, and interface quality of user interfaces.

The PSSUQ comprises 19 items, targeting five system usability characteristics: swift work completion, simplicity of learning, excellence of documentation and online information, functional adequacy, and rapid usability acquisition [13]. Employing PSSUQ in medical interface design can facilitate assessing user satisfaction, recognizing issues and refining opportunities, comparing diverse design approaches, validating interface enhancements, and encouraging continuous improvements for a more satisfactory user experience and satisfaction (Fig. 4).

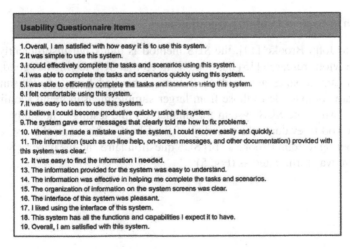

Fig. 4. Usability Questionnaire Items.

4   FURS Robot Control Console Interface Usability Evaluation

4.1   Interface Design

The FURS robot control console interface design at Zhejiang Laboratory prioritizes robot functionality. The design adheres to the principle of consistency and draws inspiration from the Avicenna FURS robot interface. The design scheme follows usability design methods, tailored for a 24-inch screen and prioritizes real-time information feedback and visual design strategies. Surgical process analysis identified eight functional requirements for the flexible scope device: bending, holmium laser, forward/backward movement, rotation, elevation, pitch, communication settings, and camera image display. Control buttons and data displays are designed to accommodate surgical operation steps and feedback information, promoting the substitution of manual labor with machine automation. The FURS robot control console interface was developed in two versions utilizing User-Centered Design, Information Architecture, and Visual Design principles.

4.2   Experimental Design

This study evaluated the usability of Interface 1 and Interface 2, the 1st and 2nd generation, respectively, of the Zhejiang Laboratory FURS robot interface. Interface 1 is the first-generation interface developed using functional products, while Interface 2 is a second-generation interface improved upon by designers based on user needs and design concepts. The usability evaluation assesses the usability and learnability of both interfaces, providing guidance and insights for future optimization of the FURS robot interface. Participants included 6 males and 2 females, ratio 3:1, comprising urologists and researchers from different hospitals and laboratories involved in clinical work. Ages ranged from 27 to 37, and all participants had a basic understanding of both generation interfaces' functionality and operation. Interface 1 and Interface 2 were each evaluated by 8 urologists and researchers.

4.3   Design of System Usability Questionnaire

According to John Brooke [14], the SUS method is quick but insufficiently detailed. However, previous research [15] has demonstrated that SUS testing has good reliability when small sample sizes are used. SUS scores obtained from smaller sample measurements are comparable to those from larger sample measurements, confirming the feasibility of using the SUS system for smaller sample testing. The study will utilize the SUS method to evaluate the usability of the FURS robot control console interface design. Adhering to John Brooke's [14] SUS questionnaire and the paper's Sect. 3.1, the questionnaire was formulated as (Fig. 5):

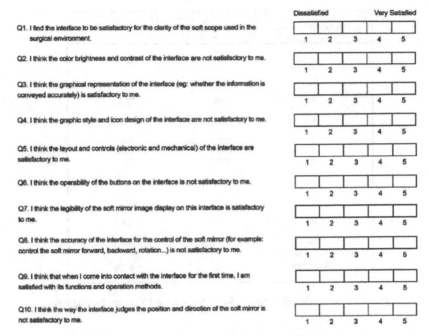

Fig. 5. SUS Based on the Design of the Control Console Interface.

10 questions were designed, with 1, 3, 5, 7, and 9 being positive statement sentences, and 2, 4, 6, 8, and 10 being negative statement sentences. As per Sect. 3.1 of this article and references [10, 11], questions 1–8 addressed usability-related indicators and questions 9 and 10 addressed learnability-related indicators.

4.4 System Quantitative Usability Score Analysis

The evaluation of the second version interface was carried out with the same set of par ticipants. The experimental results were analyzed using Bangor's classification method for interpreting SUS questionnaire scores, as references have outlined [16]. SUS scores below 50 indicate poor usability, while scores between 50 and 70 suggest acceptable levels. SUS scores above 70 indicate highly acceptable usability.

The usability score for the first version interface is 32, as shown in Fig. 6, which is unacceptable for users. The average usability score for the second version interface is 59.75, which falls within the acceptable range of 50–70, indicating that it is acceptable to users, albeit at the lower threshold level. Therefore, some users find the second generation interface of the FURS robot control panel to be acceptable in terms of usability. There is a significant difference between the SUS scores of the two interface versions. The overall score for interface 1 is relatively low, with only marginally better scores of 47.5 for button convenience. In addition, the average SUS score is mainly in the range of 27.5– 32.5, which is below 50 and unacceptable to users. The weakest aspects are the display and clarity of the software mirror, which only received 12.5 points. On the other hand, Interface 2 has a relatively high overall score, with graphic design style, icon design,

Questionnaire	Interface 1	Interface 2
1	12.5	65
2	30	62.5
3	30	72.5
4	30	75
5	32.5	55
6	47.5	60
7	32.5	60
8	27.5	42.5
9	40	55
10	37.5	50
Average	32	59.75

Fig. 6. System Usability Scale (SUS) Scores for Usability Evaluation.

and feedback graphics all receiving high scores of 75 and 72.5 respectively, indicating a level of acceptability by users. However, aspects of logical judgment of software mirror position and orientation, as well as software mirror control precision, only scored 50 and 42.5, placing them at the lower threshold of user acceptability, rather than being fully recognized.

4.5 Analysis of Usability and Learnability Indicators

Following the previous setup, the interface usability score can be determined by summing and averaging the scores of questions 1 to 8. By adding and averaging the scores of questions 9 and 10, the interface learnability score can be obtained. Figure 7 illustrates the comparison of usability and learnability for the second version interface.

For Interface 1, the SUS scores are 30.3125 for usability and 38.75 for learnability; for Interface 2, the SUS scores are 61.5625 for usability and 52.5 for learnability. Interface 2 has higher absolute scores than Interface 1 for both usability and learnability, which is consistent with the overall usability situation. However, when comparing usability and learnability within each interface, Interface 1 has superior learnability to usability, whereas Interface 2 has better usability than learnability. Through design analysis, it is found that Interface 1 focuses solely on functional implementation as its design objective, which lowers the learning cost but lacks consideration for user perspectives, resulting in a higher learnability than usability score. On the other hand, Interface 2 takes user experience into account, significantly improving usability by incorporating a guided design. As a result, the learnability score is higher than that of Interface 1. However, the reconstruction of interface logic leads to increased learning costs. Although there is some optimization compared to Interface 1, the improvement is not significant.

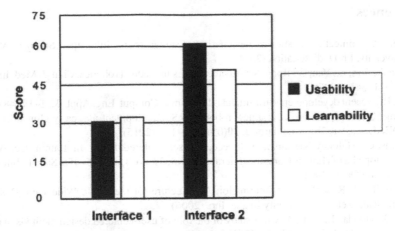

Fig. 7. Average SUS Scores for Interface Usability and Learnability.

4.6 Overall Analysis of System Quantitative Usability Testing

Using SUS, the FURS robot control panel interface design usability evaluation was conducted for the second version, resulting in an overall reliability of 0.92, a usability reliability of 0.91, and a learnability reliability of 0.7. The following points can be concluded: SUS is effective in evaluating the usability of the FURS robot control panel interface design. The data analysis shows that the SUS scores for the second version interface fall within the unacceptable range for users (<50) when compared to the first version interface. The second version demonstrates significant improvement, indicating the effectiveness of interface design in optimizing the FURS robot interface. After optimizing to the second version interface, the SUS scores generally fall within the acceptable range for users (50–70). However, this suggests that there are still issues to be addressed, such as considering both usability and learnability of the interface to reduce learning costs associated with interface use for medical staff. The strengths of this experiment are its focus on the Zhejiang Lab project and the involvement of frontline urological surgical medical staff as research subjects, which provided accurate feedback. However, the limitations of this study include the small sample size, suggesting that further experimentation is necessary in the future.

5 Conclusion

Interface design can provide richer functionality and interactive experiences with the continuous development of medical and robotic technologies. Designers and researchers should always leverage the advantages of SUS for conducting usability testing quickly. The FURS robot control panel interface can be more efficiently integrated with frontline medical staff's work, offering more flexible and natural operating methods, driving interface development, and achieving higher usability.

Acknowledgement. The authors would like to acknowledge the support from the Scientific Research Item of Zhejiang Lab under Grant No. 2022NB0AC01.

References

1. Wen, Z.: Clinical application and evaluation of ureteroscopic lithotripsy. Southern Medical University, Ph.D. dissertation (2014)
2. Gao, L., Lin, L., Yan, G., Rong, R.: Advancements in medical robotics. Chin. J. Med. Instrum. **06**, 341–344 (1997)
3. Lu, R.: Recent developments in artificial intelligence. Comput. Eng. Appl. **04**, 1–14+48 (1987)
4. Long, Q.: European urology: a new robot FURS: development and early clinical research (IDEAL stage 1–2b). Mod. Urol. J. **20**(02), 131–132 (2015)
5. Abras, C., Maloney-Krichmar, D., Preece, J.: User-centered design. In: Bainbridge, W. (ed.) Encyclopedia of Human-Computer Interaction, vol. 37, no. 4, pp. 445–456. Sage Publications, Thousand Oaks (2004)
6. Morville, P., Rosenfeld, L.: Information Architecture for the World Wide Web: Designing large-scale web sites. O'Reilly Media, Inc. (2006)
7. Lai, J., Honda, T., Yang, M.C.: A study of the role of user-centered design methods in design team projects. Ai Edam **24**(3), 303–316 (2010)
8. Wilson, C.: Interview techniques for UX practitioners: a user-centered design method. Newnes (2013)
9. Lynch, P.J.: Visual design for the user interface, Part 1: design fundamentals. J. Biocommun. **21**, 22 (1994)
10. Bangor, A., Kortum, P.T., Miller, J.T.: An empirical evaluation of the system usability scale. Int. J. Human-Comput. Interact. **24**(6), 574–594 (2008)
11. Lewis, J.R., Sauro, J.: The factor structure of the system usability scale. In: Kurosu, M. (ed.) HCD 2009. LNCS, vol. 5619, pp. 94–103. Springer, Heidelberg (2009). https://doi.org/10. 1007/978-3-642-02806-9_12
12. Lund, A.M.: Measuring usability with the use questionnaire12. Usability Interface **8**(2), 3–6 (2001)
13. Fruhling, A., Lee, S.: Assessing the reliability, validity and adaptability of PSSUQ. In: AMCIS 2005 Proceedings, p. 378 (2005)
14. Brooke, J.: SUS-A quick and dirty usability scale. Usability Eval. Ind. **189**(194), 4–7 (1996)
15. Bangor, A., Kortum, P., Miller, J.: Determining what individual SUS scores mean: adding an adjective rating scale. J. Usability Stud. **4**(3), 114–123 (2009)
16. Tullis, T.S., Stetson, J.N.: A comparison of questionnaires for assessing website usability ABSTRACT: introduction. In: Usability Professional Association Conference

Knowledge-Based Robot
Decision-Making and Manipulation

Obstacle-Avoidance State Characterization Models Based on Hybrid Geometric Descriptions for Mobile Manipulators

Jingjing Xu, Long Tao, Zhifeng Liu$^{(\boxtimes)}$, Qiang Cheng, Jianzhou Chen, and Yanhong Cheng

Beijing University of Technology, Beijing 100124, China
lzf@bjut.edu.cn

Abstract. With advantages of large working space and high flexibility, mobile manipulators has been rapidly developed and applied to manufacturing system and assembly shop etc. But how to ensure their motion safety is the key problem in practical applications. To accurately predict the obstacle-avoidance state of the mobile manipulator can provide important information for its motion trajectory/path planning. For the above problem, this work proposes three distance estimation models to characterize the obstacle-avoidance state based on hybrid geometric descriptions (polygon/polyhedron, polygonal/circular slices) for three motion stages, which are the motion of the mobile device, pre-operating pose adjustment motion and operating motion of the manipulator. Three models are respectively the rough estimation model, the general estimation model and the fine estimation model of the shortest distance between robot and surrounding obstacles for each motion stage. The calculation accuracy and efficiency are analyzed during simulation. This work can provide algorithm basis for the safe motion control of mobile manipulators under open three-dimensional (3D) environments.

Keywords: Mobile Manipulator · Distance Estimation Models · Obstacle Avoidance

1 Introduction

When the mobile manipulator are applied to multi-state manufacturing system, and with a continuous trajectory operational task, its motion process can be divided into three motion stages, which are respectively mobile platform motion for multi-station conversion (Motion-1), pre-operating pose adjustment motion from the initial pose (Motion-2) and operating motion of the manipulator (Motion-3), as shown in Fig. 1. Motion-1 is two-dimensional motion, and its safety depends on the obstacle avoidance between the whole robot and surrounding environmental structure. During motion-2, the end-effector of the manipulator is far away from the operating target, which makes the manipulator have a certain flexible movement area. In motion-3, the end effector is gradually approach or contacting the operating target, which usually has a small operating space or more surrounding constraints. During this motion, the accurate prediction of the shortest distance can help search for the feasible motion trajectory for the manipulator. The completely collision-free motion planning of the mobile manipulator has been an major problem for its application. For this problem, the estimation of the shortest distance between robot and surrounding obstacles can provide quantifiable data for the motion planning, which can be used to detect the collision or find the potential collision danger, which can be called the obstacle-avoidance state. And the shortest distance between the robot and its obstacles is taken as the obstacle-avoidance state characteristic index in this work.

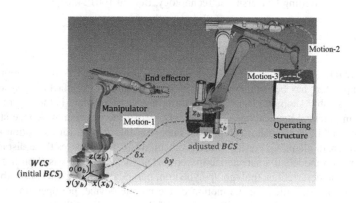

Fig. 1. Motion stages of mobile manipulators

In recent studies, distance measurement mainly uses kinds of visual sensors, and generally used for local collision-free motion planning of the mobile device. And the mobile device and its obstacles were always assumed as points or enveloped by a circle [1]. But the above simple way is not applicable to manipulators due to their multiple links and complex spatial poses. To ensure its motion safety, the force or micro-pressure sensors are used in real applications, but the effect largely relies on the accuracy and reliability of sensors. Therefore, the distance estimation is still a major way to solve this problem. Previously, lines [2, 3], capsule [4], basic geometrical bodies [5, 6], and hierarchical bounding volumes (HBVs) [7] were used to simply describe the structure of the manipulator or surrounding obstacles in the working environment. In the above descriptions, the basic geometrical bodies and the hierarchical bounding box can be used to more tightly envelope the structure of the manipulator, but they both need a large amount of calculations to obtain the shortest distance. For the former one, the calculation is based on Gilbert-Johnson-Keerthi (GJK) algorithm [8, 9]. In the GJK-based algorithm, the geometrical bodies need be further divided into a large number of monomers, which largely reduces the execution efficiency of the algorithm [10]. HBVs has the high efficiency when it is used to detect collisions, but is limited to calculate the distance due to the calculation difficulty of the distance between prisms and the extremely low execution speed due to the iterative construction of the 3D model.

Overall, in previous studies, the shortest distance was always predicted based on the simplified envelope description of the robot. The overly simplified loose envelope can improve the calculation speed, but the estimation accuracy is poor, more easily resulting in the non-contact state being determined as a collision. Thus, the feasible solution space of the robotic motion may be largely reduced. The under-simplified tight envelope can improve the estimation accuracy, and ensure the feasible solution space as much as possible, which will be quite helpful for the application to narrow spaces of the robot, but the computational difficulty and efficiency are largely increased.

For mobile manipulators, the loose envelope way of the whole robot can be used in the path planning of Motion-1, which can largely improve the calculation speed of the shortest distance; the general envelope way of links and joints of the manipulator can be used for Motion-2, which can better ensure the computation speed and motion space before the robotic end effector reaches its pre-operating pose; the tight envelope way of the manipulator needs to be used for Motion-3, which can largely increase the feasible motion space under the limited working space. In this method, the robot and its obstacles can be divided into several sub-structures, and convex polygonal planes and circular planes are selected to envelop each sub-structure according to its geometric feature as tightly as possible.

For the above problem, this work provides three distance models according to different requirements of three motion stages and based on envelope description with different degree of tightness, as well as the basic distance calculation functions proposed in our previous works [11]. Three models are respectively the rough estimation model, the general estimation model and the fine estimation model of the shortest distance. These models can be used to predict the shortest distance and then characterize the obstacle-avoidance state of the mobile manipulator during its motion planning.

The remainder of this paper is organized as the following three sections: Sect. 2 proposes three shortest distance models between mobile manipulator and obstacles based on hybrid geometric descriptions. Section 3 verifies the computational speed and accuracy of three models. Section 4 gives the main conclusions of this work and the future works.

2 Shortest Distance Models Between Mobile Manipulator and Obstacles

In this work, the shortest distance models are established based on two basic distance functions, which are respectively used to calculate the shortest distance between the spatial circular plane and convex polygonal plane Dis_{cTp}, and the shortest distance between two convex polygonal planes Dis_{pTp}. Two calculations have been presented in detail in our previous work and their algorithms are shown in sub-algorithm 3 and 4 of the reference report [11]. Herein, the detailed processes will not be repeated, and two functions $fun_1(\cdot)$ and $fun_2(\cdot)$ have been defined in MATLAB and quoted directed here, and they are represented as follows.

$$Dis_{cTp} = fun_1(\rho_C, \rho_P) \tag{1}$$

$$Dis_{pTp} = fun_2(\rho_{P,1}, \rho_{P,2}) \tag{2}$$

where ρ_C and ρ_P represent the spatial information of the circular plane and the convex polygonal plane, respectively. And ρ_C includes the 3D location of the circular center, radius and normal vector to the circular plane. ρ_P includes 3D locations of vertexes of the polygon. $\rho_{P,1}$, $\rho_{P,2}$ represent the spatial information of two polygons.

2.1 Rough Estimation Model of The Shortest Distance

For motion-1 (the multi-station conversion motion), the rough estimation model of the shortest distance between the whole robot and environmental obstacles is established. During this motion, the robot as a whole moves within a 2D plane. The robot and obstacles are enveloped by series of convex polygons and circles, as shown in Fig. 2.

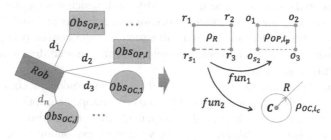

Fig. 2. Rough envelope description

Based on the above envelope description, set $\rho_R = (r_1, r_2, \cdots, r_{s_1})$, $\rho_{OP,i_p} = (o_1, o_2, \cdots, o_{s_2})$, wherein r_i and o_i represent the polygonal vertex locations of the enveloping robot and that of the i_p enveloping obstacles. s_1 and s_2 are vertex numbers of two polygons. $\rho_{OC,i_c} = (C, R)$ is set as the i_c circular representation of surrounding obstacles. C, R are the location of the circular center and the radius. The above locations are all 2D coordinates in oxy plane of the world coordinate system. For the ease of calculation, they are extended into 3D coordinates by setting z as zero. Finally, the rough estimation model can be defined as follows,

$$DIS_1 = min\{fun_2(\rho_R, \rho_{OP,i_p}), fun_1(\rho_R, \rho_{OC,i_c})\} \tag{3}$$

where $1 \leq i_p \leq I_p$, $1 \leq i_c \leq I_c$, I_p and I_c are the numbers of convex polygonal obstacles and circular obstacles respectively, existed in the open environment.

When the model is applied into motion planning, spatial information of all polygons and circles are necessary input, which can be determined by positioning sensors, like camera. And 3D location of the robotic polygon changes with the motion of the mobile device and can be calculated according to the transformation matrix determined by its motion parameters. Set R_M as the transformation matrix, and the original coordinate of one vertex of the robotic polygon is r_0, the current coordinate can be written as $r_1 = R_M r_0$.

2.2 General Estimation Model of the Shortest Distance

During motion 2, the end-effector path is not strictly limited. Therefore, some transitional path points can be set according to environmental obstacles, that is, the manipulator can operate with the large operational space and high flexibility. Under this condition, although the loose envelope description will reduce some feasible solution space of the manipulator's motion planning, the optimal trajectory is still easy to obtain. Then, for this motion stage, convex polygons with variable pose are used to envelop and describe links and other structures of the manipulator, as shown in Fig. 3. The pose of the manipulator can be determined by forward kinematics based on angular displacements of all joints θ. In order to model the distance, the structure of the mobile manipulator is divided into several sub-structures, and enveloped by convex polygons, which are represented by $Rob = (Cuboid_k, \rho_{Ri,k})$, wherein $Cuboid_k$ and $\rho_{Ri,k}$ are the kth convex polyhedron and its ith convex polygonal plane. $1 \leq i \leq 6$, $1 \leq k \leq K$, K means the number of polyhedrons obtained by dividing the robot.

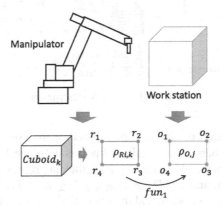

Fig. 3. General envelope description

The working space of the manipulator can be described as several convex polygonal obstacle planes. Set $WorkS = (\rho_{O,j}, 1 \leq j \leq J)$, the general estimation model can be defined as follows,

$$DIS_2 = min\{fun_1(\rho_{Ri,k}, \rho_{O,j})\} \tag{4}$$

During the calculation, 3D coordinates of all vertexes of the convex polygonal plane $\rho_{Ri,k}$, $\rho_{O,j}$ under the world coordinate system are input of this function. Since the motion of mobile device leads to that the manipulator's base changes with variables δx, δy and α, and poses of convex polyhedrons changes with the joint motion of the manipulator. That is, each vertex coordinate of $\rho_{Ri,k}$ can be calculated based on the station conversion matrix R_M and the manipulator's pose θ.

2.3   Fine Estimation Model of the Shortest Distance

In real applications, the end effector of the manipulator generally faces the requirement of definite path points or continuous motion trajectory, which means that the feasible solution space of the motion trajectory of the manipulator is largely limited. Under this case, the tight envelope description can enlarge the solution space, so as to find the optimal trajectory. Therefore, the manipulator's structure is divided into some sub-structures, which are then enveloped by convex polyhedron, prism or cylinder with certain or variable cross section. Then the manipulator is represented by $Rob_f = (PolyHD_l, PolyHDV_m, CyLD_n)$, wherein $1 \leq l \leq L$, $1 \leq m \leq M$ and $1 \leq n \leq N$, L, M and N are numbers of polyhedrons, prisms and cylinders, respectively. For ease of the calculation of the shortest distance, prisms with variable cross section and cylinders are divided into slices along their one axis, as shown in Fig. 4.

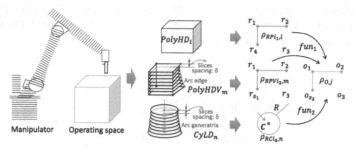

Fig. 4. Tight envelope description

For ease of modelling, the lth convex polyhedron is represented by $PolyHD_l = (\rho_{RPi_1,l}, 1 \leq i_1 \leq I_1)$, wherein $\rho_{RCi_1,l}$ is its i_1th polygonal plane. For prisms with variable cross section and cylinders, taking spacing as δ, they are represented as $PolyHDV_m = (\rho_{RPVi_2,m}, 1 \leq i_2 \leq I_2)$, and $CyLD_n = (\rho_{RCi_3,n}, 1 \leq i_3 \leq I_3)$, wherein I_2 and I_3 are numbers of slices of the mth prism and the nth cylinder, respectively. Based on slices-based representation, the spacing δ has the major influence on the prediction accuracy of the distance. From Fig. 4, the fine estimation model can be written as follows,

$$DIS_3 = min \left\{ \begin{array}{c} fun_1(\rho_{RPi_1,l}, \rho_{O,j}), fun_1(\rho_{RPVi_2,m}, \rho_{O,j}), \\ fun_2(\rho_{RCi_3,n}, \rho_{O,j}) \end{array} \right\} \tag{5}$$

Noted that, this model is used to determine whether the manipulator collides with surrounding obstacles. But when the manipulator is required to perform the contact operational task, it means that the shortest distance between the manipulator and the target surface is zero. In order to avoid its effect on the abnormal collisions detection, the end effector of the manipulator can be shortened along the working direction by a certain length, which can be equal to the safety distance threshold during the construction of space constraints, during the structure representation.

3 Analysis of Efficiency and Accuracy of Three Models

In this section, the efficiency and accuracy of three proposed estimation models are analyzed through numerical simulation, the running environment is shown in Table 1.

In the simulation case, the mobile KUKA robot is used as the research object. And, the two-station operational environment is designed as Fig. 5. The world coordinate system is established by taking the current location of the mobile device as its center.

Table 1. Running Environment

CPU	CPU Memory	System	Software
Intel(R) Core(TM) 2.6GHz	8GB	Windows10	MATLAB R2018a

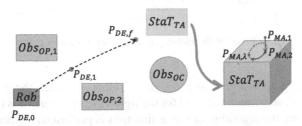

Fig. 5. Two-station operational environment

In Fig. 5, centers of rectangle obstacles $Obs_{OP,1}$ and $Obs_{OP,2}$ are set as (625, 2000, 0) and (4000, 0, 0) mm, and their length and width are set as 2500 mm and 1000 mm, respectively; the center location and radius of the circular obstacle Obs_{OC} are set as (7000, 1000, 0) and 600 mm. According to the size of the manipulator, the length and width of the rectangular shape Rob are 1250 mm and 500 mm. Based on the proposed obstacle-avoidance state characteristic, the rough estimation, general estimation and fine estimation of the shortest distance can be obtained. Under the given environment, the efficiency of three models can be analyzed through changing poses of the mobile device and the manipulator. Under each pose, the calculation is executed 10 times, and their average value is taken to be compared.

The location of the mobile device was changed by motion variables including linear displacements along axes x and y of the world coordinate system and angular displacement about the axis z, namely $P_{DE} = [x(mm), y(mm), \alpha(deg)]$. Taking three way points as $P_{DE,0} = (0, 0, 0)$, $P_{DE,1} = (2000, 1000, 20)$ and $P_{DE,f} = (6000, 2500, 0)$, the rough estimation is executed. Table 2 gives the estimation result and execution time under each way point. From Table 2, estimation distances is consistent with the distance shown in Fig. 6, which indicates that the results are accurate. Under three way points, average execution times are 0.0135, 0.0129 and 0.0151s, the difference is mainly caused by condition judgment and calculation process existed in the algorithm. Overall, they are smaller than 0.015s, that is, the calculation time based MATLAB codes is at the level of 10 ms.

Table 2. Rough estimation result and efficiency

Way Point	Point 1	Point 2	Point 3
Execution time (s)	0.0135	0.0129	0.0141
Distance (mm)	1250	262.5988	250

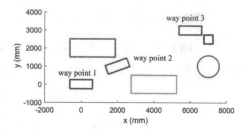

Fig. 6. Poses of the mobile device under three way points

Based on the proposed general and tight envelope methods, the general and fine estimation results can be obtained. And for the tight envelope, when δ is taken as 10, 15, 20, 25 and 30 mm, the algorithm of fine estimation is performed, respectively. Taking the pose of the mobile device as $P_{DE} = [6000, 2500, 0]$, and angular displacements of joints of the manipulator as $\theta_1 = [0, 0, 0, 0, 0, 0]deg$, $\theta_2 = [10, 10, 10, 10, 10, 10]deg$ and $\theta_3 = [20, 20, 20, 20, 20, 20]deg$. Under the general envelope, from Table 3 and Fig. 7, the estimation results are accurate, and the average execution times based on MATLAB codes are 0.4333, 0.4632 and 0.4527s for three poses, respectively.

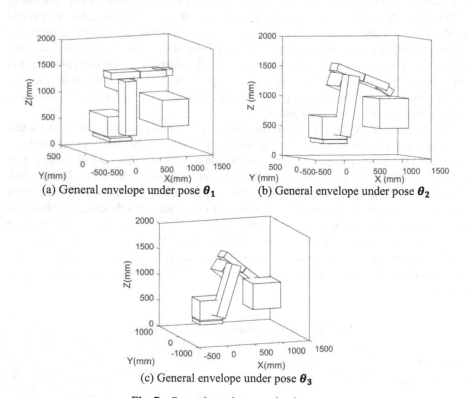

(a) General envelope under pose θ_1

(b) General envelope under pose θ_2

(c) General envelope under pose θ_3

Fig. 7. General envelopes under three poses

Under the tight envelope, from Table 4 and Fig. 8, the estimation results with different slices spacing are accurate, and the average execution times when $\delta = 10\,\text{mm}$ are 2.1501, 2.1433 and 2.1308 s for three poses, which are about 2 s. Compared with the general estimation, the execution efficiency obviously reduces. Under three poses, computational times increase 1.7168, 1.6801 and 1.6781 s, respectively. And under pose 2, the estimation results are quite different, and they are 0.1499 and 83.0448 mm, respectively. The above analysis means that when the estimation model based on the general envelope is used, the calculated distance is much smaller than the fine estimation under the tight envelope due to the excessive envelope of the manipulator.

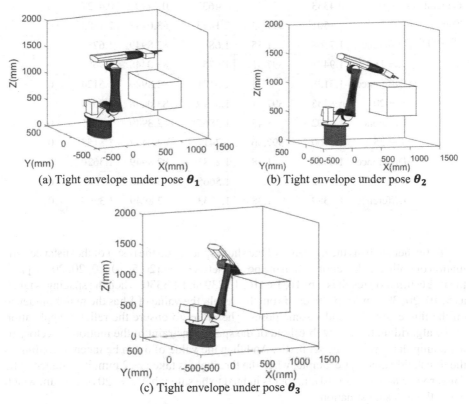

(a) Tight envelope under pose θ_1

(b) Tight envelope under pose θ_2

(c) Tight envelope under pose θ_3

Fig. 8. Tight envelopes under three poses ($\delta = 10\,\text{mm}$)

From Table 3, the following conclusion can also be obtained. (1) Under pose θ_1, the influence effect is relatively large, and compared with the result when $\delta = 10$, the difference does not increase or decrease over the variation of δ; (3) Under pose θ_2, the estimation result is basically unchanged. From Fig. 7(b), the shortest distance under this pose is the distance between the end effector and task surface, but the end-effector pose cannot be affected by the value of δ, so the distance remains unchanged; (4) Under pose θ_3, the collision can be detected under different values of δ. From Fig. 7(c), the forearm of the manipulator collides with the target, and the contact is large, so the collision detection are not affected by the value of δ. (5) The execution time gradually reduces when the spacing δ increases. It is reduced by about 0.6s due to the decrease of the number of slices.

Table 3. Estimation result and efficiency under general envelope and tight envelope

Pose		Pose θ_1		Pose θ_2		Pose θ_3	
Index		Execution time/s	Distance /mm	Execution time/s	Distance /mm	Execution time/s	Distance /mm
General envelope		0.4333	395.98	0.4632	0.1499	0.4527	0
Tight envelope	$\delta = 10$	2.1501	397.33	2.1433	83.0448	2.1308	0
	Difference	1.7168	1.35	1.6801	82.8949	1.6781	0
	$\delta = 15$	1.9471	397.31	1.9753	83.0448	1.9651	0
	Difference	1.5138	1.33	1.5121	82.8949	1.5124	0
	$\delta = 20$	1.8335	397.41	1.8499	83.0448	1.9014	0
	Difference	1.4002	1.43	1.3867	82.8949	1.4487	0
	$\delta = 25$	1.7760	397.36	1.7417	83.0448	1.8153	0
	Difference	1.3427	1.38	1.2785	82.8949	1.3626	0
	$\delta = 30$	1.6722	397.36	1.5665	83.0448	1.7925	0
	Difference	1.2389	1.38	1.1033	82.8949	1.3398	0

To further analysis the influence of the slices spacing on the result of the distance estimation or collision detection, when the pose is set as $\theta_3 = [20.5, 20, 20, 20, 20, 20]deg$, the fine estimation result is 1.6416, 1.6416, 4.3239 and 4.3330, when the spacing is taken as 5, 10, 20, 30 mm, respectively. From this result, the value of δ has the major influence on the fine estimation under some poses. Therefore, to ensure the reliably application of the algorithm, the safety threshold of the space constraint of the motion trajectory of the manipulator should be set firstly. And then the value of δ can be taken according to the threshold value, for example, when the threshold is taken as 2 mm, it is judged to be dangerous when $\delta = 5 or 10$ mm, but is judged to be safe when $\delta = 20 \ or \ 30$ mm, which is not the real safe situation.

4 Conclusions

This paper proposes three estimation models of the shortest distance to characterize the obstacle-avoidance state for mobile manipulators. In detail, the motion of the mobile manipulator includes the multi-station transfer motion of the mobile device, the pre-operating pose adjustment motion and operating motion of the manipulator; The rough estimation model, the general estimation model and the fine estimation model are established for three motion states, based on two basic distance calculation functions presented in our previous work [11]. Three estimation models can provide spatial constraint conditions for the motion planning of the mobile manipulator. Through numerical simulation, we can obtain the following conclusions:

(1) The estimation result is consistent with the relative spatial pose between the whole robot and the surrounding obstacles, and the average execution time based on MATLAB codes is at the level of 10 ms.
(2) The general estimation model can accurately calculate the shortest distance between structures based on general envelope, and under three poses of the manipulator, the average execution times based on MATLAB codes are 0.4333, 0.4632 and 0.4527 s, respectively, which are all less than 0.5 s.
(3) The fine estimation model can accurately calculate the shortest distance between structures enveloped tightly. The spacing value has also major influence on the execution time. Taking the spacing as 10 mm, under three poses, the average execution times are 2.1501, 2.1433 and 2.1308 s, respectively, which are larger than the general estimation.

In real applications, the value of the spacing should be determined according to the estimation precision requirement (safety threshold) and computational efficiency of the algorithm.

In future works, we will further focus on the improvement of the execution time of each model, through the optimization of codes and the introduction of intelligent algorithms. Meanwhile, we will apply these models into the safe motion planning problem of mobile manipulator, to further verify the significance of this work.

References

1. Li, H., Savkin, A.V.: An algorithm for safe navigation of mobile robots by a sensor network in dynamic cluttered industrial environments. Robot. Comput.-Integr. Manuf. **54**, 65–82 (2018)
2. Bhattacharjee, T., Bhattcharjee, A.: A study of neural network based inverse kinematics solution for a planar three joint robot with obstacle avoidance. Assam Univ. J. Sci. Technol. **5**(2), 1–7 (2010)
3. Zhou, T.: Research on motion planning and control System of seven degrees of freedom fruit harvesting manipulator. China Jiliang University (2015)
4. Safeea, M., Neto, P.: Minimum distance calculation using laser scanner and IMUs for safe human-robot interaction. Robot. Comput.-Integr. Manuf. **58**, 33–42 (2019)
5. Rubio, F., Llopis-Albert, C., Valero, F., et al.: Industrial robot efficient trajectory generation without collision through the evolution of the optimal trajectory. Robot. Auton. Syst. **86**, 106–112 (2016)
6. Han, D., Nie, H., Chen, J., et al.: Dynamic obstacle avoidance for manipulators using distance calculation and discrete detection. Robot. Comput.-Integr. Manuf. **49**, 98–104 (2018)
7. Li, M.Y.: Research on collision detection algorithm based on progressive intersecting bounding box. Lanzhou Jiaotong University (2015)
8. Ong, C.J., Gilbert, E.G.: Fast versions of the Gilbert-Johnson-Keerthi distance algorithm: additional results and comparisons. IEEE Trans. Robot. Autom. **17**(4), 531–539 (2001)
9. Cameron, S., Culley, R.: Determining the minimum translational distance between two convex polyhedral. In: Proceedings 1986 IEEE International Conference on Robotics and Automation, vol. 3, pp. 591–596. IEEE (1986)

10. Montanari, M., Petrinic, N, Barbieri, E.: Improving the GJK algorithm for faster and more reliable distance queries between convex objects. ACM Trans. Graph. (TOG), **36**(3), 1–17 (2017)
11. Xu, J.J., Liu, Z.F., Yang, C.B., et al.: Minimal distance calculation between the industrial robot and its workspace based on circle/polygon-slices representation. Appl. Math. Model. **87**, 691–710 (2020)

Performance Optimization of Robotic Polishing System with a 3-DOF End-Effector Using Trajectory Planning Method

Yaohua Zhou[1,2,3], Chin-Yin Chen[1,2(✉)], Guilin Yang[1,2], and Chi Zhang[1,2]

[1] Ningbo Institute of Materials Technology and Engineering, Chinese Academy of Sciences, Ningbo 315201, China
chenchinyin@nimte.ac.cn
[2] Zhejiang Key Laboratory of Robotics and Intelligent Manufacturing Equipment Technology, Ningbo 315201, China
[3] University of Chinese Academy of Sciences, Beijing 100049, China

Abstract. A robotic polishing system is usually composed of an industrial robot (macro-robot) and an end-effector (micro-robot), called a macro-micro robotic system. The macro-robot is mainly responsible for path tracking, while the micro-robot implements force control for polishing. This combination has the advantages of large workspace and fast response. However, the traditional end-effector usually has only one degree of freedom (DOF). It can hardly provide optimization space for trajectory planning of the macro-robot, which affects the polishing quality to some extent. Therefore, we developed a 3-DOF end-effector to compensate for the motion of the macro-robot, especially for curved surface polishing. The trajectory planning is modeled as an optimal control problem, and Gauss pseudospectral method is used as the corresponding solution strategy. Finally, in polishing simulations of the arc path, the 3-DOF end-effector is proved to be superior to the traditional 1-DOF one in trajectory planning.

Keywords: Macro-micro robotic system · End-effector · Trajectory planning

1 Introduction

Polishing is a key technology to improve the quality of workpiece in precision engineering [1,2]. However, many polishing tasks are still performed manually by experienced workers, resulting in low efficiency and inconsistent product quality. To address the problem of manual polishing, robotic polishing is a promising strategy, which has gradually attracted the attention of experts and scholars in recent years [3].

There are mainly two robotic polishing strategies, i.e., "through-the-arm" and "around-the-arm", to achieve polishing force control [4]. Since the industrial robots used for surface polishing applications usually have large inertia and low response rate, it is difficult to achieve accurate force control by "through-the-arm" method. In contrast, the "around the arm" method based on an additional force-controlled end-effector is a more suitable for achieving active force control. This is because the end-effector has faster response rate and higher control accuracy.

Traditionally, polishing quality can be improved by a 1-degree-of-freedom (1-DOF) end-effector (shown in Fig. 1(a)), which can implement relatively precise force control. Some approaches based on mechanical/electromagnetic design or control have been proposed for its performance enhancement: layout improvement of mechanical components [5], design of an additional eddy current damper for vibration suppression [6], application of a disturbance observer based on generalized momentum [7] and design of an averaged sub-gradient integral sliding mode controller [8]. However, these approaches can only be applied to end-effector (micro-robot) and cannot improve the performance of industrial robot (macro-robot), while the latter almost dominate the comprehensive performance of this macro-micro robotic system (MMRS). In fact, for MMRS, the industrial robot is mainly responsible for path tracking, while the end-effector implements force control. Therefore, the performance of the macro-robot can only be enhanced by considering the aspect of trajectory planning.

For some common curved surface polishing tasks, it is meaningful to reduce the velocity of the macro-robot through macro-micro coordinated trajectory planning, while the 1-DOF end-effector is not ideal in this aspect. Therefore, we developed a 3-DOF two-rotational one-translational (2R1T) end-effector [4] (shown in Fig. 1(b)), to compensate for the trajectory of the macro-robot, especially in curved surface polishing. Figure 1(c) shows the prototype of our MMRS: it consists of ABB IRB 4400 (macro-robot) and the 3-DOF 2R1T end-effector (micro-robot).

(a)   (b)   (c)

Fig. 1. (a) A traditional 1-DOF end-effector. (b) The prototype of the 3-DOF 2R1T end-effector. (c) The prototype of our MMRS.

As for the trajectory planning algorithm, it is usually an offline link for polishing tasks, so the global trajectory optimization method is worth considering. This study adopts the modeling method based on optimal control. In addition, Gauss pseudospectral method (GPM) is selected as the solution strategy of optimal control due to fast convergence speed and simple operation [9].

The rest of this paper is organized as follows: Sect. 2 describes the relevant configuration and kinematics modeling of MMRS. Section 3 gives the trajectory planning framework based on optimal control, including the definition of variables, constraints and objective functions. Section 4 gives the algorithm flow of GPM concisely. Section 5 carries out numerical simulations and discussions. Section 6 summarizes the full paper.

2   Kinematic Modeling

2.1   Configuration Description

Figure 2 displays the comprehensive configuration of our MMRS: Fig. 2(a) describes the models of the macro-robot and micro-robot, and Fig. 2(b) gives mechanism diagrams for them.

In Fig. 2(b), the macro-robot is a general industrial manipulator whose three joint axes at the end intersect at a point. {B} and {T} represent the base and tool frame, respectively. The micro-robot is a 3-prismatic-prismatic-spherical (3PPS) parallel mechanism. It consists of a base platform, three identical PPS branch chains and a moving platform. These two platforms can be regarded as identical equilateral triangles, and {T} (it is also the tool frame of the macro-robot) and {M} are built at the center. The prismatic joint directly connected to the base platform in each branch chain is active, which is practically driven by a voice coil motor. The other two joints in each branch chain are passive. Among them, the passive prismatic joints are installed horizontally, with their directions pointing to the center. The relationship between joint serial number and frame is also shown in Fig. 2(b), which is used to analyze the mapping between joint displacements and micro-robot's pose in numerical simulations. In addition, when the three active joints exert force simultaneously, the 3-DOF 2R1T effector can achieve the same force-controlled effect as the 1-DOF one. Remarkably, those existing improvement strategies (e.g., based on mechanical/electromagnetic design or control) for the 1-DOF end-effector are also applicable to the 3-DOF 2R1T end-effector.

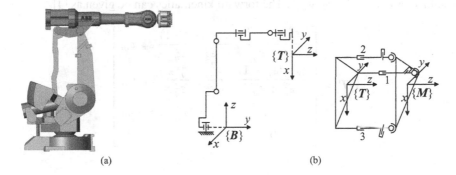

(a)   (b)

Fig. 2. Our MMRS: (a) A comprehensive model; (b) Mechanism diagrams for the macro-robot and micro-robot.

2.2   Kinematics of the Macro-Robot

Forward Kinematics. Since the macro-robot (IRB 4400) is a traditional serial industrial robot, the local exponential product method is used to establish the forward kinematics model:

$$
{}_T^B T = e^{\theta_1 \hat{\xi}_1} {}_2^1 T_0 e^{\theta_2 \hat{\xi}_2} {}_3^2 T_0 e^{\theta_3 \hat{\xi}_3} {}_4^3 T_0 e^{\theta_4 \hat{\xi}_4} e^{\theta_5 \hat{\xi}_5} e^{\theta_6 \hat{\xi}_6} {}_T^6 T_0.
\tag{1}
$$

${}_i^j T$ represents the homogeneous transformation matrix of the frame $\{i\}$ (or i-th joint) respect to $\{j\}$ (or j-th joint), and the subscript "0" represents the initial pose. ξ_i is the screw of the i-th joint. $q_M = [\theta_1, \theta_2, ..., \theta_6]^\mathrm{T}$ is defined as the joint displacement of the macro-robot.

Inverse Kinematics. The macro-robot has a special configuration with three joint axes at the end intersecting at the same point. For this robot satisfying the Pieper criterion [10], it is efficient to use the analytical inverse kinematics. The corresponding theoretical analysis is omitted due to the generality of the method. In addition, although multiple solutions can be obtained, there is usually only one effective solution when considering joint limit constraints.

2.3   Kinematics of the Micro-Robot

The kinematics of the 3-PPS parallel mechanism was deduced in detail in the previous work [4]. For simplicity, this paper gives the relevant formulas directly.

Forward Kinematics. Assume that the length of the equilateral triangle of the moving platform is a (as well as the base platform). The joint displacement of the micro-robot is defined as $q_m = [\vartheta_1, \vartheta_2, \vartheta_3]^\mathrm{T}$. The forward kinematics can be given as [4]

$$
{}_M^T T = \begin{bmatrix}
\dfrac{\varepsilon_x^2 \varepsilon_z + \varepsilon_y^2}{\varepsilon_x^2 + \varepsilon_y^2} & \dfrac{\varepsilon_x \varepsilon_y (\varepsilon_z - 1)}{\varepsilon_x^2 + \varepsilon_y^2} & \varepsilon_x & x_m \\[2ex]
\dfrac{\varepsilon_x \varepsilon_y (\varepsilon_z - 1)}{\varepsilon_x^2 + \varepsilon_y^2} & \dfrac{\varepsilon_x^2 + \varepsilon_y^2 \varepsilon_z}{\varepsilon_x^2 + \varepsilon_y^2} & \varepsilon_y & y_m \\[2ex]
-\varepsilon_x & -\varepsilon_y & \varepsilon_z & z_m \\[1ex]
0 & 0 & 0 & 1
\end{bmatrix}.
\tag{2}
$$

where ε_x, ε_y, ε_z, x_m, y_m and z_m are intermediate variables. They have the following linear relationship with the three joint displacements:

$$
\begin{cases}
\varepsilon_x = \dfrac{\vartheta_2 - \vartheta_3}{l} \\[2mm]
\varepsilon_y = \dfrac{-2\vartheta_1 + \vartheta_2 + \vartheta_3}{\sqrt{3}l} \\[2mm]
\varepsilon_z = \sqrt{1 - \varepsilon_x^2 - \varepsilon_y^2} \\[2mm]
x_m = \dfrac{\varepsilon_x \varepsilon_y l}{\sqrt{3}(\varepsilon_z + 1)} \\[2mm]
y_m = \dfrac{(\varepsilon_y^2 - \varepsilon_x^2)(\varepsilon_z - 1)l}{2\sqrt{3}(\varepsilon_y^2 + \varepsilon_x^2)} \\[2mm]
z_m = \dfrac{\vartheta_1 + \vartheta_2 + \vartheta_3}{3}
\end{cases}
\tag{3}
$$

where l is the side length of the base/moving platform. Therefore, two steps are required to solve the forward kinematics of the micro-robot: i) Use (3) to calculate the intermediate variables; ii) Obtain ${}_M^T T$ via (2).

Inverse Kinematics. The inverse kinematics of the micro-robot is to solve q_m when ${}_M^T T$ is known, which can be effortlessly achieved when observing the forms of (2) and (3):

$$
\begin{cases}
\vartheta_x = z_m - \dfrac{\varepsilon_y l}{\sqrt{3}} \\[2mm]
\vartheta_y = \dfrac{\sqrt{3}\varepsilon_x l + \varepsilon_y l + 2\sqrt{3}z_m}{2\sqrt{3}} \\[2mm]
\vartheta_z = \dfrac{-\sqrt{3}\varepsilon_x l + \varepsilon_y l + 2\sqrt{3}z_m}{2\sqrt{3}}
\end{cases}
\tag{4}
$$

3 Optimal Control Framework

3.1 Variable Definition

Optimal control provides a channel for solving the global optimal trajectory of MMRS. Through reasonable variable allocation, we can make this problem conform to the optimal control framework. In this study, we define the joint displacement of the macro-robot as the state variable and that of the micro-robot as the control variable:

$$
\begin{cases}
x = [q_M^{\mathrm{T}}, \dot{q}_M^{\mathrm{T}}, \ddot{q}_M^{\mathrm{T}}]^{\mathrm{T}} \\[2mm]
u = [q_m^{\mathrm{T}}, \dot{q}_m^{\mathrm{T}}, \ddot{q}_m^{\mathrm{T}}]^{\mathrm{T}}
\end{cases}
\tag{5}
$$

which is due to the following two considerations: i) The macro-robot has a complete 6-DOF Cartesian space motion. ii) As mentioned in Sect. 2, the forward/inverse kinematics of macro-robot and micro-robot have bijective properties. Therefore, given the task frame (i.e., a homogeneous transformation matrix) and the joint displacement of the micro-robot, the displacement of the macro-robot can be uniquely determined. This kinematic characteristic of MMRS is the basis for establishing an effective optimal control model. In addition, velocity and acceleration are introduced to make the derivatives of state and control variables not explicitly appear in constraints.

3.2 Constraints

The state equation constraint is fundamental for the optimal control problem (OCP). In this study, the state equation in integral form is adopted instead of the one in differential form like $\dot{x}(t) = f(x(t), u(t), t)$. There are three considerations: i) The state equation in integral form and differential form are equivalent when using GPM [11], which means that the properties of the original OCP can be maintained. ii) Truncation errors arising from numerical integration (such as Euler and Runge-Kutta methods) can be avoided when evaluating the state variable. iii) The integral form is compatible with the offline programming and displacement input of the industrial robot. For MMRS, the state equation in integral form is the kinematic constraint at the displacement level, which can be described as

$$\text{Log}(FK_M(q_M) \cdot FK_m(q_m) \cdot {}^{B}_{G}T^{-1}) = 0, \tag{6}$$

$\text{Log}(\cdot)$ is a logarithmic mapping from $\text{SE}(3) \in \mathbb{R}^{4 \times 4}$ to $\text{se}(3) \in \mathbb{R}^{6 \times 1}$. $FK_M(q_M)$ and $FK_m(q_m)$ are forward kinematics of the macro-robot and micro-robot, respectively. $\{G\}$ represents the frame along the task path. Thus, (6) can be considered as the state equation since it has the standard integral form $f(x(t), u(t), t) = 0$ (${}^{B}_{G}T$ can be regarded as a function of t).

Attaching path constraints and boundary constraints to the OCP is also reasonable. For path constraints, the following two points are mainly considered: i) joint displacement; ii) joint velocity and acceleration. The former is used to avoid joint limits, while the latter improves the smoothness of the trajectory. Therefore, the path constraints have a box form:

$$\begin{cases} |q_M| \leq q_{M,\max}, |\dot{q}_M| \leq \dot{q}_{M,\max}, |\ddot{q}_M| \leq \ddot{q}_{M,\max} \\ |q_m| \leq q_{m,\max}, |\dot{q}_m| \leq \dot{q}_{m,\max}, |\ddot{q}_m| \leq \ddot{q}_{m,\max} \end{cases} \tag{7}$$

which has a standard form $C(x(t), u(t)) \leq 0$. For boundary constraints, to enhance the stability of the robotic system at startup/stop phase, we limit the velocity and acceleration at these two moments to zero:

$$\begin{cases} \dot{q}_M(t_0) = \ddot{q}_M(t_0) = \dot{q}_M(t_f) = \ddot{q}_M(t_f) = 0 \\ \dot{q}_m(t_0) = \ddot{q}_m(t_0) = \dot{q}_m(t_f) = \ddot{q}_m(t_f) = 0 \end{cases} \tag{8}$$

which can also be simplified into the following form: $E(x(t_0), u(t_0), x(t_f), u(t_f)) = 0$.

3.3 Objective Function

Compared with a single industrial robot, the micro-robot provides 3-DOF redundancy for the MMRS. In practical, for the polishing tasks of complex surfaces, the swing of the macro-robot can be effectively attenuated by planning the orientation of the micro-robot. Therefore, making full use of the motion of the micro-robot can reduce the operation burden of the macro-robot and improve the stability of the whole system. In this work, we approach this goal by minimizing the joint velocity of the macro-robot, thus the objective function can be expressed as

$$J = \frac{1}{t_f - t_0} \int_{t_0}^{t_f} \sqrt{\frac{\dot{q}_M^{\mathrm{T}} W \dot{q}_M}{\mathrm{tr}(W)}} \, \mathrm{d}t. \tag{9}$$

t_0 and t_f are the starting time and the final time, respectively. W is a constant diagonal matrix representing the weights of different joints. $\mathrm{tr}(\cdot)$ represents the trace of a matrix. It can be seen from (9) that J reflects the global average joint velocity of the macro-robot. According to the form, (9) has a general expression: $J = \int_{t_0}^{t_f} g(x(t)) \, \mathrm{d}t$.

3.4 Formulation of OCP

Based on the constraints and objective function presented above, the final OCP can be formulated as

$$\min J = \int_{t_0}^{t_f} g(x(t)) \, \mathrm{d}t$$

$$s.t. \begin{cases} f(x(t), u(t), t) = 0 \\ C(x(t), u(t)) \leq 0 \\ E(x(t_0), u(t_0), x(t_f), u(t_f)) = 0 \end{cases} \tag{10}$$

It can be seen that the trajectory optimization problem of MMRS can be summarized as an OCP, which has the objective function, state constraints, path constraints and boundary constraints.

4 Application of GPM

Generally, using the direct method (e.g., Pontryagin's minimum principle) to solve OCP can obtain an accurate optimal trajectory. However, due to the high dimension and non-linearity of the trajectory planning problem in this work, the direct method usually has no desired convergence effect. Instead, GPM is adopted in this work because of its large convergence radius and high computational efficiency.

Essentially, GPM approximates the OCP as a nonlinear programming (NLP) problem at Legendre-Gaussian (LG) points, which is the zero points of N-degree Legendre polynomial (N is also the number of LG points). To accommodate LG points, the time interval $[t_0, t_f]$ needs to be linearly transformed into $[-1, 1]$:

$$t = \frac{t_f - t_0}{2} \tau + \frac{t_f + t_0}{2}. \tag{11}$$

where $\tau \in [-1, 1]$ is the time interval after transformation. Then, the state and control variables are approximated as a global interpolation polynomial respectively:

$$
\begin{cases}
\boldsymbol{x}(\tau) \approx \boldsymbol{X}(\tau) = \sum_{i=0}^{N} L_i(\tau)\boldsymbol{X}_i \\
\boldsymbol{u}(\tau) \approx \boldsymbol{U}(\tau) = \sum_{i=1}^{N} L_i'(\tau)\boldsymbol{U}_i
\end{cases}
\tag{12}
$$

where $\boldsymbol{X}$ and $\boldsymbol{U}$ are variables after approximation, L_i and L_i' are the bases of Lagrange polynomials and the subscript "i" means the i-th LG point.

In order to obtain a high-precision solution, the objective function is approximated by Gaussian quadrature:

$$
\int_{t_0}^{t_f} g(\boldsymbol{x}(t))\, \mathrm{d}t \approx \frac{t_f - t_0}{2} \sum_{i=1}^{N} w_i g(\boldsymbol{X}_i).
\tag{13}
$$

where w_i is the quadrature weight at the i-th LG point, with the following expression:

$$
w_i = 2 / \left[(1 - \tau_i^2)\dot{\mathcal{L}}_N^2(\tau_i) \right]
\tag{14}
$$

where $\mathcal{L}_N$ is the N-degree Legendre polynomial.

In summary, the final Gauss Pseudospectral NLP problem can be described as

$$
\min J = \frac{t_f - t_0}{2} \sum_{i=1}^{N} w_i g(\boldsymbol{X}_i)
$$
$$
s.t. \begin{cases}
\boldsymbol{f}(\boldsymbol{X}_i, \boldsymbol{U}_i, \tau_i) = \boldsymbol{0}, \ i = 1, ..., N \\
\boldsymbol{C}(\boldsymbol{X}_i, \boldsymbol{U}_i) \leq \boldsymbol{0}, \ i = 1, ..., N \\
\boldsymbol{E}(\boldsymbol{X}_0, \boldsymbol{U}_0, \boldsymbol{X}_f, \boldsymbol{U}_f) = \boldsymbol{0}
\end{cases}
\tag{15}
$$

It can be observed that (15) is a constrained NLP problem, which can be solved by the Quasi-Newton method with interior penalty functions.

The overall algorithm flow is designed as follows:

  i) Enter necessary parameters and a proper initial N.
 ii) Transform the OCP into a discrete NLP problem using GPM.
iii) Solve the NLP problem using the Quasi-Newton method.
 iv) Compute the trajectory tracking error of MMRS.
  v) If the error satisfies the given tolerance, output the results of joint trajectories; Otherwise, increase N and return ii).

5   Numerical Simulations and Discussions

In this section, we mainly display the gap between the proposed 3-DOF end-effector and the traditional 1-DOF end-effector in trajectory planning. The strokes of both end-effectors are set to be equal (3 cm). To present the results of curved surface polishing, an arc task path is designed, as shown in Fig. 3. The arc path is installed latitudinally or longitudinally (the x-axis is the initial positive direction of the macro-robot), as shown in Fig. 3(a) (Case A) and Fig. 3(b) (Case B), to show the diversity of velocity optimization (for macro-robot's different joints). It is worth noting that the task path installed longitudinally is only half an arc, which is to avoid the macro-robot passing through the singular configuration. In addition, the influence of the end-effectors' strokes are also discussed.

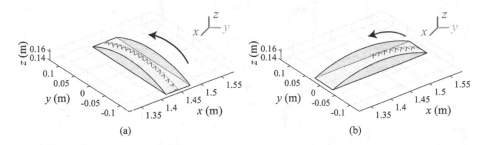

(a)   (b)

Fig. 3. Predefined arc task path. (a) Case A: Horizontal workpiece. (b) Case B: Vertical workpiece (to avoid singularity, it is only half an arc).

5.1 Results of Case A

For Case A, simulation results are: $J_{1-\text{DOF}} = 0.0322$ rad/s and $J_{3-\text{DOF}} = 0.0138$ rad/s. For the given task path, the overall joint velocity of the macro-robot is almost reduced by 57.1%. Figure 4 shows the specific simulation curves. Theoretically, the 3-DOF end-effector indirectly reduces joint velocities of the macro-robot by compensating its Cartesian space motion (mainly for the rotation around the x-axis/y-axis and the translation along the z-axis). Figure 4(a) and (b) show the results of angular and linear velocities (expressed in the body frame $\{T\}$) of the macro-robot in Cartesian space, respectively. The subscripts "1" and "3" denote 1-DOF and 3-DOF end-effectors, respectively. Intuitively, the 3-DOF end-effector makes more considerable compensation for ω_x, which results from the frame distribution in Case A. This also leads to the differences in v_x and v_y between the 3-DOF and 1-DOF end-effectors. Remarkably, since the optimization algorithm mainly considers the weighted joint velocity of the macro-robot, the 3-DOF end-effector does not strictly rotate around x-axis (ω_{y3} is not equal to 0). This can be explained by the joint displacement curves of 3-DOF end-effector in Fig. 4(c): ϑ_2 is not exactly equal to ϑ_3. In addition, ω_{z3} and v_{x3} have extremely small fluctuations around zero, which is caused by the parasitic motion of the 3-DOF end-effector and can be considered insignificant.

Figure 4(d)–(i) show the comparison results of six joint velocities of the macro-robot. Generally, the decrease of velocity in Cartesian space (described in Fig. 4(a) and (b)) leads to the expected lower joint velocities: The reduction rates are about 31%, 47%, 70%, 95% and 57% for joint 1, 2, 4, 5 and 6. It is worth noting that the velocity increase of joint 3 caused by the 3-DOF end-effector can be considered insignificant because it only has an order of 10^{-3}. In addition, since the task path is installed latitudinally, the macro-robot mainly moves in the y-z plane (described in $\{B\}$). Therefore, when comparing 1-DOF and 3-DOF end-effectors, the velocity difference between joint 2 and joint 3 (mainly responsible for the motion in the x-z plane) is small.

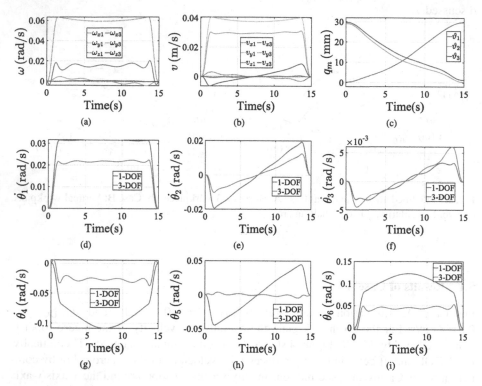

Fig. 4. Results of Case A. (a) Angular velocity in Cartesian space of macro-robot (the subscript "1" means 1-DOF end-effector, while "3" means 3-DOF end-effector). (b) Linear velocity in Cartesian space of macro-robot. (c) Joint displacements of the 3-DOF end-effector. (d)–(i) Comparison of joint velocities of the macro-robot.

5.2 Results of Case B

For Case B, the simulation results are: $J_{1-\mathrm{DOF}} = 0.0213\,\mathrm{rad/s}$ and $J_{3-\mathrm{DOF}} = 0.0063\,\mathrm{rad/s}$. For the given task path, the overall joint velocity of the macro-robot is almost reduced by 70.5%. Figure 5 shows the specific simulation curves (the description is consistent with Case A). Compared with Case A, Case B is easier to analyze, since the macro-robot can almost be seen as a planar three-link robot. From Fig. 5(a), we can see that the angular velocity compensation of 3-DOF end-effector to the macro-robot changes the direction of ω_x, which is to obtain lower joint velocities. In addition, for the given weight matrix $\boldsymbol{W}$, the cognition that $\omega_{x3} \equiv 0$ is the optimal trajectory seems to be untenable. The reduction of v_y in Fig. 5(b) also benefits from the orientation compensation of the 3-DOF end-effector. Due to the accurate rotation around the x-axis, the curves of ϑ_2 and ϑ_3 are identical, as shown in Fig. 5(c), which is different from Fig. 4(c).

Figure 5(d)–(i) show the comparison results of six joint velocities of the macro-robot. As mentioned above, the macro-robot in Case B can be regarded as a three-link robot in the x-z plane. Therefore, the task path is almost completed by joint 2, 3 and 5. Due to the orientation compensation of the 3-DOF end-effector, the velocities of these three joints are reduced by 60%, 51% and 93%, respectively. It is worth noting that the insignificant velocity fluctuations of $\dot{\theta}_1$, $\dot{\theta}_4$ and $\dot{\theta}_6$ are derived from the parasitic motion of the 3-DOF end-effector, which can be ignored.

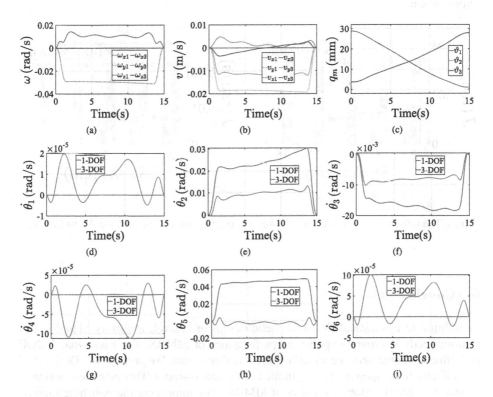

Fig. 5. Results of Case B. (a) Angular velocity in Cartesian space of macro-robot. (b) Linear velocity in Cartesian space of macro-robot. (c) Joint displacements of the 3-DOF end-effector. (d)–(i) Comparison of joint velocities of the macro-robot.

5.3 Discussions of Stroke

This part presents the optimization results of changes in strokes: Fig. 6(a) for Case A and Fig. 6(b) for Case B. It is worth noting that we do not change the size of the base/moving platform of the 3-DOF end-effector to maintain the uniqueness of variable. Thus, under large stroke (12 cm and 15 cm), the optimization results of it are not given due to the singularity of the mechanism.

Overall, large stroke does not significantly enhance the trajectory planning performance of the 1-DOF end-effector (within 4%), as the position scale of macro-robot is significantly larger than that of micro-robot. However, in terms of an orientation scale, macro-robot and micro-robot are almost equal. A special phenomenon is that in Fig. 6(a), the increase in stroke leads to an improvement in the optimization effect of the 3-DOF end-effector. This is because the range of the 2-DOF rotation increases from 18.2° (3 cm) to 69.6° (9 cm). In Fig. 6(b), due to the particularity of the workpiece's installation pose, the rotation range of 18.2° is almost saturated. Therefore, even for the 3-DOF end-effector, an increase in stroke can not lead to a significant performance improvement.

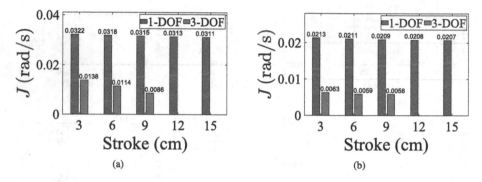

Fig. 6. The influence of end-effectors' strokes on optimization results. (a) Case A; (b) Case B.

6   Conclusion

In addition to mechanical/electromagnetic design or control, trajectory planning can also indirectly improve the polishing performance of MMRS. The traditional 1-DOF end-effector cannot produce a marked effect in this aspect. We propose a 3-DOF 2R1T end-effector to compensate for the motion of the macro-robot. This practice can significantly enhance the motion stability of MMRS, thus improving the polishing quality. The polishing simulations of the arc path show that the proposed 3-DOF end-effector is superior to the 1-DOF one in compensating for the velocity of the macro-robot.

Acknowledgment. This work was supported by National Key Research and Development Program of China (2022YFB4702500), the Key Research and Development Program of Zhejiang Province (2022C01101, 2022C01096), the Natural Science Foundation of Zhejiang Province (LD22E050007) and the Ningbo Key Project of Scientific and Technological Innovation 2025 (2022Z037, 2021Z020, 2022Z065).

References

1. Ochoa, H., Cortesao, R.: Impedance control architecture for robotic-assisted mold polishing based on human demonstration. IEEE Trans. Industr. Electron. **69**, 3822–3830 (2021)
2. Tian, F., Lv, C., Li, Z., Liu, G.: Modeling and control of robotic automatic polishing for curved surfaces. CIRP J. Manuf. Sci. Technol. **14**, 55–64 (2016)
3. Xiao, M., Ding, Y., Yang, G.: A model-based trajectory planning method for robotic polishing of complex surfaces. IEEE Trans. Autom. Sci. Eng. **19**(4), 2890–2903 (2021)
4. Yang, G., Zhu, R., Fang, Z., Chen, C.Y., Zhang, C.: Kinematic design of a 2R1T robotic end-effector with flexure joints. IEEE Access **8**, 57204–57213 (2020)
5. Mohammad, A.E.K., Hong, J., Wang, D.: Design of a force-controlled end-effector with low-inertia effect for robotic polishing using macro-mini robot approach. Robot. Comput.-Integr. Manuf. **49**, 54–65 (2018)
6. Chen, F., Zhao, H., Li, D., Chen, L., Tan, C., Ding, H.: Contact force control and vibration suppression in robotic polishing with a smart end effector. Robot. Comput.-Integr. Manuf. **57**, 391–403 (2019)
7. Van Damme, M., et al.: Estimating robot end-effector force from noisy actuator torque measurements. In: 2011 IEEE International Conference on Robotics and Automation, pp. 1108–1113. IEEE (2011)
8. Chertopolokhov, V., Andrianova, O., Hernandez-Sanchez, A., Mireles, C., Poznyak, A., Chairez, I.: Averaged sub-gradient integral sliding mode control design for cueing end-effector acceleration of a two-link robotic arm. ISA Trans. **133**, 134–146 (2023)
9. Li, Y., Chen, W., Yang, L.: Multistage linear gauss pseudospectral method for piecewise continuous nonlinear optimal control problems. IEEE Trans. Aerosp. Electron. Syst. **57**(4), 2298–2310 (2021)
10. Pieper, D.L.: The Kinematics of Manipulators Under Computer Control. Stanford University (1969)
11. Garg, D., Patterson, M., Hager, W.W., Rao, A.V., Benson, D.A., Huntington, G.T.: A unified framework for the numerical solution of optimal control problems using pseudospectral methods. Automatica **46**(11), 1843–1851 (2010)

KGGPT: Empowering Robots with OpenAI's ChatGPT and Knowledge Graph

Zonghao Mu[1,2], Wenyu Zhao[1,2], Yue Yin[1,2], Xiangming Xi[1,2], Wei Song[1,2(✉)], Jianjun Gu[1,2], and Shiqiang Zhu[1,2]

[1] Research Center for Intelligent Robotics, Research Institute of Interdisciplinary Innovation, Zhejiang Lab, Hangzhou 311100, China
[2] Zhejiang Engineering Research Center for Intelligent Robotics, Hangzhou 311100, China
{muzonghao,wyuzhao,yinyue,xxm21,weisong,jgu,zhusq}@zhejianglab.com

Abstract. This paper presents a study on using knowledge graph with ChatGP for robotics applications, called KGGPT. Traditional planning methods for robot tasks based on structured data and sequential actions, such as rosplan, have limitations such as limited data range and lack of flexibility to modify behaviors based on user feedback. Recent research has focused on combining AI planning with large language models (LLMs) to overcome these limitations, but generated text may not always be consistent with real-world physics and the robot skills to perform physical actions. To address these challenges, we propose KGGPT, a system that incorporates prior knowledge to enable ChatGPT for a variety of robotic tasks. KGGPT extracts relevant knowledge from the knowledge graph, generates a semantic description of the knowledge, and connects it to ChatGPT. The gap between the knowledge of ChatGPT and actual service environments is addressed by using the knowledge graph to model robot skills, task rules, and environmental constraints. The output is a behavior tree based on robot skills. We evaluate our method in an office setting and show that it outperforms traditional PDDL planning and a separate ChatGPT planning scheme. Additionally, our system reduces programming effort for applications when new task requirements arise. This research has the potential to significantly advance the field of robotics.

Keywords: ChatGPT · Knowledge graph · AI planning

1 Introduction

Robotic task planning is an important aspect of artificial intelligence with a wide range of applications in industry and services. However, traditional planning approaches based on structured data and sequential operations (e.g. Rosplan

Supported by "Pioneer" and "Leading Goose" R&D Program of Zhejiang (2022C01130) and Key Research Project of Zhejiang Lab (No. G2021NB0AL03).
Z. Mu and W. Zhao—Contribute equally to this work.

[2]) have several limitations, including limited data range and lack of flexibility to modify behaviors based on user feedback. Recent researches [1,14] has focused on overcoming these limits with LLMs can flexibly generate lists of key actions required to complete tasks, opening up the possibility of building general-purpose robot intelligence systems. However, the text generated by large language models may not always be consistent with real-world physics and the robot skills to perform physical actions. In this paper, we propose a system called KGGPT to bridge the gap between generated text and actual task execution. As shown in Fig. 1, the entire process of KGGPT can be divided into three stages:

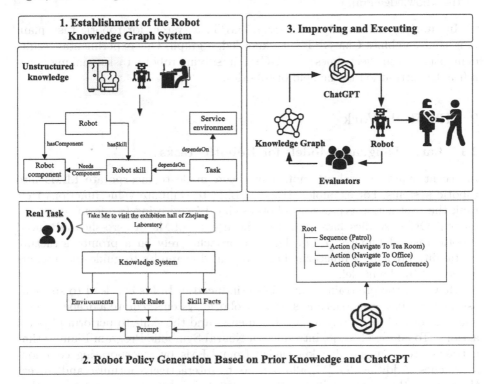

Fig. 1. Overview of KGGPT

- Establishment of the robot knowledge graph system: The system organizes unstructured knowledge into a knowledge graph, including robot, robot component, robot skills, service environment, and task.
- Robot Policy Generation Based on Prior Knowledge and ChatGPT: Convert the task-oriented knowledge extracted from the knowledge graph into appropriate semantic hints, enabling ChatGPT to plan tasks effectively and efficiently. The output is a behavior tree with robot skills as nodes.
- Improvement and execution: During the test process, according to the feedback of the applicable person, modify the task rules in the knowledge graph, so as to improve the planning effect until the requirements are met.

Therefore, KGGPT can make full use of the robot skills and task rules to constrain the task strategy generated by ChatGPT, thus handling various real tasks.

The contributions of this paper mainly include the following three aspects:

- Development of a knowledge graph, including robot, robot component, robot skills, service environment, and task.
- Provide a new way to design general-purpose robot task planning.
- Provision of a scheme to continuously improve the execution logic by updating the knowledge graph.

In summary, our study proposes KGGPT, a system for robotic task planning that combines ChatGPT with knowledge graph. Our experimental results demonstrate the effectiveness of KGGPT in solving robotic tasks, making a significant contribution to the field of robotics.

2   Related Work

2.1   Large Language Models for Robotic Tasks

In recent years, several attempts have been made to incorporate LLMs into robotic systems. For example, [1] uses LLMs to compute value functions that rank the best action types in a robot-specific library using free-form text commands. Other studies have explored the use of LLMs in zero-shot advanced robotic task planning [5,7,14]. These approaches rely on a prompt structure containing predefined functions, behaviors, and examples to guide the answers generated by the model.

However, the pre-training knowledge induced in LLMs can lead to spurious associations between goals and steps, as robotic systems require a deeper understanding of real-world physics, environments, and the skills to perform physical actions. To address this, [8] introduces a Neural Symbolic Program Planner that extracts program planning knowledge from LLMs by incorporating commonsense cues. Additionally, [17] allows users to interactively optimize and correct the plan, rather than modifying the prompt from scratch to generate another zero-shot response. These approaches rely on prior knowledge to modify the planning of the LLMs.

Overall, the use of prior knowledge and commonsense cues can improve the accuracy and effectiveness of LLM-based planning, providing a new way to design general-purpose robot task planning.

2.2   Knowledge Graph and Robotic Task Planning

In the field of robotics, prior knowledge can be expressed through knowledge graph, and there have been many studies. Research on knowledge graphs such as RoboEarth [18], KnowRob [15], and RoboBrain [12] has yielded outstanding results, highlighting the growing importance of knowledge methodologies.

Therefore, it is very common to use knowledge graph to organize the information required for robot task planning. Previous research has attempted to use knowledge graph to store the underlying task planning and semantic representation of robots, including object affordances [16], robot action trees [11], and dynamic capabilities [9]. This knowledge can then guide planning modules, such as the Model of PDDL structure [6] and neural networks [3], in planning new tasks. Recent experiments that combine task planning and knowledge graph have demonstrated the effectiveness of incorporating knowledge in robotic tasks [4,10].

In the task planning process, it is critical to understand what the task needs to do and what the robot is capable of doing. It seems feasible to infer from the robot's components whether it can perform the task. But it is tedious to infer robot tasks directly from components because components vary between robots. To address this problem, modeling tasks as a set of basic skills to be performed and reasoning about the availability of the modeling [19] or potential representations of these skills [13] has proven successful in integrating planning algorithms and generalizing to various task domains. In this study, an ontology approach to modeling robot tasks, skills, and components is used to enable the task planning module to understand the robot's capabilities better and thus improve the effectiveness of task planning.

3   Method

The workflow of KGGPT consists of three stages, 1) Establishment of Robotic Knowledge Graph system, 2) Robot Policy Generation Based on Prior Knowledge and ChatGPT, and 3) Improving and Executing.

3.1   Establishment of Robotic Knowledge Graph System

When planning for a task, the task planning system needs to understand not only what it needs to do in the servicing environment but also what it is capable of doing. Therefore, we use a task-oriented ontology, including a multi-layered framework: robot, robot component, robot skills, service environment, and task to guide task planning with the related knowledge. As shown in Fig. 2, in our system, the completion of robot tasks depends on the robot skills and the service environment. Task class semantic descriptions are independent of the robot class and are adapted to robot component classes through robot skills classes. The following sections provide a detailed description of the ontology of the robot, robot component, robot skills, service environment, and task.

Robot and Robot Component. The robot ontology defines the attributes of the robot, such as name, dimensions, and so on. The robot component ontology is defined to describe all that a robot contains, including hardware and software. Robot components are represented in the knowledge graph as instances of component classes to capture their component types and specific robots.

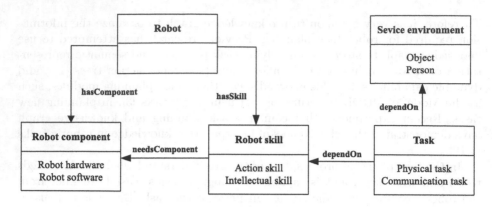

Fig. 2. The Ontology of KGGPT

Robot Skills. Robots and their components are specific, and different robots may require different components to perform the same task. There are many limitations if each component is a necessary element in the task planning process. Thus, robot skills are needed to serve as a bridge between robot components and tasks. Robot skills represent the ability of a robot to perform certain tasks. The ontology of robot skills is crucial. The ability of a robot to perform a task in a given situation depends on its skills. A task requires a set of skills, while a set of components gives the robot certain skills that help us to plan tasks more flexibly without the limitations of the robot software and hardware.

Service Environment. The service environment ontology is designed to describe people, objects, and their relationships in the scene, to provide support for task planning. In the process of task execution, the robot not only needs to perceive the items in the environment but also needs to identify the service object. For example, for service robots, map information is very important in the process of completing tasks. Map information is required for many robot actions, such as moving, manipulating objects, and finding objects. Therefore, we semantically describe the space information in the map, mainly including the positional relationship between locations and the coordinates of the locations.

Task. The tasks that robots can complete are mainly divided into two categories: communication tasks and physical tasks. A communication task is a task in which two or more agents exchange information. Physical tasks include the tasks in which a Physical Agent affects some physical object, such as Interacting, Manipulating, Navigating, and so on.

The task ontology semantically describes the relevant content and execution rules of robot tasks. In our knowledge system, task ontology has a mutual relationship with robot ontology to define and reflect the skills information required in the task. In addition to skills, tasks also depend on the service environment. The dependency relationship is specified using the object attribute "dependOn".

By using these relationships in knowledge reasoning, complex knowledge can be generated and provided to determine which robots can complete specific tasks.

In addition, the knowledge graph also includes logical rules for task execution. These rules enhance the ability of the task planner to derive the corresponding optimal plan when determining that a specific robot can complete a task. Once it is determined that a robot has the skills to complete a task, this information will be extracted and used to help the task planning system.

3.2 Robot Policy Generation Based on Prior Knowledge and ChatGPT

To plan a robot task, KGGPT needs to extract relevant knowledge from the knowledge graph and input it into ChatGPT. This requires converting structured knowledge into a suitable semantic description to facilitate ChatGPT's understanding and planning. KGGPT extracts the required knowledge from the three types of knowledge related to the robot, task, and service environment mentioned above, and semantically describes them in the form of facts and rules.

The robot knowledge graph provides the semantic description, code specification, and robot components on which the skills of the robot are based, which are stated as known facts. Robot skills has their own limitations, such as their scope of use and necessary components required, which are described as rules. The task knowledge graph provides the semantic description of the task, the list of parameters required for task execution, and the task dependencies that define the prerequisite tasks required for execution. The rules mainly impose common constraints on the completion of tasks. The service environment knowledge includes various objects and their attributes that robots can visually perceive in the service environment.

The output of ChatGPT task planning is generally semantics or code. Semantic methods are not suitable for robots to understand, while code methods are difficult for humans to understand, and it is not easy to handle tasks that require parallel operations. Behavior trees are a common method for robot task planning, which is easy for users to understand and can perform tasks. Therefore, KGGPT requires ChatGPT to output skills as behavior tree nodes, enabling the system to plan tasks effectively and efficiently, ensuring that the robot can understand and complete tasks smoothly.

Figure 3 provides an example of the notification policy generation process in the office scenario, demonstrating the skills to generate robot task processes and content. In this scenario, the user commands the robot to notification Sam that he can take leave tomorrow, which falls under the notification task type. For the notification task, the robot must have two skills: search for people and communicate. The system extracts the semantics of the notification task from the knowledge graph, along with the general rules of tasks and skills. Then, based on the skills requirements, the system searches for component information, evaluates the feasibility of the task and sends it to ChatGPT.

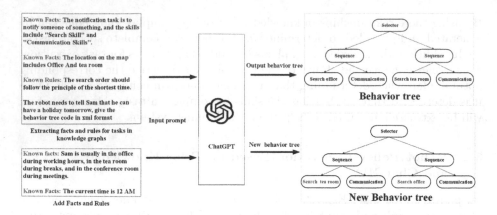

Fig. 3. Notification policy generation process

3.3 Improving and Executing

During actual testing, various practical problems may arise, but unlike traditional task processes that require recoding, KGGPT can adapt to these problems by changing the knowledge in the knowledge graph and generating new solutions accordingly. As shown in Fig. 3, we add two known facts: Sam is usually in the office during working hours, in the tea room during breaks, and in the conference room during meetings, while the current time is 10 AM. Using this information, the regenerated behavior tree will search the office first and the tea room last. This approach can be used as a strategy by designers to improve the efficiency and effectiveness of task planning. In the next chapter, we conduct method tests and comparisons to evaluate the performance of KGGPT in handling robotic tasks.

4   Experiments and Results

To demonstrate the effectiveness of our proposed strategy for improving robotic systems, we evaluate it on real robots, as shown in Fig. 4. To evaluate the effectiveness of our method, we design three different types of tasks: patrolling, notification and delivery. We compare our method with rosplan-based planning methods (which is a ROS package that includes PDDL-based planning methods) and proposals generated directly based on ChatGPT (input task description and given the robot's API), all of which are under the same task information conditions. We evaluate these methods in terms of success rate and time required to complete the task.

4.1   Patrol Task

We design a patrol task to evaluate the effectiveness of our proposed method, which requires the robot to individually visit all specified points on the map

Fig. 4. The robot in our system is equipped with a mobile base, two 6-DOF arms, a depth camera, and a speaker.

within a given time limit for the task to be considered successful. To make the task more challenging, we randomize the initial position of the robot, which means that the robot has to prioritize the remaining points for patrolling according to the current situation.

Table 1. Patrol task success rate and average time

Project	Approach	Success Rate	Avg. Time (s)
Patrol	Our approach	100%	55
	rosplan	100%	72
	Only ChatGPT	100%	75

In the patrol task, the general facts of the task include its current location, and the coordinates of the marked points, and our method obtains the main rule from the knowledge graph is to complete the patrol as quickly as possible, and the shortest path principle can be considered. Our proposed method exploits common sense in large language models and combines the positions of multiple markers with the robot's current position, as shown in Fig. 5. In contrast, the solutions provided by rosplan and ChatGPT patrol according to the order of the given points on the map, regardless of the location of the robot. This is because rosplan does not have the function of planning the navigation order according to the length of the path, but only in a predetermined order. ChatGPT, on the other hand, does not emphasize time and only treats it as a secondary factor. As shown in Table 1, although all tasks are completed within the specified time, it is clear that our method outperforms other solutions in terms of time efficiency.

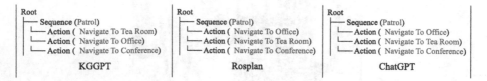

Fig. 5. The nearest point of the robot's real-time position is the tea room, which we use as the starting point of the patrol, and give priority to unvisited marked points according to the shortest path principle.

4.2 Notification Task

Another task we designed to evaluate our proposed strategy is the notification task, in which a robot is assigned to notify a specific individual of a specific event within a specified time frame. To add to the difficulty of the task, we do not provide the exact location of the person, only possible locations. Therefore, the robot must adjust its search strategy according to the current situation.

Table 2. Notification task success rate and average time

Project	Approach	Success Rate	Avg. Time (s)
Notification	Our approach	100%	38
	rosplan	100%	58
	Only ChatGPT	70%	35

In this task, the known facts of the task include the possible location of the human being, such as in the office, tea room, or conference room, and the time when the task starts. What our method obtains from the knowledge graph includes the people are usually in the office during working hours and in the tea room during breaks.

Fig. 6. The current time is 10:00 am, our scenario starts the search in the office, and if the person cannot be found, continues the search in other rooms.

Our method prioritizes search locations according to the current time, as shown in Fig. 6. On the other hand, the solution provided by Rosplan searches each room in turn and does not take into account the most likely location of the person. As a result, the search takes a long time, and some tasks may fail. The solution given by ChatGPT only searches the most likely room. If no one is found in that room, it will not search in other areas. As shown in Table 2, our proposed method outperforms other solutions in terms of time efficiency and task completion rate.

4.3   Delivery Tasks

The last task we designed to evaluate our proposed policy was the delivery task, in which the robot was required to transport 4 drinking glasses from the office to the tea room within a specified time limit. To make the task more challenging, we randomly assign the weight of each item between 0–500 g, and the weight of each delivery of the robot is limited to 500 g. Since our robot does not have dexterous hands, human assistance is required for the grasping part.

Table 3. Delivery task success rate and average time

Project	Approach	Success Rate	Avg. Time (s)
Delivery	Our approach	100%	138
	rosplan	0%	521
	Only ChatGPT	80%	228

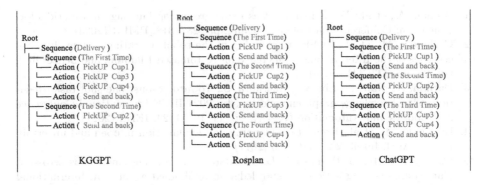

Fig. 7. In this example the office has the following cups: Cup No. 1 (230 g), Cup No. 2 (430 g), Cup No. 3 (130 g), Cup No. 4 (30 g). Our method delivered cups 1, 3, and 4 for the first time, and cup 2 for the second time, significantly outperforming the other methods

In this task, the known facts include the weight of each drinking glass and the total mass of each delivered item, which cannot exceed 500 g. Our method extracts the rule required to complete delivery tasks from the knowledge graph is that the robot can carry more than one cup at a time and should carry as much weight as possible. To complete the delivery task, KGGPT employs a greedy algorithm to select the delivery method with the least number of times, as shown in Fig. 7. In contrast, rosplan does not have its own plan, and the water glasses are delivered one by one, which leads to exceeding the time limit. ChatGPT delivers the drinking glasses in the given order until the weight limit of 500g is reached. As shown in Table 3, our method outperforms both of these methods in terms of success rate and time required to complete the task.

5   Conclusion

This paper presents KGGPT, a system that uses a knowledge graph to link LLMs with actual robotic tasks. LLMs act as the robot's brain and plan tasks into a behavior tree composed of multiple skills nodes based on the robot and actual scene information. The gap between the knowledge of ChatGPT and actual service environments is addressed by using the knowledge graph to model robot skills, task rules, and environmental constraints. Experimental results demonstrate that KGGPT outperforms conventional task planning algorithms and pure ChatGPT planning effects in handling robot tasks. Our design can inspire the entire robotics industry and open a new path toward general-purpose robotic intelligence. In the future, we hope to explore the use of ChatGPT for multi-modal information understanding and task planning to achieve general robot intelligent operation.

References

1. Brohan, A., et al.: Do as i can, not as i say: grounding language in robotic affordances. In: Conference on Robot Learning, pp. 287–318. PMLR (2023)
2. Cashmore, M., et al.: ROSPlan: planning in the robot operating system. In: Proceedings of the International Conference on Automated Planning and Scheduling, vol. 25, pp. 333–341 (2015)
3. Daruna, A., Nair, L., Liu, W., Chernova, S.: Towards robust one-shot task execution using knowledge graph embeddings. In: 2021 IEEE International Conference on Robotics and Automation (ICRA), pp. 11118–11124. IEEE (2021)
4. Hanheide, M., et al.: Robot task planning and explanation in open and uncertain worlds. Artif. Intell. **247**, 119–150 (2017)
5. Huang, W., Abbeel, P., Pathak, D., Mordatch, I.: Language models as zero-shot planners: extracting actionable knowledge for embodied agents. In: International Conference on Machine Learning, pp. 9118–9147. PMLR (2022)
6. Kootbally, Z., Schlenoff, C., Lawler, C., Kramer, T., Gupta, S.K.: Towards robust assembly with knowledge representation for the planning domain definition language (PDDL). Robot. Comput.-Integr. Manuf. **33**, 42–55 (2015)
7. Liang, J., et al.: Code as policies: language model programs for embodied control. arXiv preprint arXiv:2209.07753 (2022)
8. Lu, Y., et al.: Neuro-symbolic procedural planning with commonsense prompting. arXiv preprint arXiv:2206.02928 (2022)

9. Munawar, A., et al.: MaestROB: a robotics framework for integrated orchestration of low-level control and high-level reasoning. In: 2018 IEEE International Conference on Robotics and Automation (ICRA), pp. 527–534. IEEE (2018)

10. Nyga, D., et al.: Grounding robot plans from natural language instructions with incomplete world knowledge. In: Conference on Robot Learning, pp. 714–723. PMLR (2018)

11. Puig, X., Ra, K., Boben, M., Li, J., Wang, T., Fidler, S., Torralba, A.: VirtualHome: simulating household activities via programs. In: Proceedings of the IEEE Conference on Computer Vision and Pattern Recognition, pp. 8494–8502 (2018)

12. Saxena, A., et al.: RoboBrain: large-scale knowledge engine for robots. arXiv preprint arXiv:1412.0691 (2014)

13. Silver, T., Athalye, A., Tenenbaum, J.B., Lozano-Perez, T., Kaelbling, L.P.: Learning neuro-symbolic skills for bilevel planning. arXiv preprint arXiv:2206.10680 (2022)

14. Singh, I., et al.: ProgPrompt: generating situated robot task plans using large language models. arXiv preprint arXiv:2209.11302 (2022)

15. Tenorth, M., Beetz, M.: KNOWROB-knowledge processing for autonomous personal robots. In: 2009 IEEE/RSJ International Conference on Intelligent Robots and Systems, pp. 4261–4266. IEEE (2009)

16. Varadarajan, K.M., Vincze, M.: AfRob: the affordance network ontology for robots. In: 2012 IEEE/RSJ International Conference on Intelligent Robots and Systems, pp. 1343–1350. IEEE (2012)

17. Vemprala, S., Bonatti, R., Bucker, A., Kapoor, A.: ChatGPT for robotics: design principles and model abilities (2023)

18. Waibel, M., et al.: Roboearth. IEEE Robot. Autom. Mag. **18**(2), 69–82 (2011)

19. Xu, D., Mandlekar, A., Martín-Martín, R., Zhu, Y., Savarese, S., Fei-Fei, L.: Deep affordance foresight: planning through what can be done in the future. In: 2021 IEEE International Conference on Robotics and Automation (ICRA), pp. 6206–6213. IEEE (2021)

Robot Trajectory Optimization with Reinforcement Learning Based on Local Dynamic Fitting

Ji Liang[1,2](✉), Shuo Yan[2], Guangbin Sun[2], Ge Yu[2], and Lili Guo[2]

[1] University of Chinese Academy of Sciences, Beijing, China
liangji@csu.ac.cn
[2] Key Laboratory of Space Utilization, Technology and Engineering Center for Space Utilization, Beijing, China
yanshuo@csu.ac.cn

Abstract. With the development of artificial intelligence, reinforcement learning plays an increasingly important role in the robot operation filed. In this paper, a trajectory optimization method based on local dynamic model fitting is proposed to improve sample utilization and reduce the difficulty of dynamic model learning. Firstly, the Gaussian mixture model of the robot was constructed, and based on this, the accurate local dynamics model was obtained through the Normal-inverse-wishart distribution. Secondly, LQR optimization algorithm was used to optimize the robot trajectory, and the optimal control strategy was obtained during the grasping process of the robot. Finally, the effectiveness of the proposed algorithm is verified on the dynamic simulation platform. The experimental results show that the method proposed in this paper can significantly improve sample utilization and learning efficiency.

Keywords: Trajectory Optimization · Reinforcement Learning · Robot Learning

1 Introduction

More and more domains are using robots to assist humans in daily life, such as space/underwater missions, invasive surgeries [1], remote patient monitoring [2], as it provides a low-cost solution for the dangerous or tedious tasks. These robot controllers are mostly designed and tuned by human beings so far, which is a tedious task and may requires years of experience and high degree of expertise. The programmed controllers are based on assuming exact models of both the robot's behavior and its environment. Consequently, these kinds of robot controllers has its limitations when a robot has to adapt to new situations or when the robot/environment cannot be modeled sufficiently accurately [3, 4]. Hence, there is a gap between the robots currently used and the vision of incorporating fully autonomous robots.

Machine learning methods which extract relevant information from data provide us with a new way to solve the robot autonomous operation task. Using the flexibility and power of modern machine learning techniques, the field of robot control may

H. Yang et al. (Eds.): ICIRA 2023, LNAI 14271, pp. 352–364, 2023.
https://doi.org/10.1007/978-981-99-6495-6_30

be further automated, and the gap toward autonomous robots, can be narrowed substantially [5]. However, machine learning algorithms also suffer from three main challenges: high-dimensional continuous state and behavior, high real-time requirements and time-consuming interaction between robot and environment. At present, the most widely used machine learning method for robotics is reinforcement learning algorithm, which is divided into model free method and model based method [6].

J. Kober [7] improved the actor critical algorithm and put forward the eNAC algorithm to learn the complex skills with human like limbs. And the algorithm was verified in the example of 7-DOF robot hitting baseball. To further improve learning performance, J. Kober [8] proposed the policy learning algorithm by weighting exploration with the returns. By the use of this algorithm the ball-in-the-cup task is successfully completed in the simulation and real environment. P. Kormushev [9] incorporated a mechanism of learning local coupling information into PoWER algorithm, and verified it in pancake flipping task on the Barrett WAM 7-DOF robot. J. Kober [10] extended the reward weighted regression policy to cost regularized kernel regression, and verified the algorithm through dart throwing and table tennis experiments. C. Daniel [11] proposed hierarchical relative entropy policy search method, which can learn the parallel solution of a motor skill task. Therefore, the local degradation of the solution space will not prevent the successful completion of the task. This method significantly improves the robustness of robot applications and makes their motion library more like human beings, which is verified by rope ball experiment. C.Yang [12] employ a random network distillation method to train a series of neural networks and then use the SAC algorithm to maximize the return of the policy designed to capture a known object in space. Chase Frazelle [13] explore the application of policy optimization methods through Actor-Critic gradient descent in order to optimize a continuum manipulator's search method for an unknown object.

Since the model free policy search method directly learns from the real world, the policy function should not be too complex (the parameters should not be too many, which should be less than 100 [5]). In addition, model free method belongs to local search method, it is necessary to set the initial value of parameters as reasonably as possible. Otherwise the searched policy is likely to fall into local optimization.

Another kind of reinforcement learning method is model based method which samples the interaction between the robot and the environment first, then fits the dynamic model of the interaction between the robot and the environment according to the sampled data, and finally trains the robot with the dynamic model as the simulation environment. As a result of the policy interacts directly with the dynamic model, this kind of method greatly improves the efficiency of policy search.

Ng et al. [14, 15] used locally weighted Bayesian regression to learn the dynamic model of helicopter autonomous hovering. Considering the noise and inaccuracy of the model, they randomized the original deterministic model and added Gaussian noise to the dynamic model to improve the system stability.

Bagnell and Schneider [16] clearly described the uncertainty of the learning model through the posterior distribution, and selected the trajectory from these hybrid models with Pegasus (policy evaluation of goodness) method, which improved the robustness of the controller and verified it in helicopter control.

M. P. Deisenroth [17] proposed probabilistic influence for learning control policy search framework, and used Gaussian process to describe the uncertainty of manipulator dynamic model. The strategy parameters were updated by gradient descent method and verified in building block experiment.

Although model-based reinforcement learning method is efficient in policy search, the construction of accurate environmental dynamics model is challenging. What's more, the policy is easy to be affected by the errors of dynamics model.

To address these issues, we proposed a robot trajectory optimization method with reinforcement learning based on local dynamic fitting. In order to improve the learning efficiency of the dynamic model when robot interact with environment, a coarse to fine dynamic model fitting algorithm is constructed in this paper. On the bases of the dynamic model, the robot controller is optimized by LQR algorithm which improved the optimization efficiency.

This paper is organized as follows: In the first part, the linear time-varying Gaussian dynamic model and linear Gaussian controller is proposed to formulate the robot manipulation and motion process. Then to obtain the precise dynamic model a coarse to fine algorithm based on GMM is proposed. Subsequently, linear quadratic regulator algorithm is use to optimize the robot end-effector trajectory. To verify the validity and efficiency of the algorithm, a dynamic simulation verification platform based on ROS is constructed and based which a catch task is designed. Finally, the conclusion.

2 Approach

2.1 Definitions and Problem Formulation

In this paper, the manipulation and motion process of the robot is considered as a Finite Horizon Markov Decision Process [18]. There are five elements in the model: the robot and environment state s, the robot action a, the state transition distribution P_{sa} (also can be known as system dynamics), the reward, and mission duration time T. Usually, the robot and object both has six degree-of-freedom which can be shown as $\theta \in \mathbb{R}^{1 \times 6}$ and $\phi \in \mathbb{R}^{1 \times 6}$ respectively, where θ represents the robot six rotating joint angles and ϕ represents the six degree-of-freedom pose of the object based on the robot base coordinate system. The robot action is defined as $a = [\tau]^T$, where $\tau \in \mathbb{R}^{1 \times 6}$ represents the robot six rotating joint torque. The state transition distribution P_{sa} is defined as a conditional probability density function $p(s_{t+1}|s_t, a_t)$. The reward function $R(s_t, a_t)$ and mission duration time T varies according to the task. Our goal is to find an optimal controller or policy $p(a_t|s_t)$ to maximum the value function which is shown as follows:

$$V_p(s_0) = E_p \left[\sum_{t=0}^{T} R(s_t, a_t) \right] \tag{1}$$

where p represents the policy $p(a_t|s_t)$, s_0 represents the initial state of the system, and $E_p \left[\sum_{t=0}^{T} R(s_t, a_t) \right]$ represents the expected value of the total reward during time T.

S.M.Khansari-Zadeh [19] noted that the dynamics of contact between multiple rigid bodies can be roughly represented by a set of segmented, time-dependent linear models.

Therefore, in this paper, we use linear time-varying Gaussian model to formulate the dynamic model and controller. The dynamic model is shown as follows:

$$p(s_{t+1}|s_t, a_t) = N\left(F_{sat}\begin{bmatrix} s_t \\ a_t \end{bmatrix} + f_t, \delta_{st}\right) \tag{2}$$

where $F_{sat} = \begin{bmatrix} F_{st} & F_{at} \end{bmatrix}$, F_{st}, F_{at}, are the coefficients of the dynamic linear model at time t, f_t is the linear increments of the dynamic linear model at time t, and δ_{st} is the covariance matrix of the dynamic linear model at time t.

The controller is described as follows:

$$p(a_t|s_t) = N(K_t s_t + k_t, \delta_{at}) \tag{3}$$

where K_t is the coefficient, k_t is the linear increments and δ_{at} is the covariance matrix of the controller at time t respectively.

2.2 Local Dynamic Model Fitting Based on GMM

Based on the formulations above, by collecting a large number of samples of the robot's trajectory for the task, a linear regression can be used to fit the dynamics model of the robot's interaction with the environment. But for a system with multiple degrees of freedom like a robotic arm, a huge sample size is needed to get a better fit. What's more, these samples need to be sampled in a real environment using a physical robot arm, the wear and tear on the equipment and the time overhead is huge, so a direct fit is not practical.

Considering that under the same operation task and controller, the dynamics models at different moments of the robot arm movement have certain correlation, we fit the global dynamics through a Gaussian mixture model. This global model is used as a priori knowledge to fit the linear time-varying dynamic model of each step in the trajectory of the robot, so as to reduce the complexity of the local dynamic model fitting process. It is worth noting that this global dynamic model is only valid in a neighborhood where the initial state of the operating environment is at s_0.

Under the guidance of the above ideas, we first fit the global dynamic model of the interaction between the robot and the environment. We initialize a random Gaussian controller with zero control coefficient and linear increment, and control the robot to obtain a nominal trajectory $\tau = [s_0, a_0, s_1, a_1, ...s_t, a_t, ...s_T, a_T]$. At the same time, the state and action of each step is recorded $z_t = [s_t, a_t, s_{t+1}]$. To ensure the model accuracy, we can increase the number of nominal trajectories which are sampled under same controller and initial state. Then the samples are combined together to fit the global dynamic model.

The probability density function of Gaussian Mixture Model(GMM) is formulated as follows:

$$p(z_t|\mu, \delta) = \sum_{k=1}^{K} a_k \varphi(z_t|\mu_k, \delta_k) \tag{4}$$

where K is the number of sub Gaussian model of GMM,

$\varphi_k(z|\mu_k, \delta_k)$ is the probability density function of the kth Gaussian distribution, and a_k is the weight coefficient of probability of sub Gaussian model.

The log-likelihood function can be shown as:

$$Log(L(\mu, \delta)) = \sum_{t=1}^{T} \log p(z_t|\mu, \delta)$$

$$= \sum_{t=0}^{T} \log[\sum_{k=1}^{K} a_k \varphi(z_t|\mu_k, \delta_k)] \tag{5}$$

In this paper, we use EM algorithm [20] to solve GMM. As EM is a mature algorithm, we omitted its implementation details. The global GMM provides us with a good prior for fitting the dynamic model, so that we do not need to fit the linear time-varying dynamic model of each step in a large number of samples. We only need to find an precise dynamic model within the framework of GMM.

The calculation process needs three steps:

Firstly use GMM to calculate the Normal-inverse-Wishart distribution of random variable z_t.

Secondly, as Normal-inverse-wishart distribution is the conjugate prior of z_t, it's convenient to obtain the distribution of z_t.

Finally, the precise linear time-varying dynamic model is got, according to z_t distribution.

To get the Normal-inverse-wishart distribution, we need to obtain the posterior probability estimation of each sample with each sub Gaussian model. The posterior probability estimation can be calculated as follows:

$$\gamma_{tk} = \frac{a_k \varphi_k(z_t|\mu_k, \delta_k)}{\sum_{k=1}^{K} a_k \varphi_k(z_t|\mu_k, \delta_k)} \tag{6}$$

Then use the posterior probability estimation as the mean and covariance weight of each sub model Gaussian model, we can get the mean and covariance of Normal-inverse-wishart distribution of z_t (Fig. 1).

$$\overline{\mu}_t = [\mu_1, \mu_2 \ldots \mu_k][\gamma_{t1}, \gamma_{t2} \ldots \gamma_{tk}] \tag{7}$$

$$\overline{\sum}_t = \sum_{k=1}^{K} \gamma_{tk} \left[\delta_k + (\mu_k - \overline{\mu}_t)(\mu_k - \overline{\mu}_t)^T\right] \tag{8}$$

where $\overline{\mu}_t$ and $\overline{\Sigma}_t$ are the mean and covariance of Normal-inverse-wishart distribution of z_t respectively, μ_k and δ_k are the mean and covariance value of the kth sub Gaussian model respectively. In this paper we assume that state and action both have six dimensions, therefore z_t has eighteen dimensions, $z_t \in \mathbb{R}^{18 \times 1}$, $\mu_k \in \mathbb{R}^{18 \times 1}$, $\delta_k \in \mathbb{R}^{18 \times 18}$, $\overline{\mu}_t \in \mathbb{R}^{18 \times 1}$, and $\overline{\Sigma}_t \in \mathbb{R}^{18 \times 18}$.

Then we can get the mean and covariance value of z_t by the following equations:

$$\Sigma_t = \frac{\overline{\Sigma}_t + N\hat{\Sigma} + (\hat{\mu} - \overline{\mu})(\hat{\mu} - \overline{\mu})^T}{N} \tag{9}$$

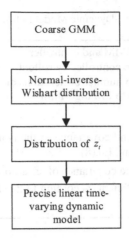

Fig. 1. The linear time-varying dynamic model fitting process

$$\mu_t = \frac{\overline{\mu} + \hat{\mu}}{2} \tag{10}$$

where N is the number of samples at time t, $\hat{\mu}$ and $\hat{\Sigma}$ are unbiased estimation of the mean and covariance respectively. In this paper, μ_t is a eighteen dimensions vector and Σ_t is a matrix with eighteen rows and eighteen columns. Σ_t and μ_t can be divided as follows:

$$\Sigma_t = \begin{bmatrix} \Sigma_Y & \Sigma_{YX} \\ \Sigma_{XY} & \Sigma_X \end{bmatrix} \tag{11}$$

$$\mu_t = \begin{bmatrix} \mu_Y & \mu_X \end{bmatrix} \tag{12}$$

where $\Sigma_Y \in \mathbb{R}^{12 \times 12}, \Sigma_{YX} \in \mathbb{R}^{12 \times 6}, \Sigma_{XY} \in \mathbb{R}^{6 \times 12}, \Sigma_X \in \mathbb{R}^{6 \times 6}$,
$\mu_Y \in \mathbb{R}^{12 \times 1}, \mu_X \in \mathbb{R}^{6 \times 1}$.

According to the following formulations, we can obtain the coefficients of precise linear time-varying dynamic model:

$$F_{sat}^T = \Sigma_Y^{-1} \Sigma_{YX} \tag{13}$$

$$f_t = \mu_X - F_{sat} \mu_Y \tag{14}$$

$$\delta_{st} = \Sigma_X - F_{sat} \Sigma_Y F_{sat}^T \tag{15}$$

We describe the derivation process of formulations above in Appendix A.1.

The procedure of local dynamic model fitting algorithm based on global GMM is shown as follows (Table 1):

Table 1. Local Dynamic Model Fitting Algorithm.

1: Initialize the parameters of GMM and controller
2: Generate samples $\hat{\tau}$ from the controller by rollout
3: **for** iteration i=1 to maximum number of iterations **do**
4:    Fit global GMM according to EM algorithm
5: **end for**
6: **for** iteration t=1 to T **do**
7:    calculate the mean value and covariance of the Normal-inverse-wishart distribution of z_t according to Eq.(7) and Eq.(8)
8:    calculate the mean value and covariance of z_t according to Eq.(11) and Eq.(12)
9:    calculate the dynamic coefficients according to Eq.(13), Eq.(14) and Eq.(15)
10: **end for**

2.3 LQR Based Trajectory Optimization

In the previous section, the local dynamic model is derived based on the Gaussian mixture model prior. On the bases of the dynamics, this section solves the optimal linear Gaussian controller at each time step through the linear quadratic regulator algorithm.

The linear quadratic regulator optimization algorithm needs two preconditions: the first is that the dynamic model needs to be linear which is consistent in our situation, and the second is that the reward function needs to be quadratic which is easy to ensure by second-order Taylor expansion. In this paper we assume that the reward function has the quadratic format as follows:

$$R(s_t, a_t) = \frac{1}{2}\begin{bmatrix} s_t \\ a_t \end{bmatrix}^T R_t \begin{bmatrix} s_t \\ a_t \end{bmatrix} + \begin{bmatrix} s_t \\ a_t \end{bmatrix}^T r_t \tag{16}$$

where $R_t = \begin{bmatrix} R_{sst} & R_{sat} \\ R_{ast} & R_{aat} \end{bmatrix}$ and $r_t = \begin{bmatrix} r_{xt} \\ r_{ut} \end{bmatrix}$.

According to the LQR algorithm, the value-function, the Q-function and the controller coefficients can be represented as follows:

$$V^*(s_t) = \frac{1}{2}s_t^T V_t s_t + s_t^T v_t \tag{17}$$

where $V_t = R_{sst} + R_{sat} K_t + K_t^T R_{ast} + K_t^T R_{aat} K_t$ and $v_t = r_{st} + R_{sat} k_t + K_t^T r_{at} + K_t^T R_{aat} k_t$.

$$Q(s_{t-1}, a_{t-1}) = \frac{1}{2}\begin{bmatrix} s_{t-1} \\ a_{t-1} \end{bmatrix}^T Q_{t-1} \begin{bmatrix} s_{t-1} \\ a_{t-1} \end{bmatrix} + \begin{bmatrix} s_{t-1} \\ a_{t-1} \end{bmatrix}^T q_{t-1} + const \tag{18}$$

where $Q_{t-1} = R_{t-1} + F_{t-1}^T V_t F_{t-1} = \begin{bmatrix} Q_{ss(t-1)} & Q_{sa(t-1)} \\ Q_{as(t-1)} & Q_{aa(t-1)} \end{bmatrix}$ and

$$q_{t-1} = r_{t-1} + F_{t-1}^T V_t f_{t-1} + F_{t-1}^T v_t = \begin{bmatrix} q_{s(t-1)}, q_{a(t-1)} \end{bmatrix}^T$$

$$K_{t-1} = -Q_{aa(t-1)}^{-1} Q_{as(t-1)} \tag{19}$$

$$k_{t-1} = -Q_{aa(t-1)}^{-1} q_{a(t-1)} \tag{20}$$

The procedure of LQR based trajectory optimization algorithm is shown as follows (Table 2):

Table 2. LQR based trajectory optimization algorithm.

1: Initialize the parameters of controller and reward function
2: **for** iteration $t = T$ to 1 **do**
3:    calculate the Q-function according to Eq.(18),
4:    calculate the controller coefficients according to Eq.(19) and Eq.(20)
5:    calculate the value-function according to Eq.(17)
6: **end for**
7: update controller coefficients

After get the new controller, utilize it to drive the robot. If the value-function $V_p(s_0)$ has not reach the expectation, a new iteration is needed according to algorithm 1 and 2.

3 Experiment and Evaluation

We constructed a dynamic simulation verification platform by simulating the real environment with gazebo to verify our approach. The robot arm uses IRB 120 industrial robot developed by ABB, and its CAD model, collision detection model and the dynamic parameters are obtained through ROS wiki [21]. The objects manipulated are got from MARVIN project [22] which is designed by Cranfield University.

The dynamic simulation verification platform is built on ROS framework, including autonomous control software which is based on the model based reinforcement learning and gazebo dynamic simulation software. The two parts communicate through ROS topic. Firstly, the linear Gaussian controller of the autonomous control software uses the random strategy to generate the control instructions of the robot. The simulated robot in gazebo moves according to the instructions and releases the state after executing the instructions through ROS topic. After multiple sampling, the dynamic model fitting module outputs the fitted dynamic time-varying linear Gaussian model, and the linear quadratic regulator gives the optimized linear Gaussian controller according to the fitted dynamic model. After the linear Gaussian controller is obtained, it will enter the next cycle to drive the robot in the simulation again to obtain samples and fit a better model until convergence (Fig. 2).

3.1 Experiment Tasks

In the simulation scene, the base coordinate system of the robot is taken as the world coordinate system, the center of the circular rod is taken as the operating coordinate system, and the pose of the circular rod relative to the world coordinate system is initialized

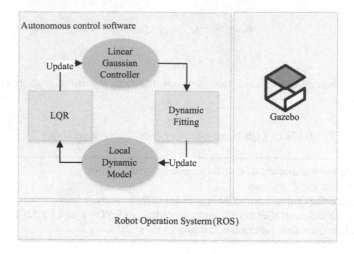

Fig. 2. Dynamic simulation verification platform

as $\begin{bmatrix} 0.3m & 0.3m & 0.06m & 0rad & 0rad & 0rad \end{bmatrix}$. The robot arm initial joint angles are zero. The initial scene is shown as follows (Fig. 3):

Fig. 3. The initial scene in Gazebo

We expected the robot to catch the circular rod from the initial state, so the reward function is designed as:

$$R(s_t, a_t) = -\frac{1}{2}\omega_a \|a_t\|^2 - \frac{1}{2}\omega_s \|s_{des} - s_t\|^2$$

where $\omega_a = 10^{-2}$, and $\omega_s = 1$.

In order to make the robot grasp the operating object as soon as possible, the value of its reward function is always negative at each time step. In addition to ensure that the closer the actual pose is to the expected pose, the higher reward the system obtain, we utilized $\|s_{des} - s_t\|^2$. Furthermore, in order to ensure the system can obtain higher reward under small torque to make the motion of the robot more smooth, the torque term

$-\frac{1}{2}\|a_t\|^2$ is added to the reward function. And $\omega_a = 10^{-2}$ ensures that the moment item and the state item have the same order of magnitude.

3.2 Result and Evaluation

According to the initial state above, the trajectory diagram of the end of the robot in the first iteration is shown as follows (Fig. 4):

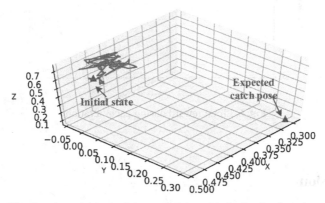

Fig. 4. The trajectory of the end of the robot in the first iteration

It can be seen that through the initial controller, the robot basically makes random motion in the initial position. After nine iterations, the value function tends to converge. Figure 5 shows the trajectory diagram of robot end effector after 9 iterations:

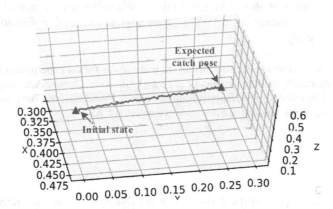

Fig. 5. The trajectory of the end of the robot in the nineth iteration

It can be seen that after nine iterations, the robot can move to the desired pose, which fully shows that the model base reinforcement learning algorithm has obvious advantages in sample utilization and convergence efficiency. The following figure shows the growth trend of the value function during each iteration. It can be found that it gradually increases from the initial −90.21 to gradually approach the maximum value of the reward function (Fig. 6).

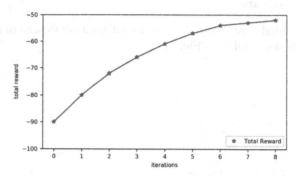

Fig. 6. Total reward during each iteration

4   Conclusion

In this paper a robot trajectory optimization algorithm based on local dynamic fitting is proposed. The global Gaussian mixture model is used as a dynamic model priori, which reduces the difficulty of model fitting. By using of LQR, the optimization efficiency of the policy is improved. Finally, the algorithm proposed in this paper is verified on the dynamic simulation software. However, there are also some problems which will be addressed in the future. As the controller we used is a linear model, when the initial state is changed the controller should be reoptimized. We will use deep neural network to construct a more commonly controller, to adjust a wider range of application scenarios in the following study.

Acknowledgment. We would like to thank all the participants for the experiments in this paper. This work is supported by the Key Laboratory of Space Utilization, Chinese Academy of Sciences under the grant Y7031661SY, the National Natural Science Foundation of China under the grant No. 61502463 and Youth Innovation Promotion Association CAS.

Appendix

In this appendix, we present the derivation of the dynamic model coefficients. Firstly, we need to define some temporary variables.

The random variable $[s_t, a_t]$ and s_{t+1} are represented by Y and X respectively. μ_X and Σ_X represent the mean value and covariance of X, and $\Sigma_X = \delta_X \delta_X^T$. μ_Y and Σ_Y represent the mean value and covariance of Y, and $\Sigma_Y = \delta_Y \delta_Y^T$.

Secondly, we prove $F_{sat}^T = \Sigma_Y^{-1} \Sigma_{YX}$.

$$\Sigma_Y F_{sat}^T - \Sigma_{YX}$$

$$= \delta_Y \delta_Y^T F_{sat}^T - \delta_Y \delta_X^T$$

$$= \iint p(x,y) \Big[(y - E(y))(y - E(y))^T F_{sat}^T - (y - E(y))(x - E(x))^T \Big] dxdy \quad \text{Where}$$

$$= \int_y (y - E(y)) dy \int_x p(x,y) \Big[F_{sat}y - F_{sat}E(y) - x + E(x) \Big]^T dx$$

$p(x,y) = p(s_t, a_t, s_{t+1})$.

As $E(X) = E(F_{sat}y + f_t) = F_{sat}E(y) + f_t$, substitute this into equation above we can get:

$$\Sigma_Y F_{sat}^T - \Sigma_{YX}$$

$$= \int_y (y - E(y)) dy \int_x p(x,y) \Big[F_{sat}y - F_{sat}E(y) - x + F_{sat}E(y) + f_t \Big]^T dx$$

$$= \int_y (y - E(y)) dy \int_x p(x,y) \Big[F_{sat}y - x + f_t \Big]^T dx$$

$$= \int_y (y - E(y)) p_y(y) dy \Big[(F_{sat}y + f_t - E(x|y)) \Big]$$

$$= \int_y (y - E(y)) p_y(y) dy * 0$$

$$= 0$$

Thirdly, we prove $f_t = \mu_X - F_{sat}\mu_Y$.
As $E(X) = E(s_{t+1}) = \mu_X, E(Y) = E(s_t, a_t) = \mu_Y$, we can obtain:

$$f_t = \mu_X - F_{sat}\mu_Y$$

Finally, we prove $\delta_{st} = \Sigma_X - F_{sat}\Sigma_Y F_{sat}^T$.
As we know that $E(X|Y = y) = F_{sat}y + f_t$, we can derive that:

$$D(E(X|Y)) = D(F_{sat}y + f_t) = F_{sat}D(Y)F_{sat}^T = F_{sat}\Sigma_Y F_{sat}^T$$

And because of $D(X|Y) = \delta_{st}$, we can derive that:

$$E(D(X|Y)) = \delta_{st}$$

As $D(X) = D(E(X|Y)) + E(D(X|Y))$, we can get:

$$\Sigma_X = F_{sat}\Sigma_Y F_{sat}^T + \delta_{st}$$

References

1. Lanfranco, A.R., Castellanos, A.E., Desai, J.P. and Meyers, W.C.: Robotic surgery: a current perspective. Ann. Surg. **239**(1), 14–21 (2004)

2. Wyrobek, K.A., Berger, E.H., Van der Loos, H.M., Salisbury, J.K.:Towards a personal robotics development platform: rationale and design of an intrinsically safe personal robot. In: International Conference on Robotics and Automation (ICRA), pp. 2165–2170 (2008)
3. Haarnoja, T., et al.: Soft actor-critic algorithms and applications. arXiv preprint arXiv:1812. 05905 (2018)
4. Hwangbo, J., et al.: Learning agile and dynamic motor skills for legged robots. Sci. Robot. 4(26), eaau5872 (2019)
5. Deisenroth, M.P., Neumann, G., Peters, J.: A survey on policy search for robotics. Found. Trend Robot. 2, 1–142 (2013)
6. Hoppe, S., Giftthaler, M., Krug, R., Toussaint, M.:Sample-efficient learning for industrial assembly using Qgraph-bounded DDPG. In: 2020 IEEE/RSJ International Conference on Intelligent Robots and Systems (IROS), pp. 9080–9087 (2020)
7. Kober, J., Mohler, B.J., Peters, J.: Learning perceptual coupling for motor primitives. Intell. Robots Syst. 834–839 (2008)
8. Kober, J., Peters. J.: Policy Search for Motor Primitives in Robotics. Mach. Learn. 1–33 (2010)
9. Kormushev, P., Calinon, S., Caldwell, D.G.: Robot motor skill coordination with EM-based reinforcement learning. In: Proceedings of the IEEE/RSJ International Conference on Intelligent Robots and Systems, pp. 3232–3237 (2010)
10. Kober, J., Oztop, E., Peters, J.: Reinforcement learning to adjust robot movements to new situations. In: Proceedings of the 2010 Robotics: Science and Systems Conference, pp. 301–312 (2010)
11. Daniel, C., Neumann, G., Peters, J.: Learning concurrent motor skills in versatile solution spaces. In: IEEE/RSJ International Conference on Intelligent Robots and Systems, pp. 3591–3597 (2012)
12. Yang, C., Yang, J., Wang, X., Liang, B.:Control of space flexible manipulator using soft actor-critic and random network distillation. In: 2019 IEEE International Conference on Robotics and Biomimetics (ROBIO), pp. 3019–3024 (2019)
13. Frazelle, C., Rogers, J., Karamouzas, I., Walker, I.: Optimizing a continuum manipulators search policy through model-free reinforcement learning. In: 2020 IEEE/RSJ International Conference on Intelligent Robots and Systems (IROS), pp. 5564-5571 (2020)
14. Kim, H., Jordan, M., Sastry, S., Ng, A.: Autonomous helicopter flight via reinforcement learning. In: Advances in Neural Information Processing Systems (2004)
15. Ng, A.Y., et al.: Autonomous inverted helicopter flight via reinforcement learning. In: Ang, M.H., Khatib, O. (eds.) Experimental Robotics IX. Springer Tracts in Advanced Robotics, vol. 21, pp. 363–372. Springer, Heidelberg (2006). https://doi.org/10.1007/11552246_35
16. Bagnell, J.A., Schneider, J.G.: Autonomous helicopter control using reinforcement learning policy search methods. In: Proceedings of the International Conference on Robotics and Automation, pp. 1615–1620 (2001)
17. Deisenroth, M.P., Rasmussen, C.E., Fox, D.: Learning to control a low-cost manipulator using data-efficient reinforcement learning. In: Proceedings of the International Conference on Robotics: Science and Systems (2011)
18. Edition, R.L.A.I.S.: Richard S. MIT Press, Sutton (2019)
19. Khansari-Zadeh, S.M., Billard, A.: BM: an iterative algorithm to learn stable non-linear dynamical systems with Gaussian mixture models. In: 2010 IEEE International Conference on Robotics and Automation (ICRA), pp. 2381–2388 (2010)
20. Dempster, A.P:. Maximum likelihood from incomplete data via the EM algorithm (1977)
21. http://wiki.ros.org/abb_irb1200_support
22. https://github.com/tlund80/MARVIN/tree/9fddfd4c8e298850fc8ce49c02ff437f139309d0/ src/swcomponents/marvin/models/cranfield-40

ChatGPT for Robotics: A New Approach to Human-Robot Interaction and Task Planning

Bing Xie, Xiangming Xi, Xinan Zhao, Yuhan Wang, Wei Song$^{(\boxtimes)}$, Jianjun Gu, and Shiqiang Zhu

Zhejiang Lab, Hangzhou 311100, Zhejiang Province, China
{xiebing,xxm21,zhaoxa,wangyuhan,weisong,jgu,
zhusq}@zhejianglab.com

Abstract. ChatGPT, released by OpenAI, has garnered academic interest due to its powerful natural language processing capabilities. It can accurately understand conversations and generate high-quality responses. This paper explores the potential of applying ChatGPT to two significant research topics in robotics: Human-Robot Interaction and Task Planning. Human-Robot Interaction involves studying the interactions between humans and robots. ChatGPT is well-suited for this purpose as it enables robots to communicate with humans. However, ChatGPT has shortcomings such as outdated knowledge and fabricating answers, making it unsuitable for direct use in Q&A. To address these issues, we propose an architecture called FRC that combines FAQ, retrieval module, and ChatGPT. In this architecture, ChatGPT is used for rephrasing questions and reading comprehension. Experiments show that the architecture can combine multiple rounds of dialogue to answer incomplete questions or questions that need coreference resolution. Task planning involves using an internal model to reason about the world and create a plan of actions to achieve a specific goal. Traditional approaches to robotic task planning rely on search while using ChatGPT for task planning is a novel approach based on generation. Existing methods using ChatGPT do not consider the state of the robot. We propose a method that enables ChatGPT to perform task planning based on the state of the robot and have verified its feasibility through experiments. We also discuss the limitations of ChatGPT in multi-party talk and motion control.

Keywords: ChatGPT · Human-Robot Interaction · Task Planning · FRC architecture

1 Introduction

ChatGPT [1] is an AI chatbot developed by OpenAI and released in November 2022. Built on top of OpenAI's GPT-3.5 large language models, it has been fine-tuned using supervised and reinforcement learning techniques. ChatGPT interacts in a conversational way, allowing it to answer follow-up questions, admit mistakes, challenge incorrect premises, and reject inappropriate requests.

H. Yang et al. (Eds.): ICIRA 2023, LNAI 14271, pp. 365–376, 2023.
https://doi.org/10.1007/978-981-99-6495-6_31

There are many applications for ChatGPT [2], including serving as an alternative to search engines like Google or Bing, roleplaying, writing high-quality copy and code, serving educational purposes, and brainstorming ideas. It can also be used to create virtual assistants for businesses to handle tasks such as scheduling appointments, sending emails, and managing social media accounts [3]. With these successful applications, it is natural to apply ChatGPT to robots for human-robot interaction. However, ChatGPT has its limitations. Its training data only goes up until September 2021 and it may lack specialized knowledge or make up answers to questions it can't answer. To fully utilize ChatGPT's capabilities and avoid its shortcomings in human-robot interaction, this paper proposes a question-answering architecture that takes full advantage of ChatGPT.

There has been some interesting work applying ChatGPT to task planning. AutoGPT [4] can generate a task list from just one user prompt, while HuggingGPT [5] uses Chat-GPT to analyze user requests and break them down into sub-tasks, selecting and invoking appropriate models hosted on HuggingFace to execute them. Microsoft's Autonomous Systems and Robotics Division has extended ChatGPT's capabilities to robotics, using language to intuitively control robotic arms, drones, home assistant robots, and more [6].

However, these experiments all use skill APIs to complete instructions without considering the impact of the robot's state on instruction execution. We propose providing ChatGPT with the robot's state through APIs so that ChatGPT can get the latest status and combine it when doing task planning. We have designed a drone-controlled experiment to validate this method.

We also discuss the performance of ChatGPT on multi-party talk and motion control. In summary, our contributions are as follows:

(1) We propose a question-answering architecture that combines ChatGPT with an FAQ module and text retrieval module to answer questions based on multi-round dialogue and customized knowledge. This architecture takes advantage of ChatGPT's ability to rephrase questions into a canonical form and perform reading comprehension based on retrieved content.

(2) We propose providing ChatGPT with the state of the robot through APIs. ChatGPT can then get the latest status of the robot and be prompted to combine it when doing task planning. We design a drone-controlled experiment to validate this method.

(3) We discuss the performance and shortcomings of ChatGPT in multi-party talk scenarios and limitations in task planning and motion control.

2   Human-Robot Interaction with ChatGPT

Human-Robot Interaction can be divided into physical embodied tasks, question-answering tasks, and chatting tasks [7]. For question-answering, ChatGPT has limitations such as outdated knowledge, lack of knowledge, and fabricating answers, making it unsuitable for direct use in Q&A. However, by selecting appropriate existing or novel techniques to overcome these limitations, it may be possible to answer questions seriously and accurately.

We propose a novel question-answering architecture called the FRC architecture, which integrates an FAQ module, retrieval module, and ChatGPT to overcome these limitations. This architecture is shown in * MERGEFORMAT Fig. 1.

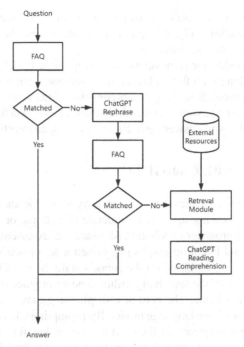

Fig. 1. Illustration of the proposed FRC architecture for Q&A

The proposed FRC architecture works as follows. The FAQ module processes input question and attempts to find a suitable answer. If it fails, the rephrase module uses ChatGPT to rephrase the question into a canonical and complete form. The FAQ module then tries again to find an answer to the rephrased question. If it still fails, the retrieval module retrieves relevant information from external resources. This information, along with the rephrased question, is input into the reading comprehension module, which uses ChatGPT to find an answer through reading comprehension.

The FAQ module in the FRC architecture maintains a set of frequently asked question-answer pairs. For an input question, the FAQ module encodes it into a vector and calculates its similarity to pre-defined questions in the set. If the maximum similarity is below a certain threshold, the input question cannot be answered. Otherwise, the answer to the most similar question in the set is used to answer the input question.

The ChatGPT rephrase module rephrases questions into a canonical and complete form based on recent dialogue. A prompt is designed to require ChatGPT to rephrase the last question asked by the user based on a recent conversation. The rephrased question should be standardized and complete and will be input into the FAQ module again. With this module, the system can obtain information from recent conversations to understand incomplete questions or questions that need coreference resolution.

The retrieval module in the FRC architecture retrieves content related to the question from external resources such as company documents and search engines. By placing customized knowledge into these external resources, the system can possess domain-specific knowledge. Additionally, by updating the resources, the system can answer questions based on the latest information.

The content retrieved by the retrieval module is input into the ChatGPT reading comprehension module along with the rephrased question and designed prompt. ChatGPT answers the question through reading comprehension. This module not only prevents ChatGPT from fabricating answers but also fully utilizes its powerful text understanding and reasoning capabilities to answer new, difficult, and open questions.

3   Task Planning with ChatGPT

Robot task planning involves autonomous reasoning about the state of the world using an internal model and coming up with a sequence of actions, or a plan, to achieve a goal [8]. Traditional approaches to robotic task planning are essentially search, such as Plan-space planning and Planning graphs [9]. Given a set of actions a robot can take, it searches for the best action based on the robot's state. Most of the studies focus on improving the efficiency of the search algorithm. The emergence of ChatGPT provides an innovative research scheme. The core of task planning may not be searching in the space, but generative as a large language model. By prompting ChatGPT with skill APIs, it can generate a calling sequence of these APIs to complete the task. ChatGPT's rich knowledge allows it to combine basic functions to complete tasks. There are applications such as AutoGPT, HuggingGPT, and Plan4MC [10] that use ChatGPT for task planning. And Microsoft designed experiments to demonstrate it too. In Microsoft's experiments, task planning did not take the state of the robot into account. Changes in the robot's state during autonomous operation can affect the execution of the task plan. For example, when the robot's left hand has a mechanical failure, some tasks may need to be performed with the right hand.

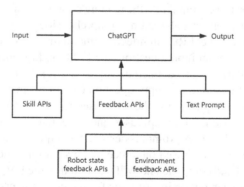

Fig. 2. Illustration of task planning with feedback using ChatGPT

So how can ChatGPT combine the state of the robot for task planning? Drawing on the successful cases of AutoGPT, HuggingGPT, and Microsoft experiments, we can provide ChatGPT with the robot's state through APIs and prompt ChatGPT to make a task plan with the robot's state. ChatGPT should be able to call these APIs to get the robot's state and make a task plan based on it. Since the robot's state changes as an action executed, it can be considered as a kind of feedback information. Other feedback information like environmental feedback can also be provided to ChatGPT in this way. The method can be summarized as Fig. 2.

4 Experiments

4.1 FRC architecture

In our experiments, we implement the FRC architecture. We collect some question-answer pairs to build FAQ, then encode the questions into vectors with Sentence-BERT[11,] and store them in Milvus[12] database. For the input question, use the same Sentence-BERT to encode into a vector, and then query the most similar question from the Milvus database. We set the similarity threshold to 0.9. When the maximum similarity is greater than or equal to 0.9, the answer corresponding to the matched question is returned.

To implement question rephrasing using ChatGPT, we designed the following prompt:

"There is a dialogue as follows: {{dialogue}}, in order to help the robot understand the question, please rewrite the last question into a standardized and complete question, start with "User:", and output the rewritten question."

The "{{dialogue}}" in the prompt will be replaced with recent dialogue content. The rephrased question would start with "User:", which can be stripped before being input into FAQ again.

We implemented the search module using ElasticSearch [13], which stores documents about our company and projects. We also integrated the Baidu [14] search engine API into the retrieval module, so that the retrieval module can search for resources on the Internet. When retrieving information, we first use ElasticSearch. If no relevant documents are found, we will use the Baidu search engine to retrieve and extract the top results.

To use ChatGPT for reading comprehension, we designed the following prompt:

"There is the following information:{{information}}. Please answer the question: {{question}}. If you can answer, start with "Answer:" and output the answer; if you can't answer, output "Insufficient information to answer"."

In the prompt, "{{information}}" is replaced with the context retrieved by the retrieve module, and "{{question}}" is replaced with the rephrased question. If ChatGPT can answer the question based on the given information, the output starts with "Answer:", otherwise it outputs "Insufficient information to answer".

Our system works well. It can extract and answer questions from multiple rounds of dialogue. Such questions are often incompletely formulated or require coreference resolution and cannot be answered by a single FAQ module. For example, in this dialogue:

User: Is this robot dog a product of your company?

Robot: Yes, it is.

User: How much.

The question "How much" can't be answered by FAQ alone, but can be answered by our system. Figure 3 shows examples of ChatGPT rephrase results.

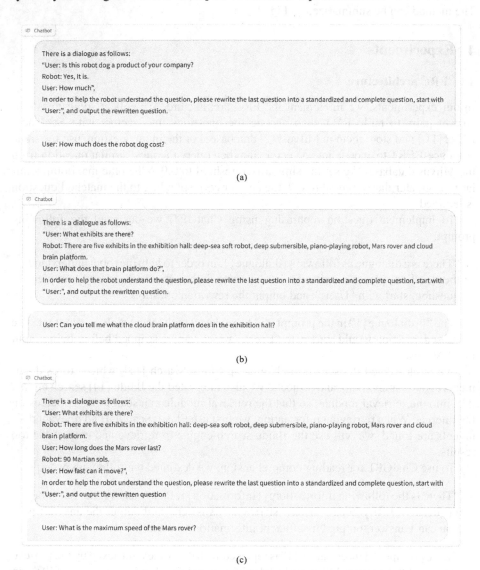

Fig. 3. Examples of ChatGPT rephrase results

The format of the rephrased questions is standardized and the components are complete, which is easier for FAQ to match questions with the same semantics.

Our system is also easy to customize. By adding custom content to the retrieval module, the system can use this content to answer relevant questions. For example, if you ask ChatGPT when Zhejiang Lab was founded, it will make up an answer. However, if you ask our FRC system, it can provide the correct answer because the relevant content has been added to the system's retrieval module. Figure 4 demonstrates that our system can answer domain-specific questions through reading comprehension and won't make up answers if there isn't enough information.

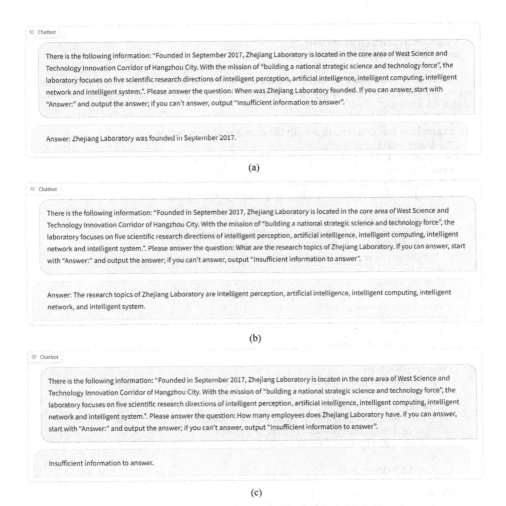

Fig. 4. ChatGPT reading comprehension examples

4.2 Drone control

We designed a drone control experiment to verify the proposed method of task planning with a robot state. Every time the drone acts, it will consume a certain amount of power. If the power of the drone is too low to fly back to the charging pile after acting, the drone should not act but fly back to the charging pile to charge. The power needed to fly back to the charging pile is related to the distance between them. To simplify the experiment, we set the drone to return to charging when the power is less than a certain threshold. We modified the PromptCraft-Robotics [15] project to implement our design. The following key information is added to the basic prompt of PromptCraft-Robotics:

> "......
>
> aw.get_battery_level: get battery level
>
> aw.charge: charge battery level to full level
>
> ......
>
> As a drone, every command you execute will consume a certain amount of battery power, and you must pay attention to it. When your battery power is lower than 3, return to the origin to charge, otherwise execute the command."

An example of our conversation with the drone is shown below.

(The drone's initial battery level is 10)

User: move 5 units up

Drone: ```python

```python
current_pos = aw.get_drone_position()
target_pos = [current_pos[0], current_pos[1], current_pos[2]+5]

if aw.get_battery_level() < 3:
    print("Battery level too low. Going back to the origin to charge.")
    aw.fly_to([0, 0, 0]) # Go back to the origin to charge
    aw.charge() # Charge the battery to full level
else:
    aw.fly_to(target_pos)
```

(After execution, the battery level is 7)

User: move to turbine2

Drone: ```python

```python
target_pos = aw.get_position("turbine2")

if target_pos is None:
    print("Could not find turbine2!")
else:
    if aw.get_battery_level() < 3:
        print("Battery level too low. Going back to the origin to charge.")
        aw.fly_to([0, 0, 0]) # Go back to the origin to charge
        aw.charge() # Charge the battery to full level
    else:
        aw.fly_to(target_pos)
```

(After execution, the battery level is 3)

User: go to a place where I can see both car and solarpanels

Drone: ```python

```python
car_pos = aw.get_position("car")
solarpanels_pos = aw.get_position("solarpanels")

if car_pos is None or solarpanels_pos is None:
    print("Could not find car or solarpanels!")
else:
```

```
center_pos = [ (car_pos[0] + solarpanels_pos[0])/2,
               (car_pos[1] + solarpanels_pos[1])/2,
               max(car_pos[2], solarpanels_pos[2]) ]
target_pos = [center_pos[0], center_pos[1], center_pos[2]+10]

if aw.get_battery_level() < 3:
    print("Battery level too low. Going back to the origin to charge.")
    aw.fly_to([0, 0, 0]) # Go back to the origin to charge
    aw.charge() # Charge the battery to full level
else:
    aw.fly_to(target_pos)
```

(After execution, the battery level is 0)
User: move 5 units up
Drone: (same as the first command)

(a) Initial state, battery=10   (b) Move 5 units up, battery=7   (c) Move to turbine2, battery=3

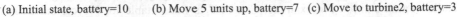

(d) Execute the third command, battery=0   (e) Execute the fourth command, battery=10

Fig. 5. The drone's position after executing commands

In this case, we set the drone's initial position at the origin, with battery level of 10. First, the user asks the drone to go up 5 units, and then ChatGPT replies with a code to be executed. This code first checks the current battery level. If the battery level is below 3, it will fly back to the origin to charge. Otherwise, it will get the current position of the drone with the Z coordinate increased by 5, and then fly the drone to this new position. After execution, the battery level is 7. The user then commands the drone to go to turbine2 and ChatGPT generates a similar code. After execution, the battery level is 3. The user then wants the drone to fly to a place where the user can see both the car and the solar panels. To determine the destination, ChatGPT obtains the location of the car and the solar panels respectively, and calculates the midpoint as the destination. After execution, the battery level is 0. The user asks the drone to go up 5 units again. ChatGPT generates the same code as the first time. However, since the drone's battery power is less than 3, the drone does not execute the user's command but returns to the origin to charge. The positions of the drone after executing the codes are shown in Fig. 5.

5 Discussion

In human-robot interaction, it often happens that many people stand in front of the robot and talk with each other, including with the robot. This situation which we call multi-party talk is very different from a one-on-one conversation. Some utterances in the conversation are spoken to the robot, some are not. Robots need to listen to conversations, but can't reply to every utterance. So for robots, some utterances do not need to be replied to. So user utterances in human-robot interaction should be classified into four categories: chat, question, command, and no reply. It is important for robots to recognize no-relay utterances. Some no-reply utterances can be distinguished by their semantics, such as "Look, that robot is great" and "Remember to charge the robot before you leave". But some utterances can't be recognized by semantics only. Like "Hello", "Good Bye". The speaker's facial orientation and gaze information are essential in this case. This task requires multi-modal information, which is beyond ChatGPT's grasp. As ChatGPT's follow-up model GPT4 [16] is a multi-modal model, its performance in the multi-party talk is of interest.

In task planning, ChatGPT also has limitations. ChatGPT may output incorrectly formatted code, causing errors when executing the task plan. ChatGPT takes a long time to respond. ChatGPT is usually called multiple times during task planning, which leads to a long time to finish it. ChatGPT can only do high-level task planning but can't handle motion control. For example, ChatGPT is not suitable for bicycle balancing. Reinforcement learning is more suitable for motion control. How to combine ChatGPT with reinforcement learning so that the robot can do both high-level task planning and detailed motion control is a topic worthy of research.

6 Related Work

Large Language Models: A language model is a probability distribution over sequences of words. Language models generate probabilities by training on text corpora. A large language model (LLM) is a language model consisting of a neural network with many parameters (typically billions of weights or more), trained on large quantities of unlabeled text using self-supervised learning or semi-supervised learning. Google's Transformer [17] model drove the development of BERT, GPT-2, GPT-3, and ChatGPT. Large language models like PaLM [18], LLaMa [19], and ChatGPT have transformed natural language processing with their impressive abilities. To make better use of large language models, there is an increasing amount of research on prompts. Chain-of-thought [20] prompting improves reasoning by setting up case examples. But some problems cannot be solved by prompts such as ChatGPT will make up the answer. We propose an architecture to address this problem.

Task Planning with Large Language Models: Large language models have been used for robotics task planning using prompting structures with pre-defined functions and examples. Interactive planning for error correction [21] has been explored using techniques such as environment feedback and descriptors and explainers. Recently, AutoGPT [4] and HuggingGPT [5] use ChatGPT to call various functional interfaces to complete tasks proposed by users, and Plan4MC [10] uses GhatGPT to fulfill complex tasks in

Minecraft. These applications give us a glimpse into the promise of ChatGPT in task planning. We further use ChatGPT for task planning while considering the state of the robot.

7 Conclusion

In this paper, we explored the potential of using ChatGPT for Human-Robot Interaction and Task Planning in robotics. We propose the FRC architecture to address ChatGPT's shortcomings in Q&A. The proposed FRC architecture uses an FAQ module to try to find an answer to the input question. If it fails, ChatGPT is used to rephrase the question and the FAQ module tries again. If it still fails, a retrieval module retrieves related information from external resources, and ChatGPT is used for reading comprehension to answer the rephrased question. To enable ChatGPT to combine the state of the robot for task planning, we propose providing ChatGPT with the state of the robot through APIs. ChatGPT can then get the latest status of the robot and be prompted to combine it with the state of the robot when doing task planning. APIs for obtaining environmental feedback can also be provided to ChatGPT if needed. We verified the feasibility and effectiveness of the proposed method through experiments. We also discussed ChatGPT's limitations in multi-party talk and motion control. We hope that our work will inspire more exploration of large language model applications in robots and accelerate the development of intelligent robots.

Acknowledgment. This paper is supported by the Key Research Project of Zhejiang Lab (No. G2021NB0AL03).

References

1. OpenAI, ChatGPT. https://openai.com/blog/chatgpt. Accessed 10 May 2023
2. Top 12 Interesting ChatGPT Applications and Examples. https://savvycomsoftware.com/blog/top-interesting-chatgpt-applications-and-examples/. Accessed 17 May 2023
3. Best ChatGPT Use Cases: 8 Industry Applications with Examples – Emeritus. https://emeritus.org/blog/ai-and-ml-chatgpt-use-cases/. Accessed 17 May 2023
4. Auto-GPT. https://news.agpt.co/. Accessed 10 May 2023
5. Shen, Y., Song, K., Tan, X., Li, D.S., Lu, W., Zhuang, Y.T.: HuggingGPT: solving AI tasks with ChatGPT and its friends in HuggingFace. arXiv abs/2303.17580 (2023)
6. Vemprala, S., Bonatti, R., Bucker, A., Kapoor, A.: Chatgpt for robotics:Design principles and model abilities. Technical report MSR-TR-2023-8, Microsoft,February 2023. https://www.microsoft.com/en-us/research/publication/chatgpt-for-robotics-design-principles-and-model-abilities/
7. Xi, X., Xie, B., Zhu, S., Jin, T., Ren, J., Song, W.: A general framework of task understanding for tour-guide robots in exhibition environments.In: 2022 WRC Symposium on Advanced Robotics and Automation (WRC SARA), Beijing, Chin, pp. 197-202 (2022). https://doi.org/10.1109/WRCSARA57040.2022.9903960
8. Robotic Sea Bass, Task Planning in Robotics. https://roboticseabass.com/2022/07/19/task-planning-in-robotics. Accessed 10 May 2023

9. Jiang, Y., Zhang, S., Khandelwal, P. et al.: Task planning in robotics: an empirical comparison of PDDL- and ASP-based systems. Front. Inf. Technol. Electron. Eng. **20**, 363–373 (2019). https://doi.org/10.1631/FITEE.1800514

10. Yuan, H., et al.: Plan4MC: skill reinforcement learning and planning for open-world minecraft tasks. arXiv abs/2303.16563 (2023)

11. Reimers, N., Iryna, G.: Sentence-BERT: sentence embeddings using siamese BERT-networks. In: Conference on Empirical Methods in Natural Language Processing (2019)

12. Vector database – Milvus. https://milvus.io/. Accessed 21 May 2023

13. Elastic/elasticsearch. https://github.com/elastic/elasticsearch. Accessed 21 May 2023

14. Baidu. https://www.baidu.com/. Accessed 21 May 2023

15. Microsoft/PromptCraft-Robotics.   https://github.com/microsoft/PromptCraft-Robotics. Accessed 21 May 2023

16. OpenAI: GPT-4 Technical Report. arXiv abs/2303.08774 (2023)

17. Vaswani, A.: Attention is All you Need. NIPS (2017)

18. Chowdhery, A., et al.: PaLM: scaling language modeling with pathways. arXiv abs/2204.02311 (2022)

19. Touvron, H., et al.: LLaMA: Open and Efficient Foundation Language Models. arXiv abs/2302.13971 (2023)

20. Wei, J., et al.: Chain of thought prompting elicits reasoning in large language models. In: Conference on Neural Information Processing Systems (NeurIPS) (2022)

21. Zihao, W., Cai, S., Liu, A., Ma, X., Liang, Y.: Describe, explain, plan and select: interactive planning with large language models enables open-world multi-task agents. arXiv abs/2302.01560 (2023)

Precision Control and Simulation Verification of Hydraulic Manipulator under Unknown Load

Qixian Wang, Manzhi Qi, Yangxiu Xia, and Zheng Chen[✉]

Ocean College, Zhejiang University, Zhoushan 316021, Zhejiang, China
{qxwang_m,manzhi.q,yx.xia,zheng_chen}@zju.edu.cn

Abstract. Hydraulic manipulators with multiple degrees of freedom have an increasing range of applications in industrial production, and have the potential to complete various complex tasks. Nowadays, the complex and precision-demanding working environment often requires the hydraulic manipulators to have high control accuracy, which limits their usage. The inherent high-order nonlinearity and uncertainty of hydraulic systems greatly affect the precise control of hydraulic manipulators. High order dynamics such as friction and vibration also have a significant impact on their controlling. Additionally, manipulator typically operates in complex environments with large loads, the end load has always been an important external factor affecting their control accuracy. In this paper, a direct/indirect adaptive robust controller (DIARC) is developed. By incorporating nonlinear and uncertain terms into the dynamic modeling, the control accuracy can be improved. In addition, the end load of the manipulator is incorporated into the parameter space, which makes end load estimation possible. Simulation is constructed using MATLAB Simscape and the performance of the controller is attested. Results shows that the controller can not only improve the tracking accuracy when the end load is heavy, but precisely identify the mass of end load precisely.

Keywords: Hydraulic manipulator · Adaptive robust control · End load estimation

1 Introduction

Hydraulic manipulator with multiple degrees of freedom (DOF), as the combination of hydraulic system and automation technology, has been increasingly used. They enjoy many advantages such as convenient maintenance and strong load-bearing capacity. However, with the development of industrial intelligence, the complexity of tasks is increasing and the required operational accuracy is improving, which to some extent limits the application of hydraulic manipulators due to their lack of control accuracy.

The main reason for the limited application of hydraulic manipulators is the lack of control accuracy. Nowadays, most hydraulic manipulators are open-loop operated, and closed-loop control often uses PID controller. Due to the influence of the manipulator

---

Q. Wang and M. Qi—These authors contributed equally to this work.

© The Author(s), under exclusive license to Springer Nature Singapore Pte Ltd. 2023
H. Yang et al. (Eds.): ICIRA 2023, LNAI 14271, pp. 377–388, 2023.
https://doi.org/10.1007/978-981-99-6495-6_32

flexibility, vibration, inter-joint clearance, combined friction and temperature inside the hydraulic cylinder, complex external interference and so on, it is difficult to effectively improve control accuracy [1, 2].

In order to pursue more accurate control, Yao et al.combined the RISE-based controller with parameter adaptive control to decrease the system tracking error, which can effectively suppress parameter uncertainty and reduce tracking error of hydraulic system [3, 4]. Xia estimated the viscous friction coefficient and coulomb friction coefficient of hydraulic system, and achieved high tracking accuracy [5]. However, the experimental object of the above methods is hydraulic single push rod, and the effect on the manipulator still needs to be verified. In recent years, research on hydraulic manipulators has gradually deepened. Mattila et al. proposed virtual decomposition control (VDC) control method, which achieved impressive effect on multi-DOF hydraulic manipulator [6, 7]. And many scholars have studied the influence of various environmental parameters and mechanical structure parameters on the performance of hydraulic manipulator, and proposed different kinds of controllers [8–11]. However, these studies mainly focus on laboratory environments. In actual production, hydraulic manipulators often face complex time-varying loads.

The end load is also an important factor that seriously affects the accuracy and control effect of operations. But in many engineering tasks, such as excavation and logging, the idea of using a force/torque sensor at the end-effector is difficult due to the nature of the contact task [12]. Therefore, designing a specific control law for load estimation is a practical and feasible solution. The load variation of the end-effector on electric rigid manipulator were studied. Duan et al. proposed a variable structure robust control method with feedforward compensator based on equivalent control for robots with load uncertainty, which can adapt to end-load changes under the condition of powerless sensors and achieve better control effect [13]. Scholars like Zeng et al.also discussed the method of estimating load conditions for electric rigid body robots [14, 15]. However, most of the above research focuses on industrial robots, there is still little research on load estimation of hydraulic manipulators with more complex dynamic characteristics.

In this paper, to achieve precise control under unknown loads, a direct/indirect adaptive robust controller (DIARC) focusing on the time-varying end load is proposed. The controller overcomes the nonlinearity and uncertainty of hydraulic systems and can achieve considerable improvement in tracking accuracy. It also incorporates end-load into the dynamic system to achieve accurate estimation of end load. The load will be integrated into the control law afterwards, further improving the control effect under variable and unknown loads. Finally, simulation is conducted to attest the tracking accuracy and end load estimation precision. The new method is expected to be applied to goods sorting, construction engineering, mining and other industries which have high requirements for load recognition.

2 Problem formulation

2.1 Dynamic modeling

The hydraulic manipulator analyzed in this article is a two DOF manipulator. Only the swing joint which is connected to the base and the wrist joint at the end will be considered. Figure 1 shows the structure diagram of the manipulator and identified the controlled joints.

Supposing the centroid is at the center of each rod, the dynamic model of a manipulator is established using the Lagrange method and described as follows,

$$H(q)\ddot{q} + C(q,\dot{q})\dot{q} + G(q) + f_1 s(\dot{q}) + f_2 \dot{q} = T + \Omega_1 \tag{1}$$

where q_1 and q_2 are the angle of swing joint and wrist joint, respectively, $H(q) \in \mathbb{R}^{2 \times 2}$ is the mass matrix, $C(q,\dot{q}) \in \mathbb{R}^{2 \times 2}$ the matrix of inertia, $G(q) \in \mathbb{R}^{2 \times 1}$ the matrix of gravity, $f_1 = diag(f_{v1}, f_{v2})$ the viscous friction matrix and $f_2 = diag(f_{c1}, f_{c2})$ the coulomb friction matrix, $s(\dot{q}) = 2 \arctan(900\dot{q})/\pi$, $T \in \mathbb{R}^2$ the matrix of torque, $\Omega_1 \in \mathbb{R}^2$ the modeling uncertainty. $H(q)$, $C(q,\dot{q})$ and $G(q)^T$ can be expressed as Eqs. 2, 3 and 4, respectively.

$$H(q) = \begin{pmatrix} (L_1 m_2 + L_1 m_t + L_2 m_t \cos(q_2))(L_1 + L_2 \cos(q_2)) & 0 \\ 0 & J + L_2^2 m_t \end{pmatrix} \tag{2}$$

$$C(q,\dot{q}) = \begin{pmatrix} -\frac{1}{2}L_2\dot{q}_2 x & -\frac{1}{2}L_2\dot{q}_1 x \\ \frac{1}{2}L_2\dot{q}_1 x & 0 \end{pmatrix}, \; x = \sin(2q_2)L_2 m_t + L_1 \sin(q_2)(m_2 + 2m_t) \tag{3}$$

$$G(q)^T = \left(0, \frac{1}{2}gL_2 \cos(q_2)(m_2 + 2m_t)\right) \tag{4}$$

where L_i ($i = 1.2$) is the length of the two arms, $J_t = L_2^2 m_t$, J is the moment of the wrist arm, m_t is the mass of the end load, m_2 the mass of wrist arm. The hydraulic dynamics of a manipulator are expressed in the following form,

$$\frac{V_1}{\beta_e}\dot{p}_1 = A_1 \frac{\partial X_L}{\partial q}\dot{q} + Q_1 + \Omega_2, \; \frac{V_2}{\beta_e}\dot{p}_2 = A_2 \frac{\partial X_L}{\partial q}\dot{q} - Q_2 + \Omega_3 \tag{5}$$

where $V_1 \in \mathbb{R}^{2 \times 2}$ and $V_2 \in \mathbb{R}^{2 \times 2}$ are the volume matrixes of the chambers, $A_1 \in \mathbb{R}^{2 \times 2}$ and $A_2 \in \mathbb{R}^{2 \times 2}$ the area matrixes of the chambers. $\frac{\partial X_L}{\partial q} = diag(\frac{\partial x_1}{\partial q_1}, \frac{\partial x_2}{\partial q_2})$ can be used to represent the driving force arm of the joints. $Q_1 \in \mathbb{R}^2$ is the input flow matrix and $Q_2 \in \mathbb{R}^2$ is the return flow matrix. Based on Eq. 5, the control force can be written as,

$$F_L = P_1 A_1 - P_2 A_2$$
$$\vartheta_8 \dot{F}_L = \vartheta_8 (\dot{P}_1 A_1 - \dot{P}_2 A_2) = -\lambda_A \cdot \frac{\partial X_L}{\partial q} \cdot \dot{q} + Q_L + \lambda_B \Omega_2 + \lambda_C \Omega_3 \tag{6}$$

where $\lambda_A = diag(\lambda_{A1}, \lambda_{A2})$, $\lambda_B = diag(\lambda_{B1}, \lambda_{B2})$ and $\lambda_C = diag(\lambda_{C1}, \lambda_{C2})$ are used to facilitate equation expression and $Q_L \in \mathbb{R}^2$ is the control flow.

Then, the relation between the control flow and the valve input voltage can be expressed as,

$$Q_L = k_v u \sqrt{\Delta p} \tag{7}$$

where k_v is the conversion coefficient, $u = diag(u_1, u_2)$ the matrix of valve input voltage and $\sqrt{\Delta p} \in \mathbb{R}^2$ the matrix of pressure difference of the valve ports.

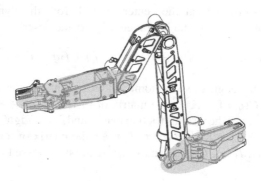

Fig. 1. Structure diagram of the hydraulic manipulator

2.2 Parameterization of dynamic models

Equation 1 can be further written in the form of a regression matrix as,

$$T = \frac{\partial X_L}{\partial q} F_L = \phi_1^T \vartheta \tag{8}$$

where ϑ is the matrix of uncertain parameters. ϑ can be expressed in the following form,

$$\vartheta = [\vartheta_1, \vartheta_2, \vartheta_3, \vartheta_4, \vartheta_5, \vartheta_6, \vartheta_7, \vartheta_8, \vartheta_9, \vartheta_{10}, \vartheta_{11}, \vartheta_{12}, \vartheta_{13}, \vartheta_{14}]^T \tag{9}$$

$$\vartheta = [m_t, J, m_2, F_{v1}, F_{v2}, F_{s1}, F_{s2}, \frac{1}{\beta_e}, \overline{\Omega}_{11}, \overline{\Omega}_{12}, \overline{\Omega}_{21}, \overline{\Omega}_{22}, \overline{\Omega}_{31}, \overline{\Omega}_{32}]^T \tag{10}$$

where $\overline{\Omega}_i$, $i = 1, 2, 3$ is the calculable parts of Ω_i. At this point, the parameterization of the dynamic models is complete, it is clear that m_t has been parameterized separately.

Subsequently, the main aim is designing a virtual control flow Q_{Ld} so that an appropriate valve input voltage can be generated to drive the hydraulic system to track the given trajectory. Additionally, another aim is to propose an adaptation law to accurately estimate m_t.

3   Controller design

3.1   Basic DIARC controller construction

In this section, a DIARC controller is designed so that the precise control of the manipulator can be realized. The algorithm flow chart of the controller is shown in Fig. 2. In the following parts of the paper, $\hat{\bullet}$ represent the estimation of $\bullet$, and $\tilde{\bullet} = \hat{\bullet} - \bullet$ is the error between the two values.

Step I

The angular error and the angular velocity error are defined as,

$$e_1 = q - q_d, \; e_2 = \dot{e}_1 + k_1 e_1 = \dot{q} - \dot{q}_{eq} \tag{11}$$

where $\dot{q}_{eq} = \dot{q}_d - k_1 e_1$ is the slip modulus and $k_1 \in \mathbb{R}^{2 \times 2}$ a positive definite diagonal matrix. Similar to Eq. 8, Eq. 1 can be described with q_{eq} as Eq. 12. Therefore, the difference between Eq. 12 and Eq. 1 can be written as Eq. 13.

$$H(q)\ddot{q}_{eq} + C(q, \dot{q})\dot{q}_{eq} + G(q) + f_1 s(\dot{q}) + f_2 \dot{q} = \phi_2^T \vartheta + \Omega_1 \tag{12}$$

$$H(q)\dot{e}_2 + C(q, \dot{q})e_2 = -\phi_2^T \vartheta + \frac{\partial X_L}{\partial q} F_L \tag{13}$$

Then a virtual control force used to replace F_L can be written as,

$$F_{Ld} = F_{Lda} + F_{Lds}, \; F_{Lda} = F_{Lda1} + F_{Lda2}, \; F_{Lds} = F_{Lds1} + F_{Lds2}$$
$$F_{Lda1} = \frac{\partial q}{\partial X_L} \varphi_2^T \hat{\theta}, \; F_{Lds1} = -k_2 e_2 \frac{\partial q}{\partial X_L} \tag{14}$$

where F_{Lda1} can compensate for nonlinear terms in dynamic equations, F_{Lds1} can ensure the error of tracking force converges exponentially if k_2 is a positive diagonal matrix. F_{Lda2} and F_{Lds2} are designed in the following step.

Step II

The error between the real output force and the virtual output force is written as Eq. 15, and its differentiation can be written as Eq. 17.

$$e_3 = F_L - F_{Ld} \tag{15}$$

$$\dot{F}_{Ld} = \dot{F}_{Ldc} + \dot{F}_{Ldi}, \; \dot{F}_{Ldc} = \frac{\partial F_{Ld}}{\partial q} \dot{q} + \frac{\partial F_{Ld}}{\partial \dot{q}} \hat{\ddot{q}} + \frac{\partial F_{Ld}}{\partial t} \tag{16}$$

$$\vartheta_8 \dot{e}_3 = \vartheta_8 \dot{F}_L - \vartheta_8 \dot{F}_{Ld}$$
$$= \phi_3^T \vartheta + Q_L - \vartheta_8 \dot{F}_{Ldi} \tag{17}$$

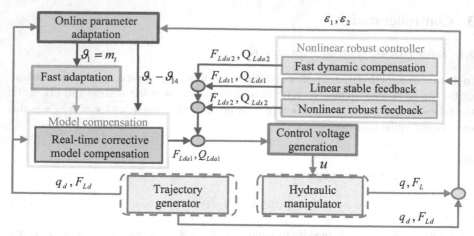

Fig. 2. Algorithm flow chart of the controller

where $\dot{F}_{Ldc}$ and $\dot{F}_{Ldi}$ is the calculable part and incalculable part of $\dot{F}_{Ld}$ respectively.
$\hat{\dot{q}} = \hat{H}(q)^{-1}(\frac{\partial x_L}{\partial q}F_{Ld} + \Omega_1 - \hat{C}(q,\dot{q})\dot{q} - \hat{G}(q) - \hat{f}_1s(\dot{q}) - \hat{f}_2q)$. ϕ_3^T is also a regression
matrix.

In Eq. 17, Q_L is substituted by the virtual control flow Q_{Ld} and can be expressed as,

$$Q_{Ld} = Q_{Lda} + Q_{Lds}, \; Q_{Lda} = Q_{Lda1} + Q_{Lda2}, \; Q_{Lds} = Q_{Lds1} + Q_{Lds2}$$
$$Q_{Lda1} = -\phi_3^T \hat{\vartheta} + \mu, \; Q_{Lds1} = -k_3 e_3 \tag{18}$$

where $\mu = -\frac{\partial X_L}{\partial q}\frac{\omega_1}{\omega_2}e_2$ can be used to balance the order of magnitude of F_{Ld} and Q_{Ld}, so
that they have the same effect in the controller. Q_{Lda1} can compensate for nonlinear terms
in hydraulic dynamic equations. Q_{Lds1} can ensure the error of control flow converges
exponentially if k_3 is a positive diagonal matrix. The dynamic equations in Eq. 13 and
Eq. 17 are expressed as follows,

$$H(q)\dot{e}_2 + C(q,\dot{q})e_2 = -k_2e_2 - \phi_2^T \tilde{\vartheta} + \frac{\partial X_L}{\partial q}e_3 + \frac{\partial X_L}{\partial q}F_{Lda2}$$
$$\vartheta_8 \dot{e}_3 = -k_3e_3 - \phi_3^T \tilde{\vartheta} + Q_{Lda2} - \vartheta_7 \dot{F}_{Ldi} + \mu \tag{19}$$

In Eq. 19, the fast-dynamic compensation items are expressed as,

$$F_{Lda2} = -\frac{\partial q}{\partial X_L}\gamma_1, Q_{Lda2} = -\gamma_2 \tag{20}$$

where γ_1 is the low frequency part of $-\phi_2^T \tilde{\vartheta}$, γ_2 the low frequency part of $-\phi_3^T \tilde{\vartheta} - \vartheta_7 \dot{F}_{Ldi} + \mu$. They are updated by the following updating law,

$$\dot{\gamma}_i = \begin{cases} 0, & if \; |\hat{\gamma}_i| = \gamma_{iM} \; and \; \hat{\gamma}_i(t)e_{i+1} > 0 \\ \kappa_i e_{i+1}, & else \end{cases} \tag{21}$$

where κ_i is a positive diagonal matrix. F_{Lds2} and Q_{Lds2} are described as,

$$F_{Lds2} = -k_{2s1}e_2, \quad k_{2s1} = \frac{1}{4\eta_1}(\gamma_{1M} + \|H_M\|\|\vartheta_1\|)^2$$
$$Q_{Lds2} = -k_{2s2}e_3, \quad k_{2s2} = \frac{1}{4\eta_2}(\gamma_{2M} + \|\vartheta_{8M}\|\|\vartheta_2\|)^2 \tag{22}$$

where H_M means that each term in the matrix take the maximum value. η_1 and η_2 are constants that fit the following robust condition,

$$e_2(\frac{\partial X_L}{\partial q}F_{Lds2} - \gamma_1) \leq \eta_1, \quad e_3(\frac{\partial X_L}{\partial q}Q_{Lds2} - \gamma_2) \leq \eta_2 \tag{23}$$

3.2 Parameter estimation

Since one of the main objectives of this paper is to accurately estimate the mass the the end load, a first-order differentiation device is proposed. Two intermediate matrixes are designed as follows,

$$\delta_{si} = -\overline{\Phi}_i^T \vartheta_{si}, \quad \delta_{s1} = \frac{\partial X_L}{\partial q}F, \quad \delta_{s2} = Q_L - \frac{\partial X_L}{\partial q}\lambda_A \dot{q} \tag{24}$$

Differentiate both sides of Eq. 24 simultaneously, we have

$$\delta_{sif} = -\overline{\Phi}_{if}^T \vartheta_{si}, \quad \hat{\delta}_{sif} = -\overline{\Phi}_{if}^T \hat{\vartheta}_{si}, \quad \varepsilon\ominus_i = \hat{\delta}_{sif} - \delta_{sif} = -\overline{\Phi}_{if}^T \tilde{\vartheta}_{si}, \quad i = 1, 2 \tag{25}$$

where $\varepsilon\ominus_i$ is the error of intermediate matrixes. Then, the projective law is eventually generated as shown in Eq. 26,

$$\dot{\Psi}_i = \begin{cases} \alpha_i\Psi_i - \zeta_i\Psi_i\overline{\Phi}_{if}\overline{\Phi}_{if}^T\Psi_i, & if \; \Lambda_{imax}(\Psi_i(t)) \leq \rho_{iM} \\ 0, & otherwise \end{cases}, \quad i = 1, 2 \tag{26}$$

where $\zeta_i = (1 + v_i\Phi_{if}^T\Psi_{if}\Phi_i)^{-1}, \Lambda = \min\{2k_2/\vartheta_{1\max}, 2k_3/\vartheta_{8\max}\}$, v_i is a positive parameter and ρ_{iM} the upper bound of $\Psi_i.\alpha_i$ is the forgetting factor which partly determines the speed of the parameter adaptation. In this paper, this figure will be set to be a comparatively large value.

The adaptive law for unknown parameters is as follows,

$$\dot{\hat{\vartheta}}_{si} = Proj_{\hat{\vartheta}}(\Psi_i\tau), \quad \tau = \zeta_i\Phi_{if}\varepsilon_i \tag{27}$$

where Ψ_i is a positive-definite matrix and determines the speed of parameter estimation. For this least square adaptive law, each term of Ψ_1 has an impact on the estimation speed of m_t. In order to estimate m_t as quickly and stably as possible, the value of Ψ_1 should be carefully adjusted and should be as large as possible.

Equation 27 will be used to update $\vartheta_1 = m_t$, the accuracy and speed of the adaptation will be attested in the next section.

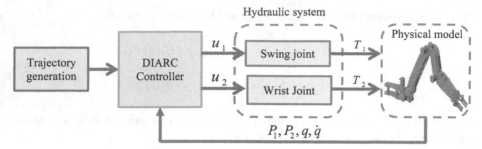

Fig. 3. Scheme diagram of simulation

4   Simulation setup and results

4.1   Simulation setup

A simulation is conducted using MATLAB Simulink. The scheme diagram of the simulation system is shown in Fig. 3, and the picture of the manipulator can be seen in Fig. 4. The physical model of the manipulator is built by Simscape Multibody, which takes the joint coupling into consideration. The trajectory generator can generate the required trajectory, which is third-order differentiable. To simplify the simulations, both joints run the same P2P trajectory as shown in Fig. 5. The sensor noise amplitude is set to 5×10^{-5} radians.

The simulation selected three groups for comparison, 1) PID controller, 2) DIARC controller without end load compensation, 3) DIARC with end load compensation.

The manipulator is installed with a 3 kg end load, and the tracking accuracy of the three groups is compared first. Afterwards, the end load of the manipulator is changed to detect whether DIARC with end load compensation can accurately perceive the mass of the end load. The end load will be set as 0 kg, 2.5 kg, 5 kg, 7.5 kg and 10 kg.

Fig. 4. The analyzed hydraulic manipulator

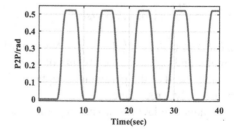

Fig. 5. Trajectory used in simulation

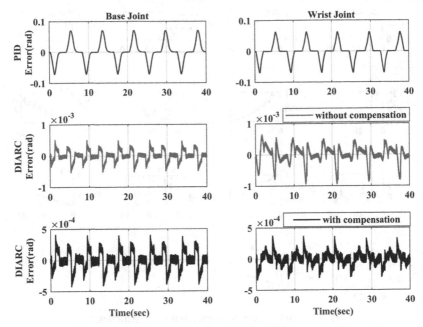

Fig. 6. Angular error of each joint with different controllers

4.2 Simulation results

In the simulation, a spherical weight of 3 kg is placed in the gripper of the wrist joint, 0.4 m away from the joint rotation axis. Under certain circumstances, the error curves of each joint using the three kinds of controllers are shown in Fig. 6. The tracking accuracy of the proposed DIARC controller has been significantly improved. The PID controller does not consider the complex dynamics of the hydraulic system. The error of each joint reached 0.06 rad. DIARC controller achieved far better control performance. The error of swing joint by DIARC controller without end load compensation is between -5.5×10^{-4} and 5.5×10^{-4} rad. Wrist joint error is between -1×10^{-3} and 6×10^{-4} rad. When the acceleration of the angle approaches the extreme value, there is a spike in tracking error due to the influence of the end load. Evidently, this is significantly reduced by DIARC with end load compensation. Due to the precise estimation of the end load, the calculation of the moment of inertia of the swing joint is also more accurate, which improves its tracking accuracy to a certain extent. The error of swing joint is between -4×10^{-4} and 4×10^{-4} rad, improved by 27%. The error of wrist joint is between -3×10^{-4} and 4×10^{-4} rad. The error amplitude has been significantly reduced by 56.3%.

The adaptive curves for each unknown parameter are shown in Fig. 7. Each of the parameters tend to converge to a certain value which can be regarded as the real value. It can be found that the DIARC controller has the ability to accurately estimate unknown parameters. Therefore, the controller has the potential to accurately estimate the mass of the end load.

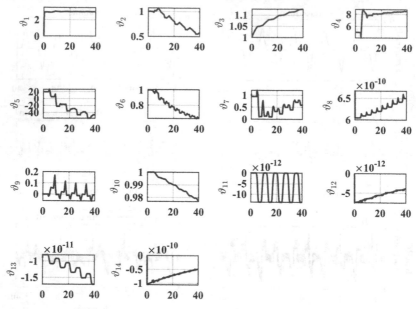

Fig. 7. Adaptive curves for each unknown parameter

The end load of the manipulator is also estimated. A spherical weight is installed at the same location, but its weight is variable. Figure 8 shows the adaptive curve with five sets of end masses. The result indicate that the controller can quantitatively estimate the weight of the end load. More accurate data can be found in Table 1. It can be seen that the controller has a high accuracy in estimating the end load. At the same time, due to the emphasis on improving the speed of end load adaptation in the early design, it only takes about 1s to obtain comparative accurate estimation of the load.

Table 1. Comparison of real and estimated weight

No.	Real value(kg)	Estimated value (kg)	Error (kg)
1	0	0.005	0.005
2	2.5	2.496	0.004
3	5	4.995	0.005
4	7.5	7.493	0.007
5	10	9.988	0.012

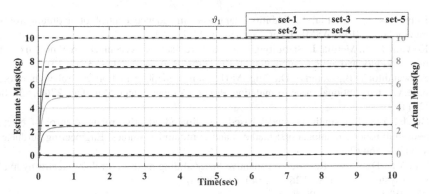

Fig. 8. The adaptive curves of end load

5 Conclusions

This developed a direct/indirect adaptive robust controller (DIARC), which can compensate for the influence of the end load on hydraulic manipulators and can effectively estimate the mass of the end load. Besides, the end load of hydraulic manipulator can be estimated online. Then, a co-simulation method is developed using MATLAB Simulink and Simscape to test the effectiveness of this controller. The maximum error of the swing joint and the wrist joint is only 73% and 43.7% of that of a conventional DIARC controller, respectively. At the same time, the controller also has high accuracy in estimating the end load, with the estimation error being only 0.012 kg when the actual load is 10 kg. The controller can effectively compensate for the additional torque caused by the gravity of the end load and the tracking accuracy is significantly enhanced. This proves potential of the DIARC controller proposed in this paper, which has a high guiding effect on industrial production.

Acknowledgement. This work is supported by National Natural Science Foundation of China (Nos. 52075476), Zhejiang Provincial Natural Science Foundation of China (No. LR23E050001), and Fundamental Research Funds for the Central Universities (226–2023-00029).

References

1. Hu, J., Li, C., Chen, Z., Yao, B.: Precision motion control of a 6-dofs industrial robot with accurate payload estimation. IEEE/ASME Trans. Mechatron. **25**(4), 1821–1829 (2020)
2. Huang, Y., Pool, D.M., Stroosma, O., Chu, Q.: Long-stroke hydraulic robot motion control with incremental nonlinear dynamic inversion. IEEE/ASME Trans. Mechatron. **24**(1), 304–314 (2019)
3. Yao, J., Deng, W., Jiao, Z.: RISE-based adaptive control of hydraulic systems with asymptotic tracking. IEEE Trans. Autom. Sci. Eng. **14**(3), 1524–1531 (2017)
4. Yao, Z., Yao, J., Sun, W.: Adaptive RISE control of hydraulic systems with multilayer neural-networks. IEEE Trans. Industr. Electron. **66**(11), 8638–8647 (2019)
5. Xia, Y., Nie, Y., Chen, Z.: Motion control of a hydraulic manipulator with adaptive nonlinear model compensation and comparative experiments. Machines **10**(3), 214 (2022)

6. Koivumäki, J., Mattila, J.: Stability-guaranteed impedance control of hydraulic robotic manipulators. IEEE/ASME Trans. Mechatron. **22**(2), 601–612 (2017)
7. Koivumäki, J., Mattila, J.: Stability-guaranteed force-sensorless contact force/motion control of heavy-duty hydraulic manipulators. IEEE Trans. Rob. **31**(4), 918–935 (2015)
8. Soewandito, D.B., Oetomo, D., Ang, M.H.: Neuro-adaptive motion control with velocity observer in operational space formulation. Robot. Comput. Integr. Manufact. **27**(4), 829–842 (2011)
9. Bu, F., Yao, B.: Nonlinear model based coordinated adaptive robust control of electro-hydraulic robotic manipulators: methods and comparative studies. Engineering.purdue.edu **4**, 3459–3464 (2000)
10. Liu, Y.F., Dong, M.: Research on adaptive fuzzy sliding mode control for electro-hydraulic servo system. Proc. CSEE **26**(14), 140–144 (2006)
11. Zhu, W.H., Dupuis, E., Piedboeuf, J.-C.: Adaptive output force tracking control of hydraulic cylinders. In: Proceedings of the 2004 American Control Conference, pp. 5066–5071. Boston, MA, USA (2004)
12. Kamezaki, M., Iwata, H., Sugano, S.: Condition-based less-error data selection for robust and accurate mass measurement in large-scale hydraulic manipulators. IEEE Trans. Instrum. Meas. **66**(7), 1820–1830 (2017)
13. Duan, S., Chen, L., Ma, Z., Lu, G.: Variable structure control with feedforward compensator for robot manipulators subject to load uncertainties. In: 2010 11th International Conference on Control Automation Robotics & Vision, pp. 2367–2372. Singapore (2010)
14. Zeng, A., Song, S., Lee, J., Rodriguez, A., Funkhouser, T.: TossingBot: learning to throw arbitrary objects with residual physics. IEEE Trans. Rob. **36**(4), 1307–1319 (2020)
15. Colomé, A., Pardo, D., Alenyà G., Torras, C.: External force estimation during compliant robot manipulation. In: 2013 IEEE International Conference on Robotics and Automation, pp. 3535–3540, Karlsruhe, Germany (2013)

Experience Adapter: Adapting Pre-trained Language Models for Continual Task Planning

Jiatao Zhang[1,2], Jianfeng Liao[2], Tuocheng Hu[3], Tian Zhou[1], Haofu Qian[1,2],
Haoyang Zhang[1,2], Han Li[1,2], LanLing Tang[2,4], Qiwei Meng[2], Wei Song[1,2(✉)],
and Shiqiang Zhu[1,2(✉)]

[1] Zhejiang University, Hangzhou, China
{weisong,zhusq}@zhejianglab.com
[2] Research Center for Intelligent Robotics, Zhejiang Lab, Hangzhou, China
[3] University of Electronic Science and Technology of China, Chengdu, China
[4] Hangzhou Institute for Advanced Study, University of Chinese Academy of
Sciences, Hangzhou, China

Abstract. In this paper, we investigate the challenge of Pre-trained Language Models (PLMs) for continual task planning. PLM-based planner is difficult to incorporate incremental experience without risking catastrophic forgetting or overwhelming the model parameters. Inspired by human cognition, we propose the Experience Adapter, a novel method that avoids the need for model re-training or fine-tuning. The adapter continually collects experiences externally, including observation memory and human feedback, represented in memory graph and rules. Using these, the adapter directs task planning and corrects behavior not aligning with human expectations. Our method, not relying on the planner's inherent structure, pairs easily with various foundational planning methods. In experiments on everyday tasks within the VirtualHome environment, we show that our approach significantly improves task success rate from 47% to 64%. This non-invasive method fits seamlessly within existing model-serving pipelines without altering the model training.

Keywords: Task Planning · Pre-trained Language Models · Adapter

1 Introduction

Task planning is a high-level decision-making process, which is widely used in various robotics applications such as decision making [14], manipulation [7] and navigation [9]. Traditional task planning settings focus on the execution of individual tasks. In many scenarios, such as everyday household tasks, robots are required to perform a series of diverse tasks consecutively. The accumulated experience from previous tasks can be employed to optimize subsequent tasks. Continual task planning [12] focuses on accumulating experience and refining models, making robots more efficient in executing subsequent tasks.

J. Zhang and J. Liao—Contribute equally to this work.

H. Yang et al. (Eds.): ICIRA 2023, LNAI 14271, pp. 389–400, 2023.
https://doi.org/10.1007/978-981-99-6495-6_33

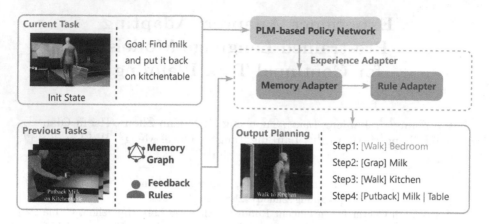

Fig. 1. The Experience Adapter collects observations and human feedback from previous tasks, and represents this experience as a memory graph and feedback rules. This experience is then utilized by the memory adapter and rule adapter to enhance subsequent tasks without the need for fine-tuning the model.

Recently, Pre-trained Language Models (PLMs) have emerged [20]. PLMs are trained on extensive unsupervised text corpora, possess substantial parameter structures, and demonstrate considerable knowledge of common sense and logical reasoning abilities across many applications, including code writing [2], math problem solving [13] and question answering [6]. But how can we harness the capabilities of PLMs to benefit continual task planning?

Using PLMs to perform continual task planning is a nontrivial problem. Planners that use PLMs as backbones demonstrate strong task planning capabilities [5,10,11,14], as these models can understand complex commands and handle tasks involving multiple steps due to their inherent reasoning abilities. Although these methods exhibit promising capabilities in traditional task planning, applying them to continual task planning settings poses challenges.

One major challenge is that the experience accumulated from memory and human feedback is difficult to incorporate into these methods to optimize subsequent tasks. This is mainly because PLMs typically have a large number of parameters, and the accumulated experience compared to the training data is relatively sparse. Besides, fine-tuning the model may result in catastrophic forgetting, which could negatively impact their performance [4] (Fig. 1).

We argue that it is not always necessary to embed experience into model parameters via re-training or fine-tuning. This experience can be stored externally, and invoked when necessary. It aligns with human intuition, as humans usually store experiences in note-taking instead of memorizing them to reduce cognitive burden, and review them only when needed.

We propose an Experience Adapter for continual task planning that can continuously accumulate experience from memory and human feedback to enhance the execution of subsequent tasks. Specifically, This adapter is composed of two components: the Memory Adapter and the Rule Adapter. The memory adapter continuously accumulates environmental observations, organizing this information into a memory graph. The memory graph then directs the planner, guiding the exploration for new tasks. The rule adapter converts human feedback into conditional rules, which are employed to correct planner behavior that deviates from human expectations. Our method can be easily paired with different planning frameworks without the need to re-train the planner.

To validate the effectiveness of our proposed method, we conducted experiments in everyday tasks within VirtualHome [17] environment. By utilizing our adapter to bias the model generation, the success rate improves from 47% to 64%, without any invasive modifications to model parameters. This approach offers advantages as it does not require any modifications to the model training procedure and seamlessly fits within existing model-serving pipelines.

2 Related Works

PLMs for Planning. The advancement of PLMs [20] has led to numerous studies exploring their use as planners in open-ended environments. For instance, SayCan [1] merges PLMs with skill affordances to generate viable plans. LID [14] fine-tunes PLMs using tokenized interaction data. Inner Monologue [11] proposes the inclusion of environmental feedback into the planning process. DEPS [19] introduces the concepts of descriptor, explainer, and selector to enable PLMs to generate plans. These techniques primarily focus on how to utilize PLMs for individual task planning. Our research, however, explores the application of PLMs in continual task planning, leveraging previously accumulated experience to enhance the performance of subsequent tasks.

Adapter. Adapters, initially introduced within the Natural Language Processing (NLP) community [8], serve as a scalable model for fine-tuning PLMs to downstream task. The potential for multi-task learning with shared task-specific parameters within a single BERT model was examined in [18]. Within the domain of computer vision, minimal modifications were proposed for fine-tuning the Vision Transformer (ViT) for object detection [15]. The concept of adapters was further used by ViT-Adapter [3] to facilitate a plain ViT's performance on various downstream tasks. Despite these advancements, no previous studies have endeavored to apply adapters to pre-trained task planning models.

3 Preliminaries

Task Planning. A task τ can be structured as $\langle S, I, G, T, A \rangle$, where S is a set of possible states, I represents the initial state, G denotes the goal state, A represents the set of possible actions. T is the transition model, formally defined as $T : S \times A \rightarrow S$, which illustrates the environmental changes that occur in response to the implementation of an action within a given state.

Continual Task Planning. Continual task planning can be represented as a sequence of tasks, denoted as $\langle \tau_1, \tau_2, ..., \tau_n \rangle$. Each task shares a common $\langle S, T, A \rangle$.

In contrast to conventional task planning that concentrates on individual tasks, continual task planning underscores the significance of past experiences and feedback from preceding tasks to augment the subsequnent tasks.

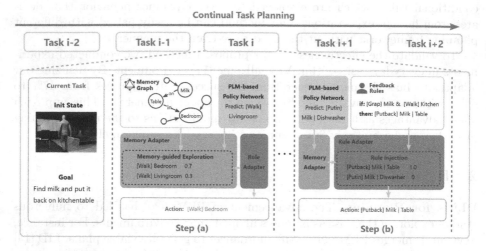

Fig. 2. The framework of Experience Adapter: The memory graph captures historical observations, while the feedback rules represent human feedback from previous tasks. At each step of a subsequent task, the PLM-based policy network predicts an initial action. In step (a), the memory adapter guides the agent's exploration using the memory graph. In step (b), the rule adapter adjusts the current planning prediction by utilizing the feedback rules to align the action with human feedback.

4   Method

In this study, we propose Experience Adapter capable of consistently gathering experience in a continual task planning setting. The gathered experience can then be utilized in subsequent task planning without the need for model retraining.

As shown in Fig. 2, our method comprises three components: a PLM-based policy network, responsible for the overall planning; an memory adapter tasked with the continuous collection of environmental observation; and a rule adapter ensuring that the planner's behavior adheres to human feedback rules.

4.1   PLM-Based Policy Network

Recent works have experimented with using PLMs as backbone for task planning. These PLMs are trained on extensive unsupervised text corpora, encapsulating a wealth of common sense information, and several studies have demonstrated the potential of PLMs to serve as policy networks for long-term planning.

In this paper, we use LID [14] as the PLM-based policy network. LID is a GPT-2 based model that has been fine-tuned on a planning dataset. Specifically, LID is parametric as $\pi(a_{t+1} \mid s_t)$, where current state s_t includes task goal g, history actions h_t and partial observation o_t. LID translates observations, goals, and historical actions as sequences of words. These sequences are then tokenized by the PLM. The resultant tokens are averaged for action prediction. The PLM-based policy network have the capability for common-sense understanding and logical reasoning, demonstrating a promising ability to plan for individual tasks.

4.2 Memory Adapter

We have chosen LID as PLM-based policy network. However, this model mainly focuses on planning individual tasks. The historical observations, which are important prior knowledge about the environment accumulated from previous tasks, cannot be effectively utilized for subsequent tasks. To address this, we propose the memory adapter, consisting of two components: Memory Graph and Memory-guided Exploration.

Memory Graph. The memory graph primarily collects environmental observations accumulated during continuous execution. For a given task sequence $\langle \tau_1, \tau_2, ..., \tau_n \rangle$, we collect partial observations o_t^i at each step t during the execution of each task τ_i. We organize these observations into a graph format, referred to as the memory graph. Formally, memory graph consists of $\{V, R\}$, where V represents the set of nodes (observed objects), and R represents the relationships between these objects(e.g., on and in). With each step executed by the agent, we incorporate its observation o_t^i into the memory graph. The memory can also be considered an extension of partial observations.

Memory-Guided Exploration. We have observed that planning failures often occur due to partial observations of the environment and ineffective exploration. Specifically, due to limited observations, planners may not know where to find the necessary objects and may take many steps to explore the environment, resulting in failure. For instance, in the task "find mike and put him on the table," the agent may fail to complete the task if it cannot locate the mike.

The memory graph stores environmental observations accumulated from previous tasks, recording the locations where objects have previously appeared. This can help the agent reduce ineffective exploration and quickly find the object's location. Inspired by the ϵ-greedy in reinforcement learning [16], we propose memory-guided exploration, which can efficiently direct the agent to explore the environment based on the memory graph. Particularly, when the action provided by the PLM-based policy network is '[walk]', we modify the walk target with a certain likelihood. The target location is chosen from the memory graph in relation to the task goal as follows:

$$loc_t = \begin{cases} \arg\max_{loc} \pi([\text{walk}] \ loc \mid s_{t-1}) & with \ probability \ 1 - \epsilon \\ \text{Mult}(loc \mid \text{Memo}(loc \mid g)) & otherwise \end{cases} \quad (1)$$

where $\epsilon \in [0, 1]$ denotes the probability of exploration, Mult represents the process of sampling from a multinomial distribution, while $\text{Memo}(loc|g)$ signifies the distribution over target location loc given the task goal g. The distribution is calculated based on the co-occurrence frequency of the object tied to the goal and distinct locations in the memory graph.

To balance between exploration based on memory and utilization based on policy, we design the ϵ as follows:

$$\epsilon = \alpha \, \frac{\#steps_{current}}{\#steps_{max}}, \tag{2}$$

where $\alpha \in [0, 1]$ is a hyper-parameter, $\#steps_{current}$ represents the current step number, and $\#steps_{max}$ represents the maximum step number allowed for task execution. The main idea is to encourage the agent to utilize the PLM-based policy in the early stages of task execution. As the number of execution steps increases, if the task is still not completed, it indicates that the PLM-based policy is facing difficulties. In such cases, we gradually increase the probability of memory intervention to improve exploration efficiency.

Through memory-guided exploration, the memory adapter can employ the memory graph as prior knowledge of the environment, directing the planner to explore the environment more effectively, thereby enhancing the accuracy and efficiency of task planning.

4.3   Rule Adapter

As discussed earlier, PLM-based policy network accumulates environmental observations through the memory adapter. During continual task planning, planners may exhibit various errors or actions that do not meet human expectations. As the model parameters cannot be adjusted in real-time, human feedback cannot be promptly incorporated into the model, leading to the repeated occurrence of similar errors in subsequent tasks. To address this, we propose a Rule Adapter that can accumulate human feedback rules during continual task planning, enabling the planner to align its planning results with user rules.

Human Feedback Rules. We employ conditional rules to represent the human feedback. Rules, being an inductive structure, offer a solution to the sparsity issue of error data and can easily act as a form of user feedback. A conditional rule consists of two parts: The **if** part of the statement describes a condition or set of conditions that must be met, while the **then** part describes the resulting action that will occur if the conditions are met.

Rule Injection. Given a set of rules, we employ rule injection to synthesize these rules with the current situation for task planning.

The rule adapter utilizes rule-based reasoning. If the condition is met, the action specified in the **then** clause is selected. Formally, we represent this process as the probability of choosing an action based on the history actions h_t and observation o_t:

$$P(a_i|h_t, o_t) = \frac{\#rule[\mathbf{if} : (h_t, o_t) \rightarrow \mathbf{then} : a_i]}{\Sigma_j \#rule[\mathbf{if} : (h_t, o_t) \rightarrow \mathbf{then} : a_j]}, \tag{3}$$

where $\#rule$ denotes the number of rules whose **if** part are satisfied.

Rule adapter enhances task planning by collecting human feedback during the continuous task planning process, utilizing these feedback rules for inference. This process can correct errors in the task planner and ensures that the planning outcomes align with human expectations.

5   Experimental Evaluation

Environment. We conducted an evaluation on VirtualHome [17], a realistic 3D environment. VirtualHome is characterized by partial observability, expansive action spaces, and extended time horizons. It offers a collection of realistic 3D homes and objects that can be manipulated to carry out household tasks.

Data Sets. We conduct experimental testing on three datasets provided by [14]. The first is **In-Distribution**, in which the task goals are randomly sampled from the same distribution as the training data. The objects are initially situated in the environment according to standard layouts. The second is **Novel Scenes**, in which the objects are positioned randomly in the initial environment, devoid of standard constraints. The third is **Novel Tasks**, in which the components of all goals were not observed together during training, only appear in the test set.

Metrics. To evaluate the performance of our methods, we use two metrics: The first is **Success Rate**, which measures whether the planning generated by the model could achieve the task goal within the maximum steps. The second is **Average Steps**, which measures the average number of steps required to complete all the tasks in the datasets.

Experimental Setup. To conduct hyper-parameter tuning, we searched for the optimal value of the hyper-parameter α from values in the range of [0-1] at intervals of 0.05. For In-Distribution, Novel Scenes, and Novel Task, we respectively choose 0.8, 0.85, and 0.95 as the values for α. For the baseline model LID, we reported the results using their provided pre-trained model. Following the approach in [14], we set the maximum number of steps to 70 for all datasets. The construction of the memory graph relies on environmental observations during continual task planning. The observation in VirtualHome is a graph that outlines a list of objects and their relations (e.g., on, inside). At every step, the agent updates its memory graph based on the latest observation.

Table 1. Success rates for various methods under continual task planning settings. The proposed method outperforms all baselines.

	In-Distribution	Novel Scenes	Novel Tasks
LID	87.00 ± 2.00	47.00 ± 5.57	58.00 ± 1.00
w/o Memo	92.00 ± 1.00	60.30 ± 4.73	72.00 ± 2.00
w/o Rule	94.00 ± 0.00	53.33 ± 2.31	62.33 ± 0.58
Ours	**95.33 ± 1.53**	**64.70 ± 6.11**	**75.33 ± 1.53**

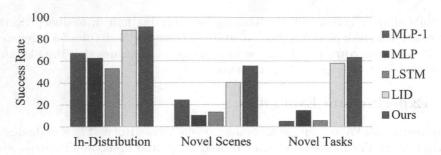

Fig. 3. Comparisons of the proposed method and baselines under individual task planning settings. Our method outperforms all baselines.

Table 2. Average steps for various methods under continual task planning settings. Our method outperforms all baselines.

	In-Distribution	Novel Scenes	Novel Tasks
LID	26.76 ± 1.25	54.34 ± 2.04	48.37 ± 0.44
w/o Memo	23.78 ± 0.99	**50.44 ± 2.22**	43.07 ± 0.59
w/o Rule	22.98 ± 0.31	54.41 ± 0.92	47.46 ± 1.00
Ours	**22.17 ± 1.54**	50.73 ± 1.89	**42.51 ± 1.01**

5.1 Results

Continual Task Planning. To simulate the scenario of continual task planning, we have modified the three test sets provided by LID, maintaining consistent item distribution within the test set to simulate continuous operation within the same space.

The results of success rate under continual task planning settings are show in Table 1. We see that our method consistently outperforms existing methods across all datasets. On the Novel Scenes dataset, the success rate of LID is the lowest, with only 47.00% of task goal have been finish. While, our method achieves 64.70%, effectively increasing the success rate of task execution. This is attributed to the fact that our method continually optimizes subsequent work effects through the accumulation of memory and the application of human feedback rules. On the Novel Tasks dataset, LID's planning success rate is 58%. It's evident that the PLM method can achieve satisfactory results on tasks unseen in the training set. Our method also realizes a performance of 75.33% for these tasks, which indicates our method's substantial effect on improving new tasks. On the In-Distribution dataset, all methods can achieve good results, as the task distribution of In-Distribution is trained based on the training set. This indicates that LID can maintain good performance on the training set, and our method also slightly improves these methods.

Efficiency Analysis. To further probe the effectiveness of our method, we also conducted experiments on task execution efficiency, where we observed the aver-

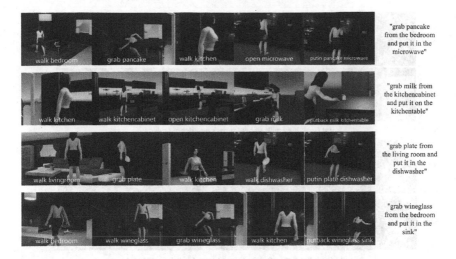

Fig. 4. Example evaluation planning for our method across various tasks.

age number of steps taken to complete tasks. The results are show in Table 2. Our method outperforms LID in terms of the average number of steps taken across all three datasets. This indicates that our method can accomplish tasks with fewer operations. On the Novel Tasks, our method achieved an average of 42.51 steps, a 5.86 improvement over LID. This suggests that the experience accrued from continual task performance can effectively enhance execution efficiency. It also demonstrates that the experience gained from other tasks can generalize to unseen tasks. On the Novel Sences, our method achieved an average of 50.73 steps, a modest 3.61 improvement over LID. In terms of the In-Distribution, the average steps required are the least compared to other datasets, with our method achieves 22.17 and LID achieves 26.76. This finding is consistent with the success rate indicator, suggesting that when the tasks being performed are covered by the training data and stored in the network parameter structure, PLM-based model can achieve good results. Conversely, if new tasks have not been trained, the model's success rate and execution efficiency may decrease significantly.

Individual Task Planning. To demonstrate the planning effectiveness of the Experience Adapter in traditional Individual Task Planning settings, we conduct evaluations on three test sets: In-Distribution, Novel Scenes, and Novel Tasks. In our comparisons, we consider MLP, LSTM, and LID. MLP utilizes a simple multi-layer neural network structure for action prediction, while LSTM incorporates the encoding of historical information. MLP and MLP-1 both employ multilayer neural networks (MLPs) to predict actions, with MLP-1 possessing three additional average-pooling layers compared to MLP.

The results shown in Fig. 3. The results of MLP-1, MLP, and LSTM were obtained from [14]. It can be seen that under Individual Task Planning settings, our method consistently outperforms all other approaches in terms of success rate. This performance is particularly pronounced in Novel Scenes, where

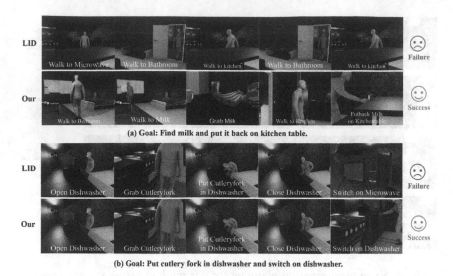

(a) Goal: Find milk and put it back on kitchen table.

(b) Goal: Put cutlery fork in dishwasher and switch on dishwasher.

Fig. 5. Case study in two different tasks.

our method achieves a 15% improvement over LID. These results suggest that, even in Individual Task Planning settings, the Experience Adapter can leverage within-task memory and human feedback rules to enhance planning performance.

Ablation Study. To demonstrate the effectiveness of various components, we conducted an ablation study. The results are also shown in Table 1 and Table 2. The **w/o Rule** approach exclusively incorporates the memory adapter while omitting the use of the rule adapter.

The results indicate that the success rate of w/o Rule surpasses that of LID across all data sets. Furthermore, this improvement is also reflected in the model's execution efficiency. These findings substantiate the effectiveness of memory adapter in enhancing the success rate of the model. Memory adapter enables the incorporation of observed insights from previous tasks, leveraging past experience to avoid errors in the planning model's expansion.

Similarly, in **w/o Memo** we solely employ the rule adapter without incorporating the memory adapter. This approach outperforms LID in terms of success rate and execution efficiency. This can be attributed to the utilization of human feedback and corrective rules derived from previous tasks, which effectively enhance the success rate and efficiency of subsequent task execution.

5.2 Case Study

In this case study, we present the quantitative analysis. Figure 4 highlights our method's capability to provide planning for various tasks. In continuous task planning, LID often fails due to three main issues: 1) the agent fails to find target object within the limited number of steps; 2) repetitive or cyclical actions leading to premature step exhaustion; 3) difficulty in executing specific actions due to inadequate training data, leading to environmental interaction errors.

Our adapter addresses these issues by incorporating experience and feedback rules. As shown in Fig. 5(a), the LID method cycles between the kitchen and bathroom in its quest to find milk. By intervening with experience, we enable the agent to deduce in advance the location where the target object is most likely to be found. Consequently, the agent chooses to search in the bedroom, where it successfully locates the milk and completes the subsequent tasks. In Fig. 5(b), the LID method finds the fork and places it in the dishwasher. However, after closing the dishwasher, it fails to switch it on and instead activates the microwave, which is irrelevant to the task. This is a typical example of an error in interaction with the environment. To address such issues, we introduce some feedback rules to prevent these errors.

6   Conclusion

In conclusion, this paper presented an innovative approach to continual task planning by introducing an Experience Adapter. This methodology facilitates efficient accumulation and utilization of environmental observations and human feedback in continual setting, thereby enhancing the effectiveness of task planning. The PLM-based policy serves as the backbone of this approach, providing an overall planning and information handling mechanism. The memory adapter plays a pivotal role in the continual collection of environmental observation, while the rule adapter ensures the conformity of planner behavior to human feedback rules. The success of our methodology was demonstrated across multiple tasks, with substantial improvements in planning efficiency and error correction.

Acknowledgement. This research was supported by Key Research Project of Zhejiang Lab (Grant No. G2021NB0AL03) and National Natural Science Foundation of China (Grant No. U21A20488).

References

1. Brohan, A., et al.: Do as i can, not as i say: grounding language in robotic affordances. In: Conference on Robot Learning, pp. 287–318 (2023)
2. Chen, M., et al.: Evaluating large language models trained on code. arXiv preprint arXiv:2107.03374 (2021)
3. Chen, Z., et al.: Vision transformer adapter for dense predictions. arXiv preprint arXiv:2205.08534 (2022)
4. De Lange, M., et al.: A continual learning survey: defying forgetting in classification tasks. IEEE Trans. Pattern Anal. Mach. Intell. **44**(7), 3366–3385 (2021)
5. Driess, D., et al.: PaLM-E: an embodied multimodal language model. arXiv preprint arXiv:2303.03378 (2023)
6. Goyal, Y., Khot, T., Summers-Stay, D., Batra, D., Parikh, D.: Making the V in VQA matter: elevating the role of image understanding in visual question answering. In: Conference on Computer Vision and Pattern Recognition, pp. 6325–6334 (2017)

7. Guhur, P.L., Chen, S., Pinel, R.G., Tapaswi, M., Laptev, I., Schmid, C.: Instruction-driven history-aware policies for robotic manipulations. In: Conference on Robot Learning, pp. 175–187. PMLR (2023)
8. Houlsby, N., et al.: Parameter-efficient transfer learning for NLP. In: International Conference on Machine Learning, pp. 2790–2799 (2019)
9. Huang, C., Mees, O., Zeng, A., Burgard, W.: Visual language maps for robot navigation. arXiv preprint arXiv:2210.05714 (2022)
10. Huang, W., Abbeel, P., Pathak, D., Mordatch, I.: Language models as zero-shot planners: extracting actionable knowledge for embodied agents. In: International Conference on Machine Learning, pp. 9118–9147 (2022)
11. Huang, W., et al.: Inner monologue: embodied reasoning through planning with language models (2022)
12. Lesort, T., Lomonaco, V., Stoian, A., Maltoni, D., Filliat, D., Díaz-Rodríguez, N.: Continual learning for robotics: definition, framework, learning strategies, opportunities and challenges. Inf. Fusion **58**, 52–68 (2020)
13. Lewkowycz, A., et al.: Solving quantitative reasoning problems with language models. arXiv preprint arXiv:2206.14858 (2022)
14. Li, S., et al.: Pre-trained language models for interactive decision-making. Adv. Neural Inf. Process. Syst. **35**, 31199–31212 (2022)
15. Li, Y., Mao, H., Girshick, R., He, K.: Exploring plain vision transformer backbones for object detection. In: Avidan, S., Brostow, G., Cissé, M., Farinella, G.M., Hassner, T. (eds.) ECCV 2022. LNCS, vol. 13669, pp. 280–296. Springer, Cham (2022). https://doi.org/10.1007/978-3-031-20077-9_17
16. McFarlane, R.: A survey of exploration strategies in reinforcement learning. McGill University (2018)
17. Puig, X., et al.: Virtualhome: simulating household activities via programs. In: IEEE Conference on Computer Vision and Pattern Recognition, pp. 8494–8502 (2018)
18. Stickland, A.C., Murray, I.: Bert and pals: projected attention layers for efficient adaptation in multi-task learning. In: International Conference on Machine Learning, pp. 5986–5995 (2019)
19. Wang, Z., Cai, S., Liu, A., Ma, X., Liang, Y.: Describe, explain, plan and select: interactive planning with large language models enables open-world multi-task agents. arXiv preprint arXiv:2302.01560 (2023)
20. Zhao, W.X., et al.: A survey of large language models. arXiv preprint arXiv:2303.18223 (2023)

Nonlinear Disturbance Observer-Based Continuous Fixed-time Tracking Control for Uncertain Robotic Systems

Yi Li[1(✉)], Wenjun Zhang[1], Yufei Zhou[2], Yongting Tao[1], and Mingchao Zhu[2]

[1] School of Mechanical Engineering, Ningxia University, Yinchuan 750021, China
liyi173@nxu.edu.cn
[2] Changchun Institute of Optics, Fine Mechanics and Physics, Chinese Academy of Sciences, Changchun 130033, China

Abstract. This paper proposes a nonlinear disturbance observer-based continuous fixed-time tracking control scheme for uncertain robotic systems. A nonlinear disturbance observer is constructed to estimate and reject the lumped disturbance of the control systems in real-time. It exhibits good results in terms of disturbance estimating and computational cost. Based on the disturbance observer, a fixed-time tracking control scheme for the uncertain robotic system is presented. Compared with the existing fast nonsingular integral terminal sliding mode controller, the proposed controller ensures local fixed-time convergence of both velocity tracking error and position tracking error. The stability and fixed-time convergence of the proposed controller are analyzed using the Lyapunov theory. Finally, comparative simulations of both the numerical and application examples are conducted to verify the proposed control schemes' effectiveness, indicating that the continuous fixed-time tracking control scheme can be used effectively for robotic systems.

Keywords: Fixed-time Convergence · Disturbance Observer · Robotic Systems

1 Introduction

In recent years, many researchers have focused on sliding mode control (SMC) for its strong robustness, fast convergence, and computational simplicity. The method has been employed to design controllers for many systems [1]. Among these applications, SMC can facilitate achieving the desired tracking performance without complex hardware requirements. On this aspect, it has obtained tremendous popularity in high-precision tracking tasks of robotic systems, including robotic manipulators [2], underwater vehicles [3], and mobile robots [4].

In conventional SMC, the sliding surface is designed linear; therefore, the sliding motion to the origin is accomplished asymptotically. Although the convergence rate may be arbitrarily fast by adjusting appropriate control gains, stabilizing dynamical systems cannot be achieved in finite time. To obtain a faster convergence rate, a fast nonsingular integral terminal SMC (FNITSMC) [5] was designed by introducing a boundary-like

© The Author(s), under exclusive license to Springer Nature Singapore Pte Ltd. 2023
H. Yang et al. (Eds.): ICIRA 2023, LNAI 14271, pp. 401–412, 2023.
https://doi.org/10.1007/978-981-99-6495-6_34

function to the integral fractional terms. Furthermore, a new form of adaptive FNITSMC (AFNITSMC) [3] is proposed for robust tracking control of underwater vehicles. It promotes the system trajectory to converge to the equilibrium with a fast convergence rate. Although AFNITSMC is faster than conventional NITSMC, it also remains the following shortcomings. First, the control law is not continuous, which may cause chattering. Second, the position tracking errors converge to the sliding surface asymptotically, which relies heavily on the initial condition and cannot remain zero within a finite time [6]. To further improve the control performance, fixed-time tracking control schemes for uncertain robotic manipulators were proposed in [7]. These methods ensure fixed-time convergence of tracking errors such that the convergence time is uniformly bounded a priori without requirements of the upper bound of lumped disturbance. The minor shortcoming for these fixed-time control methods is that the control law is not continuous, and there is a tradeoff between the robustness and chattering of the control system.

Recently, disturbance observer-based control schemes are designed to overcome the lumped disturbance and reduce the chattering in the control law. In [8], a nonlinear disturbance observer (NDOB) for robotic manipulators was presented. Subsequently, an improved NDOB based SMC [9] was utilized for tracking control of robotic manipulators. In [10] and [11], sliding mode disturbance observers were proposed to reject disturbance for uncertain nonlinear systems. However, these disturbance rejection control methods still need the inverse of the inertia matrix. It will inevitably increase the computational burden of the controller.

For this reason, a momentum observer [12] was proposed for robotic manipulators to estimated the disturbance. The method removes the acceleration signal requirement and inverse of inertia matrix, which was initially used to estimate disturbances and detect possible collisions. Based on its superior disturbance detection performance, a reduced-order ESO was proposed by [13] and developed in [9] to compensate for disturbance in robot control. In these disturbance observer-based control methods, the estimated lumped disturbance can be feedforward compensation to the controller.

Motivated by the above discussion, we propose nonlinear momentum observer (NMOB) based continuous fixed-time tracking control for uncertain robotic systems. To our knowledge, little researches focus on the disturbance observer-based fixed-time tracking control. Compared with [8] and [10], the proposed NMOB does not require the inverse of inertia matrix and improves the estimation accuracy. Additionally, compared with the AFNITSMC [3], the proposed novel NITSMC tracking control could promote both the position tracking error and velocity tracking errors to converge in fixed-time. In this way, the proposed method can be appealing for uncertain robotic systems.

2 Problem Formulation

2.1 Preliminaries

The dynamics of an n-link rigid robotic manipulator can be written as:

$$M(q)\ddot{q} + C(q, \dot{q})\dot{q} + G(q) + F_f(\dot{q}) + \tau_d = \tau \tag{1}$$

where $q, \dot{q}, \ddot{q} \in R^n$ are joint angular position vectors, velocity vectors, and acceleration vectors of the manipulator, respectively; $M(q) \in R^{n \times n}$ is the symmetric and positive definite inertia matrix; $C(q, \dot{q}) \in R^{n \times n}$ is the effect of centrifugal and Coriolis and centrifugal forces; $G(q) \in R^{n \times 1}$ is the gravity vector; $F_f(\dot{q}) \in R^{n \times 1}$ represents the friction forces. And $\tau_d \in R^{n \times 1}$ denotes an unknown vector of bounded external disturbance and $\tau \in R^{n \times 1}$ is the torque input vector. Practically, these parameters are laborious to identify accurately due to uncertainties in the center of nonlinear friction, payload variations, and other inherent factors.

Considering the system uncertainty in the obtained dynamic model, the Eq. (1) can be rewritten as:

$$M_0 \ddot{q} + \Omega_0(q, \dot{q}, \ddot{q}) + f(q, \dot{q}, \ddot{q}, t) = \tau \tag{2}$$

where $\Omega_0(q, \dot{q}) := C_0(q, \dot{q})\dot{q} + G_0(q) + F_{f0}(\dot{q})$ is the modeled nominal term and $f(\cdot) = \Delta M(q)\ddot{q} + \Delta C(q, \dot{q})\dot{q} + \Delta G(q) + \Delta F_f(\dot{q}) + \tau_d$ denotes the lumped system uncertainty.

Assumption 1: The uncertainties and the external disturbances $f(\cdot)$ is unknown and bounded, i.e., $\|f(.)\| \leqslant \rho_1$ with unknown bounded constant ρ_1.

3 Control Development

In this section, we design a position tracking controller using NMOB based NITSMC scheme for the robotic system in (2). To overcome the lumped disturbance with strong robustness and free-chattering properties, we propose an NMOB to estimate $f(\cdot)$. The NMOB achieves the required monitoring bandwidth with better disturbance tracking performance. Then, the estimated lumped disturbance is feedforward compensation to the NITSMC, which guarantees the finite-time convergence of the tracking error.

3.1 NMOB Formulation

The first-order generalized momentum-based observer to detect external torque was proposed and concluded in [12]. It is worth noting that the generalized momentum-based form is a kind of dynamic model-based equation. Therefore, the estimated lumped disturbance involves complex unknown friction forces, unmodelled dynamics, and external disturbances. In this way, we further explore the potential of the generalized momentum-based observer and apply it to the sliding mode controller design. Compared with the general state observers, the method avoids the inverse operation of inertia matrix and requirement of the acceleration signal. Thus, it is practical and superior to be applied to the lumped disturbance estimation of the uncertain robotic systems with more freedom degrees [13]. The general momentum and its time derivate are defined as

$$p_0 = M_0(q)\dot{q}, \ \dot{p}_0 = \dot{M}_0(q)\dot{q} + M_0(q)\ddot{q}. \tag{3}$$

Then, combine (2) and Property 1, a first-order dynamic equation can be obtained as

$$\dot{p}_0 = \tau_p + f(\cdot), \ \tau_p(t) = \tau + C_0^T(q, \dot{q})\dot{q} - G_0(q) - F_{f0}(\dot{q}). \tag{4}$$

In this way, the dynamic terms can be obtained, and the generalized momentum-based first-order state-space equation can be constructed as

$$x_1(t) = M_0(q), \ \dot{x}_1(t) = \tau_p(t) + f(\cdot), \ y(t) = \hat{x}_1(t), \tag{5}$$

where $\hat{x}_1(t)$ is the estimated state. If we consider the $f(\cdot)$ as an extended state of (12), then a new second-order state-space form equation can be written as:

$$z_1(t) = M_0(q), \ \dot{z}_1(t) = \tau_p(t) + z_2(t), \ \dot{z}_2(t) = \varphi(t), \ y(t) = z_1(t), \tag{6}$$

where $z_2(t) := \hat{f}(\cdot)$, $\varphi(t)$ is an unknown bounded function. According to (13), an NMOB can be designed as:

$$z_1(t) = M_0(q)\dot{q}, \ \dot{\hat{z}}_1 = \hat{z}_2 - \lambda_1 \ \mathrm{fal}(e_1, \alpha_1, \delta) + \tau_p(t), \ \dot{\hat{z}}_2 = -\lambda_2 \ \mathrm{fal}(e_1, \alpha_2, \delta),$$

with

$$\mathrm{fal}(e_1, \alpha_i, \delta) = \frac{e_1}{\delta^{1-\alpha_i}}, \ |e_1| \le \delta; \ e_1^{\alpha_i}, \ |e_1| > \delta. \tag{7}$$

where $e_1 = \hat{z}_1 - z_1$, $0 < \alpha_i < 1$ and δ is a small positive scalar. $\lambda_1 = \mathrm{diag}(2\omega_1, 2\omega_2,..., 2\omega_n)$ and $\lambda_2 = \mathrm{diag}(\omega_1^2, \omega_2^2,...,\omega_n^2)$ are assigned such that the matrix $G_1 = [\lambda_1 I; \lambda_2 0]$ is Hurwitz. Besides, ω_i is the NMOB's initial bandwidth of the ith joint. It can be parameterized by the pole-placement method. Figure 1 illustrates the Block diagram of the NMOB. $\hat{f}(\cdot)$ is the output of the disturbance observer.

Additionally, the NMOB is a kind of nonlinear extended state observer (NESO) from the active disturbance rejection control scheme. Based on numerous computer simulations and engineering practices, Han [14] claimed that the observer with non-linear function (7) is quite effective for the lumped disturbance estimation, improving the estimation accuracy and achieving the required monitoring bandwidth with higher noise immunity. Additionally, [15] provided a detailed certification process of the system state's boundedness, and the estimation error of NESO converges asymptotically. Readers can refer to the literature [14, 15] for more details and choose δ and α_i.

Remark 1. Compared with the nonlinear disturbance observers for robotic manipulators in [8], the proposed NMOB does not require the inverse or differentiation of the inertia matrix. On this aspect, the computation burden can be further reduced, and the NMOB is applicable to robots with more freedom degrees. Additionally, benefiting from the fractional power function, the peaking phenomenon is alleviated, and estimation accuracy is improved in the proposed NMOB.

3.2 Control Formulation

The AFNITSMC was proposed and simulation verified in [3]. It can ensure local finite-time convergence of the velocity tracking errors and the exponential convergence of the position tracking errors. Based on the work, we proposed a NITSMC tracking control to promote both the position tracking error and velocity tracking errors to converge in a fixed time.

From (2), the simplified dynamic model can be written as:

$$\ddot{q} = M_0^{-1}[\tau - \Omega_0(q, \dot{q}) - f(\cdot)]. \tag{8}$$

The position tracking error and the auxiliary velocity are defined as

$$e_1 = q - q_r, \ e_2 = \dot{q} - \dot{q}_c(\dot{q}_c = \dot{q}_r - K_1 e_1^p) \tag{9}$$

where $0 < p < 1$, $K_1 \in R^{n \times n}$ is a positive-definite diagonal matrix. Then, the error dynamics of the robot manipulator with the lumped disturbance can be expressed as:

$$\dot{e}_1 = \dot{q} - \dot{q}_r, \ \dot{e}_2 = \ddot{q} - \ddot{q}_c = M_0^{-1}[\tau - \Omega_0(q, \dot{q}) - f(\cdot)] - \ddot{q}_c. \tag{10}$$

Additionally, a nonsingular fast integral terminal sliding mode (FNITSM) surface [3] is introduced as follows:

$$s_v = \int_0^t e_2 d\tau + K_2 \left(\int_0^t e_2 d\tau \right)^{\alpha_1/\alpha_2} + K_3 e_2^{\beta_1/\beta_2}, \tag{11}$$

where $K_2 \in R^{n \times n}$, $K_3 \in R^{n \times n}$ are all positive-definite diagonal matrices; $1 < \beta_1/\beta_2 < 2$, $\alpha_1/\alpha_2 > \beta_1/\beta_2$ are odd integers which need to be designed. It was analyzed and concluded in [3] that the FNITSM increases the convergence rate of the system states. For the error dynamic nonlinear systems in (8)–(10), we will further illustrate that the tracking error $(e_1, \dot{e}_1)$ will convergence to zero in a fixed time.

To ensure the sliding motion occurs, the derivates of the sliding surface $\dot{s} = 0$ should be satisfied such that

$$\dot{s}_v = e_2 + \frac{\alpha_1}{\alpha_2} K_2 \left(\int_0^t e_2 d\tau \right)^{\alpha_1/\alpha_2 - 1} e_2 + \frac{\beta_1}{\beta_2} K_3 e_2^{\beta_1/\beta_2 - 1} \dot{e}_2 \tag{12}$$

Substitute (10) into (12), one obtains

$$\dot{s}_v = e_2 + \frac{\alpha_1}{\alpha_2} K_2 \left(\int_0^t e_2 d\tau \right)^{\alpha_1/\alpha_2 - 1} e_2 + \frac{\beta_1}{\beta_2} K_3 e_2^{\beta_1/\beta_2 - 1} \left(M_0^{-1}[\tau - \Omega_0(q, \dot{q}) - f(\cdot)] - \ddot{q}_c \right). \tag{13}$$

Thus, the equivalent control law can be obtained from $\dot{s}_v = 0$ and $f(\cdot) = 0$ as

$$\tau_{eq} = M_0 \left(\ddot{q}_c - \frac{\beta_2}{\beta_1} \frac{e_2^{2-\beta_1/\beta_2}}{K_3} \left(1 + \frac{\alpha_1}{\alpha_2} K_2 \left(\int_0^t e_2 d\tau \right)^{\alpha_1/\alpha_2 - 1} \right) \right) + \Omega_0(q, \dot{q}) \tag{14}$$

Then, the estimated $\hat{f}(\cdot)$ by the NMOB is used to offset the lumped disturbance. The feedforward compensation to the controller is $\tau_{ob} = \hat{f}(\cdot)$.

Additionally, define the NMOB's estimation error as $\tilde{f} = f(\cdot) - \hat{f}(\cdot)$. Considering the existence of $\tilde{f}$, an auxiliary controller is needed to eliminate the effects of approximation errors. In this way, the common fractional-order robust term is adopted as

$$\tau_{au} = M_0 \left[-ks - \hat{K}(s)\text{sig}^{\alpha_3}(s) \right], \tag{15}$$

where k is a constant diagonal positive matrix, $0 < a < 1$; $\hat{K}(s) \geqslant \tilde{f}$. However, it is not easy to get the upper bound of $\tilde{f}$ due to the complexity of the lumped disturbance. Usually, during the design process, the overestimated upper gain is used to guarantee that sliding motion will take place. This conservatism may exacerbate chattering because the chattering is not totally eliminated with the general continuous robust term. On this aspect, we adopted an adaptive upper gain to avoid overestimate of upper bound and minimize the estimation error. $\hat{K}(s)$ is a time-varying gain matrix for the robust term, which is updated by the following adaptive law:

$$\dot{\hat{K}}_i = \begin{cases} -\eta_i, & \text{if } \hat{K}_i \geqslant K_{\max,i}, \\ \vartheta_i sig^{\alpha_3}(\iota), & \text{if } K_{\min,i} \leqslant \hat{K}_i \leqslant K_{\max,i}, \\ \eta_i, & \text{if } \hat{K}_i \leqslant K_{\min,i}, \end{cases} \tag{16}$$

where $\iota = |s_i| - \zeta_i$; $0 < b < 1$, η_i, ϑ_i, and ζ_i are constant parameters to be tuned through simulations or experiments. $K_{\min,i}$ and $K_{\max,i}$ are the bounds of the disturbances which can be determined according to the approximate range of $\tilde{f}$. In this way, $\hat{K}(s)$ is growing with the s and will not be overestimated.

Based on the above analysis, the proposed NMOB based NITSMC is as follows:

$$\tau_{tol} = \tau_{eq} + \tau_{ob} + \tau_{au}. \tag{17}$$

To further reduce chattering, a fractional sigmoid function (FSF) based robust term is designed as follows

$$\dot{s} = -c_1 s(t) - \hat{K} \tanh\left(b \cdot sig^{\alpha_3}(s)\right) \tag{18}$$

Theorem 1: Consider the error dynamic systems (8)–(10) with the error dynamics, the control law (17) ensures local fixed-time convergence of the velocity tracking errors and position tracking errors to zero.

Proof: To ensure the NITSM surface can converge to zero in a fixed time, the following Lyapunov function is considered.

$$V = 0.5 s^T s$$

$$\dot{V} = s^T \dot{s} = s^T \left[e_2 + \frac{\alpha_1}{\alpha_2} K_2 \left(\int_0^t e_2 d\tau \right)^{\alpha_1/\alpha_2 - 1} e_2 + \frac{\beta_1}{\beta_2} K_3 e_2^{\beta_1/\beta_2 - 1} \dot{e}_2(t) \right]. \tag{19}$$

Substituting (17) into (19), one obtains:

$$\dot{V} = s^T \left(-k_1 s - \hat{K}(s) sig^a(s) + \frac{\beta_1}{\beta_2} K_3 e_2^{\beta_1/\beta_2 - 1} M^{-1} \tilde{f} \right)$$

$$\leqslant -\left(\hat{K}(s) \| s \|^{2a+1} - \frac{\beta_1}{\beta_2} K_3 e_2^{\beta_1/\beta_2 - 1} M^{-1} \tilde{f} \right) \| s \|. \tag{20}$$

Referring to Theorem 2.1 in [15], the estimation error $\tilde{f}$ ultimately converges into a small bounded ball for any $t > t_r$. If we keep, $\eta = \hat{K}(s) \| s \|^{2a+1} - \frac{\beta_1}{\beta_2} K_3 e_2^{\beta_1/\beta_2 - 1} M^{-1} \tilde{f} \geq$

0 one obtains that $\dot{V} \leqslant -\eta\sqrt{2}V^{0.5}$. Based on Lemma 1, the sliding mode s consequently converges to zero in a finite time, and the converge time is less than $t_s = \frac{\sqrt{2}}{\eta}V(0)^{0.5}$.

On the sliding mode $s = 0$, the error dynamic is

$$\dot{e}_{2I}(t) = -\left(\frac{e_{2I}(t) + K_2 e_{2I}(t)^{\alpha_1/\alpha_2}}{K_3}\right)^{\beta_2/\beta_1}, \tag{21}$$

where $e_{2I}(t) = \int_0^t e_2(\tau)d\tau$. Then, the convergent time $t_{e_{2I}}$ can be calculated as

$$t_{e_{2I}} = \int_0^{|e_{2I}(t_s)|} \frac{K_3^{\beta_2/\beta_1}}{\left(e_{2I} + K_2 e_{2I}^{\alpha_1/\alpha_2}\right)^{\beta_2/\beta_1}} de_{2I} \leqslant \int_0^{|e_{2I}(t_s)|} \frac{K_3^{\beta_2/\beta_1}}{e_{2I}^{\beta_2/\beta_1}} de_{2I}. \tag{22}$$

Solving the above inequality, we can get

$$t_{e_{2I}} \leqslant \frac{e_{2I}^{(1-\beta/\beta_1)}(t_s)}{K_3^{\beta_v/\beta}(1 - \beta_2/\beta_1)}. \tag{23}$$

Furthermore, when $t \geqslant t_{e_{21}} + t_s$, we can also obtain $e_2 = 0$ and $\dot{q} = \dot{q}_c$. Combine (9), we have that $\dot{e}_1 = -k_1 e_1^p$. On this aspect, the convergent time t_{e_1} cost for position tracking errors $e_1(t)$ to reach $e_1(t_{e_{2I}} + t_{e_1}) = 0$ from $e_1(t_{e_2})$ is calculated as

$$t_{e_1} = \frac{\left|e_1(t_{e_{21}})\right|^{(1-p)}}{k_1(1 - p)}. \tag{24}$$

Therefore, we can have that the variables in (9) is globally fixed-time-stable to the equilibrium point $(e, \dot{e}) = (0, 0)$. And the total convergence time is

$$t_{tol} = t_s + t_{e_{2I}} + t_{e_1}. \tag{25}$$

Besides, in case $s \neq 0$, there may be a potential singularity problem in $\ddot{q}_c$ when $e_1 = 0, e_2 \neq 0$. To tackle this problem, a novel two-phase approach strategy is proposed to avoid the singularity in the control law. Subsequently, the auxiliary velocity is redefined as

$$\dot{q}_c = \begin{cases} \dot{q}_r - k_1 e_1^p, & \text{if } |e_1| \geqslant \varepsilon, \\ \dot{q}_r - k_2 e_1 - k_3 \int_0^t e_1 d\tau, & \text{if } |e_1| \leqslant \varepsilon, \end{cases} \tag{26}$$

where ε is a small positive constant vector. If $t \geqslant t_{e_{21}} + t_s$, we have that $(e_1, e_2) = (\varepsilon, 0)$

$$e_1 + k_2 e_1 + k_3 \int_0^t e_1 d\tau = 0, \tag{27}$$

where k_2 and k_3 are positive parameters, satisfying the relationship of $k_2^2 \geqslant 4k_3$. Then, the e_1 can exponentially converge to zero from $e_1 = \varepsilon$. Therefore, the (26) ensure a relatively fast convergence rate without singularity, and it also makes the e_1 converge into zero domain in a fixed time. Subsequently, the (27) promotes the exponential convergence of the position tracking errors to zero.

4   Numerical Simulations

There three simulation studies are presented in this section. First, to evaluate the efficiency of the proposed disturbance observer, comparative simulations between the
NMOB, MESO [13], and NDOB [8] are conducted to estimate the lumped disturbance
of a two-link robot manipulator. Then, an application of the NMOB based NITSMC to
the tracking control of the robot is presented. Finally, the proposed control scheme is
compared with the existing controllers in [3, 5], and the simulation results are further
illustrated to demonstrate the effectiveness of the scheme. MATLAB is used to perform
all simulations, and the sampling time is set to 10^{-3}s.

Then, we consider a two-link robot manipulator for the robust fixed time tracking
control in an uncertain environment. The dynamic parameters of the robot manipulator
and the desired reference signals in [5] are utilized for simulation. Then, we further
compare and prove the validity of the offered observer and control scheme. The tuning
parameters of the NMOB based NITSMC are chosen as:

$K_3 = \text{diag}(1, 1), \cdot k_1 = \text{diag}(2, 2), \cdot k_2 = \text{diag}(0.5, 0.5), \cdot k_3 = \text{diag}(0.01, 0.01), b = 80, \cdot$
$k = c_1 = \text{diag}(20, 20), \alpha_1/\alpha_2 = 13/3, \cdot \beta_1/\beta_2 = 5/3, p = 0.9, \alpha_3 = 0.5, K_{\min} = 5,$
$K_{\max} = 20, \cdot \vartheta = 2, \cdot \varsigma = 0.05, \cdot \eta = 0.8, K_1 = \text{diag}(2, 2), K_2 = \text{diag}(1.2, 1.2).$

4.1   Disturbance Tracking Simulation

To prove the validity of the disturbance observer, two other types of existing observers
are also considered in disturbance tracking simulation for the purpose of comparison,
which are momentum-based reduced-order extended state observer (MESO) in [13] and
a nonlinear disturbance observer (NDOB) in [8].

To illustrate the performance of the observers, we assume that the robot manipulator's
dynamic model is fully known, which means that the system's lumped disturbance
only contains the external disturbance. The applied external disturbance is defined as
$\tau_{d1} = 6 \sin(t), \tau_{d2} = 6 sign(\sin(t))$ Then, the NMOB, MESO, and NDOB are used to
estimate the disturbance, together with the parameters NMOB: $\omega_1 = \omega_2 = 20, \alpha_1 =$
0.5, $\alpha_2 = 0.25, \delta = 0.1$; MESO: $\omega_1 = \omega_2 = 20$; NDOB: $\mu = 9.3, \sigma_2 = 1.3, \kappa = 6.$
Considering the impact of measurement noise on the actual velocity and torque signals,
Gaussian white noise with zero mean value, a variance of 0.0005, and a sampling time
of 0.001 s is applied. The disturbance tracking performance is displayed as follows.

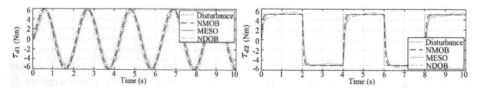

Fig. 1. Estimated external disturbance of joint1 and joint2.

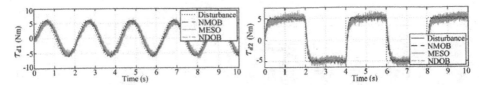

Fig. 2. Estimated external disturbance of joint 1 and joint 2 in the presence of the same measurement noise.

Simulation results are depicted in Figs. 1, 2. The estimated external disturbance of joint1 and joint2 in comparison with the real ones are illustrated in Fig. 1. It is clear that the NMOB is better than NDOB in terms of convergence rate and estimation error. On this aspect, the NMOB can improve the estimation accuracy of the disturbance. Figure 2 exhibits the estimated external disturbance of joint 1 and joint 2 in the presence of the same measurement noise, where one can observe that NMOB has strong robustness of measurement noise. These simulation results verify that the NMOB has good performance and the noise-immunity of the disturbance tracking.

Note that the NDOB requires the inverse of the inertia matrix. For this reason, the NMOB is proposed to estimate the lumped disturbance and alleviate the computation burden. Additionally, NMOB can further improve the estimation accuracy and convergence rates with higher noise-immunity.

4.2 Trajectory Tracking Simulation

Based on the output of the proposed disturbance observer, a continuous NITSMC scheme for the uncertain robotic system is presented. The unknown dynamics of the manipulator are regarded as 20% of the actual dynamics, and the external disturbances considered are $\tau_{d1} = 2\sin(t) + 0.5\sin(200\pi t)$, $\tau_{d2} = \cos(2t) + 0.5\sin(200\pi t)$, it represents the lumped disturbance includes dynamic uncertainties, external disturbance, and high-frequency measurement noise in robot manipulator control.

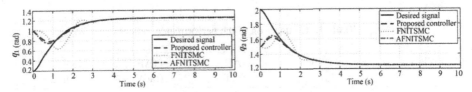

Fig. 3. Comparison of position tracking responses with three types of controllers.

Then, the comparative simulations are conducted to demonstrate the effectiveness of the proposed control scheme. The simulation results of the FNITSMC presented in [5] are considered for the purpose of comparison. Besides, the AFNITSMC laws in [3] are redesigned for the simulation verification model in this paper. The parameters for the control laws are chosen the same values as the proposed controller, and the constant adaptive gains are designed as $\chi_i = 0.05$, $(i = 0, 1, 2)$. Subsequently, $IAE :=$

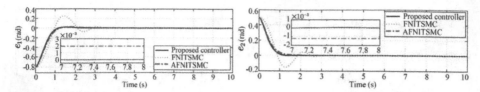

Fig. 4. Comparison of position tracking errors with three types of controllers.

$\int_0^{t_f} |e_1(t)|dt$, $ITAE := \int_0^{t_f} t \cdot |e_1(t)|dt$ and ISV $= \int_0^{t_f} \tau^2 dt$ are applied to quantitative the three types of controllers' tracking performances.

The position tracking performance is shown in Fig. 3 and 4. We can see that the proposed controller is better than the two other controllers in terms of convergence speed and steady errors. And it promotes both the position tracking error and velocity tracking errors to converge in a fixed time. Moreover, benefit from the disturbance rejection of the NMOB, the designed method exhibits strong robustness and does not need the exact dynamic model of the robot manipulator. As plotted in Fig. 5, the proposed scheme indicates a chattering-free property as well as the continuous NITSMC in [11]. The comparison of the tracking performance indices is summarized in Table 1. It can be seen that the proposed controller provides small IAE and ITAE values than the existing methods with lower control energy consumption. In this way, the proposed control scheme can be used effectively for robot tracking control in the presence of the lumped disturbances and provides a faster convergence rate, strong robustness without chattering.

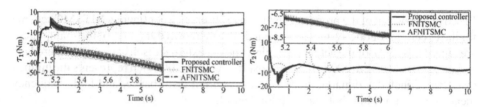

Fig. 5. Comparison of input torques with three types of controllers.

Table 1. Comparison of the performance indices

Controllers	Joints	IAE (rad)	ITAE (rad)	ISV (Nm)2
Proposed controller	Joint1	0.4070	0.1514	276.3
	Joint2	0.2211	0.0685	590.5
AFNITSMC [3]	Joint1	0.4610	0.2850	280.5
	Joint2	0.2651	0.1443	601.4
FNITSMC [5]	Joint1	0.7106	0.5743	526.1
	Joint2	0.3787	0.2667	658.5

5 Conclusion

In this paper, NMOB based NITSMC is proposed for trajectory tracking of uncertain robotic systems. The NMOB is constructed to estimate and compensate for the lumped disturbance of the control systems in real-time. It does not require an explicit dynamic model of the robot or high computing costs. Moreover, the time-varying gain and continuous robust term are designed to approximate the upper bound of the estimation error. Based on the Lyapunov function, a novel NITSMC is presented to ensure local fixed-time convergence of the velocity tracking errors and the position tracking errors. Finally, the designed controller is applied to control a two-link robotic manipulator in simulation, and the comparative results demonstrate the superiority of the designed control scheme. It is noteworthy that the NMOB has good disturbance tracking performance, and it can also be adopted to control other Euler–Lagrange systems. Future work will focus on more application fields of the proposed method including high-precision surgical robots, and mobile robots.

Acknowledgements. This research was supported by the National Natural Science Foundation of China (Grant No. 62173047).

References

1. Yao, X., Park, J.H., Dong, H., Guo, L., Lin, X.: Robust adaptive nonsingular terminal sliding mode control for automatic train operation. IEEE Trans. Syst. Man Cybern. Syst. **49**(12), 2406–2415 (2019)
2. Rahmani, M., Rahman, M.H.: Adaptive neural network fast fractional sliding mode control of a 7-DOF exoskeleton robot. Int. J. Control. Autom. Syst. **18**(1), 124–133 (2020)
3. Qiao, L., Zhang, W.: Trajectory tracking control of AUVs via adaptive fast nonsingular integral terminal sliding mode control. IEEE Trans. Ind. Inf. **16**(2), 1248–1258 (2020)
4. Ren, C., Li, X., Yang, X., Ma, S.: Extended state observer-based sliding mode control of an omnidirectional mobile robot with friction compensation. IEEE Trans. Ind. Electron. **66**(12), 9480–9489 (2019)
5. Li, P., Ma, J., Zheng, Z., Geng, L.: Fast nonsingular integral terminal sliding mode control for nonlinear dynamical systems. In: Proceedings of the IEEE Conference on Decision and Control, vol. 2015, pp. 4739–4746, February 2014
6. Su, Y., Zheng, C., Mercorelli, P.: Robust approximate fixed-time tracking control for uncertain robot manipulators. Mech. Syst. Signal Process. **135** (2020)
7. Su, Y., Zheng, C.: Fixed-time inverse dynamics control for robot manipulators. J. Dyn. Syst. Meas. Control Trans. ASME **141**(6), 1–32 (2019)
8. Mohammadi, A., Tavakoli, M., Marquez, H.J., Hashemzadeh, F.: Nonlinear disturbance observer design for robotic manipulators. Control. Eng. Pract. **21**(3), 253–267 (2013)
9. Homayounzade, M., Khademhosseini, A.: Disturbance observer-based trajectory following control of robot manipulators. Int. J. Control. Autom. Syst. **17**(1), 203–211 (2019)
10. Sun, T., Cheng, L., Wang, W., Pan, Y.: Semiglobal exponential control of Euler-Lagrange systems using a sliding-mode disturbance observer. Automatica **112**, 108677 (2020)
11. Rabiee, H., Ataei, M., Ekramian, M.: Continuous nonsingular terminal sliding mode control based on adaptive sliding mode disturbance observer for uncertain nonlinear systems. Automatica **109**, 108515 (2019)

12. Haddadin, S., De Luca, A., Albu-Schäffer, A.: Robot collisions: a survey on detection, isolation, and identification. IEEE Trans. Robot. **33**(6), 1292–1312 (2017)
13. Ren, T., Dong, Y., Wu, D., Chen, K.: Collision detection and identification for robot manipulators based on extended state observer. Control Eng. Pract. **79**, 144–153 (2018)
14. Han, J.: From PID to active disturbance rejection control. IEEE Trans. Ind. Electron. **56**(3), 900–906 (2009)
15. Zhao, Z.L., Guo, B.Z.: A nonlinear extended state observer based on fractional power functions. Automatica **81**, 286–296 (2017)

Optimized Adaptive Impedance Control Based on Robotic Seven-Axis Linkage Grinding Platform

Yilin Mu, Ziling Wang, Size Liang, and Lai Zou(✉)

The State Key Laboratory of Mechanical Transmissions, Chongqing University, No. 174, Shazhengjie, Shapingba, Chongqing 400044, China
zoulai@cqu.edu.cn

Abstract. In order to achieve control of the seventh axis during the robotic belt grinding, the adaptive impedance control algorithm has been proposed. By comparing the steady-state error of adaptive impedance controller (AIC) and impedance controller (IC) from simple step signals, slope signals, to complex trigonometric function signals, the performance of controller is analyzed. The Simulink simulation model of AIC is constructed, through simulation analysis, the impact of key parameters ϕ and b_d in the AIC on controller performance is obtained, and the two parameters are optimized through the improved cat swarm optimization (ICSO) algorithm. During the optimization process, the two mutually constrained optimization objectives of minimum contact force tracking error and shortest response time are constructed into the final objective function through weight coefficient variation method, ultimately achieving the improvement of controller performance. The optimized controller is transformed from continuous domain to discrete domain through backward difference dispersion method, ultimately achieving the control of seventh axis.

Keywords: Robotic belt grinding · Robotic seventh axis · Adaptive impedance controller · Parameter optimization

1 Introduction

Automated grinding schemes are generally divided into CNC grinding and robotic grinding [1, 2]. Compared to CNC grinding, robotic belt grinding has advantages such as strong flexibility and low equipment cost, and has become the main processing method for complex workpieces [3]. Based on the feedback adjustment of whether there is contact force during the processing, the robotic belt grinding method is divided into two categories: passive force control strategy and active force control strategy [4].

The passive control strategy usually depends on the end effector to achieve contact force control. Wang et al. [5] designed a novel force-controlled end effector that can effectively control workpiece vibration, whose effectiveness was verified through grinding experiments. Wei et al. [6] proposed a conceptual design of a new robotic grinding end effector based on a constant force mechanism. The actuator was installed at the end

H. Yang et al. (Eds.): ICIRA 2023, LNAI 14271, pp. 413–423, 2023.
https://doi.org/10.1007/978-981-99-6495-6_35

of the robot and passively adjusted the contact force based on its internal structure. Chen et al. [7] designed an eddy current damper to suppress chatter during robotic processing. The designed eddy current damper was installed on the milling spindle to suppress tool tip vibration. However, the accuracy of force control is difficult to ensure, so it is usually used as an auxiliary device in the robotic belt grinding process.

For the active force control strategy, it greatly improves the control accuracy of contact force. According to the different active force control strategies of the controlled object, they are divided into the robot based active force control strategy and the force control device based active force control strategy. The former adjusts the robot body through sensors to achieve control of contact force, while the latter achieves control of contact force by adjusting the additional actuator. For the robot based active force control strategy, Li et al. [8] proposed a new impedance controller that the reference trajectory of the robot was adjusted to limit mutual forces and maintain them at the desired level. Zhao et al. [9] proposed an asymmetric nonlinear impedance control method, and a comparative study was conducted with symmetric linear impedance control. Zhang et al. [10] designed a controller using radial basis function neural networks, which had the ability to effectively approximate arbitrary bounded and continuous function. For the force control device based active force control strategy, Chen et al. [11] used an intelligent end effector as the actuator for contact force control. The proposed force controller included a gravity compensation module, a force prediction module, and a force position controller. Liao et al. [12] designed an adaptive controller to track the pressure of the pressurized cutting head. This was a new polishing control method that combines adaptive control theory with contact model constant stress theory. At present, due to the advantages of fast response speed and no coupling between force and position during the control process, the active force control strategy based on the force control device has become the mainstream solution for the contact force control strategy.

The control of the robotic seven-axis linkage grinding platform belongs to the active force control strategy based on the force control device. The advantage of this processing method is that it decouples the force-position control problem in the process of robotic belt grinding. The robot is used for motion control to meet the precise grinding position and pose requirements, and the seventh axis of the robot is used for contact force control to meet the precise contact force control requirements. Due to the fact that the seventh axis is driven by a servo motor to drive the screw nut pair, which drives the contact wheel to move, it has high position control accuracy. Therefore, position based adaptive impedance control is chosen as the controller for the robotic seventh axis.

2   Robotic Seven Axis Linkage Grinding Platform

In our self-built robotic seven axis linkage grinding platform, the robot and the seventh axis are two independent mechanisms, and the linkage is achieved through robotic machining code. Force control is achieved through the seventh axis, and position control is achieved by the robot. The sensor, as the sensing tool, collects force signals during actual machining processes, with filtering and gravity compensation carried out in the host computer. The final contact force error value Δf of each cutter-contact (CC) point can be converted into displacement compensation value Δz through our proposed force control algorithm, which is real-time transmitted by the host computer to the seventh axis for adjustment, thus achieving the control of contact force. The schematic diagram of robotic seven axis linkage force control is shown in Fig. 1.

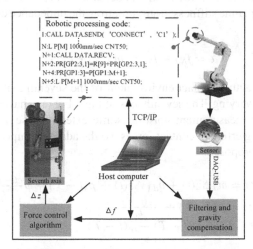

Fig. 1. Schematic diagram of robotic seven axis linkage force control.

3   Adaptive Impedance Control Algorithm

During the grinding process of the robotic seventh axis, the deviation value of the force generated is converted into the deviation value of the displacement through the proposed adaptive impedance controller. The deviation value of the displacement is transmitted to the robotic seventh axis. The robotic seventh axis has high position control accuracy because it is driven up and down by the servo motor to complete the movement of the contact wheel, so the gain of the seventh axis motion controller can be simplified to 1. The simplified closed-loop system diagram between the seventh axis and environment is shown in Fig. 2.

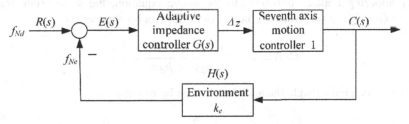

Fig. 2. Simplified system for closed-loop transmission between the seventh axis and the environment.

In Fig. 2, f_{Nd} represents the ideal contact force, f_{Ne} represents the actual contact force, and $G(s)$ represents the transfer function of the controller. For the complex and unstructured contact environment of robotic belt grinding, the precise values of environmental stiffness k_e and environmental reference position z_e cannot be known. If the expected stiffness k_d is not set to 0, the contact force tracking error of the controller always exists. In order to meet the ideal and accurate contact force tracking conditions for environmental dynamic stiffness in any situation, the impedance control (IC) equation is obtained:

$$e = f_{Nd} - f_{Ne} = m_d \Delta \ddot{z} + b_d \Delta \dot{z} \tag{1}$$

However, in the actual contact environment of the seventh axis, the environmental parameters are time-varying. The seventh axis of the robot may have signal transmission or control delays or measurement noise to some extent. These will directly or indirectly lead to tracking errors in contact forces, so the adaptive impedance control (AIC) algorithm has been proposed:

$$\begin{cases} e(t) = m_d \Delta \ddot{z}(t) + b_d \left(\Delta \dot{z}(t) + \rho(t - T) + \phi \frac{c(t-T)}{b_d} \right) \\ \rho(t) = \rho(t - T) + \phi \frac{c(t-T)}{b_d} \\ c(t - T) = f_d(t - T) - f_e(t - T) \end{cases} \tag{2}$$

From the purpose of the adaptive algorithm, it can be seen that the position deviation uncertainty caused by the above factors is compensated in the damping term, where ρ is the compensation value, T is the sampling period, ϕ is the update rate.

3.1 Controller Performance Analysis

It can know from the adaptive compensation rate in formula (2) that as the update rate ϕ increases, the more obvious the compensation effect, but at the same time, it inevitably leads to significant contact force overshoot.

According to the principle of dispersion, it is assumed that after nT cycles, the system is in a stable state. Formula (2) can be rewritten as:

$$e(t) = m_d \Delta \ddot{z}(t) + b_d \Delta \dot{z}(t) + \phi(c(t - nT) + \cdots + c(t - T)) \tag{3}$$

By applying Laplace transform to the above equation, the steady-state transfer function $G(s)$ of the adaptive impedance controller can be obtained as:

$$G(s) = \frac{1 + \phi(e^{-nTs} + \cdots + e^{-Ts})}{m_d s^2 + b_d s} \tag{4}$$

When n is large enough, the additive part can be rewritten as:

$$e^{-nTs} + \cdots + e^{-Ts} = \sum_{n=1}^{\infty} e^{-nTs} = \frac{e^{-Ts}}{1 - e^{-Ts}} \tag{5}$$

Due to the large sampling frequency and small sampling period T, the time term obtained after Taylor expansion is $e^{-Ts} \cong 1 - Ts$. The steady-state transfer functions of impedance control (IC) and adaptive impedance control (AIC) can be ultimately obtained:

$$\begin{cases} G(s) = \frac{1}{m_d s^2 + b_d s} \ (IC) \\ G(s) = \frac{1 + \phi \frac{1-Ts}{Ts}}{m_d s^2 + b_d s} \ (AIC) \end{cases} \tag{6}$$

After considering the environmental stiffness k_e, the transfer function $\Phi(s)$ of the entire closed-loop system is:

$$\begin{cases} \Phi(s) = \frac{1}{1+G(s)H(s)} = \frac{m_d s^2 + b_d s}{m_d s^2 + b_d s + k_e} \ (IC) \\ \Phi(s) = \frac{1}{1+G(s)H(s)} = \frac{m_d s^2 + b_d s}{m_d s^2 + b_d s + k_e + \phi k_e \frac{1-Ts}{Ts}} \ (AIC) \end{cases} \tag{7}$$

The steady-state error e_{ss} of the closed-loop system is calculated using the terminal value theorem, where the input signal $R(s)$ of the system selects the most common step signal $1/s$ and slope signal $1/s^2$:

$$e_{ss} = \lim_{s \to 0} s\Phi(s)(1/s) = \begin{cases} \lim_{s \to 0} s \frac{m_d s^2 + b_d s}{m_d s^2 + b_d s + k_e} (1/s) = 0 \ (IC) \\ \lim_{s \to 0} s \frac{m_d s^2 + b_d s}{m_d s^2 + b_d s + k_e + \phi k_e \frac{1-Ts}{Ts}} (1/s) = 0 \ (AIC) \end{cases} \tag{8}$$

$$e_{ss} = \lim_{s \to 0} s\Phi(s)(1/s^2) = \begin{cases} \lim_{s \to 0} s \frac{m_d s^2 + b_d s}{m_d s^2 + b_d s + k_e} (1/s^2) = \frac{b_d}{k_e} \ (IC) \\ \lim_{s \to 0} s \frac{m_d s^2 + b_d s}{m_d s^2 + b_d s + k_e + \phi k_e \frac{1-Ts}{Ts}} (1/s^2) = 0 \ (AIC) \end{cases} \tag{9}$$

For more complex input signals, sine signal $r(t) = \sin \omega t$ and cosine signal $r(t) = \cos \omega t$. The long division method is used to calculate the steady-state error of two controllers (taking the first three terms):

$$e_{ss}(t) = \sum_{i=0}^{l} \frac{1}{i!} \Phi^{(i)}(0) r^{(i)}(t) = \begin{cases} 0 - \omega \frac{b_d}{k_e} \sin \omega t - \omega^2 \frac{mk_e - b^2}{k_e^2} \cos \omega t + \cdots \ (IC) \\ 0 + 0 - \omega^2 \frac{2bT}{\phi k_e} \sin \omega t \ (AIC) \end{cases} \tag{10}$$

$$e_{ss}(t) = \sum_{i=0}^{l} \frac{1}{i!} \Phi^{(i)}(0) r^{(i)}(t) = \begin{cases} 0 + \omega \frac{b_d}{k_e} \cos \omega t - \omega^2 \frac{mk_e - b^2}{k_e^2} \sin \omega t + \cdots \ (IC) \\ 0 + 0 - \omega^2 \frac{2bT}{\phi k_e} \cos \omega t \ (AIC) \end{cases} \tag{11}$$

It can be clearly seen that as the input signal gradually becomes more complex, the steady-state tracking error of the impedance controller goes from 0 to unstable and ultimately fails. The steady-state error of the adaptive impedance controller is relatively stable, even if the input is a more complex trigonometric function signal, it still maintains a small steady-state error.

3.2 Simulink Simulation Experiment

The Simulink simulation model is built for the proposed adaptive impedance controller, as shown in Fig. 3. The expected position z_d is set to 0, and the expected contact force f_{Nd} is set to 30N. In the adaptive impedance model, there are three parameters m_d,

b_d, and ϕ. During the process of robotic belt grinding, due to the small change in the acceleration of the seventh axis and the corresponding small change in the dynamic response of the system, the change in the inertia coefficient m_d is also relatively small, so the optimization of parameter m_d does not significantly improve the performance of the controller. However, there is significant uncertainty in the selection of parameter b_d and parameter ϕ.

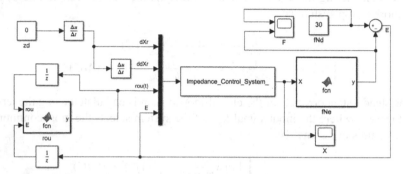

Fig. 3. Simulation model of adaptive impedance controller.

In order to explore the impact of two key parameters on the adaptive impedance controller, the simulation experiments are conducted separately on the parameter b_d and parameter ϕ. As shown in Fig. 4, The experimental results indicate that: with the remaining parameters unchanged, as the damping coefficient b_d decreases, the overshoot and oscillation of the system can increase. Increasing the damping coefficient b_d can reduce the overshoot of the system to 0, but the adjustment time can become longer; with the remaining parameters unchanged, as the update rate ϕ increases, the adaptive impedance controller has smaller contact force tracking error, but at the same time, if the update rate ϕ is too large, the system can oscillate.

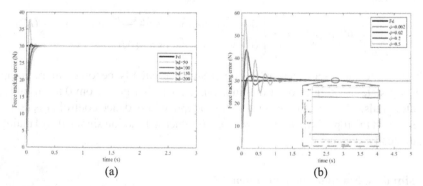

Fig. 4. Simulation results of the key parameters b_d and ϕ. (a) Force tracking curves under different b_d. (b) Force tracking curves under different ϕ.

4 Controller Parameter Optimization

4.1 Determination of Fitness Function

The primary objective of parameter optimization is to ensure the minimum force tracking error of the seventh axis during machining, and the slow response time of impedance control becomes the main constraint for its stable fitting to its moving surface. Therefore, the secondary objective of optimization is to minimize the response time of the single point contact process.

(1) Primary constraint objective:

$$J = \sum_{k=1}^{N} \left[f_{Nd}(k) - f_{Ne}(k) \right]^2 \tag{12}$$

In the above equation, N represents the total number of CC points, and $f_{Nd}(k)$ and $f_{Ne}(k)$ represent the expected contact force and actual contact force on each CC point of the seventh axis, respectively.

(2) Secondary constraint objective:

$$t_r = \frac{2m_d \left(\pi - \arccos \frac{b_d}{2\sqrt{m_d k_e (1+\phi)}} \right)}{\sqrt{4m_d k_e (1+\phi) - b_d^2}} \tag{13}$$

The rise time t_r of the system refers to the time when the response curve first from 0 reaches steady state, The rise time of the adaptive impedance controller is shown in the above formula.

The realization of two optimization goals is to some extent mutually constrained. The small tracking error of the force pursues stability of the control, while the short rise time pursues fast responsiveness of the control. Therefore, it is necessary to balance the importance of two factors. The weight coefficient change method is used to find the optimal value.

$$u = \sum_{i=1}^{n} \omega_i \cdot f_i(x) \tag{14}$$

where, u represents the fitness value, n represents the number of multi-objective optimization, ω_i represents the weight coefficient, and $f_i(x)$ represents the sub objective function.

The final fitness function $u(i)$ is:

$$u(i) = \omega_1 \frac{1}{J'} + \omega_2 \frac{1}{t_r'} \tag{15}$$

4.2 Parameter Optimization Algorithm

The improved cat swarm optimization (ICSO) algorithm is adopted to optimize ϕ and b_d, and the algorithm flowchart is shown in Fig. 5. Firstly, the range of the optimization variables ϕ and b_d is determined, and the initial parameters is set, and then perform binary discrete encoding. In the predetermined range, the initial population is generated by random initialization, and the fitness value of each individual in the population is calculated. By using the MR operator to divide population behavior patterns partition, the population is divided into two types of individuals for search mode (global search) and tracking mode (local search). At different stages of the cycle, the weight of behavior pattern division is controlled through MR parameters. In the early stages of the loop, the algorithm tends to focus more on global search, and as the number of loop algebras increases, the algorithm will tend to focus more on local search. Finally, when the set maximum cycle algebra is reached, the parameter optimization ends.

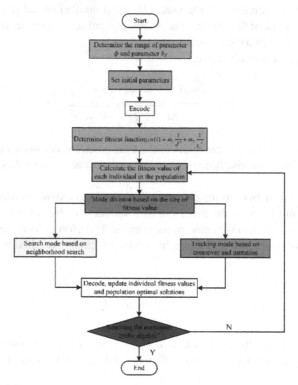

Fig. 5. The flowchart of parameter optimization algorithm.

The genetic algorithm (GA) and particle swarm optimization (PSO) algorithm are selected as comparative algorithms, and the algorithm iteration graph is shown in Fig. 6. From the experimental results, it can be seen that within the specified number of iterations, the ICSO algorithm converges and finds the optimal value in the 86th iteration, achieving the best performance among the three algorithms. Compared to the ICSO algorithm and the PSO algorithm, The GA algorithm exhibits poor search ability in the continuous optimization problem. Especially when approaching the optimal value, the search efficiency significantly decreases and there is no convergence in the finite algebra. At the beginning of the iteration, The PSO algorithm exhibits strong global search ability, but as the number of iterations increases, the optimization efficiency decreases, and ultimately does not converge within the specified number of iterations, only achieving better results compared to GA.

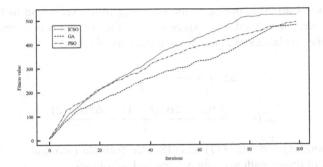

Fig. 6. Iterative graph of optimization algorithms.

During the parameter optimization process, the initial iteration parameters, intermediate iteration parameters, and final iteration parameters are selected for Simulink simulation. The force tracking curve after simulation is shown in Fig. 7. It can be seen that the optimized adaptive impedance controller is more stable and performs better than the controller without optimization.

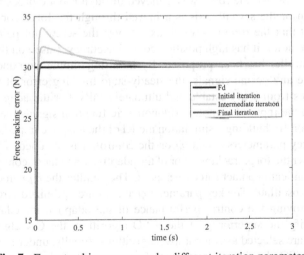

Fig. 7. Force tracking curves under different iteration parameters.

5   Implementation of Control Algorithm

The time-domain expression of the second-order impedance equation under zero initial value conditions is:

$$\Delta f(t) = m_d \Delta \ddot{z}(t) + b_d \Delta \dot{z}(t) \tag{16}$$

Due to the fact that the seventh axis, like the robot, also operates in the discrete time domain. In order to facilitate the application on the seventh axis, the control algorithm should be discretization according to the sampling time. According to the backward difference dispersion method, the expressions of the first derivative and the second derivative of the displacement in the discrete state are obtained:

$$\Delta \dot{z}(t) = \frac{\Delta z(t) - \Delta z(t-1)}{T} \tag{17}$$

$$\Delta \ddot{z}(t) = \frac{\Delta z(t) - 2\Delta z(t-1) + \Delta z(t-2)}{T^2} \tag{18}$$

By incorporating formulas (17) and (18) into formula (16), the end displacement compensation of the seventh axis can be obtained as follows:

$$\Delta z(t) = \frac{T^2}{m_d + b_d T} \Delta f(t) + \frac{2m_d + b_d T}{m_d + b_d T} \Delta z(t-1) - \frac{m_d}{m_d + b_d T} \Delta z(t-2) \tag{19}$$

6   Conclusion

For the seventh axis in the robotic seven axis linkage platform, the linkage between the robotic seventh axis and the robot was achieved through robotic processing code. The control problem of the seventh axis is achieved through the force control algorithm. Due to the fact that the robotic seventh axis drives the screw nut pair up and down through a servo motor, it has high position control accuracy. Based on this, an adaptive impedance controller has been proposed. By inputting simple step and ramp signals to complex sine and cosine signals, the steady-state tracking error of the impedance controller ranges from 0 to unstable and ultimately fails. For the adaptive impedance controller, even the input of complex trigonometric function signals maintains a small steady-state error. By building a simulation model of the adaptive impedance controller, the impact of key parameters ϕ and b_d on the controller is obtained. The larger the ϕ value, the smaller the force tracking error of the adaptive impedance controller, but it can bring about significant contact force overshoot. The smaller the b_d value, the more the system tends to oscillate. The key parameter ϕ and b_d are optimized through the ICSO algorithm, improving the control performance of the adaptive impedance controller. In order to verify the superiority of the ICSO algorithm, the GA algorithm and the PSO algorithm are selected as comparative algorithms. Finally, under the set number of iterations, the ICSO algorithm can converge faster and obtain the optimal solution. The final optimized controller is transformed into a discrete domain through the backward difference dispersion method, achieving the control of seventh axis.

Acknowledgements. This study was supported by the National Natural Science Foundation of China (Grant No. 52075059) and the Innovation Group Science Fund of Chongqing Natural Science Foundation (No. cstc2019jcyj-cxttX0003).

References

1. Zhu, D., et al.: Robotic grinding of complex components: a step towards efficient and intelligent machining – challenges, solutions, and applications. Robot. Comput. Integr. Manuf. **65** (2020)
2. Mu, Y., Lv, C., Li, H., Zou, L., Wang, W., Huang, Y.: A novel toolpath for 7-NC grinding of blades with force-position matching. Int. J. Adv. Manuf. Technol. **123**(1–2), 259–270 (2022)
3. Ji, W., Wang, L.: Industrial robotic machining: a review. Int. J. Adv. Manuf. Technol. **103**, 1239–1255 (2019)
4. Lv, C., Zou, L., Huang, Y., Li, H., Wang, T., Mu, Y.: A novel toolpath for robotic adaptive grinding of extremely thin blade edge based on dwell time model. IEEE-ASME Trans. Mechatron., 1–11 (2022)
5. Wang, Q., Wang, W., Zheng, L., Yun, C.: Force control-based vibration suppression in robotic grinding of large thin-wall shells. Robot. Comput. Integr. Manuf. **67** (2021)
6. Wei, Y., Xu, Q.: Design of a new passive end-effector based on constant-force mechanism for robotic polishing. Robot. Comput. Integr. Manuf. **74** (2022)
7. Chen, F., Zhao, H., Li, D., Chen, L., Tan, C., Ding, H.: Robotic grinding of a blisk with two degrees of freedom contact force control. Int. J. Adv. Manuf. Technol. **101**, 461–474 (2018)
8. Li, Y., Ganesh, G., Jarrasse, N., Haddadin, S., Albu-Schaeffer, A., Burdet, E.: Force, impedance, and trajectory learning for contact tooling and haptic identification. IEEE Trans. Robot. **34**, 1170–1182 (2018)
9. Zhao, X., Tao, B., Qian, L., Yang, Y., Ding, H.: Asymmetrical nonlinear impedance control for dual robotic machining of thin-walled workpieces. Robot. Comput. Integr. Manuf. **63** (2020)
10. Zhang, S., Lei, M., Dong, Y., He, W.: Adaptive neural network control of coordinated robotic manipulators with output constraint. IET Contr. Theory Appl. **10**, 2271–2278 (2016)
11. Chen, F., Zhao, H.: Design of eddy current dampers for vibration suppression in robotic milling. Adv. Mech. Eng. **10** (2018)
12. Liao, L., Xi, F., Liu, K., Adaptive control of pressure tracking for polishing process. J. Manuf. Sci. Eng. Trans. ASME **132**(1), 165–174 (2010)

Decision-Making in Robotic Grasping with Large Language Models

Jianfeng Liao[1,2], Haoyang Zhang[3], Haofu Qian[3], Qiwei Meng[1,2], Yinan Sun[1,2], Yao Sun[1,2], Wei Song[1,2(✉)], Shiqiang Zhu[1,2], and Jason Gu[4]

[1] Research Center for Intelligent Robotics, Zhejiang Lab, Hangzhou, China
weisong@zhejianglab.com
[2] Zhejiang Engineering Research Center for Intelligent Robotics, Hangzhou, China
[3] Zhejiang University, Hangzhou, China
[4] Department of Electrical and Computer Engineering, Dalhousie University, Halifax, Canada

Abstract. Recent advances in large language models have highlighted their potential to encode massive amounts of semantic knowledge for long-term autonomous decision-making, positioning them as a promising solution for powering the cognitive capabilities of future home-assistant robots. However, while large language models can provide high-level decision, there is still no unified paradigm for integrating them with robots' perception and low-level action. In this paper, we propose a framework centered around a large language model, integrated with visual perception and motion planning modules, to investigate the robotic grasping task. Unlike traditional methods that only focus on generating stable grasps, our proposed approach can handle personalized user instructions and perform tasks more effectively in home scenarios. Our approach integrates existing state-of-the-art models in a simple and effective way, without requiring any fine-tuning, which makes it low-cost and easy to deploy. Experiments on a physical robot system demonstrate the feasibility of our approach.

Keywords: Large Language Model · Robotic Grasping · Decision-making

1 Introduction

Home-assistant robot capable of performing a variety of daily tasks is a long-term goal of robotics research [1–3]. In this paper, we investigate the fundamental task of home-assistant robot manipulation: grasping objects that meet user's requirements in the scenario (Fig. 1). Performing this task is faced with two major challenges: (1) the unstructured home environment introduces uncertainty for the robot's perception and control, for instance, target objects have varying shapes and random poses, which may lead to failure in manipulation; (2) natural language can be ambiguous and vague, which presents challenges for the robot to understand users' intentions, for example, the phrase "I'm thirsty" could refer to a water glass or a soda can.

H. Yang et al. (Eds.): ICIRA 2023, LNAI 14271, pp. 424–433, 2023.
https://doi.org/10.1007/978-981-99-6495-6_36

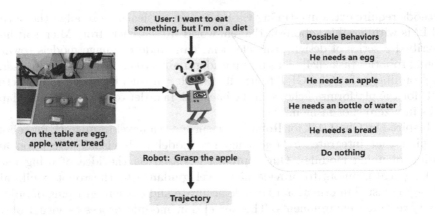

Fig. 1. Robot needs to grasp an object that aligns with the user's intention in unstructured environments through visual observation and language model decision-making.

Early approaches to robotic grasping would assume that assume full 3D prior knowledge of the objects, use analytic methods to find a gripper configuration [4–6], then generate a trajectory base on planning algorithms [7,8]. This paradigm cannot handle both of the above challenges. With the rapid development of deep learning, many researchers focused on building large-scale dataset [9–11] and applied supervised learning to directly output grasp poses from visual observation like RGBD images [12] or point clouds [13,14]. Data-driven paradigm shows great performance and generalization in grasping unseen and cluttered objects, even demonstrated almost human-level grasping capabilities in unstructured environments [14]. However, these methods are task-irrelevant, which means they don't care about the purpose of objects being grasped.

Natural language can provide an intuitive interface for specifying goals and implicitly transferring concepts across tasks. Recently, researchers have investigated the problem of generating language-conditioned policies for robots using both imitation learning and reinforcement learning [15–17]. Language models [18–20] are applied to provide high-level knowledge about the procedures required to perform complex language instructions. These methods combine broad semantic understanding with precise spatial action, enabling robots to follow a rich variety of language instructions. However, they still require precise linguistic instructions, such as "put the blue blocks in a green bowl" [17], and are unable to handle the vagueness and ambiguity of natural language.

Recent progress in large language models (LLMs) [21] has shown amazing potential in generating complex and reliable text based on prompts, which can be applied to a wide variety of downstream robotic tasks. Google and Every Robots have proposed a framework called SayCan [22], which extracts and leverages high-level knowledge from LLMs for physically-grounded tasks. Lin et al. [23] have proposed a language-based planning framework that enables robots to solve sequential manipulation tasks requiring long-horizon reasoning. However, these methods require extra fine-tuning via reinforcement learning to align the output of LLMs with feasible actions in the real world. Researchers from Microsoft have described a series of design principles that can guide language models towards solving robotics tasks [24]. This new paradigm aims to create a simple high-level function library for ChatGPT to handle, which can then be linked to the actual APIs for the platforms of choice in the backend, in order to solve robotics-related tasks in a zero-shot fashion.

Inspired by ChatGPT for Robotics, we propose a novel framework for robotic grasping that integrates a large language model with visual perception and motion planning modules. Our approach is based on the idea of using natural language prompts to provide high-level guidance to the robot, while also leveraging visual information to enable accurate and efficient grasping of objects in unstructured environments. The perception module processes visual observations in the scene, extracting semantic information that is fed to the large language model as prompts along with user instructions. The large language model then produces decisions based on the input, which are used by the perception module to calculate the grasping pose of the robot end-effector. The motion planning module generates a trajectory to complete the corresponding action, allowing the robot to grasp the target object. One of the key advantages of our proposed framework is its ability to understand imprecise language commands, enabling it to grasp objects in the task environment without requiring fine-tuning or demonstration. This approach significantly lowers the deployment cost of the framework, making it well-suited for real-world applications. We evaluated the effectiveness of our proposed framework through a series of real-world robot experiments.

2   Method

We utilize large language models to enable robots to understand user's intent and make autonomous decisions in an open world. Below, we describe how to integrate large language models with visual perception and manipulation, and deploy the approach on a real-world robotic grasping system in Fig. 2.

2.1   Problem Formulation

Given a random natural language instruction l_t, like "I'd like to eat something, but I'm on a diet", and RGBD images as visual observation o_t, our goal is to use a large language model as the optimal policy $\pi(a|s)$, in order to output the best action that matches the user's intention.

2.2   Visual Perception

Object Detection in Open World. To enable robots to perform detection tasks in open environments, it is essential to convert visual information in the scene into semantic information. Traditional object detection methods are

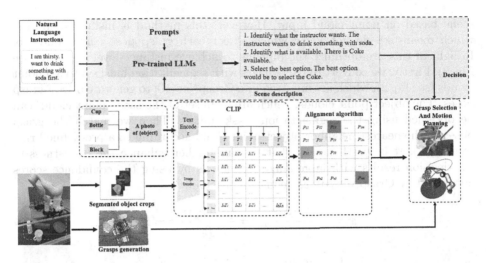

Fig. 2. Our framework consists of three components: (a) a perception module that locates potential target objects in the scene from visual observations and generates grasp poses while evaluating the feasibility of execution; (b) a LLM decision-making module that combines the object prompts and user instructions to select the most suitable and feasible target object; (c) a motion planning module that generates the trajectory of the robotic arm based on the decision result.

trained on closed-set datasets and require fine-tuning for specific tasks. To mitigate this limitation, we leverage the CLIP model [20] to perform visual-semantic matching. Firstly, we use the pre-trained Mask2former model [25] for object detection, setting ts confidence threshold to zero, in order to output a series of N image crops that potentially contain objects. We maintain a list of M common object classes in parallel, and fill each name into a prompt template "A photo of xxx". Using the CLIP model [20], we jointly encode the image crops and text prompt in an embedding space to determine their cosine similarity (see Eq. 1), which indicates the degree of matching between the image crop and text prompt. We convert the similarity matrix to a probability matrix using the softmax function. By searching for the maximum value in each row, we determine the index of the object represented by the image crop. Additionally, we can set a probability threshold to filter out image crops that do not contain the object correctly.

$$\text{cosine similarity} = \frac{\mathbf{Vec_{text}} \cdot \mathbf{Vec_{img}}}{\|\mathbf{Vec_{text}}\|\|\mathbf{Vec_{img}}\|} \qquad (1)$$

Grasp Detection in Clutter. Home-assistant robots operating in unstructured environments need to perceive affordances of objects, i.e., 6-DOF end-effector pose for robotic grasping task. In this paper, we use the baseline model from GraspNet [10], which can densely generate 6-DoF grasp poses in clutter scene based on point cloud input. However, this method is instance-agnostic, which means we do not know which object each grasp pose corresponds to. In light of this, we optimize the pipeline to achieve instance-level grasping (see Fig. 3). Firstly, we convert RGBD images with segmentation masks into 3D point clouds (see Eq. 2), which are inputted into GraspNet [10] to generate 6-DoF grasp poses. The object point clouds, which are a subset of the scene point cloud, can be obtained using the segmentation mask indices. Then we match the grasp poses to the nearest neighbor object point cloud according to a pre-defined rule (see Eq. 3). It is worth noting that we can further enhance the robustness of the decision results with large language models by using the confidence scores outputted by GraspNet [10] as geometric feasibility.

$$x = \frac{(u - c_x)z}{f_x} \quad y = \frac{(v - c_y)z}{f_y} \quad z = z \tag{2}$$

$$f(p, P, d) = \begin{cases} 1, & \text{if } \min_{q \in P_{object}} ||p_{grasp} - q|| < dis_{threshold} \\ 0, & \text{otherwise} \end{cases} \tag{3}$$

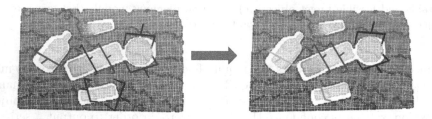

Fig. 3. We have optimized our pipeline to enable simple generation of instance-level grasp poses. The left figure represents the poses directly output by GraspNet [10], while the matched pose we have generated is displayed on the right side with corresponding colors indicating the associated objects.

2.3   Decision-Making with LLMs

By leveraging the vast semantic knowledge contained within large language models, robots can make informed and contextually appropriate decisions when faced with complex and nuanced situations, ultimately enhancing their decision-making capabilities. The quality and robustness of text generated by LLMs heavily depend on prompt engineering. Thus, effective prompt design that enables the decision of LLMs to adapt to specific robotic task scenarios should be a primary focus of robotics researchers. In this paper, we have designed a simple and effective prompt chain that generates several intermediate steps leading to the final solution of our problem. Initially, the user's natural language instruction and semantic information extracted from the perception module are presented to the large language model (LLM), which implicitly incorporates the task goal and constraints. Subsequently, we use prompts to guide the robot through a decision-making process consisting of three steps: understanding the user's intention, identifying relevant objects, and selecting the optimal solution. Further details are illustrated in the Fig. 4.

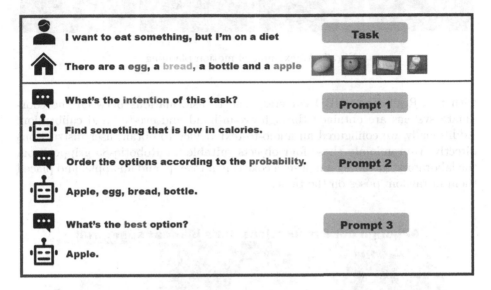

Fig. 4. We propose a hint engineering method that enhances the robustness of robot decision-making, in comparison to the direct output of results in a single step. Additionally, this method avoids failures by using use alternative when the optimal option is geometrically infeasible.

2.4 Motion Planning

In contrast to industrial robots that prioritize time or energy optimization in motion planning to increase production efficiency, home-assistant robots must prioritize smooth, collision-free trajectories to enhance manipulation safety. Once the perception and decision-making modules have completed their tasks, we can directly obtain the 6-DoF grasp pose for the object corresponding to natural language instructions. In this work, we simply employ the informed RRT* algorithm [8] from the OMPL library [26] to meet the performance requirements for the robotic grasping task.

3   Real-World Experiments

To implement our method in a real-world robot system, we used a 7-DoF robot arm Kinova Gen3 and a two-finger Robotiq-85 gripper, which is also equipped

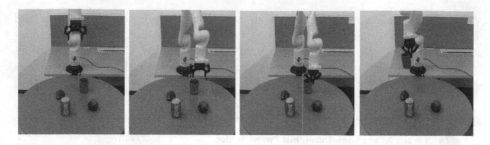

Fig. 5. An example of motion planning.

with two RealSense RGBD cameras. The transformations between the coordinate systems are obtained through eye-in-hand and eye-to-hand calibration. Additionally, we configured an audio-to-text device to obtain user instructions directly. We randomly chose four objects suitable for Robotiq-85 gripper from the laboratory, including a mouse, a coke can, a teacup, and an apple, and placed them in random poses on the table.

Fig. 6. Visualization of our framework's decision making.

During the experiment, we used the RGBD images obtained by the RealSense cameras to detect the objects and generate grasp poses. Then we input the language instruction and semantic information of the scene into the GPT-3 API [19] according to our proposed prompt format, waiting for it to output the decision result. After obtaining the target object, we sent the corresponding 6-DoF grasp pose to the motion planning node using the ROS system, which generated the trajectory and controlled the robot arm to complete the action. We conducted multiple experiments to verify the effectiveness of this framework. The visualization of the experimental process and the experimental results are presented in Fig. 6 and 7. Furthermore, to better understand the decision-making process of the large language model, we provided a robot decision-making example using the ChatGPT's [24] web page (for better visualization) in Fig. 8.

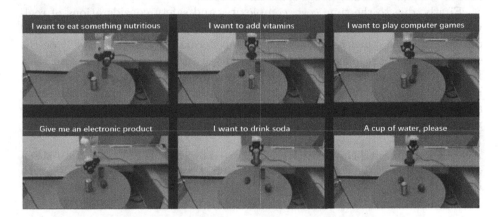

Fig. 7. Experimental results for successful complete the tasks following user's personalized language commands. These experiments validate the feasibility of our method in real-world deployment.

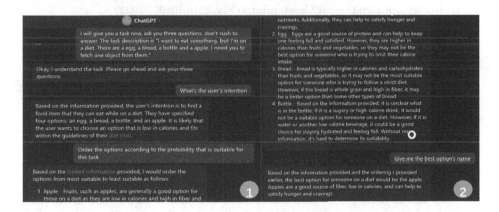

Fig. 8. An decision making example with ChatGPT

4   Conclusion

We present a robotic grasping framework that utilizes natural language commands from humans, incorporating a large language model and integrating visual perception and motion planning modules, enabling home-assistant robots to make autonomous decisions and grasp target objects in cluttered environments. Our framework has the advantages as no fine-tuning, low cost, and ease of deployment, and its effectiveness has been demonstrated in real-world experiments. Our work shows the potential of combining large language models and robots, though we acknowledge some limitations.

Firstly, due to the time cost, complexity, and safety considerations of real-world experiments, our experiments mainly focused on feasibility verification and did not establish a benchmark for evaluation. Secondly, we focused solely on the simple action of grasping, which is essentially a short-term manipulation task. Future works can investigate: (1) integrating more advanced visual modules and motion planning modules to improve whole system performance; (2) establishing an evaluation benchmark in a simulated environment; and (3) expanding the robot skill library and considering long-term manipulation.

Acknowledgement. This research was supported by Zhejiang Provincial Natural Science Foundation of China Grant No. LQ23F030009 and supported by Key Research Project of Zhejiang Lab (No. G2021NB0AL03).

References

1. Tamei, T., Matsubara, T., Rai, A., Shibata, T.: Reinforcement learning of clothing assistance with a dual-arm robot. In: 2011 11th IEEE-RAS International Conference on Humanoid Robots, pp. 733–738. IEEE (2011)
2. Lew, T., et al.: Robotic table wiping via reinforcement learning and whole-body trajectory optimization. arXiv preprint arXiv:2210.10865 (2022)
3. Wu, J., et al.: Tidybot: personalized robot assistance with large language models. arXiv preprint arXiv:2305.05658 (2023)
4. Miller, A.T., Allen, P.K.: Graspit! a versatile simulator for robotic grasping. IEEE Robot. Autom. Mag. **11**(4), 110–122 (2004)
5. Kehoe, B., Matsukawa, A., Candido, S., Kuffner, J., Goldberg, K.: Cloud-based robot grasping with the google object recognition engine. In: 2013 IEEE International Conference on Robotics and Automation, pp. 4263–4270. IEEE (2013)
6. Mahler, J., et al.: Dex-Net 1.0: a cloud-based network of 3D objects for robust grasp planning using a multi-armed bandit model with correlated rewards. In: 2016 IEEE International Conference on Robotics and Automation (ICRA), pp. 1957–1964. IEEE (2016)
7. Kuffner, J.J., LaValle, S.M.: RRT-connect: an efficient approach to single-query path planning. In: Proceedings 2000 ICRA. Millennium Conference. IEEE International Conference on Robotics and Automation. Symposia Proceedings (Cat. No. 00CH37065), vol. 2, pp. 995–1001. IEEE (2000)
8. Gammell, J.D., Srinivasa, S.S., Barfoot, T.D.: Informed RRT: optimal sampling-based path planning focused via direct sampling of an admissible ellipsoidal heuristic. In: 2014 IEEE/RSJ International Conference on Intelligent Robots and Systems, pp. 2997–3004. IEEE (2014)
9. Kumra, S., Kanan, C.: Robotic grasp detection using deep convolutional neural networks. In: 2017 IEEE/RSJ International Conference on Intelligent Robots and Systems (IROS), pp. 769–776. IEEE (2017)

10. Fang, H.S., Wang, C., Gou, M., Lu, C.: Graspnet-1billion: a large-scale bench-mark for general object grasping. In: Proceedings of the IEEE/CVF Conference on Computer Vision and Pattern Recognition, pp. 11444–11453 (2020)

11. Eppner, C., Mousavian, A., Fox, D.: Acronym: a large-scale grasp dataset based on simulation. In: 2021 IEEE International Conference on Robotics and Automation (ICRA), pp. 6222–6227. IEEE (2021)

12. Morrison, D., Corke, P., Leitner, J.: Learning robust, real-time, reactive robotic grasping. Int. J. Robot. Res. **39**(2–3), 183–201 (2020)

13. Mousavian, A., Eppner, C., Fox, D.: 6-DOF GraspNet: variational grasp generation for object manipulation. In: Proceedings of the IEEE/CVF International Conference on Computer Vision, pp. 2901–2910 (2019)

14. Fang, H.S., et al.: Anygrasp: robust and efficient grasp perception in spatial and temporal domains. arXiv preprint arXiv:2212.08333 (2022)

15. Stepputtis, S., Campbell, J., Phielipp, M., Lee, S., Baral, C., Ben Amor, H.: Language-conditioned imitation learning for robot manipulation tasks. Adv. Neural. Inf. Process. Syst. **33**, 13139–13150 (2020)

16. Shao, L., Migimatsu, T., Zhang, Q., Yang, K., Bohg, J.: Concept2robot: learning manipulation concepts from instructions and human demonstrations. Int. J. Robot. Res. **40**(12–14), 1419–1434 (2021)

17. Shridhar, M., Manuelli, L., Fox, D.: Cliport: what and where pathways for robotic manipulation. In: Conference on Robot Learning, pp. 894–906. PMLR (2022)

18. Devlin, J., Chang, M.W., Lee, K., Toutanova, K.: Bert: pre-training of deep bidirectional transformers for language understanding. arXiv preprint arXiv:1810.04805 (2018)

19. Brown, T., et al.: Language models are few-shot learners. Adv. Neural. Inf. Process. Syst. **33**, 1877–1901 (2020)

20. Radford, A., et al.: Learning transferable visual models from natural language supervision. In: International Conference on Machine Learning, pp. 8748–8763. PMLR (2021)

21. Ouyang, L., et al.: Training language models to follow instructions with human feedback. Adv. Neural. Inf. Process. Syst. **35**, 27730–27744 (2022)

22. Ahn, M., et al.: Do as i can, not as i say: grounding language in robotic affordances. arXiv preprint arXiv:2204.01691 (2022)

23. Lin, K., Agia, C., Migimatsu, T., Pavone, M., Bohg, J.: Text2motion: from natural language instructions to feasible plans. arXiv preprint arXiv:2303.12153 (2023)

24. Vemprala, S., Bonatti, R., Bucker, A., Kapoor, A.: ChatGPT for robotics: design principles and model abilities (2023)

25. Cheng, B., Misra, I., Schwing, A.G., Kirillov, A., Girdhar, R.: Masked-attention mask transformer for universal image segmentation. In: Proceedings of the IEEE/CVF Conference on Computer Vision and Pattern Recognition, pp. 1290–1299 (2022)

26. Sucan, I.A., Moll, M., Kavraki, L.E.: The open motion planning library. IEEE Robot. Autom. Mag. **19**(4), 72–82 (2012). https://doi.org/10.1109/MRA.2012.2205651

Language Guided Grasping of Unknown Concepts Based on Knowledge System

Saike Huang, Zhenwei Zhu, Jin Liu, Chaoqun Wang, and Fengyu Zhou[✉]

Center for Robotics, School of Control Science and Engineering, Shandong University, No. 17923, Jingshi Road, Jinan 250061, China
zhoufengyu@sdu.edu.cn

Abstract. Language guided grasping in cultter environment has become a hot topic for robotic arms, where the robot is supposed to grasp a specific object according to the language instruction. However, existing studies typically fail on grasping unknown objects that are not recognized by the detection model, which post higher requirements of the learning unknown objects from external knowledge. In this paper, unlike traditional target detection algorithms, our system identifies unknown objects through a knowledge-driven approach. We present a knowledge-learning driven system that guides the robot in learning new concepts to grasp unknown objects from pre-built multimodal knowledge base. Specifically, we first retrieve the image knowledge from Internet and text description knowledge from human experts to construct the multimodal knowledge base. Based on the question context, the model will query the object concept knowledge from the knowledge base. Once the concept is known, the model will ground the object by a multimodal fusion module. In contrast, to address the issue of novel concept, we propose a knowledge fusion module that combines BERT, GCN and ResNet to acquire semantic text knowledge, structured text knowledge, and image knowledge derived from the knowledge base. Subsequently, we utilized the re-calibration multimodal fusion module to ground unknown objects. Finally, conditioned on the grounding context, we employ a well-trained grasp network to derive the accurate grasping pose to perform the grasping task. Experiments conducted on the simulation and real-world scenarios demonstrate that our knowledge-learning driven system is effective in assisting robots to learn unknown concepts and achieve successful grasping tasks. A demo video is available online (https://youtu.be/Fsc4nZyY9LI).

Keywords: concept learning · grasp · unknown concept · multimodal knowledge graph

1 Introduction

The grasping function is essential for robotic arms and has been studied extensively in various fields, including household and industrial settings [1,17,18]. Current research in these fields focuses on grasping target objects based on human instructions [4,12,15]. These methods integrate human instructions and scene image features to ground the target object and generate its mask to achieve the task. However, they are limited in requiring target objects to be recognizable by the visual recognition algorithm. That's to say, once the algorithm fails to identify the target object, the manipulator cannot grasp it successfully.

These observations indicate that successfully grasping unknown objects still poses a severe challenge. To address such issue, many researchers turn to concept learning. Yang et al. [16] proposed to learn the attribute color and shape of a single object and then combine the attributes to learn unknown concepts. However, they describe unidentified objects solely by shape and color, which will neglect other critical attributes, such as material and size and limit the number of learned objects. Further, Tziafas and Kalithasan et al. [6,13] proposed neuro-symbolic methods conditioned on the concept learning to grasp unknown objects by understanding the attributes and spatial relations. However, they still focus on the known objects conditioned on the detection model. In order for the robot arm to grasp unknown objects, it is crucial for the robot arm to learn unknown concept. Recently, several concept learning methods that integrate knowledge graph have emerged for improving the robot reasoning ability. Manrique et al. [8] used a knowledge graph to learn unknown concepts, and Russo et al. [11] proposed an unsupervised knowledge construction method to improve robot cognitive ability using robot perception. Ding et al. [5] used natural language processing methods to construct a knowledge graph-based knowledge base to complete an assembly task. While these methods demonstrate the potential of knowledge integration to learn unknown concepts, they still neglect the rich semantic information from the text description and relevant image context which will limit their application domain.

To address the above issues on learning unknown objects, we propose a knowledge-learning driven system shown in Fig. 1 that guides the robot in learning new concepts to grasp unknown objects from pre-built multi-modal knowledge base. In particular, our model is available for both known and unknown concept grasping processes. Compared with the baseline method which is without utilizing any knowledge, our model obtains 20% improvements.

2   Method

In this section, we first present the overview of the task in Sect. 2.1 and then elaborately introduce our knowledge-learning driven system in Sect. 2.2.

2.1   Task Overview

Given a query Q consisting of N words and one image I from camera composed of K objects, including known objects $\{O_{u_i}\}_{i=1}^{U}$ and unknown objects $\{O_{k_i}\}_{i=1}^{K}$. Conditioned on the multimodal knowledge graph G, the task aims to grasp the specific object o from I according to the concept c (i.e., object descriptions) from

Fig. 1. When retrieving a target object, the robot arm first queries the knowledge system for the object concept. If the concept is already known, the robot arm grasps the object accordingly. However, if it is unknown, the robot arm requests input from the knowledge system until the concept is learned, and then proceeds to retrieve it.

query Q. In general, the task can be formulated as follows.

$$\hat{o} = \underset{o \in \{O_u \cup O_k\}}{\operatorname{argmax}} \mathcal{F}_\theta(o|Q, I, G) \tag{1}$$

where $\hat{o}$ denotes the object that needs to be grasped. $\mathcal{F}_\theta$ represents the modeling function with learnable parameters θ.

After obtaining the object details, a well-trained grasp network GR-ConvNet [7] is employed to pick up the object $\hat{o}$. The grasp pose can be described using formula $G_r = (P, \Theta, W, S)$, where $P = (x, y, z)$ represents the object's position, Θ is gripper orientation around the z-axis, W is the required gripper width, S is the grasp quality score and we chose the grasping pose with the highest quality score. Figure 2 shows some examples.

Fig. 2. The grasping pose examples of some objects trained by GR-ConvNet

2.2   Knowledge-Learning Driven System

Our architecture is composed of the following five parts shown in Fig. 3: a) A proposal and features extraction module, where we employ Fast-RCNN [14] to extract features of objects in the scene, explicitly known and unknown objects. b) A multimodal fusion module, where we ground the specific objects to be grasped from human instructions. c) knowledge system construction, where we develop a multimodal knowledge system through data retrieval on the internet and expert description knowledge. d) A knowledge fusion module, where we re-calibrate the knowledge for grounding the unknown concepts conditioned on the retrieval knowledge. e) A grasp execution module, where the robotic arm generates the grasping pose through GR-ConvNet and completes the grasping task of the target object.

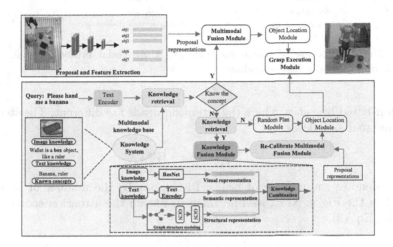

Fig. 3. The architecture of knowledge-learning driven system.

Proposal and Features Extractions. Following previous work, we utilize one fine-tuned Fast-RCNN, with an accuracy of mAP 73.16%, to extract the proposals of the scene objects. Subsequently, conditioned on the proposals, we obtain the object feature representations $\{o_i^f\}_{i=1}^M$, where M is the number of objects in the scene. Notably, the labels' information is unavailable for our model during the training and test phases.

Multimodal Fusion Module. One critical issue for the grasping process is to understand scene according to the instruction. To comprehend the instruction command, we utilize BERT [9] as the text encoder to extract the sentence-level language representation q^f and word-level language representations $\{w^f\}_{i=1}^N$, where N is the number of the words. After obtaining both the object and instruction representations, we propose a multimodal fusion module shown in Fig. 4(a) to fuse the context for better grounding the objects.

In specific, we first project the sentence-level representation q^f and concatenated object representations o^f as into the same semantic embedding space to obtain the query representation $Q^f \in \mathcal{R}^{1*D}$ and object representation $V^f \in \mathcal{R}^{M*D}$. Subsequently, the multimodal fusion module fuses them via two

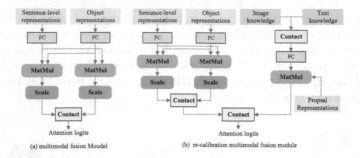

Fig. 4. The architecture of fusion Module. (a) Multimodal Fusion Module (b) re-calibration multimodal fusion module

attention-based branches, where the attention heads are different. The steps can be formulated as follows.

$$q^i = W_i^q Q_i^f, \quad k^i = W_i^k V_i^f \tag{2}$$

where i denotes the number of heads. In this study, the number of heads are set to 4 in the Fig. 4. Next, we fuse them to obtain the attention scores by the following Eq. (3).

$$\text{Attention}(Q_i, K_i) = \frac{1}{L} \sum_i^L \text{softmax}(\frac{Q^T * K_i}{\sqrt{d_k}}) \tag{3}$$

where L denotes the number of heads. After acquiring all the attentions from two branches, we combine them to obtain the final object attention scores. Conditioned on the attention score, we can obtain required object by object location module, which can be described as the following Eq. (4).

$$o^* = \text{argmax}(\text{Attention}_i^M) \tag{4}$$

To optimize the entire grounding process, we further introduce the binary cross entropy loss shown in the following Eq. (5).

$$loss = -\frac{1}{M} \sum_{i=1}^M y_i \cdot \log(p(o_i)) + (1 - y_i) \cdot \log(1 - p(o_i)) \tag{5}$$

where o_i denotes the attention logits. log is the log function. y_i denotes the ground-truth, i.e., if ground the specified object, $y_i = 1$, otherwise $y_i = 0$.

Besides, to further enhance the robustness of the model comprehension process, we provide six different types of human instructions, presented in Table 1.

During each training process, the template will be randomly selected as the instruction.

Table 1. The different types of human instructions

Instruction	Instruction
Can you offer me the [object] ?	May I ask for the [object] ?
Can you give me the [object] ?	Please hand me the [object] ?
Is there any an [object] ?	Can you grasp the [object] on the table ?

Knowledge System Construction. We construct the knowledge system using the known objects' characteristics to establish multimodality knowledge, including text and image knowledge. The knowledge system stores the concepts of known objects, efficiently facilitating retrieval after object recognition. For the textual knowledge of the unrecognizable objects, we identify the common attributes with known objects through Internet retrieval and expert opinions. This provides 2–3 instances of knowledge for each unrecognized object. For example, with regard to the unidentified object wallet, we provide two forms of knowledge: 1) the wallet and milk carton share a cuboid shape, and 2) a rope is present in both the wallet and tape measure. For image knowledge, we randomly obtain two wallet images from the internet. This technique is extended to other unidentifiable objects. Thus, a comprehensive multimodal knowledge base system is developed.

Knowledge Fusion Module. When the manipulator receives instructions and locates the object concept through grounding, it will retrieve the knowledge system to determine if the concept is known. If the concept is recognized, the Grasp Execution Module will perform grasping to complete the task. However, in the case of unknown concept objects, if the model determines not to utilize the knowledge from the knowledge system for concept learning, the system will select the object with the highest score from the previously known concepts or the attention outputs from multimodal fusion module as the target object. Otherwise, the knowledge retrieval module will be used to obtain relevant knowledge for concept learning to re-calibrate feature fusion process. In specific, as shown in Fig. 3, for the image knowledge, we utilize a pre-trained ResNet model to obtain the visual representations. For the text knowledge, we first utilize BERT to extract the sentence-level semantic representations. And then we utilize NLTK [2] to extract the noun words from the obtained text description and construct a small scale graph. Subsequently, we utilize a typical graph neural network (GNN) formulated as follows, to obtain the structural representation for the text knowledge.

$$h_i^{l+1} = \sigma(b^l + \sum_{j \in \mathcal{N}(i)} \frac{1}{c_{ij}} h_j^l W^l) \tag{6}$$

where $\mathcal{N}(i)$ denotes the neighbor for specific object i. b^l is the bias item. h^l denotes the representation for the object. W^l is the weight matrix for learning representation. $c_{ij} = \sqrt{|\mathcal{N}(i)|}\sqrt{|\mathcal{N}(j)|}$ is the regularization item. In this paper, we utilize a two-layer GNN network to obtain the structural representations, i.e.,

$l = 2$. Next, we combine the visual representation, semantic representation and structural representation as the final knowledge representation.

After obtaining the knowledge, we utilize re-calibration multimodal fusion module to ground the object as shown in Fig. 4(b). In specific, the knowledge representation and visual object representations are first fused by the attention component in Eq. 3 to obtain the re-calibrated attention scores. Subsequently, the re-calibrated attention scores and the original attention scores which are obtained by the multimodal fusion module are combined to get the final attention logits. Then the object location module is used to ground the object, leading to the execution of a grasping action. If the robotic arm fails to learn the concept, the system continues coding the next piece of knowledge until the concept is learned. Notably, the learned concept is matched with the corresponding scene object, and the knowledge system is updated once the concept is learned.

Grasp Execution Module. In this work, we utilized the previously mentioned GR-ConvNet network to generate grasping poses. By fine-tuning the network, the targeted object can be grasped effectively in both simulation and real environments.

3   Experiment

In this section, we first introduce our experimental environment settings in Sect. 3.1. And then we conduct experiments in Sect. 3.2 on both V-REP [10] simulation and real world environments to verify the effectiveness of our model.

3.1   Data Collection

Due to the specific task requirements of this paper, we are unable to find a publicly available dataset that meets our needs. Therefore, we collect our own dataset for the task. In specific, we first select 20 real objects including 6 from real scene and others from the YCB dataset [3], which is shown in Fig. 5. Besides, we set the camera parameters to be the same as realsenseD435 to capture images in the simulation environment V-REP, where the image size is 640 × 480. In the real world environment, we use the same settings as above.

Fig. 5. 20 common objects selected in the dataset. (a) 10 known objects selected into the training dataset (b) 5 unknown objects selected into the evaluation dataset (c) 5 unknown objects selected into the test dataset

To make the experiments more convinced, we construct two scenarios with different-level of difficulty for concept learning according to the number of unknown objects that exist in the scene, shown in Fig. 6. Specifically, as for the easy scene, we set all the concepts for the objects to known state. While in the hard scene, we set 50% of object concepts are unknown.

Finally, we place them at random positions and angles, and obtain 500 RGB images. After randomly paired with human instructions (i.e., we select 4–6 sentences to pair with image), we can get about 2.5k image-query pairs, where 80% of the datasets are utilized to train the model and 10% are for validation, and 10% for test.

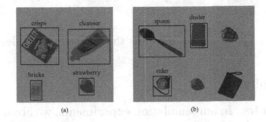

Fig. 6. Scenarios with different levels of difficulty. (a) easy level (b) hard level

We set the simulation working area to 0.65 m × 0.37 m, which is the same as our real scene. For robot motion planning, we employ the internal inverse kinematics module of V-REP. We modify the friction coefficient of the object to simulate object interactions as similar to the real world as possible. The computation is finished on Ubuntu18.04 and Pytorch 1.13 with Intel(R) Xeon(R) Silver 4314 CPU and one NVIDIA Geforce GTX 3090 GPU. In each test process, the optimizer is Adam and learning rate is 0.0001 for 100 epochs with batch size 8. We conduct 10 runs and measure the success rate as the proportion of successful grasp with the given instructions. Table 2 reports the results of the grasping success rate for model variants, i.e., model with no knowledge (as baseline), model with image knowledge, model with text knowledge, model with image and text knowledge (as our full model). As can be observed from the results in Table 2, we find that knowledge brings a small improvement to the performance of the model in easy scene, where the concepts of the objects are already known. However, the model performance drops significantly on the hard scene, where the novel concepts are introduced. We find that when model is incorporated with external knowledge, the model performance can be improved compared with baseline model. In other words, knowledge indeed helps the model to learn novel concepts. Further, to better view the grasping process in simulation environment, we display one qualitative result of grasping one object with known concept "cleanser" in Fig. 7.

Table 2. The grasping success rate of different learning modes in different scenarios

Learning modes	Hard scene	Easy scene
No knowledge	55%	95%
Only image Knowledge	69%	98%
Only text Knowledge	61%	98%
Image and text Knowledge	75%	98%

Fig. 7. The process of grasping the known objects cleanser

3.2   Main Results

Simulation Results. In our simulation experiments, we observe that the grasp accuracy didn't overly depends on the grasp network in the simulation environment. Therefore, in the next section, we will conduct real world experiments and explore the effectiveness of grasping network.

(a)   (b)   (c)   (d)   (e)

Fig. 8. The process of grasping in response to the query "Can you hand me the wallet?". a) setting the initial pose of the robot arm, b) commencing the grasp movement, c) utilizing the knowledge system to learn the concept of wallet and then moving the robot arm towards the top of the wallet, d) adjusting the pose of the robot arm based on the grasping pose generated by GR-ConvNet, and e) successfully grasping the wallet

Real-World Experiments. We evaluate the proposed method in real-world scenarios, using a UR3e robotic arm with a robotiq140 gripper. Just above the working area is a realsense D435 camera that can be used to capture RGB-D images. We transfer the model trained in the simulation to the real environment with a small fine-tuning process. In the real environment, our scene settings are consistent with the simulation environment. We perform grasping experiments on known and unknown objects respectively. The quantitative results are reported in Table 3. Our model obtains 90% accuracy on the easy scene while only get 65% accuracy on the mixed scene. We have found that several failed cases are caused by grasping network even though our model can clearly find the object. Such phenomenon reveals that our model still has room for improvement in the learning of unknown concepts and grasping process. One possible solution is to introduce a large model, e.g., DINO, to provide more multimodal context alignment information for improving the grasping performance. The qualitative results of our grasping process on UR3e are illustrated in Fig. 8. As shown in the figure, we can find that our model can grasp the unknown objects with extra knowledge assistance.

Table 3. The success rate of grasping known and unknown objects in real environment

State	Easy Scene	Hard Scene
our model	90% (18/20)	65% (13/20)

4 Conclusion

In this paper, we propose a knowledge-learning driven system to assist the robot to learn and grasp unknown concepts by leveraging multimodal knowledge. Specifically, conditioned on the built multimodal knowledge base, our proposed method utilizes a Multimodal Fusion Module to facilitate the fusion of scene features and human instructions for known object concept grounding. As for the unknown concepts, we propose a knowledge fusion module followed by the re-calibrating fusion module to ground the objects. Finally, empirical results carried on simulation and real world scenes verify the effectiveness of our system in grasping known and unknown objects.

In the future, we plan to expand the scope of our study to encompass multiple identical, unknown objects for multi-object disambiguation, which would enhance the overall intelligence of the robotic arm.

References

1. Andronas, D., et al.: On the perception and handling of deformable objects-a robotic cell for white goods industry. Robot. Comput.-Integr. Manuf. **77**, 102358 (2022)
2. Arora, G.: iNLTK: natural language toolkit for Indic languages. arXiv preprint arXiv:2009.12534 (2020)
3. Calli, B., Singh, A., Walsman, A., Srinivasa, S., Abbeel, P., Dollar, A.M.: The YCB object and model set: towards common benchmarks for manipulation research. In: 2015 International Conference on Advanced Robotics (ICAR), pp. 510–517. IEEE (2015)

4. Cheang, C., Lin, H., Fu, Y., Xue, X.: Learning 6-DoF object poses to grasp category-level objects by language instructions. In: 2022 International Conference on Robotics and Automation (ICRA), pp. 8476–8482. IEEE (2022)
5. Ding, Y., Xu, W., Liu, Z., Zhou, Z., Pham, D.T.: Robotic task oriented knowledge graph for human-robot collaboration in disassembly. Procedia CIRP **83**, 105–110 (2019)
6. Kalithasan, N., et al.: Learning neuro-symbolic programs for language guided robot manipulation. arXiv preprint arXiv:2211.06652 (2022)
7. Kumra, S., Joshi, S., Sahin, F.: Antipodal robotic grasping using generative residual convolutional neural network. In: 2020 IEEE/RSJ International Conference on Intelligent Robots and Systems (IROS), pp. 9626–9633. IEEE (2020)
8. Manrique, R., Pereira, B., Marino, O., Cardozo, N., Wolfgand, S.: Towards the identification of concept prerequisites via knowledge graphs. In: 2019 IEEE 19th International Conference on Advanced Learning Technologies (ICALT), vol. 2161, pp. 332–336. IEEE (2019)
9. Nitish, S., Darsini, R., Shashank, G., Tejas, V., Arya, A.: Bidirectional encoder representation from transformers (BERT) variants for procedural long-form answer extraction. In: 2022 12th International Conference on Cloud Computing, Data Science & Engineering (Confluence), pp. 71–76. IEEE (2022)
10. Rohmer, E., Singh, S.P., Freese, M.: V-rep: a versatile and scalable robot simulation framework. In: 2013 IEEE/RSJ International Conference on Intelligent Robots and Systems, pp. 1321–1326. IEEE (2013)
11. Russo, C., Madani, K., Rinaldi, A.M.: An unsupervised approach for knowledge construction applied to personal robots. IEEE Trans. Cogn. Dev. Syst. **13**(1), 6–15 (2020)
12. Tang, C., Huang, D., Meng, L., Liu, W., Zhang, H.: Task-oriented grasp prediction with visual-language inputs. arXiv preprint arXiv:2302.14355 (2023)
13. Tziafas, G., Kasaei, H.: Enhancing interpretability and interactivity in robot manipulation: a neurosymbolic approach
14. Wang, X., Shrivastava, A., Gupta, A.: A-fast-RCNN: hard positive generation via adversary for object detection. In: Proceedings of the IEEE Conference on Computer Vision and Pattern Recognition, pp. 2606–2615 (2017)
15. Xu, K., et al.: A joint modeling of vision-language-action for target-oriented grasping in clutter. arXiv preprint arXiv:2302.12610 (2023)
16. Yang, Y., Liu, Y., Liang, H., Lou, X., Choi, C.: Attribute-based robotic grasping with one-grasp adaptation. In: 2021 IEEE International Conference on Robotics and Automation (ICRA), pp. 6357–6363. IEEE (2021)
17. Zhang, X., Domae, Y., Wan, W., Harada, K.: Learning efficient policies for picking entangled wire harnesses: an approach to industrial bin picking. IEEE Robot. Autom. Lett. **8**, 73–80 (2022)
18. Zhu, X., Zhou, Y., Fan, Y., Sun, L., Chen, J., Tomizuka, M.: Learn to grasp with less supervision: a data-efficient maximum likelihood grasp sampling loss. In: 2022 International Conference on Robotics and Automation (ICRA), pp. 721–727. IEEE (2022)

A Review of Nonlinear Systems Based on Optimal Control Theory

Xiaodan Lu(✉)

Shanghai Maritime University, Shanghai 201306, China
853752832@qq.com

Abstract. Many common objects in daily life can be described by the form of a system. The control systems in actual production life are all primarily nonlinear due to the presence of disruptions, errors, diverse human and environmental elements, and there are also a sizable number of nonlinear phenomena. Studying the optimal control problem of nonlinear systems is therefore extremely important from a practical standpoint under the presumption of guaranteeing the system's stable operation. This essay explores the nature of existing methodologies and conclusions while summarizing the results of previous studies based on the evolution of nonlinear systems and their optimum control theory.

Keywords: Nonlinear systems · Optimal control · Lyapunov stability theory · Dynamic programming

1 Introduction

A system is made up of several of parts that work together and are connected by specific rules to create a whole that is capable of carrying out a specific defined function. The majority of systems in actual manufacturing can be categorized as nonlinear systems, and the nonlinear phenomena they display are unclear. In order to better utilize the control system, increase the precision of the control action, and enhance the function of the control system, it is crucial to understand nonlinear systems.

The system design will often also include other goals, such as requirements for the transient response [1, 2] or restrictions on the control inputs [3, 4]. These criteria may compete with one another, and trade-offs must inevitably be made between the many competing requirements. The issue of nonlinear systems' optimal control is impacted on by this trade-off and optimization.

After a period of development, control theory has achieved great advances since its inception in the 1930s, particularly in the analysis and design of linear systems, and has developed into a number of mature, somewhat independent theories. However, due to the practical process, most systems show different degrees of nonlinear characteristics, the theoretical methods of linear systems are difficult to be applied. If nonlinear control can be used, it is not only able to analyze strong nonlinearity, deal with model uncertainty, and improve the performance of the system, but also to simplify the design of the control

H. Yang et al. (Eds.): ICIRA 2023, LNAI 14271, pp. 445–455, 2023.
https://doi.org/10.1007/978-981-99-6495-6_38

system. At the same time, it has superior performance in dealing with system disturbances, uncertainties and other characteristics [5–7]. Therefore, the scientific research topic of nonlinear system control theory has received increasing attention in the field of control and is one of the more active research directions today.

2 Overview

2.1 Nonlinear Systems

Humans are capable of learning new things that are simple to complicate, low-level to high-level, and specialized to general. Control science and technology have advanced quickly since the turn of the 20th century, and through the ongoing realization and improvement of the physical description and mathematical solution of linear systems, the theory of linear systems has gradually matured and formed a full set of linear system theory and analysis research methods, leading to numerous accomplishments. Taking linear system as the research object, classical control theory based on frequency domain analysis and modern control theory based on state space analysis and differential equations as the main mathematical tools have been formed. The characteristics of classical control theory in terms of computational methods and mathematical theoretical basis are closely related to the mature application of computer technology and integral transformation methods at the primary stage. Classical control theory has promoted the development of automation technology and is still indispensable in many technical fields today. Modern control theory originated around the 1960s when the maturity of electronic computer technology and its widespread use and the need for control of air and space systems had a profound impact on the development of modern control theory. Both in-depth and breadth, modern control theory has entered a new phase of development compared to classical control theory.

Linear systems are, after all, idealized models of actual systems, and actual control systems are mostly nonlinear systems. For example, the positioning and attitude adjustment of an underwater vehicle cannot be described by a linearized model, but only by nonlinear differential equations. Phenomena that occur in the system such as chaos and attractors are nonlinear problems. The combination of several linear components does not produce essentially different functions, but the combination of several nonlinear components can make a qualitative change in the function of the whole network, such as neuronal networks, where several neurons with similar functions form a neural network with functions such as memory and self-learning [8, 9].

As control systems become more complex and their nonlinearities become stronger, the performance of the controller is required to be higher and higher. Most nonlinear system control problems are approximated and reduced to linear system control problems for analysis, leading to a significant reduction in control accuracy. Although there are sound theoretical and analytical research methods for linear systems, these are not suitable for nonlinear systems, and the study of nonlinear systems and nonlinear problems has become an inescapable reality in the development of control theory.

The research methods of nonlinear systems are used for different types of systems with different methods to study and solve problems. Early control theories and methods on nonlinear systems are established for a particular system. The phase plane method is only applicable to low-order systems; the object of study of the description function method can be any order system, but the system only has nonlinear characteristics of the actuator. On this basis, some advanced control methods also came into being, such as sliding mode variable structure control, fuzzy control, adaptive control, etc. Methods are also used in the control analysis of nonlinear systems.

In the process of system operation, there are a large number of disturbance signals, some of these disturbance signals are deterministic, but most of them belong to the random disturbance signals. Ignoring these disturbance signals simplifies the control analysis process of the system, but also reduces the control accuracy of the system. To obtain a high control accuracy, the description of the actual problem must be increasingly close to the current situation of the system operation, and various random factors cannot be easily ignored.

In addition, there are various forms of constraints in actual operating nonlinear systems, such as physical stops, saturation, and performance and safety specifications. If these conditions are violated during system operation, the performance of the system may deteriorate, and in severe cases, the system may become unstable and unable to operate properly resulting in property damage or even human casualties. Traditional controller design methods do not ensure that the closed-loop system is stable while still satisfying the constraints. In addition to the constraints, there are various uncertainties in nonlinear systems due to measurement noise, model errors, model simplifications, perturbations, etc. These uncertainties from within or outside the system have a significant impact on the stability of the control system, and these uncertainties are collectively referred to as unmodeled dynamics. Driven by theoretical innovations and practical needs, the analysis and study of controllers for nonlinear systems with con-straints and unmodeled dynamics have become one of the hot spots of interest for researchers [10, 11].

2.2 Optimal Control

Optimal control theory is a very important branch of modern control theory. The central problem of optimal control research is: how to find the optimal control scheme or the optimal control law among all possible control schemes according to the dynamic characteristics of the controlled system, so that the system operates according to certain technical requirements, and makes a certain "index" describing the performance or quality of the system reach the optimal value in a certain sense.

It is well known that processes occurring in the field of engineering and technology, including physical or chemical processes, are usually controllable, i.e. they can be realized in different forms according to the needs of people. Thus, the problem of choosing the best way to implement it under certain conditions arises, i.e., the problem of the so-called optimal control process. For example, optimality under fast-acting conditions, i.e. the requirement to reach the destination of the process in the shortest possible time, or it may be that the destination of the process is reached with the least amount of energy consumed.

Optimal control theory has a long history of research. As early as the early 1950s, Bushuaw studied the problem of time-optimal control of servo systems, and he proved geometrically that relay-type control could adjust the error of the servo system to zero in the shortest possible time. In the 1950s, space technology began to develop rapidly.

The research of optimal control theory in this period was mainly in the context of guidance of space vehicles. Missiles and satellites are complex multi-input and multi-output nonlinear systems with strict performance requirements, and this requirement in engineering stimulated the development of optimal control theory. Optimal control by its nature can be seen as a function of extreme value problems and variational problems. From 1953 to 1957, the American scholar Bellman founded the theory of dynamic programming and developed the Hamilton-Jacobi theory in variational. From 1956 to 1958, the Soviet scholar Pontryagin and others founded the maximum principle, these two methods became the present-day two cornerstones of optimal control theory.

The development of optimal control theory is largely due to the development of digital computers - the increase in computing speed, the expansion of storage capacity, the reduction in size, and the widespread use of the software. Digital computers are not only powerful tools for control system analysis and design but are gradually becoming one of the main components of automatic control systems. In the past 20 years, the development results of optimal control theory mainly include optimal control of distributed parameters, stochastic optimal control, optimal control of large systems, and differential countermeasures. Optimal control theory has formed a relatively complete system and has made more adequate preparation for modern control engineering [12–16].

3 Mathematical Models of Nonlinear Systems

According to the expression form of the mathematical model of the system, the system can usually be divided into nonlinear and linear systems. If the mathematical equations of the model contain only linear differential or difference links (i.e., satisfying the superposition principle), then the system is called a linear system. If the mathematical equations of the model contain nonlinear differential or difference links (i.e., not satisfying the superposition principle), then the system is called a nonlinear system.

In general, a class of continuous nonlinear systems can be represented by the following differential equations

$$\begin{cases} \dot{x} = f(x(t), u(t), t) \\ y = g(x(t), u(t), t) \end{cases} \tag{1}$$

where $x(t) \in R^n$ denotes the state variable, and $u(t) \in R^m$ denotes the control variables, and f and g denote the nonlinear function, and t denotes the time.

However, in practical engineering, many nonlinear systems, such as spacecraft soft landing problems, inverted pendulum systems, helicopter auto-control systems, and robotic systems, can be represented by equations of state of the form (2).

$$\begin{cases} \dot{x}_1 = f_1(x_1, x_2, \cdots, x_n) + g_{11}(x_1, x_2, \cdots, x_n)u_1 + \cdots + g_{m1}(x_1, x_2, \cdots, x_n)u_m \\ \dot{x}_2 = f_2(x_1, x_2, \cdots, x_n) + g_{12}(x_1, x_2, \cdots, x_n)u_1 + \cdots + g_{m2}(x_1, x_2, \cdots, x_n)u_m \\ \qquad\qquad\qquad\qquad \cdots \\ \dot{x}_n = f_n(x_1, x_2, \cdots, x_n) + g_{1n}(x_1, x_2, \cdots, x_n)u_1 + \cdots + g_{mn}(x_1, x_2, \cdots, x_n)u_m \end{cases} \tag{2}$$

The output equation is

$$\begin{cases} y_1 = h_1(x_1, x_2, \cdots, x_n) \\ y_2 = h_2(x_1, x_2, \cdots, x_n) \\ \qquad \cdots \\ y_3 = h_3(x_1, x_2, \cdots, x_n) \end{cases} \tag{3}$$

Abbreviate (2) and (3) as

$$\begin{cases} \dot{x}(t) = f(x(t) + \sum_{i=1}^{m} g_i(x(t))u_i(t) \\ \qquad y(t) = h(x(t)) \end{cases} \tag{4}$$

We refer to nonlinear systems represented by such forms as (4) as affine nonlinear systems, and it is not difficult to find that the system has this feature of exhibiting nonlinear relations for the state variables, yet linear relations for the control variables. Earlier work on radiative nonlinear systems by American scholars accounted for a larger proportion of the research work and is now widely valued by scholars in various countries.

4 Analytical Methods for Nonlinear Systems

After decades of development, the study of nonlinear system control theory has made great achievements with the participation and support of many scholars. At present, in the field of nonlinear control, the main analytical methods used are phase plane analysis, descriptive function method, and Lyapunov stability theory.

4.1 Phase Plane Analysis Method

Phase plane analysis is a graphical method proposed in 1885 by the French mathematician Henri Poincaré and is a relatively simple and intuitive method of design and analysis. An important step in this method is the ability to accurately graph the phase plane of a system based on its state, which is used to some extent for nonlinear systems to avoid solving differential equations. However, since this is an approximate graphical method, it is limited to application in second-order systems and simple third-order systems.

4.2 Descriptive Function Method

The descriptive function analysis method was first proposed in 1940 by Professor Daniel in England. This method is not limited by the order of the system, and its main idea is: according to certain assumptions, the output response of the nonlinear part of the system under the action of a sinusoidal signal is approximated by using the first harmonic component. This method is mainly used to analyze the stability and self- oscillation of nonlinear systems in the absence of external action. Because it is an approximate method of analysis, there are certain restrictions on its application and it can only be used to analyze the frequency response characteristics of the system and cannot be used to analyze deterministic information about the time response.

4.3 Lyapunov's Stability Theory

The method was proposed in 1892 by the Russian mathematician Lyapunov, and there are two types of Lyapunov's first method (also known as the indirect method) and Lyapunov's second method (also known as the direct method). The indirect method is a method to analyze the stability of a system by solving its equations, so it is generally applicable to nonlinear systems that can be linearized; the direct method, as an important tool for analyzing nonlinear systems, has strong general applicability, and the analysis is not limited to local motion. The Lyapunov analysis method can be used not only to analyze the stability of a system, but also to accomplish the design and analysis of nonlinear system controllers.

In addition to the three methods mentioned above, new systems for nonlinear systems are developing and growing, for example, by combining nonlinear systems with differential geometry, and in addition to this, neural network methods are being used on nonlinear systems.

5 Methods for Solving Optimal Problems

After the mathematical model has been established for the corresponding optimization problem, the choice of the solution method that allows the optimization problem to be solved becomes the main problem. In general, the solution methods for solving the optimization problem can be roughly divided into four categories: analytical methods, numerical solution methods (direct methods), optimization methods combining analytical and direct methods, and network optimization methods.

The design of a technical solution to an optimization problem can generally be carried out in three steps:

a. Develop a correct mathematical model of the optimization problem, based on the optimization problem that has been formulated, while establishing the variables that
b. Then list the objective function (or performance metric) and give the constraints;
c. Selecting the appropriate optimal solution method through specific analysis and study of the model that has been developed;
d. Based on the chosen optimization solution algorithm, the computer will be used to perform simulation calculations, and the simulation results obtained will be used to evaluate the effectiveness, simplicity, calculation effect and error of the algorithm accordingly.

6 Methods for Optimal Control of Nonlinear Systems

The meaning of the nonlinear optimal control problem is: Construct the state feedback controller $u(t) = u^*(t)$ such that the performance metrics are optimal while making the system $x(t) = f(x) + g(x)u^*(t)$ eventually stable or asymptotically stable.

In general, optimization problems can be classified into unconstrained and constrained problems, deterministic and stochastic problems, linear and nonlinear problems, static and dynamic problems, and network optimization problems. In the study of optimal control problems, we also need to clarify the following issues:

a. The equation of state of the system must be given, which means that the system must be described dynamically. If the system is continuous, then we have: $x(t) = f(x(t), u(t), t)$. If the system is discrete, then we have: $x(k + 1) = f(x(k), u(k), k), k = 0, 1, \cdots, n$

b. Clarify the scope of control. In most engineering, the control variable $u(t)$ is subject to some conditions because it is not allowed to take any value. Usually, the range of values of the control variable $u(t)$ is called the control domain.

c. Specify the beginning and terminal conditions. The initial state $x(t_0)$ of the system is known and the initial moment t_0 is also known. The terminal state $x(t')$ and the terminal moment t' are given.

d. Determine the objective function of the system, which is the performance metric.

The methods often used in optimal control theory contain mainly classical variational methods, the principle of extreme values and dynamic programming, which are the basic elements of optimal control theory.

6.1 Optimal Control of Nonlinear Systems Based on the Variational Method

The variational method is a mathematical method that is mainly used to deal with the problem of finding extrema for generalized functions. This method is only valid for a class of unconstrained or constrained belongs to the open set, so the classical variational theory can only be used to deal with some relatively simple control unconstrained optimal control problems. However, in reality, there is more of a class of optimal control problems that satisfy the condition that the control domain belongs to the closed interval, and the boundary values often limit the range of values of the control function, such as the rudder can only rotate in the range of two limit values, and the motor torque can only be generated in the range of positive and negative maximum values, etc. Therefore, the classical variational method is inadequate for solving many important practical optimal control problems.

Recall the formulation of the optimal control problem, i.e., finding a permissive control $u(t) \in R^m$, $t \in [t_0, t_f]$ such that the controlled system $\dot{x} = f(x, u, t)$ from an initial state $x(t_0) = x_0$ starts and at some end-state moment t_f time shifts to a specified set of objectives such that the performance metric generalizes

$$J = \theta\left[x(t_f), t_f\right] + \int_{t_0}^{t_f} L[x(t), u(t), t]dt \tag{5}$$

reaches a minimum. Therefore, it can be considered that the optimal control problem is the variational problem of solving the extremum of the generalized function in the presence of certain constraints.

6.2 Optimal Control of Nonlinear Systems Based on the Extreme Value Principle

The extreme value principle was first introduced by the Soviet scholar Pontryagin in 1956, derived from the variational method, and a rigorous mathematical derivation of the proof of this principle and its main conclusions was subsequently given. The extreme value principle, as a fundamental element of optimal control theory, is a further extension of the classical variational method in analytical mechanics, to obtain a better treatment when the input (i.e., control) action of the system is constrained due to the limitations of external sources of forces. The extreme value principle has been widely used not only in solving optimal control problems for continuous controlled systems but has also been greatly extended in dealing with optimal control problems for discrete controlled systems.

The maximum principle of the composite optimal control problem, i.e., the equation of state for a given system

$$\dot{x} = f(x(t), u(t), t) \tag{6}$$

and the control function $u(t)$ closed-set constraints on the

$$u(t) \in \Omega, t \in [t_0, t_f] \tag{7}$$

then it is the case that the system is transferred from a given initial state to some final state that satisfies to some final state that satisfies the terminal constraint to some final state of $x(t_f)$ where t_f is variable and makes the performance generic function

$$J = \theta[x(t_f), t_f] + \int_{t_0}^{t_f} L[x(t), u(t), t] \tag{8}$$

The necessary conditions that should be satisfied by the optimal control to reach the minimal value are as follows.

Set $u^*(t)$ be the optimal control and $x^*(t)$ be the optimal control corresponding to $u^*(t)$ the optimal trajectory, then there exists an optimal trajectory with $u^*(t)$ and $x^*(t)$ corresponding to $\lambda(t)$ that $x^*(t)$ and $\lambda(t)$ satisfying the canonical equation

$$x(t) = \frac{\partial H}{\partial \lambda} = f[x(t), u(t), t], \lambda(t) = -\frac{\partial H}{\partial x} \tag{9}$$

where the Hamiltonian function

$$H = H[x(t), \lambda(t), u(t), t] = -L[x(t), u(t), t] + \lambda^T(t)f[x(t), u(t), t] \tag{10}$$

The boundary conditions for the state and covariate variables are

$$\begin{cases} x(t_0) = x_0, \Phi[x(t_f), t_f] = 0 \\ \lambda(t_f) = -[\frac{\partial \theta}{\partial x} + \frac{\partial \Phi^T}{\partial x}\mu]\Big|_{t=t_f} \\ [H + \frac{\partial \theta}{\partial t} + \frac{\partial \Phi^T}{\partial t}\mu]\Big|_{t=t_f} = 0 \end{cases} \tag{11}$$

$$\mu = [\mu_1, \mu_2, \ldots, \mu_r]^T \tag{12}$$

The Hamiltonian function H reaches its maximum on the optimal control and optimal trajectory

$$H[x^*(t), \lambda(t), u^*(t), t] = max_{u(t)\in\Omega}H[x^*(t), \lambda(t), u(t), t] \tag{13}$$

6.3 Optimal Control of Nonlinear Systems Based on Dynamic Programming Method

The dynamic programming method was gradually created in the mid- 1950s by the American scholar Bellman based on the multi-stage decision process problem, Bellman took the optimality principle as a virtue and further extended the study of the Hamilton-Jacobi theory in variational calculus, thus constituting dynamic programming. The basic idea in solving a class of multi-stage decision problems is that of inverse induction with the termination end as the beginning and the initial end as the end. This approach deals with a much wider range of problems, is suitable for solving discrete optimal control problems or continuous control problems that can be discretized, and is a method that is particularly suitable for computation using computers.

6.4 Other Approximation Methods

The quadratic optimal control problem for nonlinear systems leads to the Hamilton-Jacobi-Bellman (HJB) equation or the two-point boundary value problem, for which no analytical solution can be found except in the extremely simple case. In solving optimal control problems for nonlinear systems, it is difficult to use classical optimal control theory for this purpose. In recent years, this problem has been extensively studied by many scholars. At present, the main approximation algorithms used in the optimal control of nonlinear systems are: Power Series Expansion, Galerkin Successive Approximation, State-Dependent Riccati Equation, Approximate Sequence of Riccati Equations, General Orthogonal Polynomial Series Expansion and Successive Approximation Approach.

In addition to the above methods, other approximation methods exist that partially rely on the deterministic form of the system and the properties of the nonlinear terms [17, 18], so it is important to explore nonlinear systems in the context of engineering applications.

6.5 Approximate Linearization Design Methods for Nonlinear Systems and Their Limitations

In the design of the control system by the traditional method, firstly, a nonlinear mathematical model with fixed parameters and structure is established without considering uncertainty: Secondly, the linear equation of state or transfer function of the original nonlinear system is obtained by approximating the linearization of the system at the equilibrium state (a certain equilibrium point), i.e., the mathematical model after the approximate linearization; finally, the analysis and design of the system is carried out according to the method of linear control theory.

Of course, the limitations exhibited by this approximately linearized design method, which replaces the increment of a nonlinear system function by its fully differentiated method at a point, cannot be ignored. This is because, when designing and analyzing the linear equation of state obtained through this method, the accuracy of the conclusions drawn cannot be guaranteed if the deviation between the chosen equilibrium state and the actual operating state of the system is relatively large. Moreover, when the deviation between the equilibrium point selected in the design and the actual operating point is larger, the deviation of the design and analysis results will also be larger, therefore, if the equilibrium state selected in the design is far from the operating state of the system, then it is difficult to play the role of the controller when designing the system controller based on the mathematical model derived from this approximate linearization method; even in some special cases, it will show the opposite effect.

7 Conclusion

The optimal control of nonlinear systems includes stabilization, tracking, and disturbance rejection. Many kinds of control problems can be derived from these basic types and various combinations of them. Stabilization is to design a calibrator so that the state of a closed-loop system is stabilized around an equilibrium point, e.g., device temperature control, stabilization of an inverted pendulum, flight altitude control of an aircraft, position control of a robot arm. Tracking is to design a controller, called a tracker, so that the output of the closed-loop system tracks a given time-varying trajectory, e.g., to make an aircraft fly on a specified path, to make a robot arm draw straight lines and circles. Disturbance rejection considers how to achieve the required control in the presence of various disturbances and parameter variations.

For nonlinear systems, the solution of optimal control generally does not exist. In addition to the complexity and diversity of nonlinear systems, there are few research results in this area, and there are still many problems to be solved. From the perspective of optimal control theory, the existing research theories of nonlinear systems are elaborated in detail, and their advantages and disadvantages are objectively compared, providing a reference for further research of nonlinear optimal control theory.

References

1. Hazeleger, L., Haring, M., Wouw, N.: Extremum-seeking control for optimization of time-varying steady-state responses of nonlinear systems. Automatica **119**, 109068 (2020)
2. Zhu, F., Zhong, P., Sun, Y., et al.: A coordinated optimization framework for long-term complementary operation of a large-scale hydro-photovoltaic hybrid system: Nonlinear modeling, multi-objective optimization and robust decision-making. Energy Conversion and Management **226**, 113543 (2020)
3. Mirzaei, A., Ramezani, A.: Cooperative optimization-based distributed model predictive control for constrained nonlinear large-scale systems with stability and feasibility guarantees. ISA Transactions (2021)
4. Fu J., Tian, F.: Dynamic optimization of nonlinear systems with guaranteed feasibility of inequality-path-constraints. Automatica **127**, 109516 (2021)
5. Wen, G., Chen, C., Li, W.N.: Simplified optimized control using reinforcement learning algorithm for a class of stochastic nonlinear systems. Information Sciences **517**(1) (2019)
6. Sahoo, A., Narayanan, V.: Optimization of sampling intervals for tracking control of nonlinear systems: a game theoretic approach. Neural Networks **114**, 78–90 (2019)
7. Liu, X, Zhao, B., Liu, D.: Fault tolerant tracking control for nonlinear systems with actuator failures through particle swarm optimization- based adaptive dynamic programming. Applied Soft Computing **97**, 106766 (2020)
8. Zhang, W., Xie, X.J., Liang, J.: Neural-Network-based Optimization and Analysis for Nonlinear Stochastic Systems. Neurocomputing **452**, 779–780 (2020)

9. Bo, Z.A., Fl, B., Hl, B., et al.: Particle swarm optimized neural networks based local tracking control scheme of unknown nonlinear interconnected systems. Neural Netw. **134**, 54–63 (2021)

10. Ij, A., Mazrb, C., Mj, C., et al.: Design of evolutionary optimized finite difference based numerical computing for dust density model of nonlinear Van-der Pol Mathieu's oscillatory systems. Math. Comput. Simul. **181**, 444–470 (2021)

11. Chakrabarty, A., Benosman, M.: Safe learning-based observers for unknown nonlinear systems using bayesian optimization. Elec. Eng. Sys. Sci. Sys. Cont. (2020)

12. He, S., Fang, H., Zhang, M., et al.: Online policy iterative-based H∞ optimization algorithm for a class of nonlinear systems. Information Sciences **495** (2019)

13. Zhao, J., Zhong, Z., Lin, C.M., et al.: Tracking control for nonlinear multivariable systems using wavelet-type TSK fuzzy brain emotional learning with particle swarm optimization. Journal of the Franklin Institute **358**(1) (2020)

14. Liu, H, Tong, Z.: Robust state estimation for uncertain linear systems with random parametric uncertainties. Sci. China Info. Sci. **60**(1), 1–13 (2017)

15. Li, S., Xia, W., Zhang, F.: Synchronization of continuous-time linear systems with time-varying output couplings. IEEE Trans. Industr. Inf. **99**, 1 (2020)

16. Ji, J.Y., Man, L.W.: An improved dynamic multi-objective optimization approach for nonlinear equation systems. Information Sciences **576**, 204–227 (2021)

17. Gao, W., Luo, Y., Xu, J., et al.: Evolutionary algorithm with multi objective optimization technique for solving nonlinear equation systems. Information Sciences **541**(8) (2020)

18. Hendriks, J.N., Holdsworth, J., Wills, A.G., et al.: Data to Controller for Nonlinear Systems: an Approximate Solution (2021)

Design and Control of Legged Robots

A Locust-Inspired Energy Storage Joint for Variable Jumping Trajectory Control

Yongzun Yang[1], Zhiyuan Feng[1], Cheng Jin[1], Lingqi Tang[1], Songsong Ma[1,2,3], and Yao Li[1,2,3(✉)]

[1] School of Mechanical Engineering and Automation, Harbin Institute of Technology, Shenzhen 518052, People's Republic of China
liyao2018@hit.edu.cn

[2] State Key Laboratory of Robotics and System, Harbin Institute of Technology, Harbin 150001, People's Republic of China

[3] Guangdong Key Laboratory of Intelligent Morphing Mechanisms and Adaptive Robotics, Harbin Institute of Technology, Shenzhen 518052, People's Republic of China

Abstract. Jumping is a good solution for small robots over obstacles. Most of the current jumping robots are not energy store adjustable due to the design of the energy storage elements and structures, which limits the effective working space of the robot. The locust is good at jumping. Thanks to the excellent structure of the hind legs, the locust can change the degree of compression of the simi-lunar process (SLP) and change the energy storage while maintaining the same jumping stance. Herein, we design a locust-inspired energy storage joint and verified its function on a jumping robot. The motors and wires were used to imitate the muscles and the torsion springs were used to imitate SLP. To accurately describe the energy stored, a static model of the torsion springs was developed. Furthermore, the number of motor revolutions and the stored energy value were also calculated and could be used for subsequent precise control. Six jumping experiments with different compression angles for torsion springs proved the feasibility of the static model. This locust-inspired energy storage joint is the basis for the next robot capable of the omnidirectional, continuous autonomous jumping.

Keywords: Locust-inspired Joint · Variable Energy Storage · Jumping Trajectory Control

1 Introduction

Small-sized legged robots and wheeled robots have poor passability on uneven roads, and cannot cross obstacles or gaps larger than themselves, while the jumping robot can easily cross obstacles several times larger than itself, which even tracked robots with strong obstacle-crossing capabilities cannot do. With the jump function, the robot can easily jump from the window to the house and can climb the stairs by jumping to access the second floor. Field robots with jumping functions can easily cross boulders or swampy areas in front of the road.

© The Author(s), under exclusive license to Springer Nature Singapore Pte Ltd. 2023
H. Yang et al. (Eds.): ICIRA 2023, LNAI 14271, pp. 459–468, 2023.
https://doi.org/10.1007/978-981-99-6495-6_39

Many jumping robots have been invented, and most of them were made by imitating insects or animals skilled at jumping. A single-legged robot was built based on the click beetle, which has a maximum jump height of 4.3 times its body height [1]. A miniature froghopper-inspired jumping robot could finish a steering jump at an angle of 40° [2]. Inspired by a leafhopper, the continuous jumping robot was able to jump 100 mm in height and 200 mm in distance [3]. By imitating the multi-locomotion of trap-jaw ant, Zhakypov constructed a 10-g origami jumping robot [4]. Inspired by the vampire bat, Matthew designed the MultiMo-Bat with excellent jumping along with gliding functions [5]. Due to the design of the trigger mechanism, these robots can only store energy of a specific value.

Some jumping robots used a cam to compress the elastic elements for energy storage. The energy storage reached its maximum when the cam was rotated to its largest stroke. The advantage of using a cam was the simple structure, but the disadvantage was also obvious, the released energy could not be altered. The only way to change the energy storage was to change the energy storage components used [6, 7].

Locusts are great jumpers. The locust store 9–11 mJ energy before jumping, the maximum output power reach 36 mW, the take-off speed exceeds 3.2 m/s, and the maximum take-off acceleration reaches 180 m/s^2 [8]. The locusts need three necessary steps to complete the jump. Firstly, the tibia is fully flexed under the control of the flexor muscle. Then, the flexor muscle and the extensor muscle both contract to deform semilunar processes (SLP), which is called co-contraction. At last, the contraction of the flexor muscle disappears, and the kicking or jumping is triggered [9, 10]. Based on the excellent characteristics and hind leg structure of locusts, researchers have designed several jumping robots. Shen et al. designed a small jumping robot with a six-bar mechanism [7]. Zaitsev et al. used a simple rope-driven mechanism to imitate the effect of muscle and designed a robot with strong jumping ability, which could cover a height of 3.35 m and a distance of 1.37 m. However, those locust-inspired jumping robot can also only store energy of a specific value.

During co-contraction, the amount of stored energy can be achieved by controlling the degree of compression of SLP, which has been confirmed in our previous study [11]. This excellent feature allows locusts to control the magnitude of the take-off velocity without any change in the posture of the hind legs. Furthermore, the direction of the hind leg force also affects the direction of the take-off speed [12]. These two parameters can alter the jump trajectory in a wider range.

In this study, we designed a variable energy storage joint for the trajectory control of the jumping robot. The motor pulling the rope was used to imitate the muscle contraction and the torsion springs were used to imitate the SLP to complete the energy storage. Subsequently, a static model of the energy storage elements was developed to express the relationship between the number of turns of the motor and the energy stored in the torsion spring, which was used to precisely control the jump trajectory. Finally, the function of the designed joint was verified in a series of jumping experiments under the recording of a 3D motion capture system.

2 Variable Energy Storage Joint Design

The variable energy storage joint was designed based on the energy storage method of the locust's SLP. Figure 1 shows the energy storage process of the SLP. The tibia is firstly flexed by the flexor muscle and tightened against the fumer. The flexor and extensor muscle contract together causing deformation of the SLP and stored energy in it. The greater the deformation of the SLP, the greater the energy output of the hind legs [13]. During SLP compression, the tibia fitted to the fumer and moved slightly in the direction of compression, which contributed to the steady posture. By imitating this characteristic, four torsion springs were mounted on the rotating joint in parallel to imitate the function of the SLP. Different energy storage can be achieved by controlling the degree of torsion. Similarly, robots equipped with this joint can maintain a constant standing posture in different energy storage states.

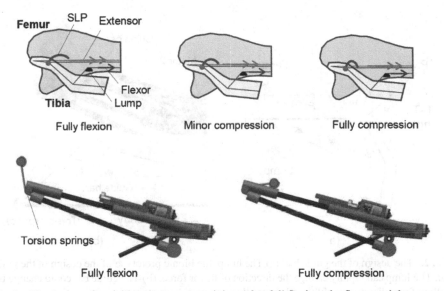

Fig. 1. The design of variable energy storage joint. After full flexion, the flexor and the extensor simultaneously compress the SLP to deform it. The greater the degree of SLP compression, the more energy is stored. The variable energy storage joint was designed by simulating the energy storage process of the locust. The robot could store different energy without changing its posture.

As shown in Fig. 2(a), locusts have a special and excellent structure inside their hind legs. The tension produced by the extensor muscle was F_e and the tension produced by the flexor muscle was F_f. The force arms of these two forces were $l_1\sin\alpha_1$ and $l_2\sin\alpha_2$, respectively. With the gradual reduction in F-T angle, angle α_1 decreased rapidly. However, with the help of the lump, the angle α_2 could increase rapidly. Therefore, the leverage ratio (flexor/extensor) changed and reached ~ 21. The flexor muscle could resist 21 times the extensor force. The distribution of the lump could be applied to the design of the joint.

We set a guide bar in the path of the pulling wire rope of motor 2, as shown in Fig. 2(b). The pulling force arms of motor 2 before and after setting the guide bar were expressed as:

$$L_1 = d_1 \sin \theta_1, \ \theta_1 \in [60, 155] \tag{1}$$

$$L_2 = d_1 \sin \theta_2, \ \theta_2 \in [40, 80] \tag{2}$$

where d_1 was the distance between the point of force and the center of rotation pivot, θ_1 and θ_2 were the angles between the wire rope and d_1.

As θ_1 increased, the force arm L_1 increased first and then decreased. In contrast, as θ_2 increased, the force arm L_2 increased continuously. With the compression of the torsion spring increased the design of the guide bar could effectively degrade the output of the motor 2.

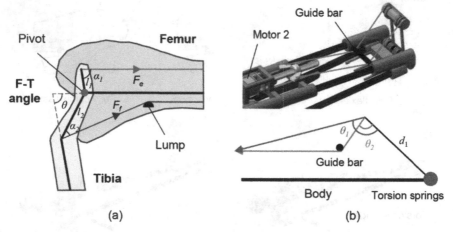

Fig. 2. The design of the guide bar. (a) The lump, the bionic prototype of the design of the guide bar. The lump can rapidly change the direction of flexor force. (b) The guide bar could change the pulling force direction rapidly, and reduce the output of the motor 2.

The designed joints were combined with other components to form a jumping robot as shown in Fig. 3. This robot mainly consisted of two motors on the body, leg, torsion springs, and trigger mechanism. First, the reel pulled the leg inward with the clockwise drive of motor 1, and the leg was locked by the trigger mechanism, which mimicked the initial flexion of the locust. Second, motor 2 drove the butterfly nut to pull the rope to achieve the compression of the torsion springs. Last, motor 1 rotated counterclockwise to release the wire, and the square nut moved backward under the limit of the guide rail. Thus, the trigger mechanism was pulled to release the leg for jumping.

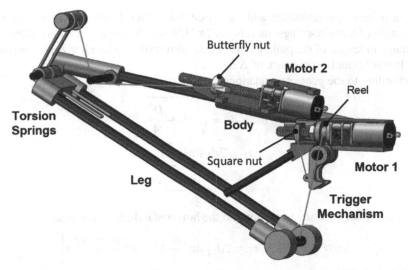

Fig. 3. The jumping robot with variable energy storage joint. This robot mainly included motor 1, motor 2, torsion springs, and leg. With the assistance of a butterfly nut, square nut, reel, and trigger mechanism, the motors pulling wires were used to mimic muscles and achieve orderly control of the robot's energy storage and release. The green lines indicated the wires (Color figure online).

3 Modeling of Energy Storage Element

The torsion springs are the main energy storage elements. Knowing the specific value of stored energy is the basis for preparing to control the jump trajectory. When storing energy, the torsion springs are compressed under the pulling force of motor 2. Two sets of left and right torsion springs are symmetrically installed, and they material are piano steel. The energy stored in the torsion spring can be expressed as:

$$E_p = 4 \times \frac{k\Delta\varphi^2}{2} = 4 \times \frac{Ed_t^4\Delta\varphi^2}{128Dn} \tag{3}$$

where E is the elastic modulus, its value is 206 GPa; d_t is the diameter of the torsion spring, its value is 1.5 mm; D is the middle diameter of the torsion spring, its value is 15 mm, n is the effective number of turns of torsion spring, its value is 2; $\Delta\varphi$ is the compression angle (the unit of angle is radian).

After substituting these data, we can obtain:

$$E_p = 1.08\Delta\varphi^2 \tag{4}$$

The compression of the torsion springs is achieved by controlling the number of revolutions of motor 2. As shown in Fig. 4, the simplified diagram of the torsion springs compression process and the size of the diameter of the guide bar are ignored. Motor 2 turns the screw and drive the butterfly nut to move left and right. The butterfly nut pulls the wire to compress the torsion springs. d is the twist arm length, d_2 is the distance between torsion springs center and the guide bar, which length equals d_1. φ_0 is the initial angle of torsion springs, its value is $2\pi/3$. When the angle of compression is $\Delta\varphi$, the change in length of the pulling wire is Δs, corresponding to a horizontal movement of the butterfly nut by a distance of Δx.

According to the geometric relationship:

$$d_1 = d_2 = \sqrt{d^2 + \frac{D^2}{4}} \tag{5}$$

$$s_1 = 2d_1 \sin(\frac{\varphi_0}{2}) \tag{6}$$

$$s_2 = 2d_1 \sin(\frac{\varphi_0 - \Delta\varphi}{2}) \tag{7}$$

The angle between the wire rope and the horizontal direction is small:

$$\Delta x \approx \Delta s = s_1 - s_2 = 2d_1 \left[\sin(\frac{\varphi_0}{2}) - \sin(\frac{\varphi_0 - \Delta\varphi}{2}) \right] \tag{8}$$

where D is the middle diameter of the torsion spring.

The relationship between the motor rotation and bolt movement is as follows:

$$\Delta x = \frac{np}{i} \tag{9}$$

where n is the number of revolutions of motor 2, i is the reduction ratio of motor 2, and p is the pitch of the thread.

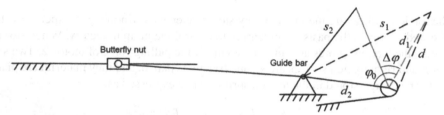

Fig. 4. Simplified diagram of the torsion springs compression process. d is the twist arm length, d_1 is the distance between the point of force and the center of rotation pivot, d_2 is the distance between torsion springs center and the guide bar, which length equals d_1, $\Delta\varphi$ is the compression angle.

Thus, we can obtain the relationship between stored energy (E_p) and the number of revolutions (n) of motor 2:

$$n = \frac{2i}{p} d_1 \left[\sin(\frac{\varphi_0}{2}) - \sin(\frac{\varphi_0 - \Delta\varphi}{2}) \right] \tag{10}$$

$$E_p = 1.08 \times \left(\frac{2\pi}{3} - 2\arcsin\frac{\sqrt{3}id_1 - np}{2id_1} \right)^2 \tag{11}$$

$$E_p = f(n) \tag{12}$$

4   Jumping Experiment and Discussion

After the variable energy storage joint was installed on the robot, the robot could complete the jump, as shown in Fig. 5. With the jump, the robot itself flipped, caused by the direction of the ground reaction force not passing through the robot's center of gravity. Two ways can avoid flipping in subsequent continuing research: the first is to adjust the structure and position of the robot's moving parts and control circuits so that the direction of the hind leg force through the robot's center of gravity; the second is to reduce the mass of the hind legs, so that the moment of inertia of the hind leg in the flight phase is as small as possible, so as not to drive the whole robot to rotate.

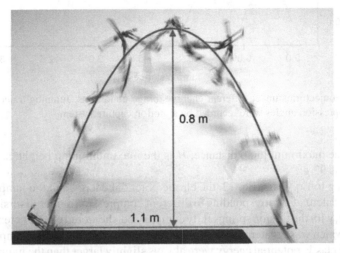

Fig. 5. The robot jumping process. The robot completed a parabolic jump with the use of torsion springs energy storage (60° compression angle). At the same time, the robot's body also flipped.

Varying the compression of the torsion springs enabled control of the robot's jumping trajectory. The pitch angle of the robot was set at a constant 60°. With full compression (90° compression angle), the robot could jump at a maximum height and distance of 2.4 m and 1.8 m, respectively. As shown in Fig. 6, the bionic jumping robot performed different trajectories under six compression angles of torsion springs. In contrast, most other jumping robots can only store a fixed amount of energy and their jumping trajectories can only be controlled by changing their pitch angle. The jumping robot in this research had a wide range of trajectory adjustment for better practice. For example, for other fixed energy jumping robots, to achieve a short horizontal jump, the robot can only achieve a smaller horizontal speed by turning up the pinch angle so that the robot consumes much energy at the jump height. Meanwhile, our robot just needs to lower its energy store.

The robot's jump trajectory was parabolic and the kinetic energy at the moment of take-off can be expressed as:

$$E_k = \frac{1}{2}m(\frac{S^2 g}{2H} + 2gH) \tag{13}$$

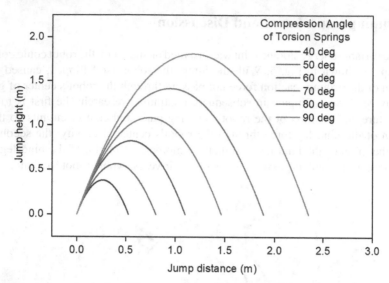

Fig. 6. Jump trajectories under different energy storage conditions. Jumping trajectories at six different compression angles were recorded by a motion capture system.

where S is the maximum jump distance, H is the maximum jump height, and the mass of the robot is 93 g.

According to Eq. 4 and Eq. 12, the elastic potential energy and the jumping kinetic energy were calculated corresponding to different compression angles of torsion springs. For example, with the torsion springs fully compressed, the stored elastic potential energy was 2.67 J, which was greater than the kinetic energy of 2.34 J during the jump. As shown in Fig. 7, the elastic potential energy were always slightly larger than the jumping kinetic energy, which main caused by two reasons: first, during the release of elastic potential energy, there was friction in the transmission of the force, resulting in a loss of energy; second, in the flight phase, the body of the robot underwent 1 to 2 revolutions (as shown in Fig. 5), which were not accounted for in the kinetic energy. There was also a potential influence of a slight elastic deformation of the twist arm during compression of the torsion springs, the amount of energy stored in this part was subject to further analysis. Although there were some differences between the two energy, the hydrostatic model could be considered feasible.

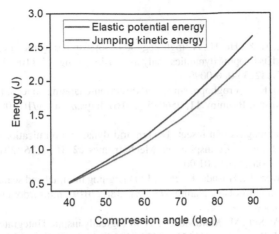

Fig. 7. The elastic potential energy and the jumping kinetic energy corresponding to different compression angles of torsion springs. The former were always slightly larger than the latter.

5 Conclusion

In this research, we designed a locust-inspired energy storage joint for variable jumping trajectory control. First, the action sequence of the hind leg flexor muscle and extensor muscle during the locust jump was analyzed, namely initial flexion, co-contraction, and trigger activity. Next, motor 1 and a wire were used to imitate the flexor, motor 2 and other transmission structures were used to imitate the extensor, and the torsion springs were used to replace the function of SLP. Then, a static model of the torsion springs was developed as shown in Eq. 10. By setting the compression angles to 40, 50, 60, 70, 80, and 90°, the corresponding potential energy and the jumping kinetic energy were calculated. Due to the energy loss in the process of force transfer and the rotation of the robot during jumping, the potential energy was larger than the corresponding kinetic energy.

This jumping robot with variable energy storage joint has excellent trajectory adjustability, but it can only complete a single jump at present. This robot cannot return to an upright position after landing. With the addition of some active regulating structures, such as the upright mechanism, turning mechanism, and pitch angle adjustment mechanism, this bionic jumping robot is capable of continuous multi-directional jumps. With the help of IMU sensor or an external motion capture system, automatic control of robot jumping can be realized.

Acknowledgment. The work was supported by Shenzhen Science and Technology Program (Grant No. RCBS20210609103901011), Shenzhen Peacock Innovation Team Project (Grant No. KQTD20210811090146075), and State Key Laboratory of Mechanical System and Vibration (Grant No. MSV202306).

References

1. Chen, G., Tu, J., Ti, X., Hu, H.: A single-legged robot inspired by the jumping mechanism of click beetles and its hopping dynamics analysis. J. Bionic Eng. **17**, 1109–1125 (2020). https://doi.org/10.1007/s42235-020-0099-z
2. Jung, G.-P., Cho, K.-J.: Froghopper-inspired direction-changing concept for miniature jumping robots. Bioinspir. Biomim. **11**, 056015 (2016). https://doi.org/10.1088/1748-3190/11/5/056015
3. Li, F., et al.: Jumping like an insect: Design and dynamic optimization of a jumping mini robot based on bio-mimetic inspiration. Mechatronics **22**, 167–176 (2012). https://doi.org/10.1016/j.mechatronics.2012.01.001
4. Zhakypov, Z., Mori, K., Hosoda, K., Paik, J.: Designing minimal and scalable insect-inspired multi-locomotion millirobots. Nature **571**, 381–386 (2019). https://doi.org/10.1038/s41586-019-1388-8
5. Woodward, M.A., Sitti, M.: MultiMo-Bat: A biologically inspired integrated jumping–gliding robot. The Int. J. Robo. Res. **33**, 1511–1529 (2014). https://doi.org/10.1177/0278364914541301
6. Kovac, M., Fuchs, M., Guignard, A., Zufferey, J.-C., Floreano, D.: A miniature 7g jumping robot. In: 2008 IEEE International Conference on Robotics and Automation, pp. 373–378. IEEE, Pasadena, CA, USA (2008). https://doi.org/10.1109/ROBOT.2008.4543236
7. Shen, Y., Ge, W., Mo, X., Hou, Z.: Design of a locust-inspired miniature jumping robot. In: 2018 IEEE International Conference on Robotics and Biomimetics (ROBIO), pp. 2322–2327. IEEE, Kuala Lumpur, Malaysia (2018). https://doi.org/10.1109/ROBIO.2018.8665287
8. Bennet-Clark, H.C.: The energetics of the jump of the locust Schistocerca gregaria. J. Exp. Biol. **63**(1), 53–83 (1975)
9. Heitler, W.J., Burrowsf, M.: I. The Motor Programme. 18
10. Cofer, D., Cymbalyuk, G., Heitler, W.J., Edwards, D.H.: Neuromechanical simulation of the locust jump. J. Exp. Biol. **213**, 1060–1068 (2010). https://doi.org/10.1242/jeb.034678
11. Ma, S., Liu, P., Liu, S., Li, Y., Li, B.: Launching of a cyborg locust via co-contraction control of hindleg muscles. IEEE Trans. Robot. **38**, 2208–2219 (2022). https://doi.org/10.1109/TRO.2022.3152102
12. Sutton, G.P., Burrows, M.: The mechanics of elevation control in locust jumping. J. Comp. Physiol. A **194**, 557–563 (2008). https://doi.org/10.1007/s00359-008-0329-z
13. Burrows, M., Morris, G.: The kinematics and neural control of high-speed kicking movements in the locust. J. Exp. Biol. **204**, 3471–3481 (2001). https://doi.org/10.1242/jeb.204.20.3471

Design and Control of a Novel Six-Legged Robot for Flat, Downhill, and Uphill Skiing

Limin Yang, Yunpeng Yin, Zelin Wang, Liangyu Wang, Feng Gao[(✉)],
Xianbao Chen, and Hong Gao

State Key Laboratory of Mechanical System and Vibration, School of Mechanical
Engineering, Shanghai Jiao Tong University, Shanghai 200240, China
{ylm20159,fengg}@sjtu.edu.cn

Abstract. This paper presents the design, control, and application of a
novel six-legged skiing robot (SLSR) on flat and slope terrains. Imitating
human skiing behavior, a unique ski with 5 degrees of freedom (DOFs)
is designed, where the front and rear legs on the same side are connected
to a ski, respectively. Each of the two middle leg tips has a ski stick. In
order to improve the locomotion ability on the flat and uphill, we utilize
a ducted-fan propulsion system (DFPS) to provide forward power. Then
a new skiing control strategy is developed, which consists of a trajectory planner and a centroid balance controller (CBC). Finally, we conducted skiing experiments on a flat snow surface and slopes. The results
show that the SLSR could successfully accelerate, decelerate, turn, and
brake. Moreover, the SLSR can slide in a large range on flat ground and
maintain a stable attitude. On the primary ski slope, the SLSR can go
downhill as well as uphill.

Keywords: Six-legged skiing robot · Centroidal dynamics · Mechanics
and control

1 Introduction

In recent years, more and more legged robots have entered public life, which
can complete various tasks such as blind guidance, safety inspection, family
companionship, etc. Similarly, in skiing, researchers have designed robots for
skiing by imitating human skiing behavior. At present, the research on ski robots
is still in its infancy and mainly focuses on humanoid robots.

Yoneyama et al. [1] developed a bipedal robot equipped with two skis and
each leg has six degrees of freedom. The authors mainly investigate the effect of
joint motions on the ski turn. Utilizing the artificial grass slope to simulate the
snow environment, the robot can produce better foot force balance and a steady
smooth turn. Iverach-brereton et al. [2] used the humanoid robot Jennifer to

This work was supported by the National Key Research and Development Program of
China under Grants 2021YFF0307900 and 2021YFF0306202.

design a skiing robot, which can realize simple turning and braking actions for alpine skiing by applying the PID controllers to adjust the body posture to ensure constant contact between the ski and the ground. In the Ski Robot Competition held at the PyeongChang 2018 Winter Olympics, some humanoid ski robots [3–5] can complete autonomous sliding and avoid the flags. The work in [6] showed a biped alpine skiing robot developed for the 2020 Beijing Ski Robot Challenge. In this work, the authors use the DDPG reinforcement learning approach to establish the relationship between the tilting angle, skateboard cutting angle, and turning radius of the robot. In particular, the first hexapod ski robot [7] was unveiled at the Beijing 2022 Winter Olympics, which can ski at a high speed on snow slopes and avoid obstacles and crowds.

In terms of applying ducted fans to robots, Huang et al. [8,9] developed a sliding gait and a method of posture optimization based on sequential quadratic programming, which was applied to the bipedal robot called Jet-HR1 with a ducted fan on its feet. Jet-HR1 could step over a ditch with a width of as much as 97% of the robot's leg length. In addition, Li et al. [10] designed a flying bipedal robot named Jet-HR2, which has four ducted fan propulsion systems fixed on the robot. Based on the thrust vector control approach, the robot achieved a successful take-off and maintain stability under low thrust-to-weight ratio conditions. The take-off height exceeded 1000 mm.

There is still a certain gap between current skiing robots and human skiing. Most ski robots can only slide down snowy slopes. This paper aims to develop the ability of robots to ski on flat ground and uphill, which will be of great significance for ski robots to perform tasks efficiently in various terrain. In order to reduce the difficulty of control, we introduced a DFPS to provide power to the SLSR (see Fig. 1).

The rest of this article is organized as follows. Section 2 introduces the mechanism design and analyzes the kinematic models of the leg and ski. Then we present a skiing control algorithm based on centroidal dynamics, which can maintain body balance and ensure effective contact between skis and snow. Sect. 3 conducts experiments to validate the motion controller. Section 4 concludes this article and discusses future work.

Fig. 1. Physical prototype of SLSR

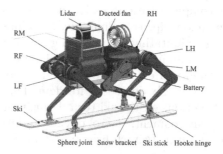

Fig. 2. Virtual prototype in NX

2   System Design

2.1   Mechanism Design and Kinematics

As shown in Fig. 2, we innovatively designed a six-legged skiing robot in the NX/UG modeling environment. For lightweight design, the main body and legs of the robot are made of aluminum alloy. The outline dimensions are about 1.12 m × 0.76 m × 0.7 m (length × width × height) and the total mass is approximately 24 kg. The robot has a body and six legs, named left front (LF) leg, left middle (LM) leg, left hind (LH) leg, right front (RF) leg, right middle (RM) leg, and right hind (RH) leg. Specifically, the LF leg and LH leg are connected to the ski through a sphere joint and a Hooke hinge, respectively. The RF leg and RH leg are connected with the ski in the same way. And each of the two middle legs is equipped with a ski stick and snow bracket. Each leg of the robot has a hip abduction/adduction (HAA) joint, a hip flexion/extension (HFE) joint, and a knee flexion/extension (KFE) joint. The leg joints are driven by direct-drive motor modules with a reduction ratio of 1.8. In order to improve the locomotion ability of the robot, a ducted fan is installed on the back of the robot to provide forward power. In addition, the vision system is used for navigation and obstacle avoidance. In this configuration, the robot can achieve stable contact with the snow surface, and can rely on the ducted fan to ski on flat snow surfaces and slopes. In addition, there are two on-board lithium polymer batteries, one for powering the robot body and the other for the ducted fan. The robot can run for about 1 h on battery power.

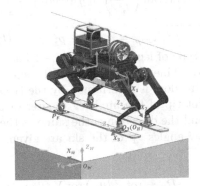

Fig. 3. Coordinate system definition of SLSR

As pictured in Fig. 3, the body coordinate frame $\{O_B - X_B Y_B Z_B\}$ of the robot is located at the center of mass. Because each leg has the same kinematic structure, we choose the LH leg for analysis. The leg coordinate frame $\{O_0 - X_0 Y_0 Z_0\}$ is located at the intersection of the HAA joint axis and the HFE joint axis. And $\{O_H - X_H Y_H Z_H\}$ is the frame of the Hooke hinge. According to the Denavit-Hartenberg (D-H) method, the transformation matrix from $i-1$ to i for the ith link can be obtained as follows:

$$
{}_{i}^{i-1}T = \begin{bmatrix} c\theta_i & -s\theta_i c\alpha_i & s\theta_i s\alpha_i & a_i c\theta_i \\ s\theta_i & -c\theta_i c\alpha_i & -c\theta_i s\alpha_i & a_i s\theta_i \\ 0 & s\alpha_i & c\alpha_i & d_i \\ 0 & 0 & 0 & 1 \end{bmatrix}
\tag{1}
$$

wheres s and c represent the sine and cosine functions.

So the D-H parameters $(\theta_i, d_i, \alpha_i, a_i)$ of adjacent links are $(\theta_1, 0, -\pi/2, 0)$, $(\theta_2, L_1, 0, L_2)$ and $(\theta_3, 0, 0, L_3)$. L_1, L_2, and L_3 are the link length of the leg, respectively. Then the transformation matrix between the tip coordinate frame and the body coordinate frame can be obtained as follows:

$$
{}^{B}T_3 = {}^{B}T_0 {}^{0}T_1 {}^{1}T_2 {}^{2}T_3
\tag{2}
$$

When the coordinate of the foot tip is known as $\boldsymbol{P} = (p_x, p_y, p_z)^T$, the rotation angles can be derived as follows:

$$
\theta_1 = -\arctan\left(\frac{p_y}{p_z}\right) - \arctan\left(\frac{L_1}{l_{yz}}\right) - \frac{\pi}{2}
\tag{3}
$$

$$
\theta_3 = -\delta \arccos\left(\frac{l_{xzp}^2 - L_2^2 - L_3^2}{2L_2 L_3}\right)
\tag{4}
$$

$$
\theta_2 = -\arctan\left(\frac{p_x}{l_{yz}}\right) + \eta \arccos\left(\frac{d + L_2}{l_{xzp}}\right)
\tag{5}
$$

where $l_{yz} = \sqrt{p_y^2 + p_z^2 - L_1^2}$, $l_{xzp} = \sqrt{l_{yz}^2 + p_x^2}$, $d = \left(l_{xzp}^2 - L_2^2 - L_3^2\right)/(2L_2)$. And η depends on the type of leg arrangement, -1 for knee and 1 for elbow.

Next, we describe the kinematics model of the ski. The ski has five DOFs and the lack of rolling freedom is determined by the HAA joint of the hind leg. Then we choose the foot tip of the hind leg (center of the hook hinge) as the coordinate origin O_S, and the direction is the same as the $\{B\}$. When the target pitch angles θ_P and yaw angles θ_Y of the ski are given, the attitude matrix of the ski is:

$$
\boldsymbol{R}_S = \operatorname{rot} Z(\theta_Y) \operatorname{rot} Y(\theta_P)
\tag{6}
$$

Then the position vector $\boldsymbol{P}_F$ of the spherical joint with respect to $\boldsymbol{O}_H = [O_{Hx}, O_{Hy}, O_{Hz}]^T$ can be obtained by the following equation.

$$
\boldsymbol{P}_F = \boldsymbol{R}_S \cdot \boldsymbol{O}_H \boldsymbol{P}_F + \boldsymbol{O}_H
\tag{7}
$$

where $\boldsymbol{O}_H \boldsymbol{P}_F = [L_S, 0, 0]^T$ and the L_S is the ski length.

By substituting the foot tip positions $\boldsymbol{O}_H$ and $\boldsymbol{P}_F$ into Eq. (3)–Eq. (5), the rotation angle of each joint can be calculated.

2.2   Control Strategy

The overall control architecture is depicted in Fig. 4. The operator provides high-level commands by giving a desired pulse width n controlled by the DFPS, the yaw angles γ_s of two skis relative to the body, and turning amplitude Δy. The input control command generates the desired joint torque after passing through modules such as trajectory planner and body balance controller, which is converted into current and sent to the joint driver. Meanwhile, the robot feeds back the joint information $\left\{\theta, \dot{\theta}\right\}$ and the body posture $\left\{\alpha, \beta, \gamma, \dot{\alpha}, \dot{\beta}, \dot{\gamma}\right\}$ detected by IMU to the controller module to participate in the control.

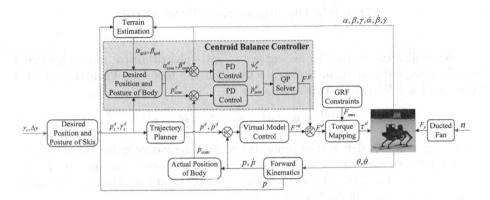

Fig. 4. Control architecture of SLSR

A. Trajectory Planner

Once the robot begins to slide with the thrust force F_P provided by the ducted fan, turning is achieved by controlling the lateral movement of the center of mass (COM) and the interaction between the ski's edge and the snow surface. This causes the ski to bend, ultimately resulting in a change of direction. As pictured in Fig. 5, when the COM of the body moves to the right, the contact force between the right ski and the snow surface increases, resulting in an increase in frictional resistance. This will make it easier for the ski to slide to the right. Similarly, if the COM of the body moves to the left, the robot will turn left.

When the target position and attitude command of two skis are given, the desired position of the foot tips connected to the skis can be calculated through Eq. (6) and Eq. (7). Then we apply PD control to track the target trajectory.

$$\begin{cases} a_{\text{cur}} = k_p \left(p_{\text{tgt}} - p_{\text{cur}} \right) + k_d \left(-v_{\text{cur}} \right) \\ v_{\text{cur}} = v_{\text{cur}} + a_{\text{cur}} dt \\ p_{\text{cur}} = p_{\text{cur}} + v_{\text{cur}} dt \end{cases} \tag{8}$$

where p_{tgt} is the tip target position given by the operator, p_{cur} and v_{cur} are the actual position and velocity of the foot tip, a_{cur} is the acceleration of tracking target trajectory, k_p and k_d represent the proportional and derivative gain coefficients, respectively. And dt is the control cycle time of the controller.

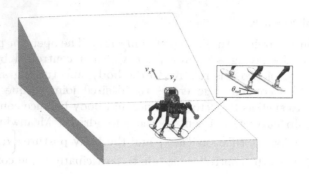

Fig. 5. Schematic diagram of SLSR turning right

We utilize the virtual model control (VMC) algorithm to impose a virtual spring damping system in three directions on the foot tip. Then the foot tip force vector $\boldsymbol{F}^{ref}$ can be expressed as

$$\boldsymbol{F}^{ref} = \boldsymbol{k}_{st}\left(\boldsymbol{p}^d - \boldsymbol{p}\right) + \boldsymbol{b}_{st}\left(\dot{\boldsymbol{p}}^d - \dot{\boldsymbol{p}}\right) \tag{9}$$

where $\boldsymbol{k}_{st}$ and $\boldsymbol{b}_{st}$ denote the proportional and derivative gains matrix of the stance leg reference tip force, both are diagonal matrices. And $\boldsymbol{p}^d$ and $\dot{\boldsymbol{p}}^d$ are desired position and velocity vector of the foot tip, $\boldsymbol{p}$ and $\dot{\boldsymbol{p}}$ are the actual position and velocity vector of the foot tip.

B. Body Balance Control

In our previous work [11], we used the CBC on a hexapod walking robot, and the robot can successfully pass through irregular terrain. Here we apply it to the SLSR. Since the contact between two skis and the snow is smooth, we assume that the thrust F_P generated by the DFPS has little influence on the body balance control.

As pictured in Fig. 4, the desired tip force $\boldsymbol{F}^d$ consists of two parts, one is the reference tip force $\boldsymbol{F}^{ref}$ calculated by the VMC, and the other is the feedforward force $\boldsymbol{F}^{ff}$ obtained by the CBC. Firstly, the linear acceleration $\ddot{\boldsymbol{p}}_{\text{com}}$ and the angular acceleration $\dot{\boldsymbol{w}}_b$ of the COM can be expressed as

$$\begin{cases} \ddot{\boldsymbol{p}}_{\text{com}} = \sum_{i=1}^{n} \frac{\boldsymbol{F}_i}{m} - \boldsymbol{g} \\ \dot{\boldsymbol{w}}_b = {}^{B}\boldsymbol{I}_b^{-1}\left(\sum_{i=1}^{n} \boldsymbol{r}_i \times \boldsymbol{F}_i\right) \end{cases} \tag{10}$$

where m is the total mass of the robot, $\boldsymbol{g}$ is the gravity acceleration vector, $\boldsymbol{F}_i$ is the ground reaction force (GRF) acting on the tip of the ith stance foot, n is the number of stance legs, ${}^{B}\boldsymbol{I}_b$ is the centroidal rotational inertia matrix with respect to $\{B\}$, $\boldsymbol{r}_i$ is the position vector from the COM of the body to the tip of the ith stance leg, and $\boldsymbol{r}_i \times \boldsymbol{F}_i$ represents the cross product of two terms.

Next, we compute the desired acceleration of the COM by PD control.

$$\begin{cases} \ddot{\boldsymbol{p}}_{\text{com}}^d = k_{pp}\left(\boldsymbol{p}_{\text{com}}^d - \boldsymbol{p}_{\text{com}}\right) + k_{dp}\left(\dot{\boldsymbol{p}}_{\text{com}}^d - \dot{\boldsymbol{p}}_{\text{com}}\right) \\ \dot{\boldsymbol{w}}_b^d = k_{pw}s\left(\boldsymbol{R}_d\boldsymbol{R}^T\right) + k_{dw}\left(\boldsymbol{w}_b^d - \boldsymbol{w}_b\right) \end{cases} \tag{11}$$

where p_{com}^d and p_{com} are the desired and actual position of the COM, respectively. $\dot{p}_{\text{com}}^d$ and $\dot{p}_{\text{com}}$ are the desired and actual velocity, respectively. k_{pp}, k_{pw} and k_{dp}, k_{dw} denote the proportional and derivative gains matrix, respectively, each of which is a diagonal matrix. R_d and R are the desired and actual rotation matrices of the body with respect to $\{W\}$, respectively. $s\left(R_d R^T\right)$ is a transformation symbol that converts the rotation matrix into the related vector.

Here we do not control the yaw angle of the body. Equation (10) is written in matrix form as

$$
\underbrace{\begin{bmatrix} I_{3\times3} & I_{3\times3} & \cdots & I_{3\times3} \\ r_1\times & r_2\times & \cdots & r_6\times \end{bmatrix}}_{A} \underbrace{\begin{bmatrix} F_1 \\ F_2 \\ \cdots \\ F_6 \end{bmatrix}}_{x} = \underbrace{\begin{bmatrix} m\left(\ddot{p}_{\text{com}}^d + g\right) \\ {}^W I_b \dot{w}_b^d \end{bmatrix}}_{b^d} \tag{12}
$$

where $I_{3\times3}$ is the identity matrix. $r_i\times$ represents the skew-symmetric matrix.

Finally, we can construct the following QP problem.

$$
\begin{aligned}
F^{ff} = \underset{f\in\mathbb{R}^{18}}{\arg\min} \left(Af - b_d\right)^T S\left(Af - b_d\right) + \delta\|f\|^2 \\
+\varphi\left\|f - f_{\text{prev}}^*\right\|^2 \\
\text{s.t.} \quad Cf \leq D
\end{aligned} \tag{13}
$$

where $f \in \mathbb{R}^{18}$ is the GRFs acting on the six stance feet. $S \in \mathbb{R}^{6\times6}$ is the coefficient matrices that control the rotational and translational motion priorities. δ and φ are the force normalization and solution filtration influence gain coefficients, respectively. C and D are force constraint matrices, which ensures that the QP problem is feasible. F^{ff} is the optimal foot force.

Then the mapping relationship between the virtual force F^d after GRF constraints at the foot tip and the joint torque τ^d can be written as

$$
\tau^d = J^T F^d \tag{14}
$$

where the force Jacobian matrix J can be obtained by taking the partial differential of the foot tip position expressed in Eq. (2), given by

$$
J = \begin{bmatrix} 0 & -L_2 c_2 - L_3 c_{23} & -L_3 c_{23} \\ -L_1 c_1 - L_2 s_1 c_2 - L_3 s_1 c_{23} & -L_2 c_1 s_2 - L_3 c_1 s_{23} & -L_3 c_1 s_{23} \\ -L_1 s_1 + L_2 c_1 c_2 + L_3 c_1 c_{23} & -L_2 s_1 s_2 - L_3 s_1 s_{23} & -L_3 s_1 s_{23} \end{bmatrix} \tag{15}
$$

C. Terrain Estimation

For the skiing robots, a slope estimation module is necessary for the control system. Specifically, based on sensor signals such as body posture angles and joint angles, the control system adjusts the robot's body posture in real-time to adapt to changes in the slope of the snow surface, thereby improving the efficiency and stability of sliding.

Based on multiple sensor data, the tip coordinates of the supporting leg connected to the skis in the world coordinate frame can be computed as P_j^W ($j = LH, LF, RH, RF$). Then, the slope equation of the robot can be written as

$$a\hat{x} + b\hat{y} + c\hat{z} + d = 0 \tag{16}$$

Equation (16) can be rewritten as

$$\frac{a}{d}\hat{x} + \frac{b}{d}\hat{y} + \frac{c}{d}\hat{z} = -1 \tag{17}$$

Substituting the tip coordinates P_j^W into Eq. (17), we can get

$$\boldsymbol{Ex} = -1 \tag{18}$$

where $\boldsymbol{E}$ is the coefficient matrix, $\boldsymbol{x}$ is the slope normal vector, which is equal to $(\frac{a}{d}, \frac{b}{d}, \frac{c}{d})$.

Due to the over-constraint of Eq. (18), there exists a least squares solution. The unit normal vector can be obtained by normalizing $\boldsymbol{x}$, which is denoted as $(\hat{a}, \hat{b}, \hat{c})$. Therefore, the slope can be expressed as

$$\begin{cases} \alpha_{\text{gnd}} = -asin(\hat{b}) \\ \beta_{\text{gnd}} = -asin(\hat{a}/cos(\alpha_{\text{gnd}})) \end{cases} \tag{19}$$

where α_{gnd} and β_{gnd} are the lateral and forward slopes of the terrain, respectively, with respect to the direction of the robot's motion.

3   Experiments

3.1   Skiing on the Flat Snow

As shown in Fig. 6, the SLSR was controlled by the operator to ski to the destination on a flat snow. The robot relied on DFPS to provide forward power and the two skis were parallel to reduce movement resistance.

Figure 7 was the intercepted time sequences, in which SLSR performed skiing actions such as acceleration, deceleration, and turning. The robot was in the acceleration phase when the thrust force F_P was always greater than the sliding friction force. Finally, SLSR returned to the vicinity of the starting point at 150 s by imitating the A-shaped braking actions, in which the front of two skis moved inward to generate greater resistance relying on the ski's inner edge. The whole process lasted about 150 s and the average sliding speed was 1.3 m/s.

The variation curve of the pulse width of the ducted fan, whose control range is from 1100 μs to 1900 μs, is pictured in Fig. 8(a). In the experiments, this pulse width value was converted to hexadecimal and sent to the DFPS via the USB serial communication protocol. Figure 8(b) shows that the orientation angle changes of the body are within $[-10°, 10°]$. The curve of the turning amplitude is depicted in Fig. 8(c), where a larger value indicates a greater turning angle. Figure 8(d) presents a comparison curve of the lateral position tracking performance of the RH leg.

Fig. 6. Experimental terrain for skiing on the flat snow

Fig. 7. The time sequence of SLSR skiing on the plane covers a sliding distance of approximately 200 m

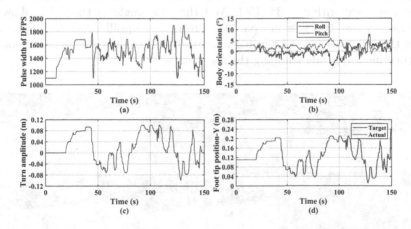

Fig. 8. (a) Pulse width of DFPS. (b) Body orientation. (c) Turn amplitude of the body. Left turn positive, right turn negative. (d) Lateral position tracking performance of the RH leg in the leg coordinate system.

3.2 Skiing on the Snow Slope

The terrain of the snow slope is illustrated in Fig. 9. Firstly, SLSR was controlled to slide down the slope, and then relied on the DFPS to slide up the slope. During the downhill process, the robot's own gravity provided the main power, and the operator controlled the yaw angles of two skis relative to the body to achieve acceleration and deceleration. Similarly, lateral movement of the body was controlled to achieve turning. Meanwhile, we can employ DFPS to accelerate downhill and improve the efficiency of task execution.

Fig. 9. Experimental terrain for skiing on the snow slope

Figure 10 and Fig. 11 are the intercepted time sequences of downhill and uphill, respectively. The variation curve of the pulse width of the ducted fan is pictured in Fig. 12(a). Compared with flat skiing, uphill requires not only overcoming friction but also gravity. Therefore, the ducted fan is required to provide greater thrust. Figure 12(b) shows that the orientation angle changes of the body are within $[-5°, 15°]$. And the yaw angle of the ski is shown in Fig. 12(c), where two skis are parallel during the uphill process. Figure 12(d) shows the change curve of turning amplitude. This shows that the robot can also turn flexibly while climbing the snow slope.

Fig. 10. The time sequences of SLSR skiing during downhill

Fig. 11. The time sequences of SLSR skiing during uphill

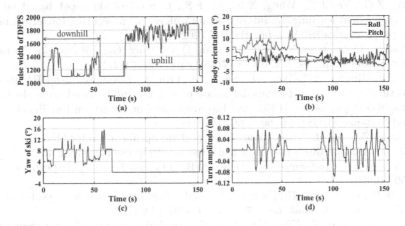

Fig. 12. (a) Pulse width of DFPS includes downhill and uphill. (b) Body orientation. (c) The yaw angle of the ski with respect to the body. (d) Turn amplitude of the body.

4   Conclusion

This paper introduces the design, modeling, control, and experimental verification of a six-legged robot equipped with two skis and a DFPS. With the help of the DFPS, we develop the ability of the SLSR to ski on both flat and snowy slopes, which SLSR can accelerate, decelerate, turn, and brake in various snow environments. Compared with the humanoid ski robots, the SLSR has higher stability and faster sliding speed.

In future work, we will develop a closed-loop speed control algorithm and conduct obstacle avoidance performance experiments utilizing the vision system. It is expected that the SLSR can be applied to ski resorts in the future to carry out tasks such as large-scale inspections and transportation of materials.

References

1. Yoneyama, T., Kagawa, H., Unemoto, M., Iizuka, T., Scott, N.W.: A ski robot system for qualitative modelling of the carved turn. Sports Eng. **11**(3), 131–141 (2009)
2. Iverach-Brereton, C., Postnikoff, B., Baltes, J., Hosseinmemar, A.: Active balancing and turning for alpine skiing robots. Knowl. Eng. Rev. **32** (2017)
3. Han, Y.H., Jeon, H.J., Cho, B.K.: Development of a humanoid robot for the 2018 ski robot challenge. Int. J. Precis. Eng. Manuf. **21**(7), 1309–1320 (2020)
4. Park, C., et al.: Carved turn control with gate vision recognition of a humanoid robot for giant slalom skiing on ski slopes. Sensors **22**(3), 816 (2022)
5. Lahajnar, L., Kos, A., Nemec, B.: Skiing robot-design, control, and navigation in unstructured environment. Robotica **27**(4), 567–577 (2009)
6. Wu, Z.G., Ye, J.T., Wang, X.R., Li, F.S.: Control of ski robot based on deep reinforcement learning. In: International Conference on Security, Pattern Analysis, and Cybernetics (SPAC), pp. 211–215 (2021)
7. Gao, F., Li, S., Gao, Y., Qi, C.K., Tian, Q.Y., Yang, G.Z.: Robots at the Beijing 2022 winter olympics. Sci. Robot. **7**(65), eabq0785 (2022)
8. Liu, B., Huang, Z.F., Wei, J.P., Shi, C.Y., Ota, J., Zhang, Y.: Jet-HR1: stepping posture optimization for bipedal robot over large ditch based on a ducted-fan propulsion system. In: IEEE/RSJ International Conference on Intelligent Robots and Systems (IROS), pp. 6010–6015 (2018)
9. Huang, Z.F., et al.: Three-dimensional posture optimization for biped robot stepping over large ditch based on a ducted-fan propulsion system. In: IEEE/RSJ International Conference on Intelligent Robots and Systems (IROS), pp. 3591–3597 (2020)
10. Li, Y.H., et al.: Jet-HR2: a flying bipedal robot based on thrust vector control. IEEE Robot. Automat. Lett. **7**(2), 4590–4597 (2022)
11. Yin, Y.P., Zhao, Y., Xiao, Y.G., Gao, F.: Footholds optimization for legged robot walking on complex terrain. Front. Mech. Eng. **18**(2), 26 (2023)

Structure Design and Fall Trajectory Planning of an Electrically Driven Humanoid Robot

Weilong Zuo[1,2], Junyao Gao[1,2(✉)], Jingwei Cao[1,2], Tian Mu[1,2], and Yuanzhen Bi[1,2]

[1] School of Mechanical Engineering, Beijing Institute of Technology, Beijing, China
gaojunyao@bit.edu.cn
[2] Beijing Advanced Innovation Center for Intelligent Robots and Systems, Beijing, China

Abstract. People have designed many different kinds of humanoid robots, but few of them have been applied to real life. On the one hand, the robot has insufficient movement ability and poor flexibility; on the other hand, there are no effective structures that can effectively buffer the impact caused by falling. Therefore, it is very important to design a robot which can detect when a fall will occur, what kinds of protective actions will be taken after a fall, and most importantly to resist the impact of the fall. In this work we present a novel humanoid robot whose design was based on the principles of bionics, high stiffness, light weight, and multipoint protections. Based on capture point theory and 3D-LIPM model, the robot can detect when it would fall down and what protective actions it would take after falling. It was verified in the actual robot, including falling, standing after a fall in outdoor environment. The experiment results show that the proposed Falling-Crawling robot can resist the impact force caused by falling.

Keywords: Humanoid Robot · Fall · Capture Point · 3D-LIPM

1 Introduction

The purpose of designing humanoid robot is to help or replace people complete various complex tasks. However, due to the complexity of the human environment, there is a risk that the robot will fall down when performing tasks. Many fall recovery methods have proposed such as modulate ZMP, regulate angular momentum and take a step forward [1–3]. However, due to the complexity of the human environment, the above methods can only work with weak disturbance, once the disturbance exceeds the adjustable area, the robot will inevitably fall. During DARPA Robotics Challenge, many robot parts were damaged because of falling and could not continue to complete the following competitions [4]. Therefore, it is very important to design a robot that can resist falls and make protective actions quickly when falling is inevitable.

To counter with the challenge, many scholars have designed various robots with protectors, such as Kajita introduced an HRP-2 robot with 30 degrees of freedom. The robot imitates the movement of UKEMI in judo to reduce the impact of falling [5]. Yohei Kakiuchi et al. have installed hard points on the possible collision points of the robot [6], which makes the robot look like a man with shackles and this design limit the working

© The Author(s), under exclusive license to Springer Nature Singapore Pte Ltd. 2023
H. Yang et al. (Eds.): ICIRA 2023, LNAI 14271, pp. 481–493, 2023.
https://doi.org/10.1007/978-981-99-6495-6_41

space, Nguyen et al. [7] installed protectors on the legs of the biped robot, since the robot has only the lower body, its actual effect cannot be seen when it falls. Authors in [8] focused on a wearable airbag developed for human safety, after falling the airbag can protect the neck, back and bottom of the robot. Meanwhile the author points out that there is deformation of the neck pitch joint. While in [9] a backpack installed on the back of the robot, when the robot falls, try to fall on its backpack. There is a risk in this method, when there are some valuable assets behind the robot, it is easy to cause the property losses if still continued.

About the fall trajectory planning and control of humanoid robot, [10] and [11] presented an algorithm to minimize the damage of humanoid falls by utilizing multiple contact points, but they verify it on a small humanoid robot. Meanwhile, many methods [12, 13] and [14] use the simplified model to obtain the falling trajectory of the robot, from their experiments we can see that the robot falls on the soft cushion, which can't convince the actual impact resistance effect. In [15], Sam et al. changed the PD parameters of the robot's arms after a fall, so that the robot has a certain flexibility when it collides with the ground, but due to the large reduction ratio and joint stiffness of the robot, it may cause great damage to the robot arm. Inspired by humanoid falling, [16] and [17] try to use biomechanical method simulate the fall of robot. In order to enable robots to fall autonomously, many researchers began to adopt reinforcement learning methods. Article [18] uses parametric modeling, and article [19] uses actor critical methods. However, these training methods require a lot of experiments, which limit the realizing in real humanoid robot.

According to the collision law $F = mv/t$, in order to reduce the impact force generated by the landing, the robot can increase the collision time or reduce the landing speed. In this article, we added corresponding protective materials to the robot for increasing the collision time, and planned the robot's fall trajectory for reducing the landing speed. Finally, fall experiments were carried out in outdoor environments, which proves our proposed Falling-Crawling robot has a relatively strong anti-fall ability. The main contributions of this paper are as follows:

(1) According to the principles of bionics, high stiffness and light weight, and multipoint protections, we design a new type of humanoid robot.
(2) The capture point and 3D-LIPM methods were used to detect when the robot will fall and what kinds of protection action the robot will take when the fall is unavoidable respectively.
(3) The proposed method was verified on the Falling-Crawling robot, and the experimental results show that the robot can resist the impact force of falling.

The remainder of the paper is organized as follows, Sect. 2 introduces the structure of our proposed humanoid robot, Sect. 3 introduces our methods, Sect. 4 introduces our simulation experiments of the robot falling forward and backward, as well as verified it in the outdoor environment, Sect. 5 concludes the paper and introduces the future work.

2 Humanoid Robot

Many humanoid robots are still in the laboratory stage, partly due to the lack of effective protection structure when they falling, so it is very important to design a structure that can resist the impact of falling. According to the research [8], the maximum acceleration generated by its fall impact exceeds 100g. If we can't effectively resist the impact when landing, it will bring huge security risks to the robot. Many methods use the landing compliance control or QP optimization to mitigate the impact, but since the fall occurs instantaneously, the effect of using above methods were minimal. Compared these, designing a humanoid robot with impact-resistant protection structure and protective actions can more effectively buffer the adverse effects of falls. Considering the short-comings which introduced above, we designed the Falling-Crawling robot according to the following principles.

- Bionic principle.
- High rigidity and lightweight principle.
- Mechanism's protective ability in collision principle.

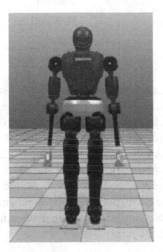

Fig. 1. Falling-Crawling robot platform. The left picture represents virtual map, the right picture represents physical map.

2.1 Bionic Principle

"Bionic principle" means that robot should be similar to humans in shape and function, and their size, mass distribution, degree of freedom distribution and limb motion range need to be consistent with the characteristics of the human body [19]. Figure 1 is a humanoid robot which we designed according to the height of an adult male, it is about 170[cm] tall and 50[kg] in weight. It is driven by motors and has a total of 22 D.O.F, including 4 D.O.F. for the arms, 2 D.O.F. for the torso and 6 D.O.F. for the legs. An inertial measurement unit (IMU) was installed on the head of the robot, a force sensor was installed on the ankle of the robot respectively, a control board was placed in the pleural. The connecting rod between each joint is made of titanium magnesium alloy material. Regarding the design of the waist joint of the robot, we use the model of the motor with the ball screw. In order to maintain the stability of the robot when walking, we installed a relatively larger soleplate on the robot's feet. Due to the relatively large impact on the head during the fall, we printed the robot's head with metal. Besides these, the basic specifications size and quality parameters of each connecting rod were shown in Table 1.

Table 1. The parameters of our robot.

Parameters	size	Mass
Thigh	361[mm]	7.36[kg]
Shank	330[mm]	5.12[kg]
Boom	350[mm]	4.15[kg]
Jib	360[mm]	2.30[kg]
others	------	31.07[kg]
Total mass	------	50[kg]

When the joints of the robot are overloaded, the traditional design structure lacks the fault tolerance and adaptability to the external high impact disturbance, which easily leads to the damage of the joints of the robot. Inspired by the phenomenon that the human body's joint will dislocate when it collides with a strong impact force, we designed a joint protection, as shown in Fig. 2.e and Fig. 2.f. A roller and a positioning slot are installed at the joint of the robot. When the robot works normally, the roller and the positioning slot work normally. Once the external impact force exceeds the threshold, the roller and the positioning slot produce relative rotation, the corresponding joint input end (motor) and output end are separated, thus showing a state similar to human dislocation, unloading the excessive impact force to protect the robot's joint.

2.2 High Rigidity and Lightweight Principle

"High rigidity and lightweight principle" mean that the robot body structure and each joint connection part should have a good rigidity and minimal transmission gap. In order to make the robot have strong flexibility and agility, its main structure also needs to reduce its own weight and moment of inertia. Relying on this principle, we have completed the structural design of the humanoid robot. The robot's arms, legs, upper body are processed with titanium magnesium alloy, which greatly reduce the weight of the humanoid robot. Meanwhile, based on the principle of human bionics, we have completed an integrated design to make it easy to maintain. As shown in Fig. 3, the robot's thigh and calf are all hollowed out, Fig. 3.a and Fig. 3.c represent the robot's thigh and calf respectively. For the convenience of viewing, we divide them, as shown

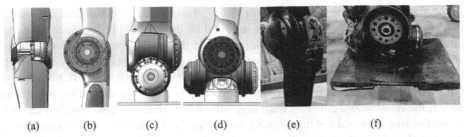

Fig. 2. Bionic passive clutch joint. (a) Front view of knee joint. (b) Side view of knee joint. (c) Front view of ankle joint. (d) Side view of ankle joint. (e) Physical of knee joint. (f) Physical of ankle joint.

in Fig. 3.b and Fig. 3.d. In the actual robot structure, as shown in Fig. 3.e and Fig. 3.f, it is an integrated structure design, which on the one hand can reduce the complexity of the robot circuit routing, on the other hand can expand the working space of the robot. Similarly, the design of arms still follows this principle.

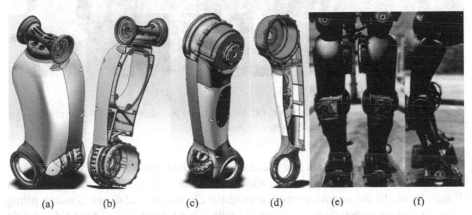

Fig. 3. Robot hollowed out parts. (a)Three-dimensional view of thigh. (b) Section view of thigh. (c) Three-dimensional view of shank. (d) Section view of shank. (e) Front view of legs. (f) Side view of legs.

2.3 Mechanism's Protective Ability in Collision Principle

"Mechanism's protective ability in collision principle" means that when the robot collided with the ground, important parts of the body should have the function of self-protection. Although the above two methods can reduce the impact force when robot falling, in the actual fall experiment we found that only relying on the first two design principles, the waist and thigh of the robot always broken.

Considering that in daily life, humans always wear a thick protective clothing to resist the impact of falling, so we also put a protective clothing on the robot, as shown in

Fig. 4.a, the protective material is made of silica gel and filled with foam material inside. Figure 4.b is a buffer block which was installed on the knee joint. Its appearance has different shapes of bulges, which not only cushion the impact force when landing, but also increase the friction between the block and the ground. This block is very important, because when doing the crawling experiment, we found that once this buffer block was removed, the robot would reverse in the crawling process, when this buffer block was added, the robot would crawl forward normally. Meanwhile, we also installed an oval protective ring at the waist of the robot, as shown Fig. 4.c. On the one hand, this protective ring can slow down the impact force caused by the collision between the robot and the ground, on the other hand, it plays a very important role in the standing of the robot, which will be introduced later. Except these, many rubber pads that are consistent with the arm structure were installed at the upper and lower arms of our robot, as shown Fig. 4.d, which plays a very important role in the process of side fall of the robot.

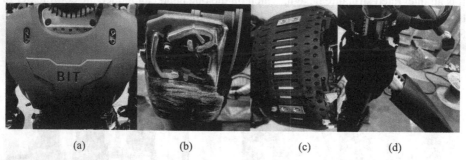

| (a) | (b) | (c) | (d) |

Fig. 4. Key protection positions of robot. (a) An integrated protective coat. (b) Buffer block. (c) Protective ring. (d) Lower arm cushion rubber pad.

During the experiment, we also found that when the robot falls, the PC104's system always crashed, the Wi-Fi communication interrupted and the IMU readings did not change. Since the above devices are placed in the chest of the robot, we consider filling some cushioning materials in it. Compared with what have used, we found that filling the chest with plastic cushion foam pad can effectively buffer the impact. The above-mentioned key protections and corresponding protective materials are obtained through repeated experiments, which have very important reference value.

3   The Fall of Robot

The fall motion of the robot are mainly divided into three parts: falling detection, falling plan, and stand after falling [21, 22], as shown Fig. 5. About the falling detection, some authors use machine learning methods, such as SVM, K-means [23, 24], some use the ZMP bias estimation methods [25]. In this article, we judge whether the robot will fall according to the values obtained by IMU and the method of Capture Point [26]. When the robot walks, the IMU which was installed on the head reads the orientation of the robot at all time. Once the robot has the risk of falling, it can judge which orientation it falls according the reading of IMU.

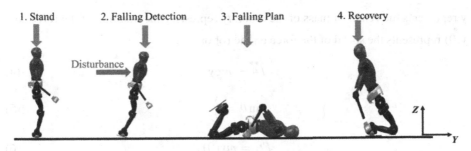

Fig. 5. Fall of humanoid robot.

Inverted pendulum model is a model which often used to simplify humanoid robot motion, since the direction of the robot's fall during walking is uncertain, it can be simplified as a 3D-LIPM, as shown Fig. 6. The dynamics of the model is given by Eqs. (1), and we study the sagittal plane of the robot's motion, so we need to we need to define a constraint surface as shown in Eq. (2), where the k represent the slope.

$$M\ddot{x} = (\frac{x}{r})f$$

$$M\ddot{y} = (\frac{y}{r})f \tag{1}$$

$$M\ddot{z} = (\frac{z}{r})f - Mg$$

$$z = z_c + ky \tag{2}$$

By Eqs. (1) and (2) and the condition that the acceleration of the center of mass is perpendicular to the normal vector of the constraining surface, we can obtain Eq. (3), Where $x(0)$, $y(0)$ respectively represent the initial position of the robot in x direction and y direction, and $(\dot{x}(0), \dot{y}(0))$ respectively represent the initial speed of the robot in x direction and y direction, g represents the gravity, z_c represents the height of the robot's centroid, which is a constant.

$$x(t) = x(0)\cosh wt + \frac{\dot{x}(0)}{w}\sinh wt$$

$$y(t) = y(0)\cosh wt + \frac{\dot{y}(0)}{w}\sinh wt \tag{3}$$

$$z(t) = kx(0)\cosh wt + k\frac{\dot{y}(0)}{w}\sinh wt + z_c$$

$$w = \sqrt{\frac{g}{z_c}}$$

Taking the forward fall of the robot as an example, the moment balance equation is established in the yz plane, as shown in Eq. (4) - Eq. (6), where I represents the inertia of the robot, F represents the force acting on the robot, L represents the height of the robot, y represents the center of mass of the robot, t_1 represents the duration of the force, and $\dot{y}(0)$ represents the speed of the force on the robot.

$$I\ddot{\theta} = mgy \tag{4}$$

$$\sin\theta = \frac{y}{L} \tag{5}$$

$$Ft_1 = m\dot{y}(0) \tag{6}$$

Let the initial position of the robot's center of mass be the origin, that is $(x(0), y(0) = (0, 0))$, simultaneous Eq. (3), (4), (5), and Eq. (6), then can get

$$\theta_{ref} = \arcsin\sqrt{1 - \frac{mgL^{-\frac{2}{3}}}{I}} \tag{7}$$

θ_{ref} represents the critical angle value when the robot is at risk of falling, since we adopt a simplified model, there will be some deviations from the actual situation, so we need to set a deviation angle ε, as shown Eq. (8). The angle θ_{real} was obtained according to the IMU which was installed in the head.

$$\theta_{real} \geq \theta_{ref} + \varepsilon \tag{8}$$

When the robot falling, we default that the foot plate is located at the origin, and the equation of the center of mass has been solved above, which can be directly brought into formula (9) to calculate the trajectory of each joint angle, where f^{-1} represents the inverse kinematics of the robot.

$$q_i = f^{-1}(P_{com}, P_{ankle})i = 1, 2, 3, 4, 5, 6 \tag{9}$$

In here, because the arm joint of the robot has relatively small impact resistance, we refer to the atlas fall video, once the robot is about to fall, the arm immediately swings back or forward.

4   Simulation and Experiments

In order to prove that our robot has strong impact resistance, we simulated the robot in CoppeliaSim software. As shown in Fig. 7, at 0.5 s, we gave the robot an impact force of 300N, last for 1 s. At this time, the robot detected that a fall was about to occur, so it immediately made a protective action according to the method described in 3. When it falling, the joints of the robot's legs start to move and the body starts to shrink, the arms of the upper body swing backward until the head touches the ground completely. Because our head is made of metal materials, there is no need to worry about the damage to the head. Beside this protective action, we did the simulation of the robot falling forward freely, Fig. 8 shows the motion of the robot. Similarly, when a backward fall was detected, the robot takes fall back protection action, as shown in Fig. 9. Figure 10 shows it falling backward freely.

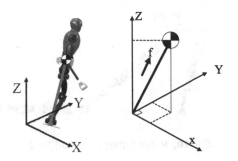

Fig. 6. 3D-LIPM model.

Fig. 7. Robot falling forward with protective action.

Fig. 8. Robot falling forward freely.

Fig. 9. Robot falling backward with protective action.

As shown in Fig. 11, here we regard the landing speed of the robot as the impact force on the ground and compared two different motions, wherein the red color indicates that the protection action was not adopted, and the blue color indicates that the protection action was adopted. It can be seen that when the robot performs an unprotected action, at 1.125 s, the robot hits the ground, and the impact speed is 5.79 m/s, the angular velocity is about 526.1°/s; when the robot performs a protective action, at 0.79 s, it hits the ground,

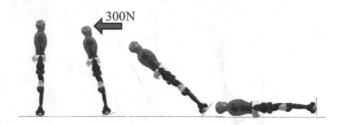

Fig. 10. Robot falling backward freely.

and the impact speed is 3.427 m/s, and the angular velocity is about 275.4°/s. Through comparison, it is found that the speed of the robot with protective action is reduced by 40%. The small protrusions after 1 s indicate that the robot has an elastic collision with the ground.

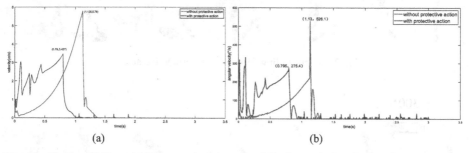

Fig. 11. Forward falling. (a) The speed of the robot falls forward. (b) The angular speed of the robot falls forward.

When the robot is in free fall backwards, it can be seen from Fig. 12 that at 0.97 s, the robot touches the ground with a landing speed of 5.795m/s and an angular velocity of 714.9°/s; when the robot falls with protective action, the landing speed is 5.52m/s, and the angular velocity is 273°/s. Compared with the forward fall, the speed of the robot is not much reduced when it falls backwards, about 4.75%, but the angular velocity is reduced more, about 61.8%. Similarly, the small protrusions after 1 s indicated that falling backward also has an elastic collision with the ground. Through the above comparison, it can be found that the materials which we choose for robot key protection points and planning of protection actions can effectively alleviate the impact force generated by robot landing. Which can prove that the trajectory planned by 3D-LIPM can effectively reduce the impact force of the robot landing.

In order to verify that our theory and the actual model of the robot can complete the fall motion in the outdoor environment, we did some fall experiments. In the experiment, the robot keeps standing until someone give it a push, when detect it was going to fall, the robot did the right protective action quickly, as shown in Fig. 13. (1) ~ (5). After completing the protective action, we hope that the robot can stand up to demonstrate the effectiveness of our structure and method. Take the front fall of the robot as an example,

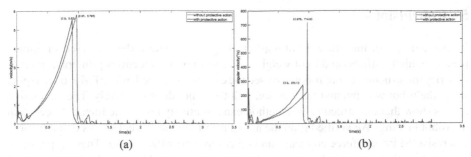

(a)   (b)

Fig. 12. Backward falling. (a) The speed of the robot falls backward. (b) The angular speed of the robot falls backward.

as shown Fig. 13. (6) ~ (10). Firstly, the arm is stretched forward, and the hip joint of the thigh is rotated backward, which drives the body to rise upward. Secondly, the arm is stretched to the longest point, and the hip joint drives the upper body to lean back. Then the knee joint and the ankle joint are used to complete the standing. We also make a test of back fall in the outdoor environment, as shown in Fig. 14. Similar to the forward fall, we gave a back push to the robot, and it take protective action immediately after detecting the fall, as shown in Fig. 14. (1) ~ (5). Figure 14 (6) ~ (10) represent that the robot makes use of the arm to driver the center of mass forward, after reaching the stable position of ZMP, it began to use the hip joint drive the upper body forward, finally use the knee joint and ankle joint to complete the standing.

Fig. 13. The front fall test in the outdoor. (1) ~ (5) represent when the robot falls down, it starts to take protective action, (6) ~ (10) represent the robot stand up after falling.

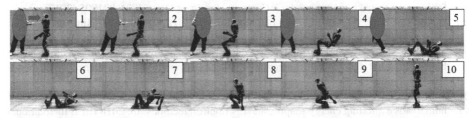

Fig. 14. The back fall test in the outdoor. (1) ~ (5) represent when the robot falls down, it starts to take protective action, (6) ~ (10) represent the robot stand up after falling.

5 Conclusions

In this article, we introduce a Falling-Crawling robot whose design based on bionic principle, high stiffness and light weight, and multipoint protections principle. In order to verify the structure of our robot, we used the capture point and 3D-LIPM model to plan when the robot will fall and what action will the robot do respectively. The simulation results show that our structure and method can effectively buffer the impact force when the robot landing. We verified it on the actual robot, and the effect shows that our robot can resist the impact force and can stand up completely after falling. These experiment results show that our robot has strong environmental adaptability. In the future, we will research the fall protection movement of humanoid robots in complex environments, which may contribute to help us design a better robot.

References

1. Nashner, L.M., Mccollum, G.: The organization of human postural movements, a formal basis and experimental synthesis. The Behavioral and Brain Science **8**(01), 135 (1985)
2. Maki, B.E., Mcilroy, W.E.: The role of limb movements in maintaining upright stance: The "change-in-support" strategy. Phys. Ther. **77**(5), 488–507 (1997)
3. Pratt, J., Carff, J., Drakunov, S., Goswami, A.: Capture point: A step toward humanoid push recovery. In: 2006 6th IEEE-RAS International Conference on Humanoid Robots (2007)
4. Atkeson, C.G., Babu, B., Banerjee, N., Berenson, D., Xinjilefu, X.: No falls, no resets: Reliable humanoid behavior in the darpa robotics challenge. In: IEEE-RAS International Conference on Humanoid Robots (2015)
5. Fujiwara, K., Kanehiro, F., Kajita, S., et al.: UKEMI: falling motion control to minimize damage to biped humanoid robot. Intelligent Robots and Systems. IEEE (2002)
6. Kakiuchi, Y., Kamon, M., Shimomura, N., Yukizaki, S., Inaba, M.: Development of life-sized humanoid robot platform with robustness for falling down, long time working and error occurrence. In: 2017 IEEE/RSJ International Conference on Intelligent Robots and Systems (IROS)
7. Nguyen, K., Kojio, Y., Noda, S., Sugai, F., Inaba, M.: Dynamic fall recovery motion generation on biped robot with shell protector. IEEE Robotics and Automation Letters **6**(4), 6741–6748 (2021)
8. Kajita, S., et al.: Impact acceleration of falling humanoid robot with an airbag. In: IEEE-RAS International Conference on Humanoid Robots, pp. 637–643 (2016)
9. Lee, S.H., Goswami, A.: Fall on backpack: Damage minimization of humanoid robots by falling on targeted body segments. J. Comput. Nonlinear Dyna. **8**(2), 021005 (2013)
10. Ha, S., Liu, C.K.: Multiple contact planning for minimizing damage of humanoid falls. In: 2015 IEEE/RSJ International Conference on Intelligent Robots and Systems (IROS) (2015)
11. Yun, S.K., Goswami, A.: Tripod fall: Concept and experiments of a novel approach to humanoid robot fall damage reduction. In: IEEE International Conference on Robotics Automation (2014)
12. Subburaman, R., Lee, J., Caldwell, D.G., Tsagarakis, N.G.: Online falling-over control of humanoids exploiting energy shaping and distribution methods. In: 2018 IEEE International Conference on Robotics and Automation (2018)
13. Fujiwara, K., Kajita, S., Harada, K., Kaneko, K., Hirukawa, H.: Towards an optimal falling motion for a humanoid robot. In: IEEE-RAS International Conference on Humanoid Robots, pp. 524-529 (2006)

14. Li, Q., Chen, X., Zhou, Y., Yu, Z., Zhang, W., Huang, Q.: A minimized falling damage method for humanoid robots. Int. J. Adva. Robo. Sys. **14**, 172988141772801 (2017)
15. Samy, V., Caron, S., Bouyarmane, K., Kheddar, A.: Post-impact adaptive compliance for humanoid falls using predictive control of a reduced model. In: 2017 IEEE-RAS 17th International Conference on Humanoid Robotics (Humanoids), pp. 655–660 (2017)
16. Meng, L., Yu, Z., Chen, X., Zhang, W., Liu, H.: A falling motion control of humanoid robots based on biomechanical evaluation of falling down of humans. In: 2015 IEEE-RAS 15th International Conference on Humanoid Robots (Humanoids) (2015)
17. Kajita, S., Sakaguchi, T., Nakaoka, S., Morisawa, M., Kanehiro, F.: Quick squatting motion generation of a humanoid robot for falling damage reduction. In: 2017 IEEE International Conference on Cyborg and Bionic Systems (2017)
18. Fujiwara, K., Kanehiro, F., Kajita, S., Kaneko, K., Yokoi, K., Hirukawa, H.: Ukemi: falling motion control to minimize damage to biped humanoid robot. In: Intelligent Robots and Systems, 2521–2526 (2002)
19. Kumar, V.C., Ha, S., Liu, C.K.: Learning a unified control policy for safe falling (2017)
20. Huang, Q., Huang., Y., Yu., Z.: Fundamental Theory and Technology of Humanoid Robots. Beijing Institute of Technology Press, Beijing (2021)
21. Kalyanakrishnan, S., Goswami, A.: Learning to predict humanoid fall. Int. J. Humano. Robo. **8**(2), 245–273 (2011)
22. Fujiwara, K., Kanehiro, F., Saito, H., Kajita, S., Hirukawa, H.: Falling motion control of a humanoid robot trained by virtual supplementary tests. In: IEEE International Conference on Robotics Automation (2004)
23. Kim, J.J., Kim, Y.J., Lee, J.J.: A machine learning approach to falling detection and avoidance for biped robots. In: Sice Conference 2011, pp. 562-567. Tokyo, Japan (2011)
24. Nho, Y.H., Lim, J.G., Kwon, D.S.: Cluster-analysis-based user-adaptive fall detection using fusion of heart rate sensor and accelerometer in a wearable device. IEEE Access **8**, 40389–40401 (2020)
25. Di, P., et al.: Fall detection for the elderly using a cane robot based on ZMP estimation. In: 2013 International Symposium on Micro-NanoMechatronics and Human Science (MHS) IEEE, pp. 1–6 (2013)

HexGuide: A Hexapod Robot for Autonomous Blind Guidance in Challenging Environments

Zelin Wang, Limin Yang, Xu Liu, Tenghui Wang, and Feng Gao[✉]

School of Mechanical Engineering, Shanghai Jiao Tong University,
Shanghai, China
zlwang_97@sjtu.edu.cn, gaofengsjtu@gmail.com

Abstract. In this paper we present the HexGuide, a hexapod guide robot designed to provide guidance to visually impaired people in challenging environments. Firstly, we propose an improved A* path planning algorithm that incorporates an artificial potential field (APF) factor into the evaluation function and optimizes the turning point to generate a safe and collision-free initial path. Moreover, we propose a Model Predictive Control (MPC)-based motion tracking controller for path tracking and a locomotion control model for the robot to manage the swing of each single leg. Furthermore, we develop an obstacle avoidance strategy and a traffic light recognition method for the robot. The experimental results show that HexGuide can excellently accomplish the task of guiding visually impaired people in challenging environments such as airports and intersections.

Keywords: Hexapod robot · Blind Guidance · Model predictive control

1 Introduction

According to the World Health Organization, at least 200 million people worldwide suffer from near or far vision disorders [1]. It is expected that population growth and aging will increase the risk of visual impairments for more people. The concept of a guide robot is derived from the utilization of guide dogs to assist individuals with visual impairments [2]. These mobile robots are designed to perceive and analyze their surroundings, generate a navigational path, and provide the user with real-time feedback [3]. The user then follows the robot through means such as tactile [4] or voice [5,6] feedback information. Based on their physical composition, guide robots are broadly classified into two categories: wheeled guide robots and legged guide robots.

Kulyukin et al. [7] proposed a wheeled robot that could effectively navigate through indoor environments. The robot utilized laser rangefinder and radio frequency identification (RFID) sensors to detect its surroundings and provide an accurate representation of the environment. Iwan Ulrich [8] designed a human-machine interactive blind robot that allowed users to interact with the robot

This work was supported by the National Key Research and Development Program of China under Grants 2021YFF0307900 and 2021YFF0306202.

using a lightweight guiding cane. The robot incorporated ultrasound sensors that detected surrounding obstacles and determined a safe direction for the user to proceed. Capi [9] developed a blind robot tailored to indoor environments. The robot was equipped with a LiDAR sensor that utilized clustering algorithms to identify obstacles in the environment.

The utilization of legged robots for blind guidance has been limited due to the complexity of their control systems, leading to a scarcity of literature in this area. Anxing Xiao et al. [10] developed a quadruped guiding robot dog that incorporated a LiDAR sensor for robot localization and a depth camera for human pose detection. NSK proposed a robot guide dog [11] that featured wheels at both ends of the dog's legs. The robot primarily used these wheels for movement, while mechanical legs enabled it to climb obstacles such as stairs. However, they do not perform guidance work in challenging environments.

This paper presents HexGuide, a guidance robot designed to assist blind people in challenging environments. To overcome the limitations of traditional path planning algorithms, an improved A* path planning algorithm is proposed by incorporating an artificial potential field factor into the evaluation function and optimizing the turning point of the path using greedy algorithms. In order to track the desired path, a motion tracking controller based on model predictive control has been developed. Additionally, a locomotion control model for the robot has been proposed to plan the swing of each leg. This paper also introduces a dynamic obstacle avoidance strategy and a traffic light identification method. Experimental results demonstrate that HexGuide can effectively guide blind people in challenging environments.

2   Robot Overview

2.1   Robot Structure

The guiding robot HexGuide is a hexapod robot, which is highly flexible and exhibits superior motion performance. As shown in Fig. 1, HexGuide has six legs, each having three degrees of freedom, and can be considered as a parallel mechanism with six support chains. To enhance its stability, HexGuide employs a tripod gait that ensures the center of gravity remains within the triangle. The robot's legs are divided into two groups, with one group lifting and stepping while the other group drives the robot's body movement until the first group lands, after which the two groups alternate. Inverse kinematics is used to obtain the movement of each joint of the leg.

Regarding the hardware, HexGuide has 18 motors, with 3 motors per leg. Each motor's rotation angle is measured by an encoder, resulting in a total of 18 encoders. The robot is also equipped with an inertial measurement unit (IMU) for body attitude measurement and localization. The tail of the robot has a retractable blind stick, which is used to guide blind people. In terms of perception, HexGuide is equipped with an Intel RealSense D435i depth camera and a RoboSense LiDAR.

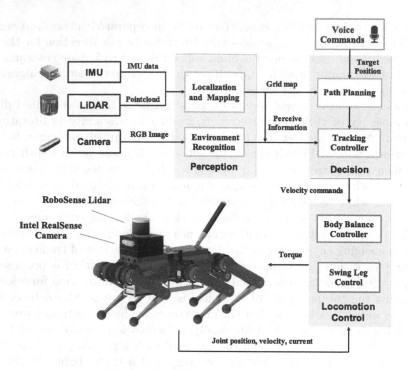

Fig. 1. Robot System Specification.

2.2   Robot Framework

The present study delineates the software framework of the robot into three distinct layers, namely the perception layer, decision layer, and locomotion control layer. As shown in Fig. 1, perception layer involves mapping the working environment using LiDAR point clouds and IMU data, alongside estimating the robot's pose on the map. Additionally, RGB camera is employed for environment recognition, such as traffic information.

In decision layer, the robot first transforms speech information into target position through a speech recognition module based on the user's voice commands. Subsequently, the robot plans a feasible path based on the previously established grid map, employing a tracking controller to track the path and steer clear of obstacles in real-time. Ultimately, the robot conveys velocity commands to the locomotion layer.

The locomotion control layer plans the robot's body pose through a body balance controller based on velocity commands, regulates the motion trajectory of the swinging leg through the swing leg controller, and conveys torque values for each joint. Furthermore, based on the robot's joint position, speed, and current values, feedback is obtained to determine if the robot has finished its motion cycle and if it has come into contact with the ground.

3   Method

3.1   Path Planning and Tracking

A popular heuristic path algorithm, A*, is often employed due to its speedy computation. However, the paths generated by this algorithm are in close proximity to obstacles and contain numerous turning points. In response to these limitations, we propose an improved version of the A* path planning algorithm, designed to enable robots to generate safer and smoother paths.

Firstly, we add the potential field cost to the evaluation function of the A * algorithm:

$$f(n) = g(n) + h(n) + p(n) \tag{1}$$

$$p(n) = -F_{rep}(n) \cdot X(n) \tag{2}$$

where $g(n)$ is the cost of moving from the initial node to node n, and $h(n)$ is the cost of the estimated optimal path from node n to the target point. The Manhattan distance can generally be used for $h(n)$. $p(n)$ refers to the potential cost, while F_{rep} denotes the potential force of the potential field and $X(n)$ represents the directional vector from the last node to the current node. The potential cost increases as the robot approaches obstacles. Incorporating this cost function is intended to find a feasible path while simultaneously minimizing the proximity of the robot to obstacles. The repulsive potential function and repulsive force function are defined as follows:

$$U_{rep}(n) = \begin{cases} \frac{1}{2}\xi_r \left(\frac{1}{\rho(n,n_{obs})} - \frac{1}{\rho_r^*}\right)^2 & \rho(n,n_{obs}) \le \rho_r^* \\ 0 & \rho(n,n_{obs}) > \rho_r^* \end{cases} \tag{3}$$

$$F_{rep}(n) = -\nabla U_{rep}(n)$$
$$= \begin{cases} \xi_r \left(\frac{1}{\rho(n,n_{obs})} - \frac{1}{\rho_r^*}\right)\frac{n_{obs}-n}{[\rho(n,n_{obs})]^3} & \rho(n,n_{obs}) \le \rho_r^* \\ 0 & \rho(n,n_{obs}) > \rho_r^* \end{cases} \tag{4}$$

where ξ_r is the repulsive coefficient, $\rho(n,n_{obs})$ is the Euclidean distance from the current position to the nearest obstacle, and ρ_r^* is the radius of the repulsive potential field. $n_{obs} - n$ is the vector from the current position to the nearest obstacle. Following the proposed improvement, the potential field cost p (n) during the heuristic search procedure undergoes a surge as the node nears the obstacle. Consequently, the search point can stay away from obstacles. Additionally, by varying the parameter ξ_r, the potential field cost can be retained at a comparable order of magnitude, and the path can be adjusted to increase or decrease the distance from the obstacle, as per the requirements.

Subsequently, to address the issue of superfluous turning points in the resultant path, a greedy algorithm is employed for path optimization. Assuming that the initial path has m inflection points, a point set T is defined, encompassing the starting point, the target point, and all inflection points:

$$T = \{T_0, T_1, \cdots T_m, T_{m+1}\} \tag{5}$$

where T_0 is the starting point and T_{m+1} is the endpoint. The methodological workflow can be explicated as follows: Firstly, the search starting point T_j and search ending point T_k are established, having initial values of $j = 0$ and $k = m$. Subsequently, if the robot is able to move forward in direction $\overrightarrow{T_j T_{j+1}}$ and reach point T_k after only passing through 0 or 1 turning point, with the final direction being $\overrightarrow{T_k T_{k+1}}$ and no collisions on the way, then the new path is used instead of the old path. Otherwise, the values of j and k are transformed (where $0 \leq j \leq m - 2, j + 3 \leq k \leq m$) and the search continues. This process is reiterated until a new path is obtained. If no new path is identified, the starting and ending positions are reversed, and the above steps are repeated.

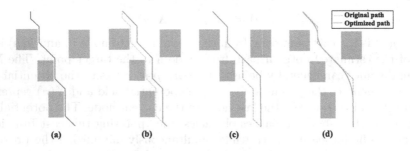

Fig. 2. Path Planning.

Finally, the Bézier curve is employed to smooth out the remaining turning points to adhere to the kinematic characteristics of the robot. Figure 2 displays an example where Fig. 2 (a) is the path produced by the original A* algorithm, and Fig. 2 (b) represents the output when incorporating potential field factors. The introduction of potential field factors facilitates the path to steer clear of obstacles and ultimately, enhances the robot's safety. Figure 2 (c) exhibits the optimized path produced by the greedy algorithm, which significantly decreases the number of turning points in the path. Figure 2 (d) illustrates the smoothed path. The improved algorithm generate a safer, faster, and smoother path, rendering it more suitable for hexapod robots.

3.2   Motion Tracking Control

The objective of the motion tracking problem is to develop a control input function to enable a robot to follow a planned path while minimizing the discrepancy between its actual and expected poses.

To achieve this, the motion error model of the robot needs to be defined. For a hexapod robot, the input speed can be described as a three-dimensional vector consisting of the forward speed v_x, the lateral displacement speed v_y, and the rotational speed v_ω, as shown in Fig. 3. The robot's locomotion control module then plans the motion of each leg based on these three speeds. The kinematics

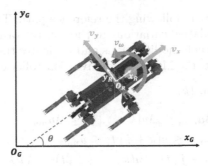

Fig. 3. An overhead view of robot coordinate system.

of the robot can be expressed as follows:

$$\dot{\chi} = f(\chi, u) = \begin{bmatrix} \dot{x} \\ \dot{y} \\ \dot{\theta} \end{bmatrix} = \begin{bmatrix} \cos\theta & -\sin\theta & 0 \\ \sin\theta & \cos\theta & 0 \\ 0 & 0 & 1 \end{bmatrix} \begin{bmatrix} v_x \\ v_y \\ v_\omega \end{bmatrix} \tag{6}$$

For the path given in the path planning, each point on it meets the kinematics equation:

$$\dot{\chi}_r = f(\chi_r, u_r) \tag{7}$$

Taylor expand Eq. (6) at reference point χ_r and subtract the two equations to obtain:

$$\dot{\tilde{\chi}} = \dot{\chi} - \dot{\chi}_r = \begin{bmatrix} \dot{x} - \dot{x}_r \\ \dot{y} - \dot{y}_r \\ \dot{\theta} - \dot{\theta}_r \end{bmatrix} = \begin{bmatrix} 0 & 0 & -(v_x)_r \sin\theta_r - (v_y)_r \cos\theta_r \\ 0 & 0 & (v_x)_r \cos\theta_r - (v_y)_r \sin\theta_r \\ 0 & 0 & 0 \end{bmatrix} \begin{bmatrix} x - x_r \\ y - y_r \\ \theta - \theta_r \end{bmatrix}$$
$$+ \begin{bmatrix} \cos\theta_r & -\sin\theta_r & 0 \\ \sin\theta_r & \cos\theta_r & 0 \\ 0 & 0 & 1 \end{bmatrix} \begin{bmatrix} v_x - (v_x)_r \\ v_y - (v_y)_r \\ v_\omega - (v_\omega)_r \end{bmatrix} \tag{8}$$

To apply this model to the tracking controller, the equation is discretized:

$$\tilde{\chi}(k+1) = A_{k,t}\tilde{\chi}(k) + B_{k,t}\tilde{u}(k) \tag{9}$$

Then, we use MPC (Model Predictive Control) to obtain the optimal control sequence. The objective function can be expressed as:

$$J(k) = \sum_{i=1}^{N_p} \|\tilde{\chi}(k+i\mid t)\|_Q^2 + \sum_{j=1}^{N_c-1} \|\Delta u(k+j\mid t)\|_R^2 \tag{10}$$

where N_p is the predictive time domain and N_c is the control time domain, Q and R are weight matrices, Δu represents the change in control input at time t. In the presented equation, the first element denotes the errors and serves as a metric of the system's proficiency in following the reference path. The subsequent component denotes the cumulative variations in the control variables, which accounts for the constraints on their modifications and mitigates the occurrence of abrupt alterations. As a result, the Model Predictive Controller can be represented as:

$$\min_{\Delta U_t} J(k) \tag{11}$$

$$s.t. \quad \Delta u_{min} \le \Delta u(k+j \mid t) \le \Delta u_{max} \tag{11a}$$

$$u_{min} \le u(k+j \mid t) \le u_{max} \tag{11b}$$

$$u(k+j \mid t) = u(k+j-1 \mid t) + \Delta u(k+j \mid t) \tag{11c}$$

$$i = 1, 2, \cdots, N_p; j = 1, 2, \cdots, N_c - 1$$

Among the constraints that govern robot control, Eq. (11a) represents the incremental constraint that is contingent upon the robot's acceleration, while Eq. (11b) captures the constraint that is imposed by the robot's maximum speed. Furthermore, Eq. (11c) denotes the relationship between the control variable and the control increment. Additionally, Eq. (9) serves as another pertinent constraint. By resolving the optimization problem presented in Eq. (17), we can obtain the optimal control sequence ΔU_t, with the first element being leveraged as the effective control increment:

$$u_{actual}(k+1 \mid t) = u(k \mid t) + \Delta u(k+1 \mid t) \tag{12}$$

This process may be repeated to effectively address the constrained optimization problem, and thus enable the robot to track the planned path.

3.3   Locomotion Control

The tripod gait is the most typical and efficient gait used by hexapod robots. This gait involves dividing the robot's legs into two groups, each with three legs. During locomotion, one group of legs is in the swing state, while the other group is in the support state. The leg in the support state maintains contact with the ground and propels the robot in the desired direction, while the leg in the swing state lifts and steps forward. Once a stride is completed, the two groups of legs alternate, with the leg previously in the swing state transitioning to the support state. Additionally, the supporting leg adjusts its posture to adapt to the terrain.

The reference trajectory for a single leg is comprised of a supporting phase and a swinging phase, each of which is composed of a cubic spline curve. In the XZ plane, as shown in Fig 4, each spline curve is constrained by five control points. The most critical control points for the supporting phase are the contact point A_0 and the lift-off point A_4. Their positions in the body coordinate system are:

$$A_{0_i} = P_{L_i} + [\frac{v_x T_{stance}}{2}, 0, -h_{body}]^T, A_{4_i} = P_{L_i} + [-\frac{v_x T_{stance}}{2}, 0, -h_{body}]^T \tag{13}$$

where i is the leg number, P_{L_i} is the position from the i-th leg to the body coordinate system, T_{stance} is the gait support time, v_x is the expected forward

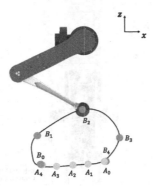

Fig. 4. Single leg reference trajectory.

speed of the robot in the x direction, and h_{body} is the expected standing height of the body. For the swinging phase, B_0 coincides with A_4, and B_4 coincides with A_0. The crucial point for control lies in B_2, which serves as the apex and determines the altitude of the robot's feet. The position of B_2 is specified in the body coordinate system:

$$B_{2_i} = P_{L_i} + [0, 0, -h_{body} + h_{step}]^T \tag{14}$$

where h_{step} is the step height. To enable lateral movement, planning can be similarly executed in the YZ plane of the leg coordinate system. This involves substituting the v_x variable in the aforementioned equation with v_y. However, when the robot necessitates turning, an additional calculation of velocity on each leg must be performed based on the leg's position relative to the center of the body. When the robot necessitates turning, an additional calculation of velocity on each leg must be performed based on the leg's position relative to the center of the body:

$$\Delta v_i = R_{L_i}^T \left(\begin{bmatrix} 0 & 0 & \omega_{body} \end{bmatrix}^T \times P_{L_i} \right) \tag{15}$$

where R_{L_i} is the rotation matrix from the coordinate system of the i-th leg to the body, and ω_{body} is the turning rate of the body. Then, add this additional velocity to the body's translation velocity:

$$v_{robot}^* = v_{robot} + \Delta v_i \tag{16}$$

Substituting the updated v_{robot}^* into Eq. (13) and Eq. (14), the turning can be realized.

3.4   Navigation in Challenging Environments

Obstacle Avoidance. Despite the meticulous planning of a safe path, the emergence of moving obstacles, such as pedestrians, during the robot's locomotion is an inevitable challenge that needs to be addressed.

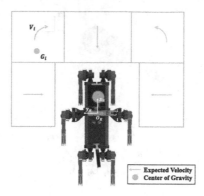

Fig. 5. Obstacle avoidance.

To this end, as shown in Fig. 5, the area surrounding the robot is partitioned into five cubic segments within the robot coordinate system. The LiDAR point cloud is utilized to instantaneously detect the number of points in each area. If the count surpasses a predefined threshold, obstacles are deemed to be present, and the center of gravity of all points in the given area is calculated and referred to as G_i. Each area corresponds to a desired obstacle avoidance speed V_i, for example, the left front area of the robot corresponds to a right turn, whereas the front area of the robot corresponds to a retreat. In the presence of obstacles within the cubic area, the robot temporarily disengages from the MPC controller and transmits the following synthesized speed:

$$v_{obs} = \sum \mathcal{K}(dist(G_i)) \times V_i \tag{17}$$

where $\mathcal{K}$ is the velocity coefficient, which is related to the distance from the center of gravity of the voxel to the center of the robot. The simple approach is to take $\mathcal{K}$ as inversely proportional to $dist(G_i)$, and for voxels without obstacles, take $\mathcal{K} = 0$. This algorithm ensures that robots can avoid dynamic obstacles around them in real-time.

Traffic Light Recongnition. Traffic light recognition plays a pivotal role in enabling robots to navigate safely in outdoor environments. To ensure compliance with the "stop at red light and go at green light" rule, RGB image captured by cameras is used for detection purposes. In particular, the low-time-cost YOLOv5 network is employed to scrutinize the image and establish the presence of traffic lights. When detected, the relevant area is stored as a candidate traffic signal region. This approach offers the notable benefit of expediting the reduction of candidate regions, thereby mitigating the computational load associated with subsequent recognition tasks.

Subsequently, template matching is applied to the candidate regions in order to identify relevant information. In this regard, pre-extracted template images of traffic lights are classified into three distinct categories, green light, green light but flashing, and red light. Specifically, let T denote the image template and I denote the input image. Standard correlation matching is utilized to gauge the similarity between the template and the candidate region, thereby enabling the identification of the pertinent information:

$$R(m,n) = \frac{\sum_{m',n'} \left[T\left(m',n'\right) \cdot I'\left(m+m',n+n'\right) \right]}{\sqrt{\sum_{m',n'} T\left(m',n'\right)^2 \cdot \sum_{m',n'} I(m+m',n+n')^2}} \qquad (18)$$

Matching the three templates with the candidate regions enables the determination of the current status of the traffic light, with the template exhibiting the highest score being selected as the definitive outcome. Note that, to enhance safety measures, robots only embark on road crossings when the recognition outcome corresponds to green. This algorithm can ensure that robots can recognize traffic signals in real time.

4   Experiments

To assess the navigational proficiency of the robot and validate the efficacy of the proposed algorithm, we performed comprehensive guidance experiments in demanding environments, including airports and intersections. In particular, the tester wears an opaque eye mask to simulate blindness, and HexGuide independently devises the optimal path and guides the individual to the intended destination.

4.1   Experiment in Airport

The Shanghai Hongqiao Airport is selected as the venue for the robot guidance experiment, and the results are presented in Fig. 6.

   The experiment is conducted by creating a point cloud map of the airport environment beforehand (Fig. 6i), and the robot receives real-time pose using the SLAM algorithm. Subsequently, the blind individual and the robot initiate their path from the arrival port (Fig. 6a) and communicate their intended destination, i.e., "baggage carousel number 9," through verbal instructions. The robot autonomously plans its path and first utilizes an accessible elevator (Fig. 6b,c). After the robot exits the elevator, the robot switches to the floor map and devises a new path, guiding the blind individual to the luggage carousel number 9 (Fig. 6d,e). When obstacles or pedestrians appear near the robot, the robot automatically avoids obstacles and continues to walk along the planned path after avoiding them (Fig. 6f). After picking up the luggage, the robot is informed of its destination ("going to the exit") through voice commands (Fig. 6g). Subsequently, the robot guides the blind person to the exit, covering a total distance of approximately 430 m (Fig. 6h). The experimental results indicate that the robot can complete challenging guidance tasks in airport environments.

Fig. 6. Blind Guide Experiment of HexGuide at Shanghai Hongqiao Airport.

4.2   Experiment in Intersection

Moreover, to evaluate the performance of the proposed algorithm, a blind guide experiment is conducted in an outdoor intersection where the robot guides the blind person through intersections with traffic lights to reach their destination, with a total path length of around 320 m. The experimental results are presented in Fig. 7.

Fig. 7. Blind Guide Experiment of HexGuide at an intersection. (Color figure online)

Prior to the experiment, a point cloud map of the environment is established (Fig. 7j), and the robot plans a feasible path based on the destination. Upon the robot reaching the intersection (Fig. 7a,b), the algorithm evaluates the traffic light status (Fig. 7c). If it is green, the robot continues moving forward (Fig. 7d), otherwise, it stops and waits (Fig. 7e,f) until the light turned green to proceed towards the destination (Fig. 7g,h,i). The experimental results show that the robot can recognize traffic signal conditions and complete challenging guidance tasks at intersections.

5   Conclusion

This paper presents HexGuide, a robot designed for guiding blind people in challenging environments. We propose an improved A* path planning algorithm that optimizes the robot's path and a motion tracking controller based on model predictive control to ensure accurate path tracking. Additionally, a motion control model is proposed for planning the swing of each leg of the robot. Furthermore, we propose a dynamic obstacle avoidance strategy and a method for recognizing traffic lights. Experimental results show the effectiveness of HexGuide in reliably guiding blind people to their destinations in challenging environments, such as airports and intersections.

References

1. World Health Organization visual impairment and blindness. http://www.who.int/mediacentre/factsheets/fs282/en/. Accessed 13 Oct 2022
2. Wachaja, A., Agarwal, P., Zink, M., et al.: Navigating blind people with walking impairments using a smart walker. Auton. Robot. **41**, 555–573 (2017)
3. Morris, A., Donamukkala, R., Kapuria, A., et al.: A robotic walker that provides guidance. In: IEEE International Conference on Robotics and Automation, pp. 25–30. IEEE (2003)
4. Wang, H.C., Katzschmann, R.K., Teng, S., et al.: Enabling independent navigation for visually impaired people through a wearable vision-based feedback system, In. IEEE International Conference on Robotics and Automation (ICRA), pp. 6533–6540. IEEE (2017)
5. Fiannaca, A., Apostolopoulous, I., Folmer, E.: Headlock: a wearable navigation aid that helps blind cane users traverse large open spaces. In: Proceedings of the 16th International ACM SIGACCESS Conference on Computers and Accessibility, pp. 19–26 (2014)
6. Saha, M., Fiannaca, A.J., Kneisel, M., et al.: Closing the gap: designing for the last-few-meters wayfinding problem for people with visual impairments. In: Proceedings of the 21st International ACM SIGACCESS Conference on Computers and Accessibility, pp. 222–235 (2019)
7. Kulyukin, V., Gharpure, C., Nicholson, J., et al.: Robot-assisted wayfinding for the visually impaired in structured indoor environments. Auton. Robot. **21**, 29–41 (2006)
8. Ulrich, I., Borenstein, J.: The GuideCane-applying mobile robot technologies to assist the visually impaired. IEEE Trans. Syst. Man Cybern. Part A Syst. Hum. **31**(2), 131–136 (2001)
9. Capi, G.: Assisting and guiding visually impaired in indoor environments. Int. J. Mech. Eng. Mechatron. **1**(2), 9–14 (2012)
10. Xiao, A., Tong, W., Yang, L., et al.: Robotic guide dog: leading a human with leash-guided hybrid physical interaction. In: 2021 IEEE International Conference on Robotics and Automation (ICRA), pp. 11470–11476. IEEE (2021)
11. NSK develops four-legged robot "guide dog". https://newatlas.com/nsk-four-legged-robot-guide-dog/20559/. Accessed 21 Nov 2011

Force-Estimation Based Interaction of Legged Robots through Whole-Body Dynamics

Yunpeng Yin⬥, Feng Gao⁽✉⁾ ⬥, Yuguang Xiao⬥, Limin Yang⬥, and Zehua Fan⬥

Shanghai Jiao Tong University, 800 Dongchuan Road, Shanghai 200240, China
gaofengsjtu@gmail.com

Abstract. External force estimation and adaptation is an assistive technology for legged robots. It enables the robot to accommodate to impacts or interferences and maintain its balance. This technology can also be used for the interaction between the robots and humans when the estimation of force is reliant. This paper presents this new interaction idea for the legged robots in the scenario of guiding visually impaired individuals. The external force is estimated through the whole-body dynamics without any extra force sensors, which enables the robot to handle the unexpected external disturbances or user manipulations in a same manner. We first demonstrate this force-estimation based interaction on a hexapod robot, using a rigid stick handler as the interface. This interaction technology not only has the advantage of being more adaptable to the environments, it also can help the robot to adjust its motions to follow the user's intention of movements.

Keywords: Legged Robot · Guide Robot · Force Estimation · Whole-Body Dynamics

1 Introduction

Legged robots have great locomotion capabilities on complex terrains and have received wide attention from researchers increasingly. Spot [1], ANYmal [2], HyQ [3], MIT Cheetah series [4, 5], and QingZhui [6, 7] have demonstrated excellent motion control performance. In addition to the inherent locomotion abilities, there are couple ways to enhance the interactive capability of the legged robot. When combined with perception and navigation technologies [8, 9], it could flexibly interact with the environment. When equipped with graphical interfaces or speech recognition devices, it could conveniently interact with humans and better meet our needs. However, the force-sensing interaction method of legged robots has not received sufficient attention, and force-based interaction is extremely important in some scenarios. For example, external force adaption can ensure the safety of the robot's balance after being disturbed by external impact; force sensing can help to interact with disabled users in a timely and effective manner.

One application of legged robots is guiding the visually impaired individuals. However, most of the relevant research [10, 11] simply hires the legged robot as a mobile platform, utilizing mapping and navigation algorithms, and then guide the user roughly through a soft leash with a force sensor. In our opinion, such a simple imitation of a guide dog lacks the interactive ability of a legged robot. For example, this soft leash cannot make the user perceive whether the robot is about to turn; similarly, the robot cannot sense the user's operational feedbacks (pushing or turning) through the leash as well.

Here we propose a new interaction method for legged guide robots based on force estimation. Firstly, we have designed a guide robot that can be handled through a rigid stick-based mechanism, which allows the user to feel the robot's motion state more comprehensively. Then, we propose an external force estimation and adaptation algorithm for the legged robot, which can enable the robot to better cope with external impacts or to understand the user's intentions, and to adjust its own behaviors through the user's operating force on the stick handler. Moreover, our external force perception algorithm is based on the proprioception of the robot rather than the additional force sensors. As the force sensor can only measure the external force after the installation position, it cannot handle unexpected interference external forces applied on other parts of the robot. Besides, free of extra force sensors can reduce production costs.

The structure of this paper is as follows. Section 2 introduces the design and control framework of our hexapod robot. Section 3 introduces the external force estimation and adaption algorithm to deal with interaction forces. Section 4 demonstrates the feasibility of the algorithm on the robot in some typical experiments. Section 5 concludes the entire work.

2 Robot Overview

2.1 Design

Little Stronger is a bionic designed hexapod robot inspired by insects, as shown in Fig. 1. The hexapod robot has better stability due to the extra two limbs compared to quadrupeds [12]. It's six legs are symmetrically distributed on both sides of the body. Each leg has 3 degrees of freedom, serially constructed as hip, thigh, and shank joints. Therefore, the robot has 18 actuating joints in total. The middle legs of the robot are installed at a position slightly farther from the sagittal plane, which not only avoids the collision of the same side legs when running in large strides, but also scales up the virtual support triangles formed by the contact legs, to enhance the stability of the robot when using a tripod-trot gait (lifting three legs in a staggered manner) [13]. It ensures that the Center of Mass (CoM) projection of the robot and the Center of Gravity (CoG) of the triangles coincide with each other. The six legs of the robot are numbered as the Back Right (BR), Back Left (BL), Middle left (ML), Front Left (FL), Front Right (FR), and Middle Right (MR). Despite of 18 actuating joints of the legs, there is a passive joint connecting the robot's back ridge and the guiding stick, which could be handled by users. It has the degree of freedom of rotating in the sagittal plane and it is retractable and lockable.

The coordinate systems are also defined in Fig. 1, where the body coordinate system {B} is fixed at the center of the robot, and world coordinate system {W} is fixed on the ground.

The robot is powered by a 24-V lithium battery. It's locomotion computer runs a GNU/Linux operation system patched with Xenomai [14] real-time kernel, and communicates with 18 drives and an Inertial Measurement Unit (IMU) through EtherCAT

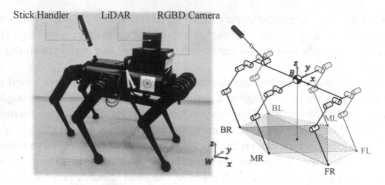

Fig. 1. Robot picture (left) and configuration (right).

protocol. The 18 joints of the robot are actuated by 18 brushless motors with planetary gear sets. Each joint's angle and angular velocity are feedback by the embedded encoder, and the joint torque is estimated from the armature current of the corresponding motor driver. The IMU is installed in the center of the robot's body and feeds back attitude, angular velocity and acceleration information. The navigation computer handles navigation tasks with the help of RGBD cameras and LiDAR. It sends motion commands to the locomotion computer through ZeroMQ [15].

2.2   Control

The control framework of the robot is shown in Fig. 2. The robot uses SLAM and our improved A* algorithm [16] for navigation, and a whole-body control algorithm [17] for locomotion. The external force estimation and adaption algorithm proposed in this work is colored in red. It produces generalized velocity adjustments to the navigation velocity commands, and they will be conducted by the gait and motion controller of the robot.

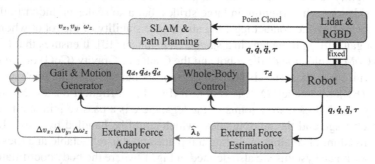

Fig. 2. Control framework for the robot.

3 External Force Estimation and Adaption

3.1 System Modeling

A legged robot is commonly described as a floating base system [18], that all limbs are arranged on a free body named floating base. With $p_b \in \mathbb{R}^3$ representing the position of the robot for the floating base, Φ standing for the Euler angles of the floating base, and the vector $q_i \in \mathbb{R}^3$ delegating joint angles for the i-th leg, where $i \in \{1, \ldots, 6\}$. Then the generalized position vector q of the system is defined as

$$q = \begin{bmatrix} p_b \\ \Phi \\ q_1 \\ \vdots \\ q_6 \end{bmatrix}. \tag{1}$$

Then the floating base dynamics of the robot can be written as:

$$M(q)\ddot{q} + h(q, \dot{q}) = \tau + J^T \lambda. \tag{2}$$

where $M(q) \in \mathbb{R}^{24 \times 24}$ is the generalized inertia matrix; $h(q, \dot{q}) \in \mathbb{R}^{24}$ is the vector of none linear terms including gravity, centripetal and Coriolis forces; $\tau \in \mathbb{R}^{24}$ is the generalized driving forces. As the floating base is a free body, the first six elements of τ are zeros, and the rest elements of it stand for the toques of each leg's joint. The external forces λ consists of the floating body term and limb term as

$$\lambda = \begin{bmatrix} \lambda_b \\ \lambda_l \end{bmatrix}, \quad \begin{cases} \lambda_b = \begin{bmatrix} F_b \\ T_b \end{bmatrix}, \\ \lambda_l = \begin{bmatrix} f_1 \\ \vdots \\ f_6 \end{bmatrix}, \end{cases} \tag{3}$$

where the floating base term λ_b is combined with the force $F_b \in \mathbb{R}^3$ and toque $T_b \in \mathbb{R}^3$ imposed on the robot's body, and the limb term λ_l is composed of the ground reaction force (GRF) [19] $f_i \in \mathbb{R}^3$ from the tip of the i-th leg. The Jacobian $J \in \mathbb{R}^{24 \times 24}$ is used to map the external forces into the floating base configurations. Relevant to the external forces, the Jacobian matrix is also combined with floating base sub term, limb sub term, and their correlation term, thus the Jacobian is stacked as

$$J = \begin{bmatrix} E_{6 \times 6} & 0_{6 \times 18} \\ J_{bl} & J_l \end{bmatrix}, \tag{4}$$

where $E_{6 \times 6} \in \mathbb{R}^{6 \times 6}$ is the identity matrix for the floating base; $J_l \in \mathbb{R}^{18 \times 18}$ is the local Jacobian for the limbs, and $J_{bl} \in \mathbb{R}^{18 \times 6}$ is their correlation matrix.

3.2 External Force Estimation

In Eq. (3), the limb term λ_l of the external forces λ is the necessary GRF that supports the robot standing on the ground. The floating base term λ_b is the interaction force with the robot that this paper interested in. Here the interaction is not distinguished between outer interference or handle forces, because the robot needs to respond to them in the same manner. As interaction force on robot cannot be measured directly, this subsection will discuss how to estimate it.

The left side of Eq. (2) indicates the dynamical features and has an invariant expression, thus here we simply rewrite left side of Eq. (2) as τ_d:

$$\tau_d = M(q)\ddot{q} + h(q, \dot{q}). \tag{5}$$

Then we expand all the vectors or matrices of Eq. (2) into the combination of floating base term and limb term. Here we introduce:

$$\begin{cases} \tau_d = \begin{bmatrix} \tau_{d,b} \\ \tau_{d,l} \end{bmatrix}, \\ \tau = \begin{bmatrix} 0_6 \\ \tau_{m,l} \end{bmatrix}, \end{cases} \tag{6}$$

where $\tau_{d,b}$ stands for the dynamical feature of the floating base, $\tau_{d,l}$ for the limbs. As the floating base is a free body so there hires a zero vector 0_6 for the actuating of the body, and $\tau_{m,l} \in \mathbb{R}^{18}$ is the vector of measured toques on the joints of each leg. Then Eq. (2) is reformed as

$$\begin{bmatrix} \tau_{d,b} \\ \tau_{d,l} \end{bmatrix} = \begin{bmatrix} 0_6 \\ \tau_{m,l} \end{bmatrix} + J^T \lambda,$$
$$= \begin{bmatrix} 0_6 \\ \tau_{m,l} \end{bmatrix} + \begin{bmatrix} E_{6\times6} & J_{bl}^T \\ 0_{18\times6} & J_l^T \end{bmatrix} \begin{bmatrix} \lambda_b \\ \lambda_l \end{bmatrix}. \tag{7}$$

Then we can solve interaction force λ_b on the body of the robot as

$$\lambda_b = \tau_{d,b} - J_{bl}^T \lambda_l,$$
$$= \tau_{d,b} - J_{bl}^T J_l^{-T} (\tau_{d,l} - \tau_{m,l}). \tag{8}$$

But, the linear algebra solution of Eq. (8) overlooked the state and measurement errors. Assuming the state noise and measurement noise are all Gaussian white noises, Eq. (7) can be rewrite as the nominal state along with the noises:

$$\begin{bmatrix} \tau_{d,b} \\ \tau_{d,l} \end{bmatrix} + \begin{bmatrix} \tilde{\tau}_{d,b} \\ \tilde{\tau}_{d,l} \end{bmatrix} = \begin{bmatrix} 0_6 \\ \tau_{m,l} \end{bmatrix} + \begin{bmatrix} 0_6 \\ \tilde{\tau}_{m,l} \end{bmatrix} + \begin{bmatrix} E_{6\times6} & J_{bl}^T \\ 0_{18\times6} & J_l^T \end{bmatrix} \begin{bmatrix} \lambda_b \\ \lambda_l \end{bmatrix}, \tag{9}$$

where $\tilde{\tau}_{d,b} \sim \mathcal{N}(0, R_b)$ stands for the normal distributed state noise of the floating base; $\tilde{\tau}_{d,l} \sim \mathcal{N}(0, R_l)$ represents the state noise of the limbs; and $\tilde{\tau}_{m,l} \sim \mathcal{N}(0, R_m)$ is the noise for the measurement. They share the same vector size with $\tau_{d,b}$, $\tau_{d,l}$, and $\tau_{m,l}$

respectively. Then by summing the nominal terms and noises terms into the same vector as

$$\begin{cases} \tau_{ob} = \begin{bmatrix} \tau_{d,b} \\ \tau_{d,l} - \tau_{m,l} \end{bmatrix}, \\ \tilde{e} = \begin{bmatrix} \tilde{e}_b \\ \tilde{e}_l \end{bmatrix} = \begin{bmatrix} \tilde{\tau}_{d,b} \\ \tilde{\tau}_{d,l} \oplus \tilde{\tau}_{m,l} \end{bmatrix}, \end{cases} \qquad (10)$$

where τ_{ob} stands for the observing values of the nominal states, and $\tilde{e}$ is the vector for the system noises. Note that the symbol "$\oplus$" stands for the addition of probability between $\tilde{\tau}_{d,l}$ and $\tilde{\tau}_{m,l}$. Then the noise in Eq. (9) can be express by the observing values as

$$\tilde{e} = J^T \lambda - \tau_{ob}. \qquad (11)$$

The target of the external force estimation is to minimize the system noises during the control prosses. In a discrete duration Δt, the current optimized estimation of external force $\hat{\lambda}_b(t_N)$ can be identified with the least squares form as

$$\begin{aligned} \hat{\lambda}_b(t_N) &= \arg\min_{\lambda(t_k)}\left(\sum_{k=1}^N \alpha^{N-k}\tilde{e}(t_k)_W^2\right), \\ &= \arg\min_{\lambda(t_k)}\left(\sum_{k=1}^N \alpha^{N-k} J^T(t_k)\lambda(t_k) - \tau_{ob}(t_k)_W^2\right). \end{aligned} \qquad (12)$$
$$\begin{cases} 0 < \alpha < 1 \\ N = \left[\frac{t}{\Delta t}\right] \end{cases}$$

where α is the forgetting factor, indicating that the past observations weight less as time goes by. The accumulation number N is the rounding of the current time t to the control interval Δt. The symbol $*_W^2$ is the square norm with the weighting matrix W. The problem in Eq. (12) can be solved in the recursive least-square fashion [20] as

$$\begin{cases} K(t_k) = P(t_{k-1}) \cdot \left(J^T(t_k)\right)^T \cdot \left(\alpha \cdot E_{24\times24} + J^T(t_k) \cdot P(t_{k-1}) \cdot \left(J^T(t_k)\right)^T\right)^{-1}, \\ P(t_k) = \frac{1}{\alpha}\left(P(t_k) - K(t_k)J^T(t_k)P(t_{k-1})\right), \\ \hat{\lambda}(t_k) = \hat{\lambda}(t_{k-1}) + K(t_k) \cdot \left(\tau_{ob}(t_k) - J^T(t_k)\hat{\lambda}(t_{k-1})\right). \end{cases} \qquad (13)$$

where $P(t_k) \in \mathbb{R}^{24\times24}$ and $K(t_k) \in \mathbb{R}^{24\times24}$ are the intermediate and updating matrices, $E_{24\times24}$ is an identity matrix.

Then as Eq. (3) shows, the interaction force/torque $\hat{\lambda}_b(t_k)$ applied on the body of the robot is extracted from the estimated external force $\hat{\lambda}(t_k)$ from its first six elements, and the interaction force $\hat{F}_b(t_k)$ and toque $\hat{T}_b(t_k)$ are separated from $\hat{\lambda}_b(t_k)$ as

$$\begin{cases} \hat{\lambda}_b(t_k) = \left[\hat{\lambda}(t_k)\right]_{1\sim6}, \\ \begin{bmatrix} \hat{F}_b(t_k) \\ \hat{T}_b(t_k) \end{bmatrix} = \hat{\lambda}_b(t_k). \end{cases} \qquad (14)$$

3.3 External Force Adaption

The robot's locomotion should respond to the interaction force. The estimated external force/torque on the robot are 3D special vectors, but the robot needn't to react in all directions. It is sufficient that the robot can adapt to user interactions for horizontal movements, which include the translation along x-axis and y-axis and rotation around z-axis. Therefore, we get the generalized impulse L from integral of the corresponding elements of as

$$L = \sum_{k=1}^{N} \beta^{N-k} \begin{bmatrix} \left[\hat{F}_b(t_k)\right]_x \\ \left[\hat{F}_b(t_k)\right]_y \\ \left[\hat{T}_b(t_k)\right]_z \end{bmatrix} \cdot \Delta t \tag{15}$$

where $\beta \in (0, 1)$ is the forgetting factor that maintains computational convergence, and $[*]_x$, $[*]_y$, and $[*]_z$ are the symbols to extract the components of a vector corresponding to the axis. Then, the generalized impulse L brought by the interaction force can be transformed into the generalized momentum variation as

$$\begin{bmatrix} m \cdot \Delta v_x \\ m \cdot \Delta v_y \\ J_z \cdot \Delta \omega_z \end{bmatrix} = L \tag{16}$$

where m is the mass of the robot and J_z is the rotational inertia around the z-axis; Δv_x, Δv_y, and $\Delta \omega_z$ are the translational and rotational velocity adjustments along the corresponding axis of the velocity commands generated by the navigation module. Then, they are sent to the locomotion controller as shown in Fig. 2, and the robot could respond to the external interaction forces.

4 Experiment

We conduct an experiment of static loading to verify the external force estimation algorithm, and two independent experiments of typical guiding scenarios to verify our force-sensing interaction algorithm with external impact forces and user manipulation forces, respectively. In both the scenarios, the participant wears an eye mask, pretending the visually impaired individual, to be led by the guiding robot.

4.1 Static force estimation

In this experiment, a payload (5 kg) is suspended and dragging onto the robot through a pulley as shown in Fig. 3. The nominal force from the payload should be about -49 N due to the local gravity. Figure 4 shows the estimated force (in blue) in the forward and backward direction. The mean value (in red) of the estimated force is -47.29 N because of the friction loss and the angle error between the belt and the pulling direction. As the robot is taking steps in place, there would be twitch accelerations inevitably, which causes the estimated force (in blue) in Fig. 4 having a standard deviation of 4.58 N. This indicates that the external force estimation algorithm is feasible and effective.

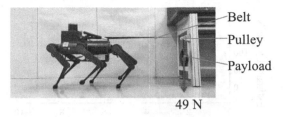

Fig. 3. Force estimation of static payload.

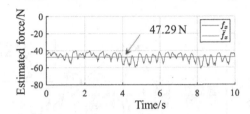

Fig. 4. Estimated force of static loading.

4.2 Impact adaptation

In this experiment, the participant is led forward by the robot. Then, a passer-by gives sidekicks to interfere with the robot. The screenshots of the experiment are shown in Fig. 5, which shows that the robot side-shifts a few steps to adapt the impacts caused by the kicks. Figure 6 shows the estimated external forces and Fig. 7 shows the motion adjustments of the translational velocity, which indicates that three times of side force impacts are detected evidently, and the adjustments have been made to the lateral speed.

Fig. 5. Screenshots of sidekick-impact adaptation.

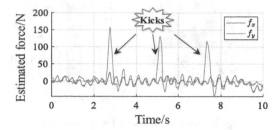

Fig. 6. Estimated external force of the sidekicks.

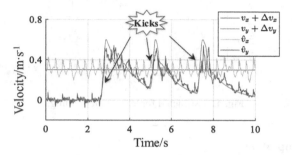

Fig. 7. The adjustments of translational velocity with the sidekicks. $\hat{v}_x$ and $\hat{v}_y$ are the estimated current translational velocity of the robot.

4.3 Manipulation adaptation

In this experiment, the robot first uses a higher speed to lead the participant around a turn, then the user drags the guide stick to slow down the robot so that he could keep up. As talked before, the guide stick is rigid so that the participant can feel the turning and then twist the robot to turn slowly. Screenshot of the scenario is shown in Fig. 8. The estimated manipulation force/toque of the drag/twist and the adjustments of forward and turning velocity are shown in Figs. 9, 10 and 11. Practically, the high-frequency noises are easy to filter, but the low-frequency noises coupled with gait steps are unavoidable, thus we set dead zones for the estimated external force/toque. The corresponding values that not exceeding the thresholds would be ignored. The robot successfully perceived the user's intent and made adjustments to its motion state. It should be note that all the variables here are expressed in body coordinate system with a left superscript {B}.

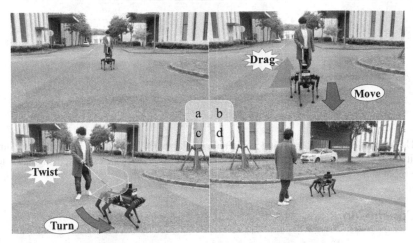

Fig. 8. Screenshots of the manipulation during a turn.

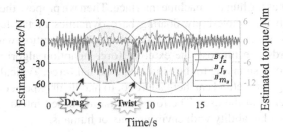

Fig. 9. Estimated external force/toque of the drag/twist. The force/toque here

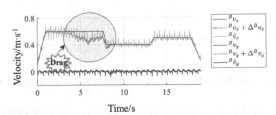

Fig. 10. The adjustments of translational velocity with the drag interaction. The planning forward velocity is in blue and the adjusted forward velocity is in red. The lateral velocity is zero.

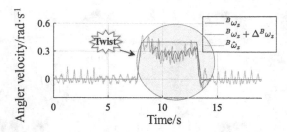

Fig. 11. The adjustments of turning velocity with the twist interaction. The planning turning velocity is in blue and the adjusted turning velocity is in red. $^{B}\hat{\omega}_z$ is the estimated angular velocity of the robot along z-axis.

5   Conclusion

This paper presents a new idea for the interaction of legged robots based on force-estimation. First, we propose a novel design of hexapod robot for guide scenario, using a rigid stick handler as the human-machine interface. Then we propose the force estimation algorithm through the whole-body floating base dynamics of the legged robot with the recursive least-square method, which based on proprioception without extra force sensors. Afterwards, we propose the external force adaption algorithm to adjust the motion of the robot responding to the estimated external force. Typical experiments are conducted proving our method can help the robot to handle unexpected external impacts and manipulations from the user. The force-estimation based interaction can enhance the legged robot's adaptability with environments or humans.

Acknowledgements. Our work is supported by the National Key Research and Development Program of China (No. 2021YFF0306202).

References

1. Boston Dynamics Spot Mini. https://www.bostondynamics.com/products/spot, accessed 1 May 2023
2. Hutter, M., et al.: ANYmal - A Highly Mobile and Dynamic Quadrupedal Robot. In: 2016 IEEE/RSJ International Conference on Intelligent Robots and Systems (IROS) (2016)
3. Semini, C., Tsagarakis, N.G., Guglielmino, E., Focchi, M., Cannella, F., Caldwell, D.G.: Design of HyQ – a hydraulically and electrically actuated quadruped robot. In: Proceedings of the Institution of Mechanical Engineers, Part I: Journal of Systems and Control Engineering (2011)
4. Bledt, G., Powell, M.J., Katz, B., Carlo, J.D., Kim, S.: MIT Cheetah 3: Design and Control of a Robust, Dynamic Quadruped Robot. In: IEEE International Conference of Intelligent Robots (IROS) 2018 (2018)
5. Katz, B., Carlo, J.D., Kim, S.: Mini Cheetah: A Platform for Pushing the Limits of Dynamic Quadruped Control. In: 2019 International Conference on Robotics and Automation (ICRA) (2019)

6. Mao, L., Gao, F., Tian, Y., Zhao, Y.: Novel method for preventing shin-collisions in six-legged robots by utilising a robot–terrain interference model. Mech. Mach. Theory **151**, 103897 (2020)
7. Zhao, Y., Gao, F., Sun, Q., Yin, Y.: Terrain classification and adaptive locomotion for a hexapod robot Qingzhui. Frontiers of Mechanical Engineering, pp. 1–14 (2021)
8. Jenelten, F., Miki, T., Vijayan, A.E., Bjelonic, M. Khe Dd Ar, A.: Perceptive Locomotion in Rough Terrain - Online Foothold Optimization. IEEE Robotics and Automation Letters **5**(4), 5370–5376 (2020)
9. Kim, D., Carballo, D., Carlo, J.D., Katz, B., Kim, S.: Vision Aided Dynamic Exploration of Unstructured Terrain with a Small-Scale Quadruped Robot. In: 2020 IEEE International Conference on Robotics and Automation (ICRA) (2020)
10. Xiao, A., Tong, W., Yang, L., Zeng, J., Li, Z., Sreenath, K.: Robotic guide dog: Leading a human with leash-guided hybrid physical interaction. In: 2021 IEEE International Conference on Robotics and Automation (ICRA), pp. 11470–11476. IEEE (2021)
11. Chen, Y., et al.: Quadruped Guidance Robot for the Visually Impaired: A Comfort-Based Approach. Computer Science Robotics (2022)
12. Yin, Y.Y.Z., Xiao, Y., Gao, F.: Footholds optimization for legged robots walking on complex terrain. Front. Mech. Eng. **18**(2), 26 (2023). https://doi.org/10.1007/s11465-022-0742-y
13. Sun, Q., Gao, F., Chen, X.: Towards dynamic alternating tripod trotting of a pony-sized hexapod robot for disaster rescuing based on multi-modal impedance control. Robotica: Int. J. Info. Edu. Res. Robo. Artif. Intelli. **36**(7), 1–29 (2018)
14. Gerum, P.: Xenomai-Implementing a RTOS emulation framework on GNU/Linux. White Paper, Xenomai, p. 81 (2004)
15. Hintjens, P.: ZeroMQ: messaging for many applications. O'Reilly Media, Inc. (2013)
16. Wang, Z., Gao, F., Zhao, Y., Yin, Y., Wang, L.: Improved A* algorithm and model predictive control- based path planning and tracking framework for hexapod robots. Indus. Robo. Int. J. Robo. Res. Appl. **50**(1), 135–144 (2023). https://doi.org/10.1108/IR-01-2022-0028
17. Bellicoso, C.D., Jenelten, F., Fankhauser, P., Gehring, C., Hutter, M.: Dynamic locomotion and whole-body control for quadrupedal robots. In: IEEE/RSJ International Conference on Intelligent Robots & Systems (2017)
18. Bellicoso, C.D., Gehring, C., Hwangbo, J., Fankhauser, P., Hutter, M.: Perception-less terrain adaptation through whole body control and hierarchical optimization. In: IEEE-RAS International Conference on Humanoid Robots (2017)
19. Focchi, M., Del Prete, A., Havoutis, I., Featherstone, R., Caldwell, D.G., Semini, C.: High-slope terrain locomotion for torque-controlled quadruped robots. Auton. Robot. **41**(1), 259–272 (2017)
20. Renner, A., Wind, H., Sawodny, O.: Online payload estimation for hydraulically actuated manipulators. Mechatronics **66**, 102322 (2020)

Lightweight Design and Property Analysis of Humanoid Robot Thigh Integrated Structure with Appearance

Daming Nie[1], Jason Gu[2], Yu Zhang[1(✉)], and Hongjian Jiang[1]

[1] Research Center for Intelligent Robotics, Zhejiang Lab, Hangzhou 310058, China
yu_zhang@zhejianglab.com

[2] Department of Electrical and Computer Engineering, Dalhousie University, Halifax B3M 1A2, Canada

Abstract. The lightweight and high stiffness leg structure of humanoid robots can effectively reduce rotational inertia and energy consumption, improving the robot's ability to quickly switch motion states. Based on the lightweight requirements of robots, this article proposes an innovative design method for humanoid robot legs based on the "structure-appearance" integration of light-alloy additive manufacturing technology. The load-bearing part of the leg structure is designed as a "shell + density-variable lattice" configuration, and the appearance part is set as a thin shell with equal thickness. The load-bearing part and the appearance one are combined together, resulting in a 20% weight reduction compared to traditional legs. The leg structure sample was processed using metal additive manufacturing method, and tested by a set of personalized fixture. When applying 200 Nm loading under pure torsion conditions, the local strain did not exceed 0.0175%, indicating that it meets the usage requirements.

Keywords: Humanoid robots · Additive manufacturing · Lightweight design · Lattice structure

1 Introduction

Humanoid robots are developed on the basis of biomimetics, which have similar height, weight, and joint flexibility to humans. Since humans have evolved over a long period of time to achieve their current limb structure and joint flexibility characteristics, humanoid robots have significant advantages over other robot types in terms of motion stability [1–4] and flexibility [5, 6]. The design goals of humanoid robot structural components could be conclude to lightweight, high-strength, low rotational inertia, and high aesthetics. Light weight can reduce the energy consumption of robots and extend their endurance [7], which should be meaningful for the application of future humanoid robots; High strength can meet the kinematic and mechanical needs of robots under various working conditions [8]; Low rotational inertia enables the robot to quickly switch actions during motion [9]; High aesthetics can improve users' positive impression on robots [10], and replace the appearance of robots when the aesthetics reach a level that can be used as appearance parts directly, thereby further reducing the overall weight of robots.

© The Author(s), under exclusive license to Springer Nature Singapore Pte Ltd. 2023
H. Yang et al. (Eds.): ICIRA 2023, LNAI 14271, pp. 518–528, 2023.
https://doi.org/10.1007/978-981-99-6495-6_44

At present many researches focus on humanoid robots [11], in which most structural components are still designed as sheets or rods manufactured by traditional machining [12–14], and connected through bolts. This connection method involves lots of screws, making it prone to connection failure during robotic impact. In this article, we propose a light-weighting approach based on the metal additive manufacturing process [15, 16], which integrates the structure and appearance into one component. The configuration of the load-bearing part of the integrated component is reconstructed through topology calculation, with the surface layer being an equal thickness shell and the core zone being density-variable lattice; Set the non load-bearing part as a thinner shell. This method can reduce the required materials on the basis of traditional topology design, meanwhile integrating the appearance components of the robot could further reduce leg weight.

This article systematically investigates the lightweight design method of "structure-appearance" integration, analyzes the performance of related 3D printed workpiece. The first part of this article introduces the design and experimental process involved in this technique, the second part elaborates the processing quality and performance of the integrated thigh. The third part is the outlook for future work, and the fourth part is the conclusion.

2 Experimental Process

2.1 Model Design

Due to the adoption of the "structure-appearance" integrated approach, the contour of the legs is determined based on the industrial design of the entire robot machine. The connection features, such as the screw holes on the upper end to connect the hip pitch joints, the bearing fitting face on the lower end to link the knee joints.

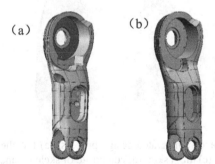

Fig. 1. Initial thigh model with connection features: (a) version with internal slots, (b) simplified version

After completing the connection features, it is also necessary to make clear the routing of the electrical and communication wires for the robotic motors, and the six dimensional force/torque sensor on foot. Therefore, internal slots need to be set at appropriate size (Fig. 1a). Extremely large slots will affect the stiffness of the structural part, and the small ones would make the ends of the wires cannot pass smoothly.

Additionally, it is necessary to note the deformation of the internal cavity during the 3D printing process [17], as well as the support introduced in printing, which may be difficult to remove in internal cavity with curvature by shot peening. In order to quickly verify the feasibility, we designed a simplified version (Fig. 1b) based on the official one of the thigh, which does not have an inner cavity.

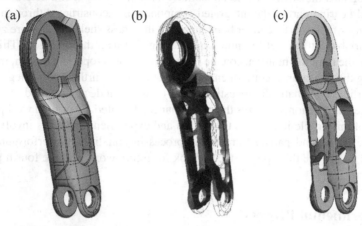

Fig. 2. Design process of skeleton model: (a) initial model, (b) material distribution after topological calculation, (c) reconstructed skeleton model

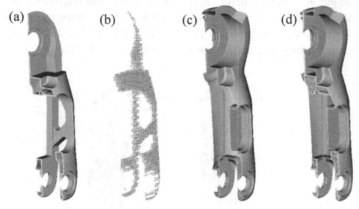

Fig. 3. "Structure-appearance" integrated design process: (a) the shell of the skeleton, (b) the lattice inside the skeleton, (c) thigh skin, (d) composite of skeleton and skin

The designed model should include the load-bearing part and the appearance one. The load-bearing part is used to undertake the main load of the thigh, and the appearance part is to complete the whole appearance of the thigh with smaller load-bearing capacity. As for the form of totally solid of the initial thigh model, topological design is used to reduce the weight of load-bearing part. Calculating the distribution characteristics of residual materials in the thighs under specific loads by method of density, the contour of load-bearing part could be reconstructed based on the calculation results (Fig. 2).

Take noting that the need of integration between load-bearing part and appearance one, the "subtraction method" is used to reconstruct the model, as shown in the Fig. 2. The four edge areas is retained based on the initial model and connected with two 45° diagonal beams in the middle, which can not only reduce weight but also integrate with the exterior components. Referring to the structure of a person's legs, this load-bearing part can be figuratively compared to a 'skeleton'.

In order to further reduce weight, the surface of the skeleton is shelled and the interior zone is filled with lattice, which help improve the stiffness of the shell to meet the usage requirements (Fig. 3). The density of the lattice is variable, meaning that the diameters of the lattice rods differs along with their location. The diameters are mapped based on the equivalent stress field of the zone. In areas with larger equivalent stresses, the diameter of the rod is set larger, correspondingly in areas with weaker equivalent stress, the diameter is smaller. However, the range of rod diameter should be particularly reasonable, with the maximum value not exceeding the cell edge length and the minimum one not lower than 1 mm, the cause is that it is difficult to be printed below 1 mm. Therefore, the mapping relationship is represented by the following equation:

$$\begin{cases} d = f(\sigma), \sigma_2 < \sigma < \sigma_1 \\ d = dmax, \sigma \geq \sigma_1 \\ d = dmin, \sigma \leq \sigma_2 \end{cases} \tag{1}$$

where, d is the rod diameter of the lattice, which is not a constant for density-variable lattice, σ is the equivalent stress in the region, σ_1, σ_2 represents the upper and lower limits of the set equivalent stress, and $dmax, dmin$ respectively represent the upper and lower limits of the rod diameter corresponding to the upper and lower limits of the equivalent stress. After process of changing lattice density supplely, the material distribution in the lattice area is more reasonable, and the stress field is more uniform. Therefore, the weight is reduced while maintaining the same stiffness.

In terms of appearance, i.e. "skin", the "skin" should contain industrial design elements and lightweight. Traditional appearance workpiece generally utilize 2 mm thick ABS or PC materials. Due to the differences in density, this article chooses an aluminum appearance with a thickness of 0.8 mm to replace plastic one, thus the weight of the two kinds of appearance parts is similar. Printing thin-walled shells is a challenge as thermal stress can cause local deformation or cracking. When combining the thin-walled shell of the "skin" with the shell of the "skeleton", sudden transition of wall thickness at the junction can also cause damage to the thinner wall during printing or use.

For those need to be connected inside the thighs, such as holes or grooves, the larger error of metal 3D printing compared to CNC is a challenge in dimensional accuracy. The holes or grooves should be first reduced and then locally thickened. In this way, the connection features can be set at the correct connection position even if there is deviation in printing. The disadvantage is that it increases the weight of the model of course.

2.2 Forming of Structural Component

The placement angle of structural component affects the final quality and weight of the model, the cause is that placement angle leads to differences in supports, and some of the supports cannot be removed, resulting in weight gain. The placement angle is affected by the stroke of the 3D printer. In this model, the structural components are placed as shown in the Fig. 4 with inclination angle of 90°. The material adopted is AlSi10Mg powder, and the average particle size of the powder is 30 μm, printing speed is 1000 mm/s, layer thickness is 30 μm.

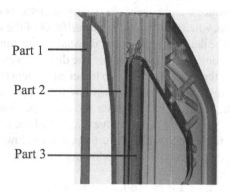

Part 1
Part 2
Part 3

Fig. 4. Distribution diagram of several types of supports

The supports can be divided into three parts (Fig. 4), the first part is exposed to the outside and can be directly removed. The second part is in the lattice part of the "skeleton". As the lattice is enclosed inside the "skeleton" shell, these supports cannot be removed and may only be reduced by optimizing the placement angle. The third part is the one between the "skin" shell and the "skeleton" shell, which cannot be removed normally. However, it can be cleverly grooved in a local area of the "skin" shell, and then pulling the internal support out of the groove. The structure should be equipped with powder cleaning holes at appropriate positions within multiple enclosed cavities.

2.3 Property Testing

Generally, the force bearing situation of the thigh during robot movement is simulated through finite element or physical methods. The hip joint pitch motor is one of the motors with the highest torque on robots, which can withstand large amounts of torque. Design a device as shown in Fig. 5 to detect the shank's property of torsional resistance, including a servo motor, torque transmission part (coupling, output shaft), thigh fixation part, and motor control part. The servo motor can control the output torque, so for the connected workpiece, the applied torque can be adjusted, with a maximum torque of 600 Nm. The torque transmission part transfers torque to the connection part of the workpiece, requiring reliable connection, especially the connection between the coupling and the motor output end. Unreliable connection may cause torque control failure and unstable torque. The fixed part of the thigh is used to fixation without rigid displacement when subjected to torsional load. The motor control part is composed of drivers from the computer, the control mode and parameter values of the motor can be adjusted by parameter input.

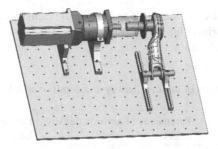

Fig. 5. Physical simulation of the working conditions of humanoid robot thigh

DIC equipment from Correlated Solutions Company is utilized to measure local strain of the thigh (Fig. 6), the basic principle of DIC is to calculate the deformation amount by comparing the specific positions before and after the deformation of two points. If the distance between the two points is small enough (<1 mm), dividing the deformation amount by the original factory can be equivalent to the strain at that location.

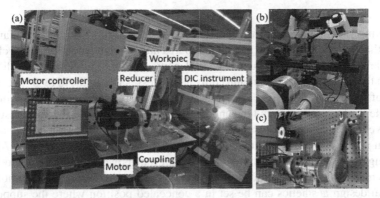

Fig. 6. "Structure-appearance" integrated thigh torsion resistance experiment: (a) overall test system, (b) DIC measurement parts, (c) machine holding part of integrated thigh

Two depth cameras can effectively calculate the deformation and location of the workpiece in three-dimensional space. DIC strain measurement needs to consider the influence of motor damping on the elastic strain of the workpiece. Due to the damping of the reducer and coupling, the workpiece undergoes elastic deformation after unloading, resulting in significant residual elastic strain. Residual elastic strain can be eliminated by rotating the motor in the opposite direction.

3 Analysis of Experimental Results

3.1 Analysis of Lightweight Effect

The density-variable lattice can obtain a more uniform stress field. This article compares the parameters of the uniform density and the selected density- variable lattice (Table 1). For the lattice region, the lattice cell belongs to BCC structure, and the rod length of the uniform density lattice is the same as that of the density-variable lattice. The rod diameters of density-variable lattice is set within the range of 1 mm–5 mm based on the equivalent stress at this location.

Table 1. Comparison of uniform density and density-variable lattice parameters

	Parameters of uniform density lattice	Parameters of density-variable lattice
Length of strut unit (mm)	10	10
Diameter of strut (mm)	3	2–5
Weight (g)	662.61	563.22
Maximum equivalent stress (MPa)	336	216
Minimum equivalent stress (MPa)	12	102

Printing is difficult when the diameter is less than 2 mm, while if the diameter is greater than 5 mm, it can cause small local pores and prevent smooth powder cleaning. Stress field analysis was conducted on a density-variable lattice, and the difference between the maximum and minimum equivalent stresses was reduced by 64% compared to that of the uniform density. The weight of the two types of lattice was reduced by 15%. The load-bearing part and the appearance one are combined together, resulting in a 20% weight reduction compared to traditional legs. The printed structural component is shown in Fig. 7, with a target weight of 662.61 g and an actual weight of 702.54 g, indicating that the weight of the remaining supports and powder inside is close to 39.93 g.

Two methods can be noted to optimize the excess weight: first, grooves or holes with industrial design aesthetics can be set in a concealed position where the supports can be removed; the second is to convert the supports to lattice that can improve the local stiffness of the structure. For example, if the supports should be set up at this location due to the need for molding, and the BCC lattice can also meet the molding requirements, then the lattice should be chosen instead of the supporters because the lattice can improve the stiffness at this location during working.

3.2 Precision Analysis of Forming Dimensions

The morphology is shown in Fig. 8, and the surface at the measurement point is flat, without warping, or distortion of appearance features. The important dimensions of the thigh are shown in Fig. 8a, and the actual measurement results of the important dimensions are shown in Fig. 8b. The diameter of the holes, and the distance between the hip and knee installation holes have evident size deviation of one level (Table 2), which requires machining to ensure the final accuracy of the thigh.

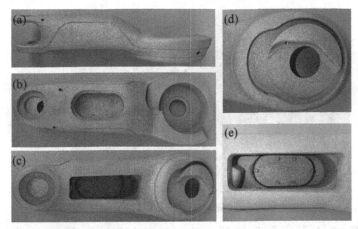

Fig. 7. "Structure-appearance" integrated thigh: (a) rear sight, (b) inner sight, (c) outer sight, (d) upper part of outer sight, (e) middle part of outer sight

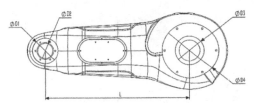

Fig. 8. Crucial structural parameters of thigh

Table 2. Comparison of target and actual sizes of thigh

	Target size	Actual size
D1	64 mm	(63.95–64.0) mm
D2	37 mm	(36.6–37.1) mm
D3	70 mm	(69.93–69.99) mm
D4	134 mm	(133.91–133.98) mm
L	350 mm	349.96 mm

3.3 Analysis of Torsional Resistance Performance

The local deformation of the thigh under the torque of 200 Nm can be visually displayed through DIC measurement. The main strain cloud map after the load reaches a stable state showing in Fig. 9, three deep purple areas indicates significant compression strain, and three green areas means the areas are subjected to tensile strain. The three deep purple areas are the transition areas 1 and 2 from the upper end to the middle, and 3 locates above the connection area of the ribs. The three green areas are the outer upper skin shell and the upper part of the rib connection. These areas inspire us to perform local thickening treatment on the transition area, where the skin takes priority over the skeleton to undergo tensile strain deformation. It is necessary to check whether the thin-walled shell will crack under high torque.

Under the action of a large load of 400 Nm, the upper thigh skin shell undergoes significant deformation, which theoretically has already undergone tearing (Fig. 10). In fact, it is intact and there is no visible plastic deformation to the naked eye. This may be

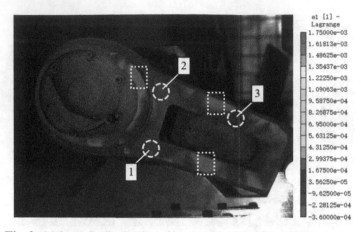

Fig. 9. Main strain distribution of humanoid robot thigh, 200 Nm loading

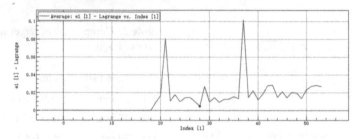

Fig. 10. Main strain distribution of humanoid robot thigh, 400 Nm loading

related to the small deformation area and the high elongation of AlSi10Mg. Compared to the skin, the deformation of the skeleton is relatively small (Fig. 11).

4 Outlook

After workpiece testing, it has been proven that the "structure appearance" integrated design method can effectively reduce the weight of structural components while maintaining the appearance and stiffness of the structure. In the future, research will be expanded on the following aspects: (1) Optimization of the "equivalent stress rod diameter" mapping algorithm for density-variable lattice. The current mapping algorithm is linear, and the subsequent use of nonlinear mapping algorithms is more in line with the changes in stress; (2) The design method with minimal residual support inside the shank that cannot be removed. The placement of the model, the setting method of process holes, and the innovative setting of the lattice can be optimized to minimize the residual support as much as possible; (3) On the basis of the density-variable lattice, the variable thickness of the skeleton and skin should be further set, the shell with variable thickness can adapt to differential stress, making the structural components closer to equal strength under load.

Fig. 11. Main strain distribution of humanoid robot thigh, 400 Nm loading

5 Conclusion

(1) The integration of structure and appearance can be achieved by setting the skeleton and skin, and then extracting shells and lattice from the skeleton to maintain stiffness while reducing the total weight compared to ordinary structural and appearance components. It has been proven to be a feasible lightweight method for humanoid robot shank.

(2) The load-bearing part and the appearance one are combined together, resulting in a 20% weight reduction compared to traditional legs. The setting of density-variable lattice can reduce the weight by 15% compared to uniform density one, and the optimization of lattice mapping algorithm requires rapid stress field simulation as the foundation.

(3) When applying 200 Nm loading under pure torsion conditions, the local strain did not exceed 0.0175%, indicating that it meets the usage requirements. The easily compressed and deformed area of the thigh is in the transition area, indicating the strength of this area should be strengthened.

(4) The thin-walled shell of the outer head is prone to significant deformation during torsional testing, it is necessary to verify the thin-walled thickness of this area.

Acknowledgement. The authors are grateful for the financial support from Zhejiang Provincial Natural Science Foundation (Grant No. LQ22E050024) and the project of "High-performance biped robot and its application" (G2021NB0AL03), founded by Zhejiang Lab.

References

1. Catherman, D.S., Kaminski, J.T., Jagetia, A.: Atlas humanoid robot control with flexible finite state machines for playing soccer. In: 2020 SoutheastCon, pp. 1–7 (2020)
2. Paredes, V.C., Hereid, A.: Resolved motion control for 3D Underactuated bipedal walking using linear inverted pendulum dynamics and neural adaptation. In: 2022 IEEE/RSJ International Conference on Intelligent Robots and Systems (IROS), pp. 6761–6767 (2022)

3. Sato, S., Kojio, Y., Kakiuchi, Y., Kojima, K., Okada, K., Inaba, M.: Robust humanoid walking system considering recognized terrain and robots' balance. In: 2022 IEEE/RSJ International Conference on Intelligent Robots and Systems (IROS), pp. 8298–8305 (2022)

4. Yuan, H., Song, S., Du, R., Zhu, S., Gu, J., Zhao, M., Pang, J.: A capturability-based control framework for the underactuated bipedal walking. In: 2021 IEEE International Conference on Robotics and Automation (ICRA), pp. 6804–6810 (2021)

5. Anson, J.M., Leo, L., T, J.M., Milton, R., Davies, J., Devassy, D.: Exode: humanoid healthcare robot. In: 2023 International Conference on Sustainable Computing and Data Communication Systems (ICSCDS), pp. 967–972 (2023)

6. Radeaf, H.S., Al-Faiz, M.Z.: Inverse kinematics optimization for humanoid robotic legs based on particle swarm optimization. In: 2023 15th International Conference on Developments in eSystems Engineering (DeSE), pp. 94–99 (2023)

7. Klas, C., Asfour, T.: A compact, lightweight and singularity-free wrist joint mechanism for humanoid robots. In: 2022 IEEE/RSJ International Conference on Intelligent Robots and Systems (IROS), pp. 457–464 (2022)

8. Chong, Z.H., Hung, R.T.W., Lee, K.H., Wang, W., Ng, T.W.L., Newman, W.: Autonomous wall cutting with an Atlas humanoid robot. In: 2015 IEEE International Conference on Technologies for Practical Robot Applications (TePRA), pp. 1–6 (2015)

9. Du, R., et al.: Design and analysis of the leg configuration for biped robots' spring-like walking. In: 2021 IEEE International Conference on Robotics and Biomimetics (ROBIO), pp. 1052–1057 (2021)

10. Rahem, R., Wong, C.Y., Suleiman, W.: Human-humanoid robot cooperative load transportation: model-based control approach. In: 2022 IEEE/RSJ International Conference on Intelligent Robots and Systems (IROS), pp. 8306–8312 (2022)

11. Kirtay, M., Hafner, V.V., Asada, M., Oztop, E.: Trust in robot-robot scaffolding. In: IEEE Transactions on Cognitive and Developmental Systems, p. 1 (2023)

12. Kouchaki, E., Palhang, M.: Balance control of a humanoid robot using deepreinforcement learning. In: 2023 28th International Computer Conference, Computer Society of Iran (CSICC), pp. 1–5 (2023)

13. Shu, X., et al.: A multi-configuration track-legged humanoid robot for dexterous manipulation and high mobility: design and development. In: IEEE Robotics and Automation Letters, pp. 3342–3349 (2023)

14. Yi, S.J., Lee, D.D.: Dynamic heel-strike toe-off walking controller for full-size modular humanoid robots. In: 2016 IEEE-RAS 16th International Conference on Humanoid Robots (Humanoids), pp. 395–400 (2016)

15. Gargalis, L., et al.: Additive manufacturing and testing of a soft magnetic rotor for a switched reluctance motor. In: IEEE Access, pp. 206982–206991 (2020)

16. Liu, Y., Dong, Q., Sun, X., Tian, L., Du, F., Li, B.: Collaborative robotic arm-based arc additive manufacturing system and part forming control study. In: 2022 5th World Conference on Mechanical Engineering and Intelligent Manufacturing (WCMEIM), pp. 620–623 (2022)

17. Liu, C.Y., et al.: Design and test of additive manufacturing for coating thermoplastic PEEK material. In: 2016 IEEE International Conference on Industrial Technology (ICIT), pp. 1158–1162 (2016)

Joint Torque and Ground Reaction Force Estimation for a One-Legged Hopping Robot

Weigang Zhou, Qiang Hua, Chao Cheng, Xingyu Chen, Yunchang Yao, Lingyu Kong, Anhuan Xie[✉], Shiqiang Zhu, and Jianjun Gu

Research Center for Intelligent Robotics, Research Institute of Interdisciplinary Innovation, Zhejiang Lab, Hangzhou 311100, China
xieanhuan@zhejianglab.com

Abstract. Robot force control performs better than position control in terms of dynamic and compliant control when interacting with complex environments. However, adding torque sensors to the robot's joints or feet for precise torque control can significantly increase volume and weight. Furthermore, torque sensors are prone to be damaged during long-term robot walking, potentially making it impossible to control the robot. This paper proposes a method to estimate joint torque and ground reaction force for a one-legged hopping robot. The method involves analyzing the robot joint dynamics model, compensating for joint friction torque, and estimating joint torque. Nonlinear factors such as joint motor model errors and gearbox backlash can lead to errors in joint torque estimation. To address this issue, nonlinear errors are compensated through BP neural network training, resulting in more accurate estimation of joint torque. Based on the estimated joint torque, the ground reaction force is calculated. The effectiveness of the proposed method was verified by comparing external force measurement data during a one-legged hopping robot jumping to the ground with the estimated ground reaction force.

Keywords: torque estimation · ground reaction force · robot joint · hopping robot

1 Introduction

Legged robots have a strong adaptability to ground environments, which is better than position control in terms of dynamic and compliant control when interacting with complex environments [1]. However, robot force control requires accurate force feedback information, usually achieved by installing force or torque sensors at the robot joints or feet [2]. Although torque sensors at joints enhance the accuracy of force feedback, they significantly increase the weight and volume of the robot and are expensive. Furthermore, force sensors are susceptible to damage during long-term walking that may affect the robot's ability to maintain control.

H. Yang et al. (Eds.): ICIRA 2023, LNAI 14271, pp. 529–541, 2023.
https://doi.org/10.1007/978-981-99-6495-6_45

Robots such as DLR (German Aerospace Center) [3–5] typically integrate torque sensors into their joints. Kawakami et al. estimated torque by detecting the torsional angle of elastic components using a linear method [6]; However, the method of adding elastic links can damage the robot's mechanical structure, introduce more flexibility, and increase controller design difficulty.

In joints equipped with harmonic reducers, the motor side and joint output side encoders can detect and estimate torque due to the flexibility [7]. However, significant estimation errors can still arise from nonlinear stiffness in harmonic reducers and encoder measurement noise. Series Elastic Actors (SEA) also face challenges estimating joint torque [8–10]. Alternatively, some studies propose torque estimation without introducing new mechanical structures. John W.L Simpson combined current and position information from servo motors along with system models to estimate joint torque [11], while A.Alcocer added a torque observer to estimate external torque within the joint model [12].

The parameters of the robot joint model can be initially determined by design specifications, such as the torque constant of motor, rotational inertia of joints, and reducer reduction ratio. Yet in practical applications, due to errors stemming from component design and assembly process, parameters such as the torque constant of motor, stiffness, damping and friction can only be identified through experiments. This research first identifies these parameters for a one-legged hopping robot's joints while accounting for challenging non-linear modeling errors. BP neural networks are implemented to train and compensate for these errors towards achieving greater accuracy in joint torque estimation. The estimated joint torque and relevant linking rod parameters are then utilized to estimate ground reaction force upon landing of a one-legged hopping robot.

2   Structure and Joint Composition of the One-Legged Hopping Robot

The structure of the one-legged hopping robot consists of two joints and two Carbon fiber links in series, as shown in Fig. 1. By controlling joint torque and planning the robot's motion trajectory, a one-dimensional vertical jumping motion can be achieved.

Each joint is comprised of a high torque density motor and a two-stage planetary reducer with a reduction ratio of 16. The angle is measured using a 17-bit high-precision position encoder installed on the joint motor side. The motion of the joint motor is controlled via the driver, while real-time current data is collected using the current sensor inside the driver.

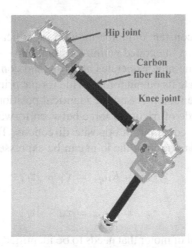

Fig. 1. Structure composition of the one-legged hopping robot.

3   Joint Torque Estimation

To accurately estimate the joint torque, a joint dynamics model is established that identifies the torque constant of motor and joint friction model.

A. *Joint dynamics model*

The robot joint is primarily composed of a motor, a reducer transmission, and a link. The transmission in this study is comprised of a two-stage planetary reducer; its input end connects to the motor output shaft, while the output end directly connects to the joint output link side. The robot joint can be viewed as having a dual mass system configuration. The dynamic equation can be obtained:

$$M(q)\ddot{q} + C(q, \dot{q}) + g(q) = \tau + \tau_{ext} \tag{1}$$

$$B\ddot{\theta} + \tau = \tau_m - \tau_f \tag{2}$$

The Eq. (1) is calculated from the Lagrange dynamics equation [13]. q represents the position of the link measured by a encoder on the link side. $M(q)$ represents the inertia matrix. $C(q, \dot{q})$ represents the Coriolis and Centrifugal force. $g(q)$ represents the gravitational term The right side of the Eq. (1) represents the combined force exerted on the link side, including the joint torque τ and the environmental external torque τ_{ext}. Equation (2) is composed of the dynamic equation of the motor, and the right end of the expression represents the combined force acting on the motor, which is the motor input torque τ_m and the friction torque τ_f. B represents the inertia of the motor, θ represents the motor angle measured by the motor's encoder. The above parameters are all based on the perspective of the link side, and relevant parameters need to be converted accordingly based on the joint deceleration ratio. Due to the fact that the reducer of the robot joint in this article is a two-stage planetary reducer with high stiffness, stiffness identification will not be conducted here. For joints using harmonic reducers, it is necessary to perform stiffness identification due to their flexibility.

B. *Joint torque estimation*

To identify the torque constant of motor, indirect identification calculations are necessary since the motor is integrated within the joint and cannot directly measure its output torque. When the motor operates at a low and constant speed, Eqs. (3) and (4) is applied to calculate its output torque. This torque primarily overcomes friction and load torques of the motor. Assuming identical positions and speeds under similar loads, the magnitude of frictional force between forward and reverse directions of joint movement are equal but in opposite directions. The dynamic equation for forward and backward rotation of the joint can be expressed as:

$$\tau_{m+} = K_t i_{q+} = \tau_+ + \left| \tau_f \right| \tag{3}$$

$$\tau_{m-} = K_t i_{q-} = \tau_- - \left| \tau_f \right| \tag{4}$$

The torque constant of motor that needs to be identified is denoted as K_t, where i_q is the input current of the motor, and the positive and negative signs represent forward and reverse motor rotation, respectively. By adding Eqs. (3) and (4), we obtain:

$$K_t i_{q+} + K_t i_{q-} = \tau_+ + \tau_- \tag{5}$$

The equation for calculating the torque constant of motor to be identified is:

$$K_t = \frac{\tau_+ + \tau_-}{i_{q+} + i_{q-}} \tag{6}$$

To accurately estimate joint output torque, it is also necessary to identify joint friction forces which can be classified as dynamic or static. The existence of static friction makes it easy for the current to overflow during the start and stop of the motor, which affects the speed of the system.Dynamic friction additionally affects the tracking error of systems. Thus, compensating for friction is an essential aspect of robot joint control. The identification of the torque constant of motor in prior text have established a foundation for identifying friction forces. In the case of uniform motion without load, we can calculate the friction force by measuring the motor current. This article uses the Stribeck friction model for identification and compensation of friction.

$$\tau_f = \left[F_c + (F_s - F_c)e^{-|v|/v_s} \right] sgn(v) + \delta v \tag{7}$$

where F_c and F_s represent the Coulombic and static friction forces of the motor in forward and reverse rotation, while v_s represents the Stribeck speed, which is related to the rate at which the friction force decreases with increasing speed at low speeds. δ represents the viscous friction coefficient of the system. Therefore, Eq. (7) mainly consists of Coulomb-viscous friction,static friction,and low-speed friction with Stribeck characteristics.

After the joint friction torque identification is completed, the small rotor inertia of the motor used in the joint can be ignored. The estimation of joint torque can thus be expressed as:

$$\tau = K_t i_q - \tau_f \tag{8}$$

Nonlinear factors such as joint motor model errors and gearbox backlash can result in errors in joint torque estimation. To address this issue, BP neural network training can be employed to compensate for these deviations and estimate joint torque more accurately, given that torque sensors can accurately measure joint torque on the experimental platform. BP neural networks possess strong nonlinear approximation capabilities [14]. The inputs of the neural network include joint angle, speed, motor current, and torque estimation error based on the model while the outputs contain the present joint torque estimation error. The block diagram for the overall joint torque estimation algorithm is illustrated in Fig. 2.

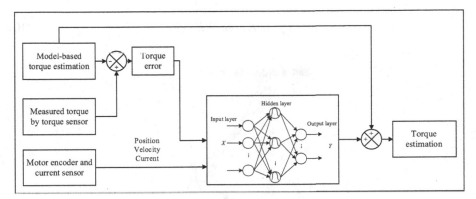

Fig. 2. The block diagram for the overall joint torque estimation.

4   Hopping Robot Control and Ground Reaction Force Estimation

A. *Hopping robot Control*

The leg flexibility control is achieved through the adoption of the virtual model control method. Virtual Model Control is a motion control framework that employs virtual components simulation to produce necessary joint torque. This control approach facilitates true execution torque (or force) generation through the simulation of virtual mechanical components, thereby creating a viscoelastic model similar to robot legs and muscle systems without requiring installation of springs or damping devices. The advantage of Virtual Model Control lies in its compactness and relatively low computational complexity, which allows for implementation in a distributed manner [15, 16]. In addition, the upper controller can be designed as a state machine to enable simple transitioning between virtual states by modifying either the virtual component connection mode or component parameters. Inverse dynamics is not employed in virtual model control to alter the behavior of robots due to computational complexities associated with matrix calculations required by inverse dynamics computation, resulting in low actual control efficiency. Complex tasks that are difficult to accomplish using traditional control methods can be achieved through virtual model control. This makes it a viable approach when the robot interacts with unknown environments. Virtual model control finds wide application in both robotic arms and foot-robots, such as bipedal walking robots [17], one-legged hopping robots [18], among others.

The virtual leg impedance system is represented in the polar coordinate system, as in Fig. 3. It utilizes a linear spring system to govern the leg length between the center of mass and foot, corresponding to the polar diameter of the polar coordinate; and a torsion spring system to regulate the leg angle, maintaining it within an intended target value, as represented by the polar angle of the polar coordinate. Virtual force and torque can be expressed as:

$$F_{spr} = K_{p,r}e_r + K_{d,r}\dot{e}_r \tag{9}$$

$$\tau_{spr} = K_{p,\theta}e_\theta + K_{d,\theta}\dot{e}_\theta \tag{10}$$

Fig. 3. The virtual leg impedance system.

Where $K_{p,r}$ is the stiffness of the virtual linear spring, $K_{d,r}$ is its damping coefficient, and $K_{p,\theta}$ and $K_{d,\theta}$ are the corresponding stiffness and damping of the virtual torsion spring, respectively; where e_r, $\dot{e}_r$, e_θ, and $\dot{e}_\theta$ are radial position error, radial velocity error, angular position error and angular velocity error.

The control block diagram for the one-legged hopping robot is presented in Fig. 4.

Conversion of the Cartesian coordinate system's position velocity error into the polar coordinate system's error and transformation of virtual force in the polar coordinate system into joint torque in the Cartesian coordinate system are essential in the overall control process.

$$\begin{bmatrix} \tau_{hip} \\ \tau_{knee} \end{bmatrix} = J_{polar}(q)^T \begin{bmatrix} F_{spr} \\ \tau_{spr} \end{bmatrix} \tag{11}$$

By utilizing joint angle to calculate the leg length, and identifying when leg lengths fall below a specific threshold while vertical speed is zero, the leg state machines can switch from landing to jumping on the ground. Through switching state machines and precise controlling of vertical virtual forces, continuous jumping of the leg can be achieved.

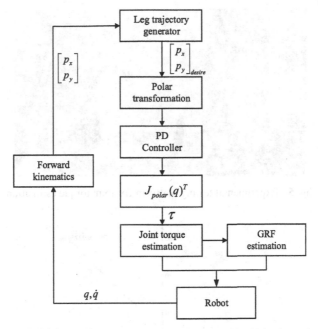

Fig. 4. The control block diagram for the one-legged hopping robot.

Ground reaction force estimation

When the leg touches the ground, the force at the end of the leg is equal to the ground reaction force(GRF), in the opposite direction. Jacobian matrix and joint torque can be used to calculate the GRF according to Eq. (12).

$$F_{GRF} = -(J^T(q))^{-1} \begin{bmatrix} \tau_{hip\_est} \\ \tau_{knee\_est} \end{bmatrix} \tag{12}$$

where, F_{GRF} is the ground reaction force, J is the Jacobian matrix from the hip joint to the foot end of the leg in Cartesian coordinate system, τ_{hip_est} and τ_{knee_est} are the actual estimated torques of the hip and knee joints, respectively (see Fig. 5).

5 Experiment

A. *Joint Torque Estimation Experiment*

We recorded the current and torque of the joint when rotating at a constant speed of ± 1 rpm with load. We did this by recording both forward and reverse direction values at the same position. Using Eq. (6), we calculated the sum of forward and reverse currents and torque, as represented in Fig. 6.

The experimental results show that motor current and torque have an excellent linear relationship, regardless of whether it is forward or reverse loading. The estimated torque constant of motor K_t is 3.74 differs significantly from the value of 2.72 given by the joint product manual.

Fig. 5. Experimental testing platform for joint torque estimation.

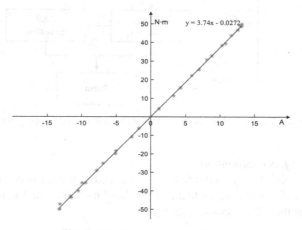

Fig. 6. The torque constant of motor.

Once the torque constant of motor calibration is complete, we can calculate the motor side torque through the motor current. When rotating at a constant speed without load, all the torque generated by the motor current is used to overcome joint friction. The joint friction force can be calculated by testing joint motor current at different rotational speeds. When the joint moves uniformly at different speeds, the friction force obtained by calculating the torque through the joint motor current is shown in Fig. 7. The Stribeck friction model is used for fitting, and the fitting curve equation is (13) and (14).

$$\tau_{f+} = 1.75 + 0.392e^{-2.912|v|} + 0.0375v \tag{13}$$

$$\tau_{f-} = -1.78 - 0.4764e^{-2.21|v|} + 0.0392v \tag{14}$$

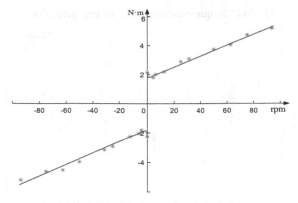

Fig. 7. The friction curve of the joint.

Through this method, we can calculate the friction force of the joint at various rotational speeds based on the above model. We then calculate joint output torque using torque generated by joint motor and friction force for different speeds.

When the joint is rotating, a varying load was applied. Figure 8 a) shows the joint torque estimated by the torque constant of motor in the joint product manual and the actual measured torque curve, which has a root mean square error of 6.84 Nm for torque estimation. Figure 8 b) shows the estimated joint torque curve after joint current torque identification and friction compensation, reducing the root mean square error to 2.29 Nm. By using BP neural network training to compensate for nonlinear errors, Fig. 8 c) shows joint estimated and actual measured torque curves obtained with a root mean square error of 0.86 Nm.After identification, the estimation accuracy of joint torque has improved by 87% compared to before identification (see Fig. 9).

B. *Ground reaction force estimation experiment*

When the robot jumps up and lands in contact with the ground, the ground reaction force can be estimated using joint torque and joint angle information by Eq. (12). We conducted an experiment in which the leg continuously performs vertical takeoff on a force measuring platform. The measured ground reaction force was compared to the estimated ground reaction force to verify this estimation. The results show good matching between the ground reaction obtained through joint estimation and the experimental data measured by the force measuring platform, as shown in Fig. 10.

a) Joint torque estimation before compensation

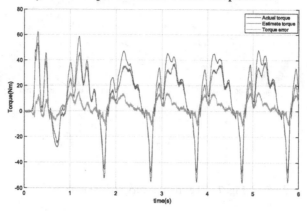

b) Joint torque estimation based on model identification

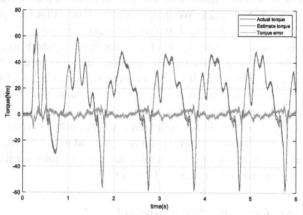

c) Joint torque estimation based on BP neural network

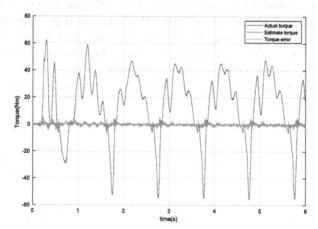

Fig. 8. a) Joint torque estimation before compensation; b) Joint torque estimation based on model identification;c)Joint torque estimation based on BP neural network

Fig. 9. Experimental for the one-legged hopping robot on a force measuring platform.

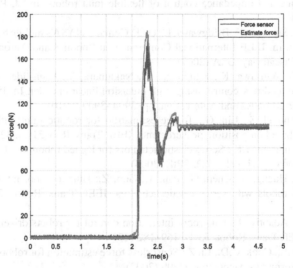

Fig. 10. Comparison of estimation GRF and force sensor measurement data in the vertical direction.

6 Conclusion

This article presents a method for joint torque estimation without torque sensors, and allows for estimation of the ground reaction force for a one-legged hopping robot. We first established a dynamic model of the joint and applied a more accurate friction model. For challenging nonlinear errors that are difficult to compensate, we employed BP neural network training to enhance accuracy. The experiments has verified the precision of our method in estimating both joint torque and ground reaction. Our method offers great practicality, providing promising conditions for force control and state estimation in one-legged hopping robots.

Acknowledgment. This work is supported by National Natural Science Foundation of China (Grants 52205034), "Pioneer" and "Leading Goose" R&D Program of Zhejiang (No. 2023C01177), Key Research Project of Zhejiang Lab (No. G2021NB0AL03), the National Natural Science Foundation of China (Grant No. 52205076).

References

1. Sayyad, A., Seth, B., Seshu, P.: Single-legged hopping robotics research—a review. Robotica **25**(5), 587–613 (2007)
2. Zeng, G., Hemami, A.: An overview of robot force control. Robotica **15**(5), 473–482 (1997)
3. Albu-Schaffer, A., Eiberger, O., Grebenstein, M., et al.: Soft robotics. IEEE Robot. Autom. Mag. **15**(3), 20–30 (2008)
4. Albu-Schaffer, A., Ott, C., Hirzinger, G.: A unified passivity-based control framework for position, torque and impedance control of flexible joint robots. Int. J. Robot. Res. **26**(1), 23–39 (2007)
5. Mehling, J.S., Strawser, P., Bridgwater, L., et al.: Centaur: NASA's mobile humanoid designed for field work. In: IEEE International Conference on Robotics and Automation, pp. 2928–2933. IEEE, Piscataway, USA (2007)
6. Kawakami, T., Ayusawa, K., Kaminaga, H., Nakamura, Y.: High-fidelity joint drive system by torque feedback control using high precision linear encoder. In: IEEE International Conference on Robotics and Automation, pp. 3904–3909 (2010)
7. Zhang, H., Ahmad, S., Liu, G.: Torque estimation for robotic joint with harmonic drive transmission based on position measurements. IEEE Trans. Rob. **31**(2), 322–330 (2015)
8. Pratt, J.E., Benjamin, T.K.: Series elastic actuators for legged robots. In: Unmanned Ground Vehicle Technology Vi, vol. 5422. SPIE (2004)
9. Haoyong, Y., Huang, S., Chen, G., Pan, Y., Guo, Z.: Human–robot interaction control of rehabilitation robots with series elastic actuators. IEEE Trans. Robot. **31**(5), 1089–1100 (2015)
10. Li, X., et al.: Adaptive human–robot interaction control for robots driven by series elastic actuators. IEEE Trans. Robot. **33**(1), 169–182 (2016)
11. Simpson, J.W.L., Cook, C.D., Li, Z.: Sensorless force estimation for robots with friction. In: Faculty of Informatics-papers, pp. 94–99 (2002)
12. Alcocer, A., Robertsson, A., Valera, A., Johansson, R.: Force estimation and control in robot manipulators. Ifac Proceedings Volumes **36**, 55–60 (2003)
13. Albu-Schaffer, A., Hirzinger, G.: Parameter identification and passivity based joint control for a 7 DOF torque controlled light weight robot, In: Proceedings 2001 ICRA. IEEE International Conference on Robotics and Automation (Cat. No. 01CH37164), vol. 3. IEEE (2001)
14. Goh, A.T.C.: Back-propagation neural networks for modeling complex systems. Artif. Intel. Eng. **9**(3), 143–151 (1995)
15. Pratt, J., Dilworth, P., Pratt, G.: Virtual model control of a bipedal walking robot. In: Proceedings of International Conference on Robotics and Automation, pp. 193–198 (1997)
16. Winkler, A., et al.: Path planning with force-based foothold adaptation and virtual model control for torque controlled quadruped robots. In: 2014 IEEE International Conference on Robotics and Automation (ICRA). IEEE (2014)

17. Pratt, J., Chew, C.-M., Torres, A., et al.: Virtual model control: an intuitive approach for bipedal locomotion. Int. J. Robot. Res. **20**(2), 129–143 (2001)
18. Kalouche, S.: GOAT: A legged robot with 3D agility and virtual compliance. In: 2017 IEEE/RSJ International Conference on Intelligent Robots and Systems (IROS), pp. 4110–4117 (2017)

Predefined-Time External Force Estimation for Legged Robots

Peiyuan Cai[1][(✉)], Danfu Liu[1][(✉)], and Lijun Zhu[1,2]

[1] School of Artificial Intelligence and Automation,
Huazhong University of Science and Technology, Wuhan 430074, China
cpy_3566@163.com, 2757086769@qq.com
[2] Key Laboratory of Imaging Processing and Intelligence Control,
Huazhong University of Science and Technology, Wuhan 430074, China
ljzhu@hust.edu.cn

Abstract. Legged robots have recently received widespread attention, and the online measurement/estimation of external torque/force places a vital role on the robust and stable controller design for legged robots. Although the external torque/force can be measured by installing force sensors, the reliability, cost and mechanical feasibility are concerning issues. This paper proposed a sensor-less external torque/force estimation for legged robot based on measurable joint position, velocity and torque. A predefined-time momentum observer (PTO) is proposed to achieve the convergence of the estimation error within the predefined time. Finally, a series of simulations and experiments are implemented to show the effectiveness of the proposed algorithm.

Keywords: Legged robots · Torque/Force estimation · Predefined-time momentum observer (PTO)

1 Introduction

Multi-legged robots have recently received widespread attention in the field of robotics research [1–4]. Compared with wheeled robots, quadruped robots have better flexibility and mobility, and can be used to accomplish complex tasks, such as navigation in complex environments, underground mining area patrols, stair climbing, planets exploring, etc. Estimating the ground reaction force and the contact status are very important for designing a robust and stable controller [5,6].

The approaches for contact force estimation and contact detection can be divided into three categories: 1) Adding an external force sensor [7,8]; 2) Learning based approaches [9,10]; 3) Model-based observer design [11–16]. In practical applications, the first type of method is not suitable since reliable force sensors are often very expensive and mechanically difficult to install at the place. Some sensors are prone to the impact and tend to degrade or even damage. The learning based approaches often requires a large amount of trusted data set and ground truth labeling that is often difficult to obtain. On the contrary, the third type of method is not limited by the above issues and has very good estimation performance when the robot model is given with certain accuracy. In [12], two nonlinear disturbance observers are employed to estimate external forces for a quadruped robot and [11,13,14] proposed a series of methods for state estimation based on Kalman Filter. Besides, Viviana Morlando et al. [15] presents a momentum-based observer and devises a whole-body controller for legged robots.

The convergence time sometime is an important factor to be considered in the observer design. In the literature, finite-time observers [17,18], fixed-time observers [19,20], and predefined-time observers [21] have bee designed. Compared to traditional asymptotically convergent observers, the aforementioned observers have faster convergence speed, higher accuracy and robustness to uncertainties. It is note that the settling time of a finite-time observer depends on the observed parameters and the initial value of the system, while a fixed-time case can remove the dependence on the initial value of the system but still be parameter dependent. On the other hand, the predefined-time observer is recently proposed and can completely eliminate all dependencies. The convergence time can be arbitrarily given by the observer.

In this paper, a novel predefined-time momentum observer (PTO) is proposed. Different from [15], we use a second-order observer model based on super-twisting algorithm (STA) [22] to estimate external forces of quadruped robots. To summarize, our main contributions are as follows:

1) First, a momentum based second-order standard observer form is derived and novel predefined-time observer(PTO) based on standard form is proposed. It demonstrates better convergence and less sensitive to the measure noise, compared to SOSM observer and HGO observer.
2) Based on the standard observer form, the high gain observer (HGO) are proposed. First-order momentum observer, second-order sliding mode momentum observer, HGO and PTO are compared in the simulated quadruped robots.
3) The stability and predefined time convergence of the proposed observer are theoretically guaranteed.

The rest of this paper is organized as follows. In Sect. 2, some necessary definitions and lemmas are reviewed. And a novel predefined-time observer(PTO) based on momentum is introduced in Sect. 3. Then, in Sect. 4, numerical simulations are carried out to verify the effectiveness of the proposed PTO algorithm. Finally, Sect. 5 concludes the paper.

2   Preliminaries and Problem Formulation

Consider the dynamics of a legged robot as follows

$$M(q)\ddot{q} + C(q,\dot{q})\dot{q} + g(q) = u + \tau_e \tag{1}$$

where $q, \dot{q} \in \mathbb{R}^{n_b+n_j}$ denote the generalized state and velocity, respectively, with n_b being the degree of freedom (DoF) of the floating base and n_j the number of the actuated joints. In dynamics (1), $M(q)$, $C(q, \dot{q})\dot{q}$ and $g(q)$ represent the inertia matrix, the generalized Coriolis force and the gravity force, respectively. The generalized force $u = S^{\mathsf{T}}\tau$ results from the joint actuation τ where S is the selection matrix determining the fully and under-actuated parts. The external force/wrench $\tau_e = \sum_{i\in S} J_i^{\mathsf{T}} F_i$ where $S := \{1, \cdots, s\}$ is the set for the end-effectors that are in the contact with the environment with s being its cardinality, and F_i and J_i are the force/wrench and corresponding Jacobian matrix at the ith contact. It can be further written as $\tau_e = J^{\mathsf{T}}F$ with $J = [J_1^{\mathsf{T}}, \cdots, J_s^{\mathsf{T}}]^{\mathsf{T}}$ and $F = [F_1^{\mathsf{T}}, \cdots, F_s^{\mathsf{T}}]^{\mathsf{T}}$.

By estimating τ_e using dynamics (1), the external force/wrench F is calculated as $F = (J^{\mathsf{T}})^{\dagger}\tau_e$ when it is assumed that J is of full row rank. One way to estimate τ_e is to use the measurement q, $\dot{q}$ and its numerical differentiation $\ddot{q}$ as well as the control command u to calculate τ_e directly with (1). The numerical differentiation method results in noisy $\ddot{q}$ and thus worsens estimation performance. The momentum based method avoids the use of $\ddot{q}$ and uses the following fact of the Euler-Lagrange system [23],

$$\dot{M}(q) = C^{\mathsf{T}}(q, \dot{q}) + C(q, \dot{q}). \tag{2}$$

The generalized momentum of the legged robot is defined as

$$p = M(q)\dot{q}. \tag{3}$$

The derivative of the generalized momentum can be obtained using Eqs. (1) and (2) and given as follows

$$\begin{aligned} \dot{p} &= \dot{M}(q)\dot{q} + M(q)\ddot{q} \\ &= u + C^{\mathsf{T}}(q, \dot{q})\dot{q} - g(q) + \tau_e \end{aligned} \tag{4}$$

Based on (4), a first-order (FO) momentum observer is proposed in [15] as

$$\hat{\tau}_e = K_o\left(p - \int_0^t (u + C^{\mathsf{T}}(q, \dot{q})\dot{q} - g(q) + \hat{\tau}_e)\mathrm{d}s - p(0)\right) \tag{5}$$

with the gain parameter K_o which requires the knowledge of the initial $p(0)$. The FO is prone to the measurement noise and only achieves the exponential convergence. The second-order momentum observer is proposed in [24] to achieve the finite-time convergence. A common assumption to derive the second-order momentum observer is given as follows.

Assumption 2.1. The external torque τ_e is differentiable and its time derivative are bounded L, i.e., there exist some function $\phi(t)$ and a known constant such that

$$\dot{\tau}_e = \phi(t), \ |\phi(t)| \le L.$$

In this paper, we aim to propose a prescribed-time momentum observer rather than a finite-time observer. The predefined-time stability is defined as follows, compared with the finite-time stability given in Definition 2.1.

Consider a controlled dynamic system

$$\dot{x}(t) = g(x(t), u(t)), x(0) = x_0 \qquad (6)$$

where $x \in \mathbb{R}^n$ and $u \in \mathbb{R}^m$ are the state and control input of the system, respectively. The function $g : \mathbb{R}^n \times \mathbb{R}^m \mapsto \mathbb{R}$ satisfies $g(0,0) = 0$ and the origin is thus an equilibrium.

Definition 2.1. ([25]) The system (6) is said to be globally finite-time stable (FTS) if it is globally asymptotically stable and there exists a function $T(x_0) : \mathbb{R}^n \mapsto \mathbb{R}_+ \cup \{0\}$ depending on the initial condition x_0 such that $\lim_{t \to T(x_0)} \|x(t)\| = 0, \forall x_0 \in \mathbb{R}^n$ and $x(t) = 0$ when $t > T(x_0)$. ■

Definition 2.2. ([26]) The system (6) is said to be semi-global predefined-time stable (PTS) if for any given initial condition and prescribed constant $T_s > 0$, the system is globally finite-time stable and $T(x_0) \leq T_s$ and $\lim_{t \to T_s} \|x(t)\| = 0, \forall x_0 \in \mathbb{R}^n$ and $x(t) = 0$ for $t > T_s$. ■

The comparison between Definition 2.1 and 2.2 shows that the PTS has better and flexible convergence property than the FTS. The convergence time of the PTS is prescribed by the designer, while that of the FTS depends on the initial condition. The predefined-time momentum observer proposed in this paper can be used to estimate the ground reaction force of legged robots and then detect the contact status with the ground, which are very important for the model-based control for legged robots.

3   Main Results

In this section, we first present the general form of the second-order momentum observer, which leads to the high-gain observer, and then we propose the predefined-time momentum observer.

From Assumption 2.1, the Eq. (4) can be rewritten as a second-order dynamic model as

$$\dot{p} = H(u, \dot{q}, q) + \tau_e$$
$$\dot{\tau}_e = \phi(t) \qquad (7)$$

where $H(u, \dot{q}, q) = u + C^{\mathrm{T}}(q, \dot{q})\dot{q} - g(q)$. Let us define $\hat{q}$ and $\hat{\tau}_e$ be the estimated value for q and τ_e, respectively. Based on Eq. (7), the second-order momentum observer can be organized as a general form

$$\dot{\hat{p}} = H(u, \dot{q}, q) + \hat{\tau}_e + \kappa(e)$$
$$\dot{\hat{\tau}}_e = \tilde{\kappa}(e) \qquad (8)$$

with $e = p - \hat{p} \in \mathbb{R}^n$ where $\kappa(e)$ and $\tilde{\kappa}(e)$ are the input to be designed. Let $\tilde{e} = \tau_e - \hat{\tau}_e = [\tilde{e}_1, \cdots, \tilde{e}_n]^{\mathrm{T}}$ and decompose $e = [e_1, \cdots, e_n]^{\mathrm{T}}$. Then, the estimation error dynamics can be written as

$$\dot{e} = \tilde{e} - \kappa(e)$$
$$\dot{\tilde{e}} = -\tilde{\kappa}(e) + \phi(t). \qquad (9)$$

The aforementioned second-order momentum observers can be organized in the form of (8) with different functions $\kappa(\cdot)$, $\tilde{\kappa}(\cdot)$, e.g., SOSM momentum observer in [24] is in the form of (8) with

$$\kappa(e) = C_1 \text{sig}^{\frac{1}{2}}(e) + D_1 e$$
$$\tilde{\kappa}(e) = C_2 \text{sign}(e) + D_2 e \tag{10}$$

where $\text{sign}(\cdot)$ is the sign function, $\text{sig}^{\frac{1}{2}}(e) = \Lambda(e)\text{sign}(e)$ with $\Lambda(e) = \text{diag}\{|e_1|^{1/2}, \cdots, |e_n|^{1/2}\}$ and $C_1, C_2, D_1, D_2 \in \mathbb{R}^{n \times n}$ are positive definite diagonal matrices. Note that the sign function applies elementwisely for a vector input.

3.1   High-Gain Observer

Based on the form (8), a high-gain observer (HGO) can be designed as

$$\kappa(e) = \frac{a_1}{\varepsilon} e, \; \tilde{\kappa}(e) = \frac{a_2}{\varepsilon^2} e, \tag{11}$$

where $\varepsilon, a_1, a_2 > 0$ are the gains. Define $\tilde{e} = \tau_e - \hat{\tau}_e$. Then, the error dynamics in (9) becomes

$$\dot{e} = -\frac{a_1}{\varepsilon} e + \tilde{e}$$
$$\dot{\tilde{e}} = -\frac{a_2}{\varepsilon^2} e + \phi(t). \tag{12}$$

Let $\eta = [e^{\mathrm{T}}/\varepsilon, \tilde{e}]^{\mathrm{T}}$. The dynamics (12) is written in the vector form as

$$\varepsilon\dot{\eta} = A\eta + \varepsilon B\phi(t) \tag{13}$$

with

$$A = \begin{bmatrix} -a_1 & 1 \\ -a_2 & 0 \end{bmatrix} \otimes I_n, \; B = \begin{bmatrix} 0 \\ 1 \end{bmatrix} \otimes 1_n$$

where I_n and 1_n denote the identity matrix of the size $n \times n$ and n-dimensional column vector with all elements being 1, respectively. The matrix F is Hurwitz when $a_1, a_2 > 0$. Taking the Lyapunov candidate function as $V = \eta^{\mathrm{T}} P_0 \eta$ with the positive definite matrix P_0 satisfying $P_0 A + A^{\mathrm{T}} P_0 = -I_{2n}$, the bound of its derivative is calculated as

$$\varepsilon\dot{V} \leq -\frac{1}{2}||\eta||^2 + 2\varepsilon L||P_0 B||||\eta|| \tag{14}$$

which leads to the bound of η as $||\eta(t)|| \leq \max\{be^{-at/\varepsilon}||\eta(0)||, \varepsilon cL\}$ for some $a, b, c > 0$. The more detailed derivation is similar to that in [27]. For a sufficiently small ε, the bound of η shows that the high-gain observer has fast convergence rate. Due to the high gain used in the estimation, it is very sensitive to measurement noises.

3.2   Predefined-Time Observer

We first define a function $h : \mathbb{R} \mapsto \mathbb{R}$ as $h(x) = \frac{x}{1+|x|}$ and thus $\mathrm{d}h(x)/\mathrm{d}x = 1/(1+|x|)^2 \neq 0$. Let us decompose $\kappa(e)$ and $\tilde{\kappa}(e)$ as $\kappa(e) = [\kappa_1(e_1), \cdots, \kappa_n(e_n)]$ and $\tilde{\kappa}(e) = [\tilde{\kappa}_1(e_1), \cdots, \tilde{\kappa}_n(e_n)]$ where $n = n_b + n_j$. The momentum-based predefined-time observer is proposed in the form of (8) with functions $\kappa(e)$ and $\tilde{\kappa}(e)$ specified by their elements as

$$\kappa(e_i) = k_i \left(\frac{\mathrm{d}h(e_i)}{\mathrm{d}e_i} \right)^{-1} |h(e_i)|^{\frac{1}{2}} \mathrm{sign}(e_i)$$

$$\tilde{\kappa}(e_i) = \frac{(1 + 4|e_i|)k_i^2}{2} (1 + |e_i|)^2 \mathrm{sign}(e_i)$$

(15)

with $k_i > 0$.

Then, the error dynamics in (9) can be written elementwisely as

$$\dot{e}_i = \tilde{e}_i - k_i \left(\frac{\mathrm{d}h(e_i)}{\mathrm{d}e_i} \right)^{-1} |h(e_i)|^{\frac{1}{2}} \mathrm{sign}(e_i)$$

$$\dot{\tilde{e}}_i = -\frac{(1 + 4|e_i|)k_i^2}{2} (1 + |e_i|)^2 \mathrm{sign}(e_i) + \phi_i(t)$$

(16)

for all $i = 1, \cdots, n$, where ϕ_i is the ith element of ϕ function. Then, the predefined-time stability of the observer (8) with $\kappa(e_i)$ and $\tilde{\kappa}(e_i)$ defined in (15) is provided in the next theorem, whose proof is omitted here.

Theorem 3.1. *For a given initial value $[e_i^T(t_0), \tilde{e}_i^T(t_0)]^T$ and prescribed converge time T_s, there always exists a k_i for $i = 1, \cdots, n$ such that the predefined-time observer (15) achieve the semi-global predefined-time estimation of the external force τ_e, i.e.,*

$$\lim_{t \to T_s} \tau_e(t) - \hat{\tau}_e(t) = 0.$$

4   Simulation and Experiment

In this section, we present two simulation examples to verify the effectiveness of the proposed PTO observer. In both examples, we use the proposed observer to estimate the contact forces of the quadruped robot. In the first example, the contact force is provided by a reference signal. This example is less realistic, since the contact in reality is generated due to the interaction between the robot and environment and could be in any form. But it can effectively verify the proposed algorithm. In the second example, we use a model-based locomotion controller to control the quadruped robot and estimate its contact forces while it is moving. Both simulation examples are conducted in Gazebo with simulated Unitree A1 robot in Fig. 1.

Throughout above experiments, we compare the estimation performance of the FO (5), the SOSM (10), the HGO (11) and the proposed PTO observer (15). For Unitree A1 robot, the external torque in (1) is $\tau_e = J^T F$ where $J = $

$[J_1^T, \cdots, J_4^T]^T, F = [F_1^T, \cdots, F_4^T]^T$ with $F_i \in R^3$ and $J_i \in R^{3 \times 18}$. F_i and J_i are the force and the corresponding jacobian matrix at the ith foot. Then, for each leg of Unitree A1 robot, the contact force can be calculated by $F_i = \mathcal{S}_i (J_i^T)^\dagger \tau_e$ where $\mathcal{S}_i$ is the matrix used to select the corresponding entries for the ith foot.

Fig. 1. Unitree A1 robot in Gazebo

4.1   Single Leg Force Estimation

In the first example, we only consider one leg part of the A1 robot, which consists of three actuated joints. The robot body is fixed to the global axis and it becomes a fixed-base robot. The simple PD controller is applied to stabilize the robot to a specified posture. In this setup, the single leg structure is equivalent to a 3-DOFs robotic arm model. Then a time-varying reference external force $F(t)$ as illustrated in Fig. 1 (Left) is added to the point foot along the z-axis and it is

$$F(t) = \begin{cases} 30\,N, t \in [0,3]s \\ 50\,N, t \in (3,5]s \\ 25(t-5)N, t \in (5,7]s \\ 50 - 25(t-7)N, t \in (7,9]s \\ 0\,N, t \in (9,10]s \end{cases} \tag{17}$$

Then, we use the FO with the parameter $K_o = 300$, the SOSM with parameters $C_1 = 150, D_1 = 0, C_2 = 1000, D_2 = 0$, the HGO with parameters $a_1 = 2, a_2 = 8, \varepsilon = 0.001$ and the proposed PTO observer with the parameter $c_\lambda = 2, T_s = 0.1\,\mathrm{s}$ to estimate the external force.

As shown in Fig. 2.a, the estimation error still exists when the estimation error converges. As illustrated in Fig. 3.a, FO is very sensitive to measurement noises. In contrast, second-order sliding mode observers have better estimation performance. Among four observers, HGO has fastest response as illustrated in Fig. 2.c when ϵ is selected sufficiently small, but it becomes very sensitive to measurement noises as illustrated in Fig. 3.c. Proper parameter selection could lead to its applications on practical scenarios. As illustrated in Fig. 3, FO, SOSM

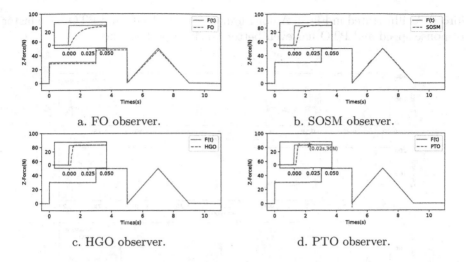

a. FO observer.   b. SOSM observer.

c. HGO observer.   d. PTO observer.

Fig. 2. Comparison of four observers for external force estimation in single leg.

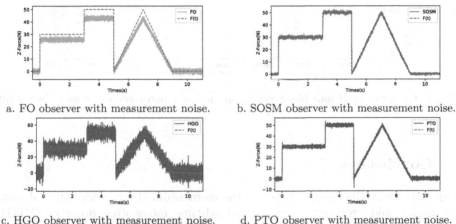

a. FO observer with measurement noise.   b. SOSM observer with measurement noise.

c. HGO observer with measurement noise.   d. PTO observer with measurement noise.

Fig. 3. Comparison of four observers for external force estimation in single leg with measurement noises $c \sim N(0, 0.1)$.

and PTO are less sensitive to the measurement noise. As shown in Fig. 2.d, our proposed PTO observer converges before the predefined time $T_s = 0.1s$ and actual settling time $t = 0.02\,\text{s} < T_s$.

4.2 Force Estimation for Unitree A1 Robot

Then, we implement an MPC controller to achieve the complete quadruped robot to achieve diagonal trot gait in Gazebo as illustrated in Fig. 1 (Right).

The parameters of the four observers were set to be the same as that in Sect. 4.1. We compare these four observers to estimate the ground reaction forces. As illustrated in Fig. 4. Among four observers, HGO and PTO have faster response speed and PTO has even better tracking performance.

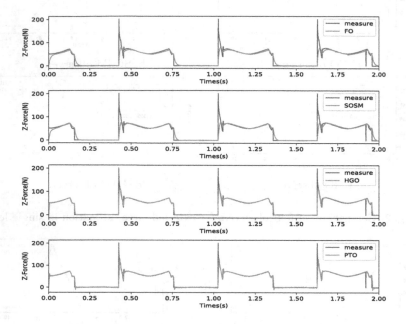

Fig. 4. Comparison of four observers for ground reaction force estimation (left front leg).

5   Conclusions

This paper uses the design method of the momentum observer for external force estimation and proposes a new predefined-time momentum observer (PTO). Compared to the current existing momentum observer, its convergence time can be arbitrarily given by the controller and estimation error is not sensitive to the measurement noise. Our algorithm requires an accurate dynamic model and therefore system uncertainty would impact the effectiveness of the proposed algorithm. In our future work, we will focus on solving the estimation problem for uncertain systems.

References

1. Kim, D., Carlo, J.D., Katz, B., Bledt, G., Kim, S.: Highly dynamic quadruped locomotion via whole-body impulse control and model predictive control. arXiv arXiv:1909.06586 (2019)
2. Klemm, V., et al.: LQR-assisted whole-body control of a wheeled bipedal robot with kinematic loops. IEEE Robot. Autom. Lett. **5**(2), 3745–3752 (2020)

3. Chao, Z.A., Tl, A., Shuang, S., Envelope, J., Qhm, B.: Dynamic wheeled motion control of wheel-biped transformable robots. Biomimetic Intell. Robot. **2**(2) (2021)
4. Grandia, R., Jenelten, F., Yang, S., Farshidian, F., Hutter, M.: Perceptive locomotion through nonlinear model predictive control (2022)
5. Aceituno-Cabezas, B., et al.: Simultaneous contact, gait, and motion planning for robust multilegged locomotion via mixed-integer convex optimization. IEEE Robot. Autom. Lett. **3**(3), 2531–2538 (2018)
6. Hereid, A., Hubicki, C.M., Cousineau, E.A., Ames, A.D.: Dynamic humanoid locomotion: a scalable formulation for HZD gait optimization. IEEE Trans. Robot. **34**(2), 370–387 (2018)
7. Kaneko, K., et al.: Slip observer for walking on a low friction floor. In: 2005 IEEE/RSJ International Conference on Intelligent Robots and Systems, pp. 634–640 (2005)
8. Maravgakis, M., Argiropoulos, D.E., Piperakis, S., Trahanias, P.E.: Probabilistic contact state estimation for legged robots using inertial information. arXiv, abs/2303.00538 (2023)
9. Liu, Q., Yuan, B., Wang, Y.: Online learning for foot contact detection of legged robot based on data stream clustering. Front. Bioeng. Biotechnol. **9** (2022)
10. Wisth, D., Camurri, M., Fallon, M.F.: Robust legged robot state estimation using factor graph optimization. IEEE Robot. Autom. Lett. **4**, 4507–4514 (2019)
11. Bloesch, M., Gehring, C., Fankhauser, P., Hutter, M., Hoepflinger, M.A., Siegwart, R.: State estimation for legged robots on unstable and slippery terrain. In: 2013 IEEE/RSJ International Conference on Intelligent Robots and Systems, pp. 6058–6064 (2013)
12. Dini, N., Majd, V.J., Edrisi, F., Attar, M.: Estimation of external forces acting on the legs of a quadruped robot using two nonlinear disturbance observers. In: 2016 4th International Conference on Robotics and Mechatronics (ICROM), pp. 72–77 (2016)
13. Varin, P., Kuindersma, S.: A constrained Kalman filter for rigid body systems with frictional contact. In: Workshop on the Algorithmic Foundations of Robotics (2018)
14. Teng, S., Mueller, M.W., Sreenath, K.: Legged robot state estimation in slippery environments using invariant extended Kalman filter with velocity update. In: 2021 IEEE International Conference on Robotics and Automation (ICRA), pp. 3104–3110 (2021)
15. Morlando, V., Teimoorzadeh, A., Ruggiero, F.: Whole-body control with disturbance rejection through a momentum-based observer for quadruped robots. Mech. Mach. Theory **164**, 104412 (2021)
16. Kim, J.-H., et al.: Legged robot state estimation with dynamic contact event information. IEEE Robot. Autom. Lett. **6**(4), 6733–6740 (2021)
17. Shen, Y., Huang, Y., Gu, J.: Global finite-time observers for lipschitz nonlinear systems. IEEE Trans. Autom. Control **56**(2), 418–424 (2011)
18. Zhang, P., Kao, Y., Hu, J., Niu, B., Xia, H., Wang, C.: Finite-time observer-based sliding-mode control for Markovian jump systems with switching chain: average dwell-time method. IEEE Trans. Cybern. **53**(1), 248–261 (2023)
19. Zhou, S., Guo, K., Yu, X., Guo, L., Xie, L.: Fixed-time observer based safety control for a quadrotor UAV. IEEE Trans. Aerosp. Electron. Syst. **57**(5), 2815–2825 (2021)
20. Moreno, J.A.: Arbitrary-order fixed-time differentiators. IEEE Trans. Autom. Control **67**(3), 1543–1549 (2022)
21. Holloway, J., Krstic, M.: Prescribed-time observers for linear systems in observer canonical form. IEEE Trans. Autom. Control **64**(9), 3905–3912 (2019)

22. Moreno, J.A., Osorio, M.: Strict Lyapunov functions for the super-twisting algorithm. IEEE Trans. Autom. Control **57**(4), 1035–1040 (2012)
23. Spong, M., Hutchinson, S., Vidyasagar, M., Skaar, S.B.: Robot modeling and control. IEEE Trans. Autom. Control **52**, 378–379 (2007)
24. Garofalo, G., Mansfeld, N., Jankowski, J., Ott, C.: Sliding mode momentum observers for estimation of external torques and joint acceleration. In: 2019 International Conference on Robotics and Automation (ICRA), pp. 6117–6123 (2019)
25. Polyakov, A.: Nonlinear feedback design for fixed-time stabilization of linear control systems. IEEE Trans. Autom. Control **57**(8), 2106–2110 (2012)
26. Jiménez-Rodríguez, E., Muñoz-Vázquez, A.J., Sánchez-Torres, J.D., Defoort, M., Loukianov, A.G.: A Lyapunov-like characterization of predefined-time stability. IEEE Trans. Autom. Control **65**(11), 4922–4927 (2020)
27. Khalil, H.K.: High-Gain Observers in Nonlinear Feedback Control. Society for Industrial and Applied Mathematics, Philadelphia, PA (2017)

Movement Analysis of a Landing Buffer Mobile Mechanism with Eccentric Load

Wei Liu[1], Zhijun Chen[2], Fei Yang[3], Yong Zhao[3(✉)], Jianzhong Yang[1], and Feng Gao[2]

[1] Beijing Institute of Spacecraft System Engineering, Beijing 100094, China
[2] School of Mechanical Engineering, Shanghai Jiao Tong University, Shanghai 200030, China
[3] School of Mechatronics Engineering, Harbin Institute of Technology, Harbin 150001, China
24048774@qq.com

Abstract. Based on the traditional four-legged landing buffer mechanism, a buffer mobile integration mechanism with landing cushioning and active movement is proposed, providing the moving capability of the lunar surface for the large mass lander of more than 1 ton. The mobile planning strategy is designed and a mobile gait planning method is provided. The kinematics model of the mechanism is established, and the movement performance of the four-leg parallel system in a symmetrical standing posture is analyzed. As for the gravity center offset of the lander, an adjustment method for the asymmetric standing posture of the four legs is proposed, and the movement characteristics of the lander after applying this method are further analyzed. The results show that the lander can successfully move uphill, flat, and downhill, solving the problem of omnidirectional movement under the uncertainty of landing terrain and orientation. The proposed buffer mobile mechanism and the adjustment method for an asymmetric standing posture of four legs provide support for future catalog buffering movement detection tasks.

Keywords: Lander · Buffer · Moving · Integration · Eccentric Load

1 Introduction

Conventional deep space exploration mission landers cannot move after landing, and can only carry out in-situ detection, limiting the detection range [1–4]. Due to the limitation of movement capacity, the inherent capacity of the lander, such as large carrying capacity, strong power supply capacity and carrying capacity of multi payload, has not been explored and utilized to the greatest extent. The rover is unable to achieve landing buffering and stable landing, which restricts the scope and effectiveness of deep space exploration tasks [5–7] Therefore, it is necessary to carry out research on integrated detection technology of buffering and movement, improving the survival and working ability of deep space detectors in complex environments [8–15].

The lander generally uses a four-legged landing buffer mechanism to achieve a stable landing, which has the foundation to realize the movement of the lander. Under the condition that the resources of the lander are occupied as little as possible and the number of legs remains unchanged, the movement after landing can be realized by relying on the landing buffer mechanism and integrating the motor drive device in the landing buffer mechanism. In the paper, a new integrated landing buffer and movement mechanism is proposed for improving the detection range of the lander. The motion characteristics of the four-legged lander are analyzed. And the method to improve the mobility of the lander in the case of centroid migration is proposed.

2 Structure and Working Principle

Figure 1 shows the layout of the landing buffer mobile mechanism. Four sets of landing buffer mobile mechanisms are uniformly installed around the lander body. Each landing buffer mobile mechanism has the same composition, forming a set of parallel systems. They play the role of buffering and energy consumption during the landing process and provide the movement ability for the lander after landing.

Lander   Landing buffer mobile mechanism

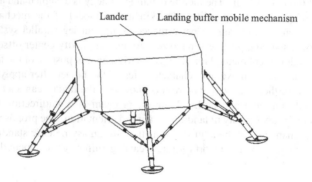

Fig. 1. The layout of the landing buffer mobile mechanism

The leg type mobile mechanisms can be divided into a series configuration, hybrid configuration, and parallel configuration. The mass of the lander is generally more than 1 ton, while the bearing capacity of series configuration and hybrid configuration is relatively weak, therefore, considering the bearing and landing safety and other factors, one of the parallel configuration, 3-UPS leg is selected as the configuration of each set of landing buffer mobile integration mechanism, as shown in Fig. 2.

Figure 3 compares the differences between the traditional landing buffer mechanism and the new landing buffer mobile mechanism. The traditional landing buffer mechanism only includes the main pillar, auxiliary pillar, and foot pad, as shown in Fig. 3(a). The main pillar and auxiliary pillar only have passive buffering functions without any active telescoping capability. Therefore, the traditional landing buffer mechanism cannot actively retract or swing for the movement of the lander. The new landing buffer mobile mechanism is shown in Fig. 3(b) and its prototype is shown in Fig. 3(c). Different from the traditional configuration, the main and auxiliary pillars not only include buffers but also incorporate a drive unit that can retract in a straight line under a motor drive, thus enabling each pillar to have active retraction capability. In order to protect the drive unit

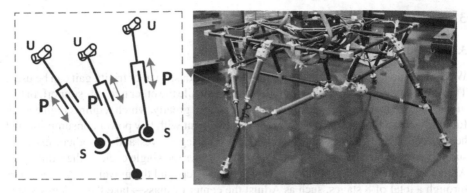

Fig. 2. 3-UPS four legged parallel system

from damage caused by landing impact loads, a locking device is installed between the drive unit and the buffer to lock the drive unit during landing. After the safe landing of the lander, the locking device will be unlocked, so as to remove the restrictions on the drive unit. A single integrated mechanism has three active degrees of freedom, which can be used to accurately plan the foot to reach any target point in its workspace. The movement of the lander can be realized under the cooperation of four sets of landing buffer mobile mechanisms.

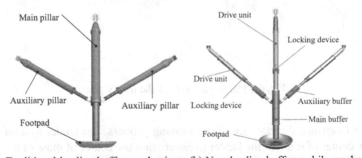

(a) Traditional landing buffer mechanism (b) New landing buffer mobile mechanism

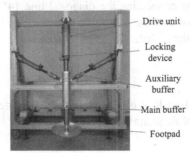

(c) Prototype of the new landing buffer mobile mechanism

Fig. 3. Comparison the differences of the two landing buffer mechanisms

3 Movement Strategy

3.1 Mobile Gait

When the four-legged parallel system moves, the biphasic gait or trinity gait can be used. The biphasic gait means two legs moving together while the other two legs support. In this mode, the gravity center height of the lander changes greatly, which requires high energy for the system and is not suitable for lander movement with low power consumption and heavy load. The trinity gait means that only one leg moves and the others maintain support during the movement process. Figure 4 shows the single cycle of the trinity gait. Adjust the center of mass position before each leg step, and the movement process goes through a total of 8 stages, such as Adjust the center of mass→take the $1^\#$ leg→adjust the center of mass→take the $2^\#$ leg→adjust the center of mass→take the $4^\#$ leg→adjust the center of mass→take the $3^\#$ leg.

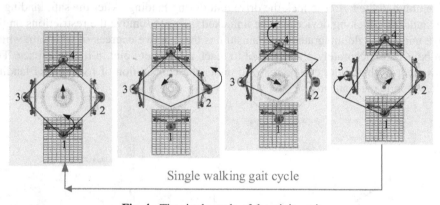

Fig. 4. The single cycle of the trinity gait

In order to ensure the stability of the moving process, the lander system needs to identify the center of mass of the lander to ensure that the center of mass of the lander is within the stable boundary. Figure 5 showsthe center of mass identification. The center of mass is located on the line connecting the diagonal line $14^\#$ of the four legs. When lifting the $2^\#$ leg, the center of mass is on a stable boundary and must be adjusted to the AB line towards the side of the $3^\#$ leg.

3.2 Mobile Planning

During the movement, the four-legs of the lander need to step alternately. Figure 6 introduces the process of mobile planning strategy.

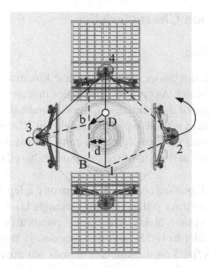

Fig. 5. Center of mass identification

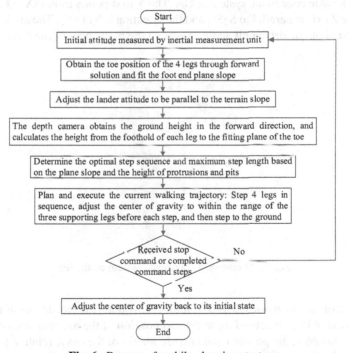

Fig. 6. Process of mobile planning strategy

4   Analysis of Motion Characteristics

4.1   Kinematics Modeling

During the movement of the lander, both the inverse kinematics and the forward kinematics of the leg are involved. As for the Kinematics inverse analysis, according to the foot pad position at the end of the mechanism, the kinematic distance of all moving pairs is obtained in reverse, which is used to plan the single leg. The Kinematics forward solution analysis is mainly used for identifying the center of mass on the device. Calculate the position of the foot pad at the end of the mechanism based on the length of the three moving pairs.

Figure 7 shows the established coordinate system on the leg. First, connect the centers of the universal joint of the three pillars to form a triangle U_1, U_2, and U_3. And establish a single-leg coordinate system at U_1. The Y-axis points from U_1 to the midpoint of U_2U_3, the Z-axis is parallel to U_2U_3, and the direction is from U_3 to U_2. The single-leg coordinate system is fixed on the lander and does not move with the movement of the strut. Connect the two spherical hinge centers with the main pillar axis to form an isosceles triangle $O_AS_2S_3$. The triangle plane is perpendicular to the main pillar axis. Establish an ankle coordinate system at OA. The Y axis points from OA to the midpoint of S_2S_3, the Z axis is parallel to S_2S_3, and the direction is S_3 to S_2. The ankle coordinate system is fixed on the drive unit and moves with the movement of the drive unit.

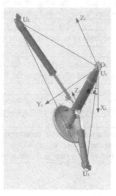

Fig. 7.   Established coordinate system on the leg.

The idea of the kinematics inverse solution is to obtain the two angles of U_1 pair and the elongation of P_1 pair according to the end position of the mechanism. According to these three variables, the position and attitude matrix of the ankle relative to the lander can be calculated. Based on this pose matrix, the position of the S pair on the ankle in the leg coordinate system can be determined, and then the elongation of P_2 and P_3 pairs can be obtained.

Based on geometric relationship analysis, it can be solved l_1, as follows:

$$l_1 = \sqrt{x^2 + y^2 + z^2 - S_{fy}^2 - S_{fz}^2} - S_{fx} \tag{1}$$

Further analysis can determine the input variables l_2 and l_3, as follows:

$$l_2 = \left| \overrightarrow{{}^L U_2^L S_2} \right| = \left| {}^L A \cdot {}^A S_2 - {}^L U_2 \right| \tag{2}$$

$$l_3 = \left| \overrightarrow{{}^L U_3^L S_3} \right| = \left| {}^L A \cdot {}^A S_3 - {}^L U_3 \right| \tag{3}$$

${}^A S_{2,3}$, and ${}^L U_{2,3}$ are size constants (the upper left label indicates the coordinate system), which have been determined during the mechanism design process. ${}^L A$ is the posture matrix of the ankle relative to the lander.

$$
{}^L A = \begin{pmatrix}
c_{\alpha 1} c_{\beta 1} & -c_{\alpha 1} s_{\beta 1} & s_{\alpha 1} & l_1 c_{\alpha 1} c_{\beta 1} \\
s_{\beta 1} & c_{\beta 1} & 0 & l_1 s_{\beta 1} \\
-s_{\alpha 1} c_{\beta 1} & s_{\alpha 1} s_{\beta 1} & c_{\alpha 1} & -l_1 s_{\alpha 1} c_{\beta 1} \\
0 & 0 & 0 & 1
\end{pmatrix} \tag{4}
$$

The idea of solving the forward solution is still to first calculate the two corners of U_1 pair based on three known inputs. Later use α_1, β_1 and l_1 can calculate the pose matrix ${}^L A$. Based on this pose matrix, the position of the end S_f pair in the leg coordinate system can be determined.

4.2 Analysis of Four Legs Symmetrical Standing Movement

The step length and speed of four-legged movement are not only limited by the workspace of a single leg but also influenced by the distance adjusted by the center of mass during movement. The center of mass must not exceed the support boundary. Considering the floating range of ± 0.02 m from the center of mass position to the coordinate origin, as well as the estimation error of the center of mass position caused by attitude measurement error (taken as $\pm 0.5°$), the sum of the two is determined as the minimum distance from the center of mass to the boundary in the motion planning.

The climbing capacity of the lander along the connecting line of the two adjacent leg pads is lower than that along the connecting line of the diagonal leg pads, so the analysis is carried out by moving along the connecting line of the diagonal leg pads. Perform the analysis in a symmetrical pattern with four legs standing in the same posture. In order to obtain the most convenient configuration for movement, the side length of the square supported by the foot pad center and the height of the lander are traversed. When the lander is lifted 0.184 m and the foot pad center is retracted 0.12 m, the movement step length is the largest.

The lander has a 0.2 m lateral eccentricity due to various factors. When the center of mass is inclined to the uphill direction, the movement ability is strong, while when the center of mass is inclined to the downhill direction, it can only adapt to the movement demand of 1.8° slope. Movement characteristics in symmetrical standing posture are listed in Table 1. In the slope, "+" means that the center of mass is offset downward and the lander moves uphill; "−" means that the center of mass is offset uphill and the lander moves downhill.

Table 1. Movement performance in symmetrical standing posture

	Slope	Step length (m)	Speed (m/h)	Swing order
1	1.8°	0.023 m	1.357	1→2→4→3
2	1.0°	0.138 m	5.481	1→2→4→3
3	0°	0.224 m	6.439	1→2→4→3
4	−1.0°	0.290 m	6.873	1→2→4→3
5	−2.0°	0.349 m	7.124	1→2→4→3
6	−3.0°	0.406 m	7.316	1→2→4→3
7	−4.0°	0.462 m	7.459	1→2→4→3
8	−5.0°	0.463 m	7.460	1→2→4→3
9	−6.0°	0.412 m	7.363	1→2→4→3
10	−7.0°	0.456 m	7.190	2→1→3→4
11	−8.0°	0.444 m	7.136	2→1→3→4
12	−9.0°	0.383 m	6.982	2→1→3→4
13	−10.0°	0.319 m	6.776	2→1→3→4
14	−11.0°	0.255 m	6.480	2→1→3→4
15	−12.0°	0.190 m	6.014	2→1→3→4
16	−13.0°	0.123 m	5.161	2→1→3→4
17	−13.7°	0.025 m	1.432	2→1→3→4

4.3 Analysis of Asymmetric Standing Movement of Four Legs

According to the analysis in Sect. 4.2, in a symmetrical standing posture with four legs, the step length is only 0.023m at a slope of 1.8°. It shows that under this condition, the lander can no longer adapt to a larger slope, and can almost only move when the center of mass is inclined to the slope and flat ground. However, in actual engineering tasks, the landing terrain and landing orientation of the lander are uncertain, which seriously restricts the mobility of the lander. When the angle θ between the orientation of the lander and the uphill direction is within 45°–90°, the two legs facing downhill cannot be lifted, as shown in Fig. 8.

The method of the asymmetric standing posture of four legs is adopted to increase the support range of the eccentric side of the leg, which can increase the adjustable range of the center of mass and improve the moving ability of the lander. During the movement process, it is also necessary to consider the influence of the height of the center of mass from the ground. As shown in Fig. 5 center of mass identification, considering the eccentricity and height of the center of mass, the center of mass must always remain within a stable boundary.

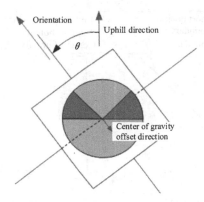

Fig. 8. Eccentric orientation and corresponding leg lifting situation

In the first stage, adjust the center of mass to the intersection point of the diagonal foot pad center line by stepping towards the two legs on the slope. Then, take four more legs to adjust to the required standing posture for the mobile turn. Figure 9 shows the relationship between the center of mass and the position of the support in the first stage (taking out two legs). We selected the most severe θ of 45° situation for analysis. By stepping on two legs on the slope, the range of support in the direction of the slope has been increased.

After completing the first stage of adjustment, the two legs in the downhill direction have legroom. Continue adjusting the two legs in the downhill direction, and then adjust the two legs in the uphill direction. Reaching the adjustment end state shown in the figure supports the quadrangle, thus completing the adjustment of the asymmetric standing posture of the lander, as shown in Fig. 10.

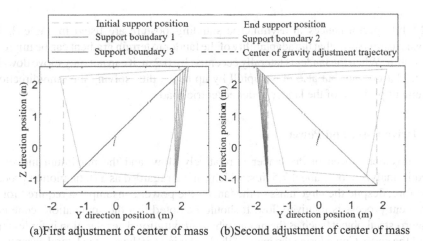

(a)First adjustment of center of mass   (b)Second adjustment of center of mass

Fig. 9. In the first stage (taking out two legs), the relationship between the center of mass and the position of the support

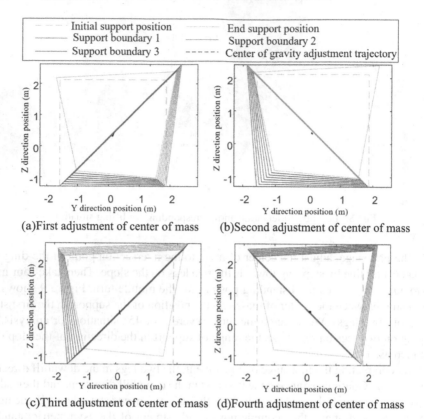

Fig. 10. In the second stage (taking out four legs), the relationship between the center of mass and the position of the support

Mobile performances in asymmetric standing posture are listed in Table 2. The analysis results show that the adaptability of the lander to terrain gradient can be improved to 9° uphill. When the lander is laterally eccentric by 0.2 m, it can not only move downhill and on flat ground, but also move uphill by up to 9°, thus solving the omnidirectional movement problem of the lander under eccentric load.

4.4 Drive Force and Power

The movement speed of the lander is relatively slow, and the maximum movement speed is analyzed to be about 7.5 m/s, which can be regarded as a static motion process. Therefore, despite the large mass of the lander, the power consumption required for the movement process is relatively low. It should be noted that the application scene is an extraterrestrial object, such as the moon, whose gravitational acceleration is far less than that of the earth. Considering the mass of the lander is 1680 kg and the lateral eccentricity of the centroid is 0.2 m, the self weight of the lander is only 2744 N in the Gravitation of

Table 2. Mobile performance in asymmetric standing posture

Slope	Step length (m)	Time consuming (s)	Speed (m/h)
9°	0.016	122.7	0.481
8°	0.087	138.2	2.260
7°	0.156	178.0	3.161
6°	0.226	221.5	3.670
5°	0.245	231.3	3.806
4°	0.262	241.1	3.907
3°	0.279	251.5	3.992
2°	0.296	261.8	4.070
1°	0.314	273.7	4.131

the Moon. By comprehensively analyzing the movement conditions of symmetric and asymmetric standing postures, the driving load and movement power consumption of each pillar are obtained as shown in Table 3.

Table 3. The supporting force and power consumption of movement

	Axial force of main pillar (N)	Axial force of auxiliary pillar (N)	Power (w)
Value	3000	2080	66

The drive unit includes a motor, harmonic reducer, and ball screw. As the driving source, the motor has a peak output torque of 0.35 Nm. Considering the influence of friction and other factors, the output torque is amplified to 12.6 Nm by a harmonic reducer with a transmission ratio of 80 times. The output torque is then converted into output force through ball screws, and the maximum output axial load can reach 6490 N, which is much greater than the required value of 3000 N, fully meeting the movement needs of the lander. In addition, as described in 3.1 Mobile gait of the paper, the movement can adopt a dynamic walking of biphasic gait, which can significantly improve the movement speed, but the required power consumption will also increase synchronously.

5   Conclusion

A new buffer mobile mechanism with landing cushioning and active movement is proposed in the paper. The movement strategy, movement modeling, and analysis are carried out, and the movement adjustment method of asymmetric standing posture is proposed for the eccentric situation of the lander. The analysis results show that under the eccentric condition, the lander can not only move downhill and on flat ground, but also move uphill. The paper solves the omnidirectional movement problem of the lander under eccentric load, which can provide a reference for the movement detection of the tonnage lander.

References

1. Zhu, W., Zeng, F., Man, J., et al.: Touchdown stability simulation of landing gear system for lunar lander. J. Astronaut. **30**(5), 1792–1796 (2009). (in Chinese)
2. Yang, J., Man, J., Zeng, F., et al.: Achievements and applications of landing gear for chang'e-3 lander. Spacecraft Recovery Remote Sens. **6**, 20–27 (2014). (in Chinese)
3. Zeng, F., Yang, J., Man, J., et al.: Study on design method of landing gear for lunar lander. Spacecraft Eng. **2**, 46–51 (2011). (in Chinese)
4. Zeng, F., Yang, J., Zhu, W., et al.: Achievements and applications of landing gear for chang'e-3 lander. Spacecraft Eng. **19**(5), 43–49 (2010). (in Chinese)
5. Bridenstine, J.: NASA's Lunar Exploration Program Overview [EB/OL]. NASA, 2020[2020–9]. https://www.nasa.gov/sites/default/files/atoms/files/artemisplan-20200921.pdf
6. Mahoney, E.: NASA's new spaceship[EB/OL]. NASA, 2018[2018–12–10]. https://www.nasa.gov/feature/ questions-na-sas-new-spaceship.
7. Lund, T.: Lunar Roving Vehicle and Exploration of the Moon: Ranger to Apollo, Luna to Lunniy Korabl (2018)
8. Han, Y., Guo, W., Gao, F., Yang, J.: A new dimension design method for the cantilever-type legged lander based on truss-mechanism transformation. Mech. Mach. Theory **142**(12), 103611 (2019)
9. Han, Y., Guo, W., Peng, Z., He, M., Gao, F., Yang, J.: Dimensional synthesis of the reconfigurable legged mobile lander with multi-mode and complex mechanism topology. Mech. Mach. Theory **155**(1), 104097 (2021)
10. Tian, X., Gao, F., Chen, X., et al.: Mechanism design and comparison for quadruped robot with parallel-serial Leg. J. Mech. Eng. **49**(6), 81–87 (2013). (in Chinese)
11. Guo, W., Tang, Y., Gao, F., et al.: Topology matrix method for gait generation of wheel-legged robots. J. Mech. Eng. **53**(21), 1–8 (2017). (in Chinese)
12. Gao, F., Yin, K., Sun, Q., et al.: Design and control of legged leaping robot in lunar exploration. Fllight Control $ Detect. **3**(4), 1–7 (2020). (in Chinese)
13. Park, J., Kim, K.S., Kim, S.: Design of a cat-inspired robotic leg for fast running. Adv. Robot. **28**(23), 1587–1598 (2014). (in Chinese)
14. Zhang, Z., Liang, L., Guo, L., et al.: Conceptual design of manned lunar lander with wheel-legged mobile system. Manned Spaceflight **22**(2), 202–209 (2016)
15. Liang, L., Zhang, Z., Guo, L., et al.: Task analysis of mobile lunar lander in crewed lunar exploration missions. Manned Spaceflight (05), 472–478 (2015) (in Chinese)

A Lightweight Manipulator Design for Quadruped Robots and Stable Locomotion Control with the Manipulator

Zishang Ji[1], Botao Liu[1,2]([✉]), Yurong Liu[1], Jiagui Zhong[1], Maosen Wang[1,2], Chunyu Hou[1], Yiwei Yang[1], and Fei Meng[1,2]

[1] Beijing Institute of Technology, Beijing 100081, China
lbt0116@bit.edu.cn
[2] Key Laboratory of Biomimetic Robots and Systems, Ministry of Education, Beijing 100081, China

Abstract. In order to enhance the manipulation capabilities of quadruped robots, numerous research have explored the integration of manipulators onto these robots. However, most manipulators encounter difficulties in harmonizing with quadruped robots, resulting in compromised locomotion performance. This paper addresses the challenge of stable locomotion and manipulation for quadruped robots equipped with manipulators. Firstly, a lightweight manipulator designed specifically for quadruped robots is introduced, featuring a generous working space and the capability to perform tasks such as torsion. Secondly, a hierarchical optimization-based whole-body control which mainly includes whole-body dynamics and trajectory tracking is proposed to enhance the stability of the quadruped robot in complex environments. Finally, the effectiveness of the proposed methodology is validated through physical prototype experiments.

Keywords: Quadruped Robot · Manipulator · Hierarchical Optimization · Locomotion

1 Introduction

In recent years, quadruped robots with walking capabilities have become a hot research topic in the field of robotics [1]. They possess superior terrain adaptation capabilities in unstructured environments compared to wheeled and tracked robots. However, quadruped robots lack capabilities of manipulation, which cannot meet the practical application requirements of humans. Equipping robots with manipulators can greatly expand their practical functions, enabling them to perform tasks such as moving objects, grabbing items, and operating tools.

Some researcher like Tsvetkov [2] and Cheng [3] propose using walking legs as manipulators, similar to how animals in nature use their front paws to grasp objects, while others propose adding an additional manipulator to the robot solely for manipulation

This work was supported by the National Key Research Program of China 2018AAA0100103.

H. Yang et al. (Eds.): ICIRA 2023, LNAI 14271, pp. 565–576, 2023.
https://doi.org/10.1007/978-981-99-6495-6_48

purposes. In some studies of the latter, quadrupedal robots are just simply equipped with commercially available manipulators. One six-degree-of-freedom Kinova arm was equipped to Anymal by [4–7], then the robot with arm can interact with their environment, such as opening a door and carrying a payload together with a human. Xie [8] equipped the self-developed robot with an arm named Gen3 lite from Kinova. The additional commercialized arm was not designed for quadruped robot and placed a heavy load on it, so Xie designed a whole-body control-based framework for whole systems to stabilize the robot's center-of-mass position and orientation. Zimmermann [9] introduced a relatively large 7-degree-of-freedom Kinova arm to Boston Dynamics Spot, and used kinematic model to optimize the joint trajectory in the planner. The robot is able to safely snatch the object off the ground and place it in the basket on the table. Commercial manipulators were used in previous studies, but there is a large amount of physical interference since the size and mechanical makeup of the manipulators are difficult to match with those of the quadruped robots.

Many researchers have specially designed manipulators suitable for quadruped robots, such as BigDog [10] and HyQ [11], they equipped the hydraulic-driven quadruped robot with hydraulic-driven manipulators. These platforms exhibit strong load-bearing capabilities and end-effector manipulation abilities. But the manipulators can only be used on hydraulic-driven quadruped robots.

For the locomotion control, the whole-body controller for dynamic motion [5] and the MPC framework [12] that combines dynamic motion and manipulation tasks for planning the motion trajectory of the entire body have been considered. With these methods, the ANYmal quadruped robot equipped with a manipulator has achieved stable coordination of upper and lower limbs, as well as collaboration with humans in tasks. However, the aforementioned research focuses primarily on the coordinated operation and stability control of quadruped robots on flat surfaces. Except for SpotMini [13], which has not disclosed any control methods or implementation approaches, there is currently scarce research on the motion stability of quadruped robots with manipulators in complex environments. The problem of decreased motion performance after attaching a manipulator to a quadruped robot remains unresolved.

In this paper, we divided the work into three parts. Firstly, a lightweight manipulator suitable for quadruped robots is designed. Secondly, a whole-body motion control framework is built based on hierarchical quadratic programing (HQP). Finally, the proposed method is verified through physical prototype experiments.

The main innovation of this work is two-fold:

(1) Aiming at the problem of mechanical mismatch between the manipulator and the quadruped robot, a lightweight manipulator suitable for quadruped robot is designed. The manipulator has a large working space and compact structure, which can complete a variety of tasks such as torsion, and has less interference with the quadruped robot.

(2) The HQP control frame-work is proposed to address the issue of reduced motion performance of the quadruped robot after the arm is added. The optimization method calculates the target joint torques based on predefined task priorities and the quadratic programming (QP) form for each subtask is standardized. Moreover, this paper discusses how to divide the priorities among different subtasks.

This paper is organized as follows. Section 2 introduces the manipulator design. The whole-body control based on HQP is described in Sect. 3. Real-world experiments and discussions are introduced in Sect. 4. The last Section summarizes this paper and proposes future work.

2 Manipulator Design

In order to enable robots to interact appropriately with objects in artificial environments, this paper has designed a five-degree-of-freedom manipulator, including shoulder yaw (SY), shoulder pitch (SP), elbow pitch (EP), wrist pitch (WP), wrist roll (WR) joints, and an active joint for controlling the gripper opening and closing. The overall structure of the manipulator is shown in Fig. 1. Although defining the end-effector pose in a three-dimensional workspace requires at least six degrees of freedom, the quadruped robot can provide an additional floating base degree of freedom, so the manipulator does not require excessive degrees of freedom, and excessive degrees of freedom will increase the complexity of the model.

The manipulator's configuration is similar in shape and proportion with the human arm. The lengths of the upper and lower arms of the manipulator are both 0.4 m. In order to reduce the weight of the manipulator, a lightweight design method for linkages based on truss structure is proposed. The total weight of the manipulator is approximately 8 kg, and the parameters of each joint are shown in Table 1.

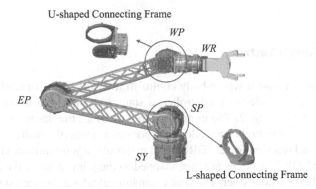

Fig. 1. The five-degree-of-freedom manipulator with shoulder yaw (SY), shoulder pitch (SP), elbow pitch (EP), wrist pitch (WP) and wrist roll (WR) joints.

The compactness of the joints is a prominent feature of the manipulator in this paper, which is mainly reflected in the integration of the shoulder and wrist joints. To achieve the integrated design of the shoulder joint, we designed an L-shaped connecting frame. The two flange faces of the L-shaped connecting frame, which are perpendicular to each other, are connected by a side rib with a certain curvature, ensuring the overall structure's strength and rigidity. The driving motor of the second joint is enveloped in the vertical semi-enclosed cavity of the L-shaped connecting frame, and its mass is arranged symmetrically along the axis of the shoulder yaw joint, reducing the overturning moment caused by the rotation of the upper limb. The integrated design of the wrist joint is reflected in the U-shaped connecting frame at the wrist. The flat end of the U-shaped connecting frame is made as thin as possible while ensuring sufficient strength, making the positions of the fourth and fifth joints more centralized and similar to the human wrist. This design allows for twisting movements such as turning doorknobs.

The installation location directly affect the system's performance. Installing the manipulator at the centroid of the quadruped robot can minimize its impact on the robot, as the center of shape can be approximated as the center of mass. However, the manipulator cannot touch the ground when it is stretched forward. When connecting the manipulator to the front-middle part of the quadruped robot, the manipulator's workspace can reach a certain circular range above the robot's body and touch the ground.

Table 1. Joint parameters of manipulator.

Joint Num	Joint Name	Range [°]	Max. Torque [Nm]	Mass [kg]
1	shoulder yaw (SY)	−180/180	170	1.53
2	shoulder pitch (SP)	−120/120	170	1.56
3	elbow pitch (EP)	−150/150	170	1.51
4	wrist pitch (WP)	−120/120	120	0.98
5	wrist roll (WR)	−180/180	120	0.87

3   Whole-Body Control

In this paper, we propose a whole-body control framework, which mainly consists of a motion planner, a whole-body controller, a state estimator, and a low-level torque controller, as shown in Fig. 2. The motion planner provides the desired state according to user input. The whole-body controller incorporates a series of constraints to solve for the optimal ground reaction forces (GRFs) and manipulator joint torques in each control cycle using the HQP. The GRFs are then mapped to the joint space of the legs and sent to the low-level torque controller. The state estimator calculates the each state to provide reliable feedback information. This paper mainly focuses on the core component of the whole-body controller.

3.1   Model Formulation

The quadruped robot with a manipulator has a total of 17 degrees of freedom, so a large amount of computation is required for the dynamic modeling and optimization. To simplify the computation, we use a simplified single rigid body model to describe the quadruped robot, as shown in Fig. 3. We set the base frame B at the center of the torso and the manipulator frame M at the connection point, while the inertial frame I can be fixed at anywhere on the ground. The entire quadruped robot can be simplified as

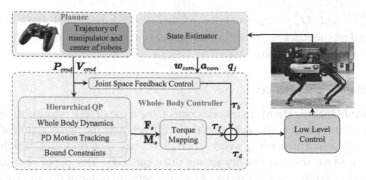

Fig. 2. Locomotion and manipulation framework based on whole-body controller.

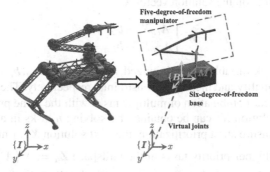

Fig. 3. Simplified dynamic model of the quadruped robot with a manipulator.

a floating base with five active joints from the manipulator (the gripper actuated joints are ignored).

The motion of the whole system can be described in the inertial frame I, where the position and orientation of the body are represented as $r_{IB} \in \mathbb{R}^3$ and $q_{IB} \in SO(3)$ respectively. The joint angles of the manipulator are described by $q_j \in \mathbb{R}^{n_j}$, where $n_j = 5$. Therefore, the generalized position vector q and generalized velocity vector $\dot{q}$ of the whole system can be expressed as

$$q = \begin{bmatrix} r_{IB} \\ q_{IB} \\ q_j \end{bmatrix} \in SE(3) \times \mathbb{R}^{n_j}, \dot{q} = \begin{bmatrix} v_{IB} \\ \omega_{IB} \\ \dot{q}_j \end{bmatrix} \in \mathbb{R}^{n_u}, \tag{1}$$

where $n_u = 6 + n_j$. v_{IB} and ω_{IB} are the linear and angular velocities of the base, respectively. The dynamic equations of the system can be simplified as

$$M(q) \cdot \ddot{q} + h(q, \dot{q}) = S \cdot T, \tag{2}$$

where $M(q) \in \mathbb{R}^{n_u \times n_u}$ is the inertia matrix, $h(q, \dot{q}) \in \mathbb{R}^{n_u}$ is the sum of gravity, centrifugal and Coriolis forces, S is a selection matrix used to select which joints are driven, and T is the set of generalized forces

$$T = \begin{bmatrix} F_s^{3 \times 1} & M_s^{3 \times 1} & \tau_j^{5 \times 1} \end{bmatrix}^T, \tag{3}$$

where $F_s^{3\times1}$ and $M_s^{3\times1}$ represent the virtual three-dimensional force and three-dimensional moment acting on the floating base, respectively. $\tau_j^{5\times1}$ represents the torque of the five joints of the manipulator.

3.2 Whole-Body Controller

Hierarchical Optimization: In robotic control, the issue of task prioritization in tracking is of great importance. However, traditional QP achieves the optimization of different targets by setting corresponding weight coefficients based on priorities, which makes it difficult to achieve absolute priority among different tasks. This paper proposes a hierarchical optimization to solve a series of QP problems in order of priority by gradually reducing the solution space. The task W can be defined as a set of linear equality or inequality constraints on the solution vector X

$$W:\begin{cases} A_{eq}X - b_{eq} = \varepsilon \\ A_{ieq}X - b_{ieq} \leq v \end{cases} \tag{4}$$

where ε, v is the slack variable to be minimized, and $A_{eq}, b_{eq}, A_{ieq}, b_{ieq}$ are the coefficient matrices for the equality and inequality constraints, respectively. The subtasks can be a single task or a linear combination of multiple tasks with the same priority.

The optimal solution X^* can be obtained by solving n tasks in a specified priority order. In order to ensure strict prioritization, the next solution X_{n+1} must have the same constraints for all higher priority tasks in the nullspace $Z_n = \mathcal{N}\left(A_{eq1}^T, A_{eq2}^T...A_{eqn}^T\right)^T$, i.e. $X_{n+1} = X_n^* + Z_n z_{n+1}$, where z_{n+1} is a vector that lives in the row space of Z_n. Therefore, solving a task W can be transformed into an iterative QP problem of Eq. (5):

$$\begin{aligned} \min_{z_{n+1}, v_{n+1}} \quad & \left\| A_{eq(n+1)}\left(X^* + Z_n z_{n+1}\right) - b_{eq(n+1)} \right\|^2 + \|v_{n+1}\|^2 \\ \text{s.t.} \quad & A_{ieq_{(n+1)}}\left(X^* + Z_n z_{n+1}\right) - b_{ieq(n+1)} \leq v_{n+1} \\ & A_{ieq_{(n)}}\left(X^* + Z_{n-1} z_n\right) - b_{ieq(n)} \leq v_n \\ & \qquad\qquad\qquad \vdots \\ & A_{ieq(1)}X^* - b_{ieq(1)} \leq v_1 \\ & v_{n+1} \geq 0. \end{aligned} \tag{5}$$

Task Formulation. We formulate the whole-body control problem as a QP problem composed of linear equality and inequality tasks, where all physical constraints and target movements must be incorporated in the form of Eq. (4). The optimization objective of the simplified floating model in motion tracking can be uniformly expressed as

$$X = \begin{bmatrix} \ddot{q}^T & T^T \end{bmatrix}^T. \tag{6}$$

Dynamical Consistency. The dynamic model represented by Eq. (2) is a mandatory requirement in the dynamic motion of robots, and is imposed as a strongly enforced equation constraint with the highest priority. The corresponding QP form is given by

$$\begin{cases} A_{eq} = \begin{bmatrix} M(q) & -S \end{bmatrix} \\ b_{eq} = -h(q, \dot{q}) \end{cases}. \tag{7}$$

Motion Tracking in Operational Space: The primary objective of robot control is to achieve precise motion tracking of desired trajectories generated by planners, which typically include the torso position tracking, torso orientation tracking and manipulation motion tracking. Motion tracking can be achieved through the following task constraints.

$$
\begin{bmatrix} I_6 & {}^M J_{arm}^{5\times5} & 0_{11} \end{bmatrix} X = \begin{bmatrix} \ddot{q}_{torso_d,p}^{3\times1} + K_{p,p}\left(p_{torso_d} - p_{torso}\right) + K_{d,p}\left(\dot{p}_{torso_d} - \dot{p}_{torso}\right) \\ \ddot{q}_{torso_d,\omega} + K_{p,\omega}log\left(R_d R^T\right) + K_{d,\omega}\left(\omega_{torso_d} - \omega_{torso}\right) \\ \ddot{q}_{arm_d}^{5\times1} - {}^M \dot{j}_{arm}^{5\times5} \dot{q}_{arm} \end{bmatrix} \tag{8}
$$

where ${}^M J_{arm}^{5\times5}$ represents the Jacobian matrix of manipulator that maps joint velocities to the end-effector velocities in operational space in the frame M. The base orientation error is obtained using exponential mapping of the rotation, where R_d and R represent the desired and actual base orientations, respectively.

Bound Constraints: The bound constraints ensure that certain parameters of the robot cannot exceed the given spatial boundaries during motion. It includes joint torque constraints and friction cone constraints.

$$
\begin{cases} \tau_{min} \leq \tau \leq \tau_{max} \\ -uF_z \leq F_{x/y} \leq uF_z \end{cases} \tag{9}
$$

where u represents the friction coefficient of the contact surface, and $F_{x,y,z}$ represents the GRFs in different directions.

Table 2. The task priorities used in HQP (1 is the highest priority).

Priority	Task	Equation
1	Dynamical consistency	(7)
	Bound constraints	(13)
	Friction cone constraints	(13)
2	Torso position tracking	(8)
	Torso orientation tracking	(8)
	Manipulator motion tracking	(8)

Table 2 presents the priority order of tasks specified in this paper. The highest priority task adheres to the dynamic consistency, boundary constraints, and friction cone constraints, followed by ensuring the tracking of expected movements. Finally, we optimize the operational capabilities of the manipulator and improve the energy efficiency of system.

3.3 Joint Torque Mapping

After getting the optimized variables X, we need to map the virtual six-dimension force $\begin{bmatrix} F_s^{3\times1} & M_s^{3\times1} \end{bmatrix}^T$ to the joint space of the legs. We obtain the optimal distribution of GRFs using Eq. (10) and then map the forces to the corresponding joints of the supporting legs through the Jacobian matrix of the legs J_{leg}.

$$\begin{bmatrix} I_3 & \cdots & I_3 \\ r_{1\times} & \cdots & r_{i\times} \end{bmatrix} \begin{bmatrix} F_{\text{leg},1} \\ \cdots \\ F_{\text{leg},i} \end{bmatrix} = \begin{bmatrix} F_s \\ M_s \end{bmatrix} \tag{10}$$

where $r_{i\times} \in \mathbb{R}^{3\times3}$ and $F_{\text{leg},i}$ represent the relative position matrix and the GRFs of the i-th leg, respectively.

The final desired joint torque is composed of two parts: the feedforward part τ_f, which is the mapping of the GRFs in joint space calculated based on Eq. (10), and the feedback part τ_b obtained through low-gain PD control in joint space.

4 Experiment

In order to verify the control methods presented in the previous sections, a series of real-world experiments were conducted. Specifically, two experiments were carried out: an independent motion of manipulator experiment and a field walking of the quadruped robot experiment. Each experiment included a baseline experiment, which served to compare against the proposed methods. For the baseline experiment, a hierarchical control method was not used. Instead, for the quadruped robot, the virtual six-dimensional force $\begin{bmatrix} \mathbf{F}_s^{3\times1} & \mathbf{M}_s^{3\times1} \end{bmatrix}^T$ was directly mapped to joint torques using Eq. (10), where the virtual six-dimensional force was obtained through PD torque feedback.

The hardware platform used in the experiment, including the quadruped robot and the manipulation, is independently developed by ourselves. The weight of the whole robot is 60 kg, the length and width are 0.6 m and 0.4 m, respectively. The dynamic equation is calculated using the open-source Pinocchio library. The HQP problem is solved using the open-source library Quadprog++. All control codes are written in C++. The computer configured in the robot system is Intel® NUC8i7BEH, whose CPU is i7-8559U. The solution time is within 1ms, which can ensure the real-time solution of the optimal force distribution. The control cycle is forced to be set to 1 kHz.

4.1 Independent Movement of Manipulator Experiment

This experiment is to explore how the movement of the manipulator affects the quadruped robot. In the experiment, the user sets the position and orientation of torso to be fixed and ensure that it is always in the four-legged support state. Only the manipulator is then moved individually. At the initial moment, the arm is in the retracted position. Then set the quadruped gait to trot and repeat the same steps.

A very intuitive fact is that the movement of the manipulator can easily cause the orientation of the torso q_{IB} to deviate. Therefore, we pay more attention to the orientation of the torso. Throughout the trajectory, the expected value of the Euler angle is set to 0. Figure 4 shows the change of the Euler angle of the torso in four-legged support state over time, while Fig. 5 shows the same in trot gait. Starting from 0s, the manipulator first stretches out from the retracted position, and mainly moves the second, third and fourth joints, as shown in Fig. 6(a). After 3.5 s, the end of manipulator moves downward in the Z direction, as shown in Fig. 6(b). After 5 s, the first joint of manipulator moves towards the right side of the torso, as shown in Fig. 6(c).

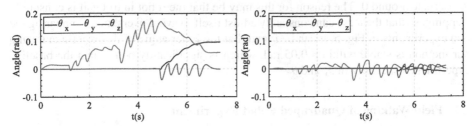

Fig. 4. The Euler angles of the torso in four-legged support state. The first figure represents the baseline experiment, while the second figure represents the experiment with our method.

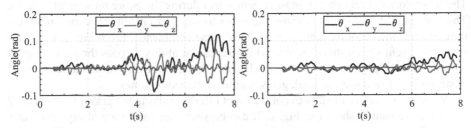

Fig. 5. The Euler angles of the torso in trot gait. The first figure represents the baseline experiment, while the second figure represents the experiment using our method.

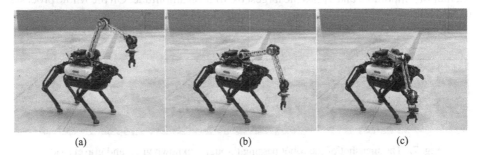

(a)   (b)   (c)

Fig. 6. A snapshot of the movement process of the manipulator.

From the baseline experiment in Fig. 4, the offsets of θ_y and θ_z are the largest, reaching 0.18 and 0.1 rad respectively. The offset of θ_x has been oscillating without a large offset. However, in the experiments using our methods, θ_x, θ_y and θ_z do not have large offsets, they are all maintained within ±0.05 rad, and the oscillation are relatively stable, which proves that our method is more robust and can weaken the movement of the manipulator's disturbance on torse.

From Fig. 5, the state in the trot gait is obviously more fluctuating than the state in Fig. 4. However, there is a big difference that the state under the trot gait just have more oscillation, but there is no absolute offset in a certain direction like in Fig. 4. For example, in the baseline experiment in Fig. 4, θ_y is always greater than 0, but in Fig. 5, θ_y oscillate around 0. The reason for this may be that the robot in trot gait is constantly stepping, so that the torse can constantly adjust itself to avoid overshoot. Comparing the two experiments in Fig. 5, it can be found that the Euler angle of the experiment using our method is stable within ±0.05 rad, which is significantly better than the baseline experiment, especially in θ_x and θ_y.

4.2 Field Walking of Quadruped Robot Experiment

This experiment can test the robustness of the robot in an unknown ground environment. We put the robot in the wild environment, let the robot pass through complex environments such as gravel roads and grass roads, as shown in Fig. 7, then observe its movement. The robot does not rely on any sensory equipment during the entire movement process. The uneven ground can easily cause the robot to slip and fall. In this experiment, the user controls the robot by sending velocity of torse commands. From Fig. 7, the physical experiment shows that this method improves the ability to pass through complex terrain under the premise of ensuring the balance of the robot, and stably passes through unstructured terrain such as mud, grass, and miscellaneous stones.

We mainly analyze the process of the robot blindly walking the gravel road in Fig. 7 and its movement is shown in Fig. 8. It can be seen that each state always oscillates around the desired value, but there is no large offset. Even if there is, it will be reset soon. On the velocity curve, when the desired velocity changes, there will be a relatively large overshoot, but it will weaken at about 0.25 s. On the angle curve, θ_z has the smallest oscillation amplitude, and θ_x has the largest oscillation amplitude. On the whole process, the movement of robot is relatively stable, and the adaptability is strong.

Fig. 7. The snapshot of the robot passing through unknown grass and gravel roads.

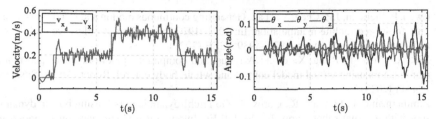

Fig. 8. The change of each state and desired state over time during the movement, in which the desired state of the Euler angle is 0.

5 Conclusions

In this paper, we present the design of a five-degree-of-freedom manipulator, which includes yaw and pitch at the shoulder, elbow pitch, wrist pitch, wrist roll. The manipulator is designed with compact joints. When attached to the front middle part of a quadruped robot, the manipulator provides a large workspace and the ability to touch the ground. Next, we propose a whole-body control based on HQP aimed at addressing the balance problem of a quadruped robot with a manipulator. A simplified single-rigid-body model is used to describe the entire system. By adopting the HQP, the whole-body controller can solve a series of QP problems according to task priorities while ensuring the robot's motion model, obtaining the ground contact forces and the manipulator joint torque. The ground reaction forces are mapped to the leg joint torque through optimal allocation, and the manipulator's joint torque is directly inputted into the manipulator motor. Experimental results show that the manipulator does not produce large disturbance on the quadruped robot and the robot has good capability to walk in complex environments while carrying the manipulator. In future work, we will consider the force at the end of the manipulator, so that the system can still maintain good locomotion and manipulation ability under the condition of external force at the end-effector.

References

1. Wang, L., et al.: Design and dynamic locomotion control of quadruped robot with perception-less terrain adaptation. Cyborg Bionic Syst. **2022** (2022)
2. Tsvetkov, Y., Ramamoorthy, S.: A novel design and evaluation of a dactylus-equipped quadruped robot for mobile manipulation. In: 2022 IEEE/RSJ International Conference on Intelligent Robots and Systems, pp. 1633–1638. IEEE (2022)
3. Cheng, X., Kumar, A., Pathak, D.: Legs as Manipulator: Pushing Quadrupedal Agility Beyond Locomotion. arXiv:2303.11330 (2023)
4. Ferrolho, H., Merkt, W., Ivan, V., et al.: Optimizing dynamic trajectories for robustness to disturbances using polytopic projections. In: 2020 IEEE/RSJ International Conference on Intelligent Robots and Systems, pp. 7477–7484. IEEE (2020)
5. Bellicoso, C.D., Krämer, K., Stäuble, M., et al.: Alma-articulated locomotion and manipulation for a torque-controllable robot. In: 2019 IEEE International Conference on Robotics and Automation (ICRA), pp. 8477–8483. IEEE (2019)
6. Ferrolho, H., Ivan, V., Merkt, W., et al.: Roloma: Robust loco-manipulation for quadruped robots with arms. arXiv preprint arXiv:2203.01446 (2022)

7. Ewen, P., Sleiman, J.P., Chen, Y., et al.: Generating continuous motion and force plans in real-time for legged mobile manipulation. In: 2021 IEEE International Conference on Robotics and Automation (ICRA), pp. 4933–4939. IEEE (2021)
8. Xie, A., Chen, T., Rong, X., et al.: A robust and compliant framework for legged mobile manipulators using virtual model control and whole-body control. Robot. Auton. Syst. **164**, 104411 (2023)
9. Zimmermann, S., Poranne, R., Coros, S.: Go fetch!-dynamic grasps using boston dynamics spot with external robotic arm. In: 2021 IEEE International Conference on Robotics and Automation (ICRA), pp. 4488–4494. IEEE (2021)
10. Murphy, M.P., Stephens, B., Abe, Y., Rizzi, A.A.: High degree-of-freedom dynamic manipulation. SPIE **8387**, 339–348 (2012)
11. Rehman, B.U., Focchi, M., Lee, J., Dallali, H., Caldwell, D.G., Semini, C.: Towards a multi-legged mobile manipulator. In: 2016 IEEE International Conference on Robotics and Automation, pp. 3618–3624 (2016)
12. Sleiman, J.P., Farshidian, F., Minniti, M.V., Hutter, M.: A unified MPC framework for whole-body dynamic locomotion and manipulation. IEEE Robot. Autom. Lett. **6**, 4688–4695 (2021)
13. SpotMini: https://www.youtube.com/watch?v=XnZH4izf_rI. Accessed May 2023

Recovery from Injury: Learning Bipedal Jumping Skills with a Motor Output Torque Limit Curriculum

Jiayi Li[1], Linqi Ye[2], Yujie Sun[3], Houde Liu[1(✉)], and Bin Liang[4]

[1] Tsinghua Shenzhen International Graduate School, Tsinghua University,
Shenzhen 518055, China
liu.hd@sz.tsinghua.edu.cn
[2] Institute of Artificial Intelligence, Collaborative Innovation Center for the Marine Artificial
Intelligence, Shanghai University, Shanghai 200444, China
[3] China North Vehicle Research Institute Postdoctoral Workstation, Beijing 100072, China
[4] Navigation and Control Research Center, Department of Automation, Tsinghua University,
Beijing 100084, China

Abstract. Bipedal robots can walk and run on different terrains and show great capacity in fast-moving. However, it's still a daunting challenge for them to achieve highly dynamic whole-body motions such as jumping. In this paper, we propose a method to learn high jump skills for humanoid robots, and the effectiveness of the method is verified through simulations on the Ranger Max humanoid robot model. Both 2D and 3D jumping locomotion for the one-legged and two-legged Ranger Max robots are generated naturally and stably with different scales of maximum motor output torque limit. A curriculum learning strategy inspired by the idea of "recovery from injury" is proposed to make the learning of the high jump more efficient for "weaker" robots, which is confirmed by the simulation results.

Keywords: Humanoid Robot · High Jump · Reinforcement Learning · Curriculum Learning

1 Introduction

The ability to demonstrate high athletic performance is one of the most attractive goals for bionic robots, and the high jump is one of the typical motions that demonstrates strength and control. The wheeled robot Handle developed by Boston Dynamics can jump 4 feet vertically [1]. A tiny robot designed by Dr. Elliot Hawkes et al. [2] weighs less than a tennis ball and can reach 31 m. Bipedal robots are often designed as general-purpose mobile robots so their physical structures are not designed for one or a few specific tasks. Therefore, how to control a robot flexibly and exert the maximum capacity of its mechanical structure and motor power in challengeable locomotion like the high jump is well worth studying.

There are mainly two ways to control a bipedal robot in general, the first one is the model-based trajectory optimization method which has led to many mature bipedal

H. Yang et al. (Eds.): ICIRA 2023, LNAI 14271, pp. 577–588, 2023.
https://doi.org/10.1007/978-981-99-6495-6_49

control algorithms. In the classical zero-moment point (ZMP) method [3], the robot is treated as a simplified model, whose stability is guaranteed by making the ZMP lie within the interior of the supporting polygon during walking. Hybrid zero dynamics is another popular framework [4]. It works by designing a set of virtual constraints that are enforced via feedback control of the actuated degrees of freedom (DoF). Model predictive control is by far the best concerned model-based optimization approach to generating bipedal locomotion [5–7]. Highly dynamic motions can be performed and robustness increases due to its previewing ability. Though notable achievements have been made on advanced humanoid robots like Atlas [8], these model-based optimization methods have their inherent defects. An accurate model is always required and the computational cost is relatively high. Planning failures may occur due to unexpected disturbances, complex environments, and model mismatches.

The data-driven method such as reinforcement learning (RL) provides a second solution. Artificial intelligence does well in solving high-dimensional, multi-input-multi-output problems. The agents continuously interact with the environment and learn from the reward feedback to update their control network automatically. However, network designing, reward setting, curriculum designing, and engineering problems of sim-to-real become the new challenges. Some effective RL frameworks have been proposed to handle continuous control tasks, such as Deep Deterministic Policy Gradients [9], Trust Region Policy Optimization [10], Actor-Critic with Experience Replay [11], and Proximal Policy Optimization (PPO) [12]. Duan et al. [13] integrated learning a task space policy with a model-based inverse dynamic controller and demonstrated a successful sim-to-real transfer on Cassie. Li et al. [14] present a model-free RL framework that can be transferred to a real robot with a gait library of diverse parameterized motions. Xie et al. [15] describe an iterative design approach with transfer learning and get robust locomotion policies. Their robot completed the 100 m in 24.73 s sprinting to 100-m World Record. Due to the advantages of the data-driven method, we choose it to design a humanoid high jump method.

2 Related Work

2.1 Proximal Policy Optimization

PPO [12] is a kind of modified policy gradient method that strikes a balance between ease of implementation, sample complexity, and ease of tuning. It tries to compute an update at each step which minimizes the cost function and ensures the deviation from the previous policy is relatively small at the same time. The objective function of PPO is given as:

$$L^{CLIP}(\theta) = \hat{E}_t[\min(r_t(\theta))\hat{A}_t, \text{clip}(r_t(\theta), 1 - \varepsilon, 1 + \varepsilon)\hat{A}_t)] \tag{1}$$

where θ is the policy parameter, $\hat{E}_t$ denotes the empirical expectation over timesteps, r_t is the ratio of the probability under the new and old policies respectively, $\hat{A}_t$ is the estimated advantage at the time t and ε is a hyperparameter. The novel clipped objective function was proven to outperform most other RL methods on almost all the continuous control problems, showing its excellent ability in the field of continuous robot motion control. We choose to do our research with a PPO trainer.

2.2 High Jump

A robot jumps by launching its body into the air with a single stroke of its joints. The amount of energy delivered in this single stroke determines the jump height and distance. The high jump focuses mainly on the maximum jump height, which is a good way to test a robot control method's explosive strength and balance ability. Xiong et al. [16] identify a spring-mass model from the kinematics and compliance of the 3D bipedal robot Cassie. Jumping and landing motions are planned based on leg length trajectories optimized via direct collocation to synthesize a control Lyapunov function based quadratic program. Whole body rotation in the underactuated flight phase is prevented through an additional centroidal angular momentum output in the control function. A ~7 inches ground clearance and ~0.423 s air-time are finally achieved. Kojima et al. [17] design a high-specific stiffness and lightweight mechanical structure for dynamic jumping motions. They achieve a 0.3 m height in the jumping test. Qi et al. [18, 19] propose a vertical jump optimization strategy for a one-legged robot. Full-body dynamics are considered to track the trajectory with virtual force control and human jumping motion capture data is collected and used as the reference center of mass (CoM) trajectory to realize a certain jumping height. A 50 cm jump is realized on a real robot platform. Chen et al. [20] clarify the mathematical modeling and motor-joint model with practical factors considered. They optimize the hopping performance of the robot by maximizing the output power of the joints.

In summary, existing control methods for jumping are mostly model-based. Among previous works, an offline whole-body trajectory is always generated before jumping, and online control algorithms are used to ensure stability. Different controllers are elaborately designed for different phases, such as trajectory optimization for the launching phase, momentum control for the flight phase, and viscoelastic control for the landing phase. Except for the difficulty of the specific controller design, inherent intractability lies in the model-based control method:

1) Model mismatch: model mismatch introduced by modeling simplification, measurement errors, and load variation causes instability of the system. Also, specialized controller designs are difficult to replicate directly with other robots with different mechanical structures;
2) Lack of flexibility: more than needed degrees of freedom are always wasted on CoM trajectory following as well as other artificial constraints instead of pursuing higher jump height;
3) Limitation of locomotion: the jumping ability is limited by the reference locomotion but not the physical properties of the robot itself. It's hard to bring out the full potential of the robot based on a manual planning trajectory;
4) Unnatural jumping posture: the relaxation of the joints is a common phenomenon in the flight phase of animal jumping. However, they are always bent to keep the robot controllable in a model-based method. It's difficult to summarize certain rules artificially that could generate natural and fluid body movements.

Considering the questions above, it's necessary to propose a relatively simple control method to achieve natural jumping movements and make the jump as high as possible. Therefore, we design a high jump learning method based on PPO, and the main contributions are as follows:

1) Presenting a RL method to generate natural and stable high jump locomotion for humanoid robots, and verifying it in the simulation on the Ranger Max robot.
2) Comparing the influence of different motor output limits on jump height and exploring a curriculum learning method to speed up locomotion generation and increase jump height based on the ideal of "recovery from injury".

3 Robot Model

The robot model used in this article is based on the open-source humanoid robot Ranger Max, which is known as Tik-Tok before [21]. We follow the original design (Fig. 1 (a)) and make some minor structural changes to our robot. One leg of the real robot has been built in our laboratory (Fig. 1 (b)). One-legged and two-legged simulation models have been built in Unity (Fig. 1 (c), (d)), and the basic specifications of Ranger Max robot hardware are shown in Table 1.

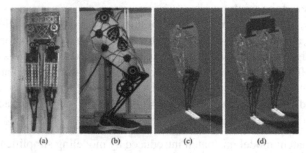

(a)   (b)   (c)   (d)

Fig. 1. Ranger Max humanoid robot. (a) The complete Ranger Max robot developed by Ruina et al. (b) One-legged Ranger Max robot we are building. (c) One-legged simulation model in Unity. (d) Two-legged simulation model in Unity.

Each leg of Ranger Max has four controllable joints. A hip abduction-adduction (HAA) joint, a hip flexion-extension (HFE) joint, a knee flexion-extension (KFE) joint and an ankle plantar flexion and dorsiflexion (APD) joint. A one-legged robot is constrained to move in a two-dimensional plane so that the HAA joint is omitted. The range of motion for each joint is indicated in Fig. 2 (a) and (b), and the detailed values are listed in Table 1. Height reference points are introduced and the vertical distance between them and their initial positions will be recorded as the jump heights as shown in Fig. 2 (c). The mass of Ranger Max is not concentrated in the pelvis but distributed on each link more evenly. Since most motors are mounted on the thigh links, they are the heaviest parts of the lower body which is quite similar to the human being.

Table 1. Table captions should be placed above the tables.

Link	Length/Width	Weight	Joint range ($°$)
pelvis	$w_1 = 0.24$ m	2 kg	–
hip	$l_1 = 0.1$ m	1 kg	$(-20, 0)$ left/$(0, 20)$ right
thigh	$l_2 = 0.4$ m	6.4 kg	$(-50, 50)$
shank	$l_3 = 0.35$ m	1.3 kg	$(-110, 10)$
foot	$l_4 = 0.05$ m $l_5 = 0.15$ m	0.3 kg	$(-50, 50)$

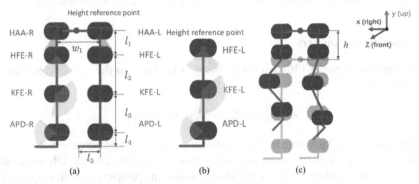

Fig. 2. Structural sketch of Ranger Max. (a) Structural sketch of the two-legged robot. (b) Structural sketch of the one-legged robot. (c) Jump height measurement method.

4 Control Method

4.1 Overview

An overview of our method is given in Fig. 3. The main objective of the presented method is to make the robot jump naturally and stably while achieving as high as possible in limited training steps. A curriculum learning (CL) [22] strategy inspired by the idea of "recovery from injury" is designed and a simple joint position PD controller with a torque limiter is proposed in the control architecture.

The idea of "starting small" and gradually presenting more complex is called curricula summarized from human education. In the high jump task that requires explosive strength, the maximum motor output torque limit is an important limiting factor on jumping height. We design our curriculum based on the phenomenon that an injured athlete always does better than people without any experience when relearning the sport that he or she is good at even with a weaker body after recovery. We assume that our robot is the injured athlete who mastered the high jump, and we believe that it has the potential to recover the jumping ability quickly with previous experience and does better than learning from the beginning. Different from other CL methods, the difficulty of the curriculum is increased by weakening the robot by constricting its joint output limit rather than making the task more difficult in this case.

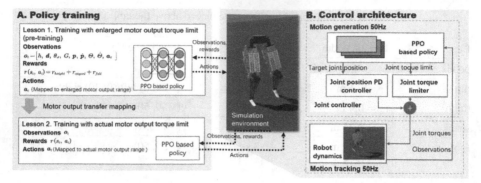

Fig. 3. Overall control framework. Left: Policy training. Right: Control architecture.

4.2 Training Parameters

An observation vector of 136 dimensions is set as the input of the network. It is defined at the time t as

$$o_t = \left[h, d, \theta_d, G, p, \dot{p}, \Theta, \dot{\Theta}, a_t\right] \tag{2}$$

where h is the vertical jumping height. d is the target direction pointing forward and θ_d is the deviation angle from the target direction. These two values are not fully used but we still put them here as they can be useful when considering jumping direction. G is a 1×9 vector of Boolean values that demonstrate if the links touch the ground. p and $\dot{p}$ denotes the positions and velocities of the leg links origin in the pelvis coordinate system. The position of the pelvis itself is not included. Θ and $\dot{\Theta}$ are the rotation quaternions and angular velocities of all links. a_t is a vector of all the joint torques. A simple flat ground without obstacles is considered.

In a high jump task, height and stability are the most concerned factors. An intensive reward in real-time allows the agent to learn faster. The reward function consists of three components: (1) a height reward r_{height} with a restriction of the horizontal speed of the pelvis. (2) a penalty r_{angvel} for pelvis shaking and (3) a penalty r_{fall} for the robot falling over.

$$r(s_i, a_i) = r_{\text{height}} + r_{\text{angvel}} + r_{\text{fall}} \tag{3}$$

$$r_{\text{height}} = \begin{cases} K_h f_1(h) & \text{if } h > H_{\text{stimulus}} \text{ and } v_x, v_z \in (-v_{\text{max}}, v_{\text{max}}) \\ K_h f_2(h) & \text{if } < H_{\text{penalty}} \text{ and } v_x, v_z \in (-v_{\text{max}}, v_{\text{max}}) \\ 0 & \text{otherwise} \end{cases} \tag{4}$$

$$r_{\text{angvel}} = - K_a \left(|\dot{\theta}_{\text{px}}| + |\dot{\theta}_{\text{py}}| + |\dot{\theta}_{\text{pz}}|\right) \tag{5}$$

$$r_{\text{fall}} = \begin{cases} -P_{\text{fall}} & \text{if } h < H_{\text{min}} \text{ or } p_{\text{yL}} < H_{\text{kmin}} \text{ or } p_{\text{yR}} < H_{\text{kmin}} \\ 0 & \text{otherwise} \end{cases} \tag{6}$$

where (s_i, a_i) is the state-action pair, K_h and K_a are the jump height reward gain and angular velocity penalty gain respectively. $f_1(h)$ refers to the reward function with the variable of pelvis height h when the robot reaches a preset jump-ready height H_{stimulus} and $f_2(h)$ refers to the reward function when the robot is squatting too much or about to fall recognized by a height constant H_{penalty}. Their expression will be introduced in Sect. 5. v_x and v_z are the pelvis velocity in the direction of x axis and z axis of the global coordinate. The action is only rewarded when linear velocities along these axes are within $\pm v_{\text{max}}$ to prevent a large horizontal movement. $\dot{\theta}_{\text{pi}}$ is the angular velocity of the pelvis about the i axis ($i = x, y, z$). P_{fall} is the penalty of the robot falling when the pelvis height h or the left and right knees height (p_{yL} and p_{yR}) is smaller than their minimum limitation H_{min} and H_{kmin}. An episode is also ended when the robot falls.

$$a_t = \left[p_{\text{target}}^{1 \times 8}, T_{\text{lim}}^{1 \times 8} \right] \tag{7}$$

The action a_t is a 16-dimensional vector that consists of two parts as shown in equation: (1) the target position p_{target} for all 8 joints and (2) a limitation of motor output torque T_{lim}. Each element in T_{lim} is normalized to $[-1, 1]$.

4.3 Curriculum Design

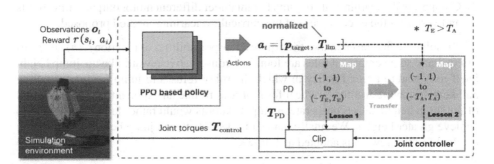

Fig. 4. Curriculum Design.

The idea of "recovery from injury" is used in the curriculum design. We implement this by taking a simple mapping from the pre-trained policy for a robot with enlarged maximum torque output to the actual "weaker" robot with smaller maximum torque output as shown in Fig. 4. The robot is first trained in lesson 1 with a relaxed motor output torque limit T_E, and after basic jumping skills are learned, mapping each element in the torque limitation part T_{lim} from $(-T_E, T_E)$ to $(-T_A, T_A)$, where T_A is the actual motor output limit.

4.4 Control Architecture

The joint torques are controlled by a simple position PD controller, while a torque limiter is added to restrict the output torques (see Fig. 3 B). Since a PD controller may lead to some sudden movements when the target joint angle is far from the current joint angle causing unnatural and dangerous behaviors. Therefore, a second control variable $T_{\lim}$ is introduced to help with a softer control method as shown in Fig. 4. Now the final torque signal used to control the joint becomes

$$T_{\text{control}i} = \begin{cases} \text{clip}(T_{\text{PD}i}, -T_{\lim i}T_E, T_{\lim i}T_E) & \text{if in stage1} \\ \text{clip}(T_{\text{PD}i}, -T_{\lim i}T_A, T_{\lim i}T_A) & \text{if in stage2 or not in training mode} \end{cases} \tag{8}$$

where $T_{\text{PD}i}$ is the ith element in the torque vector T_{PD} calculated by the target joint position and the PD parameters of the PD controller. $T_{\text{control}i}$ is the ith element in the torque vector T_{control} used to control the joints directly.

5 Simulation Results

The following problems are addressed in this section:

1) Finding a suitable reward function for high jump training and demonstrating the feasibility of our control method;
2) Comparing the learning rate of jump height under different motor output torque limits and verifying the effectiveness of the curriculum learning method proposed.

To solve the first problem, we tried quite a few possibilities of function $f_1(h)$ and $f_2(h)$ in Eq. 4 and some empirical rules are found. A conservative reward like the jump height itself may lead to a timid policy in which the robot refuses to jump for fear of falling and keep trembling in situ. A radical form of reward like an exponential transformation of the jump height causes desperate attempts. Robots would rather fall to the ground to achieve greater heights. We finally made a tradeoff between jump height and stability: a cubed form of reward is adopted as follows:

$$\begin{cases} f_1(h) = K_h(h - H_{\text{stimulus}})^3 \\ f_2(h) = K_h(h - H_{\text{penalty}})^3 \end{cases} \tag{9}$$

We first train on a one-legged robot constrained to its sagittal plane to eliminate the effects of lateral balance control. Three scales of motor torque output limit were chosen. We do training with the motor output torque limit of 50 Nm (relatively low), 100 Nm (normal), and 150 Nm (relatively high) separately. Both three training generate natural and stable continuous jumping locomotion for a one-legged robot (see Fig. 5) validating the effectiveness of our method. The maximum jump heights reach 0.226 m, 0.663 m, and 0.920 m respectively in a 30-million-step learning.

The snapshots in Fig. 5 show that not only does the jumping height differs, but also diverse jumping posture are learned with different motor output torque limit. The leaning back posture, dorsiflexion of the ankle joint in the flight phase, and the quick knee bend before touching the ground in the last line of the snapshots suggest that agents with different motor output torque limits may learn different jumping skills.

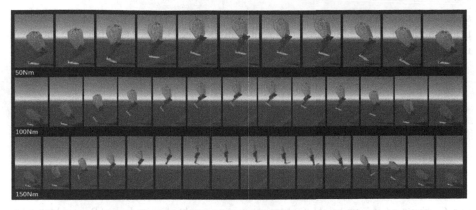

Fig. 5. Snapshots of one-legged jumping with different motor output torque limits.

We save the model once every 5 million steps and do a 30-s jump test for each model to record the maximum jump height as shown in Fig. 6 (a). The jump height learning rate shows a trend of rapid increase first and then slow growth. The agent with a greater torque limit also learns stable jumping locomotion faster. Agents with torque limits of 100 Nm and 150 Nm generate stable jumping in the first 2.5 million steps while the agent with a torque limit of 50 Nm achieves this until 5 million steps. To find out if the experience learned in the more efficient learning process with a wider range of torque limit can be utilized to help with an agent with a tighter motor output torque limit, we implement our curriculum learning method described in Sect. 0 on the robot. A 30-million-step pre-training with a motor output torque limit of 100 Nm and 150 Nm is done first, and another 30-million-step training with a limit of 50 N is done with a torque limit mapping described in Sect. 4.3. As a comparison, a 60-million-step experiment with a limit of 50 Nm from beginning to end is also completed. Results of the jumping height with and without the curriculum learning are shown in Fig. 6 (b).

It can be found that the agent with curriculum learning gets a higher jump height. A 39% height growth is made from 0.236 m to 0.391 m when a curriculum with a torque limit from 100 Nm to 50 Nm is taken. However, a smaller growth of 32% is made when a torque limit from 150 Nm to 50 Nm is made. The validity of the curriculum design is obvious while a wider pre-training limit may not lead to a better performance.

We extend the experiments to two-legged robots and design three different pieces of training: (1) A normal 30-million-step training without curriculum learning, (2) a 2-lesson curriculum learning with a 10-million-step first lesson and a 20-million-step second lesson from 100 Nm to 50 Nm, and (3) a 5-lesson curriculum learning with torque limits gradually dropping evenly from 100 Nm to 50 Nm with the training steps. Stable 3D jumping locomotion is generated successfully as shown in Fig. 7. Jump heights of 0.258 m, 0.263 m, and 0.320 m are achieved separately. The difference in final jump height between non-curriculum learning to the 2-lesson curriculum learning is inconspicuous while the 5-lesson curriculum learning makes a 24% growth. This phenomenon shows that though a "recovery from injury" curriculum learning helps with 3D locomotion generation, a suitable change of torque limit between lessons is important. The agent is more adaptable to gradual changes while an excessive gap may backfire.

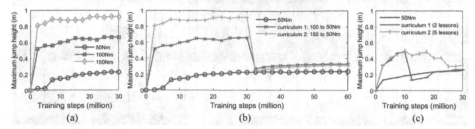

(a)   (b)   (c)

Fig. 6. The trend of jump height. (a) Maximum jump height of a one-legged Ranger Max robot with different motor output torque limit. (b) Comparison between normal training and curriculum training of a one-legged Ranger Max robot. (c) Comparison between normal training and curriculum training of a two-legged Ranger Max robot.

Fig. 7. Snapshots of two-legged jumping.

The above results demonstrate that our method works on both 2D and 3D conditions. Taking a "recovery from injury" curriculum learning with suitable lesson changes is beneficial for high jump locomotion generation and performance optimization. Our curriculum design provides a way for robots to achieve better high-dynamic performance with limited motor power.

6   Conclusion and Future Work

In this paper, we propose a method to learn high jump skills for humanoid robots, and the effectiveness of the method is validated on the Ranger Max humanoid robot model in simulation. Both 2D and 3D jumping locomotion for the one-legged and two-legged robots are generated naturally and stably with different scales of maximum motor output torque limit. A novel curriculum learning strategy from robots with relaxed motor output torque limit to actual motor output torque limit inspired by the idea of "recovery from injury" is proposed to make the learning of the high jump more efficient for "weaker" robots, which is confirmed by the simulation results.

The real robot of Ranger Max is being built in our laboratory, and the next step for our work is to verify the feasibility of our method on the real robot. This paper demonstrates a theoretical possibility of how high a robot can jump under certain drive capability constraints, while it's far more complex to achieve the jumping locomotion in the real world. Many sim-to-real problems need to be considered. The mathematical motor model should be built to imitate its real response performance in a simulation environment. Second, observations need to be filtered before being fed to the neural network and sensing errors should be introduced during training to improve the robustness of the strategy. Engineering problems like collision protection and fall protection should also be addressed.

Humans can easily relearn movements they used to excel at even though muscles deteriorate as they age. The proposed curriculum learning of "recovery from injury" may not only be beneficial for the jumping task, but also help learn other locomotion skills like balance keeping, obstacle crossing, and passive walking, which are left for exploring in the future.

Acknowledgments. This work was supported by the National Natural Science Foundation of China No.92248304 and No. 62003188, and the Shenzhen Science Fund for Distinguished Young Scholars (RCJC20210706091946001).

References

1. Introducing Handle: https://www.youtube.com/watch?v=-7xvqQeoA8c. Accessed 20 May 2023
2. World's Highest Jumping Robot: https://www.youtube.com/watch?v=daaDuC1kbds. Accessed 20 May 2023
3. Park, J., Youm, Y.: General ZMP preview control for bipedal walking. In: Proceedings 2007 IEEE International Conference on Robotics and Automation, pp. 2682–2687. IEEE (2007)
4. Hereid, A., Hubicki, C.M., Cousineau, E.A., Ames, A.D.: Dynamic humanoid locomotion: a scalable formulation for HZD gait optimization. IEEE Trans. Rob. **34**(2), 370–387 (2018)
5. Scianca, N., De Simone, D., Lanari, L., Oriolo, G.: MPC for humanoid gait generation: stability and feasibility. IEEE Trans. Rob. **36**(4), 1171–1188 (2020)
6. Romualdi, G., Dafarra, S., L'Erario, G., Sorrentino, I., Traversaro, S., Pucci, D.: Online non-linear centroidal MPC for humanoid robot locomotion with step adjustment. In: 2022 International Conference on Robotics and Automation (ICRA), pp.10412–10419. IEEE (2022)
7. Kashyap, A.K., Parhi, D.R.: Optimization of stability of humanoid robot NAO using ant colony optimization tuned MPC controller for uneven path. Soft. Comput. **25**, 5131–5150 (2021)
8. Kuindersma, S., et al.: Optimization-based locomotion planning, estimation, and control design for the atlas humanoid robot. Auton. Robot. **40**, 429–455 (2016)
9. Lillicrap, T.P., et al.: Continuous control with deep reinforcement learning. arXiv preprint arXiv:1509.02971 (2015)

10. Schulman, J., Levine, S., Abbeel, P., Jordan, M., Moritz, P.: Trust region policy optimization. In: International Conference on Machine Learning. PMLR (2015)
11. Wang, Z., et al.: Sample efficient actor-critic with experience replay. arXiv preprint arXiv: 1611.01224 (2016)
12. Schulman, J., Wolski, F., Dhariwal, P., Radford, A., Klimov, O.: Proximal policy optimization algorithms. arXiv preprint arXiv:1707.06347 (2017)
13. Duan, H., Dao, J., Green, K., Apgar, T., Fern, A., Hurst, J.: Learning task space actions for bipedal locomotion. In: 2021 IEEE International Conference on Robotics and Automation (ICRA), pp. 1276–1282. IEEE (2021)
14. Li, Z., et al.: Reinforcement learning for robust parameterized locomotion control of bipedal robots. In: 2021 IEEE International Conference on Robotics and Automation (ICRA), pp. 2811–2817. IEEE (2021)
15. Xie, Z., Clary, P., Dao, J., Morais, P., Hurst, J., Panne, M.: Learning locomotion skills for cassie: iterative design and sim-to-real. In: Conference on Robot Learning, pp. 317–329. PMLR (2020)
16. Xiong, X., Ames, A.D.: Bipedal hopping: Reduced-order model embedding via optimization-based control. In: 2018 IEEE/RSJ International Conference on Intelligent Robots and Systems (IROS), pp. 3821–3828. IEEE (2018)
17. Kojima, K., et al.: A robot design method for weight saving aimed at dynamic motions: design of humanoid JAXON3-P and realization of jump motions. In: 2019 IEEE-RAS 19th International Conference on Humanoid Robots (Humanoids), pp. 586–593. IEEE (2019)
18. Qi, H., et al.: A vertical jump optimization strategy for one-legged robot with variable reduction ratio joint. In: 2020 IEEE-RAS 20th International Conference on Humanoid Robots (Humanoids), pp. 262–267. IEEE (2021)
19. Qi, H., et al.: Vertical Jump of a Humanoid Robot with CoP-Guided Angular Momentum Control and Impact Absorption. IEEE Transactions on Robotics (2023)
20. Chen, X., Liao, W., Yu, Z., Qi, H., Jiang, X., Huang, Q.: Motion coordination for humanoid jumping using maximized joint power. Adv. Mech. Eng. 13(6), 16878140211028448 (2021)
21. Cornell Tik-Tok: Efficient, robust, and nimble open-source legged robot, http://ruina.tam.cornell.edu/research/topics/locomotion_and_robotics/Tik-Tok/. Accessed 20 May 2023
22. Wang, X., Chen, Y., Zhu, W.: A survey on curriculum learning. IEEE Trans. Pattern Anal. Mach. Intell. 44(9), 4555–4576 (2021)

Recovery Planning for the Legged Mobile Lunar Lander

Qingxing Xi[1], Feng Gao[1(✉)], Puzhen Zhang[2], Jianzhong Yang[2], and Zhijun Chen[1]

[1] Shanghai Jiao Tong University, Shanghai 200240, China
fengg@sjtu.edu.cn
[2] Beijing Institute of Spacecraft System Engineering, Beijing 100094, China

Abstract. The lander plays an important role in planetary exploration. However, most landers are immoveable and they can only detect at the same location. This paper proposes a novel recovery planning method for the legged mobile lunar lander. First, a legged mobile lunar lander with parallel mechanisms and its buffer structure are introduced. Then, the recovery planning method of the legged mobile lunar lander is addressed. Further, the footholds and body's pose are optimized to improve the adaptability by minimizing the displacements of the active joints. Finally, simulations are conducted to validate the method and its performance. The results show that the recovery planning and optimization method for the legged mobile lunar lander are effective to rough terrains.

Keywords: Legged mobile lunar lander · Recovery planning · Optimization · Gait planning

1 Introduction

With the rapid development of the aerospace field, more and more countries are committing themselves to extraterrestrial exploration. The exploration is usually completed by the lander and rover. The lander is mainly used to solve the landing and deliver the rover to the planet [1]. It cannot move and can only work in initial position. It is desirable to develop a novel lander which has the ability to move. To achieve this goal, the recovery of the buffer structure must be solved after the lander touches the ground. Methods that can solve the recovery of the buffer structure still lack.

The hard landing and soft landing are two main methods for landing. For hard landing, it has no buffer structure and will be damaged when the lander hits the surface of the planet. Therefore, this kind of lander can only explore for one time like Ranger-4 [2] and Chang'e-1 [3]. For soft landing, the lander has buffer structure, when the lander approaches the surface of the planet, the landing speed will be reduced through the buffer structure and other reduction gears to achieve a smooth landing. The soft landing can protect the lander from damage, then the lander can work for a long time and send information to the earth. According to the landing mode, the soft landing can be divided into airbag type, skycrane type and leg type. The leg type can be further divided into triangle type and cantilever type. The airbag has small bearing capacity, so it is only

H. Yang et al. (Eds.): ICIRA 2023, LNAI 14271, pp. 589–600, 2023.
https://doi.org/10.1007/978-981-99-6495-6_50

suitable for small landers like Luna-9 [4] and PathFinder [5, 6]. The skycrane type is suitable for the planet which has the atmosphere, this method is used to help the Curiosity rover to land on Mars [7, 8].

However, there still remain some issues. In order to make the lander move to get a wider range of detection, the buffer structure must be recovered. Few methods have been proposed to solve the recovery planning of the buffer structure. To solve this issue, this study proposes a novel recovery planning for the legged mobile lunar lander. The main contributions of this study are as follows:

1. The recovery planning of this study is developed for the legged mobile lunar lander.
2. The stability margin of the motion planning is larger than zero, which guarantees the stability of the lander under external disturbances.
3. The method we proposed can effectively enhance the terrain adaptability by optimizing the footholds and body's pose under the workspace constraints.

The rest of this paper is organized as follows. In Sect. 2, the legged mobile lunar lander and its buffer structure are introduced. In Sect. 3, the recovery planning of the lander is proposed. In Sect. 4, the foot-tips' position and body's pose of the lander are analyzed using the optimization method. In Sect. 5, the simulations are conducted to validate the method and its performances. In Sect. 6, this paper is concluded.

2 Legged Mobile Lunar Lander

The legged mobile lunar lander is showed in Fig. 1. It is developed to explore the moon. It has four same legs around the body, each leg is a parallel mechanism composed of a UP chain and two UPS chains. The UP chain is composed of a universal joint (U-joint) and a prismatic joint (P-joint). The UPS chain is composed of a U-joint, a P-joint and a spherical joint (S-joint). In each chain, the P-joint is the active joint and all the P-joints of the UP chain and the UPS chain have the upper and lower limits. The foot-tip is connected to the UP chain with a S-joint so that it can adapt to different terrains.

The location of the lander is described through three coordinate frames, the ground frame $O_G-X_GY_GZ_G$, the body frame $O_B-X_BY_BZ_B$ and the leg frame $O_L-X_LY_LZ_L$. The $O_B-X_BY_BZ_B$ is established at the top of the body with Z_B pointing to the front and Y_B pointing to the upside. The $O_G-X_GY_GZ_G$ is coincide with the initial body frame and it will not change as the lander moves. The leg frame $O_L-X_LY_LZ_L$ is fixed to the UP chain, O_L is established at the center of the U-joint, Z_L is parallel to the line of the other two U-joint of the leg and Y_L points to the midpoint of the line. The kinematics of the leg mechanism has been solved by Pan and Gao [9–11]. This paper is aim to solve the recovery planning of the legged mobile lunar lander, so the kinematics of the leg will not be introduced.

The buffer structure of the legged mobile lunar lander is designed to absorb the impact of landing [12, 13], as shown in Fig. 1(c). Each leg has three buffer structure, the first one is connected with the P-joint of the UP chain, it can only be compressed. The other two structures are connected with each P-joint of the UPS chain, they can be stretched or compressed. At the beginning, the buffer structures are at standard position. When the legged mobile lunar lander touches the ground of the planet, the buffer structure can change the length to absorb the energy. If the terrain for landing is rough, then the change of the buffer structure will be different, so it will result in different lengths for each leg. In order to get the best walking performance for the legged mobile lunar lander, each leg should be at a nominal length. So it is necessary to recover the buffer structure of the lander.

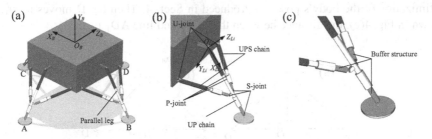

Fig. 1. The legged mobile lunar lander

3   The Recovery Planning of the Lander

The buffer structure of the leg can be recovered to the standard position when the leg is not the supporting leg. In order to implement the recovery planning, the first step is identifying the position of the center of mass (COM). The position of the four foot-tips in ground frame Pi can be got by the Eq. (1). $_{L}^{B}R_i$ is the transformation matrix from the leg frame to the body frame, $_{B}^{G}R$ is the transformation matrix from the body frame to the ground frame. The orientation of the body can be measured by IMU. The position of the four foot-tips in leg frame $^{L}P_i$ can be got by the forward kinematics. Finally, the position of the COM relative to the foot-tips can be calculated.

$$P_i = {}_{B}^{G}R \cdot {}_{L}^{B}R_i \cdot {}^{L}P_i, i = A, B, C, D \tag{1}$$

In order to solve the recovery planning of the buffer structure, the position of the COM relative to the foot-tips can be divided into two types. The first type is shown in Fig. 2(a), the position of the COM is in triangle AOB, triangle AOC, triangle BOD and triangle COD, on line OA, line OB, line OC and line OD. The second type is shown in Fig. 2(b), with the position of the COM coincident with the intersection point of line AD and line BC.

For the first type shown in Fig. 2(a), the recovery planning is developed by S_1-S_9 to recovery the length of all the buffer structures. In this part, the possible movements are analyzed, the position of the COM in triangle AOC shown in Fig. 3 is taken for example and the other situations are the same. In this situation, the landing terrain is rough and the changed length of the buffer structure in each leg is different because of the stairs and slope.

S_1-S_3: When the position of the COM is in triangle AOC, the supporting triangle is ABC, so leg D can move, raising leg D and then the buffer structure can recover to the standard position, as shown in Fig. 4(a). Now, the supporting triangle is still the ABC, in order to get enough workspace to recover the other legs, body's pose should be adjusted, as shown in Fig. 4(b). In order to keep the projection of the COM constant, the body can move along the Y_G axis and rotate around the X_G, Y_G and Z_G axis. The trajectory optimization of the body's pose is introduced in Sect. 4. Then leg D moves to D'_1, as shown in Fig. 4(c), the distance between the COM and line AD'_1 is d.

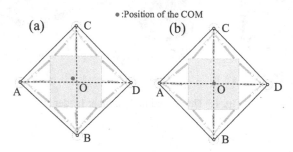

Fig. 2. Types of the position of the COM relative to the foot-tips

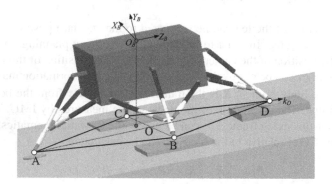

Fig. 3. The situation of the COM in triangle AOC

S_4-S_7: The supporting triangle is the ABD'_1, so leg C can raise and recover the buffer structure, then leg C moves to C', as shown in Fig. 5(a). Now the supporting triangle can be the ABC', so leg D can move to D'_2, as shown in Fig. 5(b), the distance between the COM and line AD'_2 is d. Leg B can raise and recover the buffer structure, then leg B moves to B', as shown in Fig. 5(c), the distance between the COM and line $B'C'$ is d, line $B'C'$ is parallel to line BC. Then leg D moves to D', as shown in Fig. 5(d), line AD' coincides with line AD.

S_8-S_9: The supporting triangle is $AB'C'$, rotating the body around the line $B'C'$, then the COM can move to triangle $B'C'D'$, as shown in Fig. 6(a), the distance between the COM and line $B'C'$ is d, as shown in Fig. 6(b). At last, leg A can raise and recover the buffer structure, then leg A moves to A', as shown in Fig. 6(c), line $A'D'$ coincides with line AD.

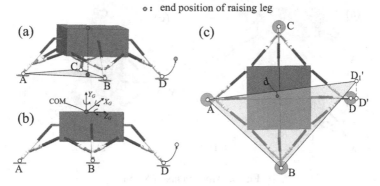

Fig. 4. Movements in S_1-S_3

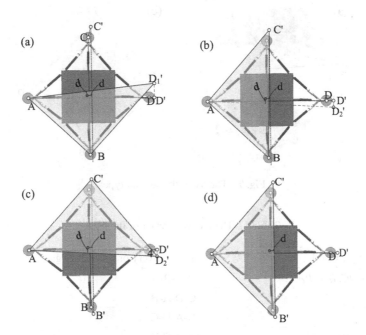

Fig. 5. Movements in S_4-S_7

For the second type, in the initial state, the COM is coincident with the intersection point of line AD and line BC, as shown in Fig. 7(a). By stretching leg D and shortening leg A, the body rotates around the line BC, moving the COM into triangle ABC. Then leg D can raise and recover the buffer structure. The following process is the same as the first type. For other situations, when the position of COM has different locations, the recovery planning is similar, the recovery order of the legs is shown in Table 1.

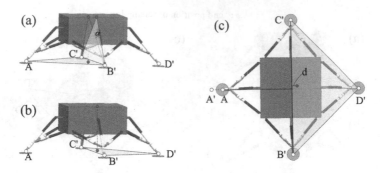

Fig. 6. Movements in S_8-S_9

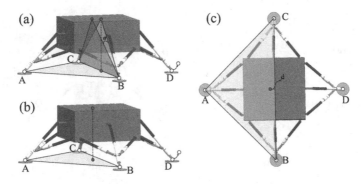

Fig. 7. The S_1 of the second type

Table 1. The recovery order of the legs

Position of the COM	The recovery order of the legs
$\triangle AOB$, $\triangle AOC$, l_{OA}, P_O	D-C-B-A
l_{OB}	C-D-A-B
l_{OC}	B-A-D-C
$\triangle BOD$, $\triangle COD$, l_{OD}	A-B-C-D

4 The Optimization of the Recovery Planning

In the process of the recovery planning, if we don't adjust the body's position and orientation and the foot-tips' position, the displacement of P-joints would be out of workspace after raising the legs and recovering the buffer structure. The optimization of the recovery planning aims to enhance the lander's ability to move under the workspace constraints. An effective way is to make the displacement of all the active joints as small as possible. In this way, the lander can recover the buffer structure better and make full use of the workspace. As a result, the optimization object is to minimize the displacement of all the P-joints. The model of the object is

$$minf(q) = \|q - q_m\|_2 \tag{2}$$

where q_m is the middle of the workspace. q can be calculated by the inverse kinematics. However, the body's pose and the footholds remain unknown and the inverse kinematics cannot be applied. q can also be calculated by using the increment,

$$q_k = q_{k-1} + \Delta q_{k-1} \tag{3}$$

The increment of the foothold in the frame $O_B\text{-}X_B Y_B Z_B$ can be expressed as

$$\Delta^B P_i = {}_B^G R^T \left[\Delta^G P_i - \Delta^G P_b + ({}^G P_i - {}^G P_b) \times \Delta^G e_b \right] \tag{4}$$

Therefore,

$$\Delta q_i = {}^L J_i {}_L^B R_i^T \Delta^B P_i = {}^L J_i {}_L^B R_i^T {}_B^G R^T \left[\Delta^G P_i - \Delta^G P_b + ({}^G P_i - {}^G P_b) \times \Delta^G e_b \right] \tag{5}$$

where ${}^L J_i$ is the Jacobian matrix in the frame $O_L\text{-}X_L Y_L Z_L$. $\Delta^G P_i, \Delta^G P_b$ is the increment of the foothold and body's position in the ground frame. ${}^G P_i, {}^G P_b$ is the foothold and body's position in the ground frame, $\Delta^G e_b$ is the increment of the body's orientation in the ground frame.

$\Delta^G P_i$ can be expressed by the swing direction k_i and the swing distance Δ_i,

$$\Delta^G P_l = \Delta_l k_l \tag{6}$$

Different legs have different k_i. Taking leg D for example, k_D is parallel to the slope, k_D's projection on the ground coincides with AD's projection on the ground, as shown in Fig. 3.

Therefore,

$$\Delta q_i = {}^L J_i {}_L^B R_i^T {}_B^G R^T \left[\Delta_i k_i - \Delta^G P_b + ({}^G P_i - {}^G P_b) \times \Delta^G e_b \right] \tag{7}$$

$\Delta^G P_b = (\Delta P_{xb}, \Delta P_{yb}, \Delta P_{zb})^T$, $\Delta^G e_b = (\Delta e_{xb}, \Delta e_{xb}, \Delta e_{xb})^T$, in the recovery planning, in order to keep the projection of the COM constant, $\Delta P_{xb}, \Delta P_{zb}$ are always known. Separating the known and unknown variables, Eq. (7) can be written as

$$\Delta q_i = A_i \Delta_{i\_unknown} + B_i \Delta_{i\_known} \tag{8}$$

If Δ_i, $\Delta^G e_b$, ΔP_{yb} are unknown,

$$A_i = \left({}^L_L J_i \, {}^B_i R^T_i \, {}^G_B R^T ({}^G P_i - {}^G P_b) \times (- {}^L_L J_i \, {}^B_i R^T_i \, {}^G_B R^T)_{C2} \, {}^L_L J_i \, {}^B_i R^T_i \, {}^G_B R^T k_i \right)$$

$$\Delta_{i\_unknown} = \begin{pmatrix} \Delta {}^G e_b \\ \Delta P_{yb} \\ \Delta_i \end{pmatrix}, B_i = \left(- {}^L_L J_i \, {}^B_i R^T_i \, {}^G_B R^T \right), \Delta_{i\_known} = \left(\Delta {}^G P_{b\_xz} \right) \qquad (9)$$

$$\Delta {}^G P_{b\_xz} = (\Delta P_{xb}, 0, \Delta P_{zb})^T$$

Combining all the four legs together,

$$\Delta q = A \Delta_{unknown} + B \Delta_{known} \qquad (10)$$

Different leg has different Δ_i, in the planning of S_1-S_7, $\Delta {}^G e_b$, ΔP_{yb}, the footholds of leg B, C and D are unknown, the foothold of leg A is known. Therefore,

$$= \begin{pmatrix} {}^L_A J_A \, {}^B_L R^T_A \, {}^G_B R^T ({}^G P_A - {}^G P_b) \times & (- {}^L_A J_A \, {}^B_L R^T_A \, {}^G_B R^T)_{C2} & 0 & 0 & 0 \\ {}^L_B J_B \, {}^B_L R^T_B \, {}^G_B R^T ({}^G P_B - {}^G P_b) \times & (- {}^L_B J_B \, {}^B_L R^T_B \, {}^G_B R^T)_{C2} & {}^L_B J_B \, {}^B_L R^T_B \, {}^G_B R^T k_B & 0 & 0 \\ {}^L_C J_C \, {}^B_L R^T_C \, {}^G_B R^T ({}^G P_C - {}^G P_b) \times & (- {}^L_C J_C \, {}^B_L R^T_C \, {}^G_B R^T)_{C2} & 0 & {}^L_C J_C \, {}^B_L R^T_C \, {}^G_B R^T k_C & 0 \\ {}^L_D J_D \, {}^B_L R^T_D \, {}^G_B R^T ({}^G P_D - {}^G P_b) \times & (- {}^L_D J_D \, {}^B_L R^T_D \, {}^G_B R^T)_{C2} & 0 & 0 & {}^L_D J_D \, {}^B_L R^T_D \, {}^G_B R^T k_D \end{pmatrix}$$

$$\Delta_{unknown} = \begin{pmatrix} \Delta {}^G e_b \\ \Delta P_{yb} \\ \Delta_B \\ \Delta_C \\ \Delta_D \end{pmatrix}, B = \begin{pmatrix} (- {}^L_A J_A \, {}^B_L R^T_A \, {}^G_B R^T) & {}^L_A J_A \, {}^B_L R^T_A \, {}^G_B R^T k_A \\ (- {}^L_B J_B \, {}^B_L R^T_B \, {}^G_B R^T) & 0 \\ (- {}^L_C J_C \, {}^B_L R^T_C \, {}^G_B R^T) & 0 \\ (- {}^L_D J_D \, {}^B_L R^T_D \, {}^G_B R^T) & 0 \end{pmatrix}, \Delta_{known} = \begin{pmatrix} \Delta {}^G P_{b\_x} \\ \Delta_A \end{pmatrix} \qquad (11)$$

In the planning of S_9, the foothold of leg A is unknown, therefore,

$$A = \begin{pmatrix} {}^L_A J_A \, {}^B_L R^T_A \, {}^G_B R^T k_A \\ 0 \\ 0 \\ 0 \end{pmatrix}, \Delta_{unknown} = (\Delta_A), \Delta_{known} = \begin{pmatrix} \Delta {}^G e_b \\ \Delta {}^G P_b \\ \Delta_B \\ \Delta_C \\ \Delta_D \end{pmatrix}$$

$$B = \begin{pmatrix} {}^L_A J_A \, {}^B_L R^T_A \, {}^G_B R^T ({}^G P_A - {}^G P_b) \times & (- {}^L_A J_A \, {}^B_L R^T_A \, {}^G_B R^T) & 0 & 0 & 0 \\ {}^L_B J_B \, {}^B_L R^T_B \, {}^G_B R^T ({}^G P_B - {}^G P_b) \times & (- {}^L_B J_B \, {}^B_L R^T_B \, {}^G_B R^T) & {}^L_B J_B \, {}^B_L R^T_B \, {}^G_B R^T k_B & 0 & 0 \\ {}^L_C J_C \, {}^B_L R^T_C \, {}^G_B R^T ({}^G P_C - {}^G P_b) \times & (- {}^L_C J_C \, {}^B_L R^T_C \, {}^G_B R^T) & 0 & {}^L_C J_C \, {}^B_L R^T_C \, {}^G_B R^T k_C & 0 \\ {}^L_D J_D \, {}^B_L R^T_D \, {}^G_B R^T ({}^G P_D - {}^G P_b) \times & (- {}^L_D J_D \, {}^B_L R^T_D \, {}^G_B R^T) & 0 & 0 & {}^L_D J_D \, {}^B_L R^T_D \, {}^G_B R^T k_D \end{pmatrix} \qquad (12)$$

Substituting Eq. (10) into Eq. (3),

$$q_k = q_{k-1} + A_{k-1} \Delta_{unknown} + B_{k-1} \Delta_{known} \qquad (13)$$

Therefore, the optimization object is

$$minf f(q_k) = \| q_{k-1} + A_{k-1} \Delta_{unknown} + B_{k-1} \Delta_{known} - q_m \|_2 \qquad (14)$$

In order to solve Eq. (14), pseudo-inverse is a quick way. Therefore,

$$\Delta_{unknown} = -A^\dagger_{k-1} (q_{k-1} + B_{k-1} \Delta_{known} - q_m) \qquad (15)$$

Obviously, Eq. (4) is an incremental expression, the iterative solving can be used to eliminate the error. The iteration algorithm is concluded in Fig. 8.

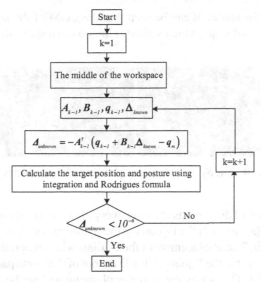

Fig. 8. The iteration algorithm

5 Simulations and Results

Two simulations were carried out to validate the recovery planning and the optimization. The first simulation illustrates the recovery planning of the legged mobile lunar lander on the slope of $8°$, as shown in Fig. 9. The second simulation illustrates the S_1 of the recovery planning of the second type, as shown in Fig. 10. In the first simulation, the initial COM of the lander is in triangle AOC, so the recovery order of the lander is D-C-B-A. The footholds of the four legs are optimized. When raising each leg, the buffer structure can recover, then the leg moves to the designated foothold. The body and foot-tips' position in each step are shown in Fig. 11. The supporting triangle means the three supporting legs in each step. The figures can illustrate the optimization of the footholds

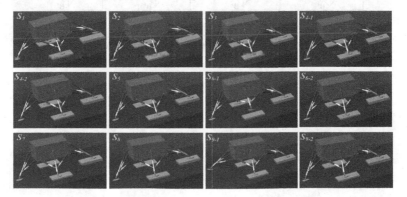

Fig. 9. The simulation of the recovery planning of the first type

and the stability of the lander. It can be seen that the COM of the lander is kept in the supporting triangle in all steps, which validates the nonzero static stability margin.

Fig. 10. The S_1 of the recovery planning of the second type

The trajectories of all the P-joints at the recovery planning are shown in Fig. 12. It can be seen that the displacement of the P-joints in the optimized method are all between the upper and lower limit. The displacement of the P-joints without optimization is shown in Fig. 13, and we can see that the P-joints of leg D are out of the workspace in the process of the recovery planning. That's why the recovery planning will not be completed without the optimization. it also validates the optimization can successfully solve the recovery planning.

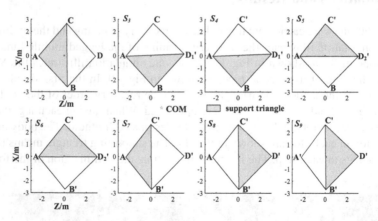

Fig. 11. The body and foot-tips' position in each step

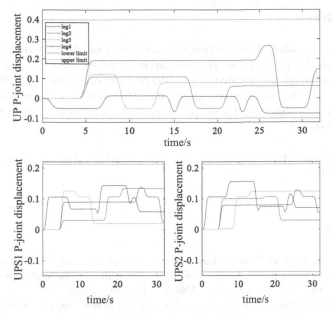

Fig. 12. Trajectories of the P-joints

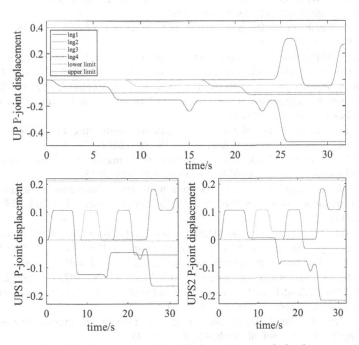

Fig. 13. Trajectories of the P-joints without optimization

6   Conclusion

In this work we introduce the legged mobile lunar lander and the recovery planning of the buffer structure. We propose a novel optimization for the recovery planning. The body's pose and the footholds are adjusted to solve the problem of insufficient workspace in the recovery process. The simulations validate the effectiveness of the recovery planning and the optimization method. The proposed method can be used on rough terrains such as slopes and steps.

Acknowledgements. This work was funded by the National Natural Science Foundation of China (No. 92248303).

References

1. Yin, K., Sun, Q., Gao, F., et al.: Lunar surface soft-landing analysis of a novel six-legged mobile lander with repetitive landing capacity. In: Proceedings of the Institution of Mechanical Engineers, Part C: J. Mech. Eng. Sci. **236**(2), 1214–1233 (2022)
2. Arnold, J.R., Metzger, A.E., Anderson, E.C., et al.: Gamma rays in space, Ranger 3. J. Geophys. Res. **67**(12) (1962)
3. Ouyang, Z.Y., Wen, W.B., Wei, B., et al.: Primary scientific results of Chang'E-1 lunar mission. Sci. China Earth Sci. **53**(11), 1565–1581 (2010)
4. Behm, H.: Results of the Ranger, Lunar 9, and Surveyor 1 missions. J. Astronaut. Sci. **14**, 101 (1967)
5. Golombek, M.P., Cook, R.A., Economou, T., et al.: Overview of the Mars pathfinder mission and assessment of landing site predictions. Science **278**(5344), 1743–1748 (1997)
6. Golombek, M.P., Bridges, N.T., Moore, H.J., et al.: Overview of the Mars pathfinder mission: launch through landing, surface operations, data sets, and science results. J. Geophys. Res. Atmos. **104**(E4), 8523–8554 (1999)
7. Welch, R., Limonadi, D., Manning, R.: Systems engineering the Curiosity Rover: a retrospective. System of Systems Engineering (SoSE) (2013)
8. Heverly, M., Matthews, J., Lin, J., et al.: Traverse performance characterization for the Mars Science Laboratory rover. J. Field Robot. **30**(6), 835–846 (2013)
9. Pan, Y., Gao, F.: Leg kinematic analysis and prototype experiments of walking-operating multifunctional hexapod robot. Proc. Inst. Mech. Eng. C J. Mech. Eng. Sci. **228**(12), 2217–2232 (2014)
10. Pan, Y., Gao, F.: A new six-parallel-legged walking robot for drilling holes on the fuselage. In: Proceedings of the Institution of Mechanical Engineers, Part C: J. Mech. Eng. Sci. (2014)
11. Pan, Y., Gao, F.: Position model computational complexity of walking robot with different parallel leg mechanism topology patterns. Mech. Mach. Theory **107**, 324–337 (2017)
12. Yang, J., Man, J., Zeng, F., et al.: Achievements and applications of landing gear for Chang'E-3 Lander. Spacecraft Recov. Remote Sens. (2014)
13. Yang, J., Zeng, F., Man, J.: Design and verification of the landing impact attenuation system for Chang'E-3 Lander. Sci. Sin Tech. 440–449 (2014)

Author Index

H. Yang et al. (Eds.): ICIRA 2023, LNAI 14271, pp. 601–603, 2023.
https://doi.org/10.1007/978-981-99-6495-6

Printed in the United States
by Baker & Taylor Publisher Services